THE CIVIL WAR

The American Iliad

CHARLESTON

MERCURY

EXTRA:

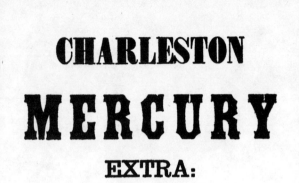

Passed unanimously at 1.15 o'clock, P. M. December 20th, 1860.

AN ORDINANCE

To dissolve the Union between the State of South Carolina and other States united with her under the compact entitled " The Constitution of the United States of America."

We, the People of the State of South Carolina, in Convention assembled, do declare and ordain, and it is hereby declared and ordained,

That the Ordinance adopted by us in Convention, on the twenty-third day of May, in the year of our Lord one thousand seven hundred and eighty-eight, whereby the Constitution of the United States of America was ratified, and also, all Acts and parts of Acts of the General Assembly of this State, ratifying amendments of the said Constitution, are hereby repealed; and that the union now subsisting between South Carolina and other States, under the name of "The United States of America," is hereby dissolved.

THE

UNION

IS

DISSOLVED!

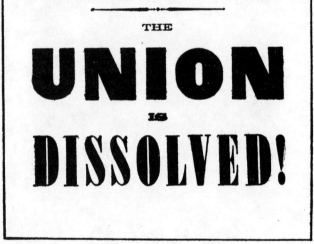

THE CIVIL WAR

THE AMERICAN ILIAD
as Told by Those Who Lived It

BY

OTTO EISENSCHIML
and RALPH NEWMAN

Introduction by
BRUCE CATTON

MALLARD PRESS

MALLARD PRESS
An imprint of BDD Promotional Book Company, Inc.
666 Fifth Avenue
New York, N.Y. 10103

Mallard Press and its accompanying design and logo
are trademarks of BDD Promotional Book Company, Inc.

Reprinted by special arrangement by William S. Konecky Associates, Inc.

This edition first published in the United States of America
in 1991 by The Mallard Press

ISBN 0-7924-5602-5

Printed in the United States of America

Foreword

This book is not intended to be just another account of the Civil War. Instead it aims to present it as a panorama, letting the events pass before the reader's eyes much as they passed before the eyes of the men and women who lived at that time.

The Civil War, beyond most wars, went deep into every aspect of life, and was more than a series of battles, cavalry raids and naval engagements. It affected every living being, both North and South, and produced many strange human experiences, some of which we have woven into this narrative as an integral part of the picture.

We did not write this book. Hundreds of people wrote it, people who witnessed a stirring contemporary scene and tell about it in their own words. They may have been commanding generals or soldiers in the ranks, newspaper reporters, statesmen or housewives. If they observed well, wrote honestly, entertainingly and with dramatic suspense, we have drawn on their contributions.

The selections we use are, for the most part, quoted verbatim. Now and then, though, we have found it desirable to make slight changes. A general may have been a fine strategist but a clumsy writer, a correspondent a good reporter but one who cluttered his sentences with commas and semicolons. We have tried to make grammar, spelling and punctuation fairly uniform throughout, except when a quaint piece of writing seemed worth preserving or else was characteristic of a well-known personage.

As a rule we have condensed our material, but at other times we have added an extra sentence or two, so as to establish continuity or to avoid the necessity of a lengthy explanation. When an autobiographical account was written in the third person, we may have changed it to the first, and where we have deviated from the original tense we have done it to fit the selection more smoothly into the balance of the text. When original wordings seemed obscure, we have clarified them. In no case, however, have we tampered with the meaning of our source material, nor have we distorted it in any way whatever.

Observations of witnesses usually differ in some particulars. Where these discrepancies or variances from accepted facts are not flagrant, we have let them stand, either as a matter of interest or as an expression of the sincere beliefs of the observers. The personal views of our authors are strictly their own, of course, not ours, and are apt to contradict one another both in sentiment and substance. Nevertheless, the reader should have little difficulty, with the evidence presented, in forming his own opinions.

In drawing our maps we have been guided by two aims: to make them simple, so that the reader may orient himself at a single glance, and to mark on them every essential locality mentioned in the text. We feel that in this manner the campaigns and battles can be most readily followed.

The scope of this volume has made it impossible to embody in it all the campaigns and engagements of the great conflict, hence we have confined ourselves to the major events of the war, all of which, we believe, are fully represented.

Books are usually dedicated to someone for whom the authors feel reverence or to whom they are especially indebted. We therefore think it entirely in order that we should dedicate this volume first, to the memory of our contributors, now long dead and buried, and second, to all men who fought in this sectional conflict, Union or Confederate, regardless of whether they paid allegiance to the Stars and Bars or to the Stars and Stripes, under which they were eventually reunited.

Credits and Acknowledgments

The authors gratefully acknowledge the following permissions to reprint material in this volume:

From *An Aide-de-Camp of Lee, being the Papers of Colonel Charles Marshall*, edited by Major General Sir Frederick Maurice, copyright, 1927, by Little, Brown and Company, reprinted by permission of General Sir Frederick Maurice.

From *Autobiographical Sketch and Narrative of the War Between the States*, with notes by R. H. Early, copyright, 1912, by J. B. Lippincott Company, reprinted by permission of the publisher.

From *Autobiography of Sir Henry Morton Stanley*, edited by his wife Dorothy Stanley, copyright, 1911, by Houghton Mifflin Company, reprinted by permission of the publisher.

From *The Campaign of Chancellorsville* by John Bigelow, Jr., copyright, 1910, by the Yale University Press, reprinted by permission of the publisher.

From *A Diary from Dixie* by Mary Boykin Chesnut, copyright, 1905, by D. Appleton and Company, reprinted by permission of the publisher.

From *The Diary of Gideon Welles*, edited by John T. Morse, Jr., copyright, 1911, by Houghton Mifflin Company, reprinted by permission of the publisher.

From *From Manassas to Appomattox* by James Longstreet, copyright, 1903, by J. B. Lippincott Company, reprinted by permission of Mrs. Helen Dortch Longstreet.

From *Home Letters of General Sherman*, edited by M. A. DeWolfe Howe, copyright, 1909, by Charles Scribner's Sons, reprinted by permission of the publisher.

From *I Rode with Stonewall* by Henry Kyd Douglas, copyright, 1940, by The University of North Carolina Press, reprinted by permission of the publisher.

From *Letters from Lee's Army or Memoirs of Life In and Out of The Army in Virginia During the War Between the States*, compiled by Susan Leigh Blackford, copyright, 1947, by Charles Scribner's Sons, reprinted by permission of the publisher.

From *Lew Wallace: An Autobiography* by Lew Wallace, copyright, 1906, by Harper & Brothers, reprinted by permission of the publisher.

From *The Life and Letters of General George Gordon Meade* by George Meade, copyright, 1913, by Charles Scribner's Sons, reprinted by permission of the publisher.

From *Life of General Ely S. Parker* by A. C. Parker, copyright, 1919, by Buffalo Historical Society, reprinted by permission of the publisher.

From *Marching with Sherman, Passages from the Letters and Campaign*

Diaries of Henry Hitchcock, edited by M. A. DeWolfe Howe, copyright, 1927, by the Yale University Press, reprinted by permission of the publisher.

From *Meade's Headquarters, 1863-1865. Letters of Colonel Theodore Lyman*, edited by George R. Agassiz, copyright, 1922, by The Atlantic Monthly Press, reprinted by permission of George R. Agassiz.

From *Military Memoirs of a Confederate* by Edward P. Alexander, copyright, 1907, by Charles Scribner's Sons, reprinted by permission of the publisher.

From *Petersburg, Chancellorsville, Gettysburg*. Volume V, Papers of Military Historical Society of Massachusetts, copyright, 1906, by The Society, reprinted by permission of the Military Historical Society of Massachusetts.

From *Recollections of a Rebel Reefer* by James Morris Morgan, copyright, 1917, by Houghton Mifflin Company, reprinted by permission of Helen Morgan Wallace.

From *Reminiscences of Peace and War. Revised and Enlarged Edition.* By Mrs. Roger A. Pryor, copyright, 1905, by The Macmillan Company, reprinted by permission of the publisher.

From *Reminiscences of the Civil War* by John B. Gordon, copyright, 1903, by Charles Scribner's Sons, reprinted by permission of the publisher.

From *Three Years with Grant, As Recalled by War Correspondent Sylvanus Cadwallader*, edited, and with an Introduction and Notes by Benjamin P. Thomas, copyright, 1955, by Benjamin P. Thomas, reprinted by permission of Alfred A. Knopf, Inc.

From *Under the Old Flag* by James Harrison Wilson, copyright, 1912, by D. Appleton and Company, reprinted by permission of the publisher.

From *A Woman's Wartime Journal* by Dolly Sumner Lunt, copyright, 1918, by The Century Company, reprinted by permission of Mrs. Louis D. Bolton.

For the help we have received in the preparation of this book we give heartfelt thanks to these friends of ours:

EVERETTE B. *"Pete"* LONG, historian and journalist, who, by his indefatigable efforts in unearthing unusual material, his criticism of historical matters and his enthusiastic co-operation, did a major share of the work that had to be done and should by all rights be considered a co-author of this work.

HARRISON PLATT, WILLIAM MORRIS, NORMAN HOSS and SHELDON MEYER, editors whose sympathetic attitude and wise counsel have helped us smooth out many a rough spot.

CARL HAVERLIN, whose superb Civil War library was made available to us and who allowed one of the authors to set up "base" in New York where final corrections in the manuscript were made, and whose uncanny bibliographical and historical knowledge was always at our disposal.

BRUCE CATTON, for constant advice and for generously interrupting a busy schedule to write an introduction to this volume.

JOSEPH L. EISENDRATH, JR., who helped us track down elusive data in the *Official Records.*

PAUL M. ANGLE, Director, and MARGARET SCRIVEN, Librarian of the CHICAGO HISTORICAL SOCIETY, who along with their associates, gave unstintingly of their time and advice, and who put at our disposal the material from the David H. Annan and Loyal Legion Civil War collections.

JAY MONAGHAN, the late HARRY E. PRATT, MARION B. PRATT and CLYDE C. WALTON, State Historians, and MARGARET A. FLINT, Reference Librarian, who made available for our use the Alfred Whital Stern Civil War collection as well as other resources of their institution.

STANLEY PARGELLIS, Librarian of THE NEWBERRY LIBRARY, who made available for our use the excellent Civil War collections of his institution.

CHARLES S. SCHWARTZ, who combined his artistic talents with interest in the Civil War in preparing the pictorial battle maps. A. P. TEDESCO, whose skill and talent is responsible for the physical appearance of this volume and who supervised the preparation of the art work on behalf of the publisher.

ARNOLD ALEXANDER, ELMER GERTZ, FRANK B. HOWARD, THOMAS I. STARR and the late F. LAURISTON BULLARD, who helped us in clearing up difficult copyright problems.

D. L. CHAMBERS, the late FOREMAN M. LEBOLD, EARL SCHENCK MIERS, ALLAN NEVINS, CARL SANDBURG, PHILIP VAN DOREN STERN, BENJAMIN P. THOMAS, WALTER TROHAN and EZRA J. WARNER, whose friendly comments, corrections and suggestions were invaluable.

MARJORIE ARNETTE BRAYE, OLIVE CARRUTHERS, RICHARD E. CLARK, VIRGINIA MAIER GOLDBERG, BARBARA LONG, WALTHER F. NAGLER, ESTELLE NEWMAN and RUTH E. TRANTINA, who read the manuscript or proofs.

MARGARET H. APRIL, VERONICA M. CARROLL, EILEEN DONOHUE, EMILY HAUSER, BEATRICE JAROS, MARION F. PALMER, CHRISTINA SARANTAKIS, the late ROSE TRIB, GERTRUD E. WADENPOHL and FRIEDA WEISBACH, whose diligence and untiring help in preparing the manuscript is beyond praise.

MARDA ALEXANDER, CHARLES M. ANTIN, ELIZABETH BRAGDON, JANE CARROLL, MILDRED CHETKIN, BEAULAH COMPTON, MILDRED CORBRIDGE, WILLIAM J. FINNERAN, WALTER HURLEY, CHARLOTTE JEANES, AL MEYER, ANNE SIEWERS and HERMAN ZIEGNER, who assisted in various ways.

All members of THE CIVIL WAR ROUND TABLE, whose advice was often sought and always cheerfully given, and whose thorough knowledge of our subject was constantly ours for the asking.

Contents

CONTENTS—*Continued*

List of Maps

Introduction

The Civil War is a common possession of all Americans. It was brought about by a succession of errors in which the whole country shared; the fearful price that was paid for it was exacted from the victors and the defeated alike; and the solemn pride with which generations of Americans have regarded the war's epic story is something that does not change when one travels from one section of the country to another. Very literally this was *our* war, a unique national experience whose ultimate significance seems heightened rather than diminished as our understanding of it increases.

There are many ways to study the Civil War. It can be viewed as a succession of military engagements, as an explosive release of accumulated industrial energy, as a convulsive forward step by a developing democracy—or, indeed, as a tragic example of the price a country can pay when both the leaders and the led become impatient with the virtues of compromise and political adjustment. The war was all of those things; it has been analyzed under each guise, and each analysis repays study.

But when all is said and done, the way to get a real understanding of what the war meant and what it did to people is to go to the men and women who were actually in it—to the participants, who may have lacked the objectivity that comes from the distant view, but who at least were in a position to say what the whole business looked and felt like while it was going on.

Under everything else—above everything else—the Civil War was an emotional experience, the profoundest one that has ever come to the American people. It still carries that emotional quality. That is to say that before it can be understood it has to be felt, and felt to the limit.

We are still trying to figure out precisely what the Civil War meant; probably we shall be at it for generations still to come. Like all truly profound human experiences, this one gains new significance as we get further and further from it in time. But the point to bear in mind is that before anyone can determine what the war meant, he must first comprehend what it cost. This chess game was played with living pieces. The enduring value of this book is that it brings together the testimony which those living pieces had to offer at the time; it is the medium through which they tell us what it was like to be in the American Civil War.

What was it like? Well, it was pretty rugged. For the most part, these participants were not conscious that they were figures in an epic. They took a short-range view of things, doing the best they could to meet an uncommonly sticky situation, facing hardship and loss and the imminent danger of sudden death with no more pleasure than we ourselves would. So the words they put down have, at times, the compelling quality of utterances wrung from men by circumstances that are greater than the people who are caught up in them. Here is testimony from the edge of the night itself. Even in the middle of the twentieth century, these words have an urgency to them.

Would this be the case if we had concluded, by this time, that this war was a terrible mistake and nothing more—that it had gained nothing of any consequence for anyone, and that the heroism and devotion that went into it were simple wastage? I do not think so. I believe that the increasing interest in the Civil War nowadays comes at least in part from a growing realization that the whole tragic experience was somehow worth what it cost. True, it might have been averted; true, many of the people involved in it were poor deluded mortals who did not accomplish, by suffering and dying, what they pathetically thought they were accomplishing; true, also, that if Providence was at work here it was occasionally making use of some extremely odd instruments.

Nevertheless, the war did provide a new concept of the unity of human society, and it did expand the boundaries of human freedom. Both achievements were imperfect; a good deal is left for us to do ourselves, and we shall unquestionably leave much for our grandchildren to do. But the gains were real. Because of the Civil War, the American ideal is a little broader, and the road that leads to it is a little less obscure. That is worth a good deal.

Meanwhile, here is what the people who were in the war have to tell us. To read their accounts is to gain a new feeling of the depth and power of America's greatest emotional experience.

Bruce Catton

New York
May 1956

CHAPTER 1

Civil War Comes to America

THE SIEGE AND FALL OF FORT SUMTER

Thursday the twentieth of December 1860 was destined to become deeply engraved in the annals of American history. At noon of that day a recently assembled Convention was to meet in Charleston for the purpose of deciding whether, after more than two generations of peaceful co-existence with the rest of the states, South Carolina should break her bonds with the Federal Union.

Long before the appointed hour crowds of people were streaming toward St. Andrew's Hall, where the meeting was to take place. It was a festival day for the citizens of the town. They had donned their holiday attire and, in conformity with the spirit of the occasion, most men wore hats adorned with a blue cockade, the kind that had been in vogue during the Nullification furore some thirty years before. Bands were playing popular airs, and flags of many novel designs were displayed in the streets; only the national colors were conspicuous by their absence. Amidst all the gay turmoil, however, the people were impatiently awaiting the official pronouncement of a single word, which all expected to hear, and which already had been cut in big, black characters into the Speaker's gavel. The word was *Secession*.

A New England surgeon named Samuel Wylie Crawford, who had recently been assigned to one of Charleston's outlying forts, closely observed the rapidly developing events, and reported them dispassionately.

The Convention was opened with a prayer to God. It was understood that the Committees were ready to report the Ordinance of Se-

I

cession, and that it would pass that day. There was no visible sign that the Commonwealth of South Carolina was about to take a step more momentous for weal or woe than had yet been known in her history. Chancellor Inglis of Chesterfield, the Chairman of the Committee to report an Ordinance of Secession, then arose and called the attention of the President. Silence pervaded the assemblage as every eye turned upon the speaker. Addressing the chair, he said that the Committee would best meet the exigencies of the occasion by expressing in the fewest and simplest words all that was necessary to effect the end proposed:

"We, the people of the State of South Carolina, in convention assembled, do declare and ordain that the Ordinance adopted by us in convention, on the 23rd day of May, in the year of our Lord, seventeen hundred and eighty-eight, whereby the Constitution of the United States was ratified, and also the acts and part of the acts of the General Assembly of this State ratifying amendments of the said Constitution, are hereby repealed, and that the union now subsisting between South Carolina and other States under the name of 'United States of America' is hereby dissolved."

The question was at once put, with the result of a unanimous vote, 169 yeas, nays none.

Edward A. Pollard, war-time editor of the *Richmond Examiner*, described the completion of the program.

A ceremony was appointed for the signing in public of the roll of parchment on which the ordinance was engrossed. The public procession entered the Hall in order: the President and members of the Convention coming first, followed by the President and members of the Senate, and House of Representatives. Their entry was greeted by loud and prolonged cheers from the spectators; the proceedings were commenced with prayer; the Attorney-General of the State then announced that the ordinance had been engrossed by order of the Convention, and the parchment roll was signed by the members who were called successively to the table. When all had signed, the parchment was raised in the sight of the assemblage, and the President announced the State of South Carolina an Independent Commonwealth.

Dr. Crawford now again takes up the story.

At once the whole audience broke out into a storm of cheers; the ladies joined in the demonstrations; a rush was made to secure mementos of the occasion. Outside, the whole city was wild with excitement as the news spread like wild-fire through its streets. Business was suspended everywhere; the peals of the church bells mingling with salvos of artillery from the citadel. Old men ran shouting down the street. Every one entitled to it appeared at once in uniform. In less than fifteen minutes after its passage, the principal newspaper of Charleston had placed in the hands of the eager multitude a copy of the Ordinance of Secession. Private residences were illuminated, while military organizations marched in every direction, the music of their bands lost amid the shouts of the people. A messenger rode with the greatest speed to the camp of the First Regiment of Rifles, South Carolina Militia, where in front of the paraded regiment the Ordinance was read amid the loud acclamations of the men.

The heart of the people had spoken.

How President Buchanan reacted to the news of South Carolina's defection is told interestingly by Mrs. Roger A. Pryor, wife of a Virginia Congressman. It happened during a wedding party to which the Chief Executive had been invited.

The President was seated in an armchair and I stood behind him, as one after another came forward to greet him. Presently he looked over his shoulder and said, "Madam, do you suppose the house is on fire? I hear unusual commotion."

I went out, and there I found Mr. Lawrence Keitt, member from South Carolina, leaping in the air, shaking a paper over his head, exclaiming, "Thank God! Oh, thank God! South Carolina has seceded!" I returned and, bending over Mr. Buchanan's chair, said in a low voice: "It appears, Mr. President, that South Carolina has seceded from the Union." He looked at me, stunned for a moment. Falling back and grasping the arms of his chair, he whispered, "Madam, might I beg you to have my carriage called?" There was no more thought of bride, bridegroom, wedding cake or wedding breakfast.

In contrast to Buchanan, influential Northern journals had foreseen the secession of South Carolina, and were in sympathy with it. Three days after Lincoln's election Greeley's *New*

York Tribune had declared that it held with Jefferson to the in-
alienable right of countries to allow or abolish governments that
had become oppressive. It then went on:

If the Cotton States shall decide that they can do better out of the
Union, we insist on letting them go in peace. The right to secede
may be a revolutionary right, *but it exists, nevertheless.*

On December 17 Greeley enlarged on this statement.

If the Declaration of Independence justified the secession of three
millions of Colonists in 1776, *we do not see why it should not JUS-
TIFY the secession of five millions of Southerners in 1861.*

The independent *New York Herald* agreed.

Each State is organized as a complete government, possessing the
right to break the tie of the Confederation. Coercion, if it were possible, is out of the question.

The *Albany Argus*, organ of Thurlow Weed, a prominent
Republican editor and politician, leaned still farther toward
the Southern point of view.

We sympathize with the South. Their rights have been invaded to
the extreme limit possible within the forms of the Constitution; their
feelings have been insulted, their interests and honor assailed by almost every form of invective. We think that all the instincts of manhood rightfully impelled them to resort to a separation from the Union.
We wish them Godspeed in the adoption of such a remedy.

The United States army officers at Fort Moultrie, the only
garrisoned work inside or on the shores of Charleston Harbor,
were less concerned about the political explosion in the city
than they were about the safety of their isolated outpost. Captain (later General) Abner Doubleday related what action was
taken by his commander to protect the property entrusted to his
care.

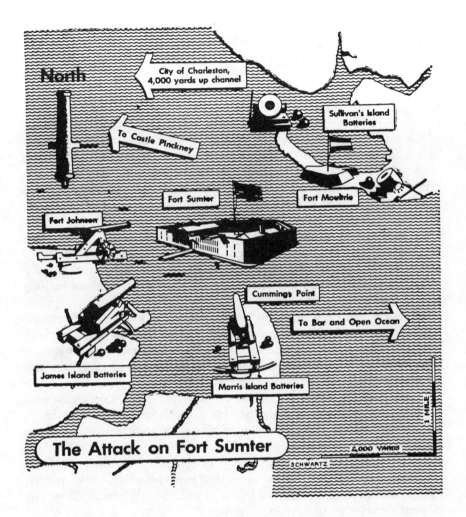

North

City of Charleston,
4,000 yards up channel

To Castle Pinckney

Sullivan's Island
Batteries

Fort Sumter

Fort Moultrie

Fort Johnson

Cummings Point

To Bar and Open Ocean

James Island Batteries

Morris Island Batteries

1 MILE

4,000 YARDS

The Attack on Fort Sumter

SCHWARTZ

This small fort in the harbor at Charleston, its unfinished
works manned by only a handful of troops and surrounded by
hostile batteries, was the prize in the first engagement
of the Civil War.

To the South Carolinians Fort Moultrie was almost a sacred spot, endeared by many precious historical associations, for the ancestors of most of the principal families had fought there in the Revolutionary War behind their hastily improvised ramparts of palmetto logs, and had gained a glorious victory over the British fleet in its first attempt to capture the city of Charleston.

The walls of the fort were but twelve feet high. The constant action of the sea breeze had drifted an immense heap of sand against the front of the work, and another in the immediate vicinity. These sand hills dominated the parapet and made the fort untenable. Our force was pitifully small, even for a time of peace. It consisted of sixty-one en- listed men and seven officers, together with thirteen musicians; whereas the work called for a war garrison of 300 men.

On November 21, 1860, our new commander, Major Robert Ander- son, arrived and assumed command. He had a hereditary right to be there, for his father had distinguished himself in the Revolutionary War in defense of old Fort Moultrie and had been confined a long time as a prisoner in Charleston.

Anderson had been urged by several of us to remove his command to Fort Sumter, but he had invariably replied that he was especially assigned to Fort Moultrie and had no right to vacate it without orders. Nevertheless, he had fully determined to make the change, and was merely awaiting a favorable opportunity.

In making his arrangements to cross over, Anderson acted with consummate prudence and ability. He only communicated his design to the staff officers whose co-operation was indispensable, and he waited until the moment of execution before he informed the others of his intention. On the last evening of our stay (December 26) I left my room to ask Major Anderson to take tea with us. He said quietly, "I have determined to evacuate this post immediately. I can allow you twenty minutes to form your company."

I dashed over to my quarters, told my wife to get ready to leave immediately, and advised her to take refuge with some family outside. Then we took a sad and hasty leave of each other.

We silently made our way to a spot where the boats were hidden. There was not a human being in sight as we marched to the rendez- vous. We found several boats awaiting us. In a low tone their crews pointed out to me the boats intended for my company, and then we pushed rapidly to the fort. Noticing that one of the guard boats was

approaching, we made a wide circuit to avoid it. As among my men
there were a number of unskillful oarsmen, we made but slow progress,
and it soon became evident that we would be overtaken in mid-
channel. The twilight had deepened, however, so that there was a fair
chance for us to escape. While the steamer was yet afar off, I took
off my cap and threw open my coat to conceal the buttons. I also made
the men take off their coats and use them to cover up their muskets.
I hoped in this way we might pass for a party of laborers returning to
the fort. The paddle wheels stopped within about a hundred yards
of us; and to our great relief, after a slight scrutiny, the steamer kept
on its way. Our men redoubled their efforts, and we soon arrived at
our destination.

As we ascended the steps of the wharf, crowds of workmen rushed
out to meet us, most of them wearing secession emblems. The majority
called out angrily, "What are these soldiers doing here?" I at once
charged my bayonets, drove the tumultuous mass inside the fort and
the disloyal workmen were shipped off to the mainland.

Major Anderson thought it best to give some solemnity to the occasion. The band played "The Star-Spangled Banner," the troops presented arms, and our chaplain offered up a fervent supplication,
invoking the blessing of Heaven upon our small command and the
cause we represented.

> There lived in Charleston at that time a member of an old
> South Carolina family, Mary Boykin Chesnut. Her husband,
> Colonel James Chesnut, was active in state and national politics
> and had until recently been United States Senator. He was to
> play a prominent part in the events which were in the making.
> Mrs. Chesnut kept a diary, and from it we gain an insight into
> the mood of the people in Charleston during the early days of
> Secession.

December 27, 1860. Mrs. Gidiere came in quietly from her market-
ing today, and in her neat, incisive manner exploded this bombshell:
"Major Anderson has moved into Fort Sumter, while our Governor
Pickens slept serenely." The row is fast and furious now. State after
state is taking its forts and fortresses. They say if we had been left
out in the cold alone we might have sulked awhile, but back we would
have had to go and would merely have fretted and fumed and quar-

reled among ourselves. We needed a little wholesome neglect. Anderson has blocked that game, but now our sister states have joined us, and we are strong. I give the condensed essence of the table talk: "Anderson has united the Cotton States." Those who want a row are in high glee. Those who dread it are glum and thoughtful.

The talk is: "Fort Sumter must be taken, and it is one of the strongest forts." How in the name of sense are they to manage it? I shudder to think of rash moves.

The narrative is now taken up by Dr. Samuel Wylie Crawford, who was the assistant surgeon of the Fort Sumter garrison.

When occupied by Major Anderson's command on the night of December 26, 1860, Fort Sumter was in no condition for defense. There were but three 24-pounders mounted on the uppermost [barbette] tier. The second tier was wholly incomplete and without embrasures [openings for guns]. There was but one gun, and that for experimental purposes, yet mounted on that tier. On the lower tier, eleven 32-pounders had been mounted. The barracks for the men were unfinished, but the officers' quarters were completed and were occupied by the garrison. A large number of wooden structures crowded the parade, while all over it lay sand and rough masonry, besides sixty-six guns with their carriages and 5,600 shot and shell. The main entrance was closed by double gates secured by bars, but they were insecure and weak.

On the thirtieth of December, all communication with the city was cut off, and no supplies of any description allowed to go to the fort, the governor having declined to change or modify his order. Storm and rain now set in. For several days the fort was enveloped in fog, and under its cover and concealment work was pushed rapidly on. Major Anderson considered that in a week he would be fully prepared for any attack that might be made.

Meantime, increased activity was visible in the harbor. Small steamers with troops and laborers were passing to and fro. Men and materials were landed on Morris Island, and preparations made for remounting the guns at Fort Moultrie and strengthening its parapet toward Fort Sumter. The harbor lights on Sullivan's and Morris Islands were put out on the night of the twentieth of December, leaving the one upon Sumter and that upon the lightship in the offing the only lights in the harbor.

By taking possession of Forts Moultrie and Castle Pinckney, which were Federal property but which the Washington government had failed to garrison, South Carolina had now committed an act which could have been construed into one of war, had Buchanan so decided. He still entertained the hope, however, that open hostilities could somehow be avoided. Nevertheless, he now tried to do what could have been done without any difficulties earlier—strengthen Major Anderson's force and provision it. On December 30, 1860, General Scott requested and obtained permission to dispatch 200 to 300 men to Fort Sumter with arms, ammunition and supplies.

Dr. Crawford tells of the supply ship's arrival off Charleston.

The general in chief was satisfied that the movement could be made with the *Star of the West* without exciting suspicion. The ship was to clear for New Orleans without formal notice and as if for her regular trip. The provisions necessary were to be bought on the ship's account, so that no public agency should be used. The arms and ammunition were to be put on board the next day. Major Anderson was also informed by letter of the character and composition of the expedition on the day it sailed, and special instructions were communicated to him that, if fire be opened upon any vessel bringing reinforcements or supplies within reach of his guns, "they may be employed to silence such fire"; and he was also to act in like manner in case his fort was fired upon.

On the morning of January 5, 1861, the *Star of the West* sailed with 250 troops on board and pursued her course toward Charleston. The weather was fine, and a skilled pilot accompanied the ship. At 1:30 on the morning of the ninth she arrived off the Charleston bar. She groped in the dark until near dawn, when the solitary light at Sumter became visible. Checking her course, she steamed slowly along under careful soundings, until she arrived off the main ship channel, where she hove to, to await the dawn.

When opposite to a group of houses near the shore, a red palmetto flag was seen, and immediately and without warning a gun battery opened upon the ship. The battery was concealed amid the sand hills, and its existence had been unsuspected. Its first shot had been fired across the bow of the ship which, nevertheless, continued on its course, when a rapid and continuous fire was opened by the battery. The firing was wild and unskillful, but one spent shot struck the ship aft near the rudder, while another struck just aft the port channels, about two feet above the water line, passing through one of the guards. As soon as the battery had opened fire, a large garrison flag was run up at the fore of the vessel, lowered and again run up as a signal to Major Anderson.

The *Star of the West* had now almost passed the battery and continued her course against a strong ebb tide, up the main ship channel. She would soon be within the range of the guns of Fort Moultrie, then distant about one and a half miles. Seeing her approach, the commanding officer of that work opened at long range with four columbiads and two 32-pounders, the shots falling wildly and in all directions. Fort Sumter was silent. It was then determined, both by the officer in command of the troops and the captain of the ship, that it was impossible to reach Fort Sumter. Had she continued upon her course, she must have exposed her broadside to the direct and close fire of the entire battery of Fort Moultrie, whose fire would have been, in all probability, fatal.

Lessening her speed, she turned around, lowered her flag and, putting on all steam, headed down the channel for the bar. The strong tide carried the ship swiftly out of range.

Major Anderson thought that General Scott would not send troops except by a vessel of war, and no arrangements had been made in anticipation of such a contingency as that with which he was suddenly confronted. He was excited and uncertain about what to do. The steamer had hoisted and lowered the national flag, when the writer reported to Major Anderson that she was making signals, but our halyards had become twisted and the flag could not be used. A lieutenant called the attention of Major Anderson to Fort Moultrie and suggested firing on the battery. Major Anderson seemed for a moment to acquiesce. Then, seeing the *Star of the West* turn, he said, "Hold on, do not fire."

The flag of the country had been fired on under our very guns, and no helping hand had been extended.

Captain Abner Doubleday next describes the gloom which settled over Fort Sumter after the *Star of the West* had departed.

Everything now looked more disheartening than before. The fort itself was a deep, dark, damp, gloomy-looking place, enclosed in high walls, where the sunlight rarely penetrated. If we ascended to the parapet, we saw nothing but uncouth state flags, representing palmettos, pelicans and other strange devices. Our glasses in vain swept the horizon; the one flag we longed to see had come at last, in a timid, apologetic way, and not as a representative of the war power of the government.

It was hard to believe the government would send to us a mercantile steamer—a mere transport, utterly unfitted to contend with shore batteries—when it could have dispatched a man-of-war. As the insurgents at this period had but few field guns and a very scanty supply of cannon powder, the *Brooklyn* alone, in my opinion, could have gone straight to the wharf of Charleston and have put an end to the insurrection then and there; for we all know what its distinguished captain, David Farragut, was able to accomplish when left to his own resources.

The remaining days of January and the month of February rolled by in tense apprehension. On February 9, the newly formed Confederate States of America had chosen Jefferson Davis of Mississippi as President. The Crittenden Compromise, on which Mr. Buchanan had built his hopes for conciliation, had been voted down, and a peace conference, called by the state of Virginia as a last-minute measure to prevent war, had failed completely.

On March 4, Abraham Lincoln became President of the United States. Almost the first difficulty which he had to face was the vexing problem of Fort Sumter. Major Anderson had sent a dispatch saying that his provisions were running low and that he could hold out only a few weeks longer. In the midst of many other pressing matters, surrounded by men whose loyalty he doubted, and harassed by a horde of office seekers, Lincoln sought council with but few. General Scott advised evacuation; Captain Gustavus Fox of the Navy urged reinforcement. The Cabinet was divided as to the political wisdom of using force.

Lincoln's Secretary of the Navy, Gideon Welles, kept a diary. He was a Connecticut journalist, a former Democrat who had joined the Republican party in 1856. His judgment was sound, his honesty and loyalty unquestioned. What he wrote in his diary shows how urgent the Fort Sumter issue had become, it being almost the very first piece of business to be laid before the newly inaugurated President.

The President had been apprised of the condition of things at Sumter on the fourth of March, and a discussion took place at the first interview at the Executive Mansion. A general and very determined opinion was expressed that Fort Sumter ought to be and should be reinforced. General Scott declared this was impracticable.

The President was averse to offensive measures and anxious to avoid them. In council, and in personal interviews with myself and others, he enjoined upon each and all to forbear giving any cause of offense. He desired that General Scott should prepare a statement, how far and long the garrison could maintain itself and repel an attack, if made.

General Scott was decidedly opposed to any attempt to relieve Major Anderson. The Navy he was confident could not do it, and an army of at least 20,000 men would be necessary to effect it. We had no such army, and the government could not collect and arm one before the garrison would starve.

In the almost daily discussions which for a time were held in regard to Sumter, the opposition to forwarding supplies gathered strength. The time had gone by. It was too late. The attempt would be attended with a useless sacrifice of blood and treasure.

Postmaster General Blair took an opposite view. He warned the President that the abandonment of Sumter would be justly considered by the people, by the world, by history, as treason to the country. With the exception of Mr. Seward, all his colleagues had concurred with Mr. Blair at the commencement but, as the impossibility and inutility of the scheme was urged, with assurance from the first military men in the country that it was a military necessity to leave Sumter to its fate, our opinions changed.

> Another of Lincoln's official advisers was Edward Bates, his Attorney General. What thoughts went through his mind is revealed by the notes he made at that time.

For several days, Cabinet consultations were held as to the feasibility of relieving Fort Sumter. The Army officers and Navy officers differ widely about the degree of danger to rapid-moving vessels passing under the fire of land batteries—the Army officers think destruction almost inevitable, where the Navy officers think the danger but slight. They believe that with light, rapid vessels they can cross the bar at high tide of a dark night, run the enemy's forts and reach Sumter with little risk.

The President has required my opinion, in writing, upon the following question: "Assuming it to be possible now to provision Fort Sumter, under all the circumstances, is it wise to attempt it?"

This is not a question of lawful right nor physical risk, but of prudence and patriotism. The right in my mind is unquestionable, and I have no doubt at all that the government has the power and means not only to provision the fort, but also, if the exigency required, to man it so as to make it impregnable.

The wisdom of the act must be tested by the value of the object to be gained and by the hazard to be encountered in the enterprise. The object to be gained by the supply of provisions is not to strengthen the fortress, so as to command the harbor and enforce the laws, but only to prolong the labors and privations of the brave little garrison that has so long held it. The possession of the fort as we now hold it does not enable us to collect the revenue or enforce the laws of commerce and navigation. It may indeed involve a point of honor or a point of pride, but I do not see any great national interest involved in the bare fact of holding the fort, as we now hold it—and to hold it at all we must supply it with provisions. It seems to me that we may in humanity and patriotism safely waive the point of pride.

I am unwilling at this moment to do any act which may have the semblance of beginning a civil war, the terrible consequences of which would, I think, find no parallel in modern times.

For these reasons I am willing to evacuate Fort Sumter.

> Inside Charleston Mrs. Chesnut kept recording the daily happenings, trying in vain to hide her womanly anxiety behind items of personal and general gossip.

March 31, 1861. General Beauregard called. He is in command here and the hero of the hour. That is, he is believed to be capable of great things. A hero worshiper was struck dumb because I said: "So far, he has only been a captain of artillery or engineers or something." I did not see him. Mrs. Wigfall did and reproached my laziness in not coming out.

Last Sunday at church beheld one of the peculiar local sights, old Negro mammies going up to communion in their white turbans and kneeling devoutly around the rail.

The morning papers say Mr. Chesnut made the best shot on the island at target practice. No war yet, thank God. Likewise they tell me Mr. Chesnut has made a capital speech in the convention.

Not one word of what is going on now. "Out of the fullness of the heart the mouth speaketh," says the Psalmist. Not so here. Our hearts are in doleful dumps, but we are as gay, as madly jolly, as sailors who break into the strong-room when the ship is going down. At first in our great agony we were out alone. We longed for some of our big brothers to come out and help us. Well, they are out, too, and now it is Fort Sumter and that ill-advised Anderson. There stands Fort Sumter, *en evidence,* and thereby hangs peace or war.

After listening to the opinions of his Cabinet and his military advisers, Lincoln arrived at a decision. Fort Sumter and the men defending it would not be abandoned. On his personal orders, an expedition carrying troops and provisions was being fitted out in secret. It consisted of several ships—the *Harriet Lane,* the *Pawnee,* the *Pocahontas,* the *Baltic,* and the tugs *Uncle Ben* and *Yankee.*

The officers at Fort Sumter had been advised of the contemplated move, and the tidings had speedily spread to Charleston. Dr. Crawford, the fort's assistant surgeon, had an opportunity to observe the impression the news made on the Confederate authorities.

The *Harriet Lane* had sailed on April 8, 1861, and was the first to arrive off Charleston bar; the tugs *Uncle Ben* and *Yankee,* together with the transport *Baltic,* with the troops and material on board, went to sea on the ninth at 8:00 A.M. The *Pawnee* sailed promptly on the ninth, the *Pocahontas* only on the tenth. She was the last to sail and the last to arrive.

The intention of the President to attempt relief to Fort Sumter, made known to the authorities at Charleston, produced an effect and action immediate and decided. A telegram was at once dispatched to the Confederate Secretary of War by General Pierre G. T. Beauregard, commanding at Charleston. The receipt of the telegram gave rise to an extended discussion in the Confederate Cabinet. While it was under discussion, Robert Toombs, the Secretary of State, came in, when the telegram was handed to him. Upon reading it, he said, "The firing upon that fort will inaugurate a civil war greater than any the world has yet seen; and I do not feel competent to advise you." Reply to the telegram was delayed until the morning of the tenth, when the following dispatch was sent to General Beauregard:

If you have no doubt of the authorized character of the agent who communicated to you the intention of the Washington government to supply Fort Sumter by force, you will at once demand its evacuation and, if this is refused, proceed in such manner as you may determine to reduce it. Answer.

L. P. WALKER, Secretary of War.

To this General Beauregard immediately replied that the demand would be made at twelve o'clock upon the following day, April 11. But the authorities at Montgomery considered that, unless there were "special reasons" connected with his own condition, the demand should be made earlier. The reasons were "special," although not communicated. The supply of powder on hand was insufficient for more than a few hours' bombardment, and the commanding general was unwilling to open his batteries unless with a supply on hand to last him for forty-eight hours. Such supply had been contracted for and only arrived that evening.

The demand for the immediate surrender of the fort was now to be made with all the formality and authority of the Confederate government. Shortly after noon on the eleventh of April a boat flying a white flag pushed off from a wharf in Charleston and made its way down the harbor toward Fort Sumter. In her stern sat three men. They were: Colonel James Chesnut, recently United States Senator from South Carolina; Captain Stephen D. Lee, a graduate of West Point, who had resigned his commission in the United States Army; and Lieutenant Colonel A. R. Chisolm, an aide-de-camp and representative of the governor of the state. At half-past three the boat arrived at Fort Sumter, and its occupants were at once conducted to the guard-room, where they were met by Major Anderson in person. They bore a communication from the Confederate general to Major Anderson demanding the evacuation of the work. Believing, he said, that an amicable settlement would be reached, and to avert war, his aides were authorized to make a demand for surrender. "All proper facilities will be afforded for the removal of yourself and command, together with company arms and property, and all private property, to any post in the United States you may select. The flag which you have upheld so long, and with so much fortitude, under the most trying circumstances, may be saluted by you on taking it down." Anderson at once summoned his officers, and submitted to them the demand of the Confederate general.

The session lasted for an hour, when the following response was made by Major Anderson and handed to the messengers:

> Fort Sumter, S. C., April 11, 1861.
>
> General:
> I have the honor to acknowledge the receipt of your communication demanding the evacuation of this fort, and to say, in reply thereto, that it is a demand with which I regret that my sense of honor and of my obligations to my government, prevent my compliance. Thanking you for the fair, manly and courteous terms proposed, and for the high compliment paid me,
>
> > Robert Anderson,
> > Major First Artillery, Commanding.

The messengers at once took their leave. Anderson accompanied them as far as the main gate and remarked that he would await the first shot, but that he would be starved out anyway in a few days, if General Beauregard did not batter him to pieces with his guns. Colonel Chesnut then asked if he might report this to General Beauregard. Anderson stated it was the fact of the case. The boat then left the work.

The refusal of Anderson, as well as his oral statement as to his condition, had been promptly telegraphed to the Confederate Secretary of War. The reply was immediate, and as follows:

> Montgomery, April 11, 1861.
> General Beauregard: Do not desire needlessly to bombard Fort Sumter. If Major Anderson will state the time at which, as indicated by him, he will evacuate, and agree that in the meantime he will not use his guns against us, unless ours should be employed against Fort Sumter, you are authorized thus to avoid the effusion of blood. If this, or its equivalent, be refused, reduce the fort as your judgment decides to be most practicable.
>
> > L. P. Walker, Secretary of War.

Anderson again summoned his officers, and a long conference took place, in which all the officers took part. The principal question considered was, how long the garrison could hold out effectually with the insufficient supply of food, now beginning to be felt by the men. It was greatly desired that the fort should hold out at least until the date specified as desirable by the government, "the 15th instant." The professional opinion of the writer, which was called for by Major Anderson, was given to the effect that the men could hold out for five days, when they would have been three days entirely without food. Major Anderson replied in a written communication to the messengers, as follows:

Fort Sumter, S. C., April 12, 1861.
General: I have the honor to acknowledge the receipt by Colonel Chesnut of your second communication of the 11th instant, and to state in reply that, cordially uniting with you in the desire to avoid the useless effusion of blood, I will, if provided with the proper and necessary means of transportation, evacuate Fort Sumter by noon on the 15th instant, and that I will not in the meantime open my fires upon your forces unless compelled to do so by some hostile act against this fort or the flag of my government, by the forces under your command, or by some portion of them, or by the perpetration of some act showing a hostile intention on your part against this fort or the flag it bears, should I not receive prior to that time controlling instructions from my government or additional supplies.

ROBERT ANDERSON, Commanding

The terms of this reply were considered by the messengers as "manifestly futile." They promptly refused them and handed to Major Anderson the following notice:

Fort Sumter, April 12, 1861, 3:30 A.M.
Sir: By authority of Brigadier General Beauregard, commanding the provisional forces of the Confederate States, we have the honor to notify you that he will open the fire of his batteries on Fort Sumter in one hour from this time.

We have the honor, &c.,
CHESNUT, LEE.

The messengers now hastily took their leave. The batteries around were lighted, their fires burning brightly, as the busy hum of preparation was borne across the water to the beleaguered fort. Anderson, accompanied by his officers, then went through the casemates where the men were quartered and sleeping; he aroused them, informing them of the impending attack, and directed them not to move until they had received orders from him; that he would not open fire until daylight, and that they were then to fire slowly and carefully.

During the next days Mrs. Chesnut heard from her husband the gist of what was going on and probably surmised the rest.

April 12, 1861. Anderson will not capitulate. Yesterday's was the merriest, maddest dinner we have had yet. Men were audaciously wise and witty. We had an unspoken foreboding that it was to be our last pleasant meeting. Mrs. Henry King rushed in saying, "The news, I come for the latest news."

While she was here, our peace negotiator, or envoy, came in—that is, Mr. Chesnut returned. His interview with Mr. Anderson had been deeply interesting, but Mr. Chesnut was not inclined to be communicative. He wanted his dinner. He felt for Anderson and had telegraphed to President Davis—what answer to give Anderson, etc. He has now gone to Fort Sumter with additional instructions.

It was the last sentence in Major Anderson's reply which had upset the negotiations, after they had almost been brought to a peaceful conclusion. It was the *if* in it—"should I not receive prior to that time controlling instructions from my government or additional supplies"—which had vitiated his acceptance of the surrender terms. With the Federal fleet rapidly approaching, the Confederate authorities suspected a ruse and broke off negotiations. Open war, so much dreaded by the far-seeing men on both sides, now was only a matter of hours.

Captain Doubleday relates what happened after the expiration of the Confederate ultimatum.

As soon as the outline of our fort could be distinguished, the enemy carried out their program. The first shot came from the mortar battery at Fort Johnson. Almost immediately afterward a ball from Cummings Point lodged in the magazine wall. In a moment the firing burst forth in one continuous roar, and large patches of both the exterior and interior masonry began to crumble and fall in all directions.

Nineteen batteries were now hammering at us, and the balls and shells from the 10-inch columbiads, accompanied by shells from the 13-inch mortars which constantly bombarded us, made us feel that the war had commenced in earnest.

When it was broad daylight, I went down to breakfast. I found the officers already assembled at one of the long tables in the mess hall. Our party was calm and even somewhat merry. We had retained one colored man to wait on us. He was a spruce-looking mulatto from Charleston, now completely demoralized. He leaned back against the wall, almost white with fear, his eyes closed and his whole expression one of perfect despair. Our meal was not very sumptuous. It consisted of pork and water, but Dr. Crawford triumphantly brought forth a little farina, which he had found in a corner of the hospital.

When this frugal repast was over, my company was told off in three details for firing purposes.

In aiming the first gun fired against the Rebellion I had no feeling of self-reproach, for I fully believed that the contest had been inevitable. My first shot bounded off from the sloping roof of the battery opposite without producing any apparent effect. It seemed useless to attempt to silence the guns there, for our metal was not heavy enough to batter the work down.

Assistant Surgeon Crawford, having no sick in hospital, volunteered to take command of one of the detachments, and I soon heard his guns on the opposite side of the fort echoing my own. They attacked Fort Moultrie with great vigor. Our firing became regular, and was answered from the Rebel guns which encircled us on four sides of the pentagon upon which the fort was built. The other side faced the open sea. Showers of balls and shells poured into the fort in one incessant stream. When the immense mortar shells, after sailing high in the air, came down in a vertical direction and buried themselves in the parade ground, their explosion shook the fort like an earthquake.

If Mrs. Chesnut had still been hoping for peace, she was quickly disillusioned.

April 12, 1861. I do not pretend to go to sleep. How can I? If Anderson does not accept terms at four, the orders are, he shall be fired upon. I count four, St. Michael's bells chime out and I begin to hope. At half-past four the heavy booming of a cannon. I sprang out of bed, and on my knees prostrate I prayed as I never prayed before.

There was a sound of stir all over the house, pattering of feet in the corridors. All seemed hurrying one way. I put on my double-gown and a shawl and went, too. It was to the housetop. The shells were bursting. In the dark I heard a man say, "Waste of ammunition." I knew my husband was rowing about in a boat somewhere in that dark bay, and that the shells were roofing it over, bursting toward the fort. If Anderson was obstinate, Colonel Chesnut was to open fire. Certainly fire had begun. The regular roar of the cannon, there it was. And who could tell what each volley accomplished of death and destruction?

The women were wild there on the housetop. Prayers came from them, and imprecations from the men. And then a shell would light up the scene. Tonight they say the forces are to attempt to land. We watched up there, and everybody wondered that Fort Sumter did not fire a shot.

Pryor, of Virginia, spoke from the piazza of the Charleston Hotel. I asked what he said. An irreverent woman replied: "Oh, they all say the same thing, but he made great play with that long hair of his, which he is always tossing aside!"

Somebody came in just now and reported Colonel Chesnut asleep on the sofa in General Beauregard's room. After two such nights he must be so tired as to be able to sleep anywhere.

> General Beauregard, who was a skillful and fluent writer, has left us his own story of the events which ushered in the War Between the States.

My men and I were ready. We had been most zealously and effectively assisted by the South Carolina authorities, and one thing only remained to be attended to, and that was the placing in position of a small Blakely rifled gun, the first ever used in America. It had just arrived from England.

At 2:00 P.M., April 11, through my aides, Captain S. D. Lee, Colonel James Chesnut, Jr., and Lieutenant Colonel A. R. Chisolm, I made a formal demand for the immediate surrender of Fort Sumter.

But Major Anderson would not consent. In consequence of which, after timely notice had been given to him, we opened fire on April 12, at 4:30 A.M.

The peaceful stillness of the night was broken just before dawn. From Fort Johnson's mortar battery, at 4:30 A.M., April 12, 1861, issued the first—and, as many thought, the too-long-deferred—signal shell of the war. It was fired, not by Mr. Edmund Ruffin, of Virginia, as has been erroneously believed, but by George S. James, of South Carolina, to whom Captain Stephen D. Lee issued the order. It sped aloft, describing its peculiar arc of fire and, bursting over Fort Sumter, fell, with crashing noise, in the very center of the parade.

Thus was "reveille" sounded in Charleston and its harbor on this eventful morning. In an instant all was bustle and activity. Not an absentee was reported at roll call. The citizens poured down to the battery and the wharves, and women and children crowded each window of the houses overlooking the sea—rapt spectators of the scene. At ten minutes before five o'clock, all the batteries and mortars which encircled the grim fortress were in full play against it.

Round after round had already been fired; and yet, for nearly two hours, not a shot in response had come from Fort Sumter. Had Major Anderson been taken by surprise? Or was it that, certain of his ability to pass unscathed through the onslaught thus made upon him, it mattered not how soon or how late he committed his flag? At last, however, near seven o'clock, the United States flag having previously been raised, the sound of a gun, not ours, was distinctly heard. Sumter had taken up the gage of battle, and Cummings Point had first attracted its attention. It was almost a relief to our troops—for gallantry ever admires gallantry, and a worthy foe disdains one who makes no resistance.

The action was now general and was so maintained throughout the day, with vigor on both sides. Our guns were served with admirable spirit, and the accuracy of our range was made evident by the clouds of dust that flew as our balls struck the fort and by the indentations hollowed in its walls. The precision with which solid shot and shells were thrown from our batteries, mainly Fort Moultrie, was such that the enemy was soon compelled to abandon the use of his barbette guns, several of which had been dismounted in the early part of the bombardment.

The ironclad battery at Cummings Point, Fort Moultrie proper, and that end of Sullivan's Island where the floating battery, the Dahlgren gun, and the enfilade or masked battery had been placed were the points which attracted Major Anderson's heaviest firing. No better proof could he have given us of the effects of our fire on his fort. An occasional shot only was aimed at Fort Johnson, as if to remind the battery there that the explosion of its first shell was not yet forgiven. Captain Butler's mortar battery, east of Moultrie, had also a share of the enemy's wrath.

The engagement was continued with unceasing vigor until nightfall, although Sumter's fire had evidently slackened before that time.

During the whole night which followed, in spite of rain and darkness, our batteries continued playing upon the fort with unvarying effect, but the shots were fired at longer intervals, in obedience to orders. It was estimated that over 2,500 shot and shell struck the fort during the first twenty-four hours.

It was expected that the Federal fleet would arrive that night and might attempt to throw troops, ammunition and supplies into Fort Sumter. To guard against such an untoward event, the keenest watchfulness was observed at our beach batteries and by the forces on Morris and Sullivan's islands. The details of men at the Drummond lights were also on the alert and ready at a moment's notice to illuminate the channels; while our cruising vessels actively patrolled the outer harbor. The fleet arrived on the morning of the thirteenth, an hour or two after the action had been renewed, but remained spectators off the bar.

Very early on that morning, all our batteries reopened on the enemy, who responded with vigor for a while, concentrating his fire almost exclusively on Fort Moultrie. The presence of the fleet outside the bar, now visible to all, no doubt inspired both officers and men of the garrison with additional courage and a renewed spirit of endurance.

Major Anderson with his officers and men did hold out; their flag was flying on the twelfth of April, and again on the thirteenth; and they were fighting in all earnest. The fleet outside thought proper, nevertheless, to abstain from all participation in the engagement.

The twelfth of April had gone by without bloodshed, and Mrs. Chesnut breathed a sigh of relief.

April 13, 1861. Nobody has been hurt at all. How gay we were last night. Reaction after the dread of all the slaughter we thought those dreadful cannon were making. Not even a battery worse for wear. Fort Sumter has been on fire. Anderson has not yet silenced any of our guns. So the aides, still with swords and red sashes by way of uniform, tell us. But the sound of those guns make regular meals impossible. None of us go to table. Tea trays pervade the corridors going everywhere. Some of the anxious hearts lie on their beds and moan in solitary misery. Mrs. Wigfall and I solace ourselves with tea in my room. These women have all a satisfying faith. "God is on our side," they say. When we are shut in, Mrs. Wigfall and I ask, "Why?" "Of course, He hates the Yankees," we are told.

Not by one word or look can we detect any change in the demeanor of our Negro servants. Lawrence sits at our door, sleepy and respectful, and profoundly indifferent. So are they all, but they carry it too far. You could not tell they even heard the awful roar going on in the bay though it has been dinning in their ears night and day. People talk before them as if they were chairs and tables. They make no sign. Are they stolidly stupid? Or wiser than we are? Silent and strong, biding their time?

The war steamers are still there, outside the bar. And there are people who thought the Charleston bar "no good" to Charleston. The bar is the silent partner, or sleeping partner, and in this fray it is doing us yeoman service.

All this time the bombardment was continuing, and Captain Doubleday reports its effect on the fort.

After three hours' firing my men became exhausted, and Captain Seymour came with a fresh detachment to relieve us. He said, jocosely, "Doubleday, what in the world is the matter here, and what is all this uproar about?"

I replied, "There is a trifling difference of opinion between us and our neighbors opposite, and we are trying to settle it."

Part of the fleet was visible outside the bar about half past 10:00 A.M. It exchanged salutes with us but did not attempt to enter the harbor or to take part in the battle.

For the next three hours a vigorous fire was kept up on both sides. A great many shots were aimed at our flagstaff, but nearly all of them passed above the fort and struck in the water beyond.

I regretted very much that the upper tier of guns had been abandoned, as they were all loaded and pointed and were of very heavy caliber. A wild Irish soldier, however, named John Carmody, slipped up on the parapet and, without orders, fired the pieces there, one after another, on his own account. One of the 10-inch balls so aimed made quite an impression on the Cummings Point battery and, if the fire could have been kept up, it might possibly have knocked the ironwork to pieces.

To my great astonishment the battery I had left recommenced firing. I could not imagine who could have taken our places. A group of workmen had been watching our motions and had thus learned the duties of a cannoneer. They could not resist the fun of trying their hand at one of the guns. We soon had them organized into a firing party.

The firing continued all through the twelfth of April, without any special incident of importance, and without our making much impression on the enemy's works. They had a great advantage over us, as their fire was concentrated on the fort, which was in the center of the circle, while ours was diffused over the circumference. Their missiles were exceedingly destructive to the upper portion of the work, but no essential injury was done to the lower casements which sheltered us.

Some of these shells, however, set the officers' quarters on fire three times; but the flames were promptly extinguished once or twice.

The night was an anxious one for us, for it was possible that the enemy might attempt an attack. We were on the alert, therefore, with men stationed at all the embrasures; but nothing unusual occurred. The batteries fired upon us at stated intervals all night long. We did not return the fire, having no ammunition to waste.

On the morning of the thirteenth, we took our breakfast—or rather our pork and water—at the usual hour, and marched the men to the guns when the meal was over.

About 8:00 A.M. the officers' quarters were ignited by shot heated in the furnaces at Fort Moultrie. The fire was put out; but at 10:00 A.M. a mortar shell passed through the roof and started the flames afresh. This, too, was extinguished; but the hot shots soon followed each other so rapidly that it was impossible for us to contend with them. It became evident that the entire block, being built with wooden partitions, floors and roofing, must be consumed, and that the magazine, containing 300 barrels of powder, would be endangered.

While the officers exerted themselves with axes to tear down and cut away all the woodwork in the vicinity, the soldiers were rolling barrels of powder out to more sheltered spots and were covering them with wet blankets. We only succeeded in getting out some ninety-six barrels of powder and then were obliged to close the massive copper door and await the result. A shot soon after passed through the intervening shield, struck the door and bent the lock in such a way that it could not be opened again. We were cut off from our supply of ammunition but still had some piled up in the vicinity of the guns.

By 11:00 A.M. on April thirteenth, the conflagration was terrible and disastrous. One-fifth of the fort was on fire, and the wind drove the smoke in dense masses into the angle where we had all taken refuge. It seemed impossible to escape suffocation. Some lay down close to the ground, with handkerchiefs over their mouths, and others posted themselves near the embrasures, where the smoke was somewhat lessened by the draught of air. Had not a slight change of wind taken place, the result might have been fatal to most of us.

I thought it would be as well to show that we were not all dead yet and ordered the gunners to fire a few rounds more. I heard afterward that the enemy loudly cheered Anderson for his persistency under such adverse circumstances.

The scene at this time was really terrific. The roaring and crackling of the flames, the dense masses of smoke, the bursting of the enemy's shells, and our own which were exploding in the burning rooms, the crashing of the shot and the sound of masonry falling in every direction made the fort a pandemonium. When at last nothing was left of the building but the blackened walls and smoldering embers, it became painfully evident that an immense amount of damage had been done. There was a tower at each angle of the fort. One of these, containing great quantities of shells, upon which we had relied, was almost completely shattered by successive explosions. The massive wooden gates, studded with iron nails, were burned, and the wall built behind them was now a mere heap of debris, so that the main entrance was wide open for an assaulting party. The sally ports were in a similar condition, and the numerous windows on the gorge side, which had been planked up, had now all become open entrances.

About 12:48 P.M. the end of the flagstaff was shot down, and the flag fell. The exultation of the enemy, however, was short-lived. One of our men found a spar in the fort, which answered very well as a temporary flagstaff.

General Beauregard noted the steady disintegration of the fort's defenses. The fire which had broken out within its walls prompted the Confederate commander to make a chivalrous offer to his enemy.

At about 8:00 A.M. on April 13, in the thickest of the bombardment, a thin smoke was observable, curling up from Fort Sumter. It grew denser and denser as it steadily rose in the air; and it soon became apparent that the barracks of the fort had been set on fire by forty rounds of red-hot shot, thrown from an 8-inch columbiad at Fort Moultrie. This sight increased the vigor of our attack; both officers and men feeling now that the garrison would soon be brought to terms. In spite, however, of this new and terrible element against which it had to contend, the fort still responded to the fire of our batteries, though at long and irregular intervals only.

Appreciating the critical position of the enemy, and carried away by their own enthusiasm, our troops, mounting the parapets in their front, cheered Major Anderson at each successive discharge that came from the fort, deriding and hooting, the while, what to them seemed the timorous inaction of the fleet outside the bar.

Matters had evidently reached a crisis for the men within the walls of Sumter. Fearing that some terrible calamity might befall them, and being informed that the United States flag no longer floated over the fort, I immediately dispatched three of my aides with offers of assistance to Major Anderson, who thanked me for my courtesy but declined to accept aid. Before the aides could get to the fort, the United States flag, which had not been hauled down, as we supposed, but had fallen from the effects of a shot, was hoisted anew.

Dr. Crawford now records the final hours of the doomed fort.

The Confederate general had noticed the absence of the flag and the burning of the quarters and had sent officers to offer assistance. Anderson declined and determined to reopen his batteries. But he was persuaded to postpone any such action until General Beauregard could be advised of the terms to which he would consent. Meantime, he reduced to writing the terms upon which he would evacuate the fort and sent them to General Beauregard by Captain S. D. Lee, one of the aides.

The formal and final terms agreed to were presented to Anderson by some messengers from General Beauregard at 7:00 P.M., April 13, in regard to which Anderson expressed his gratification; and it was arranged that he should leave in the morning, after communicating with the fleet, but that he must be responsible for the fort in the meantime, as otherwise four companies of artillery would be ordered there. The fort was a scene of ruin and destruction. For thirty-four hours it had sustained a bombardment from seventeen 10-inch mortars and heavy guns, well placed and well served. The quarters and barracks were in ruins. The main gates and the planking of the windows on the gorge were gone; the magazines closed and surrounded by smoldering flames and burning ashes; the provisions exhausted; much of the engineering work destroyed and the cartridges gone.

With only four barrels of powder available, the command at last yielded to the inevitable.

General Beauregard, who had known that the eventual fall of Fort Sumter was inevitable, showed no elation when the anticipated event became an accomplished fact, and exhibited gentle-manly restraint in his written account.

The flag over Fort Sumter at last was lowered, and a white flag sub-stituted for it. The contest was over. Major Anderson had acknowl-edged his defeat.

While final arrangements were being made for the withdrawal of the garrison, and before it was effected, I ordered a company of Regulars with two fire engines from Sullivan's Island, to repair to Fort Sumter, to put out the conflagration which, not entirely subdued, had broken out afresh. This was a harder task than was at first supposed. The two en-gines proved insufficient, and others had to be brought from Charleston with additional firemen. It was only toward dawn that the fire was at last brought under control, and the powder magazine secured from explosion.

Owing to unavoidable delays resulting from the state of confusion existing in the fort, its formal transfer to our troops did not take place until four o'clock in the afternoon on Sunday, the fourteenth of April. At that hour Major Anderson and his command marched out of the work, and we entered it, taking final possession. Then it was that, amid deafening cheers and with an enthusiastic salute from the guns of all the batteries around the harbor, the Confederate and the Palmetto flags were hoisted side by side on the damaged ramparts of the fort.

Mrs. Chesnut recorded her last remarks on Fort Sumter in her diary on April 15.

April 15. I did not know that one could live through such days of excitement. Someone called: "Come out! There is a crowd coming." A mob it was, indeed, but it was headed by Colonels Chesnut and Man-ning. The crowd was shouting and showing these two as messengers of good news. They were escorted to Beauregard's headquarters. Fort Sumter had surrendered!

The tragedy which was being enacted in Charleston Harbor was relieved now and then by a ray of humor. One such inci-dent is related by Captain Doubleday and concerns Colonel Roger A. Pryor, one of General Beauregard's emissaries to Major Anderson.

Almost a fatal accident occurred to Roger A. Pryor shortly after his arrival in the fort. He was sitting in the hospital at a table, with a black bottle and a tumbler near his right hand. The place was quite dark, having been built up all around with boxes of sand to render it shell-proof. Being thirsty and not noticing what he did, he mechanically picked up the bottle, poured some of the liquid into a glass and drank it down. It proved to be iodide of potassium, which is a poisonous compound. When I saw him, he was very pale, leaning on the shoulder of Dr. Crawford, who was taking him out on the grass to apply the stomach pump. He was soon out of danger. Some of us questioned the doctor's right to interpose in a case of this kind. It was argued that if any Rebel leader chose to come over to Fort Sumter and poison himself, the Medical Department had no business to interfere. The doctor, however, claimed that he himself was held responsible to the United States for the medicines in the hospital, and therefore he could not permit Pryor to carry any of it away.

What were the men of the United States Navy doing while their comrades inside Fort Sumter were battling against overwhelming odds?

Captain Gustavus Fox, who had conceived and accompanied the expedition, and who had been so sure that his vessels "could reach Sumter with little risk," made a short and rather cryptic statement regarding the Navy's action, or lack of action. It sounded much less heroic than his boasting forecast.

As we neared the land, heavy guns were heard, and the smoke and shells from the batteries which had just opened fire on Sumter were distinctly visible. I immediately stood out to inform Captain Rowan of the *Pawnee* but met him coming in. He hailed me and asked for a pilot, declaring his intention of standing into the harbor and sharing the fate of his brethren of the Army. I informed him that the government did not expect any such gallant sacrifice, having settled maturely upon the policy indicated by the instructions to Captain Mercer [commanding the expedition] and myself.

Horace Greeley, editor of the *New York Tribune*, made this colorless comment:

The fleet from New York, laden with provisions for the garrison, had appeared off the bar by noon of the day on which fire was opened but made no effort to fulfill its errand. To have attempted to supply the fort would have, at best, involved a heavy cost of life, probably to no purpose. Its commander communicated by signals with Major Anderson, but remained out of range of the enemy's fire till after the surrender, when he returned as he had come.

One of the active defenders of Fort Sumter condensed his criticism into two short sentences.

On Friday, before dinner, several of the vessels of the fleet, beyond the bar, were seen through the portholes. *They dipped their flag. The commander ordered Sumter's flag to be dipped in return.*

Immediately after the fall of Fort Sumter Lincoln issued a proclamation, commanding the people of the seceded states (which by now numbered seven) to disperse and return peacefully to their homes within twenty days. Simultaneously, he issued a call for 75,000 militia; as a result, four more states soon afterward joined the Confederacy.

Both sides considered the proclamation a declaration of war, and began to prepare for it.

On the outskirts of Washington, hundreds of miles away from Fort Sumter, lived another Southern lady who kept a diary. The secret fears and sorrows which she confided to it were probably shared by untold numbers of women throughout the South.

May 4, 1861. Everything is broken up. The Seminary is closed; the High School dismissed. Scarcely anyone is left of the many families which surrounded us. The homes all look desolate; and yet this beautiful country is looking more peaceful, more lovely than ever. We are left lonely indeed; our children are all gone—the girls where they may be safer, and the boys, the dear, dear boys, to the camp, to be drilled. Can it be that our country is to be carried on and on to the horrors of civil war? I shut my eyes and hold my breath when the thought of what may come upon us obtrudes itself, and yet I cannot believe it. The taking of Sumter without bloodshed has somewhat soothed my fears, though I am told by those who are wiser than I that men must fall on both sides by the score, by the hundred and even by the thousand.

Today our house seems so deserted. I go from room to room, looking first at one thing and then another. The closed piano, the locked book-case, the nicely arranged tables, the formally placed chairs, ottomans and sofas in the parlor! Oh, for someone to put them out of order! And the dinner table looked so cheerless today, as we seated ourselves one at the head, the other at the foot.

I heard distinctly the drums beating in Washington. As I looked at the Capitol in the distance, I could scarcely believe my senses. That Capitol of which I had always been so proud! Can it be possible that it is no longer *our* Capitol? Must this Union, which I was taught to revere, be rent asunder?

CHAPTER 2

America Girds for War

HOW AMERICA'S YOUTH JOINED THE COLORS

What induced the boys of America to join the colors when the tocsin sounded? Here is the story of one Massachusetts soldier named John D. Billings, who, looking back to the beginning of hostilities long after the war fever had worn off, tells us what prompted him to volunteer for service.

Young Billings, as a member of the state militia, was not an entire stranger to military ideas; yet, when the call to arms came, he was shaken by conflicting emotions.

War, that much talked-of, much dreaded calamity, was at last upon us. Could it really be so? We would not believe it; and yet daily happenings forced the unwelcome conclusion upon us.

The Governor of Massachusetts had told the militia to hold themselves in readiness to respond to a call by the President, or else resign, and this order caused the more timid to withdraw from the militia at once. A great many more would have withdrawn had they not been restrained by pride and the lingering hope that there would be no war after all. This was the final test of the militiamen's actual courage and thirst for glory, and a severe one it proved, for at this eleventh hour there was another falling out along the line. But the moment a man's declination for further service was made known, he was hooted at for his cowardice, and for a time his existence was made quite unpleasant in his own immediate neighborhood.

Possessing an average amount of the fire and enthusiasm of youth, I asked my father's consent to go. But he would not give ear to any such "nonsense," and, having been brought up to obey his orders, although of military age (eighteen years), I did not enter the service in the first rally.

31

The methods by which these regiments were raised were various. In 1861 a common way was for someone who had been in the regular army to take the initiative and circulate an enlistment paper for signatures. His chances were pretty good for obtaining a commission as its captain.

War meetings were designed to stir lagging enthusiasm. Musicians and orators blew themselves red in the face with their windy efforts. Choirs sang "Red, White, and Blue" and "Rallied 'Round the Flag" till too hoarse for further endeavor. The old veteran soldier of 1812 was trotted out and worked for all he was worth, and an occasional Mexican War veteran would air his nonchalance at grim-visaged war. At proper intervals the enlistment roll would be presented for signatures. There was generally one old fellow present who, upon slight provocation, would yell like a hyena and declare his readiness to shoulder his musket and go, if he wasn't so old, while his staid and half-fearful consort would pull violently at his coattails to repress his unreasonable effervescence ere it assumed more dangerous proportions. Then there was a patriotic maiden lady who kept a flag or a handkerchief waving with only the rarest and briefest of intervals, who "would go in a minute if she was a man." Besides these there was usually a man who said he would enlist if fifty others did likewise, when he well understood that such a number could not be obtained. And there was one more often found present who, when challenged to sign, would agree to, *provided* that A or B (men of wealth) would put down *their* names.

Sometimes the patriotism of such a gathering would be wrought up so intensely by waving banners, martial and vocal music and burning eloquence, that a town's quota would be filled in less than an hour. It needed only the first man to step forward, put down his name, be patted on the back, placed upon the platform and cheered to the echo as the hero of the hour, when a second, a third, a fourth would follow, and at last a perfect stampede set in to sign the enlistment roll. A frenzy of enthusiasm would take possession of the meeting. The complete intoxication of such excitement, like intoxication from liquor, left some of its victims (especially if the fathers of families), on the following day, with sober second thoughts to wrestle with; but Pride, that tyrannical master, rarely let them turn back.

After enlistment, what? The responsibility of the citizen for himself ceased. From then on Uncle Sam had him in charge.

Conditions in the seceded states were not much different from those prevailing in the North. A young man who enrolled in the Southern army tells about the impact of Lincoln's proclamation on the people of his home town.

In the first place let me observe, that prior to the proclamation of April 1861, in which President Lincoln warned us "to disperse to our homes in thirty [twenty] days," there were many who fondly expected that common sense would rule in the councils of the North, and that the Government would not force a war upon their "brethren" of the South. We were all mistaken; and when the proclamation was read on the bulletin boards of the telegraph offices, crowds perused the document with roars of laughter.

At the first whisper of war among these excited crowds, a hundred youths repaired to a lawyer's office, drew up a muster-roll, inscribed their names for twelve months' service, and began drilling in a concert hall. Subscriptions for arms and accoutrements began to pour in, and an emissary was dispatched Northwards post haste to get these requisites. Many among us having studied at military or semi-military colleges, the details of infantry drill were perfectly understood, so that squads were quickly placed at the command of striplings. Muskets, formerly used for holiday parades, were immediately appropriated. Banners of costly material were made by clubs of patriotic young ladies, and delivered to the companies with appropriate speeches; the men on such occasions swearing that they would perish rather than desert the flag thus consecrated.

New York City at first was slow in entering the martial arena, and some rather quaint measures had to be employed to stimulate the masses. Le Grand B. Cannon, a Union soldier who evidently had had a hand in the affair, remembered it with gusto.

Lincoln's call was received coldly in New York. The day after not a flag was visible, and there was no public response.

A few patriotic men met to determine what action should be taken. It was decided to send for a prominent politician, who had a large following in the lower wards of the city. He was to collect stevedores, laborers and people from about the docks, get a fife and drum and an American flag, and march in procession from the Battery up Broadway.

This was done. The procession immediately attracted great attention. At the top of Wall Street forty or fifty gentlemen joined. The effect was electrical. In immensely augmented numbers the procession started for the *Journal* of *Commerce* office. A demand was made that the American flag be displayed. The flag was hung out. Then the procession started for the office of the *Herald*, a dense mass of cheering enthusiasts. Within twenty-four hours the flag was flying from every church steeple, and the whole place was ablaze with patriotic enthusiasm.

Thus was the loyal sentiment of New York City aroused.

Many young men allowed an emotional wave to sweep them into the army, but while they knew that they were going to fight, very few knew why. A Frenchman, residing in the North, analyzed the situation and cited the arguments of both sides in a detached manner.

The Constitution, said the South, recognizes slavery, which is the base of our social and political organization.—No, cried the North, we tolerate slavery where it exists, but we contend against introducing it in the territories which are free.—Our fathers, said the South, founded a Union of sovereign states based upon self-government. We make use of our right, and we dissolve the Union.—The Union, replied the North, is based upon the perpetual renunciation by the states of certain rights of sovereignty. You have no right to dissolve the Union. —Above all, proclaimed the South, we owe allegiance to our respective States.—Above all, proclaimed the North, we owe allegiance to the Federal government.

Not all the men joined the Army under the pressure of public opinion. There lived in Illinois a Dr. Willis Danforth, father of two children, who left his family and his practice under the spur of pure patriotism and at great personal sacrifice.

When the war commenced in April 1861, I was anxious to go at once to the front, but Illinois put only ten regiments into the field, and I could not get into these and so waited until General Nathaniel Lyon was killed at Wilson's Creek, Missouri, some time in August of that year. This so affected me that I could not sleep nights. I felt that our cause and country would be lost if I did not go, and that, too, immediately. I wrote to my wife, who was twenty miles away on a visit, that I had laid down the lancet and taken up the sword; that if she wanted to see me, she must come quick.

General Frémont was in command at St. Louis, the Union arms were driven back from almost every field, the sky was black with death and destruction to our cause. Illinois was not raising any troops. I was practicing medicine in Joliet, Illinois, had just been expending my last dollar in assisting my brothers in Kansas to make that a free state and was in poor condition to leave my wife and two children, the elder eight years old, with no visible means of support. However, my country was bigger than my family, so I went to St. Louis to see General Frémont on September 1, 1861. I had been told it would take a week to get an audience of the general.

Nothing daunted I presented myself before headquarters, and as the guard passed the iron gate I slipped through. In a moment more I was at the general's desk, got a commission as captain of cavalry—there being no opening for a surgeon—advised General Frémont how to ration and handle his men in a better manner than he was doing and was on the *outside* in one hour from the time of running the guard.

Sometimes a volunteer recruit found it difficult to join the colors of his own choosing. A Kentucky youth, L. D. Young by name, wanted to wear the Confederate gray, but encountered some obstacles.

My history as a *real* soldier begins on September 8, 1861. I was almost twenty years old, but had been a soldier almost two years, being a charter member of that little band of Sunday soldiers—the Flat Rock Grays—which constituted an integral part of what was known at the time as the Kentucky State Guard.

This little company of citizen soldiers were in their conceit very important fellows. Invited to all gatherings and public affairs, dressed in gaudy and flashy uniforms and flying plumes, they did not know they were nursing their pride against the day of wrath.

The sixth of September found me in Paris, Kentucky, where I began preparations for the life of a soldier by substituting my pumps for brogans, which I knew would be more suitable for a soldier on the march. By night I had made my way to Louisville, a shy, cringing guest at the old Louisville Hotel, my brogans giving me more concern than anything else, being in such striking contrast to my claw-hammer broadcloth and gold buttons. Morning came, and, going up to the office, I began to turn the leaves of the register; imagine my surprise when I read the names of Generals W. T. Sherman, L. H. Rousseau, Major Anderson of Fort Sumter fame and other Federal officers.

But my fears were intensified when a gentleman put his hand on my shoulder and asked me to a corner of the room. Noticing my look of fear and trepidation, he said, "Compose yourself, young man, I *am* your friend—the shoes you wear lead me to believe you are aiming to go South to join the Confederates." I ventured to ask his name, which he readily gave me as Captain Coffee of Tennessee. Continuing, he said, "The train that leaves here this morning will likely be the last for the state line and they have guards to examine all passengers, so secure your ticket and go to the rear of the train. Take the first vacant seat and for heaven's sake, if possible, hide your brogans."

I secured the rear seat and attempted to hide my brogans. The train guards were busy examining passengers and their baggage. My heart almost leaped from my bosom as they came down the aisle. But just before they reached the rear of the car the bell rang and the train started. The guards rushed for the door, leaving me unquestioned and unmolested.

That evening I joined my schoolboy friends and soldier comrades, the Flat Rock Grays, in Camp Burnett, Tennessee.

> Here is the queer story of S. H. M. Byers, a young Iowa lawyer, who had no intention of turning soldier, yet was the first one to enlist in his home regiment.

It all came about through a confusion of names. A patriotic mass meeting was held in the courthouse of the village. Everybody was there, and everybody was excited. A new regiment had been ordered by the governor, and no town was so quick in responding as the village where I lived. Drums were beating at the mass meeting, fifes screaming, people shouting. I sat beside a Mr. Myers, one of our prominent citizens. There was a little pause in the patriotic noise, and then someone called out, "Myers to the platform!" Mr. Myers never stirred. Again the voice shouted, "Myers! Myers!" Myers turned to me and said, "They are calling you, Byers," and fairly pushed me out into the aisle.

I was young—just twenty-two—ambitious and now was all on fire with newly awakened patriotism. I went up to the platform and stood by the big drum. The American flag was hanging over my head. In a few minutes I was full of the mental champagne that comes from a cheering multitude. I was burning with excitement, with patriotism, pride and my enthusiasm lent power to the words I uttered. I don't know why nor how, but I was moving my audience.

The year before I had been on a plantation in Mississippi, and there had seen human beings flogged. Now in my excitement I pictured it all. "And the war, they tell us," I cried, "is to perpetuate this curse!" In ten minutes one hundred youths and men, myself the first, had stepped up to the paper lying on the big drum and had put down our names for the war.

Among the inducements which made men enlist, one of the most curious is told by a Southern farmer, one of whose neighbors found convincing reasons (at least convincing to himself) to join first one side and then the other.

Not far from us lived a family, father and two sons. The father was among the first to volunteer in the Southern Army and fight for his "rights," although he was utterly impecunious, having no Negroes or much of anything else. He was captured, paroled and sent home until exchanged. The Federal Army came near, and his two sons, then at man's estate, went down to the Union camp to see how things looked. They met friends there and were bountifully fed upon crackers and coffee. This last was a luxury of which they had long been deprived. They actually enlisted to get plenty of coffee and grub. When the old man heard of this performance, he started for the camp to get his sons out of the scrape. He got in, got some of that good coffee, enlisted for the war and fought it through with his two sons on the Union side.

Although, generally speaking, public opinion was as strong in the South as elsewhere, the reasons which kept her fighting gradually underwent a change; for the South soon became an invaded country, and her sons were inspired by the resolve to protect their homes and families.

This is how Carlton McCarthy, Confederate soldier and patriot, analyzed the incentives which made him and his comrades sacrifice themselves for their cause.

No man can exactly define the cause for which the Confederate soldier fought. He was above human reason and above human law, secure in his own rectitude of purpose. He dared not refuse to hear the call to arms, so plain was the duty and so urgent the call. His brethren and friends were answering the bugle call and the roll of the drum. To stay behind was dishonor and shame.

The Confederate soldier fought the cries of distress which came from his home—tales of woe, want, insult and robbery. He fought men who knew that *their* homes were safe, *their* wives and children sheltered.

The Confederate soldier was purely patriotic. He foresaw clearly and deliberately chose the trials which he endured. He was an individual who could not become the indefinite portion of a mass but fought for himself, on his own account. He fought for a principle and needed neither driving nor urging, but was eager and determined to fight.

The Confederate soldier was a monomaniac for four years. His mania was the independence of the Confederate States of America, secured by force of arms. He would not receive as gospel the dogmas of fanatics, and so he became a "Rebel." Being a Rebel, he must be punished. Being punished, he resisted. Resisting, he died.

In spite of all the noisy clamor of the recruiting platform, it was soon apparent that enthusiasm alone was not going to win battles. A multitude of peaceful citizens, farmers, clerks, mechanics and professional men had to be laboriously transformed into soldiers. Training camps sprang up everywhere.

The stories of all these camps were very much alike, and are well illustrated by the early experiences of the 36th Illinois Volunteers, a regiment known in its early days as the Young American Guards.

Mostly composed of farmers in the Fox River Valley, the volunteers were slowly turned into soldiers, and two members of the regiment, L. G. Bennett and William M. Haigh, describe the process.

The Young American Guards arrived upon the ground Saturday, August 18, 1861, being the first company in camp.

The Bristol Company was next in the order of its arrival and went into camp August 20, the Guards forming in line and according the men from Kendall County as gallant a reception as the circumstances would allow. Later in the day, the Wayne Rifles, the Oswego Rifles and the Elgin Guards put in an appearance, each preceded by the squeaking of fifes, the clangor of drums, the shout and hurrah of citizens and accompanied by little less than a brigade of anxious mothers, staid and sober fathers, devoted wives, fidgety sisters and forlorn-looking sweethearts.

But, as the declining sun began to throw a halo over camp and field, painful goodbys were said. The men then set to work with a will; tents went up as if by magic; a limited number of blankets were distributed; a meager supply of straw produced bedding; and rations, consisting of bread, beef, bacon and coffee, were issued to the men, who essayed, man fashion, to cook and eat their first meal in camp. Some of the beef passed through a cooking with little of the smell of fire about it, while huge slices of others were burned to a crisp; but whether raw or roasted, it finally went the way of all victuals, seasoned with some honest growls.

This first night in camp will doubtless long be remembered by many. Few of the men had ever before experienced the luxury of a couch of straw, or the thrilling pleasure of reclining upon the bare bosom of Mother Earth. It seemed lonely with but a thin sheet of cotton cloth between yourself and the sky, but the few who lay down to quiet rest were cruelly defrauded. Some rough from an obscure corner would give a tremendous "Baa!" Another from an adjoining tent would respond, then the chorus would be taken up along the line of tents from all parts of camp, and in ten seconds from the first yelp the whole crowd would be "baaing" with the force of a thousand calf power.

Again the lonely bark of a dog would start some human poodle in camp to bark response, and then the whole pack would take up the refrain until they had barked themselves hoarse. Then there were cat voices, turkey gobblings and cock crowings ad libitum. So it went until daylight. Few slept, some laughed, others swore, and thus the night wore away.

Next afternoon, a United States mustering officer appeared and administered the oath to the companies then in camp. It was a grand sight to see company after company, with hands uplifted to heaven, solemnly consecrate themselves to the protection and the preservation of the country. No cat squalls or cock crowing then.

The company from Elgin was particularly admired for the soldierly bearing and generally fine appearance of the men. Their officer had read up in Hardee's *Manual of Arms*. Therefore they were comparatively well drilled and had already acquired that stiffness of vertebra which the others had yet to learn. Their arms were old-fashioned rusty muskets, a sort of a cross between a cannon and a liberty pole, that had been plundered from the armory of some defunct militia company, and which they came lugging into camp very much after the fashion a person would carry a fence rail. These blunderbusses excited intense disgust in the recruits, who had been dreaming of Sharp's or Henry rifles with saber bayonets. And it was quite generally remarked that if these were a sample of what was to be our armament, our arrival in Dixie would be hailed with delight by the Johnny Rebs, for it was believed that those guns would kick further than they would shoot and were infinitely more dangerous to friend than foe.

At first our tents were scattered promiscuously, but the colonel terminated this unmilitary jumble by referring us to Hardee for instructions. The tents were taken down and put up as directed by that fascinating writer. The habitations provided were square wall tents, large and airy, and when finally arranged presented a romantic appearance, like some well-laid-out rural village, nestling like a flock of swans upon the green prairie.

The details of camp life were full of interest. The evolutions of a thousand men on drill or parade, the music of the band at reveille or tattoo, were calculated to make them fall in love with a vocation apparently full of charms. After a time the incessant drill, and standing guard beneath a broiling sun or in a drenching rain storm, washing greasy dishes, scouring rusty knives, cooking and eating stale beef, and at night wallowing down to sleep ten in a tent, pretty effectually took the romance out of camp life and left it a very plain, drudging and stupid reality.

On September 24, 1861, the long-expected day of departure dawned. Before the day the men were astir. Hurrahs would break out from some unexpected quarter, followed by scattering hurrahs all over camp. People from the country came crowding into the camp by the thousand. Eyes unused to weeping were dimmed with mistiness, and hearts throbbed heavily as the order was given to strike tents.

At 4:00 P.M. the column was formed and, headed by the band, we embarked. On the line of railroad the whole population was out, lining the track. Bonfires blazed, guns were fired and the evening air was stirred with shouting as we passed swiftly through the villages.

Daylight on the morning of the twenty-seventh found us in the city of St. Louis. It required but a short time to understand that the picnic days of camp life were over, that playing soldier was played out, and that now we were down to genuine hard work.

A Southern training camp in its early stages was visited by William Howard Russell, a London newspaperman, then traveling through America.

It was in June 1861, when the river boat on which he had taken passage arrived at the foot of Chickasaw Bluffs on the Mississippi, where the Confederate Camp Randolph was located.

On looking out of my cabin window this morning I found the steamer fast alongside a small wharf, above which rose, to the height of 150 feet, at an angle of forty-five degrees, a rugged bluff. The wharf was covered with commissariat stores and ammunition. Three heavy guns, which some men were endeavoring to sling to rude bullock carts, in a manner defiant of all the laws of gravitation, seemed likely to go slap into the water at every moment; but of the many big fellows lounging about, not one gave a hand to the working party. At the height of fifty feet above the level of the river two earthworks had been rudely erected.

A number of the soldiers, under the notion that they were washing themselves, were swimming about in a backwater of the great river, regardless of catfish, mud and fever.

After breakfast we mounted the cart-horse chargers which were waiting to receive us. It is scarcely worth while to describe the works. Certainly, a more extraordinary maze could not be conceived in the dreams of a sick engineer. They were so ingeniously made as to prevent the troops engaged in their defense from resisting the enemy's attacks, or getting away from them when assailants had got inside.

The general ordered some practice to be made with round shot down the river. An old 42-pound carronade was loaded with some difficulty and pointed at a tree about 1,700 yards distant. I ventured to say, "I think, General, the smoke will prevent your seeing the shot." To which the general replied, "No, sir," in a tone which indicated "I beg you to understand I have been wounded in Mexico and know all about this kind of thing."

"Fire!" The string was pulled, and out of the touchhole popped a piece of metal with a little chirrup. "Darn these friction tubes! I prefer the linstock and match," quoth one of the staff, "but the general will have us use friction tubes." Tube No. 2, however, did explode, but where the ball went no one could say, as the smoke drifted right into our eyes.

Slowly winding for some distance up the steep road in a blazing sun, we proceeded through the tents which were scattered in small groups on the wooded plateau above the river. The tents were of the small ridge-pole pattern, six men to each, many of whom, from their exposure to the sun and from the badness of the water, had already been laid up with illness.

By order of the general some 700 or 800 men were formed into line for inspection. Many were in their shirt sleeves, and the awkwardness with which they handled their arms showed that, however good they might be as shots, they were bad at manual platoon exercises; but such great strapping fellows, that as I walked down the ranks there were few whose shoulders were not above the level of my head. They were armed with old pattern percussion muskets, no two clad alike, many very badly shod, few with knapsacks but all provided with a tin water flask and a blanket.

From the quartermaster general I heard that each man had a daily ration of 3/4 lb. to 1-1/4 lb. of meat and a sufficiency of bread, sugar, coffee and rice; however, these military Olivers asked for more. Neither whisky nor tobacco was served out to them, which to such heavy consumers of both must have proved a source of dissatisfaction. The officers were plain planters, merchants, lawyers and the like—energetic, determined men, but utterly ignorant of the most rudimentary parts of military science.

Having gone down the lines of these motley companies, the general addressed them in a harangue in which he expatiated on their patriotism, on their courage and the atrocity of the enemy, in an odd farrago of military and political subjects. But when he wound up by assuring them, "When the hour of danger comes I will be with you," the effect was by no means equal to his expectations. The men did not seem to care much whether the general would be with them or not at that moment; and, indeed, he did not give one an idea that he would contribute much to the means of resistance.

We returned to the steamer and proceeded onward to another landing, protected by a battery, where we were received by a guard dressed in uniform, who turned out with some appearance of soldierly smartness. The general told me the corps was composed of gentlemen planters and farmers. They had all clad themselves, and came from the best families in the state of Tennessee.

On returning to the boats the band struck up the "Marseillaise" and "Dixie Land." In the afternoon we returned to Memphis.

Samuel Fiske was a clergyman who volunteered as a private soldier in the 14th Connecticut Regiment. His letters from the field were published in the *Springfield Republican* under the name Dunn Browne, and enjoyed great popularity. Among them is one which deals with the first impressions of a recruit after his training days were over but before he had been in battle.

The first observation every man would make is that the soldier's life is an eminently dirty one. Our boys slept on the dirty decks of a steamer, were packed in dirty cars and marched through dust so thick and fine that, mixed in proper proportion with perspiration, it formed a plaster cast of every man's face. Water is often too precious to waste in ablutions; linen gets dirty; and, on the whole, dirt steadily and surely prevails, till a regiment appears like a regiment of ragamuffins. Experience has already shown us, also, that a soldier's is sometimes a pretty hungry and thirsty life. For three days together, in our first week, we had nothing to eat but a few hard crackers, and once a morsel of cheese and once a slice of ham apiece served round; and for one night and part of a hot day we had no water in camp.

When we double up and crowd together at night for a bivouac, we cover the country like a cloud of locusts, as thick and as destructive. A crop of soldiers kills out any other crop in the quickest possible time. Our orders against plundering are very strict, but it seems impossible to keep an army from destroying everything through which it passes. Our soldiers very generally are, or soon become, a set of lawless plunderers.

And again ours is an amazingly uncertain life. Two nights ago we were in comfortable tents; last night and tonight we are far away, lying on the cold ground, in rainy weather. One night the camp is all alive with lights, fires, songs and shouts of laughter; the next all is silence, fires are out, men talk almost in whispers and lie on their arms. The soldier knows least of all men what a day may bring forth. His tomorrow may hold in its bosom for him starvation or plenty, a thirty miles' march or perfect idleness, the din of battle, the shout of victory, the shame of defeat, the pain of wounds—or the closing scene of death.

CHAPTER 3

The First Big Battle of the War

THE BATTLE OF BULL RUN, OR MANASSAS

Like two giant anacondas uncoiling themselves, the opposing armies began to stretch out between the hostile sections. Clashes took place in Missouri, in Kentucky, in Western Virginia and along the Potomac. But the first important battle was bound to take place where more vital issues were at stake. "On to Richmond," was the cry of the North, and sound military judgment bowed to popular ignorance. A Union army did march on Richmond. When it met a Southern force barring the way, a battle resulted near the little village of Manassas Junction, usually referred to as Manassas. The Federals were commanded by General Irvin McDowell, a veteran of the Mexican War, who had served for many years on General Scott's staff; the Confederates by General Pierre G. T. Beauregard, the hero of Fort Sumter.

The two opposing leaders had been classmates at West Point, and had learned the same fundamental lessons in strategy: first, that attack was usually better than defense; second, that it was unwise to make a frontal attack when a flank attack offered a more favorable prospect.

Hence, both generals decided on precisely the same tactics. Each feinted with his left then struck out with his right. They did this simultaneously, and if both had been successful they would have completely swung around each other. McDowell could have marched unopposed into Richmond and Beauregard into Washington. But neither was successful and, by a caprice of fortune, the less successful of the two emerged as the victor.

44

Beauregard's version of the engagement gives an excellent picture of this, the first big battle of the war.

Soon after the conflict in Charleston Harbor, I was called to Richmond, which had become the Confederate seat of government, and was directed to "assume command of the Confederate troops on the Alexandria line." Arriving at Manassas Junction, I took command on the second of June, 1861.

Although the position was strategically of commanding importance, the terrain was unfavorable. Its strategic value was that, being close to the Federal capital, it held in observation the chief enemy army then being assembled by General McDowell for a movement against Richmond. We had a railway approach in our rear for the accumulation of reinforcements, while another (the Manassas Gap) railway gave rapid communications with the fertile valley of the Shenandoah. But on the other hand, Bull Run, a petty stream, was of little or no defensive strength, for it abounded in fords. (See map, page 52.)

At the time of my arrival, a Confederate army under General Joseph E. Johnston was at Harpers Ferry, in a position from which he was speedily forced to retire, however, by a Federal army under the veteran General Robert Patterson. On my right flank a Confederate force of some 2,500 men under General T. H. Holmes occupied the position of Aquia Creek on the lower Potomac. I was anxiously aware that the sole military advantage of the moment to the Confederates was that of holding the *interior lines*. On the Federal side were all material advantages: superior numbers, decidedly better arms and equipment, and a small but incomparable body of Regular infantry as well as Regular field artillery of the highest class.

Happily, arrangements had been made which enabled me to receive regularly, from private persons at the Federal capital, most accurate information. I was almost as well advised of the strength of the hostile army in front as its own commander.

A former clerk in one of the departments in Washington had volunteered to bring me the latest information of the military and political situation. With no more delay than the writing in cipher by Mrs. Greenhow, a Southern sympathizer, of the words "Order issued for McDowell to march upon Manassas tonight," my agent was carried in a buggy with a relay of horses down the eastern shore of the Potomac. The momentous dispatch was in my hands between eight and nine o'clock that night. Within half an hour my outpost commanders were directed at the first evidence of the enemy in their front to fall back to positions already prescribed. I next suggested to President Davis that the Army of the Shenandoah should be ordered to reinforce me—a suggestion that was at once heeded. General Johnston was induced to join me; and to facilitate that movement I hastened to accumulate all possible railway transport at the eastern foot of the Blue Ridge, to which Johnston's troops directed their march.

It seemed, however, as though the deferred attempt at concentration was to go for naught, for on the morning of the eighteenth the Federal forces were massed around Centreville, only three miles from Mitchell's Ford, and soon were seen advancing upon the roads leading to that and Blackburn's Ford. My order of battle, issued in the night of the seventeenth, contemplated an offensive return, particularly from the strong brigades on the right and right center.

Our success in the first limited collision between McDowell's forces and mine was of decisive importance, by so increasing General McDowell's caution as to give time for the arrival of some of General Johnston's forces. But while on the nineteenth I was awaiting a renewed attack by the Federal army, I received a telegram from Richmond urging me to withdraw my call on General Johnston on account of the supposed impracticability of the concentration. As this was not an order and left me technically free, I preferred to keep both the situation and the responsibility, being resolved to take the offensive myself.

The Federal artillery opened in front on both fords, and the infantry, while demonstrating in front of Mitchell's Ford, endeavored to force a passage at Blackburn's. The Federals, after several attempts to force a passage, met a final repulse and retreated. The contest lapsed into an artillery duel in which the Washington Artillery of New Orleans won credit against the renowned batteries of the United States Regular Army. A comical effect of this artillery fight was the destruction of the dinner of myself and staff by a Federal shell that fell into the fireplace of my headquarters at the McLean House.

General McDowell, fortunately for my plans, spent the nineteenth and twentieth in reconnaissances; meanwhile, General Johnston brought 8,340 men from the Shenandoah Valley, with twenty guns, and General Holmes 1,265 rank and file, with six pieces of artillery, came from Aquia Creek. My force now mustered 29,188 rank and file and fifty-five guns.

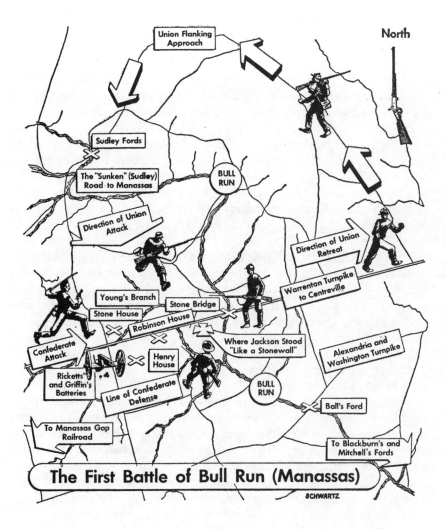

North

Union Flanking Approach

Sudley Fords

The "Sunken" (Sudley) Road to Manassas

BULL RUN

Direction of Union Attack

Direction of Union Retreat

Young's Branch

Stone House

Stone Bridge

Robinson House

Warrenton Turnpike to Centreville

Where Jackson Stood "Like a Stonewall"

Confederate Attack

Henry House

Alexandria and Washington Turnpike

Ricketts' and Griffin's Batteries

Line of Confederate Defense

BULL RUN

Ball's Ford

To Manassas Gap Railroad

To Blackburn's and Mitchell's Fords

The First Battle of Bull Run (Manassas)

SCHWARTZ

Here in the first summer two untried armies received their baptism of fire. Before the war's end the little stream of Bull Run would be red with blood again.

One of Johnston's soldiers relates how the skirmishes along
Bull Run reacted on the movements in the Shenandoah Valley.

The command of General Joseph E. Johnston numbered 11,000 men,
indifferently armed and equipped, and totally unacquainted with drill
and discipline.

For days we awaited the coming of the Federal army, but the enemy
did not advance; and the Confederate commander, fearing he was too
far from Manassas, determined to fall back to Winchester.

On July 18 General Johnston received a dispatch from General
Beauregard that he required assistance. Orders to march were immediately issued, and by four o'clock the last of the troops filed through the
streets of Winchester. It was a silent march indeed. There were no
bright smiles, no waving of handkerchiefs, no expression of joy, for all
believed that the Confederate army was retreating. The troops partook
of the same feeling, for as yet our destination had not been divulged to
them.

After marching about three miles, Colonel Arnold Elzey, our commanding officer, halted the regiment. "You are," he announced, "on the
march to meet the enemy; and, in the hour of battle, you will remember that you are Marylanders. He had better never been born who
proves himself a craven when we grapple with the foemen."

A cheer that might have been heard for miles went up and, with
flushed cheek and flashing eyes, we asked to be led against the enemy.

All that night we pressed forward, on to Piedmont Station, where we
found railroad transportation.

The troops were eagerly crowding into the cars, and all were impatiently awaiting their turn, when we met with a disaster. The engineers
of two of the trains were Yankees, and treacherously concocted a plan
to collide their trains, totally regardless of the consequences that might
ensue to the hundreds of men placed at their mercy. They consummated their wicked design, but fortunately few were hurt, and none
killed; but an engine and train were destroyed, and the road so blockaded that the utmost efforts failed to put it in running order before next
morning.

The loss was a severe blow to us, as we now had but two trains left.
However, on the morning of July 21 these two resumed their trips, and
each had made a successful run when the engine of the hindmost train
broke down, and we were consequently delayed two hours and a half.

The whole of the army should have reached Beauregard the evening before, whereas barely two-thirds actually were able to join him.

The Federal army had left its camps around Washington on July 16 for its contemplated conquest of Virginia. Soldier Warren Lee Goss drew a word picture of his first march to the front.

Our regiment was camped near Alexandria, and the whole of us grew impatient to end the war and get home. I tell you, we were glad when we were told to get ready for a march.

They gave us rations of salt junk, hardtack, sugar and coffee. Each man carried his rubber and woolen blanket, forty rounds of cartridges, a canteen, his gun and equipments and most of us a patent drinking tube. I hadn't been on the march an hour before I realized that it might not be such fun, after all. There was a 32-pound gun mooring on the road, with sixteen or eighteen horses to pull it. Finally, two or three companies were detailed to help the horses. The weather was scorching hot, but the most trying thing was the jerky way they marched us. Sometimes they'd double-quick us, and again they'd keep us standing in the road waiting in the hot sun for half an hour, then start us ahead again a little way, then halt us again, and so on. The first day we marched until after sundown, and when we halted for the night we were the tiredest crowd of men I ever saw.

The next day was the seventeenth of July. I was hungry, so I stopped at a house and asked if they would sell me something to eat. There were three Negro girls, a white woman and her daughter in the house. The white folks were proud and unaccommodating. They said the Yankees had stolen everything—all their "truck," as they called it; but when I took a handful of silver change they brought me a cold Johnnycake and some chicken. As I was leaving the house, the daughter said: "You'n Yanks are right pert just now, but you'ns'll come back soon a right smart quicker than yer'r going, I reckon!"

We marched helter-skelter nearly all night without orders to stop until, just before daylight, we halted near a little building they called a church.

The first gun of the fight I heard was when we were eight or ten miles from Centreville, on the afternoon of the eighteenth of July, the day of the engagement at Blackburn's Ford. We were hurried up at double-quick and marched in the direction of the firing until we reached Centreville, about eleven o'clock that night. Very early on the morning of the twenty-first we marched through Centreville. Near Cub Run we saw carriages and barouches which contained civilians. We thought it wasn't a bad idea to have the great men from Washington come out to see us thrash the Rebs.

> Colonel R. W. Johnson of Patterson's army, who took part in the campaign, was critical of the disposition General Scott had made of his divided forces.

General Patterson was ordered to press General Johnston so closely as to prevent him from reinforcing Beauregard, and while still at Chambersburg, a controversy arose between the general-in-chief Scott and General Patterson in regard to the point at which the command of the latter should cross the Potomac into Virginia. Patterson urged to be allowed to cross at Leesburg, but he was overruled and directed to cross at Williamsport. I shall always believe that Patterson was right. In crossing at Williamsport, McDowell and Patterson were placed on exterior lines, while Beauregard and Johnston occupied interior lines. So far as Johnston was concerned, it mattered not at which place Patterson crossed, for in either event he would have threatened the rebel line of communication, and the evacuation of Harper's Ferry would have necessarily followed. If, however, Patterson had been at Leesburg, he would have been within supporting distance of McDowell, and would have joined him sooner than Johnston could have effected a junction with Beauregard.

If Patterson's plan had been adopted, the Federal army would have been victorious at Bull Run, and not been required to suffer a humiliating defeat.

> On July 21 the army of McDowell attacked that of Beauregard, who continues his narration.

Sunday, July 21, broke brightly. My scouts had reported that the enemy was concentrating along Warrenton Turnpike. This fact caused me to apprehend that they would attack my left flank at the Stone Bridge. At half-past five o'clock the enemy was reported to be deploying a force in front of Colonel N. G. Evans, who was guarding the Stone Bridge. I immediately sent orders to my right and center to attack the Federal left flank and rear at Centreville, while my left, under Evans, would sustain the Federal attack at the Stone Bridge

[See map, page 59]. I expected a decisive victory by cutting off the Federal army from Washington.

Evans, seeing that the Federal attack at the bridge did not increase in vigor, and observing a lengthening line of dust to the left of the Warrenton Turnpike, became satisfied that the attack in his front was a feint, and that a column of enemy was moving around through the woods to fall on his left flank from the direction of Sudley Ford. He left four companies at the Stone Bridge, and led the remainder of his force across the valley of Young's Branch to the high ground beyond it.

The Federal column, about 18,000 strong, had struck to the right by a forest road to cross Bull Run at Sudley Ford, about three miles above the Stone Bridge, for the purpose of attacking my left flank. The head of the column, Colonel Ambrose E. Burnside's brigade, at about 9:45 A.M. debouched in front of Evans. Major C. R. Wheat, commanding a battalion of Louisiana Tigers, at once engaged the enemy skirmishers, and Evans' South Carolinians poured forth sudden volleys, while the howitzers flung their grapeshot upon the attacking line, which was soon driven back. Major Wheat had fallen severely wounded. Burnside's entire brigade was now sent forward in a second charge, but they encountered again the unflinching fire of Evans' line and were once more driven back to the woods, from which they continued the attack.

General B. E. Bee held a position on the high plateau in rear of Bull Run, from which it was separated by Young's Branch. On the north-western crown stood the house of Widow Henry, to its right the house of the free Negro Robinson, densely embowered in trees and shrubbery. General Bee skillfully disposed his forces. His two brigades were placed in a small depression of the plateau in advance of the Henry house. He answered Evans' request for troops by advising him to withdraw to his own position on the height; but Evans would not retreat, and renewed his appeal that the forces in rear help him hold his ground. However, the newly arrived forces had given the Federals such superiority as to dwarf Evans' means of resistance, and General Bee, generously yielding his own better judgment to Evans' persistence, led the two brigades across the valley under the fire of the enemy's artillery and threw them into action. The Federal infantry was still superior in numbers and Bee's whole line was hammered also by the enemy's powerful batteries. Against these odds the Confederate force was still endeavoring to hold its ground when W. T. Sherman's brigade came into the field upon its right. There was no choice for Bee but to retire—a movement, though, that had to be accomplished under different circumstances than when urged by him upon Evans. The troops were thrown into confusion, and the greater part soon fell into rout across Young's Branch.

Meanwhile, I had been waiting with General Johnston for the sound of conflict to open on the Federal left flank and rear, when I was

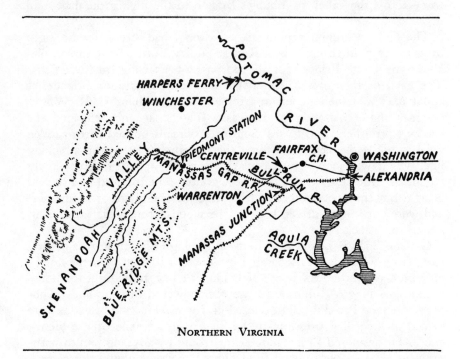

NORTHERN VIRGINIA

chagrined to hear that all troops had not come up. The firing on the left began to increase so intensely as to indicate a severe attack, whereupon General Johnston said that he would go personally to that quarter.

It appeared to me that the troops on the right would be unable to get into position before the Federal offensive should have made too much progress on our left, and that it would be better to fight the battle out in that quarter. Communicating this view to General Johnston, who approved it, I ordered our troops to make a strong demonstration all along their front on the other side of the run and ordered the reserves to move swiftly to the left. General Johnston and I now set out at full speed for the point of conflict.

The editor of the *Richmond Examiner* carries the story through the next phase.

It was half-past ten in the morning when General Beauregard learned that his advance on Centreville had miscarried. He and General Johnston had taken positions on a commanding hill to watch the movements of the enemy. The battle now was bursting and expanding its fury upon their left flank. From the hill could be witnessed the grand diorama of the conflict. The enemy's design could be no longer in doubt; the violent firing on the left showed, at last, where the crisis of the battle was; and now immense clouds of dust plainly denoted the march of a large body of troops from the Federal center.

Not a moment was to be lost. It was instantly necessary to make new combinations. The left flank of the Confederates was being overpowered. Dashing on at a headlong gallop, Generals Beauregard and Johnston reached the field just as the command of Bee and Evans had taken shelter in a wooded ravine, and Jackson's brigade had moved up to withstand the pressure of the enemy. It was a thrilling moment. General Johnston seized the colors of the 4th Alabama, and offered to lead the attack. General Beauregard leaped from his horse, and turning to his troops, exclaimed: "I have come here to die with you!"

In the meantime the Confederate reserves were rapidly moving up. Confronting the enemy General Beauregard had as yet not more than 6500 infantry, with but thirteen pieces of artillery. A force, estimated at 20,000 infantry, seven companies of cavalry, and twenty-four pieces of artillery, were bearing hotly and confidently down on their position, while heavy reserves hung in the distance.

But additional pieces of artillery came dashing up, and a new inspiration seemed to be caught by the Confederates. The line swept grandly forward. The plateau was now firmly in our possession, and the enemy, driven across the turnpike, was visibly discouraged.

Beauregard continues this chapter of the see-saw battle.

The effect of this brilliant onset was to give a short breathing spell to our troops. Reorganizing our line of battle under the unremitting fire of the Federal batteries, I prepared to meet the new attack which the

enemy was about to make. They again pushed up the slope and gradually pressed our lines back and regained possession of their lost ground
and guns. With the Henry and Robinson houses once more in their
possession, they resumed the offensive, urged forward by their commanders.

The conflict now became very severe for the final possession of this
position, which was the key to victory. The Federal numbers enabled
them so to extend their lines through the woods beyond the Sudley
Road as to outreach my left flank, which I was compelled partly to
throw back, while their numbers enabled them to outflank my right in
the direction of the Stone Bridge. I knew that I was safe if I could
hold out till the arrival of reinforcements, which was but a matter of
time; and I was determined to hold the plateau, unless my forces were
overtaken by annihilation.

> Federal troops were still arriving on the Sudley Spring Road.
> As one of the regiments approached the Henry house plateau,
> a momentary lull in the fighting led the young recruit Goss to
> an erroneous conclusion.

That day was the hottest one I ever experienced. We marched, and
marched; and double-quicked and didn't appear to get ahead at all.
Everyone of whom we inquired the distance to Manassas Junction
said five miles, and after a while they would say ten miles instead of
five. At last we arrived at Sudley Ford and rested, while several
regiments waded Bull Run. While here we could see shells bursting
in little round clouds in the air far to the left of us down the run. The
dust rising on the roads ahead was said to be the Rebel army advancing
to fight us. We were going to have a fight; there was but little doubt
about it now.

We soon followed the others across Bull Run and came to a field
where we saw dead and wounded men. It made me feel faint to look
at them. The boys began exclaiming: "Hurrah, they are running! The
Rebels are running!" We advanced to the crest, fired a volley and saw
the Rebels running toward the road below.

The next thing I remember was the order to advance, which we did
under a scattering fire; we crossed the turnpike and, ascending a little
way, were halted in a depression or cut in the road which runs from
Sudley Ford. The boys were saying constantly, in great glee: "We've
whipped them." "We'll hang Jeff Davis to a sour apple tree." "They

are running." "The war is over." We were of the opinion that the enemy had all run away.

Shortly before three o'clock in the afternoon the crux of the battle was reached.

Both contestants were worn out, and either side might break at the next impact. Beauregard threw in his last ounce of strength, but he knew that final victory or defeat depended on the arrival or nonarrival of Johnston's remaining regiments. Mr. Pollard pictures a few breathless moments preceding the end of the day's fight.

While the Federals rallied their broken line under shelter of fresh brigades, and prepared for the renewal of the struggle, telegraph signals from the hills warned General Beauregard to "look out for the enemy's advance on the left." At the distance of more than a mile, a column of men was approaching. At their head was a flag which could not be distinguished, even with the aid of a strong glass. General Beauregard was unable to determine whether it was the Federal or the Confederate flag.

Turning to Colonel Evans, the only officer with him at the time, the anxious commander directed him to proceed to General Johnston, and request him to have his reserves in readiness to protect a retreat. Evans had gone but a little way, when both officers fixed one final, intense gaze upon the advancing flag. A gust of wind shook out its folds, and General Beauregard recognized the Stars and Bars of the Confederate banner! "Colonel Evans," exclaimed Beauregard, his face lighting up, "ride forward, and order General Kirby Smith to hurry up, and strike them on flank and rear!"

It was the arrival of Kirby Smith with a portion of Johnston's army, which had been anxiously expected; and now cheer after cheer from regiment to regiment announced his welcome. General Smith knew, by the sounds of the firing, that a great struggle was in progress, and, having stopped the train, he had formed his men, and was advancing rapidly through the fields. He was directed to move on the Federal left and center. At the same time, Early's brigade, which had just come up, was ordered to throw itself on the right flank of the enemy.

Private Goss was watching Griffin's and Ricketts' batteries on the Henry plateau and saw them taken.

The batteries were in the open field near us. We were watching to see what they'd do next, when a terrible volley was poured into them. It was like a pack of Fourth of July firecrackers under a barrel, magnified a thousand times. The Rebels had crept upon them unawares, and the men at the batteries were about all killed or wounded.

The dead cannoneers lay with the rammers of the guns and sponges and lanyards still in their hands. The battery was annihilated by those volleys in a moment. Those who could get away didn't wait. We had no supports near enough to protect us properly, and the enemy were within seventy yards of us when that volley was fired.

It must have been four o'clock in the afternoon, at a time when our fire had become scattered and feeble, that the rumor passed from one to another that the Rebels had got reinforcements. Where are ours? we asked. There was no confusion or panic then, but discouragement. And at this juncture, from the woods ahead, on each side of the Sudley Ford Road, there came terrible volleys. Our men began to feel it was no use to fight, cursing their generals because no reinforcements were sent to them. The men had now in most cases been marching and fighting thirteen hours. The enemy were pressing us, and we fell back. We didn't run.

Once more the Union troops rallied, but it was their last effort, as Beauregard soon discovered.

Meanwhile, the enemy had formed a line of formidable proportions on the opposite height. They presented a fine picture as they threw forward a cloud of skirmishers, preparatory to a new assault against the plateau. But their right was severely pressed by the troops that had successively arrived; the force in the southwest angle of the Sudley and Warrenton crossroads were driven from their position.

I now gave orders to go forward in a common charge. Before the full advance of the Confederate ranks the enemy's whole line, whose right was already yielding, irretrievably broke, fleeing across Bull Run by every available direction. Major George Sykes's regulars, aided by Sherman's brigade, made a steady and handsome withdrawal, protecting the rear of the routed forces and enabling many to escape by the Stone Bridge. Having ordered in pursuit all the troops on the field, I turned over the command to General Johnston. Then, mounting a fresh horse—the fourth I had used that day— I started to press the pursuit of the enemy.

The timely arrival of Colonel Elzey's men and their active participation in the fight is related by one of them, Private W. W. Goldsborough, of the 1st Maryland Infantry.

It was nearly one o'clock when we disembarked at Manassas, where we found an officer of Johnston's staff awaiting with an order for us to push forward with all possible dispatch.

Hastily throwing off their knapsacks, the troops struck across the country in the direction of the smoke and the sound of artillery. The heat and dust were almost suffocating; but on we went, sometimes slacking our pace to a walk to recover breath, but never halting until we had made four miles and were within a mile of the battlefield.

We knew by the rapid discharges of artillery and the incessant rattle of musketry that the fight was being stubbornly contested. The enemy was made aware of our approach by the clouds of dust we raised, and several pieces of artillery were trained upon us. Wagons in great numbers were coming to the rear at headlong speed, and demoralized fugitives by the hundreds from the battlefield were rushing frantically by, crying out, "All is lost, all is lost; go back, or you'll be cut to pieces; the army is in full retreat."

But the command of our gallant Colonel Elzey was ever "Forward, pay no attention to cowards and skulkers. Charge!"

Upon that charge rested the fate of the Confederate army. At the command, with one wild, deafening yell, and amidst a perfect storm of bullets, we drove the enemy pell-mell from their strong position into the thicket in their rear.

Elzey pressed on in pursuit, and, when we came once more into the open country, we saw before us no organized force but one dense mass of fugitives. With our successful charge upon their right flank, the whole of the Federal army had given way and was rushing madly in the direction of Washington.

President Davis and Generals Johnston and Beauregard rode up to Colonel Elzey, and the former, his countenance beaming with excitement and enthusiasm, exclaimed: "*General* Elzey, you are the Blücher of the day."

Most observers agreed that the turning point of the battle was the loss of the Griffin and Ricketts batteries. According to John Nicolay, Lincoln's private secretary, this loss came about through an odd trick of fate.

When, at about half-past two o'clock, the batteries of Ricketts and Griffin were ordered to move to the top of Henry Hill, there was a complete lull in the battle. But hardly had Ricketts taken his post, before his cannoneers and horses began to fall under the accurate fire of near and well-concealed Rebel sharpshooters. Death puffed from bushes, fences, buildings, and yet the jets of flame and wreaths of smoke were the only visible enemy to assail. Officers and cannoneers held on with desperate courage. Griffin's battery came and took place alongside. But now the Rebel regiments, seeing the dangerous exposure of the Union batteries, were tempted to swarm out of their cover. They pressed cautiously but tenaciously upon Ricketts. Griffin, absorbed in directing the fire of his guns against the Rebel batteries, was suddenly startled at seeing a regiment advancing boldly on his right, in open view. Their very audacity puzzled him. Instinctively he ordered his guns to be charged with canister and trained upon them. Yet at the dreadful thought of pouring such a volley upon a Union regiment, he hesitated and held a brief colloquy with an officer standing near him. "They are Confederates," declared Griffin in tense excitement. "No," answered the officer, "I know they are your battery support." Griffin spurred forward and told his officers not to fire. The mistake proved fatal. The Confederate regiment had approached to point-blank range and leveled their muskets just as Griffin gave his order to desist. Griffin's canister would have annihilated the regiment; but now the tables were turned, and in an instant the regiment's volley had annihilated Griffin's and Ricketts' batteries. Under this sudden catastrophe the supporting regiments stood spellbound. The unexpected disaster overawed them; under the continued and still advancing volleys of the same Rebel regiment, they fired their muskets, turned and fled.

> Beauregard immediately started all available troops in pursuit of the fleeing Union army. Then, just as complete victory seemed within his grasp, he tells how he became a victim of the same delusion which a short time before had led Griffin to commit his fatal error.

I was just making arrangements to take full advantage of the situation, when I was overtaken by a courier bearing a message from General Johnston's chief of staff, informing me that a large Federal force was moving upon my depot of supplies near Manassas. I returned and communicated this important news to General Johnston. Upon consultation it was deemed best that I should take our brigades on the right, which were hastening up to the battlefield, and fall on this enemy, while reinforcements should be sent me from the pursuing forces, who were to be recalled for that purpose. To gain time, I hastily mounted a force of infantry behind the cavalrymen then present, when I learned that the news was a false alarm caught from the return of some of our own forces, the similarity of the uniforms and the direction of their march having convinced some nervous person that they were a force of the enemy. It was now almost dark and too late to resume the broken pursuit.

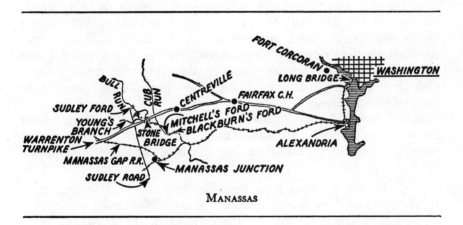

MANASSAS

Private Goldsborough, of the First Maryland, railed bitterly against the apparent lack of zeal shown by the Confederate generals in exploiting their victory.

Our column crossed the Stone Bridge and took the turnpike leading to Alexandria, confident that we were to pursue the enemy to the very gates of his capital. But we were doomed to bitter disappointment; for, after marching a mile or two, we came to a rightabout and silently retraced our steps to Manassas.

All day long this state of affairs continued. We had gained a great battle, but the demoralizing effects of countermarching an army in the moment of victory were strongly evidenced, and dissatisfaction was expressed on every side.

All day Lincoln and his entourage had been listening to reports from the front, as they came ticking in at the War Department. Two telegraph operators, William R. Plum and William B. Wilson, were eyewitnesses, and the following account is pieced together from their recollections.

During the battle a line of couriers from the Fairfax Court House to the front was established, and their reports forwarded to the War Department. These couriers were to arrive every fifteen minutes.

In the telegraph office were congregated the President, most of his Cabinet, and other celebrities, with maps before them. Hour after hour hopes beat high, and satisfaction was discernible on every brow. Suddenly a lull occurred. No courier arrived at Fairfax. What could be the matter? The most plausible reason advanced was that our victorious army was resting after the hard fighting. Every few minutes Fairfax was signaled, but only to elicit the reply, "no news." Then, after an hour, like a flash of lightning, came those chilling words: "Our army is in full retreat."

Whatever may have been the thoughts and feelings of the gentlemen present, they kept them closely veiled. All seemed to cling around the cool President, the saddened lines of whose countenance deepened.

Could the Southern army have marched into Washington on the heels of their fleeing enemies? General Johnston, who assumed full responsibility for the conduct of the battle, subsequently submitted his arguments for failing to push the pursuit.

My failure to capture Washington received general condemnation. Many erroneously attributed it to the President's prohibition; but Mr. Davis expressed neither wish nor opinion on the subject.

The conditions forbade an attempt on Washington. The Confederate army was more disorganized by victory than that of the United States by defeat.

Besides, the reasons for our course were unfitness of raw troops for assailing entrenchments; the fortifications upon which skillful engineers had been engaged since April; the Potomac, a mile wide, bearing the United States vessels of war, which commanded the bridges and the southern shores.

The Confederate army would have been two days in marching from Bull Run to the Federal entrenchments, with less than two days' rations, or not more. It is asserted that the country could have furnished food and forage in abundance. Those who make this assertion forget that a large Federal army had passed *twice* over the route in question. As we had none of the means of besieging, an immediate assault upon the forts would have been unavoidable; it would have been repelled, inevitably, and our half supply of ammunition exhausted; and the enemy, increased by the army from Harpers Ferry, could have resumed their march to Richmond without opposition.

And, if we had miraculously been successful in our assault, the Potomac still would have protected Washington and rendered our further progress impossible.

In his official report, General McDowell admitted his defeat in a manly and straightforward manner, concurring with General Beauregard in all essentials, although he ascribed to his opponent a superiority of numbers which did not exist. As a matter of fact, the Federal army of 35,000 was the larger by about 3,000 men.

McDowell's report, as quoted here, begins at the critical moment in the afternoon, when his troops were still holding the Henry house plateau.

It was now about three o'clock in the afternoon. Three times had the enemy been repulsed and driven back from the Henry house plateau. The third time it was supposed by us all that the repulse was final, for he was driven entirely from the hill, so far beyond it as not to be in sight, and all were certain the day was ours.

The enemy was evidently disheartened and broken. But we had then been fighting since ten-thirty o'clock in the morning, the men had been up since two o'clock and had made what to those unused to such things seemed a long march, though the longest distance gone over was not more than nine and a half miles; and although they had had three days' provisions served out to them the day before, many, no doubt, either had not gotten them or had thrown them away, and were therefore without food. They had done much severe fighting.

It was at this time that the enemy's reinforcements came to his aid from the railroad train. They threw themselves in the woods on our right and opened fire on our men, which caused them to break and retire down the hillside. This soon degenerated into disorder, for which there was no remedy. Every effort was made to rally them, even beyond the reach of the enemy's fire, but in vain. The battalion of regular infantry alone maintained itself until our men could get back to the position we had occupied in the morning.

The retreating current passed slowly through Centreville to the rear. The enemy followed us and, owing to the rear becoming blocked, caused us much damage, for the artillery could not pass, and several pieces and caissons had to be abandoned. In the panic the horses hauling the caissons and ammunition were cut from their traces and used for escape, and in this way much confusion was caused, the panic aggravated and the road encumbered.

By sundown it became a question whether we should endeavor to make a stand at Centreville. The condition of our artillery and its ammunition, the want of food for the men, and the utter disorganization and demoralization of the mass of the army seemed to admit of no alternative but to fall back. Our decision had been anticipated by the troops, most of them being already on the road to the rear.

The issue of this hard-fought battle, in which our troops were in conflict with an enemy ably commanded and superior in numbers, who acted on his own ground on the defensive, should not prevent full credit being given to those officers and corps whose services merited success, even if they did not attain it.

I could not have moved earlier than I did, nor could I have delayed. The best part of my forces were three-months' volunteers, whose terms of service were about expiring, but who had long enough to serve for the purpose of the expedition.

On the eve of the battle the 4th Pennsylvania and the battery of the 8th New York Militia, whose term of service expired, insisted on their discharge. I wrote to them as pressing a request as I could pen, but in vain. The next morning, while the army moved forward into battle, these troops moved to the rear to the sound of the enemy's cannon.

In the next few days, day by day, I should have lost in this way 10,000 of the best-armed, drilled, officered and disciplined troops in the army. In other words, every day would have made us weaker.

In conclusion, I desire to say that the general order for the battle to which I have referred was, with slight modifications, literally conformed to; that up to late in the afternoon, every movement ordered was carrying us successfully to our object—that of getting to the railroad leading from Manassas to the Valley of Virginia and interposing between the forces under Beauregard and those under Johnston; and could we have fought one day—yes, a few hours—sooner, there is everything to show that we should have continued successful.

> William T. Sherman, who served as a colonel in command of a brigade at Bull Run, now contributes his experiences in that short campaign.

About July 15, we moved forward leaving our camps standing. The march demonstrated the general laxity of discipline; for with all my personal efforts I could not prevent the men from straggling for water, blackberries or anything on the way they fancied.

Our men had been told often at home that all they had to do was to make a bold appearance, and the Rebels would run; and nearly all of us for the first time then heard the sound of cannon and muskets in anger and saw the bloody scenes common to all battles. We had good organization, good men, but no cohesion, no respect for authority, no real knowledge of war. Both armies were fairly defeated, and whichever had stood fast the other would have run. Though the North was overwhelmed with mortification and shame, none others, equally raw in war, could have done better than we did.

I myself had no idea that we were beaten, when I found that my brigade was almost alone, except Sykes's regulars. I then realized that the whole army was in retreat, and that my own men were individually making back for the Stone Bridge. I formed the brigade into an irregular square, but it fell to pieces; and, along with a crowd, the brigade got back to Centreville to our former camps. I saw General McDowell there, and understood that several of his divisions had not been engaged at all, that he would reorganize them at Centreville, and there await the enemy. I got my four regiments in parallel lines in a field, the same in which we had camped before the battle, and had lain down to sleep under a tree, when I was given orders to march back to our camps. It was near midnight, and the road was full of troops, wagons and batteries. We tried to keep our regiments separate, but all became inextricably mixed. The next day, about noon, we reached Fort Corcoran, our post.

> Among the many civilians who had ridden out from Washington to witness the battle was the English reporter William

Howard Russell. He did not see any of the actual fighting, but he saw its aftermath and reported it for his paper, the *London Times.*

I had ridden between three and a half and four miles, when I perceived several wagons coming from the direction of the battlefield. The drivers were endeavoring to force their horses past the ammunition carts going in the contrary direction; running by the side of the wagons were a number of men in uniform. My first impression was that the wagons were returning for fresh supplies of ammunition. But every moment the crowd increased, drivers and men crying out with vehement gestures, "Turn back! Turn back! We are whipped."

By this time the confusion had communicated itself through the line of wagons toward the rear, and the drivers endeavored to turn around their vehicles in the narrow road, which caused the usual amount of imprecations from the men and plunging and kicking from the horses. A few shells could be heard bursting not far off, but there was nothing to account for such an extraordinary scene. An officer, however, confirmed the report that the whole army was in retreat, but there was nothing in this disorder to indicate a general rout. All these things took place in a few seconds. I got up out of the road into a cornfield, through which men were hastily walking or running, their faces streaming with perspiration, and generally without arms, and worked my way for about half a mile or so, against an increasing stream of fugitives, the ground being strewed with coats, blankets, firelocks, cooking tins, caps, belts, bayonets—asking in vain where General Mc-Dowell was.

I had just stretched out my hand to get a cigar light from a German gunner, when the dropping shots which had been sounding through the woods in front suddenly swelled into an animated fire. In a few seconds a crowd of men rushed toward the guns, and the artillerymen near me seized a piece and were wheeling it round to fire, when an officer or sergeant called out, "Stop! Stop! They are our own men"; and in two or three minutes the whole battalion came sweeping past the guns at the double and in the utmost disorder. For a moment the confusion was so great I could not understand what had taken place; but a soldier whom I stopped, said, "We are pursued by their cavalry; they have cut us all to pieces."

It could not be doubted that something serious was taking place;

and at that moment a shell burst, scattering the soldiers near it. It was followed by another that bounded along the road; and in a few minutes more out came another regiment from the wood, almost as broken as the first. The scene on the road had now assumed an aspect which has not a parallel in any description I have ever read. Infantry soldiers on mules and draft horses, with the harness clinging to their heels, as much frightened as their riders; Negro servants on their masters' chargers; ambulances crowded with unwounded soldiers; wagons swarming with men who threw out the contents in the road to make room, grinding through a shouting, screaming mass of men on foot, who were literally yelling with rage at every halt.

There was nothing left for it but to go with the current one could not stem. I talked with those on all sides of me. Some uttered prodigious nonsense, describing batteries tier over tier, and ambuscades and blood running knee-deep. The names of many regiments were mentioned as being utterly destroyed. Cavalry and bayonet charges and masked batteries played prominent parts in all the narrations. Some of the officers seemed to feel the disgrace of defeat; but the strangest thing was the general indifference with which the event seemed to be regarded by those who collected their senses as soon as they got out of fire, and who said they were just going as far as Centreville and would have a big fight tomorrow.

I felt that vague sense of something extraordinary taking place which is experienced when a man sees a number of people acting as if driven by some unknown terror. As I rode in the crowd with men clinging to the stirrup leather, or holding on by anything they could lay hands on, so that I had some apprehension of being pulled off, I spoke to the men and asked them over and over again not to be in such a hurry. "There's no enemy to pursue you." But I might as well have talked to stones.

It never occurred to me that this was a grand debacle. All along I believed the mass of the army was not broken, and that all I saw around was the result of confusion created in a crude organization by a forced retreat; and knowing the reserves were at Centreville and beyond, I said to myself, "Let us see how this will be when we get to the hill." Trotting along briskly through the fields, I arrived at the foot of the slope on which Centreville stands and met a German regiment just deploying into line very well, and steadily—the men in the rear companies laughing, smoking, singing and jesting with the fugitives. One big German with a great pipe in his bearded mouth amused himself by pricking the horses with his saber point, as they passed, to the sore discomfiture of the riders. Behind that regiment came a battery of brass fieldpieces, and another regiment in column of march was following the guns. They were going to form line at the end of the slope, and no fairer position could well be offered for a defensive attitude. But it was getting too late for the enemy, wherever they were, to attempt an extensive operation.

A farewell look at the scene presented no new features. Still the clouds of dust moved onward, denser and higher; flashes of arms lighted them up at times; the fields were dotted by fugitives, among whom many mounted men were marked by their greater speed and the little flocks of dust rising from the horses' feet.

As I crossed the Long Bridge into Washington there was scarce a sound to dispute the possession of its echoes with my horses' hoofs. Little did I conceive the greatness of the defeat, the magnitude of the disaster which it had entailed upon the United States or the interval that would elapse before another army set out from the banks of the Potomac onward to Richmond.

How and why the panic started was the subject of many discussions. Private Goss, who saw its beginning and was carried away by it, offered his explanation of its origin.

The panic was the fault of the officers who had allowed the baggage wagons to come to the front. The stampede and confusion began among them first. Why, the men were so little frightened when they began to fall back that I saw them stop frequently to pick blackberries. Frightened men don't act in that way. The irresponsible teamsters, with the baggage wagons, were all crowded together. A Rebel battery began dropping shells in among them and thus demolished some of the wagons and blocked the way. The confusion and hurry and excitement then began. The drivers began to cut their traces and mount their horses and hurry away. Those who drove baggage wagons then began to desert them and gallop off. The infantry, seeing this confusion and not understanding the cause of it, quickened their pace. Soon the narrow road became filled with flying troops, horses, baggage wagons and carriages. Then the volunteers began to throw away their muskets and equipment, so as to stand an even chance in the race.

Soldiers here and there marched in groups and sorrowfully discussed the situation and its causes. The expression heard on every side among them was: "Why were not the reserves brought up from Centreville to help us?" "Why didn't they bring up the troops from Fairfax Court House?"—questions, it seems to me, hard to answer, even if they did come from private soldiers running away from the field of Bull Run.

> Colonel William T. Sherman brought his brigade through the retreat in fairly good order and relates how he, like other cool-headed officers, tried to repair the damage done. He ends by re-counting his unexpected role of battlefield guide to an illustrious visitor.

A slow, mizzling rain had set in, and probably a more gloomy day never presented itself. All organization seemed to be at an end; but I and my staff labored hard to collect our men into their proper companies. We took it for granted that the Rebels would be on our heels and accordingly prepared to defend our posts. By the twenty-fifth of July, I had my brigade as well governed as any in that army, although most of the ninety-day men had become extremely tired of the war and wanted to go home. Some of them were so mutinous, at one time, that I threatened to open fire on them, if they dared to leave camp without orders. Drills and exercises were resumed, and I ordered that at the three principal roll calls the men should keep their ranks until I in person dismissed them. One morning after reveille, when I had dismissed the regiment and was leaving, an officer said: "Colonel, I am going to New York today." I answered: "I do not remember to have signed a leave for you." He said he had engaged to serve three months and had already served more than that time; that he was a lawyer and was going home. A good many soldiers had paused to listen, and I knew that, if this officer could defy me, they also would. So I turned on him sharp, and said: "Captain, you are a soldier and must submit to orders till you are properly discharged. If you attempt to leave without orders, I will shoot you like a dog."

That same day, which must have been about July 26, I saw a carriage coming on the road and thought I recognized in it President Lincoln. I hurried, so as to stand by the roadside as the carriage passed. I was in uniform, with a sword on, and was recognized by Mr. Lincoln and Mr. Seward, who rode side by side in an open hack. I inquired if they were going to my camps, and Mr. Lincoln said: "Yes; we heard that you had got over the big scare, and we thought we would come over and see the boys." I asked if I might give directions to his coachman; he promptly invited me to jump in and to tell the coachman which way to drive. Seeing a soldier, I called to him and sent him up hurriedly to announce to the colonel that the President was coming. As we slowly ascended the hill, I discovered that Mr. Lincoln was full of feeling and wanted to encourage our men. I asked if he intended to speak to them, and he said he would like to. I asked him then to please discourage all cheering; that we had had enough of it to ruin any set of men, and that what we needed were cool, thoughtful, hard-fighting soldiers—no more hurrahing, no more humbug. He took my remarks in perfect good nature. Before we had reached the first camp, I heard the drum beating the "assembly," saw the men running for their tents, and in a few minutes the regiment was brought to order and "parade rest!"

Mr. Lincoln stood up in the carriage and made one of the neatest, best and most feeling addresses I ever listened to, referring to our late disaster at Bull Run, the high duties that still devolved on us and the brighter days to come. In winding up, he explained that, as President, he was Commander in Chief; that he was resolved that the soldiers should have everything that the law allowed; and he called on one and all to appeal to him personally in case they were wronged. In the crowd I saw the officer with whom I had had the passage at reveille that morning. His face was pale and his lips compressed. He forced his way to the carriage and said: "Mr. President, I have a cause of grievance. This morning I went to speak to Colonel Sherman, and he threatened to shoot me." Mr. Lincoln looked at him, then at me and, stooping his tall, spare form toward the officer, said to him in a loud stage whisper: "Well, if I were you and Colonel Sherman threatened to shoot, I would not trust him for, by Heaven, I believe he would do it."

Edward A. Pollard, editor of the *Richmond Examiner* during the war, writing in retrospect, outlined the effect which the victory of Manassas had on the morale of the South.

The victory was taken by the Southern public as the end of the war or, at least, as its decisive event. Nor was this merely a vulgar delusion. President Davis, after the battle, assured his intimate friends that the recognition of the Confederate States by the European Powers was now certain. The newspapers declared that the question of manhood between North and South was settled forever; and the phrase of "one Southerner equal to five Yankees" was adopted in all speeches about the war, although the rule for the precise proportion was never clearly stated. An elaborate article in *De Bow's Review* compared Manassas with the decisive battles of the world, and considered that the war would now degenerate into mere desultory affairs, preliminary to peace. On the whole, the unfortunate victory was followed by a period of fancied security and of relaxed exertions, the best proof of which was to be found in the decrease of enlistments by volunteers.

So certain, after this event, was supposed to be the term of Confederate existence, that politicians actually commenced plotting for the Presidential succession, more than six years distant. Mr. Hunter of Virginia about this time left Mr. Davis' Cabinet, because it was said that he foresaw the errors and unpopularity of this administration and was unwilling by any identification with it to damage his chances as Mr. Davis' successor in the Presidential office. There was actually a controversy between different states as to the location of the capital of a government, the existence of which they could not understand was yet imperiled by war.

All in all, the victory of Manassas proved the greatest misfortune that could have befallen the Confederacy.

CHAPTER 4

War Becomes Big Business

ORGANIZING AND REORGANIZING

The Battle of Bull Run had clearly demonstrated to the people of the North that the war against the Confederacy would be no walkover. Everyone was now agreed that the army had to be thoroughly reorganized.

After casting around for the right man to undertake this stupendous task, Lincoln chose George B. McClellan, ex-officer in the United States Army, and an engineer of high repute. McClellan, then only thirty-four years of age, had behind him a crowded and brilliant career, which had lifted him to the presidency of the Ohio and Mississippi Railroad.

As such he had been granted an early insight into the deplorable state of military unpreparedness in which the North found itself, as we are told by General Jacob D. Cox, who at that time was an Ohio State Senator.

McClellan was requested by Governor Dennison to come to Columbus for consultation. I took him to the State House, and was present at the interview the governor had with him. The destitution of the State of everything like military material, and the magnitude of building up an army out of nothing, was plainly put.

The next morning McClellan requested me to accompany him to the arsenal. We found a few boxes of smooth-bore muskets, which had once been issued to militia companies and had been returned rusted and damaged. No belts, cartridge-boxes or other accoutrements were with them. There were two or three smooth-bore brass field-pieces, 6 pounders, of which the vents had been worn out. In a heap in one corner lay a confused pile of mildewed harness, which was not worth carrying away. The arsenal was simply an empty store-house. As we

70

were leaving, McClellan turned and, looking back, remarked, half humorously and half sadly, "A fine stock on which to begin a great war!"

A record of how McClellan went to work in his new position has been left to us in his own words.

I reached Washington late in the afternoon on Friday, July 26. On the twenty-seventh I assumed command and lost no time acquainting myself with the situation.

The defeated army of McDowell was only a collection of undisciplined, ill-officered and uninstructed men, who were, as a rule, demoralized and ready to run at the first shot. Positions from which the city would be commanded by the enemy's guns were open for their occupation. The troops were as insufficient in number as in quality. The period of service of many regiments had expired or would do so in a few days. There was so little discipline that officers and men left their camps at their own will, and the city was full of drunken men in uniform. An attack by the enemy was expected from hour to hour.

The first and most pressing demand upon me was the immediate safety of the capital. This was provided for by exacting the most rigid discipline and order; by arresting all ignorant officers and men and sending them back to their regiments; by instituting and enforcing strict rules in regard to permission for leaving the camps; by prohibiting civilians from visiting the camps without permits; and by placing the troops in good defensive positions.

On the first of August, 1861, I had less than 50,000 infantry, 1,000 cavalry and 650 artillerists with thirty guns. Making the proper deduction for the sick, in arrest and on extra duty, it appears that there were not more than 37,000 infantry in the ranks. On the nineteenth of August I had less than 42,000 effective of all arms, such as they were, and the most necessary defenses still required about a week to enable them to resist assaults with tolerable certainty. On the twenty-fifth of August I had about 50,000 effectives of all arms, and perhaps 100 guns. On October 15, 1861, the troops under my command "present for duty" numbered 133,200. On the first of December there were 169,452.

The time spent in the camps of instruction produced most valuable results. The fortifications saved the capital more than once. The organization and discipline then acquired enabled the army to pass through the sanguinary conflicts necessary to terminate the war. No other army could have defeated the Confederate Army of Northern Virginia.

Behind the front of parades the unspectacular work of strengthening the core of the army went on. A fighting force had to be formed on a scale never before attempted. Specialized departments, possessing technical knowledge and skill, had to be created and trained. With millions of people arrayed against each other on both sides, war had become Big Business, as Mc-Clellan intimates.

There were but three weak companies of Engineer Troops available. These were formed into a brigade and at length became admirable pontoniers.

We had no bridge trains whatever, for the remains of the India-rubber pontoon trains constructed for the Mexican War were of no possible use.

Perhaps the greatest difficulty I encountered arose from the scarcity of thoroughly instructed staff officers. None of the officers at my disposal had ever seen large armies or the operations of war on a grand scale. Those who came from West Point had a good theoretical education, but to pass suddenly from an army of 10,000 men in peace to an army of half a million in war was no easy task.

To the corps of Topographical Engineers was entrusted the collection of topographical information and the preparation of campaign maps. Owing to the entire absence of reliable maps, the labors of this corps were difficult and arduous in the extreme. The movements of the army were sometimes unavoidably delayed by the difficulty of obtaining in advance knowledge of the country.

The obstacles to be overcome in organizing and making effective the Medical Department were very great, arising principally from the inexperience of the medical officers, who had to be instructed in their duties from the very alphabet.

A Signal Corps was formed by detailing officers and men from different regiments and instructing them in the use of the flags by day and torches by night. There was scarcely any action or skirmish in which the signal corps would not render important services.

On the first of August, 1861, the commissary of subsistence entered upon his duties. In order to realize the responsibilities pertaining to this office and the vast amount of labor, it is only necessary to consider the unprepared state of the country and our lack of practical knowledge with reference to supplying and subsisting a large army.

Great difficulty existed in the proper organization of the ordnance department for the want of a sufficient number of suitable officers. The supply of small arms was totally inadequate to the demands of a large army, and a vast proportion of those furnished were of inferior quality. The supply of artillery was more abundant but of great variety. Large quantities of small arms of foreign manufacture were contracted for, and private enterprise in the construction of arms and ammunition had to be encouraged, so that by the time the army was ordered to move again the amount of ordnance stores would be ample.

> The difficulties of the Washington government, serious as they were, loomed small in comparison with those of the seceded states. Not only did the South face a much more complex task in creating an army, because of its reverence for state rights, but it was also sadly lacking in natural and industrial resources.
>
> Twenty years later, when President Jefferson Davis wrote about his government's problems, his words still reflected the strain under which he had then labored.

The question of supplying arms and munitions of war was the first considered, because it was the want for which it was the most difficult to provide. Of men willing to engage in the defense of their country, there were many more than we could arm.

The President was authorized to receive from the several states the arms and munitions which they might desire to transfer to the Government of the Confederate States and receive the forces which should volunteer by the *consent of their state.* The arms and munitions within the limits of the states were regarded as entirely belonging to them; the forces which were to constitute the provisional army could only be drawn from them.

On the third day after my inauguration at Montgomery, an officer of high capacity was sent to the North, to make purchase of arms, munitions and machinery; and soon afterward another officer was sent to Europe, to buy and to make contracts for arms and munitions. The officer sent to the North would have been successful but for the inter-

vention of the civil authorities. The officer sent to Europe found few
serviceable arms; however, he succeeded in making contracts for large
quantities.

The difficulties which on every side met the government were but
little appreciated by the people at large.

How badly the need for arms and equipment handicapped the
Southern armies is shown by the situation which the commanding general Albert S. Johnston encountered when he took up
his duties. This is described by Mr. Davis, who again takes up the
account.

General Albert S. Johnston, on his arrival at Nashville in September
1861, found that he lacked munitions of war and the means of obtaining them. Men were ready to be enlisted, but the arms and equipments
had nearly all been required to fit out the first levies.

The chief anxiety of the commander of the department was to procure arms. On the day after his arrival he wrote to the Governor of
Alabama, "I shall beg to rely on your excellency to furnish us, as rapidly
as possible, with every arm it may be in your power to provide." The
governor replied, "It is out of the power of Alabama to afford you
any assistance in the way of arms." The Governor of Georgia replied
to the same request on September 18: "It is utterly impossible for me
to comply with your request." General Bragg, in command at Pensacola, wrote in reply on September 27: "I fear our extreme South has
been stripped of both arms and men." On September 19 General Johnston telegraphed to me: "Thirty thousand stands of arms are a necessity
to my command. I beg you to order them, or as many as can be got."

The Secretary of War replied:

The whole number received by us, by the last steamer, was 1,800,
and we purchased of the owners 1,780, of which we have been compelled to allow the Governor of Georgia 1,000 for arming troops to
repel an attack now hourly threatened at Brunswick.

We have not an engineer to send you. The whole engineer corps
comprises only six captains together with three majors, of whom one
is on bureau duty. You will be compelled to use officers from other
corps, and employ civil engineers.

These details serve as an illustration of the existing deficiencies. Much relief came from the well-directed efforts of Governor Harris of Tennessee. A cap factory, ordnance shops and workshops were established. The powder mills at Nashville turned out about 400 pounds a day. Laws were passed to impress and pay for the private arms scattered throughout the state, and the utmost efforts were made to collect and adapt them to military uses. Yet, during most of the autumn of 1861, fully one-half of General Johnston's troops were imperfectly armed, and whole brigades remained without any weapons for months.

That the South could fight at all was due to the fact that in this emergency everybody was putting his shoulder to the wheel. Even men in the highest places performed work which was far beneath their rank. General J. B. Hood, for instance, then still a first lieutenant, was greatly surprised at what he saw when he reported for duty at Richmond in the spring of 1862.

Colonel R. E. Lee had been recently promoted to the rank of Major-General. His office was in the third or fourth story of, I think, the Mechanic's Institute; and he had around him, it seemed to me, every cobbler in Richmond, giving them instructions as to the manner of making cartridge boxes, haversacks, bayonet scabbards, etc. He was studiously applying his great mind to this apparently trivial but most important work, and it may be safely asserted that his labor in this regard was the source, in a great measure, of the success of our armies in the engagements which soon followed.

Nevertheless, Jefferson Davis was apprehensive.

At the beginning there were in Richmond about 60,000 old flint muskets, and at Baton Rouge about 10,000 old rifles and carbines. There was little powder or ammunition of any kind, no serviceable field artillery. There were no mines of lead except in Virginia, and the situation of those made them a precarious dependence. The only cannon foundry existing was at Richmond. Copper, so necessary for field artillery and for percussion caps, was just being obtained in East Tennessee. There was no rolling mill for bar iron south of Richmond, and but few blast furnaces, and these, with trifling exceptions, were in the border states of Virginia and Tennessee.

As a result of all this, the troops were very poorly armed and equipped. But, poor as were the arms, enough of them, such as they were, could not be obtained to arm the troops pressing forward to defend their homes and their political rights.

The winter of 1862 was the period when our ordnance deficiencies were most keenly felt, and the equipments most needed were those we were least able to supply.

Yet, slowly and laboriously, the Confederate administration brought order out of chaos. A protégé of Jefferson Davis named Thomas C. DeLeon, who occupied a confidential position in Richmond, noted the changes which took place in the first few months of the war.

The Ordnance Department was organized, and eventually brought to a point of efficiency by Major Josiah Gorgas, a resigned officer of the United States Artillery; and it was ably seconded by the Tredegar Works in Richmond. All night long the dwellers on Gamble's Hill saw the furnaces shine with a steady glow, and the tall chimneys belch out clouds of dense, luminous smoke into the night. At almost any hour of the day horses could be seen at the door of the War Department, or dashing thence to the foundry or one of the depots. As a consequence of this energy and industry, huge trains of heavy guns and improved ordnance of every kind were shipped off to the threatened points almost daily to the full capacity of the limited rolling stock on the roads. The new regiments were rapidly armed; their old-style muskets exchanged for better ones, to be in their turn put through the improving Tredegar process. Battery equipments, harness works, forges—in fact, all requirements for the service—were at once put in operation under the working order and system introduced into the bureaus. The efficiency of the Southern artillery—until paralyzed by the breaking down of its horses—is sufficient proof how this branch was conducted.

The Medical Department, destined to play so important and needful part in the coming days of blood, was thoroughly reorganized and placed on an efficient footing. Surgeons of all ages—some of the highest reputation in the South—left home and practice, to seek and receive positions under it. Medicines, instruments, stretchers and supplies of all sorts were sent to the purveyors in the field, while the principal hospitals and depots in Richmond were put in perfect order to receive their expected tenants. The quartermaster's department, both for railroad transportation and field service, also underwent a radical change.

The commissariat alone was badly managed from its very inception. Murmurs loud and deep arose from every quarter against its numerous errors and abuses; and the sagacity of Mr. Davis, so entirely approved elsewhere, was in this case more than doubted.

> Mr. DeLeon's enthusiasm was not shared by the men who had to do the actual fighting; for in spite of all efforts, the South never could match the North in equipment, no more than it could in numbers or even the bare necessities of life. The Confederate soldiers knew the odds they had to face, but were not discouraged, to judge by the notes one of them, Carlton McCarthy, jotted down.

If the Confederate soldier had had only a disparity of numbers to contend with, he would have driven every invader from Southern soil. But the Confederate soldier fought the facilities for the transportation and concentration of troops and supplies afforded by the network of railways in the country north of him. While the South was restricted to its own territory for supplies, the North drew on the whole world for its material.

The arms and ammunition of the Federal soldiers were abundant and good—so abundant that they supplied *both* armies and were greatly preferred by Confederate officers. The equipment of the Federal armies was well-nigh perfect. Their facilities for manufacture were simply unlimited. The latest improvements were hurried to the front and adopted by both armies almost simultaneously; for hardly had the Federals bought, when the Confederates captured, and used, the *very latest*.

The Confederate soldier fought a host of ills occasioned by the deprivation of chloroform and morphia, which were excluded from the Confederacy as contraband of war. The man who has submitted to amputation without chloroform, or tossed on a couch of agony for a night and a day without sleep for the want of a dose of morphia, may possibly be able to estimate the advantages which resulted from the possession by the Federal surgeons of an unlimited supply of these.

The Confederate soldier fought bounties and regular monthly pay. He fought good wagons, fat horses and tons of quartermaster's stores; pontoon trains, of splendid material and construction; gunboats, wooden and iron, and men-of-war; illustrated papers, to cheer the "Boys in Blue" with sketches of the glorious deeds they did not do; Bibles by the carload and tracts by the million—the first to prepare them for death and the second to urge upon them the duty of dying.

The Confederate soldier fought the Sanitary Commission, whose members, armed with every facility and convenience, quickly carried the sick and wounded of the Federal army to comfortable quarters, removed the bloody garments, laid the sufferer on a clean and dry couch, clothed him in clean things and fed him on the best the world could afford and money buy.

He fought well-built, thoroughly equipped ambulances, countless surgeons, nurses and hospital stewards, and the best surgical appliances known to the medical world. He fought the commerce of the United States and all the facilities for war which Europe could supply, while his own ports were closed to the world.

A Tennessean, H. V. Redfield, whose home was on ground frequently traversed by both Federal and Confederate armies, made a comparison between the two after years of intimate observations.

The Union army was altogether the best fed. Early in 1862 the Confederates ceased to have coffee. Soon afterward meat and flour began to grow scarce. Through the whole war the superior food of the Union army was a powerful lever upon that side. In the spring of 1863, I spent two days in the camp of a Confederate cavalry brigade, and their food was simply flour and beef, nothing else. They had not an ounce of salt, and it was not to be got for love or money. They mixed the flour with water, baked it and roasted the beef on the end of a stick. I could but contrast their style of living with that of the well-fed and splendidly equipped Federal army, with their full rations of coffee, pork, beef, salt, bread and beans and convenient cooking vessels.

In clothing there was no comparison. The Southern uniform was supposed to be gray, but the soldiers wore homespun of all colors. Of overcoats they had no regular supply. Blankets were very scarce, ditto woolen shirts and socks. The splendid double-thick overcoat which every Federal soldier had was usually warmer than all articles of clothing combined that the Southern soldier had. I do not think that the Confederate government attempted to issue overcoats to their men. At least I never saw any among them that bore resemblance to uniformity. But it was in cavalry equipment that the Federal soldier stood out preeminently superior. And over all, he had an oilcloth blanket which fitted around the neck, keeping the whole person dry, as well as protecting arms and ammunition.

Much of the Southern cavalry was ridiculously equipped. In one regiment I have seen four or five different kinds of rifles and shotguns; all sorts of saddles, some with rope stirrups, many of the saddles without blankets; all sorts of bridles, and in fact a conglomerate getup fairly laughable. The horses were usually fed on raw corn on the cob. Baled hay, sacked corn and oats, such as the Union army had, was a rarity on the other side. I speak only of what fell under my own observation. The stock of the Southern army, horses and mules, never looked as well as that of the Union army. The animals of the two armies could be distinguished even if no men were about. Animals in the Union army were not only better fed, but better attended, better groomed and cared-for. Another point of difference was the superior brightness and cleanliness of the Northern arms. Their muskets and bayonets and brass ornaments upon the ammunition boxes always looked bright and clean. In the Southern army there was never this care to keep the guns bright and free from dirt and rust.

When I visited a large camp of the Union army, I was struck with the convenience of everything as compared with Southern camps. The Northern soldiers, although they might be in camp but a few days, would busy themselves constructing beds up off the ground, usually by driving forked sticks and laying rails and bits of plank across. If in the woods, they utilized small boughs and leaves in preparing beds and the larger limbs in building shelters from the sun and rain to cook in, etc. Indeed, whenever they went into camp they were as busy as bees arranging for health and comfort. On the other side the Southerners rarely troubled themselves to provide these little comforts. In camp they were usually idle. The scenes of busy industry which we always saw in the Northern camp were never duplicated in the other. And as to filth, the Union camps were almost incomparably cleaner. In the Southern camp you could hardly go twenty steps without getting into filth of some sort, while in the camp of the other side all deposits of filth were carefully removed. Much of the sickness which scourged the Southern army, particularly in the early stages of the war, is attributable, no doubt, to the filthy conditions of their camps.

In the wagon trains of the respective armies there was a great difference. I speak exclusively of the Western armies, knowing nothing whatever from observation of the Eastern armies. The wagons of the Federals were uniform in size and make and much stronger and heavier than the wagons of the Confederates; besides, there were more of them. Ordinarily, a brigade of Union troops on the march would have about twice as many wagons as a detachment of Confederates of equal size. Confederate army wagons were not uniform in size and build. They usually had the appearance of having been picked up about the country. The Federal wagons were covered with canvas, and upon it, in plain black lettering, was the brigade, division and corps to which the wagon belonged. Not so with the Confederate wagons. There was among them a lack of uniformity in build, size and style, and no general attempt was made to designate them by lettering. From the very shoes upon the mules' feet to the hat on the driver's head, the wagon-transportation system of the Federals was superior.

One of the most marked differences in the personnel of the two armies was the far greater propensity of the Federals to pillage. When the Union troops were around, we all had to look out for our money, jewels, watches, vegetables, pigs, cows and chickens. All the men, of course, would not pillage, but there were always some who laid hold of everything they could steal, whether of much use to them or not. I had in my charge a small building filled with articles usually kept in a country store. This they repeatedly broke into, carrying off what they chose and destroying what they did not want.

The remarkable difference in the pillaging propensities of the two armies may be accounted for on the ground, first, that the Federal army was in an enemy's country. Second, the foreign element in the Federal army was very large, and with them was the riffraff from the large cities. In the Southern army these conditions did not exist. The pillagers and robbers in the Federal army did not spare the Union people. The first who came to our neighborhood committed several outrageous robberies, and it happened that the victims in every instance were Union men. The officers used to say in explanation that every flock had black sheep, but the bummer element in the Union army was certainly larger than in the other. I have known regiments of Southern troops to encamp around premises for weeks and not even rob a henroost.

The discipline in the Union army, in many respects, appeared to be better. That is, there was less insubordination and more respect for officers. There was stronger individuality about the Southern soldier and he was far more apt to "talk back" to his superior.

At first the Southerners were certainly altogether the best riders. I have seen some of the Texas cavalry perform feats almost incredible, such as riding at full gallop, leaning over toward the ground, picking up a stone and throwing it, without the least abatement in speed. Inspired by such as this, the Southerners at first underrated the Northern cavalry but soon after learned to respect them.

The superiority of stockades built by the Union troops over those built by the Confederates was striking. The Union troops bestowed an immense amount of labor on theirs, making them of square timber, massive, and enduring and perfect in every particular, while those put up by the Confederates were feeble and ridiculous imitations. These little stockades were, to my mind, significant illustrations of the characteristics of the two armies. What the Northern troops built was of an enduring and substantial character and constructed with the highest skill, while Southern works of the same character were loosely thrown together, with little skill and less labor, Negroes usually being put to such service. In the construction of hospitals and warehouses the same difference was noticeable. All in all the "public works" of the Confederates were about as short-lived as the Confederacy itself.

CHAPTER 5

On to Richmond!

THE PENINSULAR AND VALLEY CAMPAIGNS

All during the winter of 1861-1862, General McClellan, who had been appointed General in Chief of all Union armies, kept drilling the troops camped around Washington, who were now officially designated as the Army of the Potomac. General Johnston with his Army of Northern Virginia still stood at Manassas, barring the way to Richmond. McClellan's immediate object was the destruction of the Confederate forces confronting him, and for this purpose he had worked out a well-considered campaign. How it came to fruition is told by himself.

As early as the beginning of December 1861 I had determined not to follow the line of operations leading by land from Washington to Richmond, but to conduct a sufficient force by water to Urbana and thence by a rapid march to West Point, hoping thus to cut off the garrison of Yorktown and all the Confederates in the Peninsula; then, using the James River as a line of supply, to move the entire Army of the Potomac across that river to the rear of Richmond.

In pursuance of this plan I did not propose disturbing the Confederate forces at Manassas, but I rather desired to hold them there to the last moment, especially until the Urbana movement was well in process of execution.

Meanwhile the preparations for operations on the lower Atlantic and Gulf coasts were progressing slowly but satisfactorily. Early in January General Burnside received final instructions for the expedition to the coast of North Carolina. The general purposes of this expedition were to control the navigation of the sounds on the North Carolina coast, thus cutting off the supplies of Norfolk by water, and at the same time covering the left flank of the main army when operating against Richmond by the line of the James River.

Toward the end of February 1862 I also gave General Butler his final instructions for the capture of New Orleans. This was accomplished chiefly by the gallant action of the naval forces, about the first of May. General Butler was ordered to secure all the approaches to New Orleans and open his communications with the column coming down the Mississippi. This being accomplished, Mobile, Pensacola, Galveston, etc., were to be attacked and occupied in turn.

On March 9, 1862, we received information of the evacuation of Manassas. I at once sent a brigade of cavalry to verify the news and do what they could against the enemy's rear-guard; but General Johnston had, as usual, masked his retreat so well that nothing could be effected.

If I had been retained in chief command, untrammeled as to time and means, I should, in the early spring of 1862, have thrown the Army of the Potomac to the James River with a strength of over 150,000 men. The fears of the administration and their inability to comprehend the merits of the scheme, or else the determination that I should not succeed in the approaching campaign, induced them to prohibit me from carrying out the Urbana movement. They gave me the choice between the direct overland route via Manassas or the route with Fort Monroe as a base. Of course, I selected the latter.

> In January 1862 Edwin M. Stanton, an Ohio lawyer of distinction, had been appointed Secretary of War. Being a novice in military matters, he looked with disdain on McClellan's plans and in a letter to the *New York Tribune* expounded his own views on war.
>
> It was a most astonishing statement, coming from a Secretary of War, particularly as it publicly ridiculed the plans of his own General in Chief.

Much has recently been said of military combinations and organizing victory. I hear such phrases with apprehension. They commenced in infidel France and resulted in Waterloo. Who can organize victory? Who can combine the elements of success on the battlefield? We owe our victories to the spirit of the Lord that moved our soldiers to rush into battle and filled the hearts of our enemies with dismay. Battles are

won now in the same manner they were won in any age since the days
of Joshua—by boldly pursuing and striking the foe.

Others besides Stanton were whispering suspicions into Lincoln's ear, while McClellan's tactlessness and vanity helped to
intensify the mistrust between the President and himself.

On January 27 Lincoln issued a War Order, the first ever
issued by a President of the United States. In it he directed Mc-
Clellan to start operations on all fronts on February 22. Alarmed
and dismayed, McClellan protested in writing, setting forth that
the weather so early in the season was bound to wreck his campaign.

My letter must have produced some effect upon the mind of the
President, since the execution of his order was not required, although
it was not revoked formally.

On the twenty-seventh of February, 1862, the Secretary of War, by
the authority of the President, instructed the Assistant Secretary of
War to procure the necessary steamers and sailing craft to transport
the Army of the Potomac to its new field of operations.

A new order, issued at this time, confined my command to the Department of the Potomac.

The instructions I gave on the sixteenth of March were to the effect
that Manassas Junction should be strongly entrenched, the immediate
approaches to Washington be covered by a strong force able to fall
back upon the city if overpowered; while, if the enemy advanced down
the Shenandoah, a force entrenched at Strasburg would be able to
hold him in check until assistance could reach them; but, unfortunately,
as soon as I started for the Peninsula this region was withdrawn from
my command and my instructions were wholly disregarded.

To make Washington safe, two armies, totalling about 60,000
men, were taken from McClellan's forces and formed into separate commands, one to protect the immediate surroundings of
the Capital, another to block the Shenandoah Valley. In a last-
minute decision, Lincoln took another 10,000 men from the
Army of the Potomac.

When McClellan's army started up the Virginia Peninsula
early in April 1862, it was split once more. One of its strongest

corps, about 40,000 men under General McDowell, was detached and ordered to take the overland route to Richmond, in compliance with Lincoln's directions to keep a strong movable force between the Confederate army and the national capital. Then, while McClellan was already engaged in combat on the Lower Peninsula, he suffered a new blow which weakened him still further. This blow came straight from the Secretary of War.

In consequence of the heavy rains the Virginia roads were very bad and the troops moved with difficulty, so that little artillery and none of the ammunition, forage and provision trains could be brought up from Fort Monroe.

It was at this moment, with the leading division of each column under a hot artillery fire and the skirmishers engaged, that I received a telegram informing me of the withdrawal of the 1st Corps (McDowell's) from my command:

Adjutant-General's Office,
April 4, 1862.

General McClellan: By directions of the President, General McDowell's army corps has been detached from the force under your immediate command, and the general is ordered to report to the Secretary of War.

L. Thomas, Adj.-Gen.

Thus the administration actually retained about twice as many men for the defense of Washington as would have been sufficient. Instead of operating with an army of 156,000 men under my immediate command, I was reduced to 85,000, because, in addition, my bases of operations—Washington and Fort Monroe [with 10,000 men]—were both removed from my control.

I had now only too good reasons to feel assured that the administration, and especially the Secretary of War, were inimical to me and did not desire my success. As further proof may be cited the fact that on the third of April, 1862, ten days after I had left Washington, there was issued General Order No. 33, closing all recruiting depots for the volunteers and stopping recruiting.

Common sense and the experience of all wars prove that when an army takes the field, every possible effort should be made at home to

collect recruits and establish depots, so that the fighting forces may
be kept up to their normal strength.

The civilian population of Richmond still viewed the war in a
frivolous spirit, which aroused the ire of a Manassas veteran.

The hotels were crowded to excess, and a great number of officers
in expensive uniforms strutted about on "sick-leave." Many of them
had never been in the army at all. Every third man was dignified
with shoulder-straps. In theatres, barrooms, and shops, on horseback
and on foot, all wore the insignia. Not one was of less rank than
captain, and as for colonels—their name was legion.

In the morning I was measured by a youth for a pair of boots, and
bought some dry-goods off another. In the evening I saw both of
them playing billiard, dressed out in brand-new uniforms with insignia
belonging to the rank of major.

Confederate spies kept General Johnston well informed.
What his plans were, he later recorded in a personal narrative.

It was ascertained, about the fifth of April, that the Federal army
was marching from Fort Monroe toward Yorktown. The President
was convinced that the entire army was then on the Peninsula. He
therefore directed me to make defensive arrangements.

General J. Bankhead Magruder was in charge of our troops in the
Lower Peninsula. That officer had estimated the importance of at
least delaying the invaders until an army capable of coping with
them could be formed, meanwhile opposing them with about one
tenth of their number. This judicious course saved Richmond.

I hastened back to Richmond to see the President. Instead of
delaying the Federal army, I proposed that it should be encountered
in front of Richmond by one quite as numerous, formed by uniting
all the available forces in the Carolinas, Georgia and Norfolk.
This great army, surprising that of the United States by an attack
when it was expecting to besiege Richmond, would be almost certain to
win, and the enemy, defeated a hundred miles from Fort Monroe,
their place of refuge, could scarcely escape destruction. Such a victory
would decide not only the campaign, but the war.

The President, who had heard me with apparent interest, replied that
the question was so important that he would hear it fully discussed

before making his decision and desired me to meet General George W. Randolph [Secretary of War] and General Lee in his office at an appointed time for the purpose; at my suggestion, he authorized me to invite Major Generals Gustavus W. Smith and James Longstreet to the conference.

In the discussion that followed, General Randolph objected to the

THE PENINSULA AND COASTAL AREA

plan proposed because it included at least the temporary abandonment of Norfolk, which would involve the probable loss of the materials for many vessels of war. General Lee opposed it because he thought that the withdrawal from South Carolina and Georgia of any considerable number of troops would expose the important seaports of Charleston and Savannah to the danger of capture. He thought, too, that the Peninsula had excellent fields of battle for a small army contending with a great one. General Longstreet took little part, which I attributed to his deafness. I maintained that all to be accomplished, by any success attainable on the Peninsula, would be to delay the enemy two or three weeks in his march to Richmond, and that success would soon give us back everything temporarily abandoned to achieve it.

At 1:00 A.M. the President announced his decision in favor of General Lee's opinion.

> The 104th Pennsylvania Infantry went through the entire Peninsular Campaign and at times took a prominent part in it. Its colonel, W. W. H. Davis, wrote up his experiences shortly afterward. They give a graphic account of the hardships which the Union army underwent during that memorable phase of the war.

The way to Richmond was a hard road to travel, and experience had not yet taught politicians the impossibility of making a winter campaign through the mud of Virginia. Strong pressure was exerted to induce General McClellan to attack the enemy forces at Manassas in the winter and fight them on their own ground, but was successfully resisted. The President, unfortunately, gave way to these influences.

Our order to march came at last. One evening I was sitting in my cold tent, looking out upon the dreary scene, when a tall and rather spare but gentlemanly young officer with captain's straps upon his shoulders entered and announced himself as aide-de-camp of General McClellan. He inquired, in broken English, whether my brigade was ready to embark when, receiving an affirmative answer, with a polite bow he withdrew. My visitor was the Duke of Chartres, the Orleans heir to the throne of France. The brigade embarked the next morning for Fort Monroe.

The army commenced its march toward Yorktown on April 4, and the next day the enemy was found to occupy the line of the Warwick

River, which stretched almost entirely across the Peninsula. Heavy fighting took place and continued for weeks, but slowly the enemy was pushed back until we found ourselves in front of Yorktown.

Upon a careful reconnaissance of the enemy's defenses they were pronounced too strong for assault, and siege operations were considered necessary, but the enemy had evacuated on the night of the third and retired up the Peninsula.

They had planted torpedoes in the road, and one was exploded by a soldier, which literally tore the poor fellow to pieces and wounded six others.

A number of Washingtonians took a holiday trip to look at Yorktown after its evacuation. What happened after their arrival is told with glee by a newspaper reporter.

Several of the sightseers asked the corporal of the guard for a pass on the plea that they were Congressmen. The corporal stated the case to the colonel.

"They are Congressmen, are they?" asked the Colonel.—"So they say."—"Well, let them pass. Let them tramp on the torpedoes, go into the magazines, and wherever there is a prospect of their being blown to the devil, for that is the quickest way to end the war."

McClellan's next goal was the Chickahominy River, a treacherous stream which was quick to turn into a rampant flood after heavy rainfalls. Inasmuch as McDowell's strong corps was scheduled to come in from the North to form the army's right wing, McClellan was forced to split his army into two parts, with the Chickahominy between them, thus placing both in a perilous position, as General Johnston was quick to perceive.

After reaching the Chickahominy, a river which separates the peninsula into a northern and southern section, General McClellan's troops advanced very slowly. Three corps were on and above the railroad on the north side of the river, and two below it, south of the river and on the Williamsburg Road. The latter, after crossing the stream at Bottom's Bridge on the twenty-second, apparently remained stationary for several days, constructing a line of entrenchments two miles in advance of the bridge. I hoped that their advance would give us an opportunity to make a successful attack upon these two corps, by increasing the interval between them and the larger portion of their army remaining beyond the Chickahominy.

By the middle of May, after having pushed steadily ahead against a series of rear guard actions, McClellan found himself within a few miles of Richmond. At the same time, the Confederate capital was threatened by a Federal fleet which had ascended the James River.

The feeling within the Confederate capital was one of grave anxiety, as is attested by the entries which a War Department clerk named J. B. Jones made in his diary.

May 14, 1862. Our army has fallen back to within four miles of Richmond. Much anxiety is felt for the fate of the city. Is there no

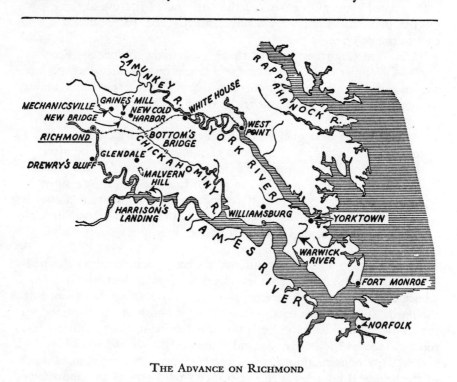

The Advance on Richmond

turning point in this long lane of downward progress? Truly it may
be said our affairs at this moment are in a critical condition. I trust in
God and the chivalry and patriotism of the South in the field. The enemy's fleet of gunboats is ascending the James River, and the obstructions are not completed. We have but one or two casemated guns in
battery, but we have brave men there.

May 15, 1862. The enemy's gunboats, *Monitor, Galena* etc. are at
Drewry's Bluff, eight miles below the city, shelling our batteries, and
our batteries are bravely shelling them. The President rode down to
the vicinity this morning and observed the firing.

The guns are heard distinctly in the city, and yet there is no consternation manifested by the people. If the enemy pass the obstructions, the city will be, it is true, very much at their mercy. They may
shell us out of it, and this may occur any hour. South of the city the
enemy has no forces, and we can find refuge there. I suppose the
government would go to Lynchburg. I shall remain with the army
and see that the tobacco be burned, at all hazards, according to law.

Our marksmen will keep up an incessant fire into the portholes of
the gunboats; and if it be at all practicable, we will board them. So
hope is by no means extinct. But it is apprehended, if the enemy gets
within shelling distance of the city, there will be an attack along our
lines by McClellan. We must beat him there, as we could never save
our guns, stores, etc., retreating across the river. And we *will* beat him,
for we have 80,000 men, and more are coming.

> But General McClellan had troubles of his own, which kept
> him from executing the attack Richmond expected and feared.
> He wrote about them to his wife, after he had reached White
> House on the Pamunkey, the place he had selected as his depot
> of supplies and temporary headquarters.

May 15, 1862. Another wet, horrid day! It rained a little yesterday
morning, more in the afternoon, much during the night, and has been
amusing itself in the same manner very persistently all day. I had expected to move headquarters to White House today, but this weather
has put the roads in such condition that I cannot do it. I think the
blows the Rebels have lately received ought to break them up; but one
can do no more than speculate. Still raining hard and dismally.

May 16. Have just arrived over horrid roads. No further movement

possible until they improve. This house is where Washington's court-
ship took place and where he resided when first married. I do not permit it to be occupied by anyone, nor the grounds around. It is a beautiful spot directly on the banks of the Pamunkey.

May 17. I am pushing on the advanced guard and reconnaisance in
various directions. We gain some ground every day; but our progress
has been slow on account of the execrable nature of the roads, as well
as their extreme narrowness and fewness in number. I am very sorry
that we could not have advanced more rapidly; my only consolation
is that it has been impossible. Just think of its requiring forty-eight
hours to move two divisions with their trains five miles! Nothing could
be much worse than that. The fastest way to move in wet weather is
not to move at all.

> While McClellan was fretting about the weather, the fears of
> the war clerk Jones were shared by a Southern woman who be-
> longed to the aristocracy of Virginia and who was at that time a
> refugee in Richmond. She also kept a diary and confided to it
> her alarm and apprehension.

May 14, 1862. The anxiety of all classes for the safety of Richmond
is now intense. A gentleman, high in position, panic-struck, was heard
to exclaim yesterday: "Norfolk has fallen, Richmond will fall, Virginia
is to be given up, and tomorrow I shall leave this city an exile and a
beggar." Others are equally despondent and, as is too frequently the
case in time of trouble, attribute all our disasters to the incompetency
and faithlessness of those entrusted with the administration of public
affairs. Even General Lee does not escape animadversion, and the
President is the subject of the most bitter maledictions. I have been
shocked to hear that a counterrevolution, if not openly advocated,
has been distinctly foreshadowed as the only remedy for our ills. The
authorities of Richmond, greatly moved by the defenseless condition
of the city, appointed a committee and appropriated funds to aid in
completing obstructions against an attack on Richmond by way of the
James River and to fortify Drewry's Bluff. The Legislature also appointed a committee to wait upon the President and ascertain the progress of the work. A member of this committee, a near connection of
mine, has given me an account of their interview with Mr. Davis. He
received them, as is his invariable custom, with marked cordiality and

respect. The subject was opened by the chairman of the Senate Committee, who made appropriate inquiries for information. The President proceeded to give a distinct narrative of the progress of the work, expressed his great desire for its early completion and regretted that the natural difficulties arising from frequent freshets in the river had rendered the progress of the work slow.

At this point the doorbell rang and General Lee was announced. "Ask General Lee in," said the President. The servant returned, saying that the General wished to see the President for a few moments in the anteroom. The President retired, met General Lee and the Secretary of the Navy and soon returned to the committee.

On the night of this meeting the river was obstructed by the sinking of the steamer *Patrick Henry* and other vessels in the channel. This, it is supposed, was the plan agreed upon by Mr. Davis and General Lee in their short interview. Several days have passed since and I trust that all is now safe. How thankful I am that I knew nothing of this until the danger was passed!

On May 15 Mr. Jones was able to make a happier entry in his diary.

May 15, 1862. Joyful tidings! The gunboats have been repulsed! A heavy shot from one of our batteries ranged through the *Galena* from stem to stern, making frightful slaughter, and disabling the ship; and the whole fleet turned about and steamed down the river! We have not lost a dozen men. We breathe freely; and the government will lose no time in completing the obstructions.

The Federal gunboats had departed but McClellan's army was still very much in evidence, and fear returned to the people of Richmond. News that McDowell's corps was about to start from Fredericksburg and close the ring about the city had filtered through the military censorship. Mr. Jones's diary expressed a strange mixture of despair and optimism, a sort of wishful hope that, all logic notwithstanding, the worst simply could not happen.

May 19, 1862. We await the issue before Richmond. It is still believed by many that it is the intention of the government to evacuate the city. If the enemy were to appear in force on the south side, and another force were to march on us from Fredericksburg, we should be inevitably taken, in the event of the loss of a battle—an event I don't anticipate. Army, government and all might, it is true, be involved in a common ruin. There would be demoralization and even insubordination in the army. Better die here! With the exception of the business portion of the city, the enemy could not destroy a great many houses by bombardment. But if defeated and driven back, our troops would make a heroic defense in the streets, in the walled graveyards and from the windows. Better electrify the world by such scenes of heroism than surrender the capital and endanger the cause.

The Legislature has passed resolutions calling upon the government to defend Richmond at all hazards, relieving the Confederate authorities, in advance, of all responsibility for any damage sustained. But every preparation has been made to abandon it. The archives have been sent to Columbia, South Carolina, and to Lynchburg. The tracks over the bridges have been covered with planks, to facilitate the passage of artillery. The Secretary of the Treasury has a special locomotive and cars, constantly with steam up, in readiness to fly with the treasure.

There is a sullen but generally calm expression of inflexible determination on the countenances of the people, men, women and children. But there is no consternation; we have learned to contemplate death with composure. It would be at least an effectual escape from dishonor.

Day after day passed, however, and McClellan's expected attack failed to materialize. The cause, unbeknown to the people in Richmond, had its roots in the constant wrangling between McClellan and the War Department regarding the disposition of McDowell's corps, which the Union commander urgently demanded for his campaign, while the administration wished to keep it stationary at Fredericksburg as additional protection to Washington. In desperation McClellan finally sent a personal telegram to President Lincoln.

May 14, 1862.

His Excellency Abraham Lincoln,
President of the United States.

I have more than twice telegraphed to the Secretary of War, but have received no reply whatever. I ask for every man that the War

Department can send me.

GEORGE B. McCLELLAN

McClellan was promised McDowell's corps, which was to march promptly. But his hopes were not to be realized. The Southern leaders were fully aware that a junction of the two Union armies had to be prevented at all hazards. The task to accomplish this was entrusted to Stonewall Jackson, who had just returned from a sortie through the Shenandoah Valley. What his plan was he kept secret even from his own staff, with the exception of a young officer named Henry Kyd Douglas, who later wrote how startled he was when told what his chief proposed to do.

About the time of the setting sun General Jackson called for me, handed me a paper, and requested me to take it to General Richard S. Ewell. He proceeded to tell me that he was on the other side of the Blue Ridge Mountains, somewhere near Culpeper Court House. While my heart stood still with amazement, he told me the contents of the paper and added that, as it was very important, he did not care to send it by a courier. He wanted it delivered by daylight in the morning.

For a moment I was paralyzed. I had never been over a foot of the country; how to get to Culpeper I could not imagine. Night was upon us; it was raining like the deluge, and I had already ridden twenty-five miles that day. But I pulled myself together quickly.

"General, I will start at once if I can get a horse."

Vision was impossible. I could feel the neck and ears of my horse, but could not see them. At times I heard the water rush across the road, and I knew we were traveling on perilous edges. At last we reached the summit of Swift Run Gap. The descent was quicker, and I had done at least thirty-seven miles on that mare. After many more miles I drew reins at General Ewell's headquarters, just as I was beginning to be exhausted beyond endurance.

The general was just up, and I handed him the crumpled and saturated dispatch. He read it, and quickly turning to me, said, "You don't say—." The sentence was not finished.

This message was designed to stop or delay the junction between the two Union armies. From all possible Confederate counter-thrusts, Stonewall Jackson's excellent plan emerged

as the best move, but it had to be made before the junction became an accomplished fact.

Mr. Jones, the Confederate war clerk, watched the developments and commented on them in his diary.

May 26, 1862. General Lee is strengthening the army. Every day
additional regiments are coming. We are now so strong that no one
fears the result when the great battle takes place. McClellan has delayed
too long, and he is doomed to defeat.

May 27. More troops came in last night and were marched to the
camp at once, so that the Yankees will know nothing of it.

May 29. More troops are marching into the city, and General Lee
has them sent out in such manner and at such times as to elude the
observations of even the spies.

May 31. Everybody is upon the tiptoe of expectation. It has been
announced (in the streets!) that a battle would take place this day, and
hundreds of men, women and children repaired to the hills to listen
and possibly to see the firing. The great storm day before yesterday, it
is supposed, has so swollen the Chickahominy as to prevent McClellan's
left wing from retreating, and reinforcements from being sent to its
relief. The time is well chosen by General Johnston for the attack,
but it was bad policy to let it be known where and when it would be
made; for, no doubt, McClellan was advised of our plans an hour or so
after they were promulgated in the streets. Whose fault is this? Johnston could hardly be responsible for it, because he is very reticent and
appreciates the importance of keeping his purposes concealed from the
enemy. Surely none of his subordinates divulged the secret, for none
but generals of divisions knew it.

May 31. The President took an affectionate leave of General Johnston, and General Lee held his hand a long time and admonished him to
take care of his life. There was no necessity for him to endanger it.
This General Johnston, I believe, has had the misfortune to be wounded
in most of his battles.

The attack on McClellan took place as advertised, and resulted
in the battles of Seven Pines and Fair Oaks. Jefferson Davis was
an eyewitness to some of the fighting.

In the forenoon of the thirty-first of May, riding out on the New
Bridge Road, I heard firing in the direction of Seven Pines. The enemy

had constructed redoubts, with long lines of rifle pits covered by abatis, from below Bottom's Bridge to within less than two miles of New Bridge, and had constructed bridges to connect his forces on the north and south sides of the Chickahominy. The left of his forces on the south side was thrown forward from the river; the right was on its bank and covered by its slope. Our main force was on the right flank of our position. There were small tracts of cleared land, but most of the ground was wooded and much of it so covered with water as seriously to embarrass the movement of troops.

When we reached the left of our line, our men had driven the enemy from his advanced encampment, and he had fallen back behind an open field to the bank of the river where, in a dense wood, was concealed an infantry line with artillery in position. Soon after our arrival, General Johnston, who had gone farther to the right where the conflict was expected and whither reinforcements from the left were marching, was brought back severely wounded and was removed from the field.

Our troops on the left made vigorous assaults under most disadvantageous circumstances, but were each time repulsed with heavy loss.

The rain during the night of the thirtieth had swollen the Chickahominy; it was rising when the Battle of Seven Pines was fought, but had not reached such height as to prevent the enemy from using his bridges; consequently, General Edwin V. Sumner, during the engagement, brought over his corps as a reinforcement. With the true instinct of the soldier to march upon fire, when the sound of the battle reached him, he formed his corps and stood under arms waiting for an order to advance. He came too soon for us and, but for his forethought and promptitude, he would have arrived too late for his friends. It may be granted that his presence saved the left wing of the Federal army from defeat.

The French Prince de Joinville, who accompanied McClellan on the Peninsular Campaign and who was a competent observer, thus described the battles of Seven Pines and Fair Oaks.

At the moment it was attacked, the Federal army occupied a position having the form of a V. The base of the V was at the Bottom's Bridge near where the railroad crosses the Chickahominy. The left arm stretched toward Richmond; it was composed of four divisions echeloned, one behind the other, between Fair Oaks and Savage's stations, and encamped in the woods on both sides of the road. The other arm of the V, the right, followed the left bank of the river. Between the two arms of the V flowed the Chickahominy. Three or four bridges had been undertaken, only one of which was serviceable on the thirty-first of May. It had been built by General Sumner, and saved the army that day from disaster.

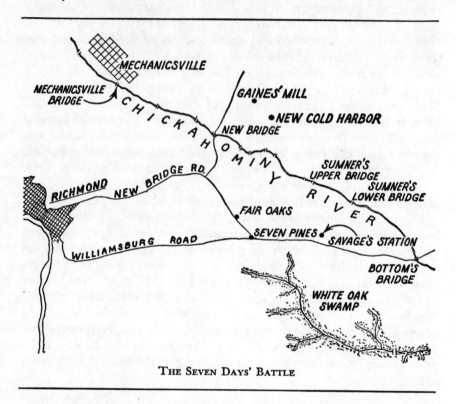

THE SEVEN DAYS' BATTLE

It was against the left wing of the army that every effort of the enemy was directed. That wing had its outposts at Fair Oaks Station and at a place called Seven Pines, on the Williamsburg Road. There the Federals had thrown up a redoubt in a clearing.

The pickets and sentries were violently driven in; the woods which surround Fair Oaks and Seven Pines were filled with clouds of the enemy. The troops rushed to arms and fought in desperation; but their adversaries' forces constantly increased, and their losses did not stop them. The redoubt of the Seven Pines was surrounded, and its defenders died bravely. In vain Generals E. D. Keyes and H. M. Naglee exhausted themselves in a thousand efforts to keep their soldiers together; they were not listened to.

S. P. Heintzelman rushed to the rescue with his two divisions. Philip Kearny arrived in good time to re-establish the fight. Hiram G. Berry's brigade advanced firm as a wall into the midst of the disordered mass which wandered over the battlefield and did more by its example than the most powerful reinforcements. About a mile of ground had been lost, fifteen pieces of cannon, the camp of the division of the advanced guard, that of General Silas Casey; but then we held our own. A sort of line of battle was formed across the woods, perpendicularly to the road and railroad, and there the repeated assaults of the enemy's masses were resisted. The left could not be turned, where the White Oak Swamp was, an impassable morass; but the right might be surrounded. At that very moment a strong column of Confederates was directed against that side. If it succeeded in interposing between Bottom's Bridge and the Federal troops, the entire left wing was lost; but precisely at this moment—at six o'clock in the evening—General Sumner, who had succeeded in passing the Chickahominy over the bridge constructed by his troops, arrived suddenly on the left flank of the column with which the enemy was endeavoring to cut off Heintzelman and Keyes.

He planted in the clearing a battery which he had succeeded in bringing with him. The rapid discharging of these pieces made terrible havoc in the opposing ranks. In vain Johnston sent against this battery his best troops. In vain he rushed on it himself; nothing could shake the Federals who, at nightfall, valiantly led by General Sumner in person, threw themselves upon the enemy at the point of the bayonet and drove him furiously, with frightful slaughter and fear, back as far as Fair Oaks Station.

Night put an end to the combat.

The 104th Pennsylvania was in the vanguard of the fighting, taking and delivering the first blows. Its colonel, W. W. H. Davis, recalls the scene.

We were in too close contact with the enemy to remain long without a battle, but it came sooner than was expected. The night of the thir-

tieth of May will long be remembered by the old Army of the Potomac
on account of the fearful storm that prevailed. The rain fell in tor-
rents; the lightning flashed with unusual vividness and the thunder was
fearful. It would have required no great stretch of the imagination to
believe a great battle going on between the opposing armies. The storm
seemed prophetic of the terrible engagement that was about to take
place.

The 104th opened the battle at Fair Oaks and was the first to receive
the overwhelming shock of the enemy. It was drawn up in advance
and stood quite alone. It delivered the first volley that sent four hundred rifle bullets whistling among the enemy. This announced to the
army that the battle was begun. The action immediately became general. The fire grew hotter and hotter, but the men stood up to the
bloody work firmly and were as cheerful as on parade. Three hours had
elapsed since the regiment had gone into action and more than one-
third of the men had fallen—our promised reinforcements did not
arrive, and we could hold the ground no longer. There was no order
given to retire, but we were literally pushed back by the superior force
of the enemy pressing against us. The regiment retired slowly and sullenly, not an officer or man running.

The regiment lost all its camp equipage and baggage, and the officers most of their personal effects. That night the enemy occupied my
headquarters cabin, which was filled with their own and our wounded.
All the concurrent testimony proves that the enemy was kind to our
wounded who fell into their hands. They carried a number of the
men of the 104th to the shade of an old building that stood near the left
of the regiment and supplied them with crackers and water. Scarcely
an officer or man had saved a blanket or overcoat or an article of clothing, except what they had on. They had nothing but tin cups to cook
their rations in, and many did not possess one of these.

The roads were fearfully bad, and it was almost impossible for the
men to make their way through the deep mud. Halfway down, the
road is crossed by a modest rivulet which, in ordinary times, will not
much more than wet the soles of one's shoes. Now, it was waist deep
and ran with the swiftness of a mountain stream. A squadron of the
8th Pennsylvania Cavalry formed a line across the stream on the lower
side, to prevent the infantry being washed down. The drummer boys,
too small to wade, were carried across on the horses. The regiment
reached its destination before dark and bivouacked in a piece of timber.

The men lay down to sleep without a particle of shelter from the storm that was descending, except such as the bushes and trees afforded.

The second day of the battle at Fair Oaks and Seven Pines was an anticlimax, so the Prince de Joinville implies in his account.

At the earliest dawn of June 1 the combat was resumed with great fury. The enemy came on in a body, but without order or method, and rushed upon the Federals, who, knowing that they were inferior in numbers and without hope of being supported, did not attempt to do more than resist and hold their ground. They fought with fierce determination on both sides, without any noise, without any cries, and whenever they were too hard pressed they made a charge with the bayonet. The artillery, placed on the eminences in the rear, fired shells over the combatants.

Toward midday the fire gradually diminished, then ceased. The enemy retreated, but the Federals were not in a position to pursue them. No one knew then what a loss the Southerners had suffered in the person of their commander, General Johnston, who was severely wounded. It was due to his absence, in a great measure, that the attacks against the Federal army in the morning were unskillful. When the firing ceased at midday the Confederates retreated in a state of inextricable confusion. The North had lost 5,000 men, the South at least 8,000; but the results were as barren on one side as on the other.

Jefferson Davis conceded that the battle was a draw. Its most important result for the Confederate side was that it brought Lee to the fore as a field commander.

General R. E. Lee was now in immediate command and thenceforward directed the movements of the army in front of Richmond. Laborious and exact in details as he was vigilant and comprehensive in grand strategy, a power, with which the public had not credited him, soon became manifest in all that makes an army a rapid, accurate, compact machine, with responsive motion in all its parts.

On the next morning, June 1, he took command of the troops. During the night our forces on the left had fallen back from their position at the close of the previous day's battle, but those on the right remained in the one they had gained, and some combats occurred there between the opposing forces.

Both combatants claimed the victory. The withdrawal of the Confederate forces on the day after the battle from the ground on which it was fought certainly gives color to the claim of the enemy, though that was really the result of a policy much broader than the occupation of the field of Seven Pines.

Our army now was in line in front of Richmond, but without entrenchments. General Lee immediately commenced the construction of an earthwork for a battery on our left flank and a line of entrenchment to the right, necessarily feeble because of our deficiency in tools. It seemed to be the intention of the enemy to assail Richmond by regular approaches, which our numerical inferiority and want of engineer troops, as well as the deficiency of proper utensils, made it improbable that we should be able to resist.

McClellan had been stopped temporarily, but all that he needed to resume the offensive was a turn in the weather and the support of McDowell's corps. McDowell had been ordered to march on May 26 and should have arrived prior to the Battle of Seven Pines. Against the combined Federal forces the Confederate chances of successful resistance would have been slim, as Jefferson Davis himself admitted.

The reason McDowell had not moved on schedule—in fact, had not moved at all and did not do so later—was due to the plan which the Confederate leaders had hatched at the beginning of May, and which had so startled General Ewell and Kyd Douglas. The plan, which was to stamp Jackson as one of the greatest military leaders of the war, had been carried into execution and had been a brilliant success. What it was, and how it worked out, is well told by a Northern officer, Major Sidney W. Thaxter, who was one of its victims.

Early in May 1862 the line of operations of the Union armies in Virginia extended from the James River, a few miles below Richmond, to the Blue Ridge, with a heavy force in the Shenandoah Valley. This line was held on the left by General McClellan with about 100,000 fine troops; in the center by General McDowell with about 40,000 troops; and on the right by General Nathaniel P. Banks with a movable force of about 15,000 men. McClellan had come to a halt before the Confederate Army of Northern Virginia, which covered Richmond and was ready to oppose his further progress. McClellan was calling for reinforcements, and the government had unwillingly determined upon moving McDowell down to join McClellan's right wing and transfer a part of Banks's force from the Shenandoah Valley to that of McDowell. This concentration of Union forces against the army under General Johnston was what the Rebel government feared, and what it bent its energies to prevent.

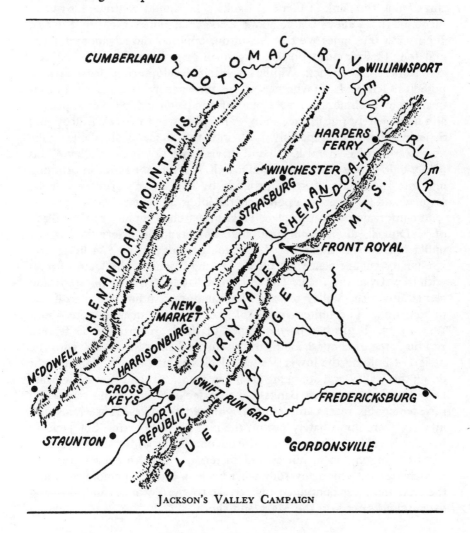

JACKSON'S VALLEY CAMPAIGN

The position of the Rebel armies was as follows: the Army of Northern Virginia of about 75,000 troops under General J. E. Johnston was within the entrenchments of Richmond; 15,000 troops under General R. H. Anderson were observing McDowell; 8,000 men under General R. S. Ewell stood near Gordonsville, ready to reinforce the army of General Johnston at Richmond or move to the support of Stonewall Jackson, who with about 8,000 troops was encamped at Swift Run Gap, threatening the flank of General Banks if he should continue his movement up the Valley; lastly, about 4,000 men under General Edward Johnson, a few miles west of Staunton, opposed the advance of General John C. Frémont who had two small brigades under R. H. Milroy and Robert C. Schenck. While awaiting developments, Jackson proposed to General Lee (who was at this time general in chief with headquarters at Richmond) a bold plan of campaign, which was approved and immediately put in execution. This plan was to attack Milroy and Schenck, then move speedily back into the Shenandoah Valley, take up the army of General Ewell and drive Banks down the Valley. This plan would at least neutralize McDowell, if it did not result in bringing him into the Valley; further progress by McClellan's army would be stopped and the pressure upon General Johnston relieved.

In conforming with this plan, Jackson marched rapidly to the village of McDowell, about twenty miles west of Staunton. Here the brigade under Milroy was encountered, and the next day, May 8, a fierce and sanguinary engagement took place. During the night the Union forces withdrew from the field. Jackson immediately retraced his steps and turned down the Valley toward Harrisonburg, sending word to Ewell to join him. The united forces of the three commands were about 18,000 men. Banks had been stripped of the larger part of his troops, and his force of about 8,000 men was entrenched at Strasburg, with the design of holding the lower Valley. Jackson, instead of going straight down the Valley and attacking Banks in front, turned off at New Market. The first news that Banks had that Jackson was on his flank, and threatening his rear, came from frightened fugitives. His trains and infantry were immediately put on the pike to Winchester; but Jackson struck his column, threw it into utter confusion and made large captures of wagons, men, horses and material. Banks, however, reached Winchester with his army somewhat broken, but not demoralized, and the next morning continued his retreat to the Potomac and, crossing over, found safety on the Maryland shore.

As the result of these operations, Milroy and Schenck were now beaten, Banks's army was routed, the fertile Valley of Virginia cleared of Union troops, Harpers Ferry in danger and Maryland and Washington threatened. In addition Washington was thrown into alarm and trepidation; McDowell's movement to connect with McClellan was suspended; he was ordered to move 20,000 men into the Valley to cut off Jackson, while Frémont with his whole force was ordered into the Valley at Harrisonburg for the same purpose. The whole plan of Union operations had been completely upset, and confusion reigned from one end of the line to the other. At no time during the war was there such dismay in the North. The government at Washington appealed to the states nearest the scene of action for help. The governors of Pennsylvania, New York and Massachusetts issued stirring appeals, the militia was called upon for services.

General Jackson himself seems to have been the only one who had not lost his head. He kept his army from May 26 to May 30 threatening Harpers Ferry and an invasion of Maryland; and gathering up the immense spoils of men and material he moved the main body of his troops on May 30 up the Valley, reaching Strasburg on the thirty-first. He was none too soon, for the advance of McDowell's troops under Shields had already crossed the Blue Ridge and had appeared at Front Royal, a distance of twelve miles from Strasburg.

Frémont, on the other side, was distant with his advance only ten miles. Two brigades of Jackson's forces had been left in front of Harpers Ferry with orders to march on the thirty-first and join the main body. Their distance from Strasburg was over fifty miles, and Jackson with his troops must keep the road open until they joined him. So, sending a part of General Ewell's division to check the advance of Frémont, with the remainder Jackson held on at Strasburg.

The night of the thirty-first brought the two rear brigades to Strasburg after an extraordinary march of thirty-six miles. Our admiration at the perfect knowledge Jackson had of the movements of the Union armies, the unexampled celerity with which he moved, the adroit manner in which he slipped through the net that had been spread to catch him, was only equaled by the shame and indignation which we felt that so much incompetency was shown on the part of our own generals.

Having started his wagon train with the spoils of his brief campaign, Jackson withdrew his army up the Valley. General Shields, instead of joining Frémont at Strasburg and pressing Jackson with their united forces, turned down the Luray Valley with the hope of crossing the south branch of the Shenandoah and striking the flank and rear of Jackson. But his movement was known to Jackson, and he destroyed every bridge crossing the south branch of the Shenandoah and defeated Shields's purpose. Frémont's pursuit resulted in no engagement of any importance until the main body of Jackson's army had reached Port Republic, where the two valleys unite. Here Jackson formed the daring plan of fighting his pursuers in detail. He directed General Ewell to oppose General Frémont, while he held Port Republic. General Ewell formed his line of battle at Cross Keys, about halfway between Port Republic and Harrisonburg, and in a sharp fight forced Frémont from the field. The following day Jackson, leaving a small force to repress Frémont, crossed the river at Port Republic, attacked the leading brigades of Shields and drove them in confusion down the Valley with large losses in killed and wounded and prisoners. Frémont came up on the opposite side of the river in time to hear the last guns of the battle and to find that the bridge had been destroyed and that he had lost his game.

Thus was finished this brilliant campaign of a little more than a month in which Jackson's army had marched more than 250 miles, fought four pitched battles and had captured more than 4,000 prisoners, guns, wagons and immense military supplies.

The story is now again taken up by McClellan, who had just received the startling news that McDowell's corps, which was to form his right wing, had been recalled to take part in the wild-goose chase after Stonewall Jackson, thereby completely ruining his plans.

Had McDowell's corps effected its promised junction, we might have turned the headwaters of the Chickahominy and attacked Richmond from the north and northwest, while we preserved our line of supply from West Point; but with the force actually left at my disposal such an attempt would simply have exposed the Army of the Potomac to destruction in detail and the total loss of its communications. The country in which we operated could supply nothing and, with our communications cut, nothing but starvation awaited us.

All the information obtained indicated that the enemy occupied all the approaches to Richmond from the east, and that he intended to dispute every step of our advance beyond the Chickahominy on our left and to resist the passage of the stream opposite our right. Strong entrenchments had been constructed around the city. Up to this time I had had every reason to expect that McDowell would commence his march from Fredericksburg on the morning of May 26, and it was only during the evening of the twenty-fourth that I had received from the President a telegram announcing the suspension of his movement. The order for the co-operation of McDowell was only suspended, not revoked; and therefore it was necessary to retain a portion of the army on the northern bank of the Chickahominy; I could not make any serious movement on the southern bank until the communications between the two parts of the army were firmly and securely established by strong and sufficiently numerous bridges.

In view of the peculiar character of the Chickahominy, and the liability to sudden inundations, it became necessary to construct eleven bridges, all long and difficult, with extensive logway approaches, and often built under fire.

> During the month of June, McClellan was forced to remain inactive, still waiting for McDowell. His predicament, with the two wings of his army separated by a treacherous river, offered Lee a rare opportunity. Moving the bulk of his army north of the Chickahominy and combining it with that of Jackson, who was hastening back from the Valley, Lee set out to crush McClellan's right wing and cut his communications with his base at White House. The resulting action became known as the Battle of Gaines' Mill.
> Jefferson Davis wrote this account of it.

General Jackson had been instructed with his whole force to move rapidly on the right flank of the enemy north of the Chickahominy. After several severe engagements, he proceeded, with that celerity which gave to his infantry its wonderful fame and efficiency, to execute the orders which General Lee had sent to him.

The whole of Jackson's command did not arrive in time to reach the point designated on the twenty-fifth. He had, therefore, more distance to move on the twenty-sixth, and he was retarded by the enemy.

Not until 3:00 P.M. on June 26 did A. P. Hill begin to move. Then he crossed the river and advanced upon Mechanicsville. After a sharp conflict he drove the enemy from his entrenchments and forced him to take refuge in his works, on the left bank of Beaver Dam, about a mile distant. This position was naturally strong, the banks of the creek in front being high and almost perpendicular, and the approach to it was over open fields commanded by the fire of artillery and infantry under cover on the opposite side. The difficulty of crossing the stream had been increased by felling the fringe of woods on its banks and destroying the bridges. Jackson was expected to pass Beaver Dam above and turn the enemy's right, so General Hill made no direct attack. Longstreet and D. H. Hill crossed the Mechanicsville Bridge as soon as it was uncovered and could be repaired, but it was late before they reached the north bank of the Chickahominy. The troops were unable in the growing darkness to overcome the obstructions and were withdrawn. The engagement ceased about 9:00 P.M.

General McClellan's position was regarded at this time as extremely critical. If he concentrated on the left or northern bank of the Chickahominy, he abandoned the attempt to capture Richmond and risked a retreat upon White House and Yorktown, where he had no reserves or reason to expect further support. If he moved to the right bank of the river, he risked the loss of his communications with White House, whence his supplies were drawn by railroad.

It would almost seem as if the Government of the United States anticipated, at this period, the failure of McClellan's expedition. On June 27 President Lincoln issued an order creating the Army of Virginia to consist of the forces of Frémont, in their Mountain Department; of Banks, in their Shenandoah Department; and of McDowell, at Fredericksburg. The command of this army was assigned to Major General John Pope. This cut off all reinforcements from McDowell to McClellan.

The battle was renewed at dawn on May 27 and continued with animation about two hours, during which the passage of Beaver Dam Creek was attempted and our troops forced their way to its banks, where their progress was arrested by the nature of the stream and the resistance encountered. They maintained their position while preparations were being made to cross at another point nearer the Chickahominy. Before these were completed, Jackson crossed Beaver Dam above, and the enemy abandoned his entrenchments and retired rapidly down the river, destroying a great deal of property, but leaving much in his deserted camps.

Pressing on toward the York River Railroad, A. P. Hill, who was in advance, reached the vicinity of New Cold Harbor about 2:00 P.M., where he encountered the foe and soon became hotly engaged. The arrival of Jackson on our left was momentarily expected, and it was supposed that his approach would cause the extension of the opposing line in that direction. Under this impression, Longstreet was held back until this movement should commence. Hill's single division met this large force with the impetuous courage for which that officer and his troops were distinguished. They drove it back and assailed it in its strong position on the ridge. The battle raged fiercely and with varying fortune more than two hours. (See map, page 115.)

When Jackson arrived, his right division took position on the left of Longstreet. At the same time, D. H. Hill formed on our extreme left, and, after a short but bloody conflict, forced his way through the morass and obstructions, and drove the foe from the woods on the opposite side. The lines being now complete, a general advance from right to left was ordered. The enemy was driven to the first line of breastworks, over which our impetuous column dashed up to the entrenchments on the crest. These were quickly stormed, fourteen pieces of artillery captured and the foe driven into the field beyond. Fresh troops came to his support, and he endeavored repeatedly to rally, but in vain. He was forced back with great slaughter until he reached the woods on the banks of the Chickahominy, and night put an end to the pursuit. Our troops remained in undisturbed possession of the field.

On the morning of the twenty-eighth it was ascertained that none of the enemy remained in our front north of the Chickahominy.

Lee's offensive had not caught McClellan unawares, as appears from his report.

To provide for the contingency of our communications with the depot at White House being severed, and at the same time for a change of our base to James River, I had made arrangements more than a week previous (on June 18) to have transports and supplies of provisions and forage sent up the James River.

The superiority of the James River route, as a line of attack and supply, is too obvious to need exposition. The dissipation of all hope of co-operation by McDowell forced an immediate change of base across the Peninsula.

Such a change of base, in the presence of a powerful enemy, is one of the most difficult undertakings in war, but I was confident in the valor and discipline of my brave army.

Information in my possession convinced me that Jackson was approaching in large force. I determined then to resist Jackson with Fitz-John Porter's 5th Corps, in order to cover the withdrawal of the trains and heavy guns.

The greater part of the heavy guns and wagons having been removed to the southern bank of the Chickahominy, the delicate operation of withdrawing the troops was commenced.

Shortly after noon on June 27, the enemy was discovered approaching in force, and it soon became evident that our entire position was to be attacked. The fire became heavy along our whole front. At 2:00 P.M. General Porter asked for reinforcements. Henry W. Slocum's division of the 6th Corps was ordered to cross to the northern bank by Alexander's Bridge and proceed to his support.

By 3:00 P.M. the engagement had become so severe, and the enemy were so greatly superior in numbers that the entire second line and reserves were moved forward.

At 3:30 Henry W. Slocum's division reached the field and was immediately brought into action. On the left the contest was for the strip of woods running almost at right angles to the Chickahominy. The enemy several times charged up to this wood, but were each time driven back with heavy loss. The regulars of Sykes's division on the right also repulsed several strong attacks.

But our own loss under the tremendous fire of such greatly superior numbers was very severe, and the troops were rapidly becoming exhausted by the masses of fresh men constantly brought against them.

When General Slocum's division arrived on the ground, it increased General Porter's force to some 35,000, who were probably contending against about 70,000 of the enemy. The line was severely pressed on several points; and, as its being pierced at any one would have been fatal, General Porter, who was required to hold his position until night, had to divide Slocum's division and send parts of it, even single regiments, to the points most threatened.

About 5:00 P.M., General Porter having reported his position as critical, other brigades were ordered to cross to his support. The enemy attacked again in great force at six but failed to break our lines, though our loss was very heavy.

About seven they threw fresh troops against us with still greater fury and finally gained the woods held by our left. This reverse, aided by the confusion that followed an unsuccessful charge by five companies of the 5th Cavalry, and followed, as it was, by more determined assaults on the remaining lines, now outflanked, caused a general retreat from our position to the hill in rear overlooking the bridge.

It was now dusk, and the enemy, already repulsed several times with terrible slaughter, failed to follow up their advantage. This gave an opportunity to rally our men and they again advanced up the hill, ready to repulse another attack. During the night our thin and exhausted regiments were all withdrawn in safety. The right wing had now joined the main body of the army.

The enemy had already turned our right and was in position to intercept the communications with our depot at White House, but he was also in large force between our army and Richmond.

I therefore concentrated all our forces on the southern bank of the river. During the night of the twenty-sixth and morning of the twenty-seventh all our wagons, heavy guns, etc., were gathered there.

It may be asked why, after the concentration of our forces on the southern bank of the Chickahominy, with a large part of the enemy drawn away from Richmond upon the opposite side, I had not, instead of striking for the James River fifteen miles below, marched directly on Richmond.

It will be remembered that at this juncture the enemy was on our rear, and there was every reason to believe that he would sever our communication with White House. We had on hand but a limited amount of rations, and if we had advanced on Richmond it would have required considerable time to carry the strong works around that place, during which our men would have been destitute of food; and, even if Richmond had fallen, the enemy could still have occupied our communications with the gunboats and turned disaster into victory. If, on the other hand, the enemy had concentrated all his forces at Richmond during our attack and we had been defeated, we must in all probability have lost our trains before reaching the flotilla.

On the evening of June 27, I assembled the corps commanders at my headquarters and informed them of the plan, its reasons and my choice of route and method of execution.

On the twenty-eighth I sent a dispatch to the Secretary of War, reading [in part] as follows:

Headquarters, Army of the Potomac,
Savage's Station, June 28, 1862, 12:20 A.M.

Hon. E. M. Stanton, Secretary of War:

I now know the full history of the day. Our men did all that men could do, but they were overwhelmed by vastly superior numbers.

I again repeat that I am not responsible for this, and I say it with the earnestness of a general who feels in his heart the loss of every brave man who has been needlessly sacrificed today.

If I save this army now, I tell you plainly that I owe no thanks to you or to any other persons in Washington.

You have done your best to sacrifice this army.

G. B. McCLELLAN

How the Battle of Gaines' Mill looked to Private J. B. Polley in Jackson's army is set forth in a letter he wrote a few days later.

On the morning of June 26, a large force of skirmishers was sent forward. I was one of them, and the distinction cost me the hardest day's work I ever did. We were formed in line, twenty feet apart, and admonished to maintain the intervals between us and to keep a sharp lookout for the Yankees. You can imagine how difficult this was in the wilderness of pine timber and matted undergrowth into which we plunged. I managed somehow, though, not to get lost and to assist in driving an outpost of the 8th Illinois Cavalry from its camp in such haste that it left cooking utensils, provisions and forage. Luckily, a cup of well-cooked rice and the best half of a ham fell to me in the distribution of eatables.

Then, noticing a party of men sitting on their horses in the road near me, I sauntered down to interview them. I was on the point of making some impertinent remark to a particularly seedy, sleepy-looking old fellow, whose uniform and cap were very dirty and who bestrode a regular Rosinante of a horse, when an officer all bespangled with lace came up in a gallop and, saluting, addressed my man as General Jackson. At first I was disposed to doubt, but was convinced by the deference paid him that it was really old Stonewall. No one offered to introduce us to each other and, as we were both bashful, we lost the best chance of our lives to become acquainted.

Friday morning, June 27, we again advanced. The Yankees fell back until they reached a strong, almost impregnable position on the ground in the vicinity of Gaines' Mill. They occupied a ridge overlooking the Chickahominy and between us and that stream, their artillery being massed behind three lines of breastworks. We began our assaults on this position about noon but were constantly beaten back.

We arrived in plain view of the Yankees, and halfway across the field men began to drop, wounded or dead, from the ranks. We passed over two regiments—said to have been Virginians—who, protected by a depression of the ground, were lying down, apparently afraid either to advance or retreat. At the crest of the hill General Hood, our brigade commander, shouted rapidly, "Fix bayonets! Make ready! Aim! Charge!" The timber between us and the enemy hid them from view, but we pulled triggers, nevertheless, and rushed down the hill at the Yankees in the first line of breastworks. They waited not for the onset, but fled like a flock of sheep, carrying with them the second and third lines. Reaching the road which ran along the summit of the hill and looking to our left, we could see large bodies of the enemy in full retreat, but they were so far behind us that, mistaken for our own troops, not a shot was fired at them.

The regiment had more work to do and gallantly did it. General Hood formed the remnant of the command in an old apple orchard while exposed to a terrific fire from batteries and once more gave the order to charge. We rushed down into a ravine and up the steep bank to find that, instead of one battery, there were three so disposed as to attack us from the front and on the flank. The enemy made no stand at the first, but supporting the second were eight companies of the 2nd United States Cavalry, among them the very company in which General Hood had served as a lieutenant. A squadron of this command charged upon us, but more than half of them were killed and wounded and the balance forced to retire in disorder. This was the last organized resistance, the third battery being easily captured and the enemy driven a mile beyond it. Then night came on and human slaughter ceased.

George Williams was a soldier in the 5th New York Volunteers and a war correspondent. He took part in the Battle of Gaines' Mill and wrote down his experiences.

My regiment formed part of the right wing under Fitz-John Porter. On the afternoon of June 26 the camps were startled by a sudden roll of musketry, and the cry, "We are attacked!" ran through the tents.

A terrific burst of artillery and musket firing broke out towards the ravine called Beaver Dam. The attacking force was evidently a strong one, for the fusillade of small arms increased in volume and intensity every moment, and our artillery now began pouring in a deadly fire of shell and solid shot. As we moved up into position, I could see Sykes's regulars pushing forward through a hollow, and it seemed quite certain that we would soon receive our share of the assault.

Our colonel indulged in a grim bit of humor. "Attention, battalion!" he shouted. "Parade rest!"

The order was promptly obeyed, though the men laughed to see the regiment thus put through holiday maneuvers in sight of the enemy. Our colonel's coolness, however, had its intended effect, for other moving columns stiffened up and passed on in excellent shape to the position assigned them.

At that instant the regulars opened a fierce volley, and we began to see the head of the attacking force. Like a swarm of angry bees, the Confederates poured out of the woods and engaged the regulars, who soon found themselves outnumbered. They stubbornly held to their own ground, however, until a battery galloped up and, rapidly unlimbering, opened on Sykes's line with solid shot.

Here came our colonel's opportunity. As yet we had not fired a bullet; and, though the men no longer stood at their absurd parade rest, the line was as steady as if on review. Dismounting, the colonel waved his hat over his head, shouting, "Forward! Double quick!"

With a cheer every man sprang forward on the run. The battery was scarcely six hundred yards away; and, as we dashed through the standing grain, the left gun was suddenly wheeled about for the purpose of giving us a round of grape. As the gunner withdrew his ramrod and stepped back to his position by the wheel, our colonel yelled out an order to lie down, at the same moment throwing himself flat upon the ground. We followed his example by instinct and the next instant the air above us was full of whistling missiles. Scarcely had the report of the gun thundered in our ears when I saw our colors rise from among the wheat stalks; then the regiment resumed its headlong career.

Before the piece could be reloaded, we were among the gunners and had it in our possession. Our fellows having been instructed in the use of artillery, several of them seized the gun and, slinging it round, sent a charge of grape into the body of Confederate infantry coming up to

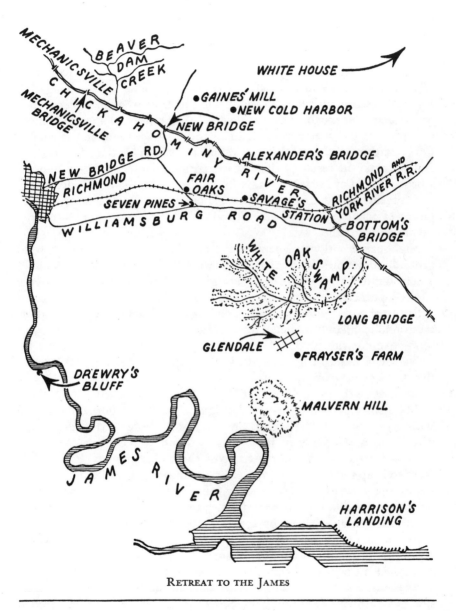

RETREAT TO THE JAMES

support their battery. A deadly volley of musketry was their reply, and I saw men falling all around me. We were for the moment in a perilous position, but our wild dash had disconcerted the battery and checked its fire, thus enabling the regulars to advance, which they soon did in splendid order.

But the battle was not yet over. The troops on our right were rapidly falling back; and soon after the regulars came up, showing that a general retreat of the entire right wing had really commenced. Then orders came for our brigade to move on. Just at that moment a column of our cavalry dashed across the plain and disappeared amid the smoke. Forgetting for the time that my regiment was in motion, I stood still and watched the result of this last despairing charge. In a few minutes a broken band of horsemen came flying back with ten or twenty riderless animals among them. As they galloped past, I also saw that three pieces of a battery were being abandoned for want of horses to drag them off.

Night came, and we maneuvered to and fro, sometimes on firm, solid ground, sometimes in treacherous swamps. None knew precisely where we were, or where we were going. The miserable roads were choked with cannon, ambulances and wagons; sometimes we were compelled to abandon a gun as it sank almost out of sight. Even the infantry found it difficult to gain a firm footing; and, for my own part, I was soon covered with mud and sand.

Just then, a bright light suddenly shot up into the sky. "What can that be?" exclaimed a corporal.

"It must be the stores on fire at White House," I replied.

The flames grew brighter and brighter, until the horizon was red with angry light. It was serious business for us, because the destruction of our stores was proof of the critical position of the army.

Orders came for our corps to cross the Chickahominy River. We were to keep the column in motion; no man being permitted to halt on the bridge even for an instant. For four long hours the troops pressed on, the trains holding the center of the road. With a few torches to define the outlines of the bridge, we stood there, urging on the laggards, or lending a helping hand to some half-wrecked vehicle. Wagons, cannon, pontoons and ambulances, artillery, cavalry and infantry all pushed on pell-mell, with that painful haste incident to a retreat.

As the first faint streaks of dawn reddened the treetops, the last division came up at a swinging gait. Scarcely had the rear guard reached the other bank of the river when the engineers began destroying the bridge. We were all safely across, and the army was once more re-united. But we had left our dead and wounded behind us, the ground where they fell being strewn with abandoned weapons.

The people of Richmond watched with rapidly beating pulses the attack on McClellan's exposed right wing. The battle was taking place almost before their eyes, and their prayerful hopes were well remembered later by T. C. DeLeon.

When the armies lay at Mechanicsville both were plainly visible from many points in the city. From the Capitol, miles of encampment could be seen, spreading out like a map; and in the dusk the red flash of each gun and the fiery trail of its fatal messenger were painfully dis-tinct. The evening before Hill's advance, the poet-librarian of the Capitol was pointing out the localities to a company of officers and ladies. A terrific thunderstorm had just passed over the hostile hosts. Not a shot disturbed the still peacefulness of the scene to give token of the wild work already shaped out for the next week. Suddenly a glori-ous rainbow shaped itself in the transparent mist over the Confederate camp, spanning it from end to end. A lady pointed it out to the poet.

"I hail the omen!" she said. And when the omen was accomplished and Richmond was safe, the poet sent the lady those classic lines so well-known in the South, "The Battle Rainbow."

Next afternoon the great fight began. The sharp, quick rattle of small arms and the dull incessant boom of artillery told of hot work even nearer than Seven Pines. So sharp and clear were the reports that it seemed the fight must be on the very edge of town, and the windows rattled at every discharge.

Almost every man worthy of the name was at the front; but the brave and steadfast women of Richmond collected in groups and— while they listened with blanched faces and throbbing hearts—still tried to cheer and comfort each other.

Day by day, as the tide of battle surged farther off, it sent into Rich-mond cheering news that nerved afresh these brave hearts for the hor-ror to come. Gaines' Mill and Cold Harbor rolled back their echoes of triumph; news came of the strait into which McClellan was driven and reports that one day more must see him a prisoner in the city he had dared—his splendid host swept away and destroyed.

Mr. Jones, the diary-keeping Richmond war clerk, also saw
the beginning of the battle and duly wrote down his impressions.

June 26, 1862. This is the day of battle! Jackson is in the rear of
McClellan's right wing! I suppose Mr. Randolph, the secretary of war,
had been previously advised of General Lee's intention to fight today;
I know some of the brigadier generals in the army do not know it. It
is characteristic of Lee's secretiveness to keep all of his officers in profound ignorance of his intentions, except those he means to be engaged.
The enemy cannot possibly have any intimation of his purpose, because
the spies here have no intelligence; and none are permitted to pass the
rear pickets in sight of the city without my passport. What a change
since the last battle!

After dinner I repaired to my old stand on the hill north of the Jews'
cemetery, and sat down in the shade to listen. Many persons, in response to my inquiries, said that distant guns had been heard in the
direction of the Pamunkey River. "That is Jackson!" I exclaimed, as
the sounds were distinctly discerned by myself. "And he is in their rear,
behind their right wing!"

The sounds grew more distinct and more frequent, and I knew he
was advancing. But how long could he advance in that direction without being overwhelmed?

This suspense continued only a few minutes. Two guns were then
heard northeast of us and in such proximity as to startle some of the
anxious listeners. These were followed by three or four more, and
then the fire continued with increasing rapidity. This was General
A. P. Hill's division in front of the enemy's right wing, and Lee's plan
of battle was developed. Hill was so near us as to be almost in sight.
The drums and fifes of his regiments, as they marched up to the point
of attack, could be easily heard; and the enemy's guns, pointed in the
direction of the city, were as plainly discerned. I think McClellan is
taken by surprise.

Another hour, and the reports come with the rapidity of seconds, or
3,600 per hour! And now, for the first time, we hear the rattle of small
arms. And lo! two guns farther to the right—from Longstreet's division, I suppose. And they were followed by others. This is Lee's grand
plan of battle: Jackson first, then Hill, then Longstreet—time and distance computed with mathematical precision! The enemy's balloons,
that innovation in warfare which they have used before, are not up

now. They know what is going on, without further investigations up
in the air. The business is upon earth, where many a Yankee will
breathe his last this night! McClellan must be thunderstruck at this
unexpected opening of a decisive battle.

As the shades of evening fall, the fire seems to increase in rapidity
and, a gentle breeze rising as the stars come out, billows of smoke are
wafted from the battlefield. And now, occasionally, we can distinctly
see the bursting of shells in the air, aimed too high by the enemy and
exploding far this side of our line of battle.

Darkness is upon us, save the glimmer of the stars, as the sulphurous
clouds sink into the humid valleys. But the flashes of the guns are visible on the horizon, followed by the deep intonations of the mighty
engines of destruction, echoing and reverberating from hill to hill and
through the vast valley of the James in the rear.

June 27, 1862. At the first dawn of day, the battle recommenced,
farther round to the east. This was enough. The enemy had drawn in
his right wing. And courier after courier announced the taking of his
batteries by our brave defenders! But the battle rages loud and long,
and the troops of Jackson's corps, like the march of Fate, still advance
upon McClellan's right flank and rear. Jackson's horse and the gallant
Stuart, with his irresistible cavalry, have cut the enemy's communications with their base on the Pamunkey. It is said they are burning their
stores!

What genius! What audacity in Lee! He has absolutely taken the
greater portion of his army to the north side of the Chickahominy,
leaving McClellan's center and left wing on the south side, with apparently easy access to the city. This is (to the invaders) impenetrable
strategy. The enemy believes Lee's main forces are here, and will never
think of advancing. We have so completely closed the avenues of intelligence that the enemy has not been able to get the slightest intimation
of our strength or the dispositions of our forces.

McClellan's decision to change his base to the James River inaugurated a series of violent rear-guard activities which, together with the struggle of the two preceding days, history has
designated as the Seven Days' Battle.

It meant marching the entire Union army past the Richmond
front. It meant a day and night retreat through swamps and over
ruined roads, while the Confederates were slashing viciously at

the flank and rear. Violent battles were fought at Glendale and
Frayser's Farm, but they were indecisive. McClellan's point of
rendezvous for his troops was Malvern Hill, an elevated plateau
adjoining the James River.

George Williams, the soldier-correspondent, gives a brief outline of the retreat.

Then we began our memorable march to the James River. For seven
weary days we fought from early dawn until far into the night, marching from the right to the left, each corps and division going into action
after traversing in turn the interior line of the army. Battle after battle
was fought, until we ceased counting the engagements. We struggled
through swamps and waded swollen streams as we charged one position after another. Amidst a hellish confusion of sounds we fought on;
we marched and countermarched, hardened in feeling, vengeful at
heart, fighting with the courage born of despair. At length, our corps
emerged from the woods, and we found ourselves in a broad, open field
of standing wheat.

"The James River!" "The James!" shouted hundreds of voices, the
welcome cry being taken up and repeated again and again.

It was indeed the James and, as we moved across the field, I could
see the gunboats lying in the stream. Soon after, we had halted for
camp.

What the retreat to the James River meant to another Union
soldier is told by the commander of the 104th Pennsylvania
Volunteers, Colonel W. W. H. Davis.

McClellan having lost all hope of assistance from McDowell, resolved to change his base to the James River. Every energy was bent
toward making the movement a success. Cars were loaded with provisions and ammunition at White House and run to Savage's Station to
the last moment; and all the wagons were loaded and sent up. On the
day and night of the twenty-eighth the supply and baggage trains
were withdrawn from Savage's Station and sent off toward the James.

The road was crowded with wagons, and the march necessarily slow.
Our brigade crossed the White Oak Swamp some time after midnight
and bivouacked on the rising ground.

The enemy pushed after us immediately and were close in our rear.

Our engineers had hardly destroyed the swamp bridge and retired before his skirmishers came up to reconnoiter. For several hours only the swamp divided the opposing forces. Without a note of warning, the enemy suddenly ran his artillery forward from behind the opposite hills and opened several batteries on our army while the men were lounging on the grass eating their dinner. The shock was so sudden that everybody seemed stunned for a moment. One division broke for the wood—the officers leaving their horses tied to the trees in the open field—but was rallied again. The teamsters were threatened with instant death if they drove faster than a walk, and guards were placed at short intervals along the road to prevent a stampede. A New York regiment broke and was leaving the field when it was charged with the bayonet by another regiment and stopped. Our guns had been placed in battery and soon thundered at the enemy in reply. The distance was hardly a mile, and they had our exact range. It was one of the most furious cannonades of the war and continued through the day. The infantry was obliged to endure this severe shelling that hot afternoon without an opportunity to reply, an ordeal more trying than any other to a soldier. Some of the batteries had to fill their ammunition chest three times, so rapid was the firing. The men serving the batteries were almost worn out, and one faithful gunner stood to his piece until he was entirely deaf. The enemy made repeated efforts to cross the swamp while this cannonading was going on, but in each case was prevented. An Irish camp woman, belonging to a New York regiment, made herself quite conspicuous during the action. She remained close to the side of her husband, and refused to retire to a place of security. Occasionally she would notice some fellow sneaking to the rear, when she would run after him, seize him by the nape of his neck and place him in the ranks again, calling him a "dirty, cowardly spalpeen," and other choice epithets. The flying shells had no terrors for her. During the hottest of the cannonade this courageous woman walked fearlessly about among the troops, encouraging them to stand up to their work. Her only weapon, offensive or defensive, was a large umbrella she carried under her arm. About the middle of the afternoon, heavy firing was heard on the left where our troops were fighting the enemy at Glendale. He had succeeded in crossing the swamp higher up, and was making an effort to fall upon our rear. This firing, so close on our left, caused considerable alarm, for should the enemy succeed in his attack, it would enable him to cut off our retreat. A brigade was sent

off to reinforce our troops. Our commander became so much interested in the progress of events in that quarter toward evening that he
rode in that direction to endeavor to obtain information. In a short
time he returned at a gallop, shouting as he came up, "All's right; we've
repulsed them."

Those who were with the rear guard that night at the White Oak
Swamp crossing will long remember it. The situation was extremely
critical. There was not a sentinel between the two armies to announce
the approach of the enemy. Our two guns threw an occasional shell
to give notice that we still occupied the ground.

It was now two o'clock on the morning of the first of July and the
march was commenced. We did not know what road to take. Those
whose business it was to know the route taken by the retreating army
had remained on the ground all day without informing themselves. The
head of the column was directed toward the right, contrary to the conviction of the most intelligent officers present, and the troops took the
direct route for the enemy. After marching some distance they passed
the pickets of another portion of our army and were again outside the
Federal lines. The road was filled with stragglers coming from the field
of Glendale. They were much demoralized, and many had thrown
away their arms.

The regiments made the march to the rear at as rapid a gait as the
men could make. Part of the time, they moved in a slow trot—as near
a "double-quick" as their fatigued bodies would permit. The column
was overtaken by a mounted officer, who advised them to "hurry up,"
as the enemy was not far off and was expected to make an attack when
daylight appeared. Scarcely a word was spoken, except now and then
a whispered command to the men to "close up." The road was still
filled with stragglers, through which our men had to force their way
—and it was often with much difficulty our wearied fellows could be
prevented from mingling with the throng of fugitives going the same
way. Several of the officers and men were really too sick to march,
and all their physical strength was taxed to keep up with the command.

The condition of the roads the last two days had been such that the
trains were got through with much difficulty. Many wagons were
abandoned and destroyed, and a number were unloaded to enable the
mules to draw them empty. Every kind of baggage was thrown into
the mud. Officers' trunks were broken open and rifled of their contents
by soldiers who were too much fatigued to carry their knapsacks, but

who could bear a few pounds of plunder. Cases of expensive surgical instruments were cast away, to be picked up by the first party that claimed them. At one point where the mud was too deep for the men to cross the road, a crossing was made of mattresses taken from a hospital wagon. In this manner thousands of dollars' worth of valuable and useful baggage was destroyed.

McClellan had succeeded in reaching Malvern Hill with most of his army intact. General Fitz John Porter, whom he had put in command, gives an account of the battle which followed.

This new position was better adapted for a defensive battle than any with which we had been favored. It was elevated, and protected on each flank by small streams or swamps; while the woods in front were marshy, and the timber so thick that artillery could not be brought up; even troops moved with difficulty. The ground in front was sloping, and over it our artillery and infantry, themselves protected by the crest and ridges, had clear sweep for their fire.

About 3 o'clock on Monday, June 30, the enemy advanced and opened fire. In return the rapid fire of our artillery was opened upon them, smashing one battery to pieces, silencing another, and driving back their infantry and cavalry. The gun-boats in the James made apparent their welcome presence and gave good support by bringing their heavy guns to bear on the enemy.

Our forces lay on their arms during the night, awaiting the attack expected on the following day. About 10 A.M. the enemy began feeling for us along our line. Until nearly one o'clock our infantry were resting, waiting for the moment when, the enemy advancing, would render it necessary to expose themselves. An ominous silence now intervened until about 5:30 o'clock, when the enemy opened with artillery from nearly the whole front, and soon afterward pressed forward his infantry, first on one side, and then on the other, or on both. As if moved by reckless disregard of life, with a determination to capture our army or destroy it by driving us into the river, regiment after regiment, and brigade after brigade, rushed at our batteries; but the artillery mowed them down with shrapnel, grape and canister, while our infantry, witholding their fire until the enemy were within short range, scattered the remnants of their columns.

The sight became one of the most interesting imaginable. The havoc made by the bursting shells was fearful to behold. The courage of our men was fully tried. The safety of the army was felt to be at stake. Determined to finish the contest, I pushed on into the woods held by the enemy. I sent messages to the commanding General, expressing the hope that we should hold the ground we occupied, but within an hour I received orders to withdraw and move to Harrison's landing.

Thus ended the memorable "Seven Days" battles. Each antagonist accomplished the result for which he had aimed: one insuring the temporary relief of Richmond; the other gaining security on the north bank of the James from whence it could renew the contest successfully.

> The attack on Malvern Hill by the Confederates was undertaken with great determination. It was a gamble which Lee had to take. If it proved a failure, it would be costly, although not disastrous; if successful, it might lead to the destruction or capture of the entire Federal army.
>
> General John B. Gordon led a Confederate brigade, and his story of the attack answers the question why the onslaught was a failure.

I found General Hill, my superior officer, in a fever of impatience for the advance upon McClellan's troops, who were massed, with their batteries, on the heights in our front. The hour for the general assault which was to be made in the afternoon by the whole Confederate army had come and passed. There had been, however, the delays usual in all such concerted movements. Some of the divisions had not arrived upon the field; others, from presumably unavoidable causes, had not taken their places in line, and the few remaining hours of daylight were passing. Finally a characteristic Confederate yell was heard far down the line. It was supposed to be the beginning of the proposed general assault. General Hill ordered me to lead the movement on the right, stating that he would hurry in the supports to take their places on both my flanks and in rear of my brigade. I made the advance, but the supports did not come. Indeed, with the exception of one other brigade, which was knocked to pieces in a few minutes, no troops came in view.

Isolated from the rest of the army and alone, my brigade moved across this shell-plowed plain toward the heights, which were perhaps

more than half a mile away. Within fifteen or twenty minutes the center regiment, the 3rd Alabama, with which I moved, had left more
than half of its number dead and wounded along its track, and the
other regiments had suffered almost as severely. My pistol had the
handle torn off; my canteen was pierced, and my coat was ruined by
having a portion of the front torn away.

At the foot of the last steep ascent, near the batteries, I found that
McClellan's guns were firing over us and, as any further advance by
this unsupported brigade would have been not only futile but fool-
hardy, I halted my men and ordered them to lie down and fire upon
McClellan's standing lines of infantry. I stood upon slightly elevated
ground in order to watch for the reinforcements, or for any advance
from the heights upon my command. In vain I looked behind us for
the promised support. Anxiously I looked forward, fearing an assault
upon my exposed position. No reinforcements came until it was too
late. At last came, also, the darkness for which I longed, and under its
thick veil this splendid brigade was safely withdrawn.

> For the first time since the beginning of the campaign, the
> South was convinced that the threat to Richmond had been ar-
> rested. A Southern lady, in her diary, gave free expression to her
> feelings, and bestowed her benedictions on the Federal army
> then resting on the James River.

Richmond is disenthralled—the only Yankees there are in the "Libby"
and the other prisons. The gunboats are rushing up and down the
river, shelling the trees on the banks, afraid to approach Drewry's
Bluff. The Northern papers and Congress are making every effort to
find out to whom the fault of their late reverses is to be traced. Our
people think that their whole army might have been captured but for
the dilatoriness of some of our generals.

McClellan and his "Grand Army" are on the James River, enjoying
mosquitoes and bilious fevers. The weather is excessively hot. I dare
say the Yankees find the "Sunny South" all that their most fervid imag-
inations ever depicted it, particularly on the marshes. So may it be,
until the whole army melts with fervent heat.

CHAPTER 6

The Navies Clash

THE *MONITOR-MERRIMAC* DUEL

On Gideon Welles, Lincoln's Secretary of the Navy, devolved the duty of keeping the Southern States from receiving vital imports from Europe, something that could only be accomplished by an efficient and up-to-date navy.

By 1861, England and France already possessed armor-clad vessels, but the United States had lagged behind in advanced naval construction. A modern fleet was needed for the blockade, an important war measure adopted at the very beginning of the war. Moreover, this fleet had to be finished before the South could construct modern warships of her own.

Welles took immediate steps to win this race for supremacy. How he did this is told in his own language.

The Navy of the United States, at the commencement of Mr. Lincoln's administration, was wholly destitute of ironclad steamers, but the attention of Congress was invited thereto, and an act was passed on the third of August, 1861, placing at the disposal of the Navy Department one and a half million of dollars. A board of naval officers was appointed to receive and report upon plans which might be submitted within twenty-five days.

Before the time limit expired, I went to Hartford. While I was there, a model was laid before me, invented by John Ericsson, for a turreted vessel, or floating battery, which impressed me favorably. I directed that the model be submitted to the Board for examination and report.

A contract for this vessel which, when built, would be called the *Monitor*, by his request, was made and signed on the fourth of October, 1861. It was stipulated that she should be ready for sea in one hundred days.

Unfortunately, there was delay on the part of the contractors, and she was not turned over to the Government until the third of March.

The *Merrimac*, a vessel then under construction by the Confederates, was being clothed with iron armor when the contract for the *Monitor* was made. We, of course, felt great solicitude, not lessened by the fact that extraordinary pains were taken by them to keep secret from us their labors. Their efforts to withhold information, though rigid, were not wholly successful, for we contrived to get occasional vague intelligence of the work as it progressed. When the contract for the *Monitor* was made, in October, with a primary condition that she should be ready for sea in one hundred days, the Navy Department intended that she should proceed up the Elizabeth River to the Navy Yard at Norfolk, place herself opposite the dry dock and with her heavy guns destroy both the dock and the *Merrimac*. This was *our* secret. The *Monitor* could easily have done what was required, for her appearance at Norfolk would have been a surprise. But the hundred days expired, weeks passed on and the *Monitor* was not ready.

The newly born Confederacy had no navy at all, nor could it, with its limited facilities, hope to build one within a reasonable length of time.

Two months after Jefferson Davis' inauguration, however, an over-aged Federal naval officer gave the South a chance to acquire the nucleus of a navy by one stroke. The editors of *Harper's Weekly*, A. Guernsey and H. M. Alden, gave a readable account of this happening.

The great naval station at Portsmouth near Norfolk, Virginia, was the most enviable place south of New York for the purpose to which it was appropriated. In April 1861, twelve vessels of war of various sizes were lying there, from the *Pennsylvania*, a four-decker of 120 guns, to the brig *Dolphin* of four. Among them was the sloop of war *Cumberland* and the *Merrimac*, the latter a steam frigate of forty guns which had been launched in 1855.

The place was entirely without protection; no measures had been taken against an attack. Commodore McCauley, in command of the yard, only was directed on April 10, to use "extreme vigilance and circumspection."

On April 12, Fort Sumter was fired on, and at last Commodore Mc-

Cauley gave orders to lose no time in loading the *Merrimac*, the *Plymouth*, the *Dolphin* and the *Germantown* with the more valuable ordnance and in putting these vessels in a position to be moved at any moment. The *Cumberland* was placed so as to command Portsmouth, the Navy Yard and Norfolk. This was not done until April 17, the day on which the ordinance of secession was passed at Richmond.

A large number of the naval officers were from slave states, and the people of Norfolk were among the bitterest secessionists. They openly declared that, if the government attempted to move any of the ships, they would attack immediately. Commodore McCauley allowed his junior officers to persuade him that delay would be prudent. On the eighteenth, they resigned their commissions. McCauley's eyes were at last opened but only to see his peril and utter helplessness. He then decided to scuttle all the vessels except the *Cumberland*.

The dry dock was mined, and combustibles were scattered through the scuttled ships. The roar of the flames, as they devoured the work of years and the wealth of a nation, was heard far and wide. The loyal officers and men took ship on the *Pawnee* and the *Cumberland*.

When the flames had subsided, it was found that little harm had been done to the yard and the ships, all of which were seaworthy. Even the *Plymouth* and the *Merrimac* eventually were raised and made serviceable. And that was how the Confederacy acquired a navy.

At least one man in the North foresaw the course of future maritime developments. He was John Ericsson, a Swedish-born engineer, who had lived in the United States since 1839 and had become a distinguished inventor. Ericsson was not satisfied with merely imitating the British and French iron-plated wooden ships. His chief improvement over them consisted of a movable gun turret, which allowed the guns to be quickly aimed in any direction desired.

Captain (later Admiral) David Dixon Porter was sent to report on Ericsson's war vessel, and gives a lifelike picture of Ericsson in his shirt sleeves.

Who was going to believe that "an iron pot," such as Mr. Ericsson had designed, would float, even if empty, much less when loaded down with guns, ammunition, machinery, provisions and men? Mr. John Lenthall, the oldest and ablest constructor in the navy, had scouted the idea. "How is the *Monitor* to ride the sea with all that weight in her?" he had inquired.

"The sea shall ride over her," replied Ericsson, "and she will live in it like a duck."

"The man is crazy!" said Lenthall.

Mr. Lenthall was a man of great ability, but he had been too many years engaged in modeling sloops of war and frigates and was too cautious and conservative to be diverted by what he considered visionary ideas.

At length it was agreed that Ericsson should build, at his own expense and at a private shipyard, an iron-turreted vessel which the Government would accept provided it fulfilled in all respects the promises of the inventor.

While "Ericsson's iron pot" was approaching completion, I received orders to make a critical examination of the vessel and report my opinion of her capabilities.

After arriving at New York, I called on Mr. Ericsson and showed him my orders. He read them, looked at me attentively and said: "Well, you are no doubt a great mathematician and know all about the calculations which enter into the construction of my vessel."

"I am no great mathematician," I replied, "but I am a practical man, and think I can ascertain whether or not the *Monitor* will do what is promised for her."

"I don't want *practical* men sent here, sir," Ericsson exclaimed. "I want men who understand higher mathematics. Men who can work out the displacements, horsepower, impregnability, endurance at sea in a gale, capacity to stow men, the motion of the vessel according to the waves, her stability as a platform for guns, her speed, actual weight—in short, everything pertaining to the subject."

"Well," said I, as the inventor paused to take a breath, "although I am not strictly what you would call a mathematician, I know the rule of three, that twice two are four, and some simple equations."

Ericsson looked hard at me, his hair bristled up, and the muscles of his brawny arms seemed to swell, as if in expectation of having to eject me from the room.

"This beats the devil," he cried. "It would be better if you knew nothing. Here's a man who tells me he knows a little of simple equations, and they send him to examine John Ericsson!

"Now what do you think of that?" continued Mr. Ericsson, handing me a small wooden model; "that's my 'iron pot,' as you navy people call it."

I regarded the model with a critical eye, holding it upside down. "This," I remarked, "is evidently the casemate—" passing my hand over the bottom—"and this—" pointing to the turret—"is undoubtedly where you carry the engine."

"O Heavens!" exclaimed Ericsson. "Well, well! Never did I see such a—— But never mind; you will learn by and by."

After learning all I could from the drawings of the *Monitor*, I proposed to the inventor to examine the simon-pure article, and we crossed the ferry to Greenpoint, where the vessel was building.

Taking my coat off, I penetrated to the innermost recesses of the *Monitor*, followed by Mr. Ericsson. After an hour spent in examining the vessel, I emerged from the hold, followed by the inventor.

"Now, sir," I said, "I know all about your machine. So I will tell you in plain terms what I think of your iron pot."

"Say what you please," exclaimed Ericsson, glaring at me like a tiger all ready to spring; "nobody will mind what you say!"

"I will say this to the government. . . ."

"Go on, sir, go on!" cried Ericsson.

"Well, then," I continued, "I will say that Mr. Ericsson has constructed the most remarkable vessel the world has ever seen—one that, if properly handled, can destroy any ship now afloat and whip a dozen wooden ships together."

Ericsson regarded me in astonishment, then seized my hand and almost shook my arm off. "My God!" he exclaimed, "and all this time I took you for a damned fool."

Rumors that the formidable *Merrimac* was being built by the Confederates had reached the Northern public, spreading fear and consternation everywhere. The *Merrimac* was a secret weapon, the more terrifying because so little was known about her. The blockade of the South, it was feared, would become a mere scrap of paper, in fact, might even be turned into a blockade of the North.

The outlook was indeed dismal. Only a select few knew of the embryonic *Monitor*, and even they doubted that it could stand up against the much larger and more heavily armed *Merrimac*.

At a later date Horace Greeley, editor of the *New York Tribune*, and T. C. DeLeon, of Richmond, pieced together the origin and construction of the *Merrimac*.

There was much discussion at one time of the question as to whom the credit for the plans of the *Merrimac* belonged. It finally was generally conceded, however, that her origin and perfection were due to Commander John M. Brooke of the Confederate Navy; and the terrible banded rifle gun and bolt she used was his undisputed invention.

When the United States warship *Merrimac*, by Commodore McCauley's orders, had been scuttled and partly sunk in Norfolk Harbor, only her rigging and upper works were burned, her hull being saved by a speedy submersion. After she had been plugged, pumped out and raised, her hull was cut down nearly to the water's edge; then a sloping roof of heavy timber, strongly and thoroughly plated with railroad iron, rose from two feet below the waterline to about ten feet above, the ends and sides being alike and thoroughly shielded. A false bow was added, and beyond this projected a strong iron beak. Thoroughly shotproof, she was armed with ten seven-inch rifled Brooke guns; and so, having been largely refitted from the spoils of the deserted Navy Yard, she became the cheapest and most formidable naval engine of destruction that the world had ever seen.

Much wonder had the good people of Norfolk expressed in their frequent visits to the strange-looking, turtlelike structure. It was the *Merrimac*, which the Confederates had rechristened the *Virginia*. Day by day she slowly grew; and at length, after weary waiting, took on her armament; then her crew was picked carefully from eager volunteers. Her captain, Commodore Franklin Buchanan, took his place, and all was ready for the trial.

John M. Brooke, a former officer in the United States Navy, to whose genius the design of the *Merrimac* was due, was a man of great daring and inventiveness. He had achieved considerable reputation by devising a depth-sounding apparatus, for which in 1860 he had received the Gold Medal of Science from the King of Prussia. He also had made important surveys for the American government. The Confederate government subsequently granted him a patent for a partially submerged war vessel, and it was on this principle and under his supervision, that an old-time vessel was transferred into an ultranovel battleship.

On March 8, 1862, the *Merrimac* steamed out of Norfolk to attempt the first break in the blockade which was fettering Southern commerce. An officer in an Indiana regiment, Lieutenant Israel N. Stiles, watching from the shore, followed the *Merrimac's* progress.

I was at that time an officer of the 20th Indiana Volunteer Infantry, stationed at one of the fortified camps guarding Hampton Roads. On the eighth of March, at about 1:00 P.M., the long roll sounded, and the cry ran through the camp, "The *Merrimac* is coming." She was now about five or six miles away and looked very much like a house submerged to the eaves, borne onward by a flood. We had been expecting her for some weeks. We had heavy guns commanding our fort; and we thought we were ready to receive her becomingly. Near by and at anchor were two of our largest sailing frigates, the *Congress* and *Cumberland*, carrying fifty and thirty guns respectively. They also were ready, prepared as well as wooden ships could be, to contend with an ironclad. A few miles away were the Union frigates *Minnesota*, *Roanoke* and *St. Lawrence* and several gunboats.

The *Merrimac* moved very slowly, accompanied by the *Beaufort* and *Raleigh*, two small boats carrying one gun each. Not until she fired her first gun was there any outward sign of life on board, or of any armament, although she bore a crew of 300 and carried ten heavy guns. She had practically no visible deck; her crew were somewhere under her roof but out of sight; her gun ports were covered by hinged lids, which were raised only when her guns were brought forward for firing and closed when they were withdrawn. She moved directly for the *Cumberland*, which had cleared for action when the enemy was first sighted, and for the last half hour had been ready with every man at his post. On her way she passed the *Congress* on her starboard side, and within easy range. The latter greeted her with a terrific broadside, to which the *Merrimac* responded but kept on her course. Soon she came within range of the shore batteries, which opened upon her, and a minute or two later the thirty guns of the *Cumberland* were doing their duty. Many of the shots struck her, but they rebounded from her sides like marbles thrown against a brick wall. Approaching the *Cumberland*, she fired her bow gun and struck her at full speed on her port bow, delivering another shot at the same time. The blow opened an immense hole in the frigate, and the force of it was so great that the *Merrimac's* iron prow, or beak, was wrenched off as she withdrew and was left sticking in the side of the ship. The two shots which were delivered

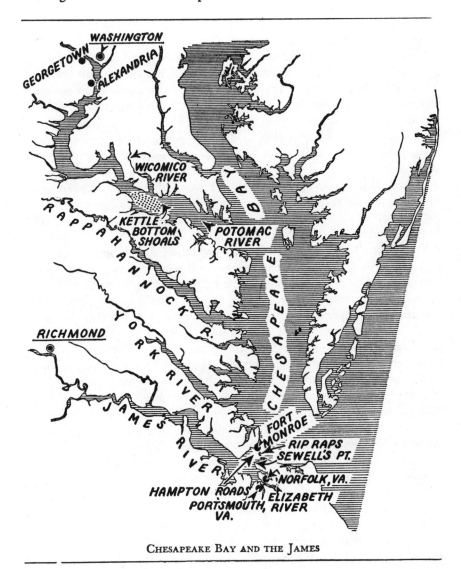

CHESAPEAKE BAY AND THE JAMES

from her bow gun had been terribly destructive. One entered the *Cumberland's* port, killing or wounding every man at one of her guns; the other raked her gun deck from one end to the other. Withdrawing from the frigate, the *Merrimac* steamed slowly up the river and, turning, chose her own position, from which she delivered broadside after broadside into the now sinking ship, and then, changing her position, raked her fore and aft with shell and grape.

Meantime the shore batteries had kept up their fire, while the *Congress* had been towed up into position and with her thirty guns pounded away at the iron monster. It was plain to us on shore that all combined were not a match for her. This must have been plain to the officers and men of the *Cumberland* as well; yet, with their ship sinking under them, they continued the fight with a courage and desperation which is recorded in no other naval battle. It was stated at that time that while her bow guns were under water, those in the after part of the ship were made to do double duty. Her commander was called upon to surrender; he refused, and his men cheered him. Still she sank, and the men were ordered to save themselves by swimming ashore. The water closed over her with her flag still flying.

While the *Merrimac* was occupied with the *Cumberland*, three Confederate steamers—the *Patrick Henry*, *Jamestown* and *Teaser*—had come down the James River, and with the two gunboats *Beaufort* and *Raleigh* had already engaged the *Congress*. On our side, the screw frigate *Minnesota* had worked her way from the fort, but had grounded a mile and a half away. For half an hour or more the *Merrimac* alternated her attentions between the *Congress* and the *Minnesota*. Owing to her great draught of water, the *Merrimac* could not get near enough to the latter to do much damage, but she chose her own position, and the utter destruction of the *Congress* became only a question of time. She had repeatedly been set on fire; her decks were covered with the dead and wounded; and the loss of life (including that of her commander) had been very great. She was run ashore, head on, and not long after hoisted the white flag. Two tugs were sent by the enemy alongside the *Congress* to take possession and to remove the prisoners, but a sharp fire of artillery and small arms from the shore drove them off. Captain Reed raised a question of military law: "Since the ship has surrendered, has not the enemy the right to take possession of her?" The question was answered by General Joseph K. Mansfield in one of the shortest and most conclusive opinions on record. "I know the damned ship has surrendered," said he, "but *we* haven't." That settled it. During the firing, Commander Buchanan of the *Merrimac* received a wound which disabled him from further participation in the fight. Being unable to take possession of the frigate, the ironclad again opened fire upon her—this time with incendiary shot—and the ship was soon on fire in several places.

It was now nearly dark, and the *Merrimac* hauled off. She had received no substantial injury and had demonstrated her ability to sink any wooden ship which might dare cope with her. Indeed, it looked that night as if the entire fleet would be wholly at her mercy on the morrow. The crew of the *Congress*, such as were able, had escaped, and during the early hours of the evening the wounded had been brought ashore. They and those of the *Cumberland* filled the little hospital. Officers and men gathered around those brave fellows and listened with moistened eyes to their accounts of the fight. One gunner, who had had both legs shot away just before the *Cumberland* sank, hobbled several steps on his bloody stumps and seized the lanyard that he might fire one more shot. An officer of the *Congress*, who had both arms shot away, cried out, "Back to your guns, boys! Give 'em hell! Hurrah for the old flag!"

I found one poor fellow, the surface of whose body was burned from head to heel. "I am all right," said he. "I have no pain. I shall get along." "His sensory nerves are destroyed," said the surgeon to me; "he will not live five hours." And so it proved.

The *Congress* continued to burn, her loaded guns discharging as the fire reached them, until about 1:00 A.M. When the fire reached her magazine, she blew up with a tremendous roar and with a shock so great that many of us on shore were prostrated, although we had retired to what we considered a safe distance. We were not sleepy that night.

Fear that the blockade could no longer be maintained quickly gave way to the far greater fear for the safety of Northern ports, of the Northern fleet, of Washington itself. Panic even penetrated the White House, as the imperturbable Secretary Welles recorded in his notes.

On Sunday morning, the ninth of March, Mr. Peter H. Watson, Assistant Secretary of War, hastily entered with a telegram from General John E. Wool at Fort Monroe, stating that the *Merrimac* had destroyed the *Cumberland* and *Congress*. Apprehensions were expressed by General Wool that the remaining vessels would be made victims the following day, and that the fort itself was in danger, for the *Merrimac* was impenetrable and could take what position she pleased for assault. I had scarcely read the telegram when a message from the President requested my immediate attendance at the Executive Mansion. The Secretary of War, on receiving General Wool's telegram, had gone instantly to the President, and at the same time sent messages to other Cabinet officers. I went at once to the White House. Mr. Seward and Mr. Chase, with Mr. Stanton, were already there, had read the telegram and were discussing the intelligence in much alarm. Each inquired what had been, and what could be done to meet and check this formidable monster which in a single brief visit had made such devastation, and would, herself uninjured, repeat her destructive visit with still greater havoc, probably, while we were in council. The Admiralty, appealed to for help, was unable to issue a reassuring statement, which tended to increase the panic.

I stated that our *Monitor*, which had left New York on Thursday, should have reached Hampton Roads on Saturday, and my main reliance was upon her.

Mr. Stanton was terribly excited and walked the room in great agitation. Mr. Seward, usually buoyant and self-reliant, overwhelmed with the intelligence, was greatly depressed, as, indeed, were all the members.

"The *Merrimac*," said Stanton, "will change the whole character of the war; she will destroy every naval vessel; she will lay all the cities on the seaboard under contribution. Likely her first move will be to come up the Potomac and disperse Congress, destroy the Capitol and public buildings. I will notify the governors and municipal authorities in the North to take instant measures to protect their harbors." He had no doubt, he said, "that the monster was at this moment on her way to Washington," and, looking out of the window, which commanded a view of the Potomac for many miles, he added, "Not unlikely we shall have a shell or cannon ball from one of her guns in the White House before we leave this room." I told the President that the *Merrimac* could not, with her heavy armor, cross the Kettle Bottom Shoals. This was a relief. I questioned the propriety of sending abroad panic missives, and said it was doubtful whether the *Merrimac* armor would venture outside of the Capes.

"What," asked Stanton, "is the size and strength of this *Monitor?* How many guns does she carry?" When I replied two, but of large caliber, he turned away with a look of mingled amazement, contempt and distress.

On the evening of that memorable Sunday, Stanton proceeded to state that he had advised the governors of the Northern States and the mayors of some cities to place rafts of timber and other obstructions at the mouths of their harbors. He had also directed the purchase of all the boats that could be procured in Washington, Georgetown and Alexandria, which were being laden with stone and earth, with a view of sinking them, in order to prevent the ascension of the *Merrimac* up the Potomac. He did procure a fleet of some sixty canal boats, which were laden, but Mr. Lincoln forbade that they should be sunk until it was known that the *Merrimac* really was approaching.

Lieutenant Stiles now continues his story. What he saw at Hampton Roads was one of the great naval battles of all time.

Before morning we heard of the arrival of "Ericsson's Battery." "It is a floating battery," said our surgeon, "lying very low in the water, with its guns enclosed in a revolving turret." He was well up in the details of the construction and had great confidence in the thing.

Morning came, and with it came into view the great hull of the *Minnesota*, also the *Merrimac* and her attendants, the *Yorktown* and the *Patrick Henry*. Alongside the *Minnesota* lay "Ericsson's Battery," a most insignificant-looking thing, a "cheese-box on a raft." The *Merrimac* and her companions were stationary and seemed to be in consultation. At seven o'clock a plan seemed to have been adopted, and the *Merrimac* steamed in the direction of the *Minnesota*. She was followed in the distance by the *Yorktown* and the *Patrick Henry*, which were crowded with troops. The *Minnesota* was still hard aground, and the *Merrimac* evidently counted upon disposing of her as she had done with the *Cumberland* and *Congress* the day before; but now a lion was in her path. The *Monitor* had steamed around the bow of the *Minnesota*, and like another David, marched out to meet this Goliath. At 8:10 o'clock the fire opened, and the first shot was fired by the *Merrimac* at the *Minnesota*. The next shot was from the *Monitor*, which struck the *Merrimac* near her water line but with little effect. The ironclads now came very near together—as it seemed to us on shore, less than one hundred feet apart—and the firing was very rapid. Occasionally the *Merrimac* varied the entertainment by a few shots at the *Minnesota* and, as often as the position would enable her to do so, the frigate would give her a broadside. Frequently the *Merrimac* would try to ram her little antagonist; but the ease with which the latter was handled enabled her to avoid a direct shock. In turn, the *Monitor* attempted to disable her enemy's screw, but without success. In vain the *Merrimac* tried to work her way up to close quarters with the *Minnesota;* the *Monitor* would not consent. The shores, which were but a few miles apart, were lined with Union and Confederate soldiers, and the ramparts of the fort and the rigging of the ships at anchor were also crowded with witnesses of the fight.

At ten o'clock no perceptible damage had been sustained by either of the contestants. With her ten guns the *Merrimac* was able to return two or three shots for every one she received. She had no solid shot, as she had expected to meet only wooden ships. Twenty-one in all of her shells struck the *Monitor,* but without doing any injury that needed repairing. The *Merrimac* presented a large mark, and during the last two hours of the fight nearly every shot of the *Monitor* struck her. Her armor was broken in several places, and in three instances, when two or more shots had struck the same place, the wood backing was badly shattered. As the fight continued, nearly all of the smaller craft ventured near enough to fire a few shots and, when at one time the batteries at Sewell's Point joined in, the soldiers declared that there was "music by the entire band." The fight continued till 12:15, when the *Merrimac* quit and steamed toward Norfolk. The commander of the *Monitor* wanted to follow her but was prevented by orders from the flag officer, who thought the risk too great. The official report of the *Merrimac* says: "Our loss is two killed and nineteen wounded. The stern is twisted, and the ship leaks. We have lost the prow, starboard anchor, all the boats; the armor is somewhat damaged, the steampipe and smokestack both riddled, and the muzzles of two guns shot away."

The *Merrimac* came down to the old fighting-ground on two or three occasions afterward and dared the *Monitor* to fight her single-handed. The *Monitor* refused to meet her, except in waters where the whole Union fleet could have pounced upon her. The *Monitor* was the only vessel that could possibly cope with her, and should some mishap befall her, the rest of the fleet would be wholly at the *Merrimac's* mercy.

What was it like to be inside the *Monitor* during the encounter? One of her crew, Samuel Lewis (alias Peter Truskitt), tells it in simple words.

The *Monitor* was a little bit the strangest craft I had ever seen; nothing but a few inches of deck above the water line, her big, round tower in the center and the pilot house at the end. We had confidence in her, though, from the start, for the little ship looked somehow like she meant business, and it didn't take us long to learn the ropes. The crew were exactly sixty strong, with the pilot.

Our first sight of the *Merrimac* was around the Rip Raps. She had been described to us and there was no mistaking her long, slanting, rakish outlines. I guess she took us for some kind of a water tank. You can see surprise in a ship just as you can see it in a human being, and there was surprise all over the *Merrimac*. She fired a shot across us, but Captain Worden, our commander, said, "Wait till you get close, boys, and then let her have it."

In a moment the ball had opened. Our guns were so low down that it was practically point-blank firing. At first the *Merrimac* was evidently trying hard to put a shell into the turret. That was impossible, however, for two reasons. The portholes were protected by heavy iron pendulums that fell of their own weight over the openings as soon as the muzzles of the guns were taken out, and when the guns were loaded they were put out at the far side, away from the *Merrimac*.

The din inside the turret was something terrific. The noise of every solid ball that hit fell upon our ears with a crash that deafened us. About that time an unexpected danger developed. The plates of the turret were fastened on with iron bolts and screwheads on the inside. These screwheads began to fly off from the concussion of the shots. Several of the men were badly bruised by them, and had anybody been hit in the face or eyes they would have been done for. Luckily this did not take place.

The immense volume of smoke made maneuvering very difficult, and at times we had hard work telling where the enemy was. Twice she tried to ram us, but we got out of the way. We looked for an attack by a boarding party and had a supply of hand grenades ready to throw out of the turret if one succeeded in gaining the deck.

The gun I served had just been pulled in and the pendulum dropped when a ball struck it a few inches from the head. The shock was so fearful that I dropped over like a dead man, and the next thing I knew

I was in the cabin with the doctor bathing my head. I soon recovered enough to go up again. Meantime the *Merrimac* had concentrated her fire upon the pilot house, giving up the turret as a bad job, and I think made an effort or two to get close and board us. I do not think that a boarding party could have been successful, even had they reached the deck, because they couldn't have penetrated the interior. There was but one hatch, and that had been closed and barred on the inside before the engagement.

The *Merrimac* turned tail after a little over four hours of fighting. The enthusiasm of our men was at fever heat.

Next day we were the heroes of the hour. The Presidential party came down with a lot of ladies, and they cheered and toasted us to the echo. The troops about the fortress all felt so proud over the victory that they started a contribution of one dollar each for the crew of the *Monitor*. The sum they raised was sent to Washington, but for some reason Congress objected, and it was never distributed.

> A midshipman on the *Merrimac* named Littlepage now gives his version of the famous duel.

I was a midshipman on the *Merrimac* when she fought the *Monitor*, and I can say that we were taken wholly by surprise when the strange vessel put in an appearance in Hampton Roads. Our first intimation was when we saw her run out to attack us before we could begin the onset upon the *Minnesota*. We thought at first it was a raft on which one of the *Minnesota*'s boilers was being taken to the shore for repairs, and when suddenly a shot was fired from her turret we imagined an accidental explosion of some kind had taken place on the raft.

In the engagement that followed, we were unable to do anything with her, though our guns were served continuously and broadside after broadside was discharged. We tried to ram her, but found that our prow had been too badly damaged by running into the *Cumberland* on the day before to inflict any harm upon the *Monitor*. She pounded us considerably, but not a shot penetrated our armor, though it was loosened, and repairs made imperative at the earliest moment. Our vessel was leaking badly, but by active efforts we were enabled to keep her from taking too much water. While we had twenty-one of our crew wounded, we thought that we had escaped losses in that respect in a remarkable degree. Had a shot from the *Monitor* entered one of our portholes it would have probably killed no less than fifty men, for there was a crew of 380 men aboard, so that there would be no lack of help when an emergency should arise, and we were quite closely packed together.

About three o'clock in the afternoon the *Monitor* withdrew from the fight and went over the bar into shallow water where we, drawing much more water than she, could not follow. We understood that she had run out of ammunition. As we were leaking badly and there was no prospect that we would be able to reach the *Minnesota* in the shallow water where she lay, our captain gave the order to return to Norfolk, where we immediately went into dry dock for repairs.

The panic in the North now subsided as quickly as it had arisen. Those who had overrated the power of the *Merrimac*, like Secretary of War Stanton, had to swallow a bitter pill, as Secretary of the Navy Welles, who was no friend of his colleague, relates with considerable relish.

In the early part of May 1862, the President, accompanied by Secretaries Chase and Stanton, took a steamer to visit Fort Monroe. While descending the Potomac, the attention of the party was directed to a string of boats nearly a mile in length on the Maryland shore, some fifty miles below Washington.

"Oh!" said the President. "That is Stanton's navy."

What happened to the *Merrimac* after the fight in Hampton Roads is told concisely by Lieutenant Stiles. Her destruction was due to the fact that with her heavy draft she could not move upriver when the Southern troops were forced to retreat in that direction.

On the tenth of May, 1862, the enemy abandoned Norfolk, on the eleventh they blew up the *Merrimac*, and on the twelfth we marched in. We talked with one of the engineers who had charge of the repairs. He stated to us that a shot from the *Monitor* had so "shivered her timbers that she never afterward could be made seaworthy. Her officers knew it when they went out and dared the *Monitor* to fight her. It was a case of pure bluff; we didn't hold a single pair."

The *Monitor* did not long outlive her opponent. The report made by her commander, J. P. Bankhead, although couched in cold official language, gives a vivid account of the tragic event.

The *Monitor* left Hampton Roads, in tow of the United States Steamer *Rhode Island*, on the twenty-ninth of December, 1862, at 2:30 P.M., wind light at southwest, weather clear and pleasant.

At 5:00 A.M., we began to experience a swell from the southward, with a slight increase of the wind, the sea breaking over the pilot house forward and striking the base of the turret, but not with sufficient force to break it. Speed at this time about five knots; ascertained from the engineer that the bilge-pumps kept her perfectly free. Felt no apprehension at the time. At 7:30 the wind increased in strength, position at this time about fifteen miles south of Cape Hatteras. At 8:00 P.M., the sea commenced to rise very rapidly, causing the vessel to plunge heavily, completely submerging the pilot house, and washing over and into the turret, and at times into the blower-pipes. Signalized several times to the *Rhode Island* to stop. The engineer reported that it would be necessary to start the centrifugal pump. About 10:30 P.M., finding the water gaining rapidly upon us, I determined to make the preconcerted signal of distress, which was immediately answered by the *Rhode Island*. I requested her commander to send boats to take off the crew. Finding that the heavy steam cable used to tow the *Monitor* rendered the vessel more unmanageable while hanging slack to her bow, and being under the absolute necessity of working the engines to keep the pumps going, I ordered it to be cut, and ran down close under the lee of the *Rhode Island*, at times almost touching her. At 11:30 my engines worked slowly, and all the pumps in full play, but water gaining rapidly, sea very heavy. Finding the vessel filling rapidly and the deck on a level with the water, I ordered all left on board, about twenty-five or thirty men, to get into two boats which were then approaching us. The boats approached very cautiously, as the sea was breaking upon our now submerged deck with great violence, washing several men overboard. Feeling that I had done everything in my power to save the vessel and crew, I jumped into the already deeply laden boat and left the *Monitor*, whose heavy, sluggish motion gave evidence that she could float but a short time longer. Shortly after we reached the *Rhode Island* she disappeared.

Before closing I must testify to the coolness, prompt obedience and absence of any approach to panic on the part of the officers and, with but few exceptions on the part of the crew, many of whom were at sea the first time and (it must be admitted) under circumstances that were calculated to appall the boldest heart.

> On the occasion of the *Monitor's* sinking, Secretary of the Navy Welles wrote a few sentences in his diary which might well be taken as a lasting memorial to the brave little war vessel and her crew.

The *Monitor* has foundered, and over twenty of her crew, including some officers, are lost. The fate of this vessel affects me. . . . She was built amidst obloquy and ridicule . . . but her prowess was exhibited in a conflict with her huge antagonist under formidable circumstances . . . and the men who were preparing to ridicule were left to admire.

> The *Merrimac*, or the *Virginia*, as the Southerners called her, had preceded the *Monitor* in death, and her demise was mourned throughout the Confederacy. It was a heavy blow to the pride as well as to the naval strength of the South, as Mrs. Jefferson Davis' parting words attest.

The evacuation of Norfolk necessitated the destruction of the *Virginia*, as she could not be brought up the James River. The consternation was great when her loss was known—coming as it did upon the heels of her triumph. The flag captured by her was brought to the Executive mansion by Colonel John Taylor Wood, a gallant participant in the fight. I found it damp with blood, and retired to my room sick of war and sorrowful over the dead and dying of both sections.

CHAPTER 7

Grant Comes to the Fore

THE CONQUEST OF FORT DONELSON

As the year 1861 drew to a close, a newly appointed brigadier general, unknown to fame, sat at a desk in his Cairo, Illinois, headquarters, studying a war map. His name was Ulysses S. Grant. At his side sat his adjutant and erstwhile neighbor from Galena, Illinois, Captain John A. Rawlins. The eyes of the two officers were focused on three rivers—the Mississippi, the Tennessee and the Cumberland. These rivers had one thing in common—they penetrated straight into the heart of the Confederacy. The possibilities which thus presented themselves were tempting, as Grant pointed out.

The enemy at this time occupied a line running from the Mississippi River at Columbus to Bowling Green and Mill Springs, Kentucky. Each of these positions was strongly fortified, as were also points on the Tennessee and Cumberland rivers. The work on the Tennessee was called Fort Henry, and that on the Cumberland Fort Donelson, at which points the two rivers approached within eleven miles of each other. These positions were of immense importance to the enemy and, of course, correspondingly important for us to possess ourselves of. With Fort Henry in our hands, we had a navigable stream open to us up to Muscle Shoals in Alabama. Fort Donelson was the gate to Nashville—a place of great military and political importance. These two points in our possession, the enemy would necessarily be thrown back to the boundary of the Cotton States.

As a result of an exploratory expedition, General C. F. Smith, one of my subordinate officers, reported that he thought it practicable to capture Fort Henry. This report confirmed views I had previously held, that the true line of operations for us was up the Tennessee and Cumberland rivers.

Flag Officer Andrew Hull Foote commanded the little fleet of gunboats then in the neighborhood of Cairo and, though in another branch of the service, was subject to the same command. He and I agreed perfectly as to the feasibility of the campaign up the Tennessee.

Grant was a newcomer on the national scene. A former captain in the army and veteran of the Mexican War, he had resigned his commission in 1854 and then had slowly drifted down to the obscurity of a clerkship in Galena, a town in northwestern Illinois. In June 1861, he had been appointed colonel of an Illinois regiment and then had been advanced to the rank of brigadier general, although he had made no outstanding record. His mild manners and stooped shoulders seemed to accentuate the failures he had suffered in the past. Yet there was something in his appearance which impressed a young army surgeon, Dr. John H. Brinton, who had been assigned to his district.

Of the many who have written of Grant, made speeches about him, applauded him and flattered him, few, very few, watched him and studied him as I did. From the very first he attracted me, and I felt very soon, and indeed wrote home, that the man had come who would finish this war, should he have the chance.

I first saw General Grant in Cairo at a dinner table. I was introduced to him and received a friendly nod from him. On the same evening I went into the bank. Behind the counter, the general and his assistant adjutant general, John A. Rawlins, or Captain Rawlins, as he was then, were seated at a little round table. I fancy that I wanted to write a letter, for I remember that the general very kindly asked me to sit down and continued his work with Rawlins. I had a good opportunity to observe him and did so very closely. He was then a very different looking man from the General Grant, or the President, of after days.

As I first saw him, he was a very short, small, rather spare man with full beard and mustache. His beard was a little long, very much longer than he afterwards wore it, unkempt and irregular, and of a sandy, tawny shade. His hair matched his beard, and at a first glance he seemed to be a very ordinary sort of a man, indeed, one below the average in most respects. But as I sat and watched him then, and many an hour afterward, I found that his face grew upon me. His eyes were gentle with a kind expression, and thoughtful. He did not, as a rule, speak a great deal. At that time he seemed to be very much occupied indeed with the work of the hour. He worked slowly, every now and then stopping and taking his pipe out of his mouth.

But this reminds me that I have not yet spoken of his pipe. The man in after days became so thoroughly identified with the cigar that people could scarcely believe that he was once an assiduous smoker of the pipe. Well, the pipe which he first used was a meerschaum with a curved stem eight or ten inches long, which allowed the pipe to hang down. He smoked steadily and slowly and evidently greatly enjoyed his tobacco.

I had been in charge of the general hospitals of the District of Cairo; General Grant was away, and General John A. McClernand commanded in his absence. One of the latter's orders was to this effect: "That all able-bodied men in the hospitals in the district should be returned to their command, irrespective of the hospital duties they were performing." The order was clearly illegal, but apart from this, its execution would have instantly paralyzed the whole hospital department of the entire District of Cairo. I accordingly instructed my surgeons to disobey it, and by my own endorsement disputed its validity. General Grant on his return sent for me, showed me my rebellious order, and added, "Doctor, this a very serious business." My answer to him was, "General, when you entrusted to me, as your medical director, the care of the invalids of your command, you said to me, 'Doctor, take care of my sick and wounded to the best of your ability, don't bother over regulations.' Now, General," I added, "I have done this to the best of my ability. If I have done right, you will support me; if I have done wrong, you know what to do with me."

The general looked at me a moment, took the paper, and put on it the endorsement which lives in my memory: "The object of having a Medical Director is that he shall be supreme in his own department. The decision of Surgeon Brinton is sustained."

I think that my veneration for his character and my strong personal affection for him dated from that interview. I doubt if another officer of his rank in the army would have so supported a medical officer under like circumstances.

The Confederate authorities were well aware of their vulnerability through the use of the Cumberland, Tennessee and Mississippi rivers, and endeavored to protect these waterways through land fortifications. President Davis explains on what principles these fortifications were built.

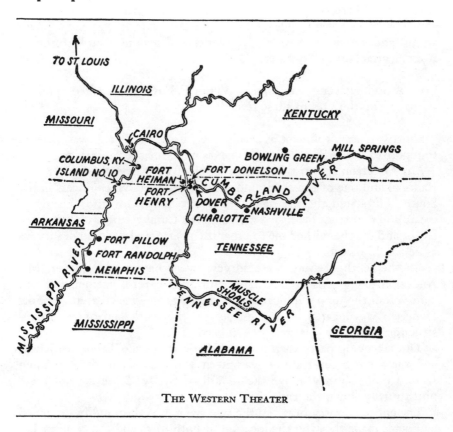

THE WESTERN THEATER

When the State of Tennessee seceded, measures were immediately adopted to occupy and fortify all the strong points on the Mississippi, such as Memphis, Fort Randolph, Fort Pillow and Island No. 10. As it was our purpose not to construct defenses for the Cumberland and Tennessee rivers on Kentucky territory, they were located within the borders of Tennessee. On these were commenced the construction of Fort Donelson on the west of the Cumberland and Fort Henry on the east side of the Tennessee, about twelve miles apart. The latter stood on the lowlands adjacent to the river above high-water mark; being just below a bend in the river and at the head of a straight stretch of two miles, it commanded the river for that distance.

Fort Donelson was placed on high ground; and with the plunging fire from its batteries was more effective against ironclads brought to attack it on the water side. But on the land side it was not equally strong and required extensive outworks and a considerable force to resist an attack in that quarter.

A Southern engineer, Major Wilbur F. Foster, was called upon to survey the sites of these river forts.

Shortly after enrollment as a volunteer, in April 1861, I was ordered to report to Mr. Adna Anderson at Nashville for special service.

Mr. Anderson at that time was receiver of the Edgefield & Kentucky Railroad and one of the ablest and most widely known engineers in the South. He stated that he had been directed by Governor Harris to locate and construct defensive works on the Cumberland and Tennessee rivers, and that he wished me to organize a party and make such surveys as he would direct.

On the tenth of May these surveys were begun near Dover, Mr. Anderson being present in person, and after careful examination and study of all the topographical details the first, or water battery, at Fort Donelson was located by Mr. Anderson, the work laid out and construction begun by a large force of men.

The surveying party then proceeded at once to the Tennessee River, and the same careful study was given and surveys made, extending from a point shortly above the mouth of Sandy Creek several miles northwardly down the river.

The entire country between the two rivers was thoroughly examined and maps made showing the location of both forts and the country between.

The work at Fort Donelson was carried forward to completion, in the main as designed by Mr. Anderson, but the point selected by him for the defensive work on the Tennessee River was not approved by Major, later General, Bushrod Johnson, who selected a location some five miles further down the river; under his direction this writer laid out Fort Henry at that place, and the work was begun by the 10th

Tennessee Regiment, commanded by Colonel Adolphus Heiman on Friday, June 14, 1861. The first gun was mounted and fired with a blank cartridge on Friday, July 12, 1861.

Before Grant could execute his contemplated move against Fort Henry and Fort Donelson, he had to obtain the approval of his department commander, Major General Henry W. Halleck, who had established his headquarters at St. Louis. Halleck had fought in Mexico and later published a book on the art of warfare which earned him the reputation of a deep student and excellent military theorist.

After resigning from the army in 1854, Halleck took up law. At the outbreak of the war he was not only head of a leading legal firm in San Francisco but also president of the Pacific and Atlantic Railroad and a prominent stockholder in the famous New Almaden quicksilver mine.

Shortly after the beginning of the Civil War Lincoln offered him a major generalship in the regular army, which Halleck accepted.

In appearance Halleck was not prepossessing. He had a large head, which he carried sideways, and during conversations his protruding eyes stared into space. His book learning was universally admitted, but whether his capacity as a commander would be equal to his reputation only future developments could determine.

In his *Memoirs* Grant relates how he attempted to secure Halleck's approval of his plans.

On January 6, 1862, I had asked permission of General Halleck, commanding the department, to go to see him at St. Louis. My object was to lay before him my plan of campaign against Fort Henry. Now that my views had been confirmed by so able a general as C. F. Smith, I renewed my request to go to St. Louis on what I deemed important military business. The leave was granted, but not graciously. I was received with so little cordiality that I perhaps stated the object of my visit with less clearness than I might have done, and I had not uttered many sentences before I was cut short as if my plan was preposterous. I returned to Cairo very much crestfallen.

On January 28, notwithstanding the rebuff I had received, I renewed the suggestion that "If permitted, I could take and hold Fort Henry on the Tennessee." This time I was backed by Flag Officer Foote, who sent a similar dispatch. On January 29 I wrote fully in support of the proposition. On February 1 I received instructions from department headquarters to move upon Fort Henry. On February 2 the expedition started.

> The President of the Confederate States reports what happened when the combined expedition of General Grant and Flag Officer Foote attacked Fort Henry.

On February 2 General Grant started from Cairo with 17,000 men on transports. Flag Officer Foote accompanied him with seven gunboats. On the fourth the landing of the troops commenced three miles or more below Fort Henry. General Grant took command on the east bank with the main column, while General Charles F. Smith, with two brigades of some five to six thousand men, landed on the left bank, with orders to take the earthwork opposite Fort Henry known as Fort Heiman. On the fifth, landing was completed, and the attack was made on the next day.

The forces of General Lloyd Tilghman, who was in command at Fort Henry, were about 3,400 men. On the fifth he intended to dispute Grant's advance by land, but on the sixth, before the attack by the gunboats, he abandoned hope of a successful defense and made arrangements for the escape of his main body to Fort Donelson, while the guns of Fort Henry should engage the gunboats. He ordered Colonel Heiman to withdraw the command to Fort Donelson, while he himself would obtain the necessary delay for the movement by standing a bombardment in Fort Henry. For this purpose he retained his heavy artillery company—seventy-five men—to work the guns, a number unequal to the strain and labor of the defense.

Noon was the time fixed for the attack; but Grant, impeded by the overflow of water and unwilling to expose his men to the heavy guns of the fort, held them back to await the results of the gunboat attack. In the meantime the Confederate troops were in retreat. Four ironclads, mounting forty-eight heavy guns, approached and took position within six hundred yards of the fort, firing as they advanced. About half a mile behind these came three unarmored gunboats, mounting twenty-seven heavy guns, which took a more distant position and kept up a bombardment of shells that fell within the works. Some four hundred of the formidable missiles of the ironclad boats were also thrown into the fort.

The officers and men inside were not slow to respond, and as many as fifty-nine of their shots were counted as striking the gunboats. On the ironclad *Essex* a cannon ball ranged her whole length; another shot, passing through the boiler, caused an explosion that scalded her commander and many of the seamen and soldiers on board.

Five minutes after the fight began, the 24-pounder rifled gun, one of the most formidable in the fort, burst, disabling every man at the piece. Then a shell exploded at the muzzle of one of the 32-pounders, ruining the gun and killing or wounding all the men who served it. About the same moment a premature discharge occurred at one of the 42-pounder guns, killing three men and seriously injuring others. The 10-inch columbiad, the only gun able to match the artillery of the assailants, was next rendered useless by a priming wire that was jammed and broken in the vent. An heroic blacksmith labored for a long time to remove it, under the full fire of the enemy, but in vain. The men became exhausted and lost confidence; and Tilghman, seeing this, in person served a 32-pounder for some fifteen minutes. Though but four of his guns were disabled, six stood idle for want of artillerists, and but two were replying to the enemy. After an engagement of two hours and ten minutes he ceased firing and lowered his flag.

Our casualties were five killed and sixteen wounded; those of the enemy were sixty-three of all kinds. Twelve officers and sixty-three noncommissioned officers and privates were surrendered with the fort. The Tennessee River was thus open, and a base by short lines was established against Fort Donelson.

With Fort Henry out of the way, General Grant lost no time in marching against Fort Donelson. His account shows that he was full of confidence, unaware of the obstacles that still awaited him.

I informed the department commander of our success at Fort Henry, and that on the eighth I would take Fort Donelson. But the rain continued to fall so heavily that the roads became impassable for artillery and wagon trains. Then, too, it would not have been prudent to proceed without the gunboats.

On the day after the fall of Fort Henry, I took my staff and made a reconnaissance to within about a mile of the outer line of works at

Donelson. I had known one of its commanders, General Gideon J. Pillow, in Mexico, and judged that with any force, no matter how small, I could march up to within gunshot of any entrenchments he was given to hold. I knew that John B. Floyd was in high command, but he was no soldier, and I judged that he would yield to Pillow's pretensions.

Fort Donelson embraced about one hundred acres of land and stood on high ground, some of it as much as a hundred feet above the Cumberland. Strong protection to the heavy guns in the water batteries had been obtained by cutting away places for them in the bluff. To the west there was a line of rifle pits some two miles back from the river at the farthest point. The ground inside and outside of this entrenched line was very broken and generally wooded. The trees outside of the rifle pits had been cut down for a considerable way out and had been felled so that their tops lay outwards from the entrenchments. The limbs had been trimmed and pointed and thus formed an abatis in front of the greater part of the line.

General Halleck commenced his efforts to get reinforcements to me immediately on my departure from Cairo. I was very impatient to get to Fort Donelson, because I knew the importance of the place to the enemy and supposed he would reinforce it rapidly. I felt that 15,000 men on the eighth would be more effective than 50,000 a month later. I asked Flag Officer Andrew H. Foote, therefore, to order his gunboats still about Cairo to proceed up the Cumberland River and not to wait.

I started from Fort Henry with 15,000 men and the advance arrived in front of the enemy by noon. That afternoon and the next day were spent in making the investment as complete as possible. General Smith occupied our left. McClernand was on the right and covered the roads running south and southwest from Dover. Our line was generally along the crest of ridges. The greatest suffering was from want of shelter. It would not do to allow campfires except out of sight of the enemy. In the march over from Fort Henry numbers of the men had thrown away their blankets and overcoats. There was therefore much discomfort and suffering.

Dr. Brinton, Grant's chief medical officer on this expedition, gave an intimate account of the ride from Fort Henry to Fort Donelson and of the housing arrangements at the point of destination.

General Grant and his staff remained at Fort Henry until about February 12. Two roads led from Fort Henry to Fort Donelson; the army moved along both, the cavalry watching the space between, so as not to allow any of the enemy to escape us. I rode near the General on my black horse, a strong, powerful beast which I had bought at Cairo. I could hardly keep him back; he particularly and persistently

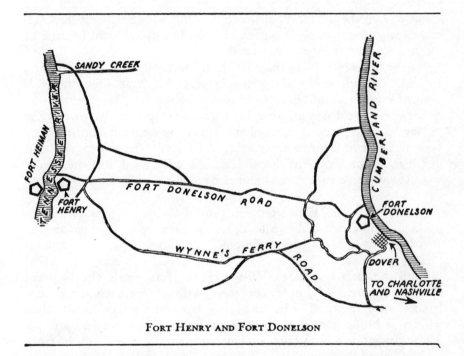

FORT HENRY AND FORT DONELSON

would pass the General who rode his old favorite stallion "Jack." Finally, he very good-naturedly said to me, "Doctor, I believe I command this army, and I think I'll go first."

We marched in battle order, ready for action. The actual luggage of the staff was represented by a few collars, a comb and brush and such toilet articles, contained in a small satchel belonging to me. General Grant had only a toothbrush in his waistcoat pocket, and I supplied him with a clean white collar. Of whisky or liquor, of which so much has been said, there was not one drop, except that in my pocket, an 8-ounce flask, which I was especially requested by the General to keep only for medical purposes, and I was further instructed by him not to furnish a drink under any pretext to any member of the staff, except when necessary in my professional judgment.

We occupied the headquarters house on the afternoon of February 12, and here we remained until after the capture of Fort Donelson. The kitchen had in it a double feather bed, and this was occupied by the General. Some small rooms in the other parts of the house were crowded by other members of the staff. I think for one night the General slept somewhere else than the kitchen, but came down because of the bed and the warmer temperature.

On the thirteenth I was busy fixing my hospitals and doing the best I could. The whole of this day was employed in establishing the positions of our forces and in strengthening their lines. We threw up no breastworks but depended upon the natural strength of the ground and its "lay" for our protection, should the enemy attempt any sortie. However, the idea of a sortie never entered General Grant's head, or if it did, it found no lodgment there. His ideas were fixed, that the enemy would stay inside their works and not readily venture out.

> The taking of Fort Donelson proved to be much more difficult than Grant had visualized, and he cites the unexpected and dangerous setbacks he encountered.

Until the arrival of Lew Wallace on the fourteenth, the National forces, composed of but 15,000 men, without entrenchments, confronted an entrenched army of 21,000, without conflict further than what was brought on by ourselves. Only one gunboat had arrived. There was no actual fighting except once, on the thirteenth, in front of McClernand's command. That general had undertaken to capture a battery of the enemy which was annoying his men. Without orders or authority he sent three regiments to make the assault. The battery was in the main line of the enemy, which was defended by his whole army. Of course the assault was a failure, and the loss on our side was great for the number of men engaged.

During the night of the thirteenth Flag Officer Foote arrived with the ironclads *St. Louis*, *Louisville* and *Pittsburgh*, and the wooden gunboats *Tyler* and *Conestoga*. Wallace, whom I had ordered over from Fort Henry, also arrived about the same time. His new division was assigned to the center, giving the two flanking divisions an opportunity to close up and form a stronger line.

The plan was for the troops to hold the enemy within his lines while the gunboats should attack the water batteries at close quarters and silence his guns, if possible. By three in the afternoon of the fourteenth Flag Officer Foote advanced upon the water batteries with his entire fleet. After coming in range of the batteries the advance was slow, but a constant fire was delivered from every gun that could be brought to bear upon the fort. The leading boat got within a very short distance of the water battery, not further off, I think, than two hundred yards, and I soon saw one and then another of them dropping down the river, visibly disabled. Then the whole fleet followed, and the engagement closed for the day. The gunboat which Flag Officer Foote was on, besides having been hit about sixty times, several of the shots passing through near the water line, had a shot enter the pilothouse, which killed the pilot, carried away the wheel and wounded the Flag Officer himself. The tiller ropes of another vessel were carried away and she, too, dropped helplessly back. Two others had their pilothouses so injured that they scarcely formed a protection to the men at the wheel.

The enemy were jubilant when they saw the disabled vessels dropping down the river entirely out of control of the men on board. The sun went down on the night of February 14, 1862, leaving the army confronting Fort Donelson anything but comforted over the prospects. The weather had turned intensely cold; the men were without tents. Two of the strongest of our gunboats had been disabled, presumably beyond the possibility of rendering any present assistance. I retired this night, not knowing but that I would have to entrench my position and bring up tents for the men or build huts under the cover of the hills.

> A young boy, Jesse Bowman Young, who served with the Union army, stole away from his camp to watch the attack of the gunboats, and thus pictured the fight between them and the river batteries.

The gunboats carefully steamed around the bend and maneuvered into position. Before they were ready to commence operations I noticed a puff of smoke appear at a certain point in one of the embankments. In a moment afterward I heard a boom and a terrible screech which filled the air.

The leading boat returned the fire, that boat being the *St. Louis*, under Flag Officer Foote. In a moment the *Louisville* also was in action, and then the other ironclads of the fleet, the *Carondelet* and the *Pittsburgh*, followed at some distance downstream by the wooden gunboats, the *Tyler* and the *Conestoga*.

When each boat arrived at the proper post, it delivered its fire and then circled around to reload and give the other boats opportunity to deliver their broadsides. Once in a while a solid shot from the fort would strike an iron-plated ship, make a deep dent in its armor and then glance off with a terrific splashing into the water. Then a shell would burst just over the deck, sending a perfect storm of iron hailstones down on the metal plates.

At the very height of the engagement I saw a well-aimed bombshell enter the porthole of the *Carondelet*, exploding just within the opening, dismantling a cannon and wounding a dozen or more men. Through the din and confusion of the conflict there could be distinguished the officers' voices giving command to the gunners, the cries of the wounded and the battering and hammering of the detail of men who at once were set to work to clear away the wreck which had been made by the shell, so as to get the decks ready for action again. Thick and fast came the shots and bombs from the batteries, crashing on the iron plates, skipping across the waves, going clean through the smokestacks, tearing down the rigging; but still the plucky Commodore Foote kept his flagship, the *St. Louis*, in the forefront of the fight, and kept signaling to the others what to do. He had been severely wounded in the ankle, but he would not leave the field without doing all that he, with his fleet, might achieve toward capturing the fort.

After an hour and a half of this sort of work a couple of the boats, the flagship *St. Louis* and the *Louisville*, were noticed to be in trouble. They moved wildly and falteringly hither and thither, and it was seen that the officers could not manage them. The signals soon told the fleet what was wrong; the steering apparatus of both boats was out of gear, the pilothouse of the *St. Louis* had been almost destroyed by round shot, and the machinery injured so that the ships could not be maneuvered and soon began to drift helplessly down the stream. The loss of these two disabled ships so weakened the fleet that it was soon found necessary to suspend the gunboat attack.

One issue was decided by this engagement: Fort Donelson could not be taken, as Fort Henry had been, by an attack on the water front by the fleet. It would need more than a mere bombardment by cannon and mortar to conquer and capture it. The land forces would have to

try their powers at it. The works would have to be stormed by the
infantry.

General Lew Wallace, commanding a brigade of some 2,500
men, had been left behind the main army to guard Fort Henry.
A few days later he was put in command of a newly formed
division, and was asked to join Grant's troops and take part in the
attack against Fort Donelson. He sketches his part in the campaign with the flair of a writer who some day would become
famous as the author of *Ben Hur*.

Fort Henry had been surrendered on February 6. On February 10
an orderly crossed the river with a note for me, sealed, informal, but
very interesting. There would be, it said, a meeting of general officers
at headquarters next day. Time—two o'clock, afternoon. My presence
was desired.

This, I saw, meant a council of war. How often had I read of such
affairs in books of war! Now I was to see one and have a voice in it.

General Grant had his headquarters on the steamboat *Tigress*. Not
an armed sentinel could be seen on the landing or on the vessel. I found
my own way into the ladies' cabin. General Grant was there, and
Rawlins, his adjutant general, sat at the table. I also recall the presence
of Generals Charles F. Smith and John A. McClernand. It struck me
that the company were in icy binding; probably because, like myself,
they were mostly new to the business. Our uniforms and swords, worn
in compliance with etiquette, may have had something to do with the
frigidity of the occasion.

After a little, General Grant stepped to the table and said ever so
quietly, "The question for consideration, gentlemen, is whether we
shall march against Fort Donelson or wait for reinforcements. I should
like to have your views." He looked first at General Smith—we were
all standing—and Smith replied, "There is every reason why we should
move without the loss of a day." General McClernand, taking the sign
next, drew out a lengthy paper and read it. He, too, was in favor of
going at once; then, as if in haste, Grant turned to me, nodding, and
said, "Let us go, by all means; the sooner the better. We will set out
immediately. Orders will be sent you. Get your commands ready."

That the opinions submitted had any influence with Grant is hardly
supposable. There is evidence that he had already determined upon the
movement.

The beginning of the impending conflict was thus described by Jefferson Davis.

The investment of Donelson was made without any serious opposition. On the thirteenth General Buckner reported that "the fire of the enemy's artillery and riflemen was incessant throughout the day; but was responded to by a well-directed fire from the entrenchments, which inflicted upon the assailant a considerable loss and almost silenced his fire late in the afternoon." The object of the enemy undoubtedly was to discover the strength and position of our forces.

On the fourteenth the entire Federal fleet of gunboats tried to subdue our water batteries, but their repulse closed the operations of the day, except a few scattering shots along the land defenses.

The plan of operations for the next day was determined by the Confederate generals about midnight. The whole of the left wing of the army except eight regiments was to move out of the trenches, attack, turn and drive the enemy's right until the Wynne's Ferry Road, which led to Charlotte through a good country, was cleared and an exit thus secured.

The troops, moving in the small hours of the night over the icy and broken roads, which wound through the obstructed area of defense, made slow progress and delayed the projected operations. At 4:00 A.M. on the fifteenth Pillow's troops were ready, except one brigade, which came late into action. By six o'clock Colonel William E. Baldwin's brigade was engaged with the enemy, only two or three hundred yards from his lines, and the bloody contest of the day began. At one o'clock the enemy's right was doubled back. The Wynne's Ferry Road was cleared, and it only remained for the Confederates to do one of two things: the first was to seize the golden moment and, adhering to the original purpose and plan of the sortie, move off rapidly by the route laid open by such strenuous efforts and so much bloodshed; the other depended on the inspiration of a mastermind, which should complete the partial victory by the utter rout and destruction of the enemy.

Here Grant takes up again the thread of the narrative.

On the morning of the fifteenth, the day chosen by the Confederates for their sortie, before it was yet broad day, a messenger from Flag Officer Foote, who was suffering from a painful wound, handed me a note expressing a desire to see me on the flagship. I directed my adjutant general to notify each of the division commanders of my absence and instruct them to do nothing to bring on an engagement until they received further orders, but to hold their positions.

When I left to visit Flag Officer Foote I had no idea that there would be an engagement on land unless I brought it on myself.

Just as I landed from my visit to the flag officer, I met Captain Hillyer of my staff, white with fear, not for his personal safety but for the safety of the National troops. He said the enemy had come out of his lines in full force and attacked and scattered McClernand's division, which was in full retreat. The attack had been made on the National right.

> The confidence which Grant had felt that the initiative was entirely in his hands is confirmed by Dr. Brinton, who was apprehensive for the safety of his patients and his medical stores.

One of my hospitals, that nearest to the Southern lines, was in a ravine, within sight of the hostile troops. It happened that some heavy skirmishing took place on the thirteenth, chiefly along General McClernand's front, our right. Indeed it was more than skirmishing, for a time in fact a very lively fight. During this, a good many wounded found their way to this particular hospital, and not only wounded, but many, a great many fainthearted ones, who disgracefully sought the hospital precinct as a shelter. This congregation hourly increased, and I began after a time to feel anxious lest the enemy, noticing so many stragglers, might sweep down and make capture of both hurt and unhurt. The hospital had only its sacred character to defend it, and this was being debased by the gathering crowd. Then, too, most of our hospital stores, I mean the reserve supplies, were here, and I did not wish them to fall into the enemy's hands. So I went to General Grant and explained to him the exposed position of the hospital. His answer was, "Yes, Doctor, I see, but they will *not* come and capture you." And back I went to the hospital. Yet things went from bad to worse. Again I saw the general. Again I told him my fears, and again heard his answer, as before, "They will not come."

As the peril increased still more, I sought him a third time, and after saying all I could, I asked him, "Am I exaggerating the risk of the loss of the medical stores of your army?" The general heard me as he always did, most patiently, and replied, "No, Doctor, you are right, but, Doctor, they won't do it; they are not thinking of anything, except holding their position."

General Lew Wallace next relates how he unexpectedly found himself in the center of stirring events and was called upon to make a historical decision.

I now was at the head of a division of seven regiments, the total of which I roughly estimated at 6,000 men. I formed the center of the line of investment, with General McClernand on my right and General Smith on my left.

"You will hold your position to prevent escape of the Confederates, without assuming the aggressive"—that was the order of the day.

The morning of the fifteenth crawled up the eastern sky as a turtle in its first appearance after hibernation crawls up a steep bank. An unusual sound off to the right front of my position attracted me. I listened. The sound broke at a jump into what was easily recognizable as a burst of musketry. What was it?

"What do you think of it?" I asked my officers. One of them thought it was McClernand assaulting the works.

"No," I replied, "the fort is here, more to our front."

Then another officer said, "The Johnnies are out pitching into McClernand." In a little while guns joined in.

"There! That settles it," I said. "Get out your horses. It looks as if we are to have it in boatloads today."

The noise over at the right had swollen in volume until it bore likeness to a distant train of empty cars rushing over a creaking bridge. But my orders were to keep my place, letting come what might.

The situation was very trying. Questions thronged in on me, all the output of imagination, but not less confusing on that account.

What, for instance, if the enemy had received reinforcements from Nashville in the night, making him once more superior to us in numbers? What if the demonstration at the moment going on over in McClernand's zone of investment were but a feint, leaving me or General Smith on my left the real object of an impending attack?

The noise kept grinding on without lull or intermission; an hour—two hours—would it never end? The suspense became torturous. At last a horseman galloped up from the rear. "I am from General Mc-Clernand," he said, "sent to ask assistance of you. The whole Rebel force in the fort massed against him in the night. Our ammunition is giving out. We are losing ground."

I dispatched a lieutenant to Grant's headquarters for permission to help McClernand. This was about eight o'clock. In good time my aide returned and reported General Grant on board the gunboat *St. Louis*, in conference with Flag Officer Foote. Nobody at headquarters felt authorized to act on my request. The battle, meantime, roared on.

After a while a second messenger came from General McClernand, a gray-haired man in uniform. His news could hardly be worse, and he spoke with tears in his eyes.

"Our right flank is turned," he said. "The regiments are being crowded back on the center. We are using ammunition taken from the dead and wounded. The whole army is in danger."

My impulse had been to send help at the first asking; that impulse was now seconded by judgment. Disaster to the first division meant that if that division were rolled back on me, a panic might ensue. In the absence of the commanding general, the responsibility was mine. I said, "Tell General McClernand that I will send him my first brigade with Colonel Charles Cruft."

Cruft acted promptly, and moved off through the woods under direction of a guide.

Shortly afterward Captain Rawlins came out to me, and I gave him an account of the messengers from General McClernand, and of what I had done with Cruft. While we talked, stragglers from the fight appeared coming on the run up a half-defined road. We scarcely noticed the fugitives, so much more were we drawn by the noise behind them. That grew in volume, being a compound of shouts and yells, mixed with the rattle of wheels and the rataplan and throbbing rumble of hoofs in undertone.

I called to an orderly, "Ride and see what all that flurry means." A suspicion of the truth broke through my wonder.

Then, as Rawlins and I sat waiting, an officer mounted and bareheaded and wild-eyed, rode madly up the road and past us, crying in shrill repetition, "We're cut to pieces!"

Now I had never seen a case of panic so perfectly defined, and it was curious, even impressive. Rawlins, however, was not disposed to view the spectacle philosophically. Jerking a revolver from his holster, he would have shot the frantic wretch had I not caught his hand. He remonstrated with me viciously, but the orderly came back at full speed and with an ominous look on his face.

"What is it?" I asked.

And he said, "The road back there is jammed with wagons, and men afoot and on horseback, all coming toward us. On the plains we would call it a stampede."

We looked at each other—Rawlins and I—and there was no need of further question. The first division was in full retreat.

"What are you going to do?" he asked.

"There's but one thing I can do."

"What is that?"

"Get this brigade out of the way. If those fellows strike my people, they will communicate the panic."

"Where will you go?"

"To take that way—" pointing to the rear—"is to retreat and carry the panic to General Smith; so I'll go up this road toward the enemy."

Then, at my word, the drummers beat the long roll. The men took arms. "By the right flank, file left!" And out in columns of companies they went.

I gave an instant to the coming mob and, believing from the sound that there would be time to get the last of my regiments clear of it and of contagion, I called to my staff and hastened forward.

The firing seemed right on us, not fifty paces away. I noticed it extending rapidly, despite the undergrowth. Instead of advancing in line of battle, the enemy had marched up the cramped road in files of four, and, meeting us unexpectedly, were trying to deploy. It was a tactical mistake with a terrible penalty in payment. All we had to do was to ply them with fire. Colonel John M. Thayer had then got the 1st Nebraska and the 58th Illinois in line, the former next the road on the right. I gave him a sign. He spoke to Colonel William D. McCord, of the 1st Nebraska. I saw their muskets rise and fall steadily as if on a parade ground. A volley—and smoke—and after that constant fire at will as fast as skilled men could load.

Then Colonel William B. Woods arrived and, without slackening speed, wheeled his first section into battery right across the road. I heard him shout, "Grape now. Double-shot them, boys!" He could not see the foemen, I knew. But why look for them; was not their fire sufficient? Almost before the wheels were stationary his guns opened; a moment more and I lost sight of guns and men in a deepening cloud of smoke. The gallant fellows were doing the right thing.

The fight was now set, and we were on the defensive. For three-quarters of an hour it went on. The Confederate artillery, having to fire uphill, was of no service. Their shot and shell flew over the trees. I would not be understood as speaking lightly of the Confederates. The struggle on their part was to get into line, and in that they were persistent to obstinacy. Twice they quit, then returned to the trial. A third time repelled, they went back to stay. From a height Colonel Cruft saw them retreat pell-mell into their works.

The success, it may as well be admitted, more than gratified me. With a brigade thrust between it and its over-confident pursuers, I had been instrumental in relieving the first division from an imminent peril. Next day, Captain William S. Hillyer, aide-de-camp, sent me a note saying, "I speak advisedly. God bless you! You did save the day on the right!"

General Grant came on the battlefield just when the force of the Confederate sortie had spent itself against Wallace's resistance. Then, he said, he decided to do some attacking himself.

I saw everything favorable for us along the line of our left and center. On the right I saw the men standing in knots talking in the most excited manner. No officer seemed to be giving any directions. The soldiers had their muskets but no ammunition, while there were tons of it close at hand. I heard some of the men say that the enemy had come out with knapsacks and haversacks filled with rations. They seemed to think this indicated a determination on his part to stay out and fight just as long as the provisions held out.

The enemy had come out in full force to cut his way out and make his escape. McClernand's division had had to bear the brunt of the attack from this combined force. When the men found themselves without ammunition, they could not stand up against troops who seemed to have plenty of it. But most of the men, as they were not pursued, only fell back out of range of the fire of the enemy. I turned to Colonel J. D. Webster of my staff, who was with me, and said, "Some of our men are pretty badly demoralized; however, the enemy must be more so, for he has attempted to force his way out but has fallen back; the one who attacks first now will be victorious." I determined to make the assault at once on our left. It was clear to my mind that if our attack could be made on the left, before the enemy could redistribute his forces along the line, we would find but little opposition except from the intervening abatis.

We rode rapidly to General Smith's quarters, where I explained the situation to him. The general was off in an incredibly short time, going in advance himself to keep his men from firing while they were working their way through the abatis. The outer line of rifle pits was passed, and during the night of the fifteenth General Smith, with much of his division, bivouacked within the lines of the enemy. There was now no doubt but that the Confederates must surrender or be captured the next day.

Jefferson Davis continues his record of the events from the time when the Confederate sortie was brought to a halt.

Of the two alternatives after his successful sortie—to march for Nashville or turn against the demoralized Union forces and try to destroy them—the Confederate commander tried neither. A fatal policy was suddenly but dubiously adopted, and not carried out. For seven hours the Confederate battalions had been pushing over rough ground and through thick timber, at each step meeting fresh troops massed, where the discomfited regiments rallied. Hence the vigor of assault slackened, though the wearied troops were still ready and competent to continue their onward movement. Fresh regiments, over 3,000 men, had then not fired a musket.

General Simon B. Buckner, third in command, had halted, according to the preconcerted plan, to allow the army to pass out by the opened road and to cover the retreat.

At this point of the fight, General Pillow heard of (or saw) preparations by General C. F. Smith for an assault on the Confederate right. He ordered the regiments which had been engaged to return to the trenches and instructed Buckner to hasten to defend the imperiled point. Buckner refused to obey and, after receiving reiterated orders, started to find General Floyd, who at that moment had joined him. He urged upon Floyd the necessity of carrying out the original plan of evacuation. Floyd assented to this view and told Buckner to stand fast until he would see Pillow. He then rode back and saw Pillow and, hearing his arguments, yielded to them. Floyd simply says that he found the retreat movement so nearly executed that it was necessary to complete it. Accordingly, Buckner was recalled. In the meantime, Pillow's right brigades were retiring to their places in the trenches, under orders from the commanders.

The conflict on the left soon ended. Three hundred prisoners, 5,000 stands of small arms, six guns and other spoils of victory had been won by our forces. But the enemy, cautiously advancing, gradually recovered most of his lost ground. It was about 4:00 P.M. when the assault on the right was made by General C. F. Smith. The enemy succeeded in carrying the advanced work which General Buckner considered the key to his position.

After nightfall a consultation of the commanding officers was held. After a consideration of the question in all its aspects, it was decided that a surrender was inevitable and that to accomplish its objects it must be made before the assault, which was expected at daylight.

The decision to surrender having been made, it remained to determine by whom it should be made. Generals Floyd and Pillow declared they would not surrender and become prisoners; the duty was therefore allotted to General Buckner. Floyd said, "General Buckner, if I place you in command, will you allow me to draw out my brigade?" General Buckner replied, "Yes, provided you do so before the enemy acts upon my communication." Floyd said, "General Pillow, I turn over the command." General Pillow, regarding this as a mere technical form by which the command was to be conveyed to Buckner, then said, "I pass it." Buckner assumed the command, sent for a bugler to sound the parley, for pen, ink and paper, and opened negotiations for surrender. General Pillow advised Colonel N. B. Forrest, who was present, to go out with his cavalry regiment and any others he could take with him through the overflow.

Dr. Brinton witnessed the receipt of the surrender offer and gives us a picture of the scene.

The enemy had made their unsuccessful sortie on the fifteenth. As I happened to be in our kitchen bedroom in the afterpart of the day, I heard General Grant give orders to aide-de-camp Captain Hillyer to get ready to go to the nearest point of telegraph and send a dispatch to General Halleck, informing him that "Fort Donelson would surrender on the following morning." When I was alone with the general

I said to him, "General, was it not a little dangerous to send so positive a message as to what the enemy will do tomorrow? Suppose he doesn't do it?" "Doctor," said the general to me, "he *will* do it. I rode over the field this afternoon and examined some of the dead bodies of his men; their knapsacks, as well as their haversacks, were full of food; they were fighting to get away, and now that they have failed they will surrender. I knew Generals Buckner and Pillow in Mexico and they will do as I have said."

The night was inclement. General Grant slept at his headquarters in the feather bed in the kitchen, and I was curled up on the floor. Early, very early, an orderly entered, ushering in General C. F. Smith, who seemed half-frozen. He walked at once to the open fire on the hearth, for a moment warmed his feet, then turned his back to the fire, facing General Grant who had slipped out of bed and was quickly drawing on his outer clothes. "There's something for you to read, General Grant," said Smith, handing him a letter. I can almost see General Smith now, erect, manly, every inch a soldier, standing in front of the fire, twisting his long white mustache. "What answer shall I send to this, General Smith?" asked Grant. Those were his actual words. Then he gave a short laugh and, drawing a piece of paper, letter size and of rather poor quality, began to write. In a short time, certainly not many minutes, he finished and read aloud, as if to General Smith but really so that we understrappers could all hear, his famous "unconditional surrender" letter.

Grant's own account of the surrender is clear and to the point.

Before daylight General Smith brought to me a letter from General Buckner asking for terms. To this I responded as follows:

Sir:-

Yours of this date, proposing armistice and appointment of Commissioners to settle terms of capitulation, is just received. No terms except an unconditional and immediate surrender can be accepted. I propose to move immediately upon your work.

Your obedient servant,

U. S. GRANT.

To this I received the following reply:

Headquarters, Dover, Tennessee,
February 16, 1862.

To Brig. Gen'l U. S. Grant, U. S. Army.

Sir:—

The distribution of the forces under my command, incident to an unexpected change of commanders, and the overwhelming force under your command, compel me, notwithstanding the brilliant success of the Confederate arms yesterday, to accept the ungenerous and unchivalrous terms which you propose.

I am sir,

Your very obedient servant,

S. B. BUCKNER, Brig. Gen. C.S.A.

General Buckner sent word to his different commanders, and white flags were stuck at intervals along the line of rifle pits.

The editor of the *Richmond Examiner* did not underrate the importance of Grant's victory, and saw in it the beginning of further disasters.

The fall of Fort Donelson was the heaviest blow that had yet fallen on the Confederacy. It opened up the whole of West Tennessee to Federal occupation, and it developed the crisis which had long existed in the west. General Johnston had previously ordered the evacuation of Bowling Green, and it was executed while the battle was fought at Donelson. Nashville was utterly indefensible; on the 6th of April the surrender of Island No. 10 had been a military necessity. The Confederates had been compelled to abandon what had been entitled, "The Little Gibraltar of the Mississippi," and experienced a loss in heavy artillery, which was nigh irreparable.

No one who lived in Richmond during the war can ever forget those gloomy, miserable days.

CHAPTER 8

The First Big Battle in the West

THE BATTLE OF SHILOH

Grant's twin victories on the Tennessee and Cumberland had
opened both rivers. On the Cumberland, Nashville was quickly
occupied by General Don Carlos Buell, commanding the Army
of the Ohio; the opening of the Tennessee, however, offered
several possibilities, all of which had to be weighed with care.

Halleck determined, before committing himself, to organize a
raiding expedition, headed by William Tecumseh Sherman who
had advanced to the rank of brigadier general since the Battle of
Bull Run.

Sherman now describes his experiences, and how, unbeknown
to himself, he selected the setting for one of the war's bloodiest
battles.

General Halleck at St. Louis must have felt that his armies were
getting away from him and began to send dispatches to me at Paducah,
Kentucky. On March 1 I received the following one, and forwarded
it to General Grant, both by telegraph and boat:

St. Louis, March 1, 1862.

To General Grant, Fort Henry:

Transports will be sent you as soon as possible, to move your column
up the Tennessee River. The main object of this expedition will be to
destroy the railroad bridge over Bear Creek, near Eastport, Mississippi;
and also the railroad connections at Corinth, Jackson and Humboldt.

Avoid any general engagements with strong forces. It will be better
to retreat than to risk a general battle. This should be strongly impressed on the officers sent with the expeditions from the river.

H. W. HALLECK, Major General.

In consequence of Halleck's instructions, General C. F. Smith, temporarily taking Grant's place, ordered me to push on under escort of two gunboats. I was to land at some point below Eastport, and break the Memphis & Charleston Railroad between Tuscumbia and Corinth. I immediately steamed up the Tennessee River, following two gunboats and, in passing Pittsburgh Landing, was told by one of the captains that, on his former trip up the river, he had found a Rebel regiment of cavalry posted there, and that it was the usual landing place for the people about Corinth, distant less than thirty miles. I sent word back to General Smith that, if we were detained up the river, he ought to post some troops at Pittsburgh Landing. (See map, page 179.)

Following my failure to destroy the railroad (due to impossible terrain), General Smith instructed me to disembark my own division and that of General Stephen A. Hurlbut at Pittsburgh Landing, to take positions well back and to leave room for the whole army.

On March 18, Hurlbut disembarked his division; on the nineteenth I disembarked mine and took post about three miles back. Within a few days Prentiss' division arrived and camped on my left, and afterward McClernand's and W. H. L. Wallace's divisions, which formed a line to our rear. Lew Wallace's division landed at Crump's, five miles downstream.

On March 17 General U. S. Grant, whom Halleck had temporarily suspended from command for alleged failure to forward reports, had been restored to command and made his headquarters at Savannah, but frequently visited our camps. We did not fortify our camps against an attack, because we had no orders to do so, and because such a course would have made our raw men timid. The position was naturally strong, with Snake Creek on our right, a deep, bold stream, with a confluent (Owl Creek) to our right front; and Lick Creek, with a similar confluent, on our left, thus narrowing the space over which we could be attacked to about a mile and a half or two miles.

At a later period of the war, we would have rendered this position impregnable in one night, but at this time we did not do it. From about April 1 we were conscious that the Rebel cavalry in our front was getting more saucy; and on Friday, April 4, it dashed down and carried off one of our picket guards. I called out a whole brigade and followed some four or five miles, when the cavalry in advance encountered artillery. I then drew back and reported the fact by letter to General Grant at Savannah; but thus far we had not positively detected the presence of infantry, and I supposed the guns that opened on us on the evening of Friday, April 4, belonged to the cavalry that was hovering along our whole front.

General Grant, somewhat more apologetically than General Sherman, explains his position, his plans and his lack of precautions against a possible enemy attack.

Knowing that the enemy was fortifying at Corinth and collecting an army there under Johnston, it was my expectation to march against that army as soon as Buell, who had been ordered to reinforce me with his nearly 40,000 men of the Army of the Ohio, should arrive; and the west bank of the river was the place to start from.

The Army of the Tennessee consisted of five divisions, commanded respectively by Generals W. H. L. Wallace, McClernand, L. Wallace, Hurlbut and Sherman. Reinforcements were arriving daily and, as they came up, they were organized into a division, and the command given to General Prentiss. Since I expected to take the initiative by marching on Corinth, I had no expectation of needing fortifications, though this subject was taken into consideration.

My apprehension was much greater for the safety of Crump's Landing than it was for Pittsburgh. I had no apprehension that the enemy could really capture either place. At this time I generally spent the day at Pittsburgh and returned to Savannah in the evening. I was intending to remove my headquarters to Pittsburgh, but Buell was expected daily and would come in at Savannah. I remained at this point, therefore, a few days longer than I otherwise should have done in order to meet him on his arrival. The skirmishing in our front, however, had been so continuous from about April 3 that I did not leave Pittsburgh each night until an hour when I felt there would be no further danger before the morning.

The fall of Fort Donelson had made General Albert S. Johnston's northern defensive line from Columbus to Bowling Green untenable, and he had withdrawn his remaining forces to northern Alabama. At the same time, the Richmond government had sent General Beauregard west as second in command, with headquarters at Corinth. The fame of Beauregard, still crowned with the laurels won by him at Bull Run, was counted on to offset whatever loss of prestige Johnston had suffered through his recent defeats.

That both the leading Confederate generals realized the precarious position Grant had chosen is shown by Beauregard's analysis of the situation and by the counterstroke he and Johnston were contemplating. (See map, page 190.)

By the middle of March, less than one month after my arrival, I had succeeded in assembling within easy concentrating distances of Corinth some 23,000 men of all arms, independently of the 14,000, more or less, I had found in the district under General Polk. I hoped to be joined before the end of March by General Johnston's command, of about 13,000 men—exclusive of cavalry from Decatur, Alabama.

The five Union divisions in front of Pittsburgh Landing were soon to be reinforced by General Buell, already on the march, with five divisions of the best organized, disciplined and equipped troops in the Federal service, numbering fully 37,000 effectives.

The united armies of Grant and Buell would have presented a well-disciplined and fully equipped force of about 84,000 men. Against this we could not possibly bring to bear more than 38,500 infantry and artillery and 4,300 cavalry. Furthermore, our forces were imperfectly armed, insufficiently drilled and only partly disciplined. They had but recently been organized into two corps, under Generals Leonidas Polk and Braxton Bragg. I believed that, under such circumstances, our only hope of success lay in striking a sudden, heavy blow before the enemy should concentrate all his forces.

General Johnston reached Corinth on the night of March 22, in advance of his army, which followed closely after him. An immediate offensive movement, I hoped, would take place at latest on April 1. This hope could not, however, be realized. As that day approached, our deficiencies in arms, ammunition and the most essential equipments were more and more felt, as was also the want in general officers.

The march to Pittsburgh was then set for the third but did not begin at the time directed, chiefly through the misapprehension of General Bragg who, instead of moving forward upon verbal instructions, held his corps under arms awaiting written orders and blocked the way. Had it not been for this deplorable loss of the afternoon of the third, the Confederate army must have made the march to the immediate vicinity of the enemy by the evening of the fourth. The attack would

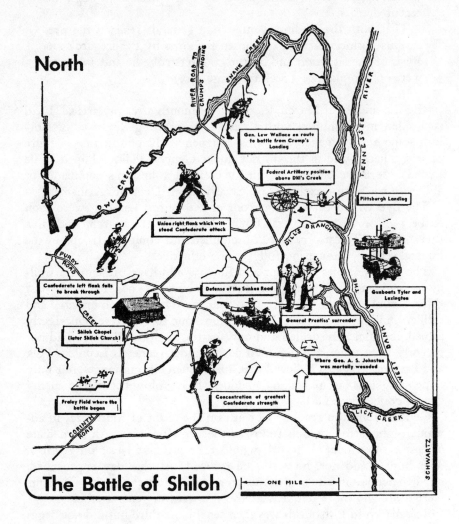

North

Gen. Lew Wallace en route to battle from Crump's Landing

Federal Artillery position above Dill's Creek

Pittsburgh Landing

Union right flank which withstood Confederate attack

Confederate left flank fails to break through

Defense of the Sunken Road

Gunboats Tyler and Lexington

General Prentiss' surrender

Shiloh Chapel (later Shiloh Church)

Where Gen. A. S. Johnston was mortally wounded

Fraley Field where the battle began

Concentration of greatest Confederate strength

RIVER ROAD TO CRUMP'S LANDING

SHAKE CREEK

TENNESSEE RIVER

OWL CREEK

DILL'S BRANCH

PURDY ROAD

PEA CREEK

THE OHIO

WEST BANK

LICK CREEK

CORINTH ROAD

SCHWARTZ

The Battle of Shiloh

|← ONE MILE →|

In the woods and broken ground near the river, generals lost contact with their commands. Shiloh was a private soldiers' battle.

172

have then been made on the morning of the fifth, as had been planned, or twenty-four hours earlier than it actually occurred.

A Confederate soldier, watching a meeting of his high command within a few miles of the Union Camp, made some interesting observations.

About eight o'clock P.M. on April 5, a Council of War was held. In an open space, with a dim fire in the midst, you could see grouped around Beauregard ten or twelve generals, as they listened to his plans and made suggestions. He walked about, gesticulating rapidly, jerking out his sentences. General Johnston stood apart from the rest, with his tall, straight form standing out like a specter against the sky. The illusion was sustained by the military cloak which folded around him. At times he drew nearer the center of the ring and said a few words. General Breckinridge lay stretched out on a blanket near the fire, and occasionally added a few words. General Bragg spoke frequently and with earnestness. General Polk sat on a camp-stool at the outside of the circle, and held his head between his hands buried in thoughts.
For two hours the council lasted, and as it broke up, I heard General Beauregard say, pointing in the direction of the Federal camp, "Gentlemen, we sleep in the enemy's camp tomorrow night."

On April 5, while the Confederate army was crouched to spring, Grant sent out a remarkably carefree message to his commanding officer, General Halleck.

I have scarcely the faintest idea of an attack . . . being made upon us . . .

The men in the rank of the Union army, including their regimental commanders, were not nearly so unmindful of impending danger as their leaders. This is proved by the report of Charles Morton, a private in the 25th Missouri Volunteers.

I was a private in Company I, 25th Missouri Infantry. On Wednesday, April 2, 1862, a part of the regiment was sent out one and a half or two miles in the direction of Corinth, on picket duty. I saw the heavens illuminated by the Confederate campfires. We were astounded at the proximity and apparently great numbers of the enemy. Our men, visiting the farmhouses near by, were warned that they ran great risk of capture.

The men who returned to camp on Friday afternoon, April 4, reported that they had not been relieved, and there was now no picket whatever between us and the enemy. Yet we had considerable cavalry in the command; why was it not screening our camp and even feeling the enemy in his own? Simply ignorance. We had no generals but in rank and authority. The Grant and Sherman of 1864 would have relieved for utter inefficiency any general who had shown no more skill than the same Grant and Sherman did at Shiloh.

On Saturday, April 5, in the afternoon, the 6th Division was reviewed near General Benjamin M. Prentiss' headquarters; and the rumor, afterward confirmed, went through the camp that night that a detachment of Confederate cavalry had ridden up to the edge of the field and witnessed the review. During the night our colonel, Everett Peabody, ordered the two reliefs to patrol the front under Major Powell, field officer of the day. This developed a force believed to be the enemy's pickets. The colonel sent out three companies, then sent out a part of the 21st Missouri Infantry to reinforce Major Powell's command.

At daybreak wounded were being brought into camp, and the companies were formed in their streets prepared for battle. No orders coming from division headquarters, Colonel Peabody ordered the "long roll" beaten, and the alarm was taken up by regiment after regiment and spread throughout the Army. Shortly afterward General Prentiss came riding rapidly down the line to our colonel, jerked up his horse and with great earnestness, if not great anger, exclaimed: "Colonel Peabody, I will hold you personally responsible for bringing on this engagement." The colonel, with severe dignity and illy concealed contempt, answered in his clear, strong voice: "General Prentiss, I am personally responsible for all my official acts." This stormy interview was seen, if the words were not heard, by hundreds of men.

The guns of the only battery in the division had not arrived. The regiment was standing at rest. Looking to the front again, I saw, coming down a gentle slope within easy range, the Confederates, massed many lines deep. Two hostile armies hunting each other without a skirmish line or advance of any kind! Our regimental commander gave the commands: "Attention, battalion—ready—aim—fire!" The moving mass was decimated and staggered. But soon our own men commenced to fall thick and fast. How long we held the enemy at bay at this time I cannot say. How we longed for field guns and lamented they did not come. Seeing a battery coming from the left at full run, I exclaimed: "We will give them hell now, a battery is coming!" My brother William had hardly finished chiding me for using such language, when it whirled into battery about two hundred yards away and opened up on us with grape and canister. We couldn't help it; we had to let go.

Could these be the guns whose reports carried the first tidings of the battle to Grant at the breakfast table at Savannah, twenty miles way?

Just in the rear of the line of field officers' tents, a knot of us made another stand. Here Colonel Peabody's horse passed us, riderless and stirrups flapping in the air. We knew our brave and noble colonel had fallen. Probably no man of our armies in our entire history had rendered his country at one time more valuable service, and yet, outside the few survivors of his regiment, his name is hardly known and is unhonored and unsung.

Whether the Union forces at Shiloh were surprised has ever been a matter of dispute. The recollection of Leander Stillwell of the 61st Illinois Infantry supports the contention that they were.

Our regiment was in camp almost on the extreme left of Prentiss' line. We had not yet got settled down to the regular drills, guard duty was light, the climate was delightful. There was a redbird that would come every morning about sunup and perch himself in the tall black oak tree in our company street, and for perhaps half an hour he would practice on his impatient, querulous note that said, as plain as a bird could say, "Boys, boys! get up! get up!" It became a standing remark among the boys that he was a Union redbird and had enlisted in our regiment as a musician to sound reveille.

So the time passed pleasantly away until that eventful Sunday morning of April 6, 1862. We had answered to roll call, and had cooked and eaten our breakfast. We had then gone to work, preparing for the regular Sunday morning inspection which would take place at nine o'clock. The boys were scattered around the company streets and in front of the company parade grounds, engaged in cleaning and polishing their muskets, brushing up and cleaning their shoes, jackets, trousers and clothing generally. It really seemed like Sunday in the country at home.

Suddenly, away off on the right, in the direction of Shiloh Church, came a dull, heavy "Pum!" then another, and still another. Every man sprang to his feet as if struck by an electric shock and we looked inquiringly into one another's faces. Those heavy booms came thicker and faster and, just a few seconds after we had heard that first dull, ominous growl off to the southwest, there came a low, sullen, continuous roar. There was no mistaking that sound. That was not a squad of pickets emptying their guns on being relieved from duty; it was the continuous roll of thousands of muskets, and told us that a battle was on.

What I have been describing just now occurred in a few seconds only, and with a roar of musketry the long roll began to beat in our camp. Then ensued a scene of desperate haste. A mounted staff officer came galloping wildly down the line from the right. The horse was flecked with foam and its eyes and nostrils were red as blood. The officer cast one hurried glance around him, and exclaimed, "My God! this regiment not in line yet! They have been fighting on the right for over an hour." Wheeling his horse, he disappeared in the direction of the colonel's tent.

Well, the companies were formed, we marched out on the regimental parade ground and the regiment was formed in line. The command was given, "Load at will; load!" We had anticipated this, however, as the most of us had instinctively loaded our guns before we had formed company. All this time the roar on the right was getting nearer and louder. Our colonel rode up close to us, opposite the center of the regimental line, and called out, "Attention, battalion!" We fixed our eyes on him to hear what was coming.

"Gentlemen," said he, in a voice that every man in the regiment heard, "remember your State, and do your duty today like brave men."

That was all. A year later in the war the old man doubtless would have addressed us as "soldiers," and not as "gentlemen," and he would have omitted his allusion to the "State," which smacked a little of Confederate notions. However, he was a Douglas democrat, and his mind was probably running on the Mexican War. By this time the roar on the right had become terrific. The Rebel army was unfolding its front, and the battle was steadily advancing in our direction. We could begin to see the blue fringe of smoke curling upward among the trees off to the right, and the pungent smell of burning gunpowder filled the air. As the roar came traveling down the line from the right it reminded me (only it was a million times louder) of the sweep of a thundershower in summertime over hard ground.

The task of the Confederates, after the advantage of the initial surprise had worn itself out, was not an easy one, as shown by the observations of Colonel B. F. Sawyer, commanding the 24th Alabama, who led his men against the Federal right center.

General Johnston's plan of battle consisted of three lines in the following order: General William J. Hardee's corps constituted the first line, extending from Owl Creek on the left to Lick Creek on the right. This line fell perpendicular to and across the Corinth Road, a distance of three miles. The second line, consisting of Bragg's corps, was drawn out parallel with and 200 yards to the rear of the first, and was to conform its movements to the first. The third line was similarly disposed, i.e., 500 yards in the rear of the second, and was to conform to its movements. This line consisted of Polk's corps. General John C. Breckinridge's corps was massed in the rear of the center of Polk's and was to move forward in column, ready to be deployed when and wherever support should be needed.

The woods in the immediate front of our brigade, through which we had to pass to reach the enemy, were a tangle of swamp, bushes and brambles, and exceedingly difficult to penetrate. Now and then a small patch of cleared ground around a cabin relieved the toilsome scramble. At sunrise we were ordered to move forward. We had not proceeded far before the roll of musketry in front told that the work of death had begun. Then came the peculiar sharp ringing report of the 12-pound Parrotts, and soon another and another, each greeted by a yell of defiance by our eager and thoroughly aroused men.

We soon reached a point opposite the Iowa camps directly in front of the enemy's right center. Before us lay an almost impenetrable thicket. Having cleared this jungle, we crossed at a double-quick the little field beyond when, rising to the crest of a sharp hill, we were brought face to face with the battle.

Never shall I forget the grandeur of that sight. The enemy's camps lay before us, spreading far and wide, dotting the well-cleared slope. McClernand's division was in our front. Dark masses of men clothed in blue were moving in soldierly precision before us, some wheeling into line, others deploying and others recumbent on the ground, awaiting in tigerlike stillness our approach, to hurl death in our faces; the deafening roar of the guns; the unearthly shriek of the shells; the rattle of musketry; the venomous "pringe" of the bullet, all conspired to make it a scene the grandest ever mortal eye beheld.

Then came the order, thrilling every heart—"By the left of companies, forward into line; double-quick, march." No order was ever more handsomely executed. Each company filed into line as deliberately as if that long line of sullen blue that lay scarcely 300 yards in front was a line of friends instead of foes. Our line moved forward until within 100 paces of the line of blue, and then we were lost in the blaze, the thunder and frenzy of battle.

The entire day was one of repeated and hard-earned triumph. After each fierce shock the Federal lines were formed, only to be broken and hurled back again. It was a fearful carnage, and none but heroes could have formed and reformed as the Federals did that day. A foeman less worthy would have been swept from the field by the first triumphant onslaught. But by noon we had driven McClernand from his tents, and by 3:00 P.M. the entire Federal force was broken.

General Johnston, who ranked Beauregard, had given in effect this battle order: "Hit hardest on the right flank and roll up the Union lines, separating them from the landing at Pittsburgh, and force them into the Snake and Owl river bottoms, where they will have to surrender." The actual field command Johnston had yielded to Beauregard, so that he himself could be with the troops and fire them on to their utmost efforts.

At half past two in the afternoon Johnston was struck by a stray bullet and died a few minutes later. The command was immediately taken over by Beauregard, whose account of the battle gives a good summary of the fight.

Before 5:00 A.M. on April 6, General William J. Hardee's pickets, driving in those of General Prentiss, encountered some companies of the Federal advanced guard, and a desultory firing began. The order to advance was now given, and at five o'clock General Hardee's entire line moved forward. Overhead was the promise of a bright day, but the aftermists of the recent storm yet hung in the valleys and woods, veiling still more thickly the forest-screened positions of the enemy,

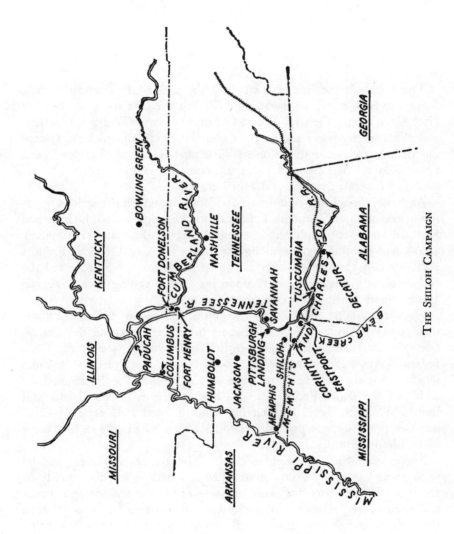

THE SHILOH CAMPAIGN

upon which the lines of battle were directed only by conjecture. General Prentiss, having hurried a reinforcement to the guard and informed Generals W. H. L. Wallace and Hurlbut of the attack, threw forward three regiments well to the front. His position was a prolongation of the elevated ground where stood the Shiloh meetinghouse, held by General Sherman, the whole bounded in front by a ravine and watercourse.

The Confederate lines of attack soon appeared. Prentiss' whole force was now thrown forward and became the first engaged. Shortly after six o'clock, General Prentiss' command was falling under fire, and the assailing wave soon struck General Sherman's pickets, sweeping them back in the direction of his camps. General Sherman called upon General McClernand for assistance and gave notice of the attack to Generals Prentiss and Hurlbut.

At seven o'clock the thunder of artillery announced the serious opening of the conflict. Generals Polk and Breckinridge were now hastened forward and were deployed in column of brigades. By this time the attack had become general along the entire front of Generals Prentiss and Sherman, though stronger as yet on the former, who received the full shock and was driven back upon his camps, calling upon Generals Wallace and Hurlbut for assistance.

Notwithstanding the noise of the conflict since dawn, General Sherman remained under the belief that no more than a strong demonstration was intended, until nearly eight o'clock when, seeing the Confederate bayonets moving in the woods beyond his front, he "became satisfied, for the first time, that the enemy designed a determined attack" on the entire Federal camp. The regiments of his division, all then under arms, were thrown into line of battle. General McClernand, responding promptly to General Sherman's call, had sent forward three Illinois regiments.

It was now half past eight o'clock. The attack was being pushed with great vigor, the Confederate lines of battle following quickly in the wake of the shells that were bursting in the enemy's camps. Prentiss' entire line gave way in confusion and disorder. It was pursued through its camps and about a half mile across a ravine to the ridge beyond.

Across the ravine and on the opposite dominating ridge were General Sherman's remaining brigades, supporting their batteries, with an infantry advance thrown out to the edge of the boggy ravine which here divided the two lines of battle. It was a swamp so overgrown with shrubs, saplings and vines thickly interwoven as to require, in many places, the use of the knife to force a passage. By a front and flank charge, General Sherman was forced to fall back, thus by ten o'clock abandoning his entire line of camps.

About the hour that General Sherman's last camps were carried and his troops were being driven back upon the line of the Purdy Road, the battle broke along the front formed by Generals Wallace and Hurlbut, who had selected strong defensive positions.

Their divisions, deliberately posted and handled with skill, maintained a stubborn resistance to the attack; consisting mostly of troops who had served at Donelson, they gallantly formed their lines, notwithstanding the surprise and disorder through which they had been ushered into the conflict.

All the forces on each side were now in action. The Confederate front line had been extended on its right and left and filled at intervening points by the troops of the second and third, or reserve lines.

The contest went on in all parts of the field, without any important incident or change, during the remainder of the morning and the early afternoon.

In the succession of ravines, ridges and woods, the Federals had, everywhere, natural defensive positions more or less strong, which their opponents were compelled to carry by assault. These were attacked with great bravery and heavy loss of life but not with that concert and massing of forces essential to decisive effects, though this fact was, in some measure, due to the concealed character of the country which, in most parts, admitted of no continuous view of any large body of troops. General officers in immediate direction of their commands were too intent upon the efforts of brigades, and even regiments, thus losing sight of the disjointed remainder and neglecting to combine efficiently the service of the artillery and infantry. Brigades and regiments, as well as batteries, were often, for this reason, at a standstill without orders; and sometimes, from the same lack of cohesion, bodies of our own troops were mistaken for the enemy and even fired into on the flank or rear and thrown into some confusion. Other commands, after casualties, remained without leadership. At two o'clock I again sent orders to General Hardee to push the enemy's right with vigor, and Sherman's and McClernand's troops now rapidly gave way, the larger part of them retiring toward Snake Creek, where they remained aside from the scene of conflict; another part retreated upon Wallace's camps.

A little before ten o'clock David Stuart's forces on the Federal extreme left had also been reached. This officer, when warned at half-past seven by General Prentiss of the presence of the Confederates, had formed his three regiments in line of battle on a ridge faced by a ravine and watercourse emptying into Lick Creek and awaited developments. It was scarcely ten o'clock when his skirmish line, thrown out on another ridge, in front, was driven in by the attacking forces, who planted a battery there and shelled his lines. Jackson's brigade opened the conflict under General Johnston's personal order. Stuart, upon going to the right, found that the 71st Ohio Regiment, together with Hurlbut's Illinois battalion and battery, had taken flight. A similar fate had overtaken the 52d Tennessee, of James R. Chalmers' brigade when, shortly before, it had received the fire of Stuart's skirmishers; and, excepting two companies of soldierly behavior, it was ordered out of the lines. Stuart's other two regiments, after being forced back some distance, were still farther withdrawn and formed along the brow of a hill numbering now a force of 800 men. His position was protected by a fence and thick undergrowth, with an open field in front and a ravine on the left; and here, without artillery, he maintained a creditable resistance against greatly superior numbers.

On the extreme left of the Federal line, as Beauregard had been correctly informed, was posted Colonel David Stuart's small brigade, almost isolated from the main body of troops. The men might well have entertained the hope that the battle would pass them by. As it happened, the brigade was fated to play an important part, quite out of proportion to its size and lack of artillery, on account of General Johnston's battle plans, which called for a strong attack against the Federal left wing in the hope of unhinging it and separating the Union army from Pittsburgh Landing.

On Stuart's brigade developed the vital task of protecting Grant's communication with the only near-by place where Buell's army could be disembarked. One of Stuart's junior officers, Lieutenant Elijah C. Lawrence, describes what befell this small body of men, who held the key position on General Johnston's battle map.

General Sherman had taken position near Shiloh Church, his right resting on Owl Creek. In order to extend the line to Lick Creek on the left, his second brigade, known as Stuart's, composed of the 54th and 71st Ohio and 55th Illinois, commanded by Colonel David Stuart of the 55th, was ordered to take position on the Hamburg Road where the Purdy Road crosses it. There was an interval of over half a mile between our right and General Prentiss' left. This gap was never filled, though many additional troops arrived at the landing previous to the battle.

The camp of the 55th Illinois, now at the extreme left of the entire army, was a peach orchard. The tents were pitched between the rows of trees which were beginning to blossom, and soon we dwelt in bowers of fragrance and beauty. An open field in front was utilized for drill ground. No effort was made to fortify at any point, and the very highest of the surrounding bluffs near by, directly in our front, were left for the enemy to occupy.

We had partaken of our breakfast when a messenger from General Prentiss came to Colonel Stuart's headquarters and announced that the enemy was approaching in force in his front. This was at 7:45 A.M. Our brigade was soon in line along the road in rear of our camp. Our battery had been ordered away from us the day before. For no apparent reason, we were advanced some little distance to a ravine in front. This move, although of no importance in itself, had a great influence on the work of that day, if not on the general result of the battle.

An officer had been dispatched by the Confederate commander, General Johnston, to find the extreme left flank of the Union line, and he arrived at the high bluff in our front just in time to see this movement. Thinking it an attempt to turn their right flank, he hastened back, and upon receiving his report, General Johnston hurriedly called Chalmers' and Jackson's brigades, who were advancing on Prentiss, and in person led them over to the bluff and ordered the charge upon us. According to their official reports, they had 4,247 muskets besides their batteries.

Not fifty feet from where we stood sat an officer on a white horse, looking toward our camp through a large field glass. I whispered to a pickett, "Joe, can't you bring that man down from his horse?" Joe raised his musket, but it went off of itself and the ball went high in the air. The officer threw himself upon the neck of his horse, which whirled like a flash and ran to the rear. But Joe's fire seemed to serve as a signal, and the whole line of skirmishers opened fire with such effect that I saw those beautiful company fronts broken and those "Johnnies" huddled together like a flock of sheep. We were afterward told that this regiment (the 52d Tennessee) then broke and ran and, with the exception of two companies, took no further part in the battle.

But we had to tear ourselves away from this interesting scene, for the retreat was sounded and we were not slow to obey it. Our skirmishers kept up a running fire, with all the rapidity possible with muzzle-loading muskets, falling back in line of and firing from behind large trees, taking deliberate aim and doing visible execution. As we entered the woods back of our camp, we saw the 71st Ohio making for the rear on the run; its great colonel (250 lbs. avoirdupois) in the lead with his horse at full gallop; and during that day nothing more was seen of them.

Our commanding officer, Colonel Stuart, was a lawyer with brains and ability but with neither military knowledge nor experience and had taken for his lieutenant colonel a Dane who professed to have had a military education. The lieutenant colonel seemed to have the idea that the main use of infantry was to repel the attacks of cavalry, and the greater part of his battalion drill had been devoted to the formation of the hollow square.

When our skirmishers returned to their places in line, Stuart's brigade had been reduced to six companies of the 54th Ohio, about 300 men, and the 55th Illinois, with 512 men, making a grand total of a little more than 800 with which to meet more than five times that number and two batteries.

Soon we were called to attention, line formed and wheel by company ordered. This seemed too much for the men's overwrought nerves, and as the wheel was started the entire line broke and ran. And now Colonel Stuart showed heroic metal. His stentorian voice resounded through those woods as he charged upon the leaders with horse and sword and commanded, "Halt, men, halt!" Finally they halted and the panic was over. Had the Colonel of the 71st Ohio been endowed with equal courage, he could undoubtedly have saved a fine regiment from disgrace. The 55th was never known to flinch again, under any circumstances, and later on were called Sherman's "pet lambs."

A new line was formed, some 500 yards back, in the woods. Our position was a good one. The men would drop down the hill to load and crawl up to the top to fire, in almost every case taking deliberate aim, with good effect. The Confederate batteries were planted on their right and on their left, partly enfilading our position, but their aim was so high they did us but slight damage. But the infantry poured such a shower of lead in upon us as rapidly to reduce our ranks to half the original number. Only the excitement of battle could sustain a man in the midst of such carnage. As man after man was shot down or mutilated, a feeling of perfect horror came over me at times, and I berated the powers which placed us in such a position and left us alone to our fate. Can it be wondered at when forty-three out of sixty-four of my own company were killed or wounded in that short space of time?

Not until our cartridge boxes were emptied and we had even borrowed from the wounded and dead was the thought of retreat entertained; then at 2:15 P.M. the retreat was ordered.

The Confederates did not follow. They claimed that their ammunition was exhausted. Of course, they could have overwhelmed us at any time, with or without ammunition, had they determined to do so. The fact that our line was so short, our resistance so determined and that we made no show of artillery deceived them. The stampede and rally, followed by "Column by file," and the hollow square in the woods, as we were told by officers captured the next day, were looked upon as Yankee tricks to draw them on to masked batteries, and repeatedly, the commanding officer, when urged to allow a charge upon us, replied, "No, you will get into a trap; no such little body of men could ever stand up and fight like that without something back of them." They never thought that that "something" was pure pluck.

What the result would have been had Jackson's and Chalmers' brigades remained with the force which attacked Prentiss in the morning cannot, of course, be conjectured, but I think it may be recorded as a fact that, by a resistance almost unparalleled, aided by a combination of favorable accidents, Stuart's brigade saved the left on that day.

Noon had passed and still the battle raged on with undiminished fury. Then came an unexpected tragedy, to which I. G. Harris, governor of Tennessee, was an eyewitness, and of which he now speaks.

General Johnston moved around to our extreme right and for about three-quarters of an hour occupied a position where a very hard fight was going on. Exposed to a galling fire, our line held its position steadily but at a very considerable cost, until finally General Johnston decided to order and lead a charge from that position upon the line of the enemy that confronted us. He rode to the front, talked to the troops a moment or two, ordered and led the charge. The enemy's line gave away before us and we advanced, I should think, three quarters of a mile and established our line on a ridge parallel to the one we had left, meeting a galling fire from the enemy while thus re-establishing our line.

Just as our line had been established and dressed, General Johnston called my attention to the fact that the sole of one of his boots had been cut by a ball. I asked him, somewhat eagerly, "Are you wounded; did the ball touch your foot?" He said, "No," and was proceeding to make an additional remark when a battery of the enemy opened fire from a position to our left, which enfiladed our line in its then position, when he said to me, "Order Colonel Statham to wheel his regiment to the left, charge and take that battery." I galloped immediately to Colonel Statham, about 200 yards distant, gave the order and galloped immediately back to General Johnston, who was sitting upon his horse where I had left him, a few feet in rear of our line of battle. Riding up to his right side, I said, "General, your order is delivered and Colonel Statham is in motion." As I was saying this, he leaned from me in a manner that impressed me with the idea that he was falling from his horse. I instantly extended my left arm around his neck, grasping his coat collar, pulling him toward me until I righted him up in the saddle and, stooping forward so that I could look him in the face, I asked him, "General, are you wounded?" He said, "Yes, and I fear seriously." At this moment his rein dropped from his hand. Holding him with my left hand, I caught up his rein with my right, in which I held my own, and guided both horses to a depression about 100 yards in rear of the line, where I took him off his horse, having asked an aide just as I was leaving the line to bring me a surgeon at the earliest moment possible. I am satisfied that General Johnston did not live exceeding thirty minutes after he was taken from his horse. I did not look at my watch at the time, but my best impression is that it was two-thirty or three o'clock when he died.

After Prentiss' men on the Union left center, the first to enter the fight, had stood bravely for two hours, they were finally forced back and might have opened a path to the pursuers had they not found unexpected refuge. About halfway between Shiloh Church and the Tennessee ran an abandoned sunken road and there they offered desperate resistance.

Here is how A. Hickenlooper, one of Prentiss' artillery officers, later brevetted a brigadier general, remembered the fateful hour he had spent in this natural trench, aptly named the "Hornet's Nest."

Slowly we retired from one defensible position to another until we finally reached a roadway termed the Sunken Road, cut for some distance through a low hill.

Thus nature had here providently supplied that which our commanders had so singularly neglected to provide, a defensive line upon which to rally with a prominent knoll upon which to place the battery and a protecting parapet only a few inches in height but enough partially to protect the infantry, with its front covered by an almost impenetrable growth of underbrush.

When the battery reached this position I was brought into closer touch with General Prentiss, had more time to contemplate his restless energy and terrible earnestness, saw the long line of determined men extending to the right and left as far at the eye could reach, observed regiments moving to the front instead of to the rear and heard the quick, sharp commands as troops were hurried into position. There was being made a systematic concentration for a mighty and possibly conclusive struggle, in which we would have to accept and bear our full share.

For this we had not long to wait. Soon the shells gave warning and the skirmish fire grew stronger and deeper. Then came long triple lines of bristling steel, whose stern-faced bearers, protected and yet impeded by the heavy undergrowth, came pressing on until our cannon's loud acceptance of their challenge and the infantry's crashing volleys caused the assailants to hesitate, break in confusion and hastily retire. We hoped they had gone for good, with that singular feeling of self-congratulation and brotherly affection which is born of the smoke of battle and dangers passed through together.

A stillness pregnant with meaning was soon broken by the rumble and roar of assembled batteries on the distant hill, which again belched forth their rain of shot and shell that indicated a renewal of the struggle.

There were inquiring glances, thoughtful countenances, blanched faces and trembling hands; but there were also evidences of readiness for a display of reckless courage and the performance of daring deeds that subordinated nervousness to pride, and by apparent lighthearted disregard of consequences encouraged the less courageous to brace themselves for another test of soldierly endurance.

The ear-piercing and peculiar Rebel yell of the men in gray and answering cheers of the boys in blue rose and fell with the varying tide of battle and, with the hoarse and scarcely distinguishable orders of the officers, the screaming and bursting of shell, the swishing sound of canister, the roaring of volley firing, the death screams of the stricken and struggling horses and the cries and groans of the wounded formed an indescribable impression which can never be effaced from memory.

Quickly came the orders sharp and clear: "Shrapnel," "Two seconds," "One second," "Canister." Then, as the enemy made preparation for their final dash, "double canister" was ordered delivered with such rapidity that the separate discharges were blended into one continuous roar. Then the supporting infantry, rising from their recumbent position, sent forth a sheet of flame and leaden hail that elicited curses, shrieks, groans and shouts, all blended into an appalling cry. Vainly, courageous Confederate leaders attempted to rally their rapidly disorganizing forces; the task assigned was too difficult for human agency to accomplish, and their lines first wavered, halted, gave way, and finally made a mad rush for cover, leaving each gun's line of fire marked by a windrow of dead and dying.

Again and again, through long and trying hours, this dance of death went on at frequent intervals from nine in the morning until four in the afternoon, thus gradually sapping the energies of these heroic men, who had borne the heat and burden of the fateful day.

One-third of our fighting force had been placed *hors de combat*, and some there were, no doubt, who in the confusion sought safety in flight; but those boys who remained with us in the Hornet's Nest were of the stuff out of which heroes are made.

The day wore on, gradually weakening our powers of resistance; the line was slowly melting away; our ammunition, several times replenished, was nearly exhausted and the Rebel lines could be plainly seen crossing the peach orchard in our rear, toward the only road over which escape seemed possible. It was then General Prentiss informed me that he feared it was too late for him to make an attempt to withdraw his infantry, but that I must pull out with the guns. I bade the general—as brave a little man as ever lived—good-by, and under whip and spur, the remnant of our battery dashed down the road, barely escaping capture. He remained with his devoted followers and with them accepted captivity rather than abandon the position he had been ordered to hold to the last.

> The drama of the first day at Shiloh was drawing to a close. Grant had been beaten along the entire front and, after the Hornet's Nest had surrendered, the Confederates were expected to sweep toward the landing and complete their victory, although two Federal gunboats now added their cannonade to the din. However, General Buell's Army of the Ohio had finally arrived across the river and was also hurrying to the scene. It was a matter of minutes who would reach the landing first—they or the Confederates.
>
> This is the way one Union participant, Jesse Bowman Young, described the end of the first day's fighting, as he, together with his regiment, hastily retreated toward the landing.

The woods were so full of smoke that scarcely anything could be seen. Here and there a battery at work, a struggling line of infantry making their last stand on the ridge that commanded the brow of the hill, at the foot of which was the wharf, an aide dashing across the bullet-swept space with messages, Grant and Sherman seemingly everywhere at the same moment, staying the retreat and re-forming the lines and directing the artillery fire and, beyond, the yelling, crowding troops of Beauregard making a final struggle to drive the Union men into the Tennessee—this was the picture that was dimly discerned through the battle smoke and tumult.

All at once a booming sound came from the river. It was the report of a gun larger than any that had been used on the field.

"Hurrah, boys, the gunboats are driving into them! The Rebels are flanked! We have 'em now," was the cry that passed along the ranks. The *Tyler* and *Lexington*, two of the ironclad fleet, had been watching

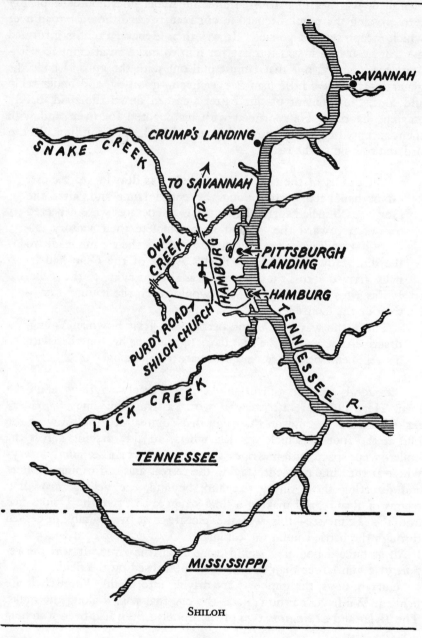

SHILOH

all day for an opportunity to help in the battle. All at once their gunners opened fire with the great cannons with which they were armed and which they had used at Fort Henry and Fort Donelson with such force.

Late in the afternoon I noticed a commotion on the other side of the river. Transports were there waiting for something or somebody. As I watched the spot, I saw a squad of men appear in sight on that side of the river. Then came a general and staff, and then on a run a regiment with its battle flags floating gaily in the air. They quickly embarked on transports and in a short time were on the Pittsburgh Landing shore. I could hardly believe my eyes as I saw the advance guard and realized that Buell's troops had come to the rescue of the Army of the Tennessee. The arriving troops cheered and were cheered in return and, nimbly marching up the steep bluff from the steamers as soon as they landed and spurning the mass of cowards that lined the banks, they went on the double-quick out to the front and into position, just in time to aid in checking the last advance of the Confederate army for the day. At the top of the bluff the advance was cheered by a gallant fellow who, with one arm shot off, heroically waved the other and shouted, "Hurrah, boys! We are glad you've come. We will whip 'em yet!"

> Another Union soldier, one L. Stillwell, wrote down his recollections of the day's ending. He did not, at that critical moment, take as pessimistic a view of the situation as did most of the other men in his army.

It must have been when we were less than half a mile from the landing in our disorderly retreat that we saw standing in line of battle at ordered arms, extending from both sides of the road until lost to sight in the woods, a long, well-ordered line of men in blue. What did that mean? And where had they come from? We did not know then that this line was the last line of battle under General Hurlbut; that on its right, at right angles to it and, as it were, the refused wing of the army, was old Sherman, hanging on with a bulldog grip to the road across Snake Creek from Crump's Landing by which Lew Wallace was coming with 5,000 men. In other words, we still had an unbroken line confronting the enemy, made up of men who were not yet ready by any manner of means to give up. Nor did we know then that our retreating mass consisted only of some regiments and isolated commands who had not been duly notified of the recession of Hurlbut and of his falling back to form a new line and thereby came very near sharing the fate of Prentiss' men. Well, we filed through Hurlbut's line, halted, re-formed and faced to the front once more. It must have been about five o'clock now. Suddenly on the extreme left and just a little above the landing came a deafening explosion that fairly shook the ground beneath our feet, followed by others in quick and regular succession. The look of wonder and inquiry that the soldiers' faces wore for a moment disappeared for one of joy and exultation as it flashed across our minds that the gunboats had at last joined hands in the dance, and we were pitching big 20-pound Parrott shells up the ravine in front of Hurlbut, to the terror and discomfiture of our adversaries. As we were lying there I heard the strains of martial music and saw a body of men marching by the flank up the road. I slipped out of ranks and walked out to the side of the road to see what troops they were. Their band was playing and the men were marching at a quickstep, carrying their guns, cartridge boxes, haversacks, canteens and blanket rolls. I saw they had not been in the fight, for there was no powder smoke on their faces. "What regiment is this?" I asked of a young sergeant marching on the flank. Back came the answer in a quick, cheery tone, "The 36th Indiana, the advance guard of Buell's army."

I did not, on hearing this, throw my cap into the air and yell. That would have given those Indiana fellows a chance to chaff and guy me, and possibly make sarcastic remarks which I did not care to provoke. I gave one big, gasping swallow and stood still, but the blood thumped in the veins of my throat and my heart fairly pounded against my little infantry jacket in the joyous rapture of this glorious intelligence. Never was the sight of reinforcing legions so precious and so welcome as on that Sunday evening, when the rays of the descending sun were flashed back from the bayonets of Buell's advance column as it deployed on the bluffs of Pittsburgh Landing.

The Confederate Lieutenant L. D. Young, who was among those who stormed the Hornet's Nest, gave vent to his feelings at the surrender and his sore disappointment that the victory of the first day was not fully exploited.

Co-operating with the troops on our left, our Kentucky brigade had the proud satisfaction of participating in the capture of Prentiss' division of more than 3,000 men, including the celebrated Waterhouse Battery of Chicago with its magnificent equipment of new guns and fine horses. This battery had been equipped by the great millionaire for whom it was named and we wondered how he would feel when he learned the fate of his pets. I never in my entire experience as a soldier saw such a humiliated and crestfallen body of soldiers as when these prisoners were driving their own magnificent battery from the field.

Their infantry formed in a hollow square stacking arms and lowering their colors; their officers dismounted and turned over their horses and side arms. We made the very Heaven and earth tremble with our triumphant shouts.

Again we moved forward to the front, expecting to deliver the last and final blow. With more than two hours of sunshine in which to deliver it, we found ourselves drawn up in the most magnificent line of battle I ever beheld, extending up and down the river bottom to the right and left as far as we could see, straight as an arrow, every man in place standing at "attention" exuberant with joy, flushed with victory, all understanding the situation, eager for the signal to be given that they knew would finish the glorious day's work. Grant's army was cowering beneath the banks of the Tennessee awaiting the final summons to surrender. What a moment of grand anticipation, and oh, how quick the heart beat!

Why, oh why, did Beauregard not allow us to finish the day's work so gloriously begun by Johnston? Beauregard did not answer this question satisfactorily to the soldiers who were engaged, whatever the opinion of the world. What, but the spirit of envy and jealousy and an overweening ambition to divide the honor of victory with Johnston, which he hoped and expected to win on the morrow, could have controlled his course? That, and that alone, answers the sad question in my mind.

The evening of the fateful sixth came, and with it the arrival of Buell, who turned the tide and sealed the fate of the Cause—the golden opportunity lost, lost forever!

Beauregard stoutly defended himself against the imputation that he had failed to make a last attack because he wanted the entire credit for the victory.

Since four o'clock Colonel J. D. Webster, an able officer of General Grant's staff, had been collecting the reserve artillery and other batteries along a ridge covering Pittsburgh Landing. In rear of Webster's guns was also Hurlbut's division, with James C. Veatch's brigade now re-attached, and two of Stuart's regiments, all of these reinforced by numbers rallied from the broken commands.

In the rear of the victorious Confederate line was a scene of straggling and pillage which, for a time, defied all remonstrance and all efforts at coercion. The disorder and plunder that followed the capture of Prentiss', Sherman's and McClernand's camps were now all the greater, as the troops, fasting since dawn—and some of them since the previous evening—were exhausted from incessant fighting and marching. The commands were broken and mixed, and among many the idea prevailed that the battle had been won and was virtually ended.

Forces were deployed again into line. Chalmers' brigade moved to the right, and, extending to the Tennessee bottom, John K. Jackson's brigade followed, without ammunition, the bayonets being their only weapon. The Federal position on the bluffs was fronted by a deep ravine and creek running into the Tennessee, filled with back water from the river, and the main ravine, which protected the Federal front, was enfiladed by the fire of the gunboats lying in its mouth. Over this ground, divided and thickly wooded, a continuous line of battle was impracticable. Seeing that nothing but a concerted and well-supported attack in heavy mass could strike the finishing blow, I ordered the corps commanders to make a hasty reorganization for a combined onslaught while I at the center should organize reinforcements for the line of attack in my immediate front.

The troops, however, were not pressed to the front in combined attack, as ordered, but in a series of disjointed assaults. These assaults were easily broken.

Jackson's brigade was led under a heavy fire from the light batteries, siege pieces and gunboats across the ravine and, with its only weapon, the bayonet, ascended the ridge nearly to the crest, bristling with guns; but, without support, it could be urged no farther. It remained for some time sheltering itself against the precipitous sides of the ravine till Jackson, seeing his men slaughtered uselessly under a raking fire without support, sought for orders from his division commander; but darkness closed the conflict before he could reach him. Chalmers' brigade, the extreme right, vainly attempted to mount the ridge against the fire from the line of batteries and infantry, assisted by the flank fire of the gunboats, till night closed in.

Meanwhile I had been weighing attentively and anxiously the premonitory signs. The strength of the Federal batteries was apparent, while the steady and heavy rolls of musketry indicated the presence either of fresh troops, the arrival of which I had feared, or of forces reorganized from the stragglers on the field. I felt not only that it was impracticable to gather up all my forces for a general and simultaneous onslaught but also that the brief space of time now remaining before nightfall must be used to collect the troops into position else the morning would find me with but a nominal army. I knew that Lew Wallace's division was near by and might, at any moment, fall upon us in flank, left or rear. I therefore resolved to withdraw the troops gradually from the front and reorganize them, to resume the offensive on the seventh and complete my victory over Grant.

> All night long Buell's crossing continued. By morning Grant's army was further swelled by the brigade of General Lew Wallace, which had arrived from Crump's Landing the night before but too late to take part in the battle.
> Of all this, however, the men in gray knew nothing, as the account written by one of their officers, Colonel B. F. Sawyer, testifies. Confident that victory was theirs, they spent a happy night and it was not until next morning that they had premonitions of a change in their fortune.

That night our army lay upon the field. So complete did we consider the victory that but little thought was given to the morrow. The night was given to plundering and richly were those camps furnished. Such a lavish abundance of good things had never been spread before unrestrained hands.

At length the morning came, not as the morning before but dark, gloomy and chill. The sun of Austerlitz had set; it was the sun of Waterloo struggling through the gloomy mist of the morn. The clouds hung dark with threatening rain. The very air seemed weighted with gloomy forebodings. It was nearly nine o'clock before the roll of musketry and the roar of artillery was heard. And when it did come it had not that animated ring which characterized the struggle of the day before. Our troops, demoralized by the night's revel, were hastily thrown together in mixed commands. All day I lay upon my back. unable to move a single muscle without a painful effort, and listened to that sham of a battle. At length about three o'clock in the afternoon the firing ceased. Then a courier came and ordered the provost guard to move off with the prisoners. Soon another came ordering all the wounded who could walk or be removed to leave, as the army was about to retreat.

It was admitted by friend and foe alike that Beauregard conducted the second day's battle with considerable skill. The hopelessness of gaining a victory was apparent even to him, as he freely admits.

At an early hour in the morning I had established my headquarters to the right of the Shiloh meetinghouse.

The enemy's boldness and the heavy roll of musketry had confirmed me in my belief that General Buell had at last formed a junction with General Grant. My depleted and exhausted forces were now facing at least 20,000 fresh troops, in addition to Lew Wallace's command, in addition also to Jacob Ammen's brigade of Nelson's division, whose timely crossing the day before had saved the Federals from annihilation. To indulge a hope of success with these fearful odds against me would have been to show a lack of judgment. The die, however, was cast. The only plan left, I thought, was to fight so as to deceive the enemy as to my real intentions, and to effect an orderly, safe and honorable retreat. I carefully kept my own counsel, because the least symptom of weakness or hesitancy on my part would necessarily increase the boldness of the opponent and correspondingly depress my new, hardly organized, and worn-out forces.

By three o'clock in the afternoon the time had evidently come when it was imperative to put the plan of retreat into execution. I ordered a company of cavalry to clear and repair the roads for any emergency. About an hour later I instructed Colonel Jordan, the adjutant general of the army, to select a position in the rear for such troops and batteries as were available to protect the retreat. I then ordered the corps commanders to be prepared to retire slowly and leisurely but, before doing so, to take the offensive again with vigor and drive back the enemy as far as possible while I established batteries and posted troops to protect our retiring forces.

The retrograde movement was being executed in a very orderly manner.

Grant was as severely criticized for not pressing his victory home on April 7, as the Confederate general had been censured for not having made a similar attempt on the previous day.

J. B. Young quite frankly expressed his opinion on why the pursuit was not undertaken.

The morning broke, giving the signal for the commencement of another death struggle. The whole army of Buell had arrived and was in position. General Grant at an early hour ordered an advance against the Rebel line. From that hour till late in the afternoon the battle continued. Cheers, now from one side and now from the other, booming of cannon and fluctuations of defeat and victory marked the day. Gradually, however, after a stubborn fight, the Confederates were pushed back until they were forced to yield all the ground hitherto occupied by them. The Rebels had been driven slowly from one point to another until finally there came a ringing cheer from our whole line. It was the token of victory. The Confederates were retreating.

Our troops were not in any condition to pursue the retreating army very far. They had as much as they could do to make him let go his hold and draw off from the attack. Probably both sides were glad enough to cry quits and stop without fighting any more just then.

Grant offered an explanation for not following up his victory, although he confessed that an immediate pursuit might have brought important results.

After the rain of the night before and the frequent and heavy rains for some days previous the roads were almost impassable. The enemy carrying his artillery and supply trains over them in this retreat made them still worse for troops following. I wanted to pursue but had not the heart to order the men who had fought desperately for two days, lying in the mud and rain whenever not fighting, and I did not feel disposed positively to order Buell or any part of his command to pursue. Although the senior in rank at the time, I had been so only a few weeks. Buell was, and had been for some time past, a department commander, while I had commanded only a district. I did not meet Buell in person until too late to get troops ready and pursue with effect; but had I seen him at the moment of the last charge I should have at least requested him to follow.

I rode forward several miles the day after the battle and found that the enemy had dropped much, if not all of their provisions, some ammunition and the extra wheels of the caissons, lightening their loads to enable them to get off their guns. About five miles out we found their field hospital abandoned. An immediate pursuit must have resulted in the capture of a considerable number of prisoners and probably some guns.

One of the most impressive pictures of the battle at Shiloh was drawn by the pen of Henry Morton Stanley, the same Stanley who some day would become famous through his journalistic triumph in locating the lost missionary Livingstone in Africa.

Although born in England, Stanley had been brought up in Arkansas and in the Battle of Shiloh fought on the Confederate side.

On April 2, 1862, we received orders to prepare three days' cooked rations. Through some misunderstanding, we did not set out until the fourth. After two days of marching, our spirits were not so buoyant at dawn on Sunday, April 6, as they ought to have been for the serious task before us.

At four o'clock in the morning we rose from our damp bivouac. Our weapons were the obsolete flintlocks, and the ammunition was rolled in cartridge paper, which contained powder, a round ball and three buckshot. When we loaded, we had to tear the paper with our teeth, empty a little powder into the pan, lock it, empty the rest of the powder into the barrel, press paper and ball into the muzzle and ram them home.

Presently we swayed forward in line, with shouldered arms. Before we had gone 500 paces our serenity was disturbed by some desultory firing in front. It was then a quarter past five. At 200 yards further a dreadful roar of musketry broke out from a regiment adjoining ours. It was followed by another further off, and the sound had scarcely died away when regiment after regiment blazed away and made a continuous roll of sound. We surged forward, for the first time marring the alignment. We tramped recklessly over the grass and young sprouts. Beams of sunlight stole athwart our course. Nothing now stood between us and the enemy. Soon we cracked into them with levelled muskets. "Aim low, men!" commanded our captain. It appeared absurd to be blazing away at shadows. But, still advancing, firing as we moved, I saw little globes of pearly smoke breaking out with spurtive quickness from a long line of blue figures in front; and simultaneously there broke upon our ears an appalling crash of sound, which suggested a mountain upheaved, with huge rocks tumbling and thundering down a slope and the echoes rumbling and receding through space.

This was how the conflict was ushered in. I looked around to see the effect on others and was glad to notice that each was possessed with his own thoughts. All were pale, solemn and absorbed; but beyond that it was impossible for me to discover what they thought, though I felt that they would gladly have preferred to be elsewhere. However, at no time were we more instinctively inclined to obey the voice of command. We had no individuality at this moment, but all motions and thoughts were surrendered to the unseen influence which directed our movements. Probably few bothered their minds with self-questionings as to the issue to themselves. That properly belongs to other moments, not when every nerve is tense and the spirit is at the highest pitch of action. We plied our arms and fired with such nervous haste as though it depended on each of us how soon this fiendish uproar would be hushed.

We continued advancing, step by step, loading and firing as we went. To every forward step we took, the enemy made a backward move, loading and firing as they slowly withdrew. Twenty thousand muskets were being fired at this stage but, though accuracy of aim was impossible owing to our laboring hearts, many bullets found their destined billets on both sides. After some time, we heard the order: "Fix bayonets! On the double-quick!" There was a simultaneous bound forward, each soul doing his best for the emergency. The Federals appeared inclined to await us; but our men raised a yell, thousands responded to it and burst out into the wildest yelling it has ever been my lot to hear. It drove all sanity and order from among us. I rejoiced in the shouting like the rest. It reminded me that there were about four hundred companies like the Dixie Greys who shared our feelings. Most of us, engrossed with the musketwork, had forgotten the fact; but the wave after wave of human voices, louder than all other battlesounds together, penetrated to every sense and stimulated our energies to the utmost.

Those savage yells and the sight of thousands of racing figures coming toward them discomfited the bluecoats; and when we arrived upon the place where they had stood they had vanished. Then we caught sight of their beautiful array of tents, before which they had made their stand. The half-dressed dead and wounded showed what a surprise our attack had been. Some precious minutes were lost in recovering our breaths, indulging our curiosity and re-forming our line. Military equipment, uniform coats, half-packed knapsacks, bedding, all of a new and superior quality, littered the company streets.

I had the momentary impression that, with the capture of the first camp, the battle was well-nigh over; but in fact it was only a brief prologue of the long and exhaustive series of struggles which took place that day.

Continuing our advance, we came in view of another mass of white tents and, almost at the same time, were met by a furious storm of bullets, poured on us from a long line of the enemy. The world seemed bursting into fragments. Cannon and musket, shell and bullet lent their several intensities to the distracting uproar. I likened the cannon, with their deep bass, to the roaring of a great herd of lions; the ripping, cracking musketry to the incessant yapping of terriers; the windy whisk of shells to the swoop of eagles, and the zipping of Minié bullets to the buzz of angry wasps. Before me was a prostrate tree about fifteen inches in diameter, with a narrow strip of light between it and the ground. Behind this shelter a dozen of us flung ourselves. The security it appeared to offer restored me to my individuality. I marveled, as I heard the unintermitting patter, snip, thud and hum of the bullets, how anyone could live under this raining death. I could hear the balls beating a merciless tattoo on the outer surface of the log, pinging vivaciously as they flew off at a tangent from it and thudding into something or other at the rate of a hundred a second. One, here and there, found its way under the log and buried itself in a comrade's body. One man raised his chest, as if to yawn, and jostled me. I turned to him and saw that a bullet had gored his whole face and penetrated into his chest. Another ball struck a man a deadly rap on the head and he turned on his back and showed his ghastly white face to the sky.

"It is getting too warm, boys!" cried a soldier, and he uttered a vehement curse upon keeping soldiers hugging the ground. He lifted his head a little too high, and a bullet skimmed over the top of the log and hit him fairly in the center of his forehead and he fell heavily on his face. The officers, with one voice, ordered the charge; and cries of "Forward, forward!" raised us, as with a spring, to our feet and changed the complexion of our feelings.

Our progress was not so continuously rapid as we desired, for the blues were obdurate; but at this moment we were gladdened at the sight of a battery galloping to our assistance. It was time for the nerve-shaking cannon to speak. After two rounds of shell and canister we felt the pressure on us slightly relaxed; but we were still somewhat sluggish in disposition, though the officers' voices rang out imperiously. We gained the second line of camps, continued the rush through them and clean beyond. It was now about ten o'clock.

The desperate character of this day's battle was presently brought home to my mind in all its awful reality. I felt curious as to who the fallen grays were and moved to one stretched straight out. It was the body of a stout English sergeant, a ruddy-faced man, conspicuous for his complexion, jovial features and good humor, who had been nicknamed "John Bull." He was now lifeless and lay with his eyes wide open, regardless of the scorching sun. Close by him was a young lieutenant who, judging by the new gloss on his uniform, must have been some father's darling. A clean bullet hole through the center of his forehead had instantly ended his career. A little further were some twenty bodies, lying in various postures, each by its own pool of viscous blood, which emitted a peculiar scent, new to me. Beyond these a still larger group lay, body overlying body, knees crooked, arms erect or wide-stretched and rigid according as the last spasm overtook them. The company opposed to them must have shot straight.

I can never forget the impression those wide-open dead eyes made on me. Each seemed to be staring out of its sockets, with a look similar to the fixed wondering gaze of an infant, as though the dying had viewed something appalling at the last moment. "Can it be," I asked myself, "that at the last glance they saw their own retreating souls?"

I cannot forget that half-mile square of woodland, lighted brightly by the sun and littered by the forms of about a thousand dead and wounded men and by horses and military equipment. For it was the first Field of Glory I had seen in my life, and the first time that Glory sickened me with its repulsive aspect, and made me suspect it was all a glittering lie.

Young Stanley here became separated from his regiment. For a time he stumbled through the bloody thickets alone or in company of others who had lost contact with their units, until he finally found himself back again among his comrades.

I overtook my regiment about one o'clock and found that it was engaged in occasional spurts of fury. The enemy resolutely maintained their ground and our side was preparing for another assault. The firing was alternately brisk and slack. We lay down and availed ourselves of trees, logs and hollows, and annoyed their upstanding ranks; battery pounded battery, and meanwhile we hugged our resting places closely. Of a sudden, we rose and raced toward the position and took it by sheer weight and impetuosity, as we had done before. About three o'clock the battle grew very hot. The enemy appeared to be more concentrated and immovably sullen but, with assistance from the reserves, we were continually pressing them toward the river Tennessee, without ever retreating an inch.

About this time, the enemy was assisted by the gunboats, which hurled their enormous projectiles far beyond us; but, though they made great havoc among the trees and created terror, they did comparatively little damage to those in close touch with the enemy.

Our officers were more urgent; dead bodies, wounded men writhing in agony and assuming every distressful attitude were frequent sights; but what made us heartsick was to see, now and then, the well-groomed charger of an officer, with fine saddle and scarlet and yellow-edged cloth and brass-tipped holsters, or a stray cavalry or artillery horse, galloping between the lines, snorting with terror, while his entrails, soiled with dust, trailed behind him.

Our officers had continued to show the same alertness and vigor throughout the day, but as it drew near four o'clock they began to abate somewhat. The pluckiest of the men lacked the spontaneity and springing ardor which had distinguished them earlier in the day. Several lagged wearily behind, and the remainder showed by their drawn faces the effects of their efforts. Yet after a short rest they were able to make splendid spurts. As for myself, I had only one wish and that was for repose. The long-continued excitement, the successive tautening and relaxing of the nerves, the quenchless thirst, made more intense by the fumes of powder and the caking grime on the lips caused by tearing the paper cartridges, and a ravening hunger, all combined, had reduced me to a walking automaton, and I earnestly wished that night would come and stop all further efforts.

Finally, about five o'clock, we assaulted and captured a large camp; the front line was as thin as that of a skirmishing body and we were ordered to retire to the tents. There we hungrily sought after provisions and I was lucky in finding a supply of biscuits and a canteen of excellent molasses, which gave great comfort to myself and friends. The plunder in the camp was abundant.

> There probably exists no description of Shiloh by a Northern man which compares in style with that of Stanley, but Andrew Hickenlooper reviewed the first day's struggle concisely.

At Shiloh there had been no order or system in camping, to begin with, no relation of one command to another; no defined front or known rear except an impassable river. There was no common directing head or superior officer beyond the rank of division commander on the firing line. There was nothing to give cohesion to the whole.

Universal had been the feeling of security before the battle; every one was in total ignorance of its meaning when it began; all was confusion during its progress and all was conjecture and rumor after the day's fighting had ceased.

There were no battle plan, no strategy, no tactical maneuvers and but few commands—certainly none that had any important bearing upon the final results. It was under such conditions that these men— many of whom had never before heard a hostile gun fired—were suddenly aroused and hastily formed in line, without food, without water or even without an adequate supply of ammunition, and were moved forward until suddenly confronted by the regiments of a vigorously pressing and determined foe.

It was a private soldiers' battle, fiercely fought by unskilled, uninstructed and inexperienced volunteers, supported by the indomitable energy, desperate courage and marvelous staying qualities of the rank and file.

> A soldier in the beaten army raised a question which gave rise to much criticism and was one of the reasons why Halleck assumed personal command of the army.

The Confederates were surprised that the victorious Federals made no more of their advantage. A rapid and persistent pursuit would have created a complete rout of the now broken, weary and dispirited Rebels. Two hours more of such fighting as Buell's fresh men could have made, would have destroyed Beauregard's army.

CHAPTER 9

The South Strikes Back

THE SECOND BATTLE OF BULL RUN, OR MANASSAS

Following McClellan's retreat to Harrison's Landing, he immediately began laying plans for his next move. Undaunted by the misfortunes which had dogged his footsteps all spring, he made ready to renew his thrust against Richmond as soon as his troops had been rested and reinforced. With the James River at his back, he need no longer worry about his lines of communication and could concentrate his entire army in front, where it belonged.

His plans, as outlined by himself, were simple and promising.

When my troops reached the James, their first want was something to eat and drink, and the next a bath in the river.

A very few days sufficed to give the men the necessary rest, and the army was then in an admirable position for an offensive movement. It was at last upon its true line of operations, which I had been unable to adopt earlier in consequence of the Secretary of War's peremptory order of the eighteenth of May, requiring the right wing to establish communication with General McDowell. General McDowell never came because, in spite of his own earnest protest, his orders to join me had been countermanded from Washington.

Had the Army of the Potomac been permitted to remain on the James, I would have crossed to the south bank and made a rapid movement on Petersburg, having gained which, I would have operated against Richmond and its communications from the west, having already gained those from the south.

Washington and Maryland would have been entirely safe under the protection of the fortifications and the troops then in that vicinity, so that a large part of the Union Army of Virginia might, with entire propriety, have been sent by water to join the army under my command.

The spirit of McClellan's army apparently had not suffered through its recent retreat, as evidenced by a letter from the pen of one Oliver Willcox Norton, a front soldier.

> Harrison's Landing, Va.,
> Sunday, July 13, 1862.
>
> We had a review by moonlight a few nights ago. "Old Abe" was down here. He did not get around to us till nine o'clock at night, but it was beautiful moonlight and, as he went galloping past beside Little Mac, everyone could tell him by his stovepipe hat and his unmilitary acknowledgment of the cheers which everywhere greeted him. His riding I can compare to nothing else than a pair of tongs on a chair back; notwithstanding his grotesque appearance, he has the respect of the army. But the real man of the army is Little Mac. No general could ask for greater love and more unbounded confidence than he receives from his men, and the confidence is mutual. He is everywhere among his boys, as he calls them, and everywhere he is received with enthusiasm. He was here yesterday about noon. The boys were getting dinner or lounging about, smoking, reading or writing, when we heard a roar of distant cheers away a mile or more. "Little Mac's a-coming," was on every tongue. The men flocked to the roadside. He rode slowly, looking as jovial and hearty as if he could not be more happy. Up go the caps, and three rousing cheers that make the old woods ring greet the beloved leader. He raises his cap in graceful acknowledgment and passes along. But what have we to say to the men who have been using their influence to prevent his being reinforced, to secure his defeat and in some way to so prolong the war as to make the abolition of slavery a military necessity? Curses loud and deep are heaped on such men. Ten thousand men have been sacrificed to that idea now, and the remainder demand that some other policy be adopted henceforth. We want 300,-000 men raised and sent down here immediately. We've been fooling about this thing long enough. No more playing at cross purposes by jealous generals, no more incompetent or traitorous officials. The army and the people demand such a vigorous prosecution of the war as shall give some hope of ending it.

Judging from the letters they wrote him, it looked as if Mc-Clellan had the full support of his superiors.

Washington, July 5, 1862.

Dear General: I can only say, my dear general . . . that there is no cause in my heart or conduct for the cloud that wicked men have raised between us for their own base and selfish purposes. No man had ever a truer friend than I have been to you and shall continue to be. You are seldom absent from my thoughts, and I am ready to make any sacrifice to aid you. . . .

Yours truly,

EDWIN M. STANTON.

Washington, July 30, 1862.

My Dear General: In whatever has occurred heretofore you have had my full approbation and cordial support. I assure you of my friendship and confidence.

H. W. HALLECK, Major General.

But McClellan wrote to his wife that he doubted the sincerity of these letters.

July 13, 1862. Sunday. You want to know how I feel about Secretary of War Stanton? . . . I *may* do the man injustice. . . . I hate to think that humanity can sink so low. . . . I ever will hereafter trust your judgment about men. I remember what you thought of Stanton when you first saw him. I thought you were wrong. I know now you were right.

July 18, 1862. I am inclined now to think that the President will make Halleck commander of the army, and that the first pretext will be seized to supersede me in command of this army.

It was not long before McClellan's suspicions were confirmed. The blow, moreover, struck not only him but also his campaign plans. The exchange of telegrams between the Washington authorities and their general shows the decision at which the War Department had arrived, and his almost piteous pleas to change it.

Washington, Aug. 3, 1862.

To Major General George B. McClellan:

It is determined to withdraw your army from the Peninsula to Aquia Creek. You will take immediate measures to effect this, covering the movement the best you can.

H. W. HALLECK, Major General.

To Major General H. W. Halleck:

I am convinced that the order to withdraw this army to Aquia Creek will prove disastrous to our cause.

The result of the movement would thus be a march of 145 miles to reach a point now only twenty-five miles distant.

Here, directly in front of this army, is the heart of the Rebellion; it is here that all our resources should be collected to strike the blow which will determine the fate of the nation.

Here is the true defense of Washington; it is here, on the banks of the James, that the fate of the Union should be decided.

GEORGE B. McCLELLAN.

To Major General George B. McClellan:

The President expects that the instructions which were sent you yesterday, with his approval, will be carried out with all possible dispatch.

H. W. HALLECK, Major General.

A few years later, Warren Lee Goss, the literary private in the Union army, reviewed the situation at Harrison's Landing and expressed his opinion on Halleck's decision.

It is an accepted maxim in war never to do that which your enemy wishes you to do. From this well-grounded maxim let us consider the withdrawal of the army from the James.

Lee's report shows what he desired: "In order to keep McClellan stationary, or, if possible, to cause him to withdraw, General D. H. Hill, commanding on the south side of James River, was directed to threaten his communications by seizing favorable positions from which to attack the transports on the river."

We have in this report the authority of Lee himself as to what he considered desirable, and it is a curious fact that Halleck's wishes were in perfect accord with the Confederate commander's in a desire to remove the Army of the James, and that he finally achieved, by reason of his high official position, that which Lee failed to attain by strategy. No more sarcastic presentation of his want of wisdom could be offered than this fact!

> Alexander Hunter, a soldier in the 17th Virginia, returning to Richmond from a Federal prison just after the Battle of Malvern Hill, described the situation he found there and how it developed before his eyes.

About the first of August the military authorities in Washington had begun to make preparations for the campaign they knew must soon commence, to guard the national capitol against a sudden flank attack by Jackson, whose name had become synonymous with rear attacks, flank approaches and all sorts of unexpected advances. Lincoln's War Department had gathered all the fag ends of armies in northern Virginia, lately under McDowell, Banks and Frémont, and consolidated them into the Army of Virginia.

The command of this force was entrusted to Major General John Pope, who assumed command in fine spirits, and used these words in a proclamation to his soldiers:

"I have come to you from the West, where we have always seen the backs of our enemies. Disaster and shame lurk in the rear."

Prophetic words! General Lee perceived that without some steps taken on his part, the combination being formed against him meant ruin and disaster. There was McClellan near to the Southern capital in an unassailable position, compelling the Rebel general to remain where he was, locking him up, as it were, in his own fortifications. At the same time another Federal army of over fifty thousand was preparing to launch itself directly in his front.

When contemplating any great undertaking or a vast strategic combination, General Lee had an abstracted manner that was altogether unlike his usual one. He would seek some level sward and pace mechanically up and down with the regularity of a sentinel on his beat; his head would be bent as if in deep meditation, while his left hand unconciously stroked his thick iron-gray beard.

When General Lee was in one of these moods, his staff and orderlies, aware of the momentous results depending on these deliberations, never approached him themselves nor allowed any one else to interrupt him.

In this emergency Jackson was summoned and came; sitting under the shadow of a tree in the cool of the evening, Lee unfolded to his lieutenant his plans.

It was General Lee's great hope that McClellan might evacuate his base at Harrison's Landing and transfer the war to Virginia. He trusted that the alarm awakened at Washington by an advance by Jackson against Pope would cause a withdrawal of McClellan's army.

How promptly Halleck fell into the trap was proved by this telegram to McClellan:

. . . The enemy is massing his forces in front of Generals Pope and Burnside . . . You must send reinforcements instantly . . . Move with all possible celerity.

Jackson's immediate task was to keep or draw Pope away from fortified Washington. While doing so, he struck Banks' isolated corps at Cedar Mountain on August 9. Banks, although commanding less than half as many men as Jackson, turned attacker and threw Jackson's troops into confusion. What happened then is vividly told by the Confederate Captain Charles M. Blackford.

Jackson came dashing across the road in great excitement. He drew his sword, took the battleflag from my man, waved it over his head, and cried: "Where is my Stonewall Brigade? Forward men, Forward!" Our men followed and drove everything before them. Jackson usually is an indifferent and slouchy looking man, but his whole person changed; his face was lit with the inspiration of heroism. Even the old sorrel horse seemed endowed with the form of an Arabian. Just as this scene was being enacted, a very handsome and hatless Yankee officer, not over twenty-one or two, whose head was covered with curls, laid his hand on my knee and said, "What officer is that, Captain?" When I told him, he seemed carried away with admiration. I leaned over, with tears in my eyes, and said, "You are too good a fellow to make prisoner; take that path to the left." He saluted me with his broken sword and disappeared. I hope he escaped.

The diary of Lincoln's Secretary of the Navy reveals what had been going on behind the scenes in Washington.

September 7, 1862. The President has heard Stanton's and Halleck's complaints about McClellan and finally was persuaded by them to recall the army from Richmond and turn the troops over to Pope. Most of this originated . . . in the War Department, Stanton and Chase being the pioneers, Halleck assenting. The recall of the army I thought wrong, and I know it was in opposition to the opinion of some of the best military men in the service. But in this Stanton had a purpose to accomplish. He succeeded in breaking down and displacing McClellan.

Who was this General Pope, on whose shoulders now rested the fate of the Northern army? A Confederate officer, Colonel (later General) E. P. Alexander, gave his opinion of the new Union leader and of the Federal War Department's strategy.

Just at the beginning of the Seven Days' Battles, President Lincoln had called from the West Major General John Pope, and placed him in command of the three separate armies of Frémont and Banks, in the Valley of Virginia, and of McDowell near Fredericksburg. The union of the three into one was a wise measure, but the selection of the commander was as eminently unwise. Pope had spent some years in Texas boring for artesian water on the Staked Plains (Llano Estacado) and making over-sanguine reports of his prospects of success. An army song had summed up his reputation in a brief parody:

> Pope told a flattering tale,
>   Which proved to be bravado,
> About the streams which spout like ale
>   On Llano Estacado.

Pope arrived early in July and began to concentrate and organize his army. In an address to his troops, July 14, dated "Headquarters in the Saddle," he said, among other things:

"Let us understand each other. I come to you from the West . . . from an army whose business it has been to seek the adversary, and beat him when he was found; whose policy has been attack and not defense. . . . I presume I have been called here to pursue the same system."

The arrogance of this address was not calculated to impress favorably officers of greater experience, who were now overslaughed by his promotion. McDowell would have been the fittest selection, but he and Banks, both seniors to Pope, submitted without a word; as did also Sumner, Franklin, Porter, Heintzelman and all the major generals of McClellan's army. Only Frémont protested, asked to be relieved and practically retired from active service.

A Northern officer, Colonel George H. Gordon of the 2nd Massachusetts, was not very enthusiastic about his new generalissimo.

Pope was a thickset man, of an unpleasant expression, about fifty years of age, average height, thick, bushy black whiskers, and wearing spectacles.

There was no reserve about General Pope; he "let out" in censure with such vigor that if words had been missiles our army would never have failed for want of ammunition. In a long talk with me at his headquarters, he attributed our want of success at Richmond to mismanagement on the part of McClellan, for whom he seemed to entertain a bitter hatred, which might have pleased the Administration but found little favor with us.

General Pope's freedom of speech infected his command. Swearing became an epidemic.

The newspapers laughed at Pope, criticized his Falstaffian pretences and dubbed him "five-cent Pope." Every man in his army wondered if he were not a weak and silly man—yet there were none who failed in their determination to do all that mortals could do to retrieve the losses sustained by the Army of the Potomac, be it under Pope or the Devil himself.

Alexander Hunter, although holding no commission in the Confederate army, was a man of sound military judgment.

In simple language he sketched the coming campaign and the inward strength of Stonewall Jackson's command, to which he belonged.

On the third of August, 1862, McClellan was ordered and soon commenced his retreat from the Peninsula to Aquia Creek, there to make a junction with Pope. (See map, page 213.)

Lee now determined to act on one of his bold conceptions—to send Jackson around in Pope's rear and cut him off from Washington, while he would attack in front. Such a step was rash and fraught with many dangers, for Pope, by turning his whole army on Jackson, might overwhelm him before Lee could assist. It was a game full of nice calculations as well as chances; and if the Rebel general had not entertained a rather poor opinion of his adversary's military talent, he would hardly have dared to divide his army into two parts with a chain of mountains between, in which there were but few gaps.

And so Jackson, with 17,300 rank and file, set off on the morning of the twenty-fifth of August from Gordonsville and moved up the western side of the Bull Run Mountains.

The drum beat the long roll for us, the 17th Virginia, and the men fell into line. The troops were all in light marching order; a blanket or oilcloth, a single shirt, a pair of drawers and a pair of socks rolled tightly therein was swung on the right shoulder while the haversack hung on the left. These, with a cartridge box suspended from the belt, and a musket carried at will, made up Johnny Reb's entire equipment. There were not two men clothed alike in the whole regiment, brigade or division; some had caps, some wore hats of every imaginable shape and in every stage of dilapidation, varied by the different shades of hair which protruded through the holes and stuck out like quills upon a porcupine; the jackets were also of different shades, ranging from light gray with gilt buttons, to black with wooden ones; the pants were for the most part of that nondescript hue which time and all weathers give to ruins; some of the men wore boots, but many were barefooted; all were dusty and dirty.

In marching, the troops had learned how to get over the ground without raising clouds of dust. The ranks would split, one half to the right and the other to the left, and then choosing untrod ground they would proceed with infinitely less trouble than in the old way of marching in solid column.

Our rations were doled out in sparing quantities; three crackers per man and a half pound of fat pork was the daily allowance. The cravings of hunger were hardly satisfied by the dole, but soon we were to get nothing at all from the commissary.

The men were becoming veteran soldiers; they had acquired the habit of implicit obedience to superior officers; they had learned how to make a pound of meat and bread go a long way by eating at stated

FROM THE JAMES TO BULL RUN

times; they had become adept in the art of foraging; they had learned
a hundred little ways of adding to their comfort, for instance, taking
off their shoes on a level stretch of sandy road, or bathing their feet in
every running brook, or carrying leaves in their hats as protection
against the sun or lying stretched out at full length at every halt instead
of sitting down. They were little things, it is true, but in the aggregate they amounted to much and were such as marked the difference
between the strong unskilled men and the trained athlete.

When a soldier had learned how to take care of himself in this manner, he rarely broke down, never grumbled, never straggled unless he
had a positive cause and with enough to eat was bound to answer to
his name at the evening tattoo.

The plan which Lee and Jackson had evolved even before Mc-
Clellan had left the James was now about to be executed with
daring and skill.

We have a short résumé of this campaign from Major Sidney
W. Thaxter, a Union officer who took part in it and who could
not help but express the greatest admiration for his adversary.

Pope was pushed back to the Rappahannock River and, while Lee
with Longstreet's corps was holding him near its banks by a constant
threat to cross, Jackson commenced that famous march around the
right flank of Pope's army and fastened himself in his rear upon his
line of communications with Washington. This movement had all the
characteristics of Jackson's genius, audacious, rapid and deliberate. All
the rules of war were set at defiance; he cut himself loose from all connection with his base of supplies; he put himself completely in rear of
the large Union army and gave Pope an easy opportunity to interpose
between him and the balance of Lee's army; he separated his corps from
the rest of his army by a two days' march.

Marching with utmost speed and secrecy on the west side of the
Blue Ridge Mountains, he emerged from them on August 26 through
Thoroughfare Gap which, as a back door to the rear of his army, Pope
should have had guarded as a matter of elementary military prudence,
but had left wide open.

While in the rear of Pope's army, he moved with the utmost coolness
and deliberation; he captured immense supplies at Manassas Junction;
he threw the government at Washington again into confusion and dis-

may, and for twenty-four hours they were without communication with Pope's army, though it was only fifty miles away. After having broken Pope's communications with Washington by rail and carried off and destroyed the great stores of commissary and other supplies at Manassas, he set himself with the utmost deliberation and good judgment to put his troops where they could again make connection with Longstreet's corps, which was on the march by the same route pursued by himself. (See map, page 225.)

If Jackson's march to the rear of Pope's army is open to any criticism by reason of its recklessness, no criticism can justly be made of his plan and movement to extricate himself from his perilous situation. It was done with the most perfect knowledge of the position and movements of Pope's army, or else with that correct insight which was a distinguishing characteristic of this great commander. No sooner did Pope know that Jackson had struck his communication at Manassas than he began to concentrate his whole army upon that point to capture Jackson but, after a march which exhausted his troops and without coming in contact with any of Jackson's divisions, he found that Jackson had escaped him. By this march he had practically opened the way of communication between the two corps of Lee's army and facilitated their junction.

Jackson brought his three divisions out of Manassas, where it would have been dangerous for him to have been attacked, into a line of battle commanding the turnpike road from Warrenton to Centreville; his right extended so as to put out its hand to the rapidly approaching forces under Longstreet; a line of retreat was open in his rear and he was ready for any attack Pope might see fit to deliver. We cannot too much admire the skill and precision with which Jackson moved his troops into this most favorable position, either for attacking or receiving an attack.

> Colonel Herman Haupt, who headed the Military Transportation Department of the Union Army, visited Union headquarters near the Rappahannock on August 22, and reported how little Pope imagined what was about to transpire.

On the afternoon of August 22 I went to the front to ascertain the condition of affairs. I found General Pope seated under a tree on a hill which overlooked the valley and the country beyond. I remained

perhaps two hours, during which reports were made to the general to
the effect that the enemy's wagons had for some time been moving up
the river.

This appeared to me to indicate a flank movement, and I asked General Pope how far he had his scouts up the river. The distance named
was not great, and I then asked, "Is that far enough? What is to prevent the enemy from going even as far as Thoroughfare Gap and getting behind you?"

He replied, "There is no danger." I did not wish to press him with
further questions, thinking he might consider me impertinent and that
his sources of information were better than mine; but I felt uneasy.

> Stuart's cavalry covered Jackson's flanks on his march and
> acted as an advance guard. At Bristoe Station, a few miles from
> Manassas, it was the first to strike Pope's railroad connection
> with Washington. One of its officers, William C. Oates, tells
> what happened at that place.

We reached the Alexandria Railroad at Bristoe Station after sunset.
A number of Yankee officers were just sitting down to an excellent
supper when they were captured. Jackson and his staff, very unwelcome and unexpected guests, took supper with them. Trains which
had been run over the Rappahannock carrying reinforcements to
Pope were now heard returning. A cross tie was put across the track,
for the purpose of throwing the train from the track, but the cowcatcher threw off the obstruction, and the train escaped and made its
way to Washington. Another obstruction was arranged. Then came
three long trains in close proximity to each other. The engine of the
first struck the obstruction, leaped into the air and then tumbled down
the embankment. The engine of the second plowed through the cars
of the first train, throwing them high in the air and overturning them,
until it was itself overturned. The engine of the third came plowing
and crashing along like its predecessor, but stopped on the track. The
engineer was captured, and also two or three other prisoners, one of
whom proved to be a civilian who had been on a visit to the army. One
of his legs was broken just above the ankle. He was laid upon the
ground near a fire. He inquired who we were and, when informed, he
expressed a desire to see Stonewall Jackson. I pointed out Jackson to
him, who just then stood at the opposite side of the fire. He requested
to be raised and surveyed the great Confederate general in his dingy

gray uniform, with his cap pulled down on his nose, for half a minute, and then in a tone of disgust exclaimed, "O my God! Lay me down!" We were ordered to remove the debris but soon found that the whole regiment could not do it without tools and proper implements. What should we do? General Jackson walked with me down to the wreck and said, "Just set fire to it and rejoin your brigade, which has gone to capture Manassas Junction." It was then after nine o'clock, and we had marched thirty miles that day, but we did as we were ordered.

The train which escaped at Bristoe carried the intelligence to Washington that a raid was being made on Pope's communications. The enemy supposed it to be only a body of Confederate cavalry and dispatched a train with a New Jersey brigade to meet the raiders. That any Confederate general with a corps of infantry would or could pass entirely around Pope's grand army and appear in his rear was not once thought of at Washington.

Had Pope been an able, enterprising general, he would have beaten the Confederates in detail; but he was only a braggart and a failure.

In Stuart's cavalry corps there served a former Prussian officer named Heros von Borcke. He took part in the attack on the Union supply depots at Manassas and left us a good picture of this episode.

Of particular interest is his allusion to the direction Jackson's troops took after they had accomplished their work of destruction. Instead of going west to join the main Confederate army, as Pope naturally expected they would, they first turned east, toward Centreville, thus misleading the Federal commander completely. Only after strong forces of the Union army had been sent the wrong way did Jackson turn back to where he wanted to go, and while Pope was looking for him in the direction of Washington, he was calmly resting far north on the Sudley Road, where no one suspected him of being.

The plateau of Manassas presents an area about three miles square, over which the Yankees had built an irregular town of storehouses, barracks, huts and tents, which was fortified on all sides by continuous redoubts. Here were collected stores and provisions, ammunition and equipment for an army of 100,000 men (besides an enormous quantity of luxuries unknown to warfare).

General Stuart had taken the troops guarding the place completely by surprise, capturing the greater part of them and twelve pieces of artillery, and had just routed infantry that had been sent from Alexandria as reinforcements.

The quantity of booty was very great, and the amount of luxuries absolutely incredible. It was exceedingly amusing to see here a ragged fellow regaling himself with a box of pickled oysters or potted lobster; there another cutting into a cheese of enormous size, or emptying a bottle of champagne; while hundreds were engaged in opening the packages of boots and shoes and other clothing, and fitting themselves with articles of apparel to replace their own tattered garments. Among other prizes of this description we had taken a Yankee sutler's wagon, and it gave me great pleasure to divide the plunder among our brave cannoneers. The different boxes were found to contain shirts, hats, pocket handkerchiefs, oranges, lemons, wines, cigars and all sorts of knickknacks.

During the afternoon we received reports that the Federal army was moving rapidly upon us, and very soon Ewell's division, which formed Jackson's rear, was hotly engaged with their advance guard. The main body of our infantry commenced now to march off quietly in the direction of Centreville, turning afterward toward the Stone Bridge and Sudley Springs, while the cavalry remained on the plains to apply the torch to the captured property. All the storehouses and depots were filled with straw and hay, and combustibles were also placed in forty-six railway cars, which had been pushed closely together.

Just as the sun was disappearing behind the range of distant hills, the flames were rising from a hundred different points of the plain.

> Jackson's soldiers had a rapturous day at Manassas Junction and gorged themselves to their heart's content. One John O. Casler tells of this pleasurable adventure with a great deal of gusto.

We remained at Manassas all day. The soldiers were at liberty to take all they wanted, except the sutler stores, which were kept under guard. But we would form in a solid mass and commence pushing one another until the guard would give way, and then we would make the good things fly until some officer would disperse us. I went to the commissary building and soon found a room filled with officers' rations, and several soldiers supplying themselves with coffee, sugar, molasses, etc. We also found a barrel of whisky, but as we had our canteens full of molasses and our tin cups full of sugar, we had nothing to drink out of. We found an old funnel, however, and while one would hold his hand over the bottom of it, another would draw it full. In this way it was passed around. But the officers soon broke up that game.

The captured trains were loaded with everything belonging to an army, and a car loaded with medical stores. Here we found fine brandy and whisky. We soon commenced throwing the medicines around in search of the bottles. Our surgeons begged us to save the morphine and chloroform, as they were scarce articles in our army. But we had no use for medicine except the whisky and brandy. They then informed General Jackson and he ordered us to save the medicines.

We now heard firing up the railroad. General Pope was coming down on us with his army like an avalanche. We remained until dark, when General Jackson started us on the march.

A soldier named John M. Gould in a Maine regiment, marching with Pope's army from the Rappahannock to Manassas while Jackson was on his rampage, kept a diary from which the following excerpts are taken. They give an insight into the mental attitude of some of the Union troops at that time.

August 27, 1862. We heard cannonading during the night toward Washington, and the story goes that they have got into our rear—a pleasant theme for consideration.

It was well that we did not know the mischief Jackson was cutting up on those lines of retreat that General Pope had left to take care of themselves. We camped a mile south of Warrenton Junction, in a place reeking with the filth from other troops, the air thick with the stench from a hundred carcasses, and no water. To give any idea of how we cursed and raved, I will not attempt.

August 28. We passed Catlett's Station and saw a few remaining evidences of the raid, and at length crossed Kettle Run, where the Rebels have lately burned the railroad bridge.

The operations of the Rebels here are worthy of praise. They have marched a respectable force half around our army and right here where we camp they yesterday morning fought our forces.

It was now the twenty-eighth of August, and new, exciting events were beginning to take shape, as Colonel E. P. Alexander of Longstreet's corps sets forth.

Jackson had now accomplished the first object of his expedition—the destruction of the Manassas Depot. Pope would, of course, move at once to crush Jackson, and his first orders were very judicious. He ordered the two corps of McDowell and Franz Sigel, with John F. Reynolds' division, about 40,000 men, to Gainesville. Gainesville was directly between Jackson and Longstreet. It behooved Pope to prevent any possible junction between these two, and now on the night of the twenty-seventh at Gainesville he held the key to the whole position.

But unfortunately for Pope, as yet he had no conception that Lee, with Longstreet's corps, would be hurrying to throw himself into the lion's den by the side of Jackson. He thought that his effort should be to bag Jackson, rather than to keep him from uniting with Lee. In some such belief, during the night all his forces were ordered to march upon Manassas at dawn on the twenty-eighth. This is the order which lost Pope his campaign.

Jackson knew that Lee and Longstreet were coming, and his most obvious move, perhaps, would have been to march for Thoroughfare Gap by some route which would avoid McDowell at Gainesville. His movement, however, had not been made solely to destroy the depot at Manassas. That was but the first step necessary to get Pope out of his strong position. Now it was necessary to bring him to battle quickly, but in detail. Jackson's decision was a masterpiece of strategy, unexcelled during the war, and the credit for it seems solely due to Jackson himself.

One of his divisions was started on the road toward Sudley Ford, to bivouac in the woods north of Groveton. Two other divisions were sent across Bull Run to Centreville and, from there, turning about and moving up toward Sudley, joined Jackson. The sending of two divisions across Bull Run was doubtless to interpose if Pope attempted to move toward Alexandria. Perhaps, also, it had in it the idea of misleading the enemy, for it certainly had that desirable effect. It entirely misled Pope as to Jackson's true location.

Jackson and his three divisions lay hidden in the woods until 5:00 P.M. of August 28. At that hour King's division of McDowell's corps—four brigades about 10,000 strong, with four batteries—appeared upon the Warrenton Pike, in front of Jackson's ambush, marching toward Centreville in pursuance of Pope's order. Jackson, about a mile from the road, might have remained hidden and allowed King to pass. Had he known that, at that moment, Lee and Longstreet were still beyond Thoroughfare Gap, and that James B. Ricketts' division of McDowell's corps was at the gap, intending to block its exit, one might suppose that he would have hesitated to disclose himself. But if Pope was allowed to withdraw behind Bull Run, the result of the whole campaign would be merely to force Pope into an impregnable position. It was the fear of this which led Jackson to attack King immediately, even though he knew that it would draw upon him Pope's whole force.

The action which now ensued was fought principally by the brigadiers on each side. For two hours and a half, without an instant's cessation of the most deadly discharges of musketry, round shot and shell, both lines stood unmoved, neither advancing and neither broken or yielding until at last, about nine o'clock at night, the enemy slowly and sullenly fell back and yielded the field to our victorious troops.

> Lee's aide-de-camp, Colonel Charles Marshall, disclosed that it had not been his chief's intention to fight a battle on the plains of Manassas, but that Jackson, whose actions had been left to his own judgment, precipitated the clash by his onslaught on King's troops.

The information which General Lee had obtained from some of General Pope's captured papers showed him that the latter would very soon receive large reinforcements from General McClellan's army. He did not wish to fight a battle and incur heavy losses which it would be difficult to replace, if General Pope's strength proved to be much greater than his own. His object was to cause General Pope to retreat by cutting the railroad behind him, and at the same time to delay the arrival of reinforcements. By placing his army on General Pope's right flank, he would be able to use the Shenandoah Valley to approach the Potomac and so cause apprehension in the Federal government for the safety of their capital. This General Lee told me himself.

The facts then seem to be that the Second Battle of Manassas did not form part of Lee's original plan. That battle was brought on by Jackson's action on the evening of August 28, in attacking King's division as it was marching across his front all unconscious of his presence. Lee, finding that the junction of Longstreet and Jackson was assured and Pope's forces scattered, allowed the battle to proceed, but he could, had he wished to do so, have avoided the battle and withdrawn Jackson by Aldie, through Snicker's Gap into the Shenandoah Valley. Then, by holding the gaps in the Valley with part of his force and marching on Harpers Ferry with the remainder, he could have caused withdrawal of the Federal army for the defense of Washington, and so achieved what he had declared to have been his purpose.

A military observer, Captain Richard Robins, looking over the situation on the evening of August 28, explains how Pope, having at last found Jackson's whereabouts through the attack on King, mapped out his battle plans on the basis of wrong premises, which naturally led to wrong results.

By the evening of the twenty-eighth, the Union army was much scattered. Ricketts' division had been sent to Thoroughfare Gap, there to contest Longstreet's passage. After dark, Ricketts disobeyed orders and retired from Thoroughfare Gap on the approach of Longstreet's column. Hearing that King was retiring to Manassas, he marched to Bristoe on the morning of the twenty-ninth, the worst move that either could have made. If they had remained in position, they would have materially aided Pope by keeping Longstreet from going into position, as they were on Jackson's right and rear.

The night of August twenty-eighth and twenty-ninth was a hopeful one for Pope. He supposed that Jackson was in full retreat toward Thoroughfare Gap, after having heard with thankfulness the guns of King's engagement in the afternoon of the twenty-eighth. He felt that Jackson was being checked, and the corps of Sigel, Samuel Heintzelman and Fitz-John Porter could now be hurled on him from the east, while the divisions of King and Ricketts were supposedly blocking his line of retreat through Thoroughfare Gap. In Pope's mind there was no escape for Jackson, except a bare possibility of his slipping through to the north. At last he felt certain that he had checkmated his wily adversary, and that before sunset of the next day Jackson would be defeated and his army captured or destroyed, long before Longstreet and Lee could join him. How different was the actual condition of affairs! Not only was Jackson not retreating but, owing to the retirement of Ricketts and King, his line of communication with Longstreet was open. Longstreet's heads of columns were actually through the Gap, and by forenoon of August twenty-ninth two of his divisions had bivouacked east of the mountains, within easy supporting distance of Jackson and with no Union troops between to molest them.

While Jackson was thus playing hide-and-seek with Pope from August twenty-sixth till the evening of August twenty-eighth, Longstreet was approaching Thoroughfare Gap which, to his surprise, was neither occupied nor seriously defended. His troops debouched into the open early on August 29, taking position on the right of Jackson, who now had placed his men behind the embankment of an unfinished railroad which cut across the plains for about half a mile.

Pope, still thinking that Ricketts' division was defending Thoroughfare Gap, and that Jackson's forces were the only ones he had to fight, threw enormous masses of troops against the railroad embankment, neglecting the remainder of the field.

J. P. Polley, a soldier in Hood's Texas brigade, part of Longstreet's corps, described his forced march to the battlefield and the Federal attack on Jackson, of which he was a witness.

At two o'clock of the twenty-sixth day of August, we began the longest and most fatiguing march we have ever made. All that evening, all that night and all the next day until sundown, it was tramp-tramp-tramp. Jackson, so we heard, was about to be surrounded and wanted help.

A message, purporting to be from General Longstreet, contained an order to our officer, who instantly halted his command but, seeing Longstreet approaching, detained the messenger. "Why have you halted, sir?" demanded Longstreet angrily. "By your order, sir," replied the officer. "Who delivered the order?" "That officer on the sorrel horse." "Who authorized you to deliver the order, sir?" demanded Longstreet of the officer. "General Longstreet," replied he without a moment's hesitation, and looking Longstreet full in the face. "Do you know General Longstreet?" "I do, sir." "Is he present?" "He is not, sir." "Arrest that man," said Longstreet turning quickly to the officer in command of his bodyguard, "then carry him to that tree over yonder and hang him—he is a spy." The fellow acknowledged that he was a Federal officer. He had played for a big stake and lost but, asking neither trial nor mercy, met his fate like a man.

At daylight of the twenty-ninth we were awakened by the noise of musketry and artillery firing. It was several miles away, but still loud enough to convince us that a terrible battle was in progress between Jackson and Pope. At sunup we were on the way to relieve old Stonewall, and about ten o'clock in the morning we took position on Jackson's right, a mile or more from the scene of the battle.

The boom of cannons broke upon our ears. It was startling to hear the simultaneous crash of a dozen batteries on our left. This was an effort of General Pope to demoralize Jackson's troops preparatory to charging and driving them in confusion from their position in a railroad cut. This cut was not more than half a mile long, but running diagonally across our line of vision. We could only see the red banks of clay behind which crouched the defiant Confederates. The Federals moved forward, a dark and threatening line of blue, in plain view. Advancing to within a hundred yards of the cut, they halted a second and then sprang forward with a long-drawn "huzzah" ringing from their 10,000 throats. On they went until half the distance to the cut and then the smoke, flash and roar of 4,000 well-aimed guns burst from the Confederate entrenchment, and a wild, reckless and terrifying Southern yell echoed and re-echoed through the woodlands. And scarcely had it ceased to reverberate when the smoke lifted and disclosed the survivors fleeing for dear life, dark blots on the greensward. That infantry struggle had lasted scarcely five minutes, but 1,000 men were killed and more than twice as many more wounded.

Three such assaults were made on the railroad before the Yanks, on that part of their line, decided they had had enough.

The Confederate soldier W. W. Goldsborough described Lee's anxiety on the twenty-eighth, as he heard the thunder of guns, while Thoroughfare Gap still separated him from Jackson.

The Gap was considered a serious obstacle, and Lee did not know then that Ricketts and King, due to a misinterpretation of Pope's orders, had withdrawn.

On the twenty-eighth day of the month we came upon the rear of Longstreet's corps a mile or two from Thoroughfare Gap. Heavy cannonading was going on in front, and we were informed the enemy in strong force was disputing the pass [which was wrong information] but that heavy columns of infantry had been sent over the mountain to flank them.

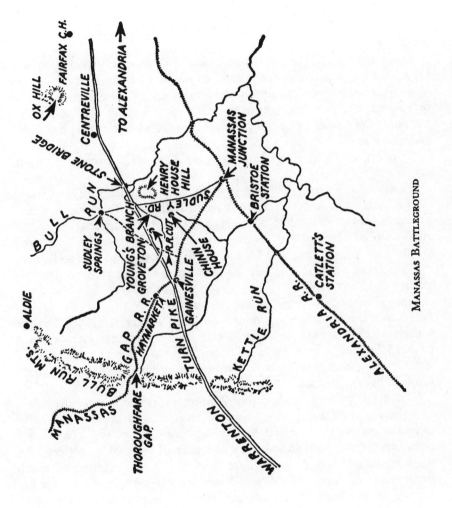

Manassas Battleground

We awoke from our slumber the next morning to find the corps of Longstreet already several miles on its way to relieve Jackson who, rumor said, had been closely pressed for two days by overwhelming numbers and with difficulty held his own. We arose feeling gloomy enough. The roar of artillery had ceased, and everything was still as death. Our poor, hapless little brigade, retiring supperless and arising breakfastless.

Resuming our march, we soon came to a neat, substantial-looking farm house, where it was determined to procure breakfast at any price. We crossed the fence and approached the house. Our commander was to be the spokesman but, just as he was about to apply his knuckles to the door, the clatter of horses feet was heard, and to our surprise General Lee and staff galloped up.

"The brigade will retreat and rally on me," was the command of our brigadier.

As we passed through Thoroughfare Gap, I could not help being struck with its vital importance. It seemed almost a Thermopylae, and it astonished me that it had not been defended by a larger force of the enemy. Had General Lee been delayed here forty-eight hours, we would have lost Jackson and his command. But no time was to be lost; the incessant peals of artillery in our front plainly told us Jackson needed our assistance.

More than once that night, as General Lee paced his room, he was heard to mutter, "The Gap must be forced at any sacrifice. On the success of this movement depends everything. General Jackson must be hard pressed; but he will hold out, or I do not know my man. Twenty-four hours behind my promise to him; forty-eight hours would result in his destruction."

Friday, the twenty-ninth day of August, 1862, was a hot, sultry day, and the corps of Longstreet, already wearied and broken down by excessive marching, dragged itself along with difficulty. Had it not been for the stimulus afforded by the roar of Jackson's artillery, the ten long miles from Thoroughfare Gap would have consumed much more time, and there would have been many more stragglers. But before noon the head of the column reached Haymarket, but a short distance from the scene of conflict. Here we received the most encouraging accounts from Jackson. He was not only holding his ground but had driven the enemy some distance before him. Nevertheless, an expression of relief must have passed over that usually stern and placid face when he observed the clouds of dust that heralded the approach of the iron Longstreet.

Rapidly the different brigades and divisions were thrown into position, and by three o'clock the line of battle was complete.

Warren L. Goss was then serving in Pope's army and surveyed the first day of the battle, August 29.

On the twenty-eighth Pope did not know, practically, where his own forces were or those of the enemy, who had so maneuvered as to mislead, elude and confuse him. His divisions, scattered by contradictory and confusing orders, were held so loosely in hand and were so isolated from each other that, so far as exercising control over them was concerned, it would almost have been as well for him to have been in the West, where he had come from, as in Virginia.

The veterans under Philip Kearny and Joseph Hooker, aroused from their bivouacs at two in the morning, were ordered to march against Jackson and an hour after were in sight of the blue hills about Thoroughfare Gap. This fragment of the army was in a destitute condition. The horses of the field officers in most instances had been left behind. The rank and file were poorly supplied with clothing and destitute of proper rations. Many were without blanket or blouse, some even without trousers; others with shoeless, blistered feet were marching over rough, hot, and dusty roads. Still they were full of enthusiasm for the fight; and as Pope, with a numerous staff, passed them on the road, he was loudly cheered. After that battle there was less cheering for the commander. At three in the afternoon Pope ordered Hooker to attack Jackson's strong position in his front. General Hooker, foreseeing that the attack promised but little chance of success, remonstrated.

Finally he gave the order to one of his brigadiers, General Cuvier Grover. "What does the general want me to do?" Grover inquired.

"Go into the woods and charge."

"Where are my supports?"

"They are coming" was the reply.

Drawing his men up in line, Grover awaited the arrival of his supports, which did not come. But receiving imperative orders to "Charge at once," the men loaded their rifles and fixed bayonets. With cheers the men dashed through the tangled woods in their front. As they stormed the railroad cut they saw wounded Confederates clutch the embankment, hold on for a moment and then, losing their grasp, roll down the steep bank. The first line of the enemy was overthrown. On they rushed upon a second line. Bayonets and swords were used at close quarters, so stubborn was the fight.

Had this attack been properly supported, it must have broken Jackson's center. The combat went on, till a new line of the enemy advanced upon our men and compelled them to fall back.

General Kearny was, at the same time, to have made an attack on Jackson's left, but for some unexplained reason he did not advance until Grover's brigade had been repulsed. Kearny, the one-armed veteran, then led his men in person. He doubled back the left of the enemy and for a short time seemed to have achieved a decisive result. The enemy hurried up two brigades acting as reserves, who came down upon Kearny's thin and exhausted line, which was driven from its hard-won position. Thus ended August twenty-ninth, the first day of the Second Bull Run, or Groveton. The enemy were readjusting their lines for another day's fighting, and Pope, misinterpreting these movements, conceived that the enemy were running away.

> The Union charge against Jackson's position had been undertaken with extreme bravery and came very close to victory. These were anxious moments in the Confederate lines, as attested by a staff officer, Major Robert Stiles.

Jackson was in the famous position in the railroad cut, and Pope's whole army moved upon him. Just as his dispositions—the best he could make for resisting such an onslaught—were complete, Jackson heard from Longstreet, who promised him aid in two hours. The shock could be delayed, however, only a few minutes, and Jackson, feeling the imminence of the crisis, started down his lines to communicate to his troops, worn with fatigue and suspense, his own heaven-born faith and Longstreet's assurance of help. I rode along the line with him, and all he said was: "Two hours, men, only two hours; in two hours you will have help. You must stand it two hours."

It was the crisis of the campaign, and both sides fully appreciated it. The enemy came right on until within two hundred yards and then broke into the rush of the charge. The officer commanding the leading center brigade, who was riding a powerful coal-black charger, carried the colors in his hand and rested the staff on the toe of his boot.

Striking his spurs deep into the flanks of his horse, at the same time rein-
ing him in, he came on, with great plunges, the standard flapping about
him and the standard bearer, cap in hand, yelling at his side. The whole
line rushed upon Jackson's men with the enthusiasm of assured victory.

A hundred yards nearer, and the full fire from Jackson's line burst
upon them, but from the inclination of the musket barrels it looked as
if the gallant fellow on the black horse would be the only man to fall.
On the contrary, while many fell and the line wavered, he was miraculously unhurt, and his men rallied and pressed on after him. For a moment it looked as if he would actually leap into the cut upon his foes;
the next moment the great horse reared wildly and fell backward, but
his heroic rider jammed the color staff into the earth as he went down,
only ten yards from the muzzles of Jackson's muskets. The spell that
held them together was broken, the advancing lines halted and wavered
throughout their length—a moment more and the whole magnificent
array had melted into a mass of fugitives.

Again Jackson rode down his lines: "Half an hour men, only half an
hour; can you stand it half an hour?"

And now it seemed as if some of his men exhaled their very souls to
him in shouts, while others, too much exhausted to cheer, took off their
hats and gazed at him in adoration as he passed.

The enemy, re-formed, began again to advance, and Jackson quickened his horse's gait. "They are coming once more, men; you must stand
it once more; you must stand it half an hour."

Could they have stood it? We shall never know—for before the
mighty wave broke again into the crest and foam of the actual charge,
Hood's Texas brigade was in on Jackson's right.

In order to ease the pressure on Jackson, General Longstreet,
late in the afternoon of the twenty-ninth, ordered an attack on
the Union center. Hood's Texas brigade spearheaded the movement, but its impetuosity brought it into a queer predicament.
The episode is told by J. P. Polley.

It was late afternoon of August 29 when orders came to us skirmishers
to drive the Yankees out of the timber beyond a meadow in front of
us. Casting a look behind to assure ourselves that our respective regiments would follow closely, we moved forward, the light of battle
in our eyes—I reckon—and fear of it in our hearts—I know.

Much to our delight, the enemy was as swift in retreat as we in advance. They did not even fire on us as we crossed the meadow and, once in the timber, our courage returned in full vigor.

Suddenly a loud voice cried, "Halt!" A single gunshot rang out on the still night air, and the command came whispered back, "Silence! We are surrounded by the enemy."

It was a pretty tale to be told on Texans who had come two thousand miles to capture the Yankee nation. But within an hour General Hood found a gap in the circumvailing lines; then he rode first to Longstreet's headquarters and next to Lee's, and asked leave to remain where he was and begin the attack at daylight. He argued that the enemy, imagining they had cooped up only one regiment, would be demoralized and easily routed when attacked by two such brigades as his and Charles J. Whiting's. Overruled by his superiors, however, he returned to the command which, led by him, marched in darkness with bated breath and without the rattle of a cup or a canteen between two Federal brigades, and at daylight confronted the foe whose clutches it had so narrowly escaped, in the same position it had occupied the day before.

Then I joined most heartily with my comrades in congratulating ourselves on having, as one fellow said, so skillfully "unsurrounded" ourselves.

Thus ended the twenty-ninth of August. Before morning both armies were fully assembled, and in the afternoon of the thirtieth, fearing that Lee's army would get away, Pope delivered his main attack. Once more the railroad cut and Jackson's corps behind it played a prominent part in the struggle.

Here are the impressions the battle left on the Union private Warren L. Goss.

The condition of Pope's army on Saturday, August 30, was such that a more cautious general would have hesitated before giving battle. His men were exhausted by incessant marching and fighting; thousands had straggled from their commands; the men had had but little to eat for two days previous; the horses of the artillery and cavalry were broken down from being continually in harness for over a week and from want of forage. But Pope believed he had gained a great victory on the day previous, when Jackson alone had fought a segment of the

Union army, and that the enemy was demoralized, while in fact his lines held the railroad embankment, and for thirty-six hours there had been nothing to prevent the union of Longstreet with Jackson.

At an early hour Pope ordered a reconnaissance made in his front. At this time the enemy, in readjusting their lines, had withdrawn their troops from some of the contested ground of the day previous. Pope interpreted this movement to mean that the enemy was in full retreat and at noon assigned McDowell to the pursuit. Porter was ordered to push forward on the Warrenton Turnpike. Upon his arrival Porter brought to General Pope the intelligence that Longstreet had joined Jackson.

To this information the general in command gave no heed, evidently regarding it as an invention of Porter's rather than as an important fact most needful for him to know.

At four o'clock in the afternoon the battle was opened by Porter. With cheers the Union force dashed up the hill, through the intervening woods, and charged the railroad cut and embankment. The fight was most obstinate and determined, and as one line was repulsed another took its place, the Confederates resisting with bayonets and stones after their ammunition had given out and sticking to the deep cut and embankment as to a fortress. Suddenly Longstreet opened with a murderous enfilading fire of shells, and under this cannonade the lines of Porter were broken and partly put to flight.

Lee had seen that Pope insisted on an attack north of the turnpike and allowed the Union army to expend its strength in that direction, relying upon Jackson to repel it, while he prepared for an attack on our left flank. When half of our troops were either in actual conflict or already discomfited, then it was that Longstreet rolled like an irresistible wave upon our left.

It was past five o'clock when his five fresh divisions, hitherto concealed in the woods, came on, giving the Rebel yell, followed by artillery which took positions from point to point in conformity to the main line of advance. When, however, the Confederates reached the position where they had hoped to intercept our line of retreat, they unexpectedly found it defended.

Then came the struggle for the Henry House Hill, the plateau which had been the scene of the hardest fighting in the first Bull Run. It was bristling with the guns of Reynolds' and Jesse L. Reno's men, and of Sykes's regulars. The enemy made a vigorous attack. At last darkness, the succor of armies hard pressed, came. The army crossed Bull Run by the Stone Bridge, and by midnight were all posted on the heights of Centreville.

It fell to McDowell to defend the line of retreat by the Warrenton Turnpike. A strong prejudice existed among the men against this able but unfortunate commander. Nothing was more common during the day than to hear him denounced. "We've got a Pope who makes more Bulls than the Pope of Rome," said one. "Sergeant," said a gray-haired officer, "how does the battle go?" "We are holding our own," replied a noncommissioned officer, "but McDowell has charge of the left." "Then God save the left!" growled the officer. "I'd rather shoot Mc-Dowell than Jackson." McDowell wore a peculiar headgear which looked like a basket. It was a common remark that "Pope had his head-quarters in the saddle, and McDowell his head in a basket." Such was the moral disadvantage under which McDowell labored.

The flank assault on Porter, which saved Jackson and turned the tide of the battle, was due to one of those quick decisions by Longstreet which made him so valuable to Lee as a battlefield tactician. Here is his own story.

About one o'clock in the afternoon of August 30, General Pope ordered an attack against Jackson's front by the corps under General Porter, supported by King's divisions, Heintzelman and Reno.

During the early part of this severe battle not a gun was fired by my troops, but about 3:00 P.M. a message came from General Jackson reporting his lines heavily pressed and asking to be reinforced. Riding forward, I came in sight of Porter's corps piling up against Jackson's right, center and left. At the same time an order came from General Lee for a division to be sent to General Jackson. Porter's masses were in almost direct line from the point at which I stood and in enfilade fire. It was evident that they could not stand fifteen minutes under the fire of batteries planted at that point, while a division marching back and across the field to aid Jackson could not reach him in an hour, more time probably than he could stand. Boldness was prudence! I called for my nearest batteries. Anticipating my call, they sprang to their places and drove at speed, saw the opportunity before it could be pointed out and went into action. Almost immediately the wounded began to drop off from Porter's ranks; the number seemed to increase with every shot; the masses began to waver, showing signs of discomfiture.

In ten or fifteen minutes Porter's men crumbled into disorder and turned toward the rear. They made brave efforts to rally; but as the new lines formed they made a new target for the batteries, which again drove them to disruption and retreat. Not satisfied, they made a third effort to rally, but by that time they had fallen back far enough to open the field to the fire of S. D. Lee's artillery. The combination tore the line to pieces and, as it broke the third time, the charge was ordered. The heavy fumes of gunpowder hanging about our ranks, as stimulating as sparkling wine, charged the atmosphere with the light and splendor of battle. The noble horses took the spirit of the riders. As orders were given, the staff pressed their spurs, and 25,000 braves moved in line as by a single impulse.

Leaving the broken ranks for Jackson to deal with, our fight was made against the lines near my front. As the plain along Hood's front was more favorable, he was ordered, as the column of direction, to push for the plateau at the Henry house, in order to cut off retreat at the crossings by Young's Branch.

At the first sound of the charge, General Lee asked me to push the battle, and himself rode to join me.

Jackson failed to pull up even on the left, which gave opportunity for some of the enemy's batteries to turn their fire across the right wing as we advanced but, we being on the jump, the fire of the batteries was not effective. It was severely threatening upon General Lee, however, who would ride under it, notwithstanding appeals to avoid it, until I thought to ride through a ravine and thus throw a traverse between him and the fire. Hood's aggressive force was well spent when his troops approached the Chinn house, a farm building on a hill near the Henry plateau.

When the last guns were fired, the thickening twilight concealed the lines of friend and foe, so that the danger of friend firing against friend became imminent. The hill of the Henry house was reached in good time, but darkness coming on earlier because of thickening clouds hovering over us, and a gentle fall of rain closely following, the plateau was shut off from view, and its ascent only found by groping through the darkening rainfall. As long as the enemy held the plateau, he covered the line of retreat by the turnpike and the bridge at Young's Branch. As he retired, heavy darkness gave safe conduct to such of his columns as could find their way through the weird mists.

The Texan J. P. Polley tells how Hood's brigade again distinguished itself on the second day of the big battle.

It was not until four o'clock on the evening of the thirtieth that our brigade again sought the foe. The same meadow was to cross, the skirt of timber to pass through. The 5th New York Battery, stationed on a commanding eminence on the other side of a deep hollow, devoted its whole attention to us and, to show our appreciation of the courtesy, we made directly for it. A Federal regiment between us and the battery fired one volley at us and fled as fast as legs could carry it. Another regiment that had been placed in a pine thicket immediately in rear of the battery as a support of it, followed suit but, undismayed, the battery fired its guns until every artillerist was shot down.

As we looked up the hill, a ghastly spectacle met our eyes. An acre of ground was literally covered with dead, dying and wounded of the 5th New York Zouaves, the variegated colors of whose peculiar uniforms gave the scene the appearance of a Texas hillside in spring, painted with wild flowers of every hue and color. Not fifty of the Zouaves escaped whole. One of their lieutenants told me that they were in the second line of the breastworks which the 4th Texas had carried at Gaines' Mill a month before; that in the mad retreat of the first line of Federals they had been swept away, and that, on learning the position in the Confederate line occupied by our brigade here at Second Manassas, they had made a special request of General Pope to be permitted to confront us on the thirtieth and regain the laurels lost at Gaines' Mill.

Then, as General Hood said, the 5th Texas "slipped its bridle and went wild." Had they not been recalled, they would have gone right on to the Potomac.

A Union officer, Colonel Daniel Leasure, thus wrote of his experiences during the battle, and of his eventual retreat.

We took position at night on the battle ground of the First Bull Run, and I tied my horse to what I supposed to be a stake, but which in the dim light of the morning I found to be a horse's leg sticking up through the grass. My brigade wagon came up in a few minutes and, after issuing rations, I crept under the wagon and slept soundly. We moved in the gray dusk of a foggy morning and debouched upon the Warrenton Turnpike about half a mile east of the Stone Bridge over Bull Run.

We met about two hundred disarmed men in blue, who informed us that Stonewall Jackson had captured them at Manassas Junction and had paroled them. They were certain that Jackson's force was completely surrounded and that before evening we would gather him in, and that if Porter would hold Longstreet for a few hours, we would have Jackson sure enough. Ah, how much depended on that *if!*

Along about four o'clock we saw fresh troops coming on the field on the other side. Our lines on that side were pushed back a short distance but still kept up a bold front.

It was now five o'clock and the enemy was again increasing his fire on our position. But our ammunition was nearly expended and I gave the order to fall back, and through the smoke and dust I saw the enemy front line not over twenty-five yards distant.

They were marching as quietly as if they were on dress parade, with their hats pulled well down over their faces and their eyes fixed on the ground ten paces in front of them, every officer in his place but only one looking ahead, and for an instant we looked into each other's eyes, and the next I started to the rear with what few men had lingered to expend their last cartridges.

But my adventures for the day were not over for, as I rode in the direction of the field hospital, I found myself all at once in close proximity of an officer whose dialect at once betrayed the land of his birth—"away down South in Dixie." Here was a fix. After a single moment's thought of a Rebel prison, I drew my revolver out of my bootleg and rode right up to the party and in a suppressed voice asked, "What are you'ns doin' here?" "A-putting out pickets," said the officer in charge. "Well," I replied, "you'ns make a hell of a noise about it, and the first thing we know you'ns 'll track the 'tention of the Yanks. Wait here half a minit till I see where to put you'ns." And I rode off into the darkness, and if they waited till I came back they are there yet.

At the end of the day, August 30, the Chinn house was a rallying point for the Federal troops, and a battery stationed there had to be taken before the Southerners could call the day a full success.

Alexander Hunter, the author-private in the 17th Virginia, participated in this struggle. He was willing to admit that some Union troops put up a good fight before retiring.

In the valley below the Chinn house, where the dust was dense and blinding, our different organizations were all mingled. Occasional glimpses of the enemy were discernible and, as the afternoon wore on, it was discovered that they were giving ground. This yielding was only temporary, though, for about a half an hour before the sun went down their reserves were brought up.

Just as the day was drawing to a close, a mighty yell arose, a cry from twice ten thousand throats, as the Rebel reserves, fresh from the rear, rushed resistlessly to the front.

It was an extended line, reaching as far as the eye could see, crescent in form. It was, in fact, a greater part of Longstreet's corps. As they swept over the plain, they took up all the scattered fighting material and nothing was left but the wounded which had sifted through, and the dead.

How the shells rained upon us; a Yankee 6-gun battery, on a hill about half a mile off, turned its undivided attention upon us, but the living wall kept on. It seemed as if we were walking on torpedoes. They crackled, split and exploded all around, throwing dirt and ejecting little spirts of smoke that for a moment dimmed the sky.

Colonel Marye, our commanding officer, dismounted, drew his sword from the scabbard and, looking the beau ideal of a splendid soldier, placed himself at the head of his men. He stopped for a moment and pointed his sword with an eloquent and vivid gesture toward the battery on the hill. A cheer answered him, and the line instinctively quickened its pace. Though the shells were tearing through the ranks, the men did not falter. The battery was now hidden by a volleying fume that settled upon the crest.

We neared the Chinn house, when suddenly a long line of the enemy rose from behind an old stone wall and poured straight in our breasts a withering volley at point-blank distance. It was so unexpected, this attack, that it struck the long line of men like an electric shock. But for the intrepid coolness of the colonel, the 17th Virginia would have retired from the field in disorder. But his clear, ringing voice was heard, and the wavering line reformed. A rattling volley answered the foe, and for a minute or two the contest was fiercely waged. Then the colonel fell with his knee frightfully shattered by a Minié ball. Now individual bravery made up for the disaster. The officers surged ahead with their swords waving in the air, cheering on the men, who kept close to their heels, loading and firing as they ran. The line of blue was not fifty yards distant and every man took a sure, close aim before his finger pressed the trigger. For ten minutes, both sides stood up gamely to their work. The left of our brigade now sent one volley into the enemy's flank. The blue line wavered and broke. In a few minutes there were none left except the dead and the wounded.

This is the way another Confederate soldier remembered the fateful afternoon of August 30.

The enemy came forward in regular battle-line. "So they are the attacking party?" said an old brigadier, as he sat on his horse, smoking a cigar. "We also are advancing, so there must be music shortly."

Our general advance was a beautiful sight. As far as the eye could range, two parallel lines of glittering bayonets were flashing in the sun; now the Federal lines halted, and the echo of their volleys was carried on the wind. Quickly the fire was returned. Then a shout, telling that our men had resumed the advance.

Prisoners, cannon, flags and other trophies were passing to the rear while in every patch of timber surgeons were plying the knife. Headless or limbless bodies were seen at every turn; riderless horses, foaming and frightened, rushed in all directions or tottered till they fell.

But the Federal army, although fighting a losing battle, did not easily give up, as Hunter discovered, when his Virginia regiment struggled for the possession of the Chinn house plateau.

There was hardly a breathing spell, and the enemy was upon us, advancing straight toward us with their steady hurrah, so different from the Rebel yell. It proved the mettle of the individual man. Some ran or, white with fear, cowered behind the Chinn house; while others stood, loaded and fired, unmindful of the hurtling shell and screaming shot.

On came the Yankees. In their front was a little drummer beating a *pas de charge*. The dauntless little fellow was handling his sticks lustily too, for the roll of the drum was heard above the noise of the guns.

It was high time to be leaving, when right behind us came a fresh Rebel brigade, and we joined them. A tremendous sheet of flame burst from our line; the weaker side went down, and the Gray swept on toward the 6-gun battery that had been sending forth a stream of death for the past hour.

Mercifully for us but not intended by our foes, the guns were elevated too high, or it would have been simply annihilation; for when those six guns poured their volley into the charging lines they were loaded to the muzzle with grape, and the distance was only about pistol shot. Of course the execution was fearful, and for a second the line was stupefied and nearly senseless from the blow. The ground was covered with victims, and the screams of the wounded rose high above the din and were awful to hear.

But the advance was not stayed long.

With a cry from every throat the Southerners kept on, officers and men together without form or order, the swiftest runners ahead, the slowest behind. Up! Still up! until we reached the crest! As the Yankees pulled the lanyards of the loaded pieces our men were among them. A terrific shock. A lane of dead in front. Those standing before the muzzles were blown to pieces like captured Sepoy rebels. I had my hand on the wheel of one cannon just as it was fired, and I fell like one dead, from the concussion. There was a frenzied struggle in the semi-darkness around the guns, so violent and tempestuous, so mad and brain-reeling that to recall it is like fixing the memory of a horrible, blood-curdling dream.

Now the mists dissolved and the panting, gasping soldiers could see the picture as it was. The battery had been captured.

Then ensued the death struggle, a last fearful grappling in mortal combat. The enemy threw forward all their reserves to meet the shock, and for a space of fifteen minutes the commotion was terrible.

At last the enemy staggered, wavered, broke and fled in utter rout. Where Longstreet was dealing his heavy blows, they were throwing away their knapsacks and rushing madly for the rear. Only one final stand was made by a brigade in the woods close by; but as the long gray line closed in on each flank they threw down their arms and surrendered with but few exceptions.

On the hill which had been occupied by the Washington Artillery of eighteen guns in the earlier part of the day, the eye took in a dim and fast-fading view of the whole surrounding country. It was unutterably grand. Jackson could be seen swinging his left on his right as a pivot, and Longstreet with his entire corps in the reverse method. The whole Yankee army was in retreat, and certainly nothing but darkness prevented it from becoming *une affaire flambée*.

The battle was over.

The Union retreat was now in full swing, and the observing Mr. Goss went through it with all-absorbing eyes.

The next day, August 31, the army occupied Centreville. The day was rainy, and the fords of Bull Run almost impassable. The Confederate commander, wishing to reap all possible benefit from the defeat inflicted upon the Union army, and judging them more demoralized than they really were, determined upon another flank movement, to break up our communications and compel another retreat. Jackson was assigned to this flanking movement, while Longstreet moved more slowly upon his track. Amid the rain on September 1, Jackson reached a crossroad which connects the little river with the Warrenton Turnpike and formed his lines with Ox Hill in his rear. The attack fell upon Reno's, Hooker's and Kearny's and a part of McDowell's troops.

The action was severe but short, and the enemy were repulsed, but not decisively. Longstreet had come up during the night, and every preparation was made by the Confederates to renew the conflict, but the authorities at Washington feared the consequences of risking another battle so near the Capital. The army was, therefore, withdrawn behind the defenses of Washington.

As the Union army fell back by squads, companies and broken parts of regiments and brigades, McClellan came out to meet them. To every brigade, regiment, or only a squad, he met, his only words were, "Boys, go back to your old camps." The regard the private soldiers felt for McClellan arose from a deep conviction that he would not needlessly throw away our lives; that, with all his faults, he understood his trade.

Lee tried to stampede the retreating Federals, but Longstreet confirmed that there was considerable fight left in the rear guard of the Union army.

By the morning of the thirty-first we were trying another move to reach the enemy's rear.

General Jackson was called to headquarters early in the morning. Upon receiving General Lee's orders to cross Bull Run at Sudley's and intercept the enemy's march, he said, "Good!" and away he went, without another word, or even a smile.

Though the suggestion of a smile always hung about his features, it was commonly said that it never fully developed, with a single exception, during his military career, though some claim there were other occasions on which it ripened, and those very near him say that he always smiled at the mention of the names of the Federal leaders whom he was accustomed to encounter over in the Valley behind the Blue Ridge. Standing, he was a graceful figure, five feet ten inches in height, with brown wavy hair, full beard, and regular features. Mounted, his figure was not so imposing. He had a habit of raising his right hand, riding or sitting, which some of his followers were wont to construe into invocation for divine aid, but they do not claim to know whether the prayers were for the slain or for the success of other fields. The fact is, he had received a shot in that hand at the First Bull Run which left the hand under partial paralysis and the circulation through it imperfect. To relieve the pressure and assist the circulation he sometimes raised his arm.

After giving orders for the day, General Lee rode out towards Centreville for personal observation, halted and dismounted at a point which seemed safe from danger of observation. Suddenly an alarm was given: "The enemy's cavalry!" The group dispersed in hot haste to have the heels of their animals under them. The rush and confusion frightened the general's horse, so that it pulled him violently to the ground, severely spraining his right wrist, besides breaking some of the bones of the hand.

Early on the first of September the Confederates resumed their march. Jackson reached Ox Hill late in the afternoon and deployed. The enemy made a furious attack, driving back the Confederate brigades in some disorder. So firm was the unexpected battle that part of Jackson's line yielded to the onslaught.

Jackson's troops were relieved as mine came up. While my reliefs were going around, General Philip Kearny rode to the line of his division. Finding himself in the presence of Confederates, he wheeled his horse, preferring the danger of musket balls to humiliating surrender. Several challenges were followed by the ring of half a dozen muskets, when he fell mortally hurt, and so perished one of the most gallant and dashing of the Union generals.

From Fairfax Court House came the report that the enemy's rear had passed in rapid retreat quite out of reach, approaching the fortifications of Alexandria and Washington City.

John M. Gould, the soldier from Maine, thus described the retreat of his regiment on August 30.

Between 4:00 and 5:00 P.M. on August 30, our turn came to retreat, and we marched steadily, profoundly thankful for the prospect of having our regular rations and a full pipe bowl again. These things were more prominent in our minds than the sadness and humiliation of our situation—but war will destroy all that is noble in man's nature.

Ten o'clock came, and no camp yet. Now came one of those times when for hours we were rushed ahead, expecting every minute to hear the welcome "Halt." We marched from nine till twelve, pulling one foot after the other, confidently expecting that the next moment would bring us to our night's camp. We had been starved till we were sick and brutish; we were chafed and raw from lice and rough clothing; we were footsore and lame; there was hardly a man of us who was not afflicted with diarrhea; we had filled our clothes with dust and perspiration till they were all but rotten; our blood was thin and heated, and now this fierce north wind searched our very marrow. We were demoralized and discouraged.

Each of us had been through the various stages of mental agony, peculiar to such marches—first a man is cheered by the prospect of a speedy camp, then this goes away and he reasons that the camp *must* now be near, because the prospect was good an hour ago, then this dies away and he rallies his strength on the positive certainty that he has only to endure a moment or two longer; then he falls to swearing, and swears himself dry, so to speak. By and by, if he does not fall out of the ranks, he is seized with a desire to laugh and cry at the same time from sheer madness.

At midnight we were halted on heights somewhere near Alexandria. We were groaning with pain, numb and shivering; then we marched on once more, then a long halt. Not a soul of us knew where we were, nor where we were going. One o'clock, and still we went on. One and a half, and our regiment had now dwindled to a few officers and a color guard; swearing and faultfinding had ceased long since. Two o'clock, and a staff officer rode up saying, "The general directs you to stack arms and rest for the night." The men dropped as if they had been shot.

It was the darkest day and the darkest hour in our regimental history.

After the actual fighting was over, a Confederate artillerist named Edward A. Moore took time to observe some of the sights of the battlefield.

Overtaking my battery, I had my attention called to a Federal soldier of enormous size lying on the ground. His head was almost as large as a half bushel and his face a dark blue color. I supposed, as a matter of course, that he was dead and considered him a curiosity even as a dead man. But, while standing near him, wondering at the size of the monster, he began to move and turned as if about to rise to his feet. Thinking he might succeed, I hurried on and joined my gun.

We had a good opportunity of observing the striking difference between the Federals and Confederates who remained unburied for twenty-four hours or more after being killed. While the Confederates underwent no perceptible change in color or otherwise, the Federals became much swollen and discolored. This was, of course, attributable to the difference in their food and drink. And while some Confederates, no doubt for want of sufficient food, fell by the wayside on the march, the great majority of them, owing to their simple fare, could endure more hardship than the Federals, who were accustomed to regular and full rations.

On Sunday, August 31, we were not averse to going over other portions of the battlefield. The area presented the appearance of an immense flower garden, the prevailing blue thickly dotted with red, the color of the Federal Zouave uniform. In front of the railroad cut, and not more than fifty yards from it, where Jackson's old division had been attacked, at least three-fourths of the men who made the charge had been killed and lay in line as they had fallen. I could have walked a quarter of a mile in almost a straight line on their dead bodies without putting a foot on the ground. By such evidences as this, our minds had been entirely disabused of the idea, "the Northerners would not fight."

It was near this scene of carnage that I also saw 200 or more citizens, whose credulity had brought them from Washington and other cities to see "Jackson bagged" and enjoy a gala day. They were now under guard, as prisoners, and responded promptly to the authority of those who marched them by at a lively pace. This sample of gentlemen of leisure gave us an idea of the material the North had in reserve, to be utilized, if need be, in the future.

A Federal Surgeon, Dr. Horace H. Thomas, who received permission from the Confederates to help the wounded of Pope's army, also visited the battlefield and made a report of what he saw.

I went to General Pope's headquarters, where leading generals were assembling. I looked through the open window, and I shall never forget the striking appearance of the commander in chief. He sat with his chair tipped back against the wall, his hands clasped behind his head, which bent forward, his chin touching his breast—seeming to pay no attention to the generals as they arrived but to be wholly wrapped in his own gloomy reflections. I pitied him then. I pity him now.

The next morning, September 1, we set out, with a flag of truce. The medical director divided us civilians into squads of eight, with two stretchers to each ambulance; and we entered upon the mournful task of gathering up our poor wounded fellows from the wide battlefield. The dead were unburied and presented a study of ghastly interest. I saw hardly a decent pair of pantaloons, a blouse, or a pair of shoes on a dead man. If any of these articles of clothing were too shabby to be worth stealing and were left on the body, the pockets were invariably turned inside out. Indeed, I saw in remote parts of the field, screened from general observation, thugs rifling the pockets of some poor fellow who had crawled into an obscure thicket to die. Everywhere these stragglers thronged, most of them boyish-appearing fellows, apparently not more than eighteen or twenty years old.

The next day, having filled all our ambulances and other available vehicles with wounded officers and soldiers, we started on our return trip to Washington.

Richmond now had its day of triumph, and celebrated it by reciting a verse which some jokester had concocted.

> Little Be-Pope, he came at a lope,
> Jackson, the Rebel, to find him.
> He found him at last, then ran very fast,
> With his gallant invaders behind him!

CHAPTER 10

Lee Invades Maryland

THE BATTLE OF ANTIETAM, OR SHARPSBURG

The Second Battle of Bull Run over, Pope's men, defeated and dispirited, were trudging into Washington. The capital itself seemed lost. Then Lincoln rose above the cabal which surrounded him, and by his independent action restored the confidence of the army and of the nation.

McClellan narrates the rapid sequence of events which followed.

On the morning of September 2, while I was at breakfast, the President and General Halleck came to my house.

Without one moment's hesitation, and without making any conditions whatever, I at once said that I would accept the command and stake my life that I would save the city. Both the President and Halleck again asserted that it was impossible, and I repeated my firm conviction that I could and would save it. The President verbally placed me in entire command of the city and of the troops.

He then left with many thanks and showing much feeling. I immediately went to work.

In the afternoon, I rode out to the most advanced of the detached works. Very soon a regiment of cavalry appeared, marching by twos, and sandwiched in the midst were Pope and McDowell with their staff officers. I never saw a more helpless-looking headquarters. Pope could give me no information. He had evidently not troubled his head about the movement of his army and had coolly preceded the troops, leaving them to get out of the scrape as best they could.

I was recognized by the men, upon which there was great cheering; but when I came to Sykes's regular division the scene was most touching. The cheers had attracted their attention, and the men at once said that it could only be for "Little Mac." As soon as I came to them the poor fellows broke through all restraints, rushed from the ranks and crowded around me, shouting, yelling, shedding tears, thanking God that they were with me again and begging me to lead them back to battle. It was a wonderful scene.

The cabinet received the news of McClellan's reappointment with much less enthusiasm than the army, so we are told by the Secretary of the Navy, Gideon Welles.

At the cabinet meeting on September 2, while affairs were growing beyond anything that had previously occurred, Stanton entered the council room a few moments in advance of Mr. Lincoln and said, with great excitement, he had just learned from General Halleck that the President had placed McClellan in command of the forces in Washington. The President soon came in and confirmed what Stanton had stated. Stanton, with some feeling, remarked that no order to that effect had issued from the War Department. The President, calmly but with some emphasis, said the order was his, and he would be responsible for it to the country. Before separating, Chase, the Secretary of the Treasury, expressed his apprehension that the reinstatement of McClellan would prove a national calamity.

In his diary Chase voiced violent disapproval of Lincoln's action:

September 2, 1862.

After the President had declared that McClellan had been placed in command of the forces to defend the capital, I remarked that this could be done equally well by the engineer who had constructed the forts.

The Secretary of War said that no one was now responsible for the defense of the capital.

I remarked . . . that I could not but feel that giving command to him was equivalent to giving Washington to the Rebels.

Montgomery Blair, Lincoln's Postmaster General, recorded to what extremes McClellan's enemies in the cabinet went in their resentment.

The bitterness of Stanton on the reinstatement of McClellan you can scarcely conceive.

The folly and disregard of public interest thus exhibited would be incredible, but the authors of this intrigue, Messrs. Stanton and Chase, *actually declared that they would prefer the loss of the capital to the restoration of McClellan to command.* Yet these are the men who have been accounted by a large portion of our countrymen as the civil heroes of the war.

McClellan had no time to reorganize the army, for Lee, anxious to reap the full benefit of his recent victory, had already invaded Maryland.

McClellan tells how the order by which he had been given a limited command placed a halter around his neck, and how this, together with the enmity of the War Department and Halleck's ineptitude, bore bitter fruit.

Before I went to the front, Secretary Seward came to my quarters one evening and asked my opinion of the condition of affairs at Harpers Ferry, remarking that he was not at ease. Harpers Ferry was not under my control, but I told Mr. Seward that I regarded the arrangements there as exceedingly dangerous; that in my opinion the proper course was to abandon the position and unite the garrison (10,000 men, about) to the main army; that Harpers Ferry would be of no use to us, and its garrison necessarily lost.

The secretary was much impressed and asked me to accompany him to General Halleck and repeat my statement. I acquiesced and we were received in the general's bedroom.

Halleck listened to me with ill-concealed contempt; said that everything was all right as it was; that my views were entirely erroneous, and soon bowed us out.

I had been expressly told that the assignment of a commander had not been decided, but I determined to solve the question for myself. It was absolutely necessary that Lee's army should be met, and there could be no hesitation on my part as to doing it promptly.

The Confederates had never been in finer spirits than when they entered Maryland, to judge from notes made by William M. Owen, an officer in the Washington Artillery. It was the first time they were the invaders, and the prospect of living in the comparative luxury of a peaceful countryside was exhilarating.

"On to Maryland!" is now the cry, and on September 6 the army forded the Potomac into Maryland. (See map, page 253.)

Every one we meet says he is a "Rebel," and we are most hospitably received wherever we go. We get plenty to eat and to drink. The young ladies are wild to see General Lee; in the afternoon a caravan is made up of all the old family carriages and filled with pretty girls, and we escort them to where "Uncle Robert" is resting. He is immediately surrounded and kissed and hugged, until the old gentleman gets very red in the face and cries for mercy. We young ones look on and only wish they would distribute those favors a little more "permiscus," so to speak; but the fair ones, though coy, are very agreeable, and we each forthwith select one whose colors we shall wear until we reach the next town. But all pleasures have an end, and the bugle sounds "Forward," and away we march. On September 7 we encamped near Frederick.

Jackson's "foot cavalry" has been here before us, and has gobbled all the plunder; but we found a grocer with Rebel sympathies, and we invested a few hundred dollars in coffee, sugar, whisky, Scotch, ale, champagne, much to the disgust of his partner, who did not take a bit of stock in Jeff Davis, and who felt remarkably sore when the last of his stock of groceries was exchanged for Confederate notes.

The engineers are destroying the railroad bridges across the river, and General Lee has issued a proclamation to the people of Maryland, asking them to come and "breathe and burn." They haven't burned much so far.

September 10 was a bright, beautiful day, and the army of Lee, with bands playing and colors flying, marched through Frederick. The citizens crowded the streets and windows to see the troops pass. Ladies were demonstrative and waved their handkerchiefs, but the men looked coolly on.

On the 12th we reached Hagerstown and found the people here more demonstrative. Many young girls approached us as we marched through the streets and presented us with beautiful flowers.

We did some shopping in Hagerstown, devoting ourselves chiefly to the dry goods line, and bought waterproof cloth and some dress patterns to present to our lady friends in Richmond, where they were in great need of such things. One merchant had upon his top shelves about one hundred old-fashioned, bell-crowned beaver hats, just the style our fathers wore. The store was soon relieved of the stock of beavers, and the streets were thronged with men with the new hats. They wore them upon the march, and went into the next battle with this most peculiar headgear for warriors.

In his diary Secretary Gideon Welles noted the current developments with considerable misgivings.

September 6. We have information that the Rebels have crossed the Potomac in considerable force, with a view of invading Maryland and pushing on into Pennsylvania. The War Department is bewildered, knows but little, does nothing, proposes nothing.

Our army is passing north. This evening some twenty or thirty thousand passed my home within three hours. There was design in having them pass McClellan's house. They cheered the General lustily, instead of passing by the White House and honoring the President.

McClellan has now been placed in a position where he may retrieve himself, or he may wilt away in tame delays. The army is, I fear, much demoralized. To have placed any other General than McClellan in command would be to risk disaster.

I have sometimes thought McClellan would better discharge the duties of Secretary of War than those of a General in the field.

McClellan had hardly left Washington, when Halleck began to shower him with messages reflecting his own never-ceasing fear for the safety of the Capital. Halleck seemed to have no idea where Lee's army was, and his telegrams show a confusion bordering on panic. Some, like the two which follow, flatly contradicted each other.

September 11. I think the main force of the enemy is in your front.

September 14. Scouts report a large force still on the Virginia side of the Potomac.

HALLECK

The acme of Halleck's ineptitude was reached on September 16. The bulk of the Confederate army then was posted in front of McClellan, and fighting already was in progress, when he received this astounding telegram.

September 16. I think you will find that the whole force of the enemy in your front has crossed the river. I fear now more than ever that they will recross at Harper's Ferry or below, thus cutting you off from Washington.

HALLECK

McClellan, refusing to be misled by his muddleheaded military chief, tried his best to convince him that Harpers Ferry should be evacuated. It still could be done, but the time was running short.

Sept. 10, 9:45 A.M.

General H. W. Halleck:

Col. Dixon S. Miles is at or near Harper's Ferry, as I understand, with 9,000 troops. He can do nothing where he is, but could be of great service if ordered to join me. I suggest that he be ordered to join me.

G. B. McCLELLAN

Gen. G. B. McClellan:

There is no way for Col. Miles to join you at present; his only chance is to defend his works.

H. W. HALLECK

On the morning of September 14, a verbal message reached me from Colonel Miles, informing me that on the preceding afternoon Maryland Heights, which, together with the other mountains encircling the town, commanded it, had been abandoned by our troops, and that all the heights had been occupied by the enemy. The messenger stated that there had been no apparent reason for the abandonment of Maryland Heights.

I directed him to make his way back with the information that I was approaching rapidly and felt confident I could relieve the place.

But Colonel Miles surrendered Harpers Ferry at 8:00 A.M. on the fifteenth.

The surrender of Harpers Ferry was sketched by Albert D. Richardson, a correspondent for the *New York Tribune*.

September 16, 1862. Last night came intelligence of the surrender of Harpers Ferry, including the impregnable position of Maryland Heights, and of our army.

Colonel Miles, who commanded, atoned for his weakness with his life, being killed by a stray shot just after he had capitulated. Colonel Thomas H. Ford, who was stationed on Maryland Heights, professed to have a written order from Miles to exercise his own discretion about evacuating; but he could not exhibit the paper and stated that he had lost it. He gave up that key to the position without a struggle. It was like leaving the rim of a teacup, to go down to the bottom for a better defensive point. He was afterward tried before a court-martial but saved from punishment and permitted to resign, through the clemency of President Lincoln. In any other country he would have been shot.

On September 13, McClellan had entered Frederick, and there ran into a strange mystery. It was that of Lee's Secret Order No. 191, usually called *The Lost Dispatch*. We have a record of John Bloss, the soldier who claimed to have found the document.

On September 13, Company F, 27th Indiana, was placed on the skirmish line and reached the suburbs of Frederick. We threw ourselves upon the grass to rest. While lying there, I noticed a large envelope. It was not sealed and when I picked it up two cigars and a paper fell out.

The cigars were readily divided and, while the needed match was being secured, I began to read the enclosed document. As I read, each line became more interesting. It was Lee's order to his army giving his plans for the next four days from that time and, if true, was exceedingly important. I carried it back to the captain of our company and together we took it to the colonel. He was at that time talking to General Nathan Kimball. They read it with the same surprise which I had felt and immediately started with it to General McClellan.

This order made known not only Lee's position, but his intent. It showed that Lee had proposed to divide his army on the tenth, and that, at this time, the thirteenth, it was really separated into five divisions, and that three divisions were far away, out to capture Harpers Ferry.

McClellan's army, on the other hand, was practically concentrated and could strike either part of Lee's army or both.

The time when I found the dispatch could not have been later than ten o'clock on the thirteenth. I saw General Kimball start with it to McClellan's headquarters, he had a good horse, understood the importance of the dispatch, and he has since told me that he carried it directly to General McClellan.

In about three-quarters of an hour we noticed orderlies and staff officers flying in all directions, and soon the whole army was rapidly moved forward, the enemy attacked and driven over the Catoctin Mountains and across the Middletown Valley, and those who knew of the Lost Dispatch attributed this movement to it.

A Confederate staff officer, Lieutenant Colonel G. Moxley Sorrel, offered the following theory for the losing of the famous dispatch.

How a document so vitally important as General Lee's order could have suffered loss has often been discussed. McClellan says it was addressed to Major General D. H. Hill. There is no disputing this, because the document is on file for evidence. General Hill and his adjutant general, Colonel Archer Anderson, both declare it impossible to have been Hill's copy. They are to be implicitly believed. In addition, Colonel Anderson is able to produce a copy addressed to his chief.

The explanation suggested is that two copies were sent to Hill. Although Hill now commanded a division, Jackson considered him under his command and sent him a copy of the order. One copy certainly reached him direct from General Lee. Jackson and Hill, although connected by marriage, had, it is said, no great personal liking for each other, and I can imagine the cross and dyspeptic Hill, with the order from Lee in his pocket, receiving another copy from Jackson with careless irritation. If this theory does not work out, we seem to be quite baffled in finding a solution.

The finder of Lee's secret order, reading Sorrel's explanation many years later, was prompted to ask a pertinent question:

How does this theory account for the two cigars within the envelope?

Lee was quickly advised that McClellan held possession of the Lost Dispatch, and saw that his scattered army was in danger of being beaten in detail. Jackson's investment of Harpers Ferry had, however, progressed too far and too favorably to be called off. McClellan must therefore be delayed at all hazards, and this

Lee decided to do at South Mountain, a range of hills which lay between him and the Federal forces. D. H. Hill's small division, some 8,000 men, was the only one immediately available and had to face McClellan's entire army of 87,000 men until the afternoon, when Longstreet's corps could come up.

Lee based his plans on McClellan's well-known caution, but even so, Longstreet considered the risk too great and, as he tells us, counseled caution.

A little after dark on September 13, General Lee received information of the advance of the Union forces to the foot of South Mountain. General Lee still held to the thought that he had ample time. He sent for me, and I found him over his map. He asked my views. I thought it too late to man the passes properly at South Mountain, and expressed preference for concentrating behind the Antietam at Sharpsburg. Lee, however, preferred to make the stand at the passes of South Mountain and ordered the troops to march next morning. The hallucination that McClellan was not capable of serious work seemed to pervade our army, even at this moment of dreadful threatening.

After retiring to my couch, I could not rest. At last I made a light and wrote to General Lee, appealing again for immediate concentration at Sharpsburg. To this no answer came, but it relieved my mind.

At daylight in the morning my column marched.

Before sunrise of September 14, General D. H. Hill had ridden to the top of the mountain to view the front. He found Garland's brigade there, and withdrew all advanced troops to the summit.

The battle was opened by Union batteries, which were posted near the foot of the mountain, in fine position to open upon the Confederates at the summit.

General Hill rode off to his right, and as he passed near Fox's Gap, two or three miles to the south, he heard the noise of troops working their way towards him, and soon artillery opened fire across the gap over his head. He hurried back and sent General Samuel Garland's brigade to meet the approaching enemy. After a severe contest, in which Garland fell, the enemy advanced in a gallant charge, part of our brigade breaking in confusion down our side of the mountain. Fortunately, General Hill had posted two batteries on the summit and they threw a destructive cross fire on the enemy.

In the afternoon the head of my column reached the top of South

Mountain, filed to the right to meet the battle, and soon after General Hood arrived with two brigades. The last reinforcement braced the Confederate front to a successful stand, and we held it till after night in hot contest.

Major General Jesse L. Reno, on the Union side, an officer of high character and attainments, was killed about 7:00 P.M. Among the

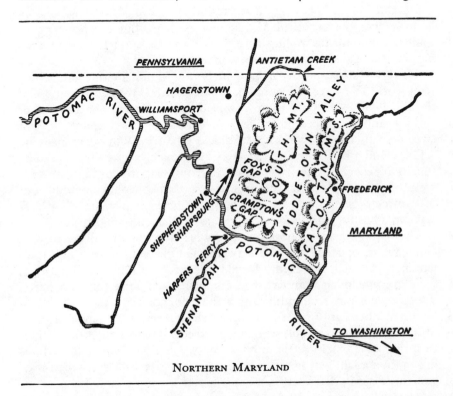

NORTHERN MARYLAND

Union wounded was Colonel Rutherford B. Hayes, afterward President of the United States.

After nightfall General Lee inquired of the prospects for continuing the fight. General Hill explained that the enemy was in great force with commanding positions on both flanks, making the cramped position of the Confederates untenable. His explanation was too forcible to admit of further deliberation. General Lee ordered withdrawal of the commands, making Sharpsburg the point of assembly.

The Confederate soldier George M. Neese, who helped in the defense of South Mountain, wrote in his diary that McClellan could have achieved a quick victory had he not mistrusted the Lost Dispatch, which disclosed how few men he was confronting.

September 14, 1862. Early dawn found us on top of South Mountain, looking over the beautiful Middletown Valley. But the booming of Yankee cannon came rolling across from the Catoctin Hills, announcing that the Yankee hosts were advancing.

There are three principal gaps in South Mountain through which roads pass. We were at Crampton's Gap, which is the southernmost of the three. We had only three companies of infantry, one brigade of cavalry, and six pieces of artillery to defend the pass against at least two, perhaps three, divisions of Yankee infantry, with accompanying artillery and a big bunch of cavalry. The whole country seemed to be full of bluecoats. They were so numerous that it looked as if they were creeping up out of the ground—and what would or could our little force of some three or four hundred available men standing halfway up a bushy, stony mountainside do with such a mighty host?

The battery held its position and, when the enemy advanced to a closer range, opened fire. We kept up the fight until nearly night; but late in the evening the enemy forced the pass by flanking and fighting, with overwhelming numbers, and compelled our little force to retire. To observe the caution with which the Yankees, with their vastly superior numbers, approached the mountain put one very much in mind of a lion, king of the forest, making exceedingly careful preparations to spring on a plucky little mouse. For we had only about three hundred men actually engaged, and they were mostly cavalry, which is of very little use in defending a mountain pass.

As usual, correspondents of Northern newspapers will say that a little band of heroic Union patriots gallantly cleaned out Crampton's Gap, defended by an overwhelming force of Rebels strongly posted and standing so thick that they had to crawl over each other to get away.

Lee had done some dangerously close reckoning. He had only half as many men as McClellan, and if he could not assemble those quickly, not even his military genius would prevail.

Harpers Ferry had surrendered to Jackson in the morning of

September 15, but two-fifths of the Confederate army had been used for that enterprise and were still many miles from the field of Antietam when McClellan's forces made their appearance there. Leaving only A. P. Hill with about 4,000 men to arrange the surrender, Jackson moved his troops at once, but could they reach Lee before he was crushed?

William M. Owen points out Lee's dangerous position on September 15.

We reached the vicinity of Sharpsburg early in the morning of September 15, and formed line of battle along the range of hills between the town and the stream, with our backs to the Potomac.

On the opposite shore of the Antietam the banks are quite steep and afford good position for artillery. All the batteries present were placed in position along the ridge. Longstreet said, "Put them all in, every gun you have, long range and short range."

A courier arrived in hot haste, with news that Jackson had captured Harpers Ferry, with its garrison of 12,000 men, 70 pieces of artillery, and 13,000 small arms.

"This is indeed good news," said General Lee; "let it be announced to the troops"; and staff officers rode at full gallop down the line, and the announcement was answered by great cheering.

Our lines were scarcely formed when the enemy appeared upon the opposite bank of the Antietam, and our artillery opened upon him with a few guns, just to let him know that we were going no further and were at bay.

Couriers were sent to Jackson and A. P. Hill to come to us as soon as possible. Our numbers in their absence were fearfully small, hardly 15,000 men, and McClellan had almost 100,000. Where did all these men come from? Pope had but 50,000 after the battle at Groveton last month.

All this day our thin line faced the whole of McClellan's army, and it closed with a little artillery practice on each side.

At daylight, on the morning of the sixteenth, the enemy was in plain view on the high ground upon the opposite bank of the Antietam. His batteries were in position. They opened fire, and we replied, but the distance was too great to make a duel effective, and the firing was stopped by order of General Lee.

Riding through the town, I met General Lee on foot, leading his horse by the bridle. It was during the artillery firing and the shells of the enemy were falling in close proximity to him, but he seemed perfectly unconscious of danger.

Colonel E. P. Alexander, Lee's trusted lieutenant, thought that Lee was unreasonable in remaining north of the Potomac.

When I arrived about noon on September 16, with my ordnance train, I was ordered to collect all empty wagons and go to Harpers Ferry and take charge of the surrendered ammunition, bringing back to Sharpsburg all suiting our calibers. The prospect of this addition to our supply was grateful, for the expenditures had been something.

It had been easily within Lee's power, all day on the fifteenth, to cross the river into Virginia, without loss, and to reunite his scattered divisions and collect his multitude of stragglers behind the Potomac. The more that one studies the situation, the more amazed he must be at the audacity which deliberately sought a pitched battle in the open field, without a yard of earthworks, against a better-equipped army of double his force, and with a river close behind him, to be crossed by a single ford, peculiarly bad and exposed in case he had to retreat. There was in the Army of the Potomac no lack of veteran troops, well organized, well led, and capable of strong offense and stubborn defense.

It must be noted, also, that the Federal equipment was far superior to that of the Confederates.

McClellan brought upon the field his 87,176 well-equipped men, against Lee's 35,255 ragged and poorly equipped. The most sanguine hope which Lee could reasonably entertain, with his inferior force, was to fight a drawn battle and then safely withdraw what was left of his army. Against it he risked its utter destruction, which would have been the speedy end of the Confederacy.

Lee took a great risk for no chance of gain except the killing of some thousands of his enemy with the loss of, perhaps, two-thirds as many of his own men. That was a losing game for the Confederacy. Its supply of men was limited; that of the enemy was not. That was not war!

Even the Prussian Major Von Borcke, who loved to fight, doubted Lee's wisdom in accepting battle on the field of Antietam.

In the morning of September 17, I discovered General Stuart and at his request rode with him along our line of battle, which stretched out nearly four miles in length. I have it from our great commander's own lips that he had less than 40,000 men with him in the conflict; and as Lafayette McLaw's division, numbering 7,000 men, and some other small detached bodies of troops did not join in the action until at a late period of the day, he commenced this tremendous struggle with not more than 30,000 men, while the Federal army, according to General McClellan's own statement, amounted to not less than 90,000. Our force had been greatly reduced by the continuous fighting of the campaign, by the long and wearisome marches it had made and the cruel hardships it had undergone. I could not help expressing to General Stuart, as we passed the thin lines of our ragged, weather-beaten soldiers, many of them without shoes, that I did not think our army equal to the impending contest; but he was in good hope and said, with his accustomed cheerfulness, "I am confident that, with God's assistance and good fighting, we shall whip these Yankees badly enough."

It was late in the afternoon of September 16 when the fighting began on the Federal right wing, but the real battle did not start until September 17, and proved a bloody slam-bang, zigzag affair, both sides alternately pushing forward and withdrawing.

Among the few buildings on the field, the Roulette farm and the Piper house were to become important as semifortified spots. The Dunker Church, a small white brick building, stood near the center of the Confederate line, and not far from it a sunken road ran across the field. Another outstanding point was the southernmost Antietam bridge which spanned the creek between the extreme left wing of McClellan's and the extreme right wing of Lee's army.

Here is McClellan's own account of the battle.

The enemy, when found in battle array again after our break-through at South Mountain, occupied a strong position on the heights, on the west side of Antietam Creek, displaying a large force of infantry and cavalry, with numerous batteries of artillery.

On September 16, I rode along the whole front and observed that the ground at the left, near what was to become known as "Burnside's Bridge," was favorable for defense on our side, and that an attack across

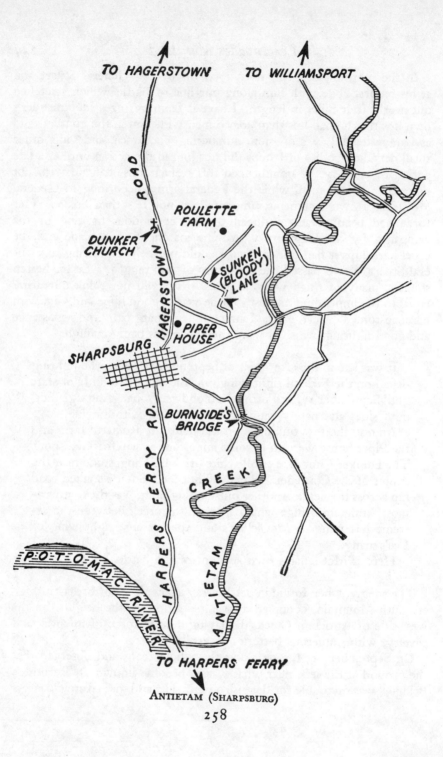

TO HAGERSTOWN

TO WILLIAMSPORT

ROAD

ROULETTE
FARM

DUNKER
CHURCH

HAGERSTOWN

SUNKEN
(BLOODY)
LANE

SHARPSBURG

PIPER
HOUSE

HARPERS FERRY RD.

BURNSIDE'S
BRIDGE

CREEK

POTOMAC RIVER

ANTIETAM

TO HARPERS FERRY

Antietam (Sharpsburg)

258

it would lead to favorable results. I therefore at once ordered Burnside to move his corps nearer the bridge, as he would probably be ordered to attack there next morning.

My plan for the impending engagement was to attack on our right with the corps of Hooker and Mansfield, supported by Sumner's and, as soon as matters looked favorable there, to move the corps of Burnside on our extreme left and, having carried the enemy's position, to press along the crest toward our right and, whenever either of these flank movements should be successful, to advance our center with all the forces then disposable.

About 2:00 P.M. on September 16, General Hooker was ordered to cross the Antietam to attack and, if possible, turn the enemy's left. It was perhaps half past three to four o'clock before Hooker got fairly in motion. I accompanied the movement until the top of the ridge was gained and then returned to headquarters.

During the night General Mansfield's corps crossed the Antietam at the same ford and bridge and bivouacked about a mile in rear of General Hooker's position.

On reaching the vicinity of the enemy's left, a sharp contest commenced by General Hooker's advance. The firing lasted until after dark, when Hooker's corps rested on their arms on ground won from the enemy.

At daylight on the seventeenth the action continued. The whole of General Hooker's corps was soon engaged and drove the enemy into a second line. This contest was obstinate, and as the troops advanced, the opposition became more determined, and the number of the enemy greater. General Hooker then ordered up the corps of General Mansfield, which moved promptly toward the scene of action.

During the deployment that gallant veteran, General Mansfield, fell mortally wounded.

For about two hours the battle raged with varied success, the enemy endeavoring to drive our troops, and ours in turn to get possession of the line in front. Our troops ultimately succeeded in forcing the enemy back. At about 9:00 A.M. the first division of General Sumner's corps arrived. At about that time General Hooker was severely wounded in the foot and taken from the field, and General George G. Meade was placed in command of his corps.

While the conflict was so obstinately raging on the right, another division was pushing against the enemy further to the left. This division was assailed by a fire of artillery, but steadily advanced, and encountered the enemy infantry in some force at the group of houses known as Roulette's farm.

The enemy was pressed back to near the crest of the hill, where he was encountered in great strength posted in a sunken road forming a natural rifle pit running in a northwesterly direction. In a cornfield in rear of this road were also strong bodies of the enemy. As our line reached the crest of the hill, a galling fire was opened on it from the sunken road and cornfield. Here a terrific fire of musketry burst from both lines, and the battle raged along the whole line with great slaughter.

The enemy attempted to turn the left of our line, but were repulsed. Foiled in this, they made a determined assault on the front, but were met by a charge from our lines which drove them back with severe loss, leaving in our hands some 300 prisoners and several stands of colors.

On the left of the center we were also hotly engaged in front of Roulette's house and continued to advance under a heavy fire nearly to the crest of the hill overlooking Piper's house, the enemy being posted in a continuation of the sunken road and cornfield. Here the brave Irish brigade opened upon the enemy a terrific musketry fire and sustained its well-earned reputation. After suffering terribly in officers and men, and strewing the ground with their enemies as they drove them back, their ammunition nearly expended, and their commander, General Meagher, disabled by the fall of his horse shot under him, this brigade was ordered to the rear.

The ground over which our center divisions were fighting was very irregular, intersected by numerous ravines, hills covered with growing corn, enclosed by stone walls, behind which the enemy could advance unobserved upon any exposed point of our lines.

Our troops on the left of this part of the line drove the enemy through a cornfield into an orchard beyond. This advance gave us possession of Piper's house, the strong point contended for by the enemy at this part of the line, it being a defensible building several hundred yards in advance of the sunken road.

One corps, General Porter's, was held in reserve. It occupied a position on the east side of the Antietam Creek, upon the main turnpike leading to Sharpsburg and directly opposite the center of the enemy's line. This corps filled the interval between the right wing and General

Burnside's command, and guarded the main approach from the enemy's position to our trains of supplies.

It was necessary to watch this part of our line with the utmost vigilance, lest the enemy should take advantage of the first exhibition of weakness here to push upon us a vigorous assault for the purpose of piercing our center and turning our rear, as well as to capture or destroy our supply trains. Once having penetrated this line, the enemy's passage to our rear could have met with but feeble resistance, as there were no other reserves to reinforce or close up the gap.

Toward the middle of the afternoon, proceeding to the right, I found that all three corps so far engaged, Sumner's, Hooker's and Mansfield's, had met with serious losses. Several general officers had been carried from the field severely wounded, and the aspect of affairs was anything but promising. At the risk of greatly exposing our center, I ordered two brigades from Porter's reserve corps, the only available troops, to reinforce the right.

General Sumner expressed the most decided opinion against another attempt during that day to assault the enemy's position in front, as portions of our troops were so much scattered and demoralized. In view of these circumstances, I directed the different commanders to hold their positions and, being satisfied that this could be done without the assistance of the two brigades from the center, I countermanded the order which was in course of execution.

This ended the battle on the right and center of the field.

The charge of the Irish Brigade formed one of the noteworthy features of the battle.

This is how a young infantryman of the 118th Pennsylvania Volunteers saw this martial spectacle.

The morning of Wednesday, September 17, our regiment, the 118th Pennsylvania Volunteers, was pushed to the front. Troops upon the ground poured in one continuous stream to where the battle was waged wickedly.

At noon the combat raged in all its fierceness. It was near this hour when General McClellan, with his large and imposing staff, rode upon the ground. The deep and abiding enthusiasm that habitually followed him promptly greeted him. Shouts, yells and cheers of appreciation rent the air. This noise, so loud that it was borne above the din of battle to the enemy's line, brought on a vigorous and persistent shelling. Regardless of the flying, bursting missiles, there he sat astride his splendid charger, glass in hand, calmly reviewing the mighty hosts.

Shortly afterward followed the famous charge of General Meagher's Irish Brigade. This charge took place in full view from the knoll occupied by our regiment. The ground over which they were about to move was rough and uneven, and in the distance appeared to be a freshly plowed field.

The enemy's line upon which the advance was to be made was in plain view just outside the edge of a belt of timber. It was flanked by several batteries, whose active work of the morning had much improved their practice. They were said to be part of the celebrated Washington Light Artillery of New Orleans. The preliminary preparations could not be concealed; the enemy caught them in their very incipiency, and gun and musket belched forth their vengeful volleys with telling accuracy. But the gallant Irishmen moved into battle array with the precision of parade. Prominent in its place beside the national standard the green harp of Erin was distinctly observed. As the scathing fire cut out its fearful gaps, the line halted with deliberation to readjust itself. The dead and wounded strewed the ground, thickening as the distance from the enemy lessened. Twice and again the green standard fell, but only to be promptly seized again. Vast curtains of smoke concealed the enemy, rising at intervals, disclosing him holding firmly to his post. The deadly moment of impact came, the lines impinged and the enemy, in irreparable confusion, broke for the friendly cover of the timber. The Irishmen, still maintaining their organization with commendable exactitude, pressed them in their helpless flight, until finally with shout and cheer, friend and foe were lost to view in the wood.

A Federal army surgeon, watching the rapidly changing fortunes of the day, admitted in open admiration that the Irish Brigade had its counterparts in Lee's army.

It is beyond all wonder how such men as the rebel troops can fight on as they do; that, filthy, sick, hungry, and miserable, they should prove such heroes in fight, is past explanation—one regiment stood up before the fire of two or three of our long-range batteries and of two regiments of infantry, and though the air around them was vocal with the whistle of bullets and screams of shells, there they stood, and delivered their fire in perfect order; and there they continued to stand. . . .

> After the left wing of Lee's and the right wing of McClellan's army had fought each other to a standstill, the battle shifted to the center, and General John B. Gordon narrates how he was trying to hold that part of the Confederate line.

From the position assigned me near the center of Lee's lines, both armies and the entire field were in view. Hooker's compact columns of infantry had fallen in the morning upon our left with the crushing weight of a landslide. The Confederate line was too weak to withstand the momentum of such a charge. Pressed back, the Southern troops reformed their lines and rushed in countercharge upon the exulting Federals, hurled them back in confusion, and recovered all the ground that had been lost. Again and again, hour after hour, by charges and countercharges, this portion of the field was lost and recovered, until the corn that grew upon it looked as if it had been struck by a storm of bloody hail.

Up to this hour not a shot had been fired in my front near the center. There was an ominous lull on the left. From sheer exhaustion, both sides seemed willing to rest. General Lee took advantage of the respite and rode along his lines on the right and center. With that wonderful power which he possessed of divining the plans and purposes of his antagonist, General Lee had decided that the Union commander's next heavy blow would fall upon our center, and we were urged to hold on at any sacrifice. My troops held the most advanced position on this part of the field, and there was no supporting line behind us. To comfort General Lee I called aloud to him as he rode away: "These men are going to stay here, General." Alas! Many of the brave fellows are there now.

The predicted assault came. The men in blue formed in my front, four lines deep. The brave Union commander, superbly mounted, placed himself in front, while his band in the rear cheered them with martial music. It was a thrilling spectacle. To oppose man against man was impossible, for there were four lines of blue to my one line of gray. The only plan was to hold my fire until the advancing Federals were almost upon my lines. No troops with empty guns could withstand the shock. My men were at once directed to lie down upon the grass. Not a shot would be fired until my voice should be heard commanding "Fire!"

There was no artillery at this point upon either side, and not a rifle was discharged. The stillness was literally oppressive, as this column of Union infantry moved majestically toward us. Now the front rank was within a few rods of where I stood. With all my lung power I shouted "Fire!"

Our rifles flamed and roared in the Federals' faces like a blinding blaze of lightning. The effect was appalling. The entire front line, with few exceptions, went down. Before the rear lines could recover, my exultant men were on their feet, devouring them with successive volleys. Even then these stubborn blue lines retreated in fairly good order.

The fire now became furious and deadly. The list of the slain was lengthened with each passing moment. Near nightfall, the awful carnage ceased; Lee's center had been saved.

> Lee had ordered no earthworks to be thrown up, but the Sunken Lane, serving as natural rampart, was used by his troops to great advantage.
> A Union soldier, T. F. DeBurgh Galwey, who took part in the fight converging on this lane, wrote of it.

As we came up, the Confederates disappeared down into an old rainworn lane that ran along through a depression in the ridge. We halted upon a slight crest from which we had a plunging fire into the lane, which looked to us then like a mere ditch and was distant about fifty or sixty yards.

We thought the Confederates in taking refuge there had put themselves into a trap, for the ground behind them, on which the corn grew, was a steep rise and, though we could see that they had reinforcements in that corn, there appeared to be hesitation among them. There were Confederate battle flags at intervals in the Sunken Lane, six or seven, I think, along our front, and more in the cornfield behind, indicating, I suppose, just so many regiments.

It is almost certain that for a very short while after our arrival we could have carried the lane and the slope beyond by a dash, though on the several occasions within the first hour when our men, by their own impulse, rose and fixed bayonets to charge, the Confederates met us with a murderous fire. It was about this time that I noticed that the Confederates in the cornfield were no longer visible; perhaps they had withdrawn. But the minutes slipped by, and the opportunity was gone.

At one time a lull occurred in the Confederate fire from the lane, and then we saw perhaps a dozen little white squares rise above the fence rails; whether they were white handkerchiefs (a luxury hardly to be expected then and there) or the white cotton haversacks used by the Confederates, we could not distinguish. It was quickly plain, however, that though there might be some in the lane who wished to surrender, these were in the minority, for we met a musketry fire so rapid and well aimed that we all unfixed bayonets and backed up step by step until we were on the old ground, where we dropped down again and resumed our fire as before.

For what seemed like an hour after our arrival on the ground, we were all alone. We could look far to the rear, but no Union troops were in sight, and we were now sadly in need of some relief. Our numbers were reduced; our ammunition was running low. Our men had all begun with sixty rounds, and now they endeavored to economize their cartridges and to gather more from the cartridge boxes of the dead or wounded.

At length the Irish Brigade came into close touch with us, an orderly sergeant kneeling down, I remember, just at my left shoulder and banging away at the enemy. He was a redheaded, red-bearded man, and the whole circumstance is impressed on my mind from the fact that he put his hand into the haversack of a dead Confederate and took therefrom a bag of coffee, which he kept for himself, handing to me a bag of sugar.

The Confederate artillery off toward the Dunker Church had now found our line and were enfilading us from right to left.

Noon came and went, and we had not yet made headway, though many times we had fixed bayonets and rushed toward the lane, but at each of these efforts the Confederates rose and drove us back. Our line of battle had now become a mere line of skirmishers; the rest lay about us wounded or dead or had gone disabled to the rear. It seemed as if we could not endure it much longer. We *must* go forward, or else altogether abandon the ground. To our rear was nothing. The Irish Brigade had moved on and left nothing on our left.

It was about this time that the captain of my company appeared, passing the order along the line as he approached, "Fix bayonets! Battalion, forward, right wheel, double quick," and the word of execution, "March!" he spoke as soon as he reached us on the knoll.

It was a good thing for us to have a voice of command, and the order was obeyed at once. It seemed like merely a hop, skip, and jump till we were at the lane, and into it, the Confederates breaking away in haste and fleeing up the slope. What a sight was that lane! I shall not dwell on the horror of it; I saw many a ghastly array of dead afterward, but none, I think, that so affected me as did the sight of the poor brave fellows in butternut homespun that had there died for what they believed to be honor and a righteous cause.

General Hood reports how his Texans received the first onslaught of the battle and then held the Confederate line in front of the Dunker Church.

During the afternoon of September 16 I was ordered, after great fatigue and hunger endured by my soldiers, to take position in an open field in front of Dunker Church. General Hooker's corps had crossed the Antietam, swung round with its right on the pike and, about an hour before sunset, encountered my division. We opened fire, and a spirited action ensued, which lasted till a late hour in the night. When the firing had in a great measure ceased, we were so close to the enemy that we could distinctly hear him massing his heavy bodies in our immediate front.

The extreme suffering of my troops for want of food induced me to ride back to General Lee and request him to send two or more brigades to our relief, at least for the night, in order that the soldiers might have a chance to cook their meager rations. He said that he knew of no command which could be spared for the purpose; but suggested I should see General Jackson and endeavor to obtain assistance from him. After riding a long time, I finally discovered him, asleep by the root of a tree. I aroused him and made known the half-starved condition of my troops; he immediately ordered relief. He exacted of me, however, a promise that I would come to the support of these forces the moment I was called upon. I quickly rode off in search of my wagons, that the men might prepare and cook their flour, as we were still without meat; unfortunately the night was then far advanced and, although every effort was made amid the darkness to get the wagons forward, dawn of the morning of the seventeenth broke upon us before many of the men had had time to do more than prepare the dough. Soon thereafter "To arms" was sounded, and quite a large number of my brave soldiers were again in camp.

Still indomitable amid every trial, they moved off by the right flank to occupy the same position we had left the night previous. We passed, about sunrise, across the pike and through the gap in the fence just in front of Dunker Church.

Not far distant in our front were drawn up, in close array, heavy columns of Federal infantry; not less than two corps were in sight to oppose my small command, numbering, approximately, two thousand effectives. However, we moved forward to the assault. Notwithstanding the overwhelming odds of over ten to one against us, we drove the enemy from the wood and cornfield back upon his reserves and forced him to abandon his guns on our left. This most deadly combat raged till our last round of ammunition was expended. Our right flank was toward the main line of the Federals. After several ineffectual efforts to procure reinforcements and our last shot had been fired, I ordered my troops back to Dunker Church.

My command remained near the church, with empty cartridge boxes, holding aloft their colors, whilst our batteries rendered most effective service further to the right, where nearly all the guns of the battalion had been disabled. Upon the arrival of reinforcements, we marched to the rear, renewed our supply of ammunition, and returned to our position near the church, which ground we held till a late hour in the afternoon, when we moved somewhat further to the right and bivouacked for the night. With the close of this bloody day ceased the hardest fought battle of the war.

> The day brought many critical moments for Lee's men. General Longstreet, who was in the thick of the fighting, shows how utter disaster to Lee's army was at times averted by the narrowest of margins.

The Federals fought with wonderful bravery and the Confederates clung to their ground with heroic courage as, hour after hour, they were mown down like grass. The fresh troops of McClellan literally tore into shreds the already ragged army of Lee, but the Confederates never gave way.

I remember at one time they were surging up against us with fearful numbers. We were under the crest of a hill, occupying a position that ought to have been held by from four to six brigades. The only troops there were J. R. Cooke's regiment of North Carolina infantry, without a cartridge. As I rode along the line with my staff, I saw two pieces of the Washington Artillery, but there were not enough gunners to man them. They had been either killed or wounded. This was a fearful situation for the Confederate center. I put my staff officers to the guns while I held their horses. It was easy to see that if the Federals broke through our line there, the Confederate army would be cut in two and probably destroyed, for we were already badly whipped and were only holding our ground by sheer desperation. Colonel Cooke sent me word that his ammunition was out. I replied that he must hold his position as long as he had a man left. He responded that he would show his colors as long as there was a man alive to hold them up. We loaded up our little guns with canister and sent a rattle of hail into the Federals as they came up over the crest of the hill.

There was more business to the square inch in that little battery than in any I ever saw, and it shot harder and faster and with a sort of human energy, as if it seemed to realize that it was to hold thousands of Federals at bay or the battle was lost. So warm was the reception we gave them that they dodged back behind the crest of the hill. We sought to make them believe we had many batteries before them instead of only two little guns. As the Federals would come up they would see the colors of the North Carolina regiment waving placidly, and then would receive a shower of canister. In the meantime General R. H. Chilton, General Lee's chief of staff, made his way to me and asked, "Where are the troops you are holding your line with?" I pointed to my two pieces and to Cooke's regiment, and replied, "There they are; but that regiment hasn't a cartridge."

Chilton's eyes popped as though they would come out of his head; he struck spurs to his horse and away he went, to General Lee. I suppose he made some remarkable report, although I did not see General Lee again until night.

While the right and center of the Federal army were fighting during the forenoon of September 17, its left wing under General Burnside had remained relatively quiet, thus enabling Lee repeatedly to shift badly needed reinforcements to his most threatened points. McClellan's anxiety about Burnside's inactivity gradually mounted to fury, and one still notes his emotion between the lines of his account, written some twenty years later.

The troops of General Ambrose Burnside held the left of the line opposite the lowest bridge. The attack on our right was to have been supported by an attack on the left.

At eight o'clock on the morning of September 17, an order was sent to Burnside to carry the bridge, then to gain possession of the heights beyond and to advance along their crest upon Sharpsburg and its rear.

After some time had elapsed, I dispatched an aide to ascertain what had been done. The aide returned with the information that but little progress had been made. I then sent him back with an order to General Burnside to assault the bridge at once and carry it at all hazards. The aide returned to me a second time with the report that the bridge was still in the possession of the enemy. Whereupon I directed Colonel Sackett, inspector general, to deliver to General Burnside my positive order to push forward his troops without a moment's delay and, if necessary, to carry the bridge at the point of the bayonet; and I ordered Colonel Sackett to remain with General Burnside and see that the order was executed promptly.

After these three hours' delay the bridge was carried at one o'clock by a brilliant charge of the 51st New York and 51st Pennsylvania Volunteers. Other troops were then thrown over and the opposite bank occupied, the enemy retreating to the heights beyond.

A halt was then made by General Burnside's advance until 3:00 P.M.; upon hearing which I directed one of my aides to inform General Burnside that I desired him to push forward his troops with the utmost vigor and carry the enemy's position on the heights; that the movement was vital to our success; that this was a time when we must not stop for loss of life, if a great object could thereby be accomplished. He replied that he would soon advance, and would go up the hill as far as a battery of the enemy on the left would permit. Upon this report I again immediately sent Colonel Key to General Burnside with orders to advance at once, if possible to flank the battery, or storm it and carry the heights; repeating that if he considered the movement impracticable, to inform me, so that his troops might be recalled. The advance was then gallantly resumed, the enemy driven from the guns, the heights handsomely carried, and a portion of the troops even reached the outskirts of Sharpsburg. By this time it was nearly dark, and strong reinforcements just then reaching the enemy from Harpers Ferry attacked General Burnside's troops on their left flank and forced them to retire to a lower line of hills nearer the bridge.

If this important movement had been consummated two hours earlier, a position would have been secured upon the heights from which our batteries might have enfiladed the greater part of the enemy's line, and turned their right and rear. Our victory might thus have been much more decisive.

We have an excellent report of Burnside's part in the battle from the pen of his opponent, General Longstreet.

General Robert Toombs was defending the crossing at the Burnside Bridge against the 9th Corps, commanded by General Burnside. Toombs's orders were, when dislodged, to retire so as to open the field to fire to all the troops on the heights behind him, the fire of his batteries to be concentrated upon the bridge, and his infantry arranged for a like converging fire.

In the forenoon the Union 2nd Maryland and 6th New Hampshire Regiments were ordered forward in double time with bayonets fixed to carry the bridge. They made a gallant, dashing charge, crowding the bridge almost to its western *débouché*, but the fire concentrated a storm that stunned their ranks and cut them down until they were forced to retire. General Burnside repeated the order to force the way at all hazards. Arrangements were made, and when concluded the 51st New York and 51st Pennsylvania Regiments found a route better covered from the Confederate fire than that of the first column.

By a dashing charge on double time they passed it, under exulting hurrahs and most gallant work, and gained the west bank. The crossing by other troops at a lower ford made our position at the bridge untenable, and General Toombs was forced to retire.

About four o'clock a strong force was over and advanced under very severe fire of artillery and infantry, increasing in force as they ascended the heights, the troops engaging in steady, brave fight as they marched. Overreaching my right, they forced it back.

When General Lee found that General Jackson had left six of his brigades under General A. P. Hill to receive the property and garrison surrendered at Harpers Ferry, he sent orders for them to join him and by magic spell had them on the field to meet the final crisis. He ordered two of them to guard against approach of other forces that might come against him by another bridge, and threw the remainder against the forefront of the battle. The strong forces concentrating against Gener-

al Burnside seemed to spring from the earth as his march bore him farther from the river.

The Union troops, assailed in front and on their flank by concentrating fires that were crushing, found it necessary to withdraw. A. P.
Hill's brigades followed. They recovered the ground that had been lost
on the right before the night dropped her mantle upon this field of sel-
dom-equaled strife.

When the 9th Corps dropped back under the crest they had so
bravely won, the Battle of Sharpsburg virtually ended.

> In the evening of September 17, firing ceased. Lee maintained
> his position all next day and then retreated.
> General Longstreet ends his account of the battle with a few
> illuminating remarks.

I rode for general headquarters to make report. All the other officers
had arrived and were lounging about. General Lee walked up as I dismounted, threw his hands upon my shoulders and hailed me with,
"Here is my old war horse at last!"

In the afternoon of September 18, General Lee was advised of new
arrivals in General McClellan's army and, thinking the few stragglers
who came up to swell his own ranks were not sufficient to justify him
in renewing the battle on the nineteenth, ordered his trains back, and
after night marched his troops across the Potomac at the ford near
Shepherdstown.

General McClellan's plan of the battle was not strong, the handling
and execution were less so. Battles by the extreme right and left, divided by a river, gave us the benefit of interior lines, and it was this that
saved the Confederate army.

> McClellan was severely criticized for not renewing the battle
> on September 18, so as to turn an indecisive struggle into unques-
> tionable victory. McClellan here presents his arguments for leav-
> ing well enough alone.

The night of September 17 brought with it grave responsibilities.
Whether to renew the attack on the eighteenth, or to defer it, even
with the risk of the enemy's retirement, was the question before me.

After anxious deliberation and a careful survey, I concluded that the success of an attack on the eighteenth was not certain. Under ordinary circumstances, a general is expected to risk a battle if he has a reasonable prospect of success; but at this critical juncture—Virginia lost, Washington menaced, Maryland invaded—the national cause could afford no risks of defeat. One battle lost, and almost all would have been lost. Lee's army might then have marched as it pleased on Washington, Baltimore, Philadelphia or New York. It could have levied its supplies from a fertile and undevastated country; extorted tribute from wealthy and populous cities; and nowhere east of the Alleghanies was there another organized force able to arrest its march.

When I was on the right on the afternoon of the seventeenth, I found the troops a good deal shaken—that is, some of them who had been in the early part of the action. I had to ride in and rally them myself.

Early next morning (September 18) Burnside told me that his men were so demoralized and beaten that were they attacked they would give way.

One division of Sumner's corps also was a good deal scattered and demoralized. It was not deemed by its corps commander in proper condition to attack the enemy vigorously the next day.

A large number of our heaviest and most efficient batteries had consumed all their ammunition on the sixteenth and seventeenth, and it was impossible to supply them until late on the following day.

Finally, reinforcements to the number of 14,000 men had not arrived, but were expected during the day.

On the night of the eighteenth the enemy, after passing troops in the latter part of the day from the Virginia shore to their position behind Sharpsburg, suddenly formed the design of abandoning their position and retreating across the river. As their line was but a short distance from the river, the evacuation was effected before daylight.

Was the Confederate army in a perilous situation on September 18, 1862? Lee himself wrote no account of his campaigns, aside from his official reports; but we can get an inkling of how he felt after the battle at Sharpsburg from a story told by one of his generals, John G. Walker, who had taken an active part in the fighting.

We had fought an indecisive battle, and General Lee determined to withdraw from Maryland. At dark on the night of September 18 the rearward movement began; and a little after sunrise next morning the entire Confederate army had safely recrossed the Potomac.

Detained in superintending the removal of the wounded, I was among the last to cross. As I rode into the river, I passed General Lee, sitting on his horse in the stream, watching the crossing of the wagons and artillery. Returning my greeting, he inquired as to what was still behind. There was nothing but the wagons containing my wounded and a battery, all of which were near at hand, and I told him so.

"Thank God!" I heard him say as I rode on.

CHAPTER 11

The War Moves to the Ohio

THE KENTUCKY AND TENNESSEE CAMPAIGNS OF 1862

On the second day of the Battle of Shiloh Grant had failed to destroy Beauregard's retreating army. He was not given another chance, for Halleck now determined to take command of the army in person and gather for himself the glory which was within such easy reach.

Grant recalled those days with ill-concealed contempt for his commander in chief.

General Halleck arrived at Pittsburgh Landing on the eleventh of April and immediately assumed command on the field. On the twenty-first General Pope arrived with an army 30,000 strong. Halleck had now three armies: the Army of the Mississippi, that of the Ohio, and that of the Tennessee.

Preparations were at once made for an advance on Corinth. Corinth was a valuable strategic point for the enemy, and consequently a valuable one for us. We ought to have seized it immediately after the fall of Donelson and Nashville, when it could have been taken without a battle, but, failing then, it should have been taken, without delay, after the Battle of Shiloh. The demoralization among the Confederates was so great that a stand for the time would have been impossible.

Beauregard was reinforced immediately after Shiloh. We estimated his strength at 70,000. Our own was, in round numbers, 120,000.

On the thirtieth of April the grand army commenced its advance from Shiloh upon Corinth. The movement was a siege from the start to the close. The National troops were always behind entrenchments. Even the commanders were cautioned "not to bring on an engagement," and "it is better to retreat than to fight."

For myself I was little more than an observer. Halleck's orders were sent directly, ignoring me. My position was so embarrassing in fact that I made several applications during the siege to be relieved.

On the twenty-eighth of May [seven weeks after Shiloh], the investment of Corinth was at last complete, or as complete as it was ever made. (See map, page 280.)

Some days before I had suggested to the commanding general that I thought if he would move the army at night, by the rear of the center and right, we would find no natural obstacle in our front and, I believed, no serious artificial one. I was silenced so quickly that I felt that possibly I had suggested an unmilitary movement.

On the twenty-eighth of May, General John A. Logan said to me that the enemy had been evacuating for several days, and that, if allowed, he could go into Corinth with his brigade. Trains of cars were heard coming in and going out of Corinth constantly. Some of his men who had been engaged on railroads said loaded trains had been going out for several days and empty ones coming in. On the thirtieth of May General Halleck had his whole army drawn up prepared for battle and announced that we were to be attacked that morning. Yet Corinth then had already been evacuated, and the National troops took possession without opposition.

I am satisfied that Corinth could have been captured in a two days' campaign commenced promptly on the arrival of reinforcements after the Battle of Shiloh.

> The newspaper correspondent Albert D. Richardson, who was there with the Federal army, made some poignant observations concerning Halleck's campaign and the way it was conducted.

The combined forces of Grant, Buell, and Pope were a grand army.

Grant nominally remained at the head of his corps but was deprived of power. He was under a cloud. Most injurious reports concerning his conduct at Shiloh pervaded the country. At the daily gatherings of eight or ten correspondents, Grant was the subject of angry discussion.

Several of these writers could demonstrate conclusively that Grant was without capacity, but a favorite of Fortune; that his great Donelson victory had been achieved in spite of military blunders which ought to have defeated him.

The subject of all this contention bore himself with undisturbed serenity. Sherman, while constantly declaring that he cared nothing for the newspapers, was foolishly sensitive to every word of criticism. But Grant, whom they really wounded, appeared no more disturbed by these paper bullets than by the leaden missiles of the enemy. He silently smoked and waited.

When the army began to creep forward, I messed at Grant's headquarters, and around the evening campfires I saw much of the general. He said little upon any subject. With his eternal cigar and his head thrown slightly to one side, for hours he would sit silently before the fire, or walk back and forth, with eyes upon the ground, or look on at our whist table, now and then making a suggestion about the play.

The journalists called him stupid. One of my confreres used to say, "How profoundly surprised Mrs. Grant must have been, when she woke up and learned that her husband was a great man!"

Grant impressed me as possessing great purity, integrity and amiability, with excellent judgment and boundless pluck. But I should never have suspected him of military genius. However, nearly every man of whom, at the beginning of the war, I prophesied a great career proved inefficient, and vice versa.

Hooker once boasted that he had the best army of the planet. One would have declared that Grant commanded the worst. There was little of order, perfect drill or pride, pomp and circumstance, but Grant's rough, rugged soldiers would fight wonderfully and were not easily demoralized. If their line became broken, every man, from behind a tree, rock or stump, blazed away at the enemy on his own account. They did not throw up their hats at sight of their general, but they were wont to remark, with a grim smile, "There goes the old man. He doesn't say much; but he's a pretty hard nut for Johnny Reb to crack."

Halleck's line was ten miles in length. The grand army was like a huge serpent, with its head pinned on our left, and its tail sweeping slowly around toward Corinth. Its majestic march was so slow that the Rebels had ample warning. It was large enough to eat up Beauregard at one mouthful; but Halleck crept forward at the rate of about three-quarters of a mile per day. Thousands and thousands of his men died from fevers and diarrhea.

There was great dissatisfaction at his slow progress. Pope was particularly impatient. One day he had a very sharp skirmish with the enemy and reported that he could hold his position against the world, the flesh and the devil; but Halleck telegraphed to him three times within an hour not to be drawn into a general engagement.

At last, Halleck's army reached Corinth, but the bird had flown. No event of the war reflected so much credit upon the Rebels and so much discredit upon the Unionists as Beauregard's evacuation. He did not disturb himself until Halleck's Parrott guns had thrown shots within

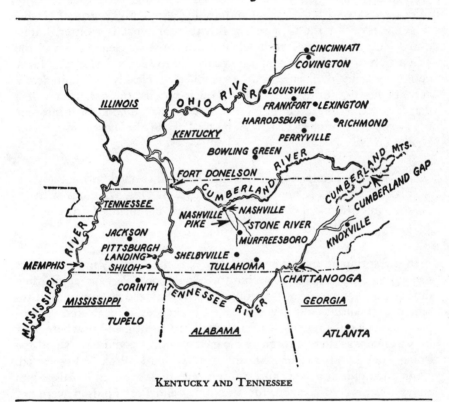

KENTUCKY AND TENNESSEE

fourteen feet of his own headquarters. Then, keeping up a vigorous show of resistance on his front, he deserted the town, leaving behind not a single gun or ambulance or even a sick or wounded man in the hospital.

Halleck lost thenceforth the name of "Old Brains," which some imaginative person had given him, and which for a time had tickled the ears of his soldiers.

A northern writer, who witnessed the occupation of Corinth by Halleck, expressed himself in bitter, denunciatory terms.

The fortifications about Corinth are plain, ordinary entrenchments, constructed of earth and logs, hardly first-rate. They are such as an army would throw up in a night. I walked around them today till my sides were sore with merriment and my lips sore with chagrin. I believe it is best now for the Commonwealth to hear what is a bitter, undisputed fact: if the attack at Shiloh was a surprise to General Grant, the evacuation of Corinth was no less a surprise to General Halleck. How could the army of Beauregard be removed so cleanly and completely and noiselessly, during one night? Did it require the concussion of a magazine explosion to get into our ears what we could not get into our eyes—the evacuation? That was the final act of the mortifying drama. Shame on us.

After the occupation of Corinth, Halleck seemed without any plan whatever. A military observer, E. A. Otis, who was with the Union army, pointed out how the commander in chief missed his splendid opportunities.

In the spring and early summer of 1862, the Civil War in the west seemed to be rapidly approaching a conclusion. Perhaps at no time during the war were so great opportunities offered as were now presented to Halleck, and never were such chances so neglected. Memphis surrendered a few days after the fall of Corinth, and nowhere west of Virginia was there a force of the enemy which could have stood for a single day before the magnificent army which Halleck had collected. With Memphis and New Orleans in our possession, the Mississippi River was practically open, for Vicksburg and Port Hudson were not then strongly fortified, and it is not surprising that the war was looked upon as nearly ended. If our army operations had been prosecuted with the same vigor and energy that were shown two years later, the "March to the Sea" might have been made by Halleck or Buell in the summer of 1862.

Grant scornfully concurred with these conclusions when he wrote:

After the capture of Corinth a movable force of 80,000 men, besides enough to hold all the territory acquired, could have been set in motion for the accomplishment of any great campaign. But the work of depletion commenced. The effects which would have resulted from prompt movements after Corinth might have been: a bloodless advance to Atlanta, to Vicksburg, or to any other desired point south of Corinth in the interior of Mississippi.

After evacuating Corinth, General Beauregard retired to Tupelo, Mississippi, about sixty miles south, but soon afterward resigned. In his place Jefferson Davis appointed General Braxton Bragg, who had commanded a Confederate corps at Shiloh. Bragg immediately chose Chattanooga for his new headquarters, from which vantage point he was in a better position to undertake offensive operations. On the Northern side, too, important changes took place. Halleck was called to Washington as general in chief and Lincoln's military adviser, and Pope soon followed him to lead the newly formed Army of Virginia. Grant was ordered into a defensive position at Jackson, Tennessee, while Buell received instructions to occupy Chattanooga, keeping the railroad behind him open for traffic. This hampered his progress to such an extent that Bragg got there ahead of him.

The historians of the 36th Illinois Volunteers, L. G. Bennett and William M. Haigh, found much cause for complaint, as they described the military developments of that period.

Our large army, broken into fragments and scattered over a wide extent of country, was now so absorbed in building railroads, maintaining long lines of communication and guarding Southern plantations as to leave little time to attend to the suppression of the Rebellion.

A column under General Buell moved leisurely eastward into Tennessee and in the direction of Chattanooga. With the exception of a small force in Eastern Tennessee, there were at that time no Confederate troops in the state, and by a little exertion on the part of General Buell both Chattanooga and Knoxville might have been captured. Instead of this, the army was halted and remained idle at Nashville.

General Bragg, who succeeded to the command of the Confederate forces, reached Chattanooga ahead of Buell, and then prepared to assume the offensive. By a bold and rapid movement into Kentucky, he intended to menace Cincinnati and Louisville and compel the withdrawal of armies which, at a cost of much treasure and blood, had obtained a firm foothold in the heart of the Confederacy. The plan was well conceived, and to carry it out successfully the whole vast energies of the South were concentrated. Everything favored the inva-

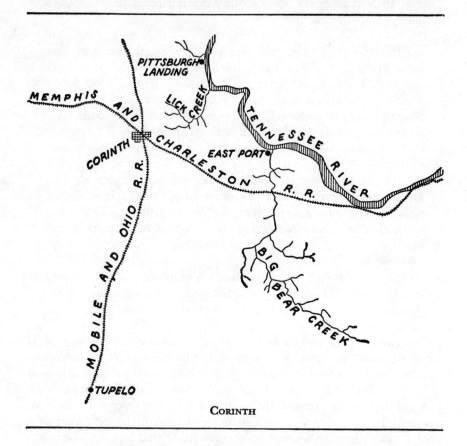

CORINTH

sion by the combined armies of Bragg and his subcommander, Kirby Smith, who, if they gained nothing, had but little to lose.

While Kirby Smith was demonstrating in the direction of Covington and Cincinnati, Bragg's army kept up a show of offensive attack upon Nashville. At the same time he pushed his way northward and succeeded in deceiving Buell as to his real object until he was far on his way to Louisville.

The country was seized with consternation at the imminent danger which menaced the cities on the Ohio River. The excitement at Cincinnati was so great as to paralyze business, and the citizens stood appalled at the threatened peril of the city. The governors of Ohio and Kentucky issued proclamations calling out the militia as well as all able-bodied citizens.

Kirby Smith, with 40,000 Rebel troops, was reported but a few miles distant from Cincinnati and marching upon the city. The excitement of the people was at fever heat. The public parks, the sidewalks and every available square inch of space were occupied by the undisciplined rabble of "squirrel hunters" and farmers fresh from field and plow, partially armed with shotguns and old rifles. Martial law was proclaimed, business houses closed and all work but that of arms suspended.

We veterans secretly were in hopes Kirby Smith would make an attack, just to give these "counter hoppers" a chance to enjoy a mixture of gunpowder and lead with their other luxuries. Imagine a charge of men with a musket in their hands, a baby on one arm and a wife clinging to the other!

For six days our troops lay in the trenches. But the sudden departure of Kirby Smith and his junction with Bragg at Frankfort threw off the mask which had so long enveloped their plans and left no room for doubt that Louisville was the real objective point of the campaign. Cincinnati being no longer menaced, we were ordered to proceed to Louisville.

The exciting and somewhat exaggerated reports which were being circulated of Bragg's near approach and the overwhelming numbers of his forces had also filled Louisville with alarm. Merchants hastily removed the contents of their stores, and household goods were carried a hundred miles into the interior of Indiana. Women, children and non-combatants generally were sent away. Earthworks were constructed, extending around the city to the banks of the Ohio. Citizens were pressed into service against their inclination and set to work in the trenches, digging, sweating and swearing, while the veterans, with arms in hand, stood by to see that each did his duty without shirking.

Each hour but intensified the terror of the people, and every preparation was made for the reception of the doughty knights under Smith and Bragg, when, to the intense relief of the population, on the twenty-fifth of September, General Buell entered Louisville instead of Bragg, he having come out ahead in the race across Kentucky.

The Confederate general, Richard Taylor, surveying the situation, was not much happier than his Northern antagonists and found much fault in the way the campaign was being handled by Bragg. He might easily have added another reproach—that, if the latter had not dawdled on the way to inaugurate a puppet governor, he probably would have beaten Buell into Louisville.

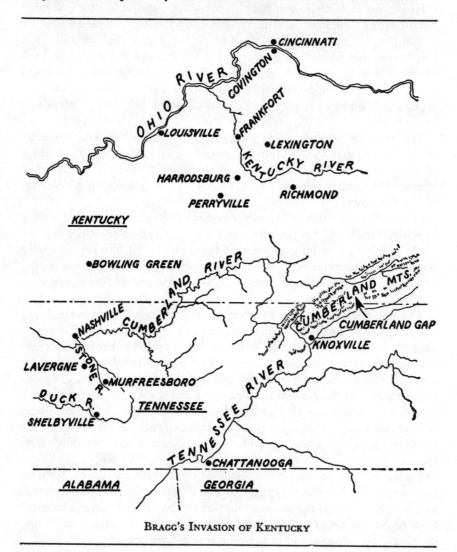

BRAGG'S INVASION OF KENTUCKY

I turned my steps toward Chattanooga, where Bragg was concentrating the Army of Tennessee. He had requested the War Department to assign me to duty with his army as chief of staff. He had reached Chattanooga in advance of his troops, who were then moving from Tupelo in northern Mississippi, and communicated to me his plan of campaign into Kentucky, which was excellent, giving promise of large results if vigorously executed.

Bragg had served long and creditably in the United States Artillery and in the war with Mexico had gained much celebrity. Possessing experience and talent, he was the most laborious of commanders, devoting every moment to the discharge of his duties. As a disciplinarian he far surpassed any of the senior Confederate generals; but his method and manner were harsh. Many years of dyspepsia had made his temper sour and petulant; and he was intolerant to a degree.

The movement into Kentucky was made as he had outlined it to me, along two lines. General Kirby Smith led a subordinate force from Knoxville, East Tennessee, through Cumberland Gap and, after defeating the Federals in spirited action at Richmond, Kentucky, reached Lexington, in the center of the state, and threatened Cincinnati. Bragg moved on a line west of the Cumberland Range toward Louisville on the Ohio River; and this movement forced the Federal commander, Buell, to march north to the same point by a parallel road, farther west. Buell had left garrisons at Nashville and other important places. Weakened by these detachments, as well as by the necessity of a retrograde movement, Bragg should have brought him to action before he reached Louisville. Defeated, the Federals would have been driven north of the Ohio to reorganize, and Bragg could have wintered his army in the fertile and powerful state of Kentucky, isolating the garrisons in his rear; but feeble health had unfitted Bragg to sustain long-continued pressure of responsibility.

While Buell's army was hurrying toward Louisville to head off Bragg, it was constantly harassed by Confederate raiders, the most dangerous of whom was John H. Morgan, a dashing cavalryman from Lexington, Kentucky. The green Union troops were no match for the wiles of this famous fighter, as we learn from Henry A. Castle, a Federal private.

Before the first of September, 1862, we were hurried south, half organized and entirely unarmed, to Louisville, Kentucky. How deficient we were in organization, and even in the knowledge of elementary military rules, one little incident will testify. At Springfield, Illinois, having shown some proficiency in making out muster-in rolls and consolidated returns, I had been temporarily detailed as a clerk. On our hasty departure the adjutant remained behind, and I, a private soldier, acted as adjutant for twenty days, signing all reports, countersigning all orders, and performing all his functions. No one, not even the twenty lieutenants eligible to promotion, questioned my right.

On my return to the regiment my friends gave me a temporary detail to fill the place of the absent quartermaster's sergeant. This secured me a horse to ride on the march, and made me ex officio regimental wagon master. Each regiment then marched luxuriously with thirteen 6-mule teams; a year later three or four amply sufficed. We were even obliged to conscript three or four additional teams every day from reluctant farmers to carry our extra baggage and accumulations of souvenirs.

One morning, I found myself so delayed by hunting fresh oxen that we lost our proper place in the long wagon train and were obliged to fall in at the extreme rear of it, at least six miles behind the marching column. Toward evening, a genteel-looking young man in semimilitary dress rode up to me from the rear and fell easily into conversation. He said he had been born and bred in that region of the country but now lived at Peoria, Illinois; that he was running a laundry for the army officers and that his apparatus was in a wagon to the rear. He was very agreeable and soon suggested that it was about time to go into camp. He spoke of a fine place on a side road that branched off a little way ahead, where there was a grove of beech trees and a large spring of excellent water. I accepted his offer to conduct us thither, and when the junction was reached filed off with my train, all those behind obediently following, like a flock of sheep. The camping spot, when reached, amply fulfilled his promises. On arrival I found myself in command of about seventy teams. My guide supped with me and shared my blanket on the hard ground. When I awoke in the morning he was missing. A few days afterwards, John Morgan captured two or three stragglers from our regiment, paroled them, and sent them in, with compliments to me, and the information that he had gone out of the laundry business, and that but for his failure to find his own men at their appointed place that night he would have returned and gobbled us all up.

But Morgan rarely wasted his time on small fry. He did not hesitate to attack isolated Union garrisons of considerable strength, and if none were near, harassed his enemies by raids which created much confusion and material damage.

As the Northern troops became more familiar with Morgan's tactics, however, their ability to take care of themselves grew, as is shown by the recollections of William E. Crane, a Union cavalryman.

About three o'clock in the afternoon the colonel came to our head-quarters and said he wanted the company to mount and go in pursuit of a body of Rebel cavalry said to be in the neighborhood. Just as the order was issued, an orderly rode up excitedly and reported that John Morgan had captured the regimental wagon train, burned the wagons and taken off teamsters, horses and mules. And this only one mile from camp—almost under our noses! Our colonel's blood was up in an instant, and in a stentorian voice he shouted, "Company C, turn out with your rifles!" This "with your rifles" had a flavor of business, and the response was quick. Then came the command, "Company C, forward!" and we dashed forward up the pike toward Nashville. In the middle of the pike were the ruins of our regimental wagon train—some wagons still burning, and some already in ashes.

As we afterward learned, the attacking party was a lieutenant colonel of John Morgan's command, with a body of Mississippi cavalry. They had first quietly taken in the pickets and then made a dash on the train. Our general himself had barely escaped capture. A halt was called, and the road examined to ascertain which way the enemy had gone. One company was sent back to get reinforcements and, with them, to try and intercept the raiders. The original party dashed into the woods, and then occurred a chase the parallel to which has seldom been seen. "Forward!" was the word, and forward it was. The woods became a thicket, sometimes apparently impassable; but the horses dashed at headlong speed through the trees, through the underbrush, under branches—thorns scratching the face and hands, projecting limbs tearing clothes and bruising bodies. Downhill and uphill, through marsh and bog, over logs and across streams, leaping obstacles, shouting, yelling, screaming and hurrahing, away we went—mud and leaves flying, and dead limbs crushing beneath horses' feet. Now the trail is lost and there is a halt. Soon it is found and the horses gallop on. The Rebel course is now marked by plunder—overcoats, canteens, saddles, blankets, the woods are full of them. Finally, we strike a narrow pike, follow it a mile or so, and learn that Morgan has divided his forces, only the smaller part having taken the course we are pursuing. We were after Morgan and the main body, so turned back. It was precious time lost, but the trail was again struck, and once more a plunge was made into the timber and cedars.

For miles the trees were so thick and the foliage so dense that it became impossible to ride other than single file; but, retarded as was our speed, the chase became hotter and more exciting than ever. The sight of an abandoned horse (and the hard-pressed enemy was now leaving his own as well as our animals) was the signal for a yell that the pursued might have heard and trembled at miles away. Then spurs were clapped into horses' flanks to urge them still faster on; and thus the column—if column it could be called—swept, dashed, plunged onward.

We had gained rapidly on the raiders and thought them almost within grasp. But they flew down the pike, scattering stones behind. We ran them into the net we had prepared. The detachment that had gone out later from camp had struck the pike opportunely and received the enemy warmly as we drove him into their arms. A brisk engagement followed, partly hand to hand. At the onset, Morgan, with his staff and a lot of blooded horses, broke away and escaped across Stone River. The enemy left four dead on the field, four sound captives in our hands and two wounded. Of the ninety-four horses taken, we recaptured seventy-five; of the forty-eight teamsters, thirty-one.

> Buell's timely arrival had saved Louisville in the nick of time, and Bragg, who had entered the environs of the city on the heels of his opponent, showed no disposition to attack the Union army in its entrenchments.
>
> It was Buell, strongly reinforced by new levies, who made the next move, with a view of driving the invaders out of Kentucky. The historians of the 36th Illinois Volunteers report on the beginning of the campaign.

Buell's army soon numbered nearly 100,000 men, a majority of whom were old soldiers, a number sufficient to have annihilated Bragg. But Buell's experienced fighters were worn down with hard marching and poorly clothed.

On the first of October, after the Rebel cavalry had quite effectually raided and devastated the country up to our picket lines, General Buell marched out with his formidable forces. The wagon trains covered over twenty-two miles in length, but averaged only about ten miles a day. All were in fine spirits and eager for an encounter with the enemy, who were slowly retiring with their plunder before the advance of our solid columns.

The summer and autumn had been unusually hot; the fields were parched, the grass withered, and thirsty soldiers looked with wearied eyes on the beds of streams and rivers either totally dry or shrunken into little, heated, tired-looking threads of water—brackish and disagreeable to taste and smell.

Both Buell and Bragg were confused as to the whereabouts of their enemy, and when a portion of the two hostile armies clashed at Perryville, it happened more by accident than by design.

Buell had in his army a young officer named Phil Sheridan, who headed a division under General Charles C. Gilbert, his corps commander. Sheridan was in the thick of the fight at Perryville and wrote an account of his acts and observations.

Orders were issued by General Buell for an advance upon the enemy, with the purpose of destroying him within the limits of the "blue grass" region, and, failing in that, of driving him from Kentucky. The army moved October 1, 1862. Bragg's troops retreated, only resisting sufficiently to enable the forces of General Kirby Smith to be drawn in closer.

Much time was consumed by Buell's army in its march, but we finally neared Perryville on the evening of October 7. The enemy was in strong force on the opposite side of a small stream called Doctor's Creek. It was very difficult to obtain water in this section of Kentucky, and the troops were suffering so for water that it became absolutely necessary that we should gain possession of Doctor's Creek. Consequently I moved out a brigade for the purpose but, after we had crossed the creek, I found that we could not hold the ground, unless we carried and occupied a range of hills called Chaplin Heights. We quickly carried the heights and entrenched.

While this was going on, General Gilbert, my corps commander, kept sending me messages not to bring on an engagement. I replied to each message that I was not bringing on an engagement, but that the enemy evidently intended to do so. Soon after I saw General A. M. McCook's corps advancing toward Chaplin River, apparently unconscious that the Confederates were present in force behind the stream. The leading regiments seemed to approach the river indifferently prepared to meet the sudden attack that speedily followed, delivered as it

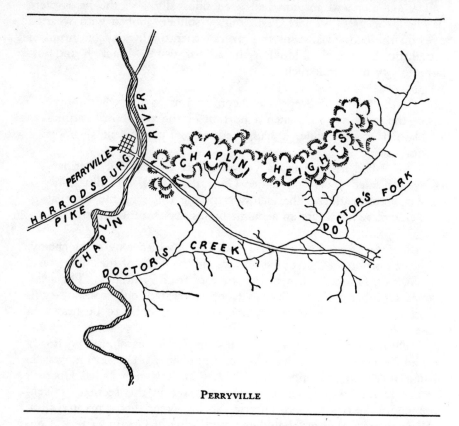

PERRYVILLE

was from the chosen position of the enemy. The fury of the Confederate assault soon threw McCook's force into confusion, pushed it back a considerable distance, and ultimately inflicted upon it such loss of men and guns as to cripple it seriously, and prevent for the whole day further offensive movements on his part.

General Gilbert, fearing that my entrenched position on the heights might be carried, directed me to withdraw. My recall was opportune, for I had no sooner got back to my original line than the Confederates attacked me furiously, advancing almost to my entrenchments, notwithstanding that a large part of the ground over which they had to move was swept by a heavy fire of canister from my batteries. Before they had quite reached us, however, our telling fire made them recoil and, as they fell back, I directed an advance. This advance pressed the enemy to Perryville, but he returned in such good order that we gained nothing.

The battle virtually ended about four o'clock in the afternoon of October 8, though more or less desultory firing continued until dark. Had the commander of the army been able to be present on the field, he could have taken advantage of Bragg's final repulse, and there would have remained in our hands more than the barren field. But no attempt was made to do anything more till next morning.

When the battle had ceased, General Gilbert asked me to join him at Buell's headquarters. I arrived just as Buell was about to sit down to his supper and, noticing that he was lame, then learned that he had been severely injured by a recent fall from his horse. Of course, the events of the day were the chief topic of discussion, but the conversation indicated that what had occurred was not fully realized, and I returned to my troops impressed with the belief that General Buell and his staff officers were unconscious of the magnitude of the battle that had just been fought.

It had been expected by Buell that he would fight the enemy on the ninth of October, but the Confederates disposed of that proposition by attacking us on the eighth. During the battle on the eighth the Second Corps lay idle the whole day for want of orders, and, moreover, a large part of Gilbert's corps was unengaged during the pressure on McCook. Had these troops been put in, success would have been beyond question; but there was no one on the ground authorized to take advantage of the situation, and the battle of Perryville remains in history an example of lost opportunities.

The enemy retired from our front the night of the eighth, falling back on Harrodsburg to form a junction with Kirby Smith.

Junius H. Browne, special war correspondent for the *New York Tribune*, fully agreed with Sheridan regarding the way Buell had fought the battle; in fact, he went Sheridan one better and did not pull his punches.

The battle of Perryville is one of the most inexplicable military events of the war. I have no disposition at this late day to find fault with anyone; but the conduct of General Buell in permitting nearly, if not all of Bragg's forces to engage a portion of ours, and refusing to give permission to our regiments to re-enforce their over-powered companions in arms, when they stood there burning to rush into the contest, is beyond the power of satisfactory explanation.

Bragg's army ought to, and could have been almost annihilated. I have never known so universal an expression of disapprobation of any General as there was of Buell after that battle. Everyone of his officers, from Generals to Second Lieutenants and privates, were so dissatisfied after they had been compelled to give up the pursuit of the enemy, that it was deemed absolutely necessary to supersede him.

Strangely, dissatisfaction with Bragg was equally strong among Southern critics, such as T. C. De Leon.

Bragg had entered Kentucky with an army re-enforced and better equipped than had been seen in that section since the war began. Once more cheering reports came to Richmond that any moment might bring news of the crushing of Buell. Great was the disappointment, therefore, when news came of the withdrawal from before Cincinnati, and that all action of Bragg's forces would be postponed until Kirby Smith's junction with him.

The fight at Munfordville [where a Union garrison had surrendered after a short fight] was not productive of any results, but that after the victory Bragg should allow Buell to escape was inexplicable, and is so still.

Why did Bragg retreat so readily after the battle of Perryville? To judge from an editorial which appeared in the *Richmond Examiner* of September 12, almost a month before Perryville, the entire Kentucky campaign had been undertaken more for economic than for military reasons.

The great and true source of meat supply is the State of Kentucky. If our armies could push over that state, the political advantages secured to the South would be of even small account compared with those she would derive from a sumptuary point of view. There are more hogs and cattle in Kentucky than are now left in all the South; and steps ought to be taken to drive back these animals, as well as mules and horses.

The pursuit of Bragg, who was taking with him herds of horses, cattle, pigs and other booty, ended at Bowling Green, Kentucky. There the Union army was placed under a new commander, General William S. Rosecrans.

General Rosecrans had become favorably known through his operations in northern Mississippi, where he had fought successfully against the Confederate Generals Earl Van Dorn and Sterling Price. In their attack on Corinth, which Rosecrans defended, they had suffered a bloody repulse but had escaped fatal damage through Rosecrans' dilatory pursuit, for which Grant, who was in command of the district, never forgave him.

With Buell out of the way, Sheridan's spirits rose.

The army as a whole did not manifest much regret at the change of commanders, for the campaign from Louisville on was looked upon generally as a lamentable failure. Buell's detractors pointed out that Bragg's retreat so jeopardized the Confederate army that, had a skillful and energetic advance of the Union troops been made, the enemy could have been destroyed before he could quit the State of Kentucky.

Bragg was now south of the Cumberland River, in a position threatening Nashville, which was garrisoned by but a small force, and it was apparent that a battle would have to be fought somewhere in Middle Tennessee. So the army was soon put in motion for Nashville.

General Rosecrans, in the reorganization of the army, had assigned Major General A. McD. McCook to command the right wing, Major General George H. Thomas the center and Major General T. L. Crittenden the left wing. The army was thus compact and cohesive, undisturbed by discord and jealousies under a commander who, we believed, had the energy and skill necessary to direct us to success. Our invincibility made us all keen for a test of strength with the Confederates. We had not long to wait.

Early on the morning of December 26, 1862, in a heavy rain, the army marched on Murfreesboro, where the enemy had made some preparations to go into winter quarters, and to hold which town it was hoped he would accept battle.

Sheridan, commanding a division in Rosecrans' center, observed with interest that, just as at First Bull Run, the two opposing generals had decided on exactly the same battle plan, when they confronted each other on the eve of December 31, 1862.

Orders received during the night revealed the fact that Rosecrans intended to attack by throwing his left on the enemy's right, with the expectation of driving it in toward Murfreesboro. From the movements of the enemy at daylight next morning, it was plainly indicated that Bragg had planned to swing his left on our right by an exactly similar maneuver, get possession of the railroad and the Nashville Pike, and if possible cut us off from our base at Nashville. The conceptions in the minds of the two generals were almost identical; but Bragg took the initiative, beginning his movements about an hour earlier than the time set by Rosecrans, which gained him an immense advantage in the earlier stages of the action.

Rosecrans had been given a rare opportunity. Grant was still lying idle at Jackson, Tennessee; Buell was in eclipse, Sherman under the cloud of malicious gossip regarding his sanity. In the East, McClellan had been summarily dismissed, and no one else had yet proved his worth. If Rosecrans could achieve a smashing victory over Bragg, he would become the man of the hour.

What happened next is told by General Milo S. Hascall, who did not take kindly to the new general in chief.

During the weeks that we had lain encamped about Nashville, I had frequent opportunities to see General Rosecrans and observe his manner, characteristics and surroundings, and had hoped to be enabled to form a more favorable opinion than I had theretofore entertained. I was sorry, however, to be forced to the conclusion that my estimate of the man had been even more favorable than the facts would justify. His head seemed to have been completely turned. Instead of the quiet dignity, orderly and businesslike methods that had formerly obtained at the headquarters of the army, the very reverse seemed to be the rule.

Having by this time surrounded himself, in addition to the usual staff, with a numerous coterie of newspaper correspondents, jobbing presses and other means of reaching the public (with the Confederate army lying immediately in our front) one could but wonder at the sublime indifference of Bragg and his army in the midst of preparations for their destruction such as these.

The enemy was in force in our front, and their fortifications were plainly visible opposite us on the right bank of the Stone River, between it and the city of Murfreesboro, and it was evident Bragg intended to accept the gage of battle.

Our army was finally concentrated, McCook, with his three divisions on the right, Thomas, with his three in the center, and Crittenden, with his three on the left. This arrangement brought my brigade on the extreme left of the entire army. We were made acquainted with the plan of the attack, which was to be made by our army in the morning of the following day, the memorable thirty-first day of December, 1862. This was for the left wing (Crittenden's) to cross Stone River—which was at that time fordable at all points—and deliver a furious attack on the enemy's extreme right, this to be followed up by a wheel to the right by other portions of our army.

This plan was well conceived and might have worked well enough perhaps—if the enemy had waited for us.

The right of our army seemed to think that, inasmuch as our plan contemplated an attack by the left, they had nothing to do in the morning but to keep a picket force out, send their artillery horses to a distant point for water and get breakfast. They did not seem to think it possible that Bragg might have plans of his own, that our attack might be anticipated or that our right might receive a desperate attack while our left was preparing to deliver one. But this is exactly what happened.

There was no great discrepancy in numbers between the two armies. If Rosecrans was to gather an overwhelming superiority on his left wing, he had to weaken his right. But could the right withstand an attack, should Bragg choose to make one? Rosecrans wanted to be sure and asked the commander of the right corps, General McCook, for his opinion. An officer named William D. Brickham, who was present, reported what transpired at headquarters on the evening prior to the battle.

At nine o'clock in the evening of December 30, the corps commanders met at headquarters, and the following plan of battle for the morrow was presented and explained:

McCook on the right was to receive the attack of the enemy or, if that did not come, to attack himself.

Thomas in the center was to gain the enemy's center and left as far as the river.

Crittenden on the left was to cross Stone River at the lower ford, and to advance on Breckinridge, who commanded the Confederate right.

This combination, ensuring us a vast superiority on our left, required for its success that General McCook should be able to hold his position for three hours; that if necessary to recede at all, he should recede slowly, refusing [bending back] his right, thereby rendering our success certain.

Having thus explained the plan, the general commanding addressed General McCook as follows:

"Tomorrow there will be a battle. You know the ground, you know its difficulties. Can you hold your present position for three hours?"

To which General McCook responded, "Yes, I think I can."

The general commanding then said, "If you don't think your present the best position, change it; it is only necessary for you to make things sure"; and the officers then returned to their commands.

The story continues with the happenings on the morning of December 31, 1862.

Breakfast was hurried. General Crittenden reported in person. The general commanding walked with him to his quarters where his first division, in pursuance of the plan of battle, was already moving to cross Stone River to sweep into Murfreesboro. Part of it had already crossed. Some firing had then been heard on the right, but not enough to indicate a battle.

Officers of the staff were grouped about little fires in the avenue between the tents. The general commanding and General Crittenden stood near the marquee conversing eagerly. It was nearly seven o'clock. Suddenly all hearts were thrilled by a sound sweeping from the right like a strong wind sweeping through a forest.

The din of battle swelled rapidly. Its volume increased, and it seemed coming nearer. It could not be! This must be hallucination! It can not be disaster! A tide of fugitives poured out of the thickets—Negroes, teamsters and some soldiers. You have seen cinders from burning building flying when the conflagration was still invisible. You could hear the roaring flames and crackling beams. Seeing the cinders you would say, "There is a fire." You had not yet felt the blast, but its avant-couriers were unmistakable. These teamsters, Negroes, soldiers, flying before it were cinders from the flames of battle.

A cocked pistol brings one squad to a halt. "We are beaten," they cry. "The right wing is broken! The enemy is sweeping everything before them!" But most soldiers cling to their muskets. The awful uproar increases and stretches swiftly now to the left. Heavy drops which precede a thunderstorm seem to be falling on the dead leaves.

At headquarters the groups have gathered into a cluster. They are talking in low, nervous tones, their eyes searchingly peering into the mysteries of the dreadful forest. The chief stalks through the avenue, obviously disturbed. Who will credit stragglers against the reliance men have in good soldiers? McCook is an approved good soldier. The army had no better general than he. The soldiers of the right wing are veterans who never turned their faces from the enemy.

An adjutant galloped back with tidings. "The right wing is broken, and the enemy is driving it back." Incredible! McCook was surely falling back with an object. "All right—never mind—we will rectify it," said the general cheerfully. Stragglers were overflowing the plain and the Murfreesboro Pike like a freshet. A staff officer from McCook confirmed evil rumors. McCook needed assistance. "Tell General Mc-Cook," said the chief vehemently, "to contest every inch of ground. If he holds them we will swing into Murfreesboro with our left and cut them off." Then to his staff, "It is working right." Alas, it was not "working right."

The frightful delusion soon was dissipated. The enemy were pressing McCook swiftly and in disorder clean back upon the center. An aide from McCook advised that reserves had better be held in hand. What! So soon! "Tell General McCook I will help him," was the instant reply, and General Rousseau from the left marched at double-quick into the cedar brakes to brace up the center under Sheridan.

Our plan of battle was crippled. The right wing had failed to hold three hours—nay, one hour. Therefore the left wing could not swing into Murfreesboro and cut the enemy off. A third of the left wing was absolutely necessary to save the right from annihilation. It was not yet eight o'clock. The battle was all against us.

The general charged through the deathly storm as if it had been no more than hail. It was wonderful that he escaped. His eyes gathered the features of the field rapidly, and his mind directed dispositions to stop the torrent which was well-nigh overwhelming. No complaint escaped him. This was no moment for reproach. But it was obvious that he was profoundly moved. His florid face had paled and lost its ruddy luster, but his eyes blazed with sullen fire. One moment's hesitation or vacillation now, and all were lost. But he was firm as iron and fixed as fate. Expostulation with him was vain. He sternly repeated, "This battle must be won."

As the right wing of the Union army gave way, the entire Federal front swung around. The pivot around which it swung was General Sheridan's division, and on its fortitude depended the outcome of the battle. If it, too, should dissolve, like the troops on its right, Rosecrans was doomed.

George H. Daggett, a private in Sheridan's division, recounts the next phase of the struggle.

When the retrograde movement commenced, we were ordered to follow the artillery and support it. We were marching at double-quick across a cotton field already swarming with the advance guard of the exultant foe who poured a storm of bullets into our ranks.

As we neared the edge of this field, we were halted by General Rousseau, who had become separated from his own division and, seeing in our regiment the only visible organized body of Union troops, proceeded to overrule the instructions we were trying to obey, and ordered the regimental commander to halt in the dense cedar thicket bordering the field we had just crossed, and hold that position until he could bring other troops to our support. Here we were sheltered by numerous stumps and trunks of trees which had been dragged to this point when the field had been cleared of its timber many years before.

A few of the more venturesome Rebels reached a rail fence less than twenty yards from the muzzles of our muskets, but none ever returned. Others paused at a distance of seventy-five to a hundred yards, delivered their fire and dropped to the ground to load and fire again. Others came up in their rear, but no human endurance could withstand the murderous fire poured into them from our well-protected line, reinforced now on the right and left by other troops who had rallied to our assistance.

Three times was the brave endeavor repeated, but each time it met with an angry repulse. Our own losses were numerous, but insignificant compared with those inflicted on the enemy. Here the victorious Confederates met the first serious opposition, and the time thus gained aided materially the efforts of General Rosecrans to reorganize his army.

For at least half an hour this bloody angle at the edge oɪ the cedars was held, and it could have been held indefinitely but for the fact that, the crumbling remnants of the defeated divisions on our right having fallen back into the cedar forest, we were likewise compelled to retreat into the depths of the wood.

This little patch of cedars, perhaps 200 acres in area, contained enough unique features to give it the prominence it has obtained in history. The surface was a confused mass of rock, lying in slabs, and boulders interspersed with holes, fissures and caverns which would have made progress over it extremely difficult even if there had been no timber; but, notwithstanding the apparent total absence of soil, a thick growth of trees covered it, seeming almost impenetrable. The trunks ran straight up into the air so near together that the sunlight was obscured, and the vision extended but a short distance horizontally, shutting out a view of what was going on outside.

As our lines of battle retreated into this maze of wood and rock, we soon lost knowledge of what was transpiring in front, in flank or in rear, except as we could gather it from the portentous avalanches of sound which assailed us from every direction. The enemy brought up their artillery and poured a furious storm of shell and grape into the woods. Musketry was also discharged somewhat at random, but in great aggregate volume, by our pursuers; then the siege guns from the defensive works of Murfreesboro opened on our right flank and added to the confusion. Our own comrades of other divisions far to the left and outside the forest were fighting vigorously to hold their part of the line and repulse charges. Thus on all sides we were stormed at and stunned by the conglomeration of fiendish noises that came seemingly from every point of the compass. Not the least terrible of these sounds was an occasional explosion of the hot, fierce, indescribable Rebel yell.

We had no possible means of knowing the result of all this fighting going on around us. We seemed to be entirely surrounded by the enemy and to be practically prisoners of war. We could do nothing for our own defense, and no one seemed able to give authentic orders or even to guide us correctly. We learned afterward that nearly all the regiments of our own division had halted and fought near us and were now moving under Sheridan's lead to an allotted place in the new line of battle, but we had no knowledge of their whereabouts. We could scarcely see the length of our short regimental line, which was often broken by the hordes of disorganized fugitives who were still pouring through, seeking safety in the rear.

A curious incident cast a ray of humor on the happenings of the day. The story is told by a Union colonel named Charles S. Greene.

In the rebel charge upon McCook's right, the rebel Third Kentucky was advancing upon one of the loyal Kentucky regiments. They came from the same county and were old friends and neighbors. As soon as they came near enough for recognition, they ceased firing, and began abusing, and cursing, and swearing at each other, calling each other the most outlandish names. All this time the battle was roaring around them without much attention from either side.

This could not last. By mutual consent they finally ceased swearing, and charged into each other with the most unearthly yell ever heard. The muskets were thrown away, and at it they went, pulling and gouging. The rebels were getting the best of it, when the 9th Ohio came up, taking a great many rebel prisoners. As the late belligerents were conducted to the rear, they were on the best terms with their captors, laughing and chatting and joking; and they all became as jolly as possible.

The rush of the Confederate left wing had reached the impetus of an avalanche, and for a time it seemed that nothing could resist it. If Bragg's men could reach the Nashville turnpike beyond the cedars, the Union army would be cut off from its base. Near that road Rosecrans had hurriedly assembled all available reinforcements from his left wing. The result of the battle depended on the efficacy of this last-minute arrangement.

A Union officer who fought in the battle on this part of the field describes it in these words:

Each minute it became more and more evident that all the reinforcements which had been hurried into the woods had been proved inadequate.

Nearer and nearer came the storm; louder and louder the tumult of battle. The immense train of wagons parked along the road suddenly seemed instinct with life, and every species of army vehicle, preceded by frightened mules and horses, rolled and rattled away. The shouts

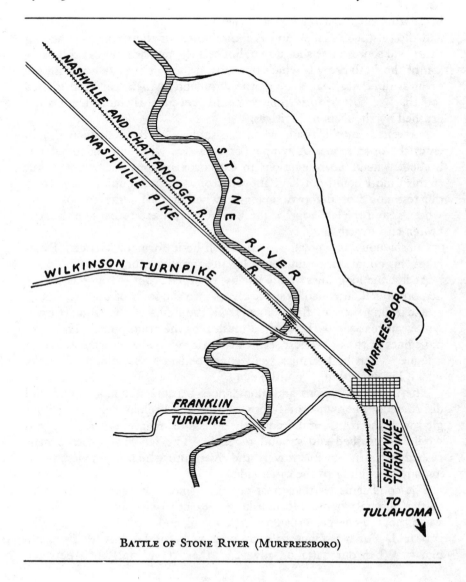

BATTLE OF STONE RIVER (MURFREESBORO)

and cries of the terrified teamsters urging their animals to the top of their speed were mingled with the billows of sound which swayed and surged over the field.

Everything now depended upon the regiments and batteries which Rosecrans had massed along the turnpike. Suddenly 10,000 fugitives burst from the cedar thickets and rushed into open space between them and the turnpike. Thick and fast the bullets of the enemy fell among them, and scores were shot down; but still the number increased by reason of the fresh crowds which burst from the thickets. It was with the greatest difficulty that some of the regiments, which had been massed together as a sort of forlorn hope, could prevent their ranks from being crushed by the mass of fugitives.

I watched for the result when the soldiers of the Rebellion should enter the open space. A tempest of iron was whistling and burst unheeded. I make no pretensions to extraordinary physical courage, but at this time I could not have moved from the spot until I knew from the testimony of my own eyesight whether or no the troops upon whom rested the last hope of the Union army were to be, like the rest, beaten and overthrown.

Conspicuous among all was the well-built form of General Rosecrans, his countenance unmoved by the tumult around him.

At last the long lines of the enemy emerged from the woods with a demoniac yell, intended to strike terror into the souls of the "Yankees."

A dazzling sheet of flame burst from the ranks of the Union forces. An awful roar shook the earth; a crash rent the atmosphere. The foremost lines of the Rebel host seemed to melt away like snowflakes before a flame. Then both armies were enveloped in a vast cloud of smoke which hid everything from the eye.

The flight of wagons and ambulances became still more rapid and disordered. Thousands of fugitives from the broken right wing mingled with the teams, and frequently a mass of men, horses and wagons would be crushed and ground together. The whole disordered mass rushed as fast as possible toward the river, into which it plunged, pushing and struggling to the other side.

The combat under that great cloud of smoke was somewhat similar to that in the woods. No one knows exactly what occurred. There was a shout, a charge, a rush of fire, a recoil, and then all for a time disappeared. For ten minutes the thunder of battle burst forth from the cloud. When our battalion advanced, they found no Rebels between the woods and the turnpike except the dead, dying and disabled. There were hundreds of these, and their blood soaked and reddened the ground. Since the annihilation of the "Old Guard" in their charge at Waterloo, there has probably not been an instance of so great a slaughter in so short a time as during this repulse of the Rebel left at Murfreesboro.

> The Union Private Henry A. Castle was made sergeant major during the battle. He was caught in the retreat and relates some queer incidents which illustrate the terrific losses sustained by the Federal army on December 31.

I soon found that the position of sergeant major in a battle is no sinecure. A staff officer dashes up with an order for the major commanding the regiment, stationed behind a tree a little to the rear. The major calls to the adjutant behind a smaller tree on his right who communicates the order to the sergeant major. He, while the bullets hum like a swarm of bees around his head, gets the order, then runs to each company commander, shakes him up and shouts it into his ear, before the line could be moved. I was the sergeant major!

About two o'clock in the afternoon we got into a hot place. My regiment was sent into a railroad cut which crossed the battle line at an oblique angle, our left well advanced toward the enemy. I was at my place on the extreme left, and while the men were firing effectively from their protected position, I naturally kept a weather eye out toward the foe on our exposed flank. After a time I saw a Rebel officer ride up to a point a few hundred yards away, gaze at us a moment and then gallop off. I soon saw a Rebel battery come up. I started promptly for the center of the regiment to notify the major, but heard that he had just been carried off wounded. I then ran to the right to find the adjutant, and learned that he, too, had retired for the same reason. I assumed the responsibility of marching the company double-quick out of the defile, trusting the rest to follow, which they did with alacrity, as just then the shells came shrieking through the straight and narrow gorge with a venom that would have left few unscathed in five minutes more. I then notified the four remaining captains that they were without a commander. Being of equal rank, they sent me to the brigade commander, sitting on his horse 200 yards in the rear, with a request to settle the matter of precedence. I started toward him, but before I had made half the distance he, the last of our brigade commanders, was shot before my eyes and fell to the ground a corpse. Finally, at four o'clock in the afternoon, our ammunition being entirely gone and the men exhausted by fatigue and thirst, we were withdrawn a short distance to the rear.

Disaster to the Union army had been averted, although it had been a close call.

When evening came, Rosecrans called a council of his generals to discuss what was to be done. An adjutant, John L. Yaryan, who was among those present, gave a graphic description of the meeting.

At the close of the first day of the battle, Rosecrans invited, as a council of war, his corps and division commanders to meet at his headquarters, an old log cabin about a mile from the battle front, in a cedar thicket. The cabin was a pioneer, single-deck old-timer, with a one-end fireplace which was filled with cedar limbs, burning and crackling, filling the room with resinous odor and yellow light. The rain was falling steadily and persistently, as if determined to wash out the red stains of battle.

When I arrived, at midnight, I found present Generals Rosecrans, McCook, Crittenden, Sheridan and Thomas, some division commanders and a few staff officers. These officers were arranged around the sides of the cabin, seated on the floor. Rosecrans, having the only campstool in the party, was in front of the fire looking intently at the curling flames, warming his hands and drying his clothes. When he heard the click of Thomas J. Wood's crutch on the puncheon floor (he had been wounded during the afternoon) he immediately rose and offered his seat, but Wood declined the thoughtful attention.

It was a weird firelit scene. These men looked as if each had been a gunner all day and had taken special pains to get himself smoked and powder-grimed. Battered as to hats, tousled as to hair, torn as to clothes and depressed as to spirits, if there was a cheerful-expressioned face present I did not see it. It was no time nor place for the glitter and tinsel of rank; it was a clear case of a demand for nerve and a fight to the death on an empty stomach and in wet clothes. Thomas looked, as he always did, calm, stern, determined, silent and perfectly self-possessed, his hat set squarely on his head. It was a tonic to look at the man.

The stillness was intense, broken only by the splash of the rain on the clapboard roof, as we sat there awaiting the action and will of one man.

After a half-hour of this silence, Rosecrans slowly turned toward his commanders with the air of having come to the crossroads, and said, beginning with the left of the row, "General McCook, have you any suggestions for tomorrow?"

"No, only I would like for Bragg to pay me for my two horses lost today."

So from man to man he went around the room, the answer of each, in substance, the same as the first. Thomas was held for the last. I had watched him closely, but he never had changed a muscle; his eye never left the bed of red coals that were now aglow on the old hearth; he did not appear to hear any of the replies; the same set, determined look I had seen when I came in was still there.

Rosecrans hesitated a little when he came to him, and said, "General Thomas, what have you to say?"

Without a word of reply Thomas slowly rose to his feet, buttoned his greatcoat from bottom to top, faced his comrades and stood there, a statue of courage chiseled out of the black marble of midnight, by the firelight, and said, "Gentlemen, I know of no better place to die than right here," and walked out of the room into the dripping night.

The council was over. No one else moved for a moment, when Rosecrans, quick as a flash, and with the dash that was a part of him, said, "If you are not attacked by six o'clock this morning, you will open the fight promptly, posted as you are, and move on to Murfreesboro. Clear the field yet tonight of all wounded and see to it that your ammunition is well up; we will whip this fight tomorrow."

> Brigadier General Milo S. Hascall retained the impression that Rosecrans' decision to renew the fight was due to an entirely different cause, and in his account General Crittenden, not General Thomas, is the hero of the occasion.
>
> If we can rely on General Hascall, Rosecrans had actually decided on a retreat and had already given orders to that effect, when something made him change his dispositions.

During the evening, I was visited by the chief of artillery on General Crittenden's staff, and informed that a council of war had been held at

General Rosecrans' headquarters, and that a general retreat to Nashville had been decided upon, and that all except General Crittenden concurred in the advisability of such movement, and he was overruled by the others. In pursuance of such determination, I was forthwith to send all the transportation of my division, except one wagon for each brigade, to the rear. The staff officer said that Crittenden had been very much incensed at the proposition for retreat; said his army was in position and on hand. However, the retreat was decided upon, and the baggage had been sent to the rear as above directed, and we were lying on our arms awaiting the further order to retreat when a very singular circumstance caused Rosecrans to change his mind, and conclude to fight it out where we were. A large number of our straggling, demoralized detachments in the rear of our army had concluded to disobey orders, and make fires and try and get something to eat. Rosecrans concluded the enemy had got in our rear and were forming line of battle by torch lights, and hence withdrew the order for a general retreat. After this, about one o'clock, I was informed that the retreat had been given up, and that I was ordered to fall back with my division about half a mile and take up a position that would there be assigned me. Accordingly I did so.

Among Bragg's troops was a brigade entirely composed of Kentucky soldiers. It had been posted at an elevation known as Swain's Hill, near the center of the Confederate line, and fought throughout the entire battle. Its experiences during the first day, as set forth by Lieutenant L. D. Young, one of its junior officers, demonstrated that, while the most dramatic events of the day took place on the Confederate left wing, other parts of the line were not left without exciting incidents.

Stone River was in some respects one of the most interesting, exciting and captivating battles of the war. On the afternoon of Monday the twenty-ninth, our Kentucky brigade took possession of Swain's Hill, which was the acknowledged key to Bragg's position of defense. Some were wicked enough to say that he wanted us all killed, hence placed us in the most perilous position. The thirtieth was spent in getting ready by both parties to the battle.

A most thrilling incident happened early on December 31, when a body of enemy cavalry swung into line with drawn sabers, gleaming and waving in the crisp, chill sunlit air, dashed down over the open fields in a grand charge upon the Confederate infantry.

We had been instructed in the formation of the "hollow square" to resist the charge of cavalry, and when I saw these regiments doubling column at half distance I knew what was coming. To see the field officers on horseback rushing within the squares as they closed and the front rank kneeling, all with fixed bayonets glittering in the frosty sunlight, and these oncoming horsemen with waving sabers and glittering helmets was a sight unsurpassed by anything I witnessed during the war. As soon as the squares were formed, the artillery in the rear opened fire through the intervening spaces made by the formation of the squares, whereupon artillery and infantry combined swept the field, and the charging column turned in confusion and rout, scurrying helter-skelter back over the field, leaving numbers of men horseless.

Soon the Rebel yell down the line told us that things were going our way, and we could see our friends moving forward.

The battle progressed steadily and satisfactorily to the Confederates until about four o'clock, when they ran against a snag. Wood's and Sheridan's divisions, with other of Rosecrans' forces which he had concentrated upon his center and left, stood in his strongest position for a final and last stand. The conflict here was desperate and bloody, neither party seeming to have much the advantage.

Both armies slept that night upon the field with the greater part of the field in possession of the Confederates, and the advantages and results of the day almost wholly in our favor.

The next day, January 1, 1863, went by without a renewal of the conflict, both sides resting on their arms. On January 2, however, the battle was resumed. This time Bragg had decided to have his right wing accomplish what his left had failed to do two days before. And General Breckinridge was chosen as the man to carry the Southern flag into the enemy camp.

Lieutenant Young tells of what he went through, and how his unit, after the close of the battle, earned its name of "The Orphan Brigade."

We spent the night in the rear of and among the artillery we had been supporting. When morning came we found that the enemy was still in our front instead of on the road to Nashville. Bragg had believed that Rosecrans' army was demolished and would surely retreat to Nashville, and so had informed President Davis.

But old "Rosy" had something else in his mind. He was planning and scheming and matured a plan for a trap, and Bragg walked right into it with the innocence of a lamb and the ignorance of a man who had never known anything of the art of war. Had he listened to the protestations of General Breckinridge and his officers, he might have saved, for the time being, his military reputation and the lives of several hundred brave and noble men.

Early on the morning of January 2, Captain William P. Bramblett, our company commander, who had served with General Breckinridge in Mexico, received orders from Breckinridge to make a thorough reconnaissance of the enemy's position. Captain Bramblett with two of his lieutenants, myself one of them, crawled through the weeds a distance of several hundred yards to a prominent point of observation from which through his field glass and even with the naked eye we could see the enemy's concentrated forces near and above the lower ford on the opposite side of the river, his artillery being thrown forward and nearest to the river. The guns appeared to be close together and covering quite a space of ground; we could not tell how many guns, but there was quite a number. The infantry was seemingly in large force and extended farther down toward the ford. Captain Bramblett was a man of no mean military genius and, after studying the situation in silence for some minutes, he said he believed Rosecrans was setting a trap for Bragg. Continuing, he said, "If he means to attack us on this side, why does he not reinforce on this side? Why concentrate so much artillery on the bluff yonder?" I accompanied Captain Bramblett to General Breckinridge's headquarters and heard him make substantially in detail a report containing these facts. General Breckinridge, to thoroughly and unmistakably understand the situation, examined it and I presume reached the same conclusion, and when he repaired to Bragg's headquarters and vouchsafed this information and suggested the presumptive plan of the enemy, Bragg said, "Sir, my information is different. I have given the order to attack the enemy in your front and expect it to be obeyed."

In furtherance of Bragg's order we were assembled about three o'clock on the afternoon of January 2, in a line north of and to the right of Swain's Hill, confronting Colonel John Beatty's and William Grose's Union brigades, with a battery or two of artillery as support, they being intended for the bait that had been thrown across the river at the lower ford, and now occupied an eminence some three-quarters of a mile to the right front of our position on Swain's Hill.

This was the force, small as it was, that Bragg was so anxious to dislodge. Between the attacking line and the Federal position was a considerable scope of open ground, fields and pastures, with here and there a clump of bushes or briers, but the entire space was in full view of and covered by the enemy's batteries to the left of the line on the opposite side of the river.

A more imposing and thoroughly disciplined line of soldiers never moved to the attack of an enemy than responded to the signal gun stationed immediately in our rear, which was fired exactly at four o'clock. Every man vied with his fellow man in steadiness of step and correct alignment, with the officers giving low and cautionary commands, many knowing that it was their last hour on earth, but without hesitating moved forward to their inevitable doom and defeat. We had got only fairly started, when the great jaws of the trap on the bluff from the opposite side of the river were sprung, and bursting shells were plunging and tearing through our columns.

On we moved, Beatty's and Grose's lines giving way seemingly to allow the jaws of the trap to press with more and ever increasing vigor upon the unfortunate and discomfited victims. But on we moved, until the survivors of the decoy had passed the river and over the lines stationed on the other side, when their new line of infantry opened on our confused and disordered columns another destructive and ruinous fire.

Coupled with this condition and correlative to it, a battery of Grose and a part of their infantry had been cut off from the ford and seeing our confused condition, rallied, re-formed and opened fire. Confronted in front by their infantry, with the river intervening, swept by their artillery from the left and now attacked by both infantry and artillery by an oblique fire from the right, we found ourselves in a helpless condition, from which it looked like an impossibility to escape; and but for the fact that two or three batteries had been ordered into position to check the threatened advance of the enemy and thereby distract their attention, we doubtless would have fared still worse.

We rallied some distance to the right of where we had started and found that many, very many, of our noblest, truest and best had fallen, a sacrifice to stupidity. Thirty-seven percent in one hour and ten minutes was the frightful summary. Breckinridge understood and was fully sensible of the unwisdom of this move. What a pity that a strict observance of military rule compelled it to be obeyed.

As he rode by the dead and dying in the rear of our lines, with tears falling from his eyes, he was heard to say in tones of anguish, "My poor Orphans! My poor Orphans!" little thinking that he was dedicating to them a name that will crown the history of that dear little band with everlasting immortality.

This is how Breckinridge's attack looked to a Northern military critic, A. F. Stevenson, who was a witness to it and subsequently gathered additional information from prisoners and other Confederate sources.

About two o'clock in the afternoon General Bragg sent for General Breckinridge to come to his headquarters for final orders.

General Breckinridge was opposed to the attack as ordered by General Bragg and tried to persuade him that it would result in disaster, as the ground occupied by the Federal troops was so much higher than the ridge which he was ordered to take that they could mass their artillery and sweep the whole field. In urging his opinions he drew, with a stick, on the ground the positions of the opposing commands. Considerable time was occupied in their discussion, but General Bragg remained firm and ordered Breckinridge to proceed. The hour for the contemplated attack drawing near, the latter galloped quickly to the extreme right of his command and sought to encourage his men by appealing to their pride and gallantry.

As Breckenridge rode past General William Preston, he beckoned the latter aside, and said, "General Preston, this attack is made against my judgment and by the special orders of General Bragg. If it should result in disaster, and I be among the slain, I want you to do justice to my memory and tell the people that I believed this attack to be very unwise, and tried to prevent it."

Promptly at four o'clock the artillery in Polk's front gave the signal for the attack. The Confederate batteries commenced their fire from the direction of the woods lining the river, for the purpose of driving out our skirmishers; while Breckinridge's division, with guns loaded and bayonets fixed, marched with steady step to the assault.

Suddenly a mass of blue-coated men arose on his front, as though they had risen from the ground, and poured into his men a fearful fire. A decidedly bloody fight ensued. Both sides fought with the utmost valor; but the two regiments who received the impact of the attack were no match for a Rebel brigade supported by artillery.

They gave way and fell back toward the second line. The enemy was checked for some minutes, disorder being visible in many places, when a new force of Rebels came pouring over the steep bank of Stone River and began their attack.

Breckinridge's division was almost wholly concentrated on these few regiments, and they were finally driven in confusion across the river.

On the west side of the river the greatest activity had prevailed in the meantime. Captain John Mendenhall, chief of artillery of the left wing, as he was riding with General Crittenden on the Nashville Pike, had observed the advance of Breckinridge. Immediately he galloped from battery to battery, and in an incredibly short time many pieces of artillery were massed on the elevated ground northwest of the position where the fighting was taking place.

Imagine the eagerness of the cannoneers of these fifty-eight guns for the moment to arrive when our troops should be out of the way, and they could open on the enemy's massed columns. Standing near one of the batteries, one could see blue-coated men running with all their might, closely followed by a dense mob of butternut-clothed troops, who were cheering and yelling and almost crazy with delight. A few shells shot over our men fell into their ranks; but they rushed wildly forward, caring nothing for the few that fell. A few moments later the Rebels had reached the river and stood face to face with our artillery.

What a carnival of death followed! What a deafening noise all around! Cheers here; yells there! Suddenly the ground shook as if rocked by a fearful earthquake, and the fifty-eight cannons emptied their double-shotted contents on this living human mass in front of them; but a few seconds intervened, and again and again the fifty-eight cannons spread death into Breckinridge's men. The enemy halted. The yells, the cheers grew fainter and fainter and at last ceased. Look at them! See how many throw up their arms; see how they fall over; see the large gaps in this mass of men where the shells and canister plow through it; look at the quivering bodies, at the streams of life's blood flowing from a thousand wounds! It was a scene that made the heart sick and touched a spring of sympathy in the souls of all, though the men that were suffering and dying were enemies.

This fight could not last long. Every effort of Breckinridge's men to take these batteries or cross the river was in vain, though the Confederate officers, after reaching the river bank, tried with great gallantry to form their men into line, preparatory to a charge.

It took but a short time, and our colonel, without waiting for orders, ordered our men started across the river.

When the Confederates saw this attack, consternation took the place of their enthusiasm of a few minutes ago, and this same great Rebel mass that had come on yelling like madmen at their supposed victory, suddenly turned and, terror-stricken, sought safety in flight.

The enthusiasm of the Union troops was unbounded. All the regiments became intermingled, and a great deal of irregular straggling, or running towards the front, was the result. Finally darkness overtook our men in the pursuit of the enemy, and the troops were halted.

Thus ended the battle on January 2; only an hour and twenty minutes had elapsed from the time of the advance of the Rebels till they reached their line again in a perfect rout.

Their infantry was so demoralized that there was nothing in the way to have prevented the Federals from marching into Murfreesboro that night.

General Hascall remained highly critical of Rosecrans' ability as displayed in this battle and, incidentally, also gave his idea as to what caused Bragg to leave his strong position and yield the town of Murfreesboro to his opponent.

On the morning of the third day, January 3, or rather, during the forenoon of that day, the stragglers from the right, from the first day's battle, who had not stopped in their flight until they reached Nashville, began to return in large numbers, in companies, and even regiments, and Bragg, observing this, concluded we were receiving large bodies of reinforcements from the north and therefore concluded to fall back and give up the contest. He accordingly did so, and on the fourth day, January 4, we took possession of Murfreesboro without the firing of a gun. Thus ended the great battle of Stone River. We had not made a single attack during the whole time; were badly beaten and well-nigh driven from the field the first day, and only saved from an ignominious retreat upon Nashville by the ridiculous misconception on the part of

Rosecrans. As it was, we lost all our transportation by sending it to the rear, that night, preparatory for the retreat, the whole having been burned by the Rebels at Lavergne, notwithstanding we were supposed to have some cavalry in our rear. Where it was at the time our transportation was being burned by the Rebel cavalry, I have never heard.

Here is the quaint story of a Southern boy, Bromfield L. Ridley, who lived near the battlefield and tried to do his part to further the downfall of the hated Yankees.

I was a boy of seventeen when the great Battle of Murfreesboro (Stone River) was fought.

The battle ground was six miles southwest from my home. The location in the disputed territory gave me a better opportunity for taking in the situation, than to one who was in the front or rear. I had brothers in Morgan's cavalry, and a brother in Bragg's army, and my father's home was, of course, the rendezvous of many on our side.

It was before the "cradle and grave act" of Congress, enlisting persons eligible to soldiers from sixteen to fifty, and I was one of what was known as the "Seed Corn of the South," too young to be called on for service, the limit being eighteen.

The result of Bragg's assault in the morning of December 31 was the rout of the Federal right wing, and it would have been of Rosecrans' whole army, had it been vigorously followed up. To show that this was so, those of us in the rear picked up stragglers fleeing in every direction. A number of us got over 200 during the battle and marched them to our pickets. They came down the west side of the river in squads, and when we would halloo, "Halt!" up would go a white handkerchief.

By the way of parenthesis, let me tell of one Yankee officer, who was different and saved the ammunition train of the Federal army from the holocaust of Wednesday's fight. He was Captain G. P. Thruston. After saving the train he met an officer of General Rosecrans' staff and told him to inform the general that the ammunition train of the right wing, seventy-five wagons, had been brought by him across the country in safety and was at the command of the army.

The staff officer, excited by the unexpected news, hastened to tell the commander, and General Rosecrans dashed down to where the captain stood. "Where is the man who said that the ammunition train was saved?"

Thruston said, "I am the man."

"Who are you?"

"G. P. Thruston, 1st Ohio Volunteer Infantry."

"Had you charge of the train and guard?"

"I had, sir."

"What is your rank?"

"Captain."

"Well sir, consider yourself promoted for gallantry to the rank of major."

General McCook was so impressed at G. P. Thruston's rescue of his ordnance train, that he had him made his chief of staff of the 20th Army Corps, with the rank of lieutenant colonel, and in this way Thruston was showered with two commissions in one day. Later, the former Captain Thruston grew to a brigadier general.

Among the stragglers whom the "Seed Corn Contingent" was picking up appeared a lieutenant colonel with his eagles and epaulets. He was on a good horse and had a pair of fine holsters. Two of us, anxious for big game, commanded him to surrender, but that fellow went for his navies, and, fearing that our little six-shooters were too small, we "withdrew" but, after picking up a few more boys, followed on and took him. That colonel was six miles from the battlefield, and a Federal officer told me after the war that he was cashiered for cowardice.

Thursday came, and every moment's delay was death to the ultimate success of Southern arms. The suspense made us restless about the result, but stragglers from the Federal lines did not diminish.

Friday night my father, who had been watching the battle, returned and said that our army would retire.

We boys went through the form of paroling our prisoners. After the war we received a letter from one of those Yanks, wanting a certificate of parole, having mislaid the one we had given him. They were accusing him up North of desertion in a race for the legislature. But we could not help him, as of course we had never been empowered to issue paroles in the first place.

Stone River was rated a great Union victory by the Northern press. General Sheridan analyzed its results coolly and pointed out to what extent the outcome of the battle influenced the future course of the war.

General Rosecrans occupied Murfreesboro on the fourth and fifth, having gained a costly victory which was not decisive enough in its character to greatly affect the general course of the war, though it somewhat strengthened and increased our hold on Middle Tennessee. The enemy in retiring did not fall back very far—only behind Duck River to Shelbyville and Tullahoma—and but little endeavor was made to follow him. Indeed, we were not in condition to pursue, even if it had been the intention at the outset of the campaign.

Rosecrans had carried into the action about 42,000 officers and men. He lost 13,230, or thirty-one and a half percent. Bragg's effective force was 37,800 officers and men; he lost 10,306, or nearly twenty-eight percent.

Though our victory was dearly bought, yet the importance of gaining the day at any price was very great. Had Bragg followed up the successful attack on our right wing—and there seems no reason why he should not have done so—the army of Rosecrans still might have got back to Nashville, but it would have been depleted and demoralized to such a degree as to unfit it for offensive operations for a long time afterward. To cap the climax of his errors, Bragg directed Breckinridge to make the assault from his right flank on January 2, with small chance for anything but disaster, when the real purpose in view could have been accomplished without the necessity of any offensive maneuver whatever.

The victory quieted the fears of the West and Northwest, destroyed the hopes of the secession element in Kentucky, renewed the drooping spirits of East Tennesseans and demoralized the disunionists in Middle Tennessee.

Nashville was firmly established as our base for future operations. Kentucky was safe from the possibility of being again overrun, and Bragg, thrown on the defensive, was compelled to give his thoughts to the protection of the interior of the Confederacy and the security of Chattanooga, rather than indulge in schemes of conquest north of the Cumberland River. While he still held on in Middle Tennessee, his grasp was so much loosened that only a slight effort would be necessary to push him back into Georgia.

A correspondent of the *Chicago Evening Journal*, Benjamin F. Taylor, visited the Stone River battlefield a year later and gave vent to some philosophical meditations.

It took ten tons of ammunition to fight the battle of Stone River, and here is Murfreesboro as calm as if it had always lain in the lap of peace. Asleep in the April sun of '64 lies the broken field of Stone River, the little thread of water working its winding way between high banks to the north.

Standing here today, I cannot clearly trace the lines of fire in the terrible geometry of battle. In this lazy air I can hardly think how right over my head the curtains of thunder had been shaken to the top of heaven.

How swiftly the plowshare follows the sword. Horses that thundered bravely on in a charge of cavalry are now going soberly to and fro along the glistening furrows.

> The Southern author De Leon was unable to take a similar view. Thirty years later he still was dismayed at the way Bragg had nullified the success of the first day's fighting by ordering Breckinridge's foolhardy attack.

On into the Valley of the Shadow they strode; thinned, reeling, broken under that terrible hail. And the crest was won! But over two thousand noble fellows lay stiff, writhing with fearful wounds, thick upon the path. And then the army fell back! Broken was the goblet of victory, wasted the wine of life; and it was small surcease to the sob of the widow and the moan of the orphan that "the retreat to Tullahoma was conducted in good order."

CHAPTER 12

Dark Days for the North

THE BATTLE OF FREDERICKSBURG

McClellan's success at Antietam in turning back Lee's invasion had not changed the hostile attitude of the War Department, but two weeks later he was given an unexpected opportunity to consult with Lincoln alone, neither Stanton nor Halleck being present.

On the first day of October the President honored the Army of the Potomac with a visit and remained several days. We had many and long consultations. He more than once assured me that he was fully satisfied with my whole course from the beginning; that he regarded me as the only general in the service capable of organizing and commanding a large army, and that he would stand by me against "all comers"; that he wished me to continue my preparations for a new campaign, not to stir an inch until fully ready, and when ready to do what I thought best, and that I should be let alone.

He had hardly reached Washington, however, before a strange order from General Halleck reached me. A singular commentary on the uncertainty of human affairs! The order was as follows:

Oct. 6. The President directs that you cross the Potomac and give battle to the enemy or drive him south. Your army must move now while the roads are good. You will immediately report what line you adopt and when you intend to cross the river; the Secretary of War and the general in chief fully concur with the President in these instructions.

Did they not know that a large part of our troops were in want of shoes, blankets, and other indispensable articles, notwithstanding all the efforts that had been made since the battle of Antietam, and even prior to that date, to refit the army?

General George Meade, who subsequently led the Union Army at Gettysburg, at that time commanded a division. In private letters to his wife and son, he hinted at his suspicion that vital supplies for the army were being withheld on purpose.

Camp near Sharpsburg, October 23, 1862.

We have been detained here by the failure of the Government to push forward reinforcements and supplies. You will hardly believe me when I tell you that as early as the 7th of this month a telegram was sent to Washington informing the Clothing Department that my division wanted 3,000 pairs of shoes, and that up to this date not a single pair has yet been received (a large number of my men are barefooted), and it is the same thing with blankets, overcoats, etc., also with ammunition and forage. What the cause of this unpardonable delay is I cannot say, but certain it is that someone is to blame, and that it is hard the army should be censured for inaction, when the most necessary supplies for their movement are *withheld*, or at least not promptly forwarded when called for.

In spite of all handicaps, however, McClellan did cross into Virginia on October 26, 1862, with a well-laid campaign plan. His first moves were propitious. Then, with unexpected suddenness, his hopes crashed. (See map, page 338.)

The plan of campaign I finally adopted was to move the army parallel to the Blue Ridge, taking Warrenton as the point of direction for the main army, seizing each pass on the Blue Ridge by detachments as we approached it, and guarding them as long as they would enable the enemy to trouble our communications.

It was my intention either to separate the enemy's army and beat them in detail, or else force them to concentrate as far back as Gordonsville, and thus place the Army of the Potomac in position either to adopt the Fredericksburg line of advance upon Richmond or to be moved to the Peninsula.

The army was thus massed near Warrenton, ready to act in any required direction, perfectly in hand and in admirable condition and spirits. I doubt whether, during the whole period that I commanded the Army of the Potomac, it was in such excellent condition to fight a great battle.

On November 7 late at night I was sitting alone in my tent, writing to my wife. Suddenly someone knocked on the tent pole, and, upon my invitation to enter, there appeared Major General Burnside and General C. P. Buckingham, both looking very solemn. After a few moments Buckingham handed me the order of which he was the bearer:

> Headquarters of the Army,
> Washington, Nov. 5, 1862.
>
> General: On receipt of the order of the President, sent herewith, you will immediately turn over your command to Maj.-Gen. Burnside, and repair to Trenton, N. J., reporting on your arrival at that place, by telegraph, for further orders.
>
> H. W. HALLECK, Gen.-in-Chief.

I read the paper with a smile, immediately turned to Burnside and said, "Well, Burnside, I turn the command over to you."

The army was so furious about McClellan's dismissal that it trembled on the verge of mutiny. This is how the action of the government affected a soldier in the 118th Pennsylvania Volunteers.

On the seventh a War Department order relieved Major General McClellan from duty in command of the Army of the Potomac. The publication of this announcement had a startling effect. With armies actively in the field the emotional is unheard of. But for McClellan there had grown such an affection that a total severance of his authority savored of disruption. No other commander ever so captured his soldiers, ever so entranced his followers. Sweeping denunciation, violent invective, were heaped without stint on the government. Subdued threats of vengeance, mutterings of insurrection slumbered in their incipiency but, restrained by good sense, patriotism and discipline, they never reached consummation in overt act. The mails teemed with correspondence to friends and relatives at home denouncing the action of the War Department, raging at the authorities.

A sadder gathering of men could not well have been assembled than that of the army drawn up to bid farewell to its beloved commander. Our corps was reviewed in the morning and, as General McClellan passed along its front, whole regiments broke and flocked around him, and with tears and entreaties besought him not to leave them, but to say the word and they would soon settle matters in Washington. Indeed, it was thought at one time there would be a mutiny, but by a word he calmed the tumult and ordered the men back to their colors and their duty. He was obliged to halt in front of us, as Meagher's Irish brigade were pressing on him so that further progress was impossible. They cast their colors in the dust for him to ride over but, of course, he made them take them up again. Another general who was riding near McClellan was forced by the crowd toward our line, and I heard him say that he wished to God that McClellan would put himself at the head of the army and throw the infernal scoundrels at Washington into the Potomac. At twelve noon McClellan met the officers and bade them goodby, and as he grasped each officer by the hand there was not a dry eye in the assemblage. Before parting he made a short address, in which he urged on us all to return to our respective commands and do our duty to our new commander as loyally and as faithfully as we had served him.

A letter from General Meade to his wife shows that the indignation of the rank was shared in higher quarters.

Camp near Warrenton, Va., Nov. 8, 1862.
The army is filled with gloom and greatly depressed. Burnside, it is said, wept like a child, and is the most distressed man in the army, openly says he is not fit for the position, and that McClellan is the only man we have who can handle the large army collected together, 120,000 men.

Burnside at once discarded McClellan's plan and substituted for it one of his own. He proposed to cross the Rappahannock and make a surprise attack on Fredericksburg, establish a bridgehead there and threaten Lee's communications. The plan received the full endorsement of the War Department as being in conformity with their pet idea of marching against Richmond in a straight line, regardless of natural and man-made obstacles.

Some strategists in the Northern army, however, were beset with grave doubts. Here is what General Meade, writing to his wife, thought of Burnside's plan.

Camp near Stafford Court House, Va.,
November 22, 1862.

It was most trying to read the balderdash in the public journals about being in Richmond in ten days. I predict, unless we have a cold spell, freezing the ground, that we will break down and if the enemy are at all energetic, meet with a check, if not disaster. All this comes from taking the wrong line of operations, the James River being the true and only practicable line of approach to Richmond. But I have always maintained that Richmond need not and should not be attacked at all; that the proper mode to reduce it is to take possession of the great lines of railroad leading to it from the south and southwest, and their army will be compelled to evacuate it and meet us on the ground we can select ourselves. The blind infatuation of the authorities at Washington, sustained, I regret to say, by Halleck, who as a soldier ought to know better, will not permit the proper course to be adopted, and we shall have to take the consequences.

The Union General Otis O. Howard was then a division commander in Sumner's corps. He describes how Burnside's campaign was muffed at its very beginning.

On November 17 our grand division, Sumner himself close to the front and full of his accustomed sanguine hope, began to descend in plain sight of Fredericksburg. Seeing our troops coming steadily on, the Confederates abandoned the shore line and fled.

An officer saw a steer wade slowly across to the north bank of the Rappahannock. This being reported to Sumner, he dispatched a letter to Burnside, asking permission to cross immediately and seize the heights beyond the city. Burnside, however, decided that the risk of crossing before his bridges were in sight would be too great. "No, Sumner," he said; "wait for the pontoons."

Forty thousand men could have crossed before dark on that day, made a strong bridgehead on the lower plane of the right bank and entrenched Marye's Heights against Lee's approach.

The story of the moving of the bridge train to our front at Falmouth is a strange one. It seems to indicate that Halleck himself was playing a part, possibly hoping to get Burnside well into winter quarters without anybody being particularly to blame.

As it required thirteen days to do a piece of work which could easily have been done in three days, it would be a marvelous stretch of charity to impute it to mere bungling.

Of course, it was now plain to Burnside that his primary plan had been defeated. Goaded by his disappointment and spurred by popular expectation, he decided to move down the river fourteen miles, surprise the enemy and effect a crossing at that point. But Lee was too vigilant for that. Seeing this, Burnside's second project also was necessarily abandoned.

Then, suddenly, our general took a new thought. It was to move straight forward upon the enemy's works.

Lee, who could hardly have dreamed of our crossing in his direct front, must have smiled at our folly

There was already murmuring among the officers. Some sharply condemned the change of commanders and openly expressed distrust of Burnside.

Thus pressed with the shafts of bitterness, having neither warm sympathy nor kindly advice, Burnside steeled himself to leave everything to the maze of battle and went on to prepare the way for the sacrifice.

When the pontoon bridges finally arrived, a brigade of Confederate sharpshooters occupying the houses on the opposite bank of the Rappahannock disputed the crossing. Thereupon Burnside served notice that he would bombard Fredericksburg and ordered immediate evacuation by the civilian population.

The cannonade began shortly, and the Confederate artillery replied, making the laying of the bridges hazardous and costly. A private in a Pennsylvania regiment was watching the progress of this military undertaking.

The engineers and pontoniers were at a difficult and perilous task. Every house on the riverbank had its riflemen, and small earthworks had been constructed for others whom the houses could not shelter. Each attempt to lay the boats was met with terrific and fatal volleys; the loss was appalling. In sheer desperation, the afternoon well spent, the engineers had sought shelter on the edge of the river. The pontoon boats, dismounted from their wagons, lay useless on the shore. Suddenly bodies of men, pelted as relentlessly as were the engineers, rushed to the shore. Regardless of their terrible loss, they took their places in the boats and pushed them into the stream.

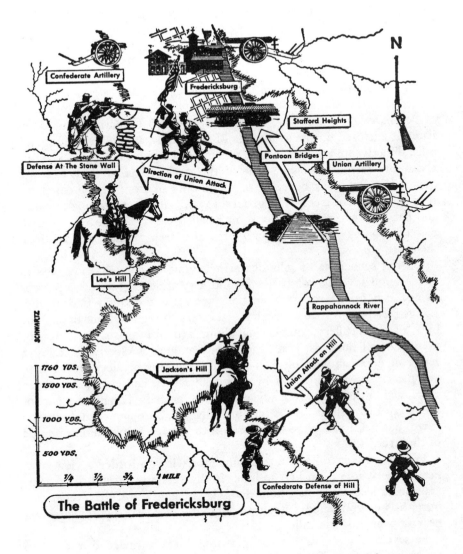

Confederate Artillery

Fredericksburg

Stafford Heights

Pontoon Bridges

Union Artillery

Defense At The Stone Wall

Direction of Union Attack

Lee's Hill

N

SCHWARTZ

Rappahannock River

1760 YDS.

1500 YDS.

1000 YDS.

Jackson's Hill

Union Attack on Hill

500 YDS.

1/4   1/2   3/4   1 MILE

Confederate Defense of Hill

The Battle of Fredericksburg

From the river, hills rise, with the forbidding Marye's Heights on
the north. Could an army scale them in the teeth of enemy artillery and rifle fire?

The laying of the bridges soon followed, but it was late in the afternoon before they were fitted for a passage.

From the hills on the opposite side of the Rappahannock, the Confederate officer Heros von Borcke viewed the situation with mixed emotions and jotted down some of his observations.

December 11, 1862. The little valley in which Fredericksburg is situated is enclosed on the south side of the Rappahannock by a range of hills, directly opposite the town, which are known as Marye's Heights and approach within half a mile of the river. Most of these hills are covered with a thick copse of oak, and only in front of the town are they quite bare of trees. The ground toward the Rappahannock is open and flat, is intersected only by some small streams and is broken immediately upon the river by several large and deep ravines, which afford shelter to troops.

On this semicircle of hills our army, numbering in all about 80,000 men, rested in order of battle behind a continuous line of entrenchments, concealed from the enemy's view by the thick underwood. Longstreet's corps formed the left, Jackson's the right of our lines. The bulk of the artillery, numbering about 250 pieces, was well distributed. On its northern bank the Rappahannock is closely lined by a range of commanding hills, on which the hostile artillery, more than 300 pieces, some of them of heavier caliber than had ever before been employed in the field, were advantageously posted. The greater part of them, especially those on the Stafford Heights, bore immediately on the town, but nearly all were in a position to sweep the plains on our side of the river.

We found General Lee on an eminence which afforded a view over nearly the whole plain before him. Longstreet and several other generals were also assembled here, looking anxiously toward Fredericksburg, as yet concealed from their sight by a dense fog which hung heavily over the little valley.

So several hours passed wearily away. Already the road leading up to the heights from Fredericksburg was thronged with a confused mass of fugitives, bearing with them such of their effects as they could bring away. Ten o'clock came, and the hammers of the church clocks were just sounding the last peaceful stroke of the hour, when suddenly, at the signal of a single cannon shot, more than 150 pieces of artillery, including some of the enemy's most ponderous guns, opened their iron mouths with a terrific roar and hurled a tempest of destruction upon the devoted town. The air shook, and the very earth beneath our feet trembled at this deafening cannonade, the heaviest that had ever yet assailed my ears. The thick fog still prevented us from obtaining a satisfactory view of the bombardment; but the howling of the solid shot, the bursting of the shells, the crashing of the missiles through the thick walls and the dull sound of falling houses united in a dismal concert of doom. Very soon the site of the unhappy town was indicated, even through the fog, by a column of smoke and dust and the flames of burning buildings. Our batteries did not respond to the guns of the enemy. It was evident that nothing could be done to save the place. The horrible din lasted two hours and was succeeded by perfect silence—the silence of solitude. About noon the sun, breaking through the clouds, seemed to mock the smoking ruins it revealed. Every heart of the thousands of brave Confederate soldiers who witnessed this spectacle burned for revenge.

General Lee knew very well that he would not be able to prevent the passage of the river by the Federal army and, having entertained from the beginning no idea of seriously contesting this, he now gave orders for Barksdale's brigade, which had furnished the sharpshooters on the shore, to withdraw gradually and to keep up only a feigned resistance. During the rest of the afternoon and evening the Federal army commenced to move over to our side of the river.

We exchanged felicitations on the great blunder of the Federal commander in preparing to attack us in a position of our own choice. Even the face of our great commander Lee, which rarely underwent any change of expression at the news of either victory or disaster, seemed to be lighted up with pleasure at every fresh report that a greater number of the enemy had crossed the river.

The Confederates questioned the military necessity of destroying Fredericksburg, and their feelings were well expressed by Major Robert Stiles, who witnessed the holocaust.

I saw then and see now no justification for the bombardment. True, the town was occupied by armed men, but the fire did not drive them out; it did drive out the women and children. I never saw a more pitiful procession than they made trudging through the deep snow as the hour drew near. I saw little children tugging along with their doll babies, holding their feet up carefully above the snow, and women so old and feeble that they could carry nothing and could barely hobble themselves. There were women carrying a baby in one arm and its bottle, clothes and covering in the other. Some had a Bible and a toothbrush in one hand, a picked chicken and a bag of flour in the other. Most of them had to cross a creek swollen with winter rains and deadly cold with winter ice and snow. We took the battery horses down and ferried them over, taking one child in front and two behind, and sometimes a woman or a girl on either side with her feet in the stirrups, holding on by our shoulders. Where they were going we could not tell, and I doubt if they could.

> On December 11 the crossing of Burnside's army was in full swing. At least one Union officer, General Regis de Trobriand, entered the battle with the vague premonition that the setting for a great slaughter could scarcely have been better chosen.

General Burnside's first plan, to force a passage several miles below Fredericksburg, having failed, he resolved to meet in front the obstacle which he could not turn.

On the evening of December 10 the order arrived to hold ourselves ready to march the next morning. "This time," it was said, "the dance is going to begin."

The night was full of suppressed agitation and of those distant rumors which denote preparations for battle. The fires remained burning longer than usual. In different directions was heard the rolling of wagons going to the rear and of cannon going to the front. Confused noises indicated the march of regiments changing position. Their bayonets flashed through the obscurity, lighted up by the bivouac fires.

We were awakened at daybreak by the sound of the cannon. Every one was quickly on foot. The men hastened to swallow their hot coffee.

At half past seven our division drew near the river and was held in reserve behind the Stafford Heights, which were crowned by artillery. Under their protection, and favored by a thick fog, the head of our columns began to occupy the city.

On the twelfth the different corps continued to cross the Rappahannock, Sumner on the right, Franklin on the left. The two corps commanded by Hooker. forming the center, were the last to cross. On both sides the sharpshooters were exchanging fire, and the artillery duel continued; no serious action occurred.

December 13, 1862, was a day as radiant as a fete day. Our brigade was already massed on the summit of the hill, arms stacked, awaiting its turn to cross the river. Some of the men, careless and with loud cries, were chasing frightened rabbits through the bushes.

From this point the view was splendid. At our feet the river was spanned by two bridges of boats, across one of which defiled the infantry, and across the other the cavalry and the artillery. We looked at the regiments as they marched out on the plain to take their place in order of battle in front of the enemy's positions, which arose by steps at the back of the picture. On the left the view extended to the horizon, which was spotted with little clouds, the nature of which we well knew. It was Franklin, who was throwing some shells at Stuart's cavalry. We could easily distinguish in that direction the crackling of the skirmishers' shots, emphasized by the firing of the cannon. And on the right a projecting hill concealed Fredericksburg from our view and we were able to see only the steeples. But farther on clearly appeared above the fog a line of heights, covered with entrenchments and bristling with cannon.

When our turn came to descend into the arena, I thought involuntarily of the gladiators of old, entering into the amphitheater in the presence of Caesar. *Morituri te salutamus!* "We who are about to die salute thee!"

Jesse B. Young kept notes of his impressions while he marched into the battle.

Early Saturday morning we were up and stirring about again in the fog. The firing had begun. The attack had been made upon the Rebel entrenchments by the troops already on the other side of the river, and orders were received from our brigade to cross and join in the action.

On the way over I noticed here and there packs of cards and empty whisky bottles strewn by the roadside. Soldiers did not relish the idea of being shot with packs of the one or flasks of the other on their persons.

Down to the bridge the command marched and were led across the river. "Boys, we are in for it now," said the soldiers one to another.

As they crossed an aide came galloping up with news from the left.

General Franklin had advanced against the hill, had not been supported aright and had been pressed back again to the river. The sounds of a fearful struggle were still heard in that direction.

Now the firing grew heavier and louder just back of the town. As the troops marched over the bridge and up into the town their faces looked serious enough. Here and there, however, was some irrepressible joker who, even amid such circumstances, would keep all about him in a roar of laughter. One of these kept up a running comment all the while: "Who would not be a soldier? Terms, 'thirteen dollars a month.' . . . They have started dancing tunes—the Confederate waltz, the Fredericksburg polka, the Stonewall Jackson round dance."

The brigade was somewhat sheltered by the houses while in the town, but every man knew that in a few moments they might be ordered out into the open fields, where the works would have to be stormed, and the dreadful heights faced and assaulted. The very thought was a trying one.

The streets in the town were deserted. Now and then for a moment a soldier would appear and then suddenly vanish. I soon found out the reason—the Confederates were sweeping the streets with artillery, having secured the range of them from the hills beyond.

On every bluff and ridge about the whole amphitheater of hills cannon were ranged, which were all firing at once. Down in the hollow—in the pit of the theater, as it were—scattered here and there over the uneven ground were detachments of Union troops. From all directions at once a rain of fire and death was sweeping in upon them.

The Confederate right wing was commanded by Stonewall Jackson. Heros von Borcke left a day-to-day description of the fighting on that part of the field.

December 12, 1862. The enemy seemed busy as bees. Interminable columns of infantry, blue in color and blurred by distance, flowed toward us like the waves of a steadily advancing sea. On and on they came, with flash of bayonets and flutter of flags, to the measure of military music, and we could distinctly observe them deploy into line of battle.

About eleven o'clock I was asked by General Stuart to accompany him on a ride along our line of battle. It was a pleasure and an encouragement to pass the extended lines of our soldiers, who were lying carelessly behind their earthworks or actively engaged in throwing up new ones—some cooking, others gaily discussing the designs of the enemy, and greeting with loud cheers of derision the enormous shells, which they called "Yankee flour barrels," as these came tumbling into the woods around them. The fog was rolling up again from the low swampy grounds.

December 13. Jackson had chosen his position on an eminence, within a few hundred yards of Hamilton's Crossing, which rose above the general elevation of the ridge in a similar manner to Lee's Hill on the left, and which has ever since borne the name of "Jackson's Hill." Jackson and Stuart concurred in the opinion that it would be the best plan to make a sudden general attack upon the enemy under cover of the fog, but General Lee had decided in council of war against any offensive movement.

Nine o'clock came, and still the vaporous curtain overhung the plateau, still the brooding silence prevailed, when suddenly it seemed as though a tremendous hurricane had burst upon us, and we became sensible upon the instant of a howling tempest of shot and shell hurled against our position from not fewer than 300 pieces of artillery. Hundreds of missiles of every size and description crashed through the woods, breaking down trees and scattering branches and splinters in all directions.

And now the thick veil of mist that had concealed the plain rolled away, like the drawing up of a drop scene at the opera, and revealed to us the countless regiments of the Federal army forming their lines of attack. At this moment I was sent by Stuart to General Jackson with the message that the Yankees were about to commence their advance. I found old Stonewall standing at ease on his hill, unmoved in the midst of the terrible fire, narrowly observing the movements of the enemy through his field glass. The atmosphere was now perfectly clear, and from this eminence was afforded a distant view of more than two-thirds of the battlefield, a military panorama the grandeur of which I had never seen equaled. On they came, in a beautiful order, as if on parade, a moving forest of steel; on they came, waving their hundreds of regimental flags, which relieved with warm bits of coloring the dull blue of the columns and the russet tinge of the wintry landscape, while their artillery beyond the river continued the cannonade with unabated fury over their heads and gave a background of white fleecy smoke, like midsummer clouds, to the animated picture.

I could not rid myself of a feeling of depression and anxiety as I saw this innumerable host steadily moving upon our lines, which were hidden by the woods, where our artillery maintained as yet a perfect silence, General Lee having given orders that our guns should not open fire until the Yankees had come within easy canister range. Upon my mentioning this feeling to Jackson, the old chief answered me in his characteristic way, "Major, my men have sometimes failed *to take* a position, but *to defend* one, never!"

In a few minutes solid shot were plowing at short range with fearful effect through the dense columns of the Federals. The boldness of the enterprise and the fatal accuracy of the firing seemed to paralyze for a time and then to stampede the whole of the extreme left of the Yankee army, and terror and confusion reigned there during some minutes; soon, however, several batteries moved into position and, uniting with several of those on the Stafford Heights, concentrated a tremendous fire upon our guns.

The thunder soon rolled all along our lines, while from the continuous roar the ear caught distinctly the sharp, rapid rattling volleys of the musketry, especially in the immediate front of General A. P. Hill, where the infantry were very hotly engaged. At intervals above the tumult of the conflict we could hear the wild hurrah of the attacking hosts of the Federals and the defiant yell of the Confederates as the assault was repulsed.

Along Jackson's lines the fury and tumult of the battle lasted all the forenoon and until two o'clock in the afternoon. A comparative quietude then succeeded, the infantry firing died away, and only an intermittent cannonade was kept up in our immediate front; but from the left opposite Fredericksburg there came to us the heavy boom of artillery and the distant rattle of small arms, and we knew the fight still raged there with undiminished vehemence.

About three o'clock there seemed to be a new movement preparing on the enemy's left, and General Stuart, suspecting it might be a movement on our right flank, ordered me to proceed with twenty couriers to our extreme right and send him a report every five minutes. The view which presented itself to our eyes far exceeded our expectations. The Yankees, not more than a thousand yards distant from us, were evidently preparing for a new advance; reinforcements were moving up at a double-quick and forming into line of battle as they arrived; we saw the Federal lines moving forward to their new attack, which was introduced and supported by a cannonade of several hundred pieces equal in fury to that of the morning.

Two hours of anxiety and doubt passed away, until at five o'clock we saw scattered fugitives straggling to the rear, their numbers augmenting every moment. Finally whole regiments, brigades and divisions, in utter confusion and bewildered flight, covered the plain before us. All discipline was lost for the moment, and those thousands of troops, whom an hour before we had seen advancing in beautiful military order, now presented the spectacle of a stampeded and demoralized mob. Off we now hastened to Jackson, who at once sent to General Lee the request that he might fall upon the enemy and render the victory complete. Our commander in chief, however, adhering to his earlier idea, still objected to a forward movement, for which, in my judgment, the golden moment had now passed, had he inclined to favor it.

About seven o'clock the battle ceased.

General Franklin's attack on Jackson's right wing was piloted by General George Meade and his Pennsylvania division. This is the way the fight looked to General Regis de Trobriand, who participated in the fighting.

It was about noon of December 13, 1862, when we deployed in line of battle in a large field.

This deploying appeared to me to be done with more ostentation than ability. But perhaps it was especially desired to draw the enemy's attention on us, who were only in the second line, and thus divert it from the attacking column, composed of Meade's division of the 1st Corps. In that case we undoubtedly succeeded, judging by the quantity of projectiles we received there while standing with arms at rest.

Soon our guns began to thunder. The shells fell with great noise in the Confederate lines among the trees. Several batteries were posted there, which hastened to reply in the same manner, one especially, the strongest and the most dangerous for our column to attack. It was important to silence it. So it became the principal target for our guns. A veritable avalanche of iron whistled, shrieked, burst and seemed to be about to destroy everything at that point. Yet the battery kept on replying behind a curtain of smoke, crossed by flashes which followed one another without slackening.

At this moment the order was given us to pile our knapsacks and get ready for action. We had scarcely left our position when a fierce musketry fire burst forth where the enemy had formed his first line of entrenchments. Our battle was commenced.

Meade's division was composed exclusively of Pennsylvania regiments. It advanced on a point of woods which extended in front of the line, entered into it without stopping and in an instant swept away everything that it found there. The 1st Brigade, which was in front, advanced then, drove back a few of the enemy's regiments, who fled in disorder, and ascended the wooded slope at their heels. It reached the crest over a second line of works, where the question now was to establish itself firmly. But there it found itself in front of an open space where General Jackson had massed his reserve. Welcomed by a terrible infantry fire in front and a cross fire from a battery, it was forced to halt and soon to fall back precipitately. The 2nd Brigade, attacked on both flanks, advanced with difficulty. The 1st carried it back on its retreat. The 3rd did not hold long, and the whole column fell back pell-mell out of the woods into which it had advanced with so firm a step.

The attack had been made too slowly: instead of rushing on as the Pennsylvanians had done, the 1st Brigade had stopped a short distance away to reply, by a useless fire, to the deadly volleys of the Confederates. The 2nd stopped in the same manner. The 3rd, however, advancing in column to the right of the two others, charged the works with the bayonet and carried them after a short but sharp resistance. It went no farther. It had lost precious time, and Meade's advance was already driven back from the summit of the hill.

When we came to take position in line with the battery, a few regiments still held on but, it was plainly seen, without any advantage. In these circumstances, the general himself being wounded, the line began to melt away and ended by breaking. It was a singular sight. The soldiers who were retiring from the fight crossed the plains to our right singly or in groups. It did not in the least resemble a flight. They marched deliberately, with their guns on their shoulders, quickening the step, but not running, to get out of reach of the balls. Convinced of the uselessness of longer effort, and seeing that the attack had failed, they retired so as not to sacrifice their lives uselessly. In one word, they had had enough of it.

Meade's division had scarcely returned, when behind it a Confederate division came out of the woods like a band of wolves. They descended the slope at a rapid pace and advanced in a confused mass. Immediately our artillery men turned their guns on them. Their élan was weakened, but they still advanced, hoping to capture the guns. At this instant we threw upon them four regiments.

The enemy halted, endeavoring to correct his line to receive them. But, being in the open field, the advantage of his entrenchments was lost. He had already paid so dearly for having left them that the temptation to return to them could not be resisted.

While our right wing pursued the flying enemy, the left found itself suddenly halted by a deep ditch. An increase of the fire proved that the enemy awaited them there. Our men, not being able to pass the ditch, hesitated. Some jumped into it, others fell killed or wounded while endeavoring to get out of it. Officers on horseback galloped right and left, looking for a crossing which did not exist. Of course, the enemy had concentrated the fire of his artillery on this point. In a very short time everything which was not in the ditch would be swept away. They must get back in any way possible, by parts of regiments and by companies. Two-thirds of those who had made the charge in the four regiments did not answer the roll call. How many remained in the ditch, we did not know.

General Longstreet watched this struggle from the opposite side, and wrote a remarkably parallel account of it.

Franklin's 40,000 men, reinforced by part of Hooker's Grand division, were in front of Jackson's 30,000. Their flags, polished arms and beautiful uniforms gave the scene the air of a holiday occasion. Off in the distance were Jackson's ragged infantry, and Stuart's battered cavalry, with their soiled hats and yellow butternut suits.

As the mist rose, Franklin advanced rapidly. Silently Jackson waited, then opened a terrific fire, which threw the Federals into confusion. They again advanced, broke Jackson's line and threatened serious trouble. Jackson's men, however, soon received reinforcements and recovered the lost ground.

Trobriand now again takes up the story.

At this moment a horrible thing happened. The cannonade had set the high grass on fire at several points, and the flames, quickened by light currents of air, extended rapidly on all sides. Despairing cries were heard. They came from the unfortunate wounded left lying on the ground and caught by the flames. Through the smoke they were seen exerting themselves in vain efforts to flee, half rising up, falling back overcome by pain, rolling on their broken limbs, grasping around them at the grass red with their blood and at times perishing in the embrace of the flames. They were between the lines, and no one could help them.

To dislodge the enemy from his position, an attack *en masse* would not have been too much; a partial attack was not enough. The fault was that, after 50,000 men had been put under the command of Franklin, *i.e.*, about half the army, his action was restricted to one single attempt, and the means of carrying it out were quite disproportionate to the result expected.

The main struggle—that part of it by which the battle of Fredericksburg is best known—took the form of an attack against Marye's Heights. Here Lee in person, accompanied by Longstreet, thrilled the men by his presence.

The famous Washington Artillery of New Orleans, the crack artillery regiment of the Southern army, was a keystone in the defense, and one of its gunners, William M. Owen, gave a vivid description of the blood bath which developed in his front.

The Washington Artillery had been assigned to Marye's Hill, which juts out toward the town, forming a sort of salient, and nearer to it than any of the other fortifications.

In front of Marye's Hill is a sunken road, and on the side toward the town is a stone wall about breast high. Before Marye's Hill is a plain, divided up into lots by board fences, with a few cottages and market gardens.

On Marye's Hill the engineers had laid out works for three of our batteries, *en barbette*—that is, with the work only as high as a man's breast, or as the muzzle of a cannon—but we improved on their work by raising the earth higher and arranging embrasures to fire through. Longstreet said, "If we only save the finger of a man, that's good enough."

Officers of other batteries had already dubbed our position a slaughter pen. It might turn out so; but the old war horse, Longstreet, said he hardly thought Burnside would cross here and make a direct attack, but go around our left flank.

The morning of the thirteenth of December we heard the movements of the enemy marching through the fog. The jingling and rattling of accouterments and the commands of the officers, "Forward! Forward, men! Guide center!" were quite distinct.

The cannoneers were at their post and the infantry were trying to peer through the fog, grasping their rifles tightly.

Almost immediately the battle opened in front of Jackson on our right, near Hamilton's Crossing, and the roar was incessant, but our view was obstructed by the fog.

At last the Federal line appeared above the ridge in front of us and advanced. What a magnificent sight it was! It seemed like some huge blue serpent about to encompass and crush us in its folds. The lines advanced at the double-quick, and the alignments were beautifully kept. The board fences enclosing the gardens fell like walls of paper. Instantly the edge of Marye's Hill was fringed with flame. The dreadful work of the Washington Artillery had begun. The boys aimed and fired coolly and deliberately. Nearer and nearer the enemy's line advanced, came within range of canister and we gave it to them. Now the Federals were near enough to the infantry in the sunken road, the Georgians and the North Carolinians, who were unseen by them, for the smoke was beginning to cover the field. All at once the gray line below us rose, and volley after volley was poured into the enemy's ranks. Great gaps appeared; we gave them canister again and again; a few left the ranks—more followed; the lines halted for an instant and, turning, were seen running in great disorder toward the town. The first assault had been met and repulsed. The field before us was dotted with patches of blue.

Another division now advanced in splendid style and, being joined by remnants of the first command, pushed on valiantly to and beyond the point previously reached, and then, in little more than fifteen minutes, like our first assailants was forced back. Of the 5,000 men led into action 2,000 fell in the charge. With them were the Zouaves and the Irish Brigade of Meagher, bearing aloft the green flag with the golden harp of Ireland. The brave fellows came within five and twenty paces of the stone wall but encountered such a fire of shot, canister and musketry as no command was ever known to live through. The result was that two-thirds of this splendid and gallant brigade were left on the field. Another division now came up and again assailed the hill. The enemy, almost massed, moved to the charge heroically and met the withering fire of the Washington Artillery and small arms with great steadiness.

On they came to within less than 150 paces of our lines, but nothing could live before the storm of lead that was hurled at them from this distance. They wavered, broke and rushed headlong from the field. A few, however, more resolute than the rest, lingered under cover of some houses and fences and annoyed us with a scattering but well-directed fire. The 25th North Carolina poured a few volleys into the enemy at a most deadly range and then dashed down the hill and took position.

The enemy, now reinforced by two new divisions, again moved forward. Our infantry held fire until it would be fatally effective. Meanwhile our artillery was again spreading havoc among the enemy's ranks. Still he advanced under the destructive fire of our line and, even more resolute than before, madly pressed on. At length, broken and dismayed, he retreated to the town.

We were fighting under the very eyes of Lee and Longstreet. "Now, boys, do your level best!" A solid rifled cannon ball tore its way through the redoubt, scattering dirt and dust in our faces. One man picked it up and said laughingly, "Boys, let's send this back to them again." An instant later it was in the gun and dispatched on its mission back to the enemy.

We were now so short of men necessary to work our guns that infantry soldiers were called in to help. The ground, which had been frozen hard, was converted into mud and slush, and all hands, officers and men, had to put their shoulders to the wheels to run the guns up to the embrasures.

The last charge against Marye's Hill was made at dusk by Sykes's division of regulars. These troops, out of sheer desperation, charged with the bayonet, but the deadly fire of the artillery and musketry broke it after an advance of fifty yards, and the united efforts of their staffs and other officers could not arrest the retiring mass. Save an occasional cannon shot or the crack of a sharpshooter's rifle, the battle in front of Marye's Hill was over.

A Pennsylvania soldier had the rare good fortune to watch the forenoon's fighting from the hills across the river. His regiment was then called into action and, after a perilous march through the desolated streets of Fredericksburg, stormed against Marye's Heights, where he had seen many previous attacks crumble under the relentless fire of the defenders.

Saturday the thirteenth dawned in an almost impenetrable fog, so dense that, with the smoke of the battle, it made objects close at hand scarcely distinguishable. There was a fear that in a close engagement friends might be mistaken for foes. To avoid such a contingency the watchword "Scott" was given to be used in an emergency.

Between nine and ten o'clock the fog lifted a little and unfolded a scene thrilling in its inspiration and awful in its terror. The streets of the city were literally packed with soldiers, pressing for the open country to seek some relief from the deadly plunge of cannon shots. But there the same batteries on Marye's Heights were again encountered, more formidable than ever and wicked in their determination to punish the temerity that dared assault these entrenchments.

About one o'clock our regiment began the movement to the bridges. It was tedious, halting and hesitating. The bridges were crowded and the streets jammed from the slow deployments under the withering fire which met the fresh victims fed to the slaughter, as the troops in advance reached the open country. It was but a short distance to the bluffs, and then the battle in all its fury was spread out to view. On the slope of Marye's Heights were long lines of blue, formed with regularity, moving with precision, disappearing as speedily as they were seen before the furious cannonade and the deadly musketry. Thought was rife and expression free with the selfish hope that some effective service might be done by those already in to save others from the terrible ordeal. The futility of open assaults was manifest. The disasters which had been plainly seen to follow one another so rapidly were woefully dispiriting. But all such hopes were in vain.

About two o'clock the regiment entered the town. The view from the other side of the river gave but a faint conception of what was within. There was a momentary, irresistible desire to seek some shelter from the havoc of the guns in the deserted houses. It was manfully conquered.

The march was continued under all the dreadful shelling and on toward the farther edge of the city. There was a halt for some time in line of battle, and we closed well up to the sidewalk.

It is seldom that the mettle of men is tested in column in crowded streets, where there can be no resistance, into which, from unseen positions, the artillery strikes its rapid, telling blows and will not and cannot be silenced.

The crucial moment was fast approaching. The head of the column must have been seen; the rapidity of the firing increased; the roar was deafening; shot and shell screeched in maddening sounds; they fell thicker and faster, dropping with wonderful accuracy right into the midst of the column. Every gun seemed trained upon this very street; and so they were, for it was afterward learned that batteries, specially planted for the purpose, raked every highway leading from the river. Two brass guns in action at the end of the street were pounding away vigorously and effectively at the enemy, the gunners holding heroically to their places in spite of the severe punishment they were receiving.

The right of the brigade had now reached an open level space on the left of the road, some 400 yards in width. At its farther edge the ground rose abruptly, as if the earth had been cut away. This perpendicular rise or cut was the extreme base of the slope that approached and terminated in the gun-capped Marye's Heights. The artillery kept playing with unintermitting vigor.

One division had just charged up the hill and, although they had failed to carry the height, hundreds of men lay prone on the ground in fair alignment, apparently too spirited to withdraw entirely from their futile effort. But a closer inspection showed all these men, hundreds in number, to be dead or too seriously wounded to move.

Our regiment still hugged the ground closely where it had first established its line. Instinctively, it began its desperate work of assault. Under the appalling musketry and amid great disorder, the advance was maintained with reasonable regularity to a brickyard, with its kiln standing, through which tore shot and shell, and from which bricks flew in every direction. The little shelter afforded by the kiln had enticed the wounded within its reach to crawl to it for cover, and their mangled, bleeding forms lay strewn everywhere, closely packed together. Sweeping by this, right into the very mouth of the cannon, upward and onward the advance continued to a board fence. The fence was about five feet high, of three boards, with intervals between them. Opposite the center and right the boards had been torn off down to the one nearest the ground. The fatality that had followed the delay in their removal was marked by the bodies of the dead lying there, one upon another. To the left the boards still remained; the men heroically seized and tore them all away, some climbing over. Thinned out, exhausted, with energies taxed to their limit in the face of such fearful odds, instinctively the line halted.

Someone said, "This is awful!"

"This is what we came here for," quietly replied our major as he dismounted.

From the place of the halt to the stone fence, behind which belched the deadly musketry, was between 200 and 300 feet. At that distance, for men halted with little or no cover, the punishment was unbearable.

There were still about two hours of daylight. Some 200 yards to the left, but no greater distance from the stone fence, there was decidedly better cover, and to this undulation, broad enough to include the entire regimental front, the command was moved within a few moments from the time it had halted.

It seems remarkable that men could live at all that close to the enemy's lines, but there the regiment remained all that night, all of Sunday's daylight and well into the night, suffering but few casualties, and those happening principally when necessity forced exposure, or temerity prompted rashness. But safety was found only in hugging the ground as tight as a human body could be made to hold onto the earth.

On Sunday night the regiment was withdrawn to the riverbank. A little after noon General Burnside and his staff rode down to the bridge and passed over. There was always a kindly feeling for Burnside, but now his presence stirred no enthusiasm; his appearance aroused no demonstration. It may have been a coincidence that, as he rode by, he drew his hat farther down over his face. Unuttered thoughts were rife that somebody had seriously blundered.

A colonel under Stonewall Jackson, William C. Oates, revealed in later years an inside story showing that, if Jackson had been allowed his way (and if some apparent good luck on Lee's part had not turned against him), the Battle of Fredericksburg might have had a different and rather sensational ending.

Sometime after dark, I suppose between eight and nine o'clock, a staff officer from General Jackson passed along our lines giving orders to regimental commanders to fix bayonets and move forward the moment that the line to the left began to move. I ordered bayonets to be fixed and the men to get up and stand in line. Within a few minutes I saw the line begin to move and ordered the regiment forward. Of course all knew it meant an attack with the bayonet in the dark, for it was a dark night. It was a desperate and hazardous undertaking. Some men remained in the trench until driven out of it, and I would have preferred to stay in it myself if I could honorably have done so.

But just as we crossed the railroad between us and the Federal lines, we were halted. I had been informed that the origin of that night movement was with General Jackson; that he set his corps in motion and then informed General Lee, who ordered a halt and summoned his generals for a consultation, which was held late that night. Jackson

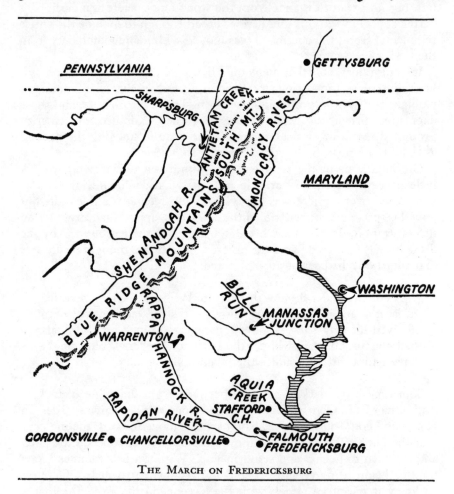

THE MARCH ON FREDERICKSBURG

slept while other generals gave their opinions, and when all were through someone slapped him on the shoulder and said, "Now, General, give us your opinion." He yawned and half asleep mumbled out, "Drive them in the river! Drive them in the river!" and the sequel proved that he was right. Had Lee's whole army advanced to that night attack it would have created a panic which would have driven the Federals into the river or forced the whole army to surrender. It would have been a bloody conflict and a great risk but would have proved an economy of human life in the end.

The reason why General Lee summoned his generals to a council of war was that at about dark one of Longstreet's scouts had captured, on the north side of the river, a courier fresh from General Burnside's headquarters bearing orders to Franklin and Sumner, commanders of two of the grand divisions of the Federal army, directing them to renew their assaults upon the Confederates at daylight the next morning. Longstreet took the captured papers to Lee, and he summoned Jackson and the Hills to a conference. It was there determined, inasmuch as the Federals would renew their attack the next morning, which the Confederates were in as comfortable a position to receive as they could desire, to act on the defensive. When the assaults were repulsed with heavy loss, as they certainly would have been, Longstreet was at that very moment to assume the offensive and throw his whole corps against the Federal right, attacking at right angles with the river, and seize the town and pontoon bridges, while Jackson's corps would advance from Hamilton's Crossing and attack the Federal line squarely in front and at short range. Stuart, with his horse artillery, would operate against the Federal left. By this combination it was believed that Burnside's army could be destroyed or captured. With this understanding they dispersed to their respective headquarters for the night.

But morning came and no attack. Sumner and Franklin had returned a protest against a renewal of the attack as ordered on the ground that their commands had already sustained very severe losses and had accomplished nothing; that to continue to assault the Confederates in their strong defensive positions would destroy the Federal army; that Marye's Heights could not be carried except at an immense sacrifice, and that the cause of the Union would not be advanced thereby. The fact that Sumner, who was always in favor of fighting whenever any possible good could be accomplished by it, protested, shook Burnside's resolution and he countermanded the order.

Burnside's corps and division commanders were convinced that a successful frontal attack against Marye's Heights was a military impossibility. Regis de Trobriand gives us the testimony

of General Sumner before the Committee on the Conduct of the
War. Sumner had commanded the Union center opposite the
heights.

There was line upon line of the fortifications in two or three tiers.
If we had carried the first line, we could not have held it, because the
second line was much stronger and commanded it. Behind that there
were, between the hilltops, great masses of infantry, and, if we had
reached the summit, we would have been obliged to fight these masses
of fresh troops and their batteries.

De Trobriand next described the futile onslaught of French's
and Hancock's divisions. Then Hooker, who had been held in
reserve, was called on to attack with his corps, and we are told
how he reacted to the order, and finally De Trobriand gives his
own opinion of Burnside's obstinacy.

General Hooker was a fighter. He went in gladly where there were
blows to receive, provided he was able to return them. But when he
saw with his own eyes the character of the enterprise entrusted to him,
he understood quickly how it would infallibly result. He took on himself to suspend the attack and sent one of his aides to ask that it should
not be made at that point. The reply was given, to attack in the same
place. Still hoping that the general in chief would yield to evidence,
Hooker himself hurried with the utmost speed to Burnside; but nothing
could affect the obstinate irritation of the latter.

Let us now give the words of General Hooker: "I then returned and
sent in advance all the disposable artillery I could find in the city, to
demolish the enemy's works. I proceeded as I would have done against
fortifications and endeavored to make a breach large enough to give
passage to a *forlorn hope*. I sent two batteries to the left of the road,
and on the right I placed some sections of batteries. All these pieces
were fired with rapidity until sundown, but without apparent effect on
the Rebels or their works.

"When the artillery fire ceased, I gave the signal to attack. General
Andrew Humphreys' men took off their knapsacks, their haversacks
and their overcoats. They received the order to advance with unloaded
muskets, for they had not time either to load or fire. At the command
they charged with the greatest impetuosity. They ran hurrahing, and I
felt encouraged by the great ardor with which they were animated.

"The head of General Humphreys' column reached a point about fifteen or twenty paces from the stone wall which formed the advance line of the Rebels and was then driven back as quickly as it had come. The time taken was probably not fifteen minutes, and it left behind 1,760 men out of 4,000."

Was that enough? No. General Burnside had butted against the obstacle. He even yet thought only of either breaking it in pieces or being utterly broken by it himself.

Night now interposed before another sacrifice could be arranged, and on the following day General Burnside was finally prevailed on to desist. His own statement on this point, made before the Committee on the Conduct of the War, is pathetic.

The two attacks were made and we were repulsed; we were still holding a portion of the ground we had fought on, but not our extreme advance.

That night I went all over the field on our right; in fact, I was with the officers and men until nearly daylight. I found the feeling to be rather against an attack the next morning; in fact, it was decidedly against it.

I returned to my headquarters and, after conversation with General Sumner, told him that I wanted him to order the 9th Army Corps— which was the corps I had originally commanded—to form the next morning a column of attack by regiments. It consisted of some eighteen old regiments and some new ones, and I desired the column to make a direct attack upon the enemy's works. I thought that these regiments, by coming quickly up after one another, would be able to carry the stone wall and the batteries in front, forcing the enemy into their next line, and by going in with them they would not be able to fire upon us to any great extent. I left General Sumner with that understanding and directed him to give the order.

The next morning, just before the column started, General Sumner came to me and said, "General, I hope you will desist from this attack; I do not know of any general officer who approves of it, and I think it will prove disastrous to the army."

Advice of that kind from General Sumner, who had always been in favor of an advance whenever it was possible, caused me to hesitate. I kept the column of attack formed and sent over for the division and corps commanders and consulted with them. They unanimously voted against the attack. I then sent for General Franklin, who was on the left, and he was of exactly the same opinion. This caused me to decide that I ought not to make the attack I had contemplated. And besides, inasmuch as the President of the United States had told me not to be in haste in making this attack; that he would give me all the support that he could, but he did not want the Army of the Potomac destroyed, I felt that I could not take the responsibility of ordering the attack, notwithstanding my own belief at the time that the works of the enemy could be carried.

> J. L. Chamberlain was a minister by profession. He served with the Federal reserves and spent the night after the battle on the bloody grounds, helping the wounded. His description of the misery following the day's fighting is a touching human document.

We had not reached the enemy's fortifications, but only that fatal crest where we had seen five lines cut to earth as by a sword swoop of fire. We had that costly honor which sometimes falls to the reserve—to go in when all is havoc and confusion, through storm and slaughter, to cover the broken and depleted ranks of comrades and take the battle from their hands. Thus we had replaced the gallant few still struggling on the crest, and we received that withering fire which nothing could withstand by throwing ourselves flat in a slight hollow of the ground within pistol shot of the enemy's works; and, mingled with the dead and dying that strewed the field, we returned the fire till it reddened into night and at last fell away through darkness into silence.

But out of that silence from the battle's crash and roar rose new sounds more appalling still—rose or fell, you knew not which, or whether from the earth or air: a strange ventriloquism, of which you could not locate the source, a smothered moan that seemed to come from distances beyond reach of the natural sense, a wail as far and deep and wide as if a thousand discords were flowing together into a keynote weird, unearthly, terrible to hear and bear, yet startling with its nearness. The writhing concord was broken by cries for help, pierced by shrieks of paroxysm. Some begged for a drop of water. Some called on God for pity, and some on friendly hands to finish what the enemy had so horribly begun. Some with delirious, dreamy voices murmured loved names, as if the dearest were bending over them. Some gathered their last strength to fire a musket so as to call attention to them where they lay he'pless and deserted. And underneath, all the time, came that deep bass note from closed lips too hopeless or too heroic to articulate their agony.

Who could sleep, or who would? Our position was isolated and exposed. Officers must be on the alert with their command. Command could be devolved, but pity, not. So with a staff officer I sallied forth to see what we could do where the helpers seemed so few. Taking some observations in order not to lose the bearing of our own position, we guided our steps by the most piteous of the cries. Our part was but little: to relieve a painful posture; to give a cooling draught to fevered lips; to compress a severed artery; to apply a rude bandage, which yet might prolong life; to take a token or farewell message for some stricken home. The farther we went the more the need deepened and the calls multiplied. Numbers, half wakening from the lethargy of death or of despair by sounds of succor, begged us to take them quickly to a surgeon and, when we could not do that, implored us to do the next most merciful service and give them quick dispatch out of their misery. Right glad were we when, after midnight, the shadowy ambulances came gliding along, and the kindly hospital stewards, with stretchers and soothing appliances, let us feel that we might return to our proper duty.

And now we were aware of other figures wandering ghostlike over the field. Some were on errands like our own, drawn by compelling appeals. Some sought a lost comrade with uncertain steps amid the unknown and ever and anon bent down to scan the pale visage closer, perhaps by the light of a brief match whose blue flickering flame scarcely could give the features a more recognizable or more human look. One man, desperately wounded, might with faltering step, before his fast ebbing blood should leave him too weak to move, be seeking to gain a quiet or sheltered spot out of sound of the terrible appeals he could neither answer nor endure, or out of reach of the raging battle that would come with the morning. Another would be creeping, scarcely moving, from one lifeless form to another, if perchance he should find a swallow of water in the canteen still swung from the dead soldier's side. Another, with just returning or just remaining consciousness, would be vainly striving to rise from a mangled heap that he might not be buried with it while yet alive. And still another, though sound of body, might be pacing the ground feverishly because in such a bivouac his spirit could not sleep.

And so we picked our way back amid the stark, upturned faces to our little living line. The night chill had now woven a misty veil over the field. Except the few sentries along the front, the men had fallen asleep—the living with the dead. At last, outwearied and depressed with the desolate scene, my own strength sank, and I lay down to sleep.

Warren Lee Goss, the observing private in the Northern ranks, tells of the battle's aftermath.

On Sunday following the battle a flag of truce was sent into our lines, and parties were permitted to bring in the wounded. The Rebels brought some of our wounded to the neutral ground, where the curious spectacle might be seen of the men of both armies engaged in friendly conversation.

"We 'uns will drive you'ns unto the river tomorrow," said one of them. "Good-by, blue bellies!" said another. "Look out for another big licking tomorrow," said a third. All of this was said in a good-natured, joking manner, rather than that of bitter earnestness.

One of the citizens I met after the battle complained bitterly of the treatment he had received from both armies. He informed me that in the town paintings, mirrors, pianos, furniture and other valuables had been wantonly destroyed, and then set forth his personal grievances by saying, "The Rebel army tuck everything I had, and the Yankees have got the rest!"

On the fifteenth our company went on picket duty. About two o'clock at night, in the sleet and rain, by whose orders I know not, we stealthily crept back toward the river, which our forces had mostly crossed, though up to this time we had had no information of the army's crossing to the opposite bank. If our artillery and heavy teams had not been moved before the rain came on, it is doubtful if they could have easily reached the northern bank, so adhesive is Southern mud. When morning dawned we were boiling our coffee on the other side of the river. In the morning the enemy advanced on the plain and began to plunder and strip the dead and gather up the fragments left in our retreat. The Union artillery opened on them and drove them back.

There was universal despondency. On the other hand, the Rebels were jubilant and believed the Southern Confederacy would be acknowledged and the fighting over in another month.

The moral condition of the army after the battle may be imagined. Gloom pervaded every rank. The feeling was deep and universal that it was of but little use to fight, unless the government could find someone to command who would not throw away our lives in useless experiments. It was evident to the most ordinary soldier in the ranks that we were not inferior in discipline and intelligence to the Rebel rank and file, and fully as brave; but that we were constantly outgeneraled rather than whipped.

That indefinable something which can be neither weighed nor measured, called the *morale* of an army, was seriously impaired. After the battle the soldiers had desire to look over the situation, and all the manifestoes of the world could not convince them that they had not been needlessly sacrificed by attacking the enemy in his chosen position, when that position could have been flanked.

In the midst of this general gloom and discontent we received boxes from home, and read newspapers and made merry over anything we could find to laugh at, with the usual careless gaiety of soldiers.

The correspondent for the *New York Tribune*, A. D. Richardson, talked with General Burnside after the battle and left a record of the interview.

I was not present at the battle but returned to the army two or three days after. Burnside deported himself with rare fitness and magnanimity. As he spoke to me about the brave men who had fruitlessly fallen, there were tears in his eyes, and his voice broke with emotion. When I asked him if anyone else was responsible for the slaughter, he replied:

"No. I understand perfectly well that when the general commanding an army meets with disaster, he alone is responsible, and I will not attempt to shift that responsibility on any one else. No one will ever know how near we came to a great victory. It almost seems to me now that I could have led my old 9th Corps into those works."

Indeed, Burnside had desired to do this. The 9th Corps would have followed him anywhere; but that would have been certain death.

Burnside was, at least, great in his earnestness, his moral courage and perfect integrity.

Every private soldier knew that the Battle of Fredericksburg had been a costly and bloody mistake, and yet I think on the day or the week following it the soldiers would have gone into battle just as cheerfully and sturdily as before. The more I saw of the Army of the Potomac, the more I wondered at its invincible spirit which no disasters seemed able to destroy.

CHAPTER 13

The War on the High Seas

THE BLOCKADE AND THE CONFEDERATE CRUISERS

A few days after his call for troops in 1861 Lincoln inaugurated the blockade—an essential part of the grand strategy of the war. If successfully instituted and maintained, this measure would inevitably strangle the Confederacy. Unable to sustain itself without exports and imports, it must eventually succumb.

To put the blockade into effect, however, was not easy. The editors of *Harper's Weekly*, A. H. Guernsey and Henry M. Alden, stated the two principal obstacles which presented themselves: the unpreparedness of the North and the countermeasures which the Confederates could be expected to adopt.

In a war whose successful termination depended on the exhaustion of the South, the blockade of the Southern ports constituted an important feature. At the beginning the successful blockade of a coast measuring more than three thousand miles seemed utterly out of reach and was not even calculated on by the South as a possible event; and, indeed, it seemed to require some miracle for a nation which, on the first of January, 1861, had but a single war steamer available for the defense of its entire Atlantic coast. But this aspect of the case was delusive. The basis of a navy consists not in ships, but in trained seamen.

However, notwithstanding the 20,000 men directly engaged in our fisheries, and the great number of seamen engaged in naval commerce, there were still great impediments to be removed. In March 1861 the number of navy vessels was only ninety, of which not more than forty-two were in commission. Nearly all those were on foreign stations, the Home Squadron consisting only of twelve vessels, and only four of these were in Northern ports.

Nevertheless, the President promptly laid an embargo on the ports of the seven states then belonging to the Confederacy. This was on the nineteenth of April. On the twenty-seventh he included within the limits of his proclamation the ports of Virginia and North Carolina. To carry these two proclamations into effect, Flag Officer Pendergrast, in command of the Home Squadron, was sent with all the ships available for the purpose of notifying foreigners of the embargo, giving them fifteen days for departure. The commandants of the navy yards in Boston, New York and Philadelphia were directed to purchase and equip suitable steamers. In the meantime the East Indian, Mediterranean, Brazilian and African Squadrons were recalled. Twelve steamers were purchased by the government, and nine more were chartered; and several small vessels which had been captured were taken into the service.

Thus, before July 4, the blockade had been rendered so effective that foreign nations were obliged to recognize its legality.

It was only through privateering that the Confederacy had the means of carrying on the war on the seas. As soon as the President's plan was made known, Jefferson Davis invited applications for letters of marque and reprisal. One difficulty in the way of successfully carrying out this scheme was the blockade, which impeded the egress of privateers, and after their escape prevented their return; the other was the refusal of neutral powers to allow these armed vessels to bring prizes into any of their ports. It was inevitable, however, that some of these cruisers would get out to sea; and this once accomplished, it became impossible for the Federal government to maintain so effective a police as to secure our commerce against the threatened danger.

Acting Master William Jennings recalled some lesser-known facts and episodes connected with the blockade.

First of all, of course, was the work of getting men by a call for volunteers. The call was answered by hosts. Captains and officers of the merchant service were a valuable part of this volunteer force, but so great was the need of officers that not a few men who had never been at sea secured appointments. As an illustration, the first ship I was ordered to on entering the navy was commanded by one who had never been to sea.

The next effort was to issue a call for ships. The department strove to buy everything that could be of service, and the prices charged were outrageously high.

The firm in whose employ I had been were large shipowners. Their ships were sold to the government at fabulous prices. They also built a good many ships and sold them to the government at about 200 percent profit. The senior member, who had known me from boyhood, would pat me on the back and say, "Billy, it is a glorious thing to be patriotic and serve one's country in the time of need." His own son, about my age, was in Europe and stayed there during most of the war. This patriotic father was worth $100,000 when the war commenced, and at the close of the war he died leaving $2,000,000.

By December 1, 1861, the government had bought 137 vessels, of which 58 were sailing vessels. During the war 420 vessels were purchased, and 600 vessels were employed in the blockade before the war ended. At the end of the year 1863 the number of guns afloat amounted to 4,443, and the tonnage of the vessels to 467,967, manned by 50,000 seamen and landsmen.

During the war 1,165 prizes were brought in, of which number 210 were fast steamers. There were also 335 vessels burned, sunk, driven on shore or otherwise destroyed, a total of 1,500. The value of these vessels and their cargoes, according to a low estimate, was equal to $30,000,000.

T. C. DeLeon, of Richmond, looking at the blockade from a Southern point of view, analyzed its possibilities, but also its long-range consequences.

A potent factor in sapping the foundations of Confederate hope and of Confederate credit was the blockade.

First held in contempt; later fruitful mother of errors as to intentions of European powers; ever the growing constrictor whose coil was to crush out our life. It became each year harder to bear.

At first Mr. Lincoln's proclamation was laughed to scorn in the South. The vast extent of South Atlantic and Gulf coast, pierced with innumerable safe harbors, seemed to defy any scheme for hermetic sealing. The limited Federal navy was powerless to do more than keep loose watch over ports of a few large cities, and, if these were effectually closed, it was felt that new ones would open.

This reasoning had good basis at first and, had the South made prompt and efficient use of opportunity and resources at hand, by placing credits abroad and running in essential supplies, the result of the first year's blockade might largely have nullified its effect for the last three. But the very inefficiency of the blockade at the outset lulled the South into false security.

The South misjudged—until error had proved fatal—the enterprise and grit of Yankee character. So gradual were appreciable results of this naval growth, so nearly imperceptible was the actual closing of Southern ports, that the masses of the people realized no real evil until it had long been an accomplished fact.

One reason why the result of the blockade, after it became actually effective, was not earlier realized in the South was that private speculation promptly utilized opportunities which the government had neglected. Private ventures, and even great companies formed for the purpose, made blockade breaking the royal road to riches. Almost every conceivable article of merchandise came to Southern ports, often in quantities apparently sufficient to glut the market and almost always of inferior quality.

Earlier ventures were content with profits of 100 or 200 percent, but as the risk increased and Confederate money depreciated, it became no unusual thing for a successful investment to realize from 1,500 to 2,000 percent on its first cost.

Still, even this profit as against the average of loss—perhaps two cargoes out of five—made the trade hazardous. Only great capital could supply the demand. Hence sprung the great blockade-breaking corporations, like the Bee Company, Collie & Company and Fraser, Trenholm & Company. With capital and credit unlimited, with branches at every point of purchase, with constantly growing orders from the departments—these giant concerns could control the market and make their own terms.

Their growing power soon became quasi dictation to government itself; the national power was filtered through these alien arteries; and the South became the victim, its treasury the mere catspaw, of the selfsame system, which clear sight and medium ability could so easily have averted from the beginning!

A Union officer on a blockading vessel, William H. Anderson, explains why life in this service was not free from vexing problems and annoyances; also how the lure of the elusive prize money tended to undermine military discipline.

It was on the strength of a few decrepit and superannuated hulks that we threw our glove to the world and declared 3,500 miles of coast line to be in a state of effective blockade. This was certainly the very apotheosis of cheek, but it was the only thing that could be done until the gaps could be filled. But filled they were; so, however, were the gaps among the blockade runners; and three years later the race between the hunters and the hunted was on under full hue and cry.

It is estimated that about sixty vessels, constructed especially for this purpose, were engaged in running the blockade off Wilmington and Charleston during the year 1864. Bermuda and Nassau were the principal points of destination and departure, at which points both the inward and outward cargoes were transshipped. These vessels were side-wheelers, from 400 to 600 tons burden, of great speed and with a carrying capacity of from 600 to 1,000 bales of cotton of 500 pounds each. They were built very low in the water, painted a dull gray color and fitted with noiseless paddles; indeed, every device was resorted to in order to make their approach as difficult as possible to discover. With cotton selling at eight cents a pound at Wilmington, and fifty cents a pound at Liverpool, it was no unusual thing to have a successful outward trip bring a clear profit of from $100,000 to $125,000, and the inward trip not very much less. This was a temptation to the cupidity of Englishmen which they could not resist, and all classes of society embarked in it; even officers of the Royal Navy, who were commonly supposed to look with contempt on any occupation that savored of trade, fell over one another in their rush to accept the command of one of these little steamers. The price paid to the commanding officer for a successful round trip was £1,000, and many a retired British naval officer lived in ease and affluence upon the proceeds of his venture in this field.

In the early part of June 1864 I received orders to report for duty on board the *State of Georgia*, then lying off the harbor of Wilmington, North Carolina. For the first time I was on the blockade. The vessels, up and down the coast, were lying in two parallel lines, lazily swinging at their moorings some four or five miles from land, and in the west the grim visage of Fort Fisher frowned on us. As I looked on the trim, clean model of my ship, visions of unlimited prize money rose before me, and, when I got aboard and was told that eight blockade runners were loading at Wilmington, a fortune seemed within my grasp. The next morning by looking across a low spot of land we could see the steamers as they came slowly down the river to wait under the guns of the fort for a favorable night and tide.

I had just turned in when I heard an unusual stirring on deck. As soon as I could get into my clothes I rushed up the companion ladder. A steamer running out had been sighted, and I got a glimpse of her as she whirled past us. Our cable had been slipped, the signal rocket fired in the direction the chase was heading to indicate the position to the other ships, and we were off. I never realized before the agony of being in a slow ship, as some of the clippers of the squadron passed us. Our only hope was in a recent order of the admiral which declared that all vessels within signal distance of the prize when she was captured should share in the prize money, and that signal distance was established at nine miles. So there was nothing for us to do but to keep going all night at our highest speed in the hope of being in at the death at daybreak; and this was the result: at daybreak the prize was about eight miles ahead, with the two fastest vessels of the squadron within a mile of her and having her well in hand. The reason why they didn't pounce on her was evident: they very well knew that three other vessels were within signal distance and would come in for their share. And so they kept the same relative distance from their victim, increasing all the time the distance between them and the three struggling followers, until the signal distance was covered, when they swooped upon their prey, gobbled her up and shut the rest of us completely out.

Earlier in the year when a blockade runner was hard pressed, she would lighten herself by throwing a dozen or more bales of cotton overboard, which we fellows could afford to pick up; and what a struggle there was for the possession of this consolatory flotsam! But even these crumbs from the table were denied us, for they soon instituted the practice of stationing a man at the gangway with an ax, who cut the hoops of the bales before they were committed to the sea, so that the track of the flying steamer was marked for miles with the snowy treasure. My share of prize money for the season was about eighty dollars, while officers of corresponding rank to my own, in faster and more fortunate vessels, realized as much as $20,000.

I can recall many incidents which relieved the dull monotony of life. Captain Dennison, who was a favorite of Admiral Porter then in charge of the squadron, had been given command of the *Cherokee*, a

captured blockade-runner. Porter, wishing some soundings made, ordered Captain Dennison on this important duty. On his way down,
the captain discovered in the gray of the morning a blockade-runner
creeping out. Should he continue on his course in obedience to his
orders, or should he haul off and give chase? He knew that Porter
was a perfect martinet in matters of duty, and he knew also that the
capture of a good fat prize would go a long way in palliation of a
deliberate disobedience of orders. He took the long chance and steered
for the open sea. Before nightfall he was headed for the squadron with
the blockade-runner in tow.

It is said that the admiral threatened to report him for neglect of
duty, but finally recommended him for promotion.

The captains of the blockade-runners usually were allowed
to undertake importations on their own account, which led at
times to queer speculations, as we may glean from an experience
of Captain A. Roberts, one of these seafaring adventurers.

Before leaving for England I met a Southern lady who, on my
inquiring what was most needed by her sex in the beleaguered states,
replied curtly, "Corsages, sir, I reckon." So I determined to buy a lot
of them and, on arriving at Glasgow, I visited an emporium and
astonished a young fellow behind the counter by asking for 1,000
pairs of stays. At the same time I bought 500 boxes of Cockle's pills
and a quantity of toothbrushes.

Well, here I was in Wilmington with all these valuables on my
hands; the corsages were all right, but the horrid little Cockles were
already bursting their cerements and tumbling about my cabin in all
directions. I began to think I was mistaken in the article recommended
by my lady friend, when an individual came on board and inquired
whether I wished to "trade." I took him into my retreat and made
him swallow three glasses of brandy, after which we commenced business. Suffice it to say that he bought all my corsages at the enormous
price of twelve shillings each—giving me a profit of nearly 1,100
percent!

I did not forget the Cockles, but to my disgust the trader told me
that he had never heard of such things. I forbore naming toothbrushes,
for what could a man who had never heard of Cockles know of toothbrushes? But he suddenly touched me and asked, "Say, Captain, have

you got any coffin screws on trade?" His question rather staggered me, but he explained that they had no possible way of making this necessary article in the Southern States, and that they positively could not keep the bodies quiet in their coffins without them, especially when being sent any distance for interment.

> Preponderance of luxuries in the cargo of blockade-runners caused the Confederate government and some individual Southern states to buy and operate ships of their own. A former naval paymaster tells about these enterprises.

One of the most successful government-owned vessels was the *Robert E. Lee*. She was an iron steamer, having a speed of 13-1/2 knots, and being considered, when new, the fastest steamer afloat. She ran the blockade twenty-one times and carried out 7,000 bales of cotton, worth $2,000,000 in gold.

The Confederate government owned three more steamers and a share in several others; all were compelled to carry out a part of their cargo in cotton, and bring in a part of supplies on government account.

The passenger rates on all vessels engaged in the contraband trade were very high, from $300 to $500 in gold per person, payable in advance; $2,500 in gold was paid as freight charge from Bermuda to Wilmington on a box of medicine small enough to put in a cabin of a steamer.

> The favorite harbor for blockade-runners was Wilmington, North Carolina, lying at the mouth of the Cape Fear River. The harbor was protected by Fort Fisher, which was considered exceptionally strong.
>
> Captain Roberts now describes the excitement of an outbound trip through the fleet of Federal guard vessels.

The time chosen for our starting was eleven o'clock, at which hour the tide was at its highest. Fortunately the moon set at about ten and, as it was very cloudy, we had every reason to expect a pitch-dark night.

Very faint lights, which could not be seen far at sea, were set on the beach and, bringing these astern into an exact line—that is, the two lights into one—we knew we were in the passage. The order was then given, "Full speed ahead," and we shot out to sea at a great pace.

Our troubles began almost immediately, for the cruisers had placed a rowing barge, which could not be seen by the forts, close to the entrance to signalize the direction which any vessel that came out might take. This was done by rockets being thrown up from the barge by a designed plan.

A minute had scarcely passed before up went a rocket. A gun was fired uncommonly close to us; but as we did not hear any shot it may have been only a signal.

We steered a mile or two near the coast and then shaped our course straight out to sea. Several guns were fired in the pitch-darkness very near us (I am not quite sure whether some of the blockaders did not occasionally pepper each other). After an hour's fast steaming we felt moderately safe.

Daylight broke with thick, hazy weather, nothing being in sight. We went on all right till about half past eight o'clock, when the weather cleared up, and there was a large paddle-wheel cruiser about six miles astern of us. The moment she saw us, she gave chase. After running for a quarter of an hour it was evident that with our heavy cargo the cruiser had the legs on us; and, as there was a long day before us for the chase, things looked bad.

It is mentioned in the *Book of Sailing Directions* that the course of the Gulf Stream is, in calm weather and smooth water, plainly marked out by a ripple on its outer and inner edges. We clearly saw about a mile ahead of us a remarkable ripple, which we rightly, as it turned out, conjectured was that referred to in the book. As soon as we had crossed it we steered the course of the current of the Gulf Stream, which here ran from two to three miles an hour. Seeing us alter our course, the cruiser did the same; but she had *not* crossed the ripple on the edge of the Stream. The result was, we dropped her rapidly astern, whereby we increased our distance to at least seven miles.

It was noon, from which time the enemy again began to close with us, and at five o'clock was not more than three miles distant. The sun set at a quarter of seven. By then she had got so near that she managed to send two or three shots over us.

Luckily as night came on the weather began to get very cloudy, and we must have been very difficult to make out though certainly not more than a mile off. All this time she kept firing away, thinking, I suppose, that she would frighten us into stopping. If we had gone straight on we should doubtless have been caught, so we altered our course two points to the eastward. After steaming a short distance we stopped quite still, blowing off steam under the water, not a spark or the slightest smoke showing from the funnel; and we had the indescribable satisfaction of seeing our enemy steam past us, still firing ahead at some imaginary vessel.

It had been a most exhilarating chase and a very narrow escape.

Roberts was one blockade-running captain who claimed that he had never been caught, which does not seem incredible, considering the boldness and skill he displayed in the following adventures.

The vessel I had charge of was one of the finest double-screw steamers that had been built, of 400 tons burden, 250 horsepower, 180 feet long and 22 feet beam; undeniably a good craft in all respects. Our crew consisted of a captain, three officers, three engineers and twenty-eight men. They were all Englishmen, and, as they received very high wages, we managed to have picked men; in fact the men-of-war on the West Indies station found it a difficult matter to prevent their crews from deserting, so great was the temptation offered by the blockade-runners.

The hull, which showed about eight feet above water, was painted so as to render her as nearly as possible invisible in the night. Coal of a nature that never smoked (anthracite) was taken on board. In order that no noise might be made, steam was blown off, in case of a sudden stop, under water. I may mention that no cocks were allowed among the fowls aboard, for fear of their proclaiming the whereabouts of the blockade-runner. This may seem ridiculous, but it was a necessary precaution.

Captain, officers and crew received a handsome bounty before starting, in order that we might not be unremunerated if captured or injured; and so we started on our voyage, rather nervous but full of hope. The distance from Bermuda to Wilmington, the port we were bound to, is 720 miles. For the first twenty-four hours we saw nothing to alarm us, but as daylight broke on the second day, there was a large American cruiser not half a mile from us. Before we could turn around she steamed straight at us and commenced firing, rapidly but very much at random, the shot and shell all passing over or wide of us.

Fortunately, according to orders to have full steam on at daylight, we were quite prepared for a run; and still more fortunately a heavy squall of wind and rain that came on helped us vastly, as we were dead to windward of the enemy; and, having no top weights, we soon dropped him astern. He most foolishly kept yawing, to fire his bow chasers, losing ground each time he did so.

By eight o'clock we were out of range, unhit, and by noon out of sight.

We were now in very dangerous waters, steamers being reported from our masthead every hour, and we had to keep moving about in all directions to avoid them, sometimes stopping to allow one to pass ahead of us, at another time turning completely round and running back on our course. Luckily we were never seen or chased. Night came on, and I had hoped that we should have made rapid progress till daybreak, unmolested. All was quiet until about one o'clock in the morning, when suddenly, to our horror, we found a steamer close alongside of us.

How she had got there without our knowledge is a mystery to me even now. However, there she was—and we had hardly seen her before a stentorian voice howled out, "Heave to in that steamer, or I'll sink you!"

It seemed as if all was over, but I answered, "Ay, ay, sir, we are stopped."

The cruiser was about eighty yards from us. We heard orders given to man and arm the quarter-boats; we saw the boats lowered into the water; we saw them coming; we heard the crews laughing and cheering at the prospect of their prize. The bowmen had just touched the sides of our vessel with their boathooks when I whispered down the tube into the engine room, "Full speed ahead"—and away we shot into the pitch-darkness!

I don't know whether the captain of the man-of-war thought that his boats had taken possession, or whether he stopped to pick up his boats. All I can say is that not a shot was fired, and that in less than a minute the darkness hid the cruiser from our view.

Shortly after, my little craft was lying about sixty miles from the entrance of the river. We determined to run straight through the blockaders and take our chances. When it was quite dark we started, steaming at full speed. It was extremely thick on the horizon but clear overhead, with just enough wind and sea to prevent the little noise made by the engines and screws being heard. Every light was out, even the men's pipes; the masts were lowered onto the deck, and if ever a vessel was invisible, we were that night.

We passed several outlying cruisers, some unpleasantly near, but still we passed them. All seemed going favorably when suddenly I saw through my glasses the long, low line of a steamer right ahead, lying as it were across our bows, so close that it would have been impossible to pass to the right or left of her without being seen. A prompt order given to the engine room (where the chief engineer stood to the engines) to reverse *one* engine, was as promptly obeyed, and the little craft spun round like a teetotum.

Having turned, we stopped to reconnoiter and could still see the faint outline of the cruiser, crawling slowly into the darkness, leaving the way open to us, of which we at once took advantage. It was now about one o'clock in the morning; a friendly star told us that we were rapidly getting near the shore. But it was so fearfully dark that it seemed almost hopeless ever to find our way to the entrance of the river, and no one felt comfortable. Still we steamed slowly on and shortly made out a small glimmer of a light right ahead. We eased steam a little and cautiously approached.

As we got nearer, we could make out the outline of a vessel lying at anchor, head to wind, and conjectured that this must be the senior officer's ship, which generally lay about two miles and a half from the river's mouth. We made a dash and, thanks to our disguise and great speed, got through without being seen.

As we were now perfectly safe, lights were at once lighted, supper and grog served out *ad libitum*, everybody congratulated everybody else, and a feeling of comfort and jollity, such as can only be experienced after three days' and three nights' intense anxiety, possessed us all.

Captain Roberts, while proud of the daring displayed by one of his confreres, was fair enough to admit that the Yankee crews of the blockading vessels could also do some quick and tricky thinking.

On the night of the first attack on Fort Fisher a blockade-runner, unaware of what was going on and finding that the blockading squadron was very near inshore, kept creeping nearer and nearer to the fort till she was near enough to make out what they were doing.

Judging rightly they would never suspect that any attempt to run the blockade would be made at such a time, she joined a detachment of gunboats and went deliberately in as one of them. When they, being repulsed, had steamed away, our friend remained at anchor under the fort, much to the astonishment of the garrison.

But, when Fort Fisher was at last taken and before its fall was known to the blockade-runners at either Nassau or Bermuda, the crafty Northerners placed the lights for going over the bar as usual. The blockade-runners came cautiously on and, congratulating themselves at seeing no cruisers, ran gaily into the port. The usual feasting and rejoicings were about to commence when a boat full of armed men came alongside and astonished them by telling them they were in the lion's mouth. This happened to four or five vessels before the news reached Nassau.

Federal guard squadrons did not constitute the only dangers to blockade-runners, to judge by the experience of James M. Morgan, a young midshipman in the Confederate navy, traveling on the *S. S. Herald*.

Our little light-draft steamer *Herald* was lying in Charleston Harbor loaded with cotton, all ready to run through the blockading fleet. Commander Maury, a famous scientist and geographer, and I went on board. About ten o'clock at night we got under way, headed for the sea. The moon was about half full, but heavy clouds coming in from the ocean obscured it. We passed between the great lowering forts of Moultrie and Sumter and were soon on the bar, when suddenly there was a rift in the clouds, and there, right ahead of us, we plainly saw a big sloop of war!

There was no use trying to hide. She also had seen us, and the order, "Hard-a-starboard!" which rang out on our boat was nearly drowned by the roar of the warship's great guns. Then friendly clouds closed again, and we rushed back to the protecting guns of the forts without having had our paint scratched.

On the night of the ninth of October, 1862, we made another attempt to get through the blockade. All lights were out except the one in the covered binnacle protecting the compass. Not a word was spoken save by the pilot, who gave his orders in whispers. The captain had no desire to be taken prisoner, as he had been proclaimed a pirate by the Federal government. He was convinced that the great danger in running the blockade was in his own engine room, so he seated himself with a revolver on the ladder leading down to it and politely informed the engineer that if the engine stopped clear of the fleet, he, the engineer, would be a dead man.

Bermuda is only 600 miles from Charleston; a fast ship could do the distance easily in forty-eight hours, but the *Herald* was slow. She had put one of her engines out of commission and we were thus compelled to limp along with one.

On the fifth day out the captain hailed a steamer and asked for latitude and longitude. He had not as yet confided to anybody that he was lost. On the sixth day, however, he told Commodore Maury that something terrible must have happened, as he had sailed directly over the Bermuda Islands! The great scientist went on deck and took observations, gave the Captain a course, and told him that he would sight the light at Port Hamilton by two o'clock in the morning. No one turned into his bunk that night. Four bells struck, and no light. Five minutes more, and still no sign of it. Then at ten minutes past two the lookout sang out, "Light, ho!"—and the learned commodore's reputation was saved.

The tricks used by the blockade-runners were numerous and varied. One which was used as a last resort is related by J. R. Soley, a Northern recorder.

Whenever a blockade-runner was hard pressed it was common practice to run her ashore, to save a fragment of his cargo. He would obtain the cooperation of infantry, often accompanied by artillery, which would harass the blockading vessels trying to get the steamer off. Sometimes the blockaders were able to prevent the people on shore from doing mischief; but at other times the latter had it all their own way. It was no easy matter to float off a steamer which had been beached intentionally, and the fire of the guns made the operation hazardous. The only course left was to burn the wreck; and even then chances were that the fire would be extinguished. In 1863 the *Kate* was run ashore and abandoned. She was set on fire, and the officer in charge reported that he had disabled her effectually. Three weeks later, however, she was floated off by the Confederates and anchored under the batteries.

The profits from blockade running and the wealth so acquired produced the same results in men which sudden riches have produced in men at all times.

The ports where the lucky sailors congregated rivaled with one another for free spending. James M. Morgan describes one of these places.

We entered the picturesque harbor of Saint George in the Bermudas on the *Herald* shortly after daylight. There were eight or ten block-ade-runners lying in the harbor, and their captains and mates lived at the same little whitewashed hotel where the commodore and I stopped. They were a reckless lot and believed in eating, drinking and being merry, for fear that they would die on the morrow and might miss something. Their orgies reminded me of the way the pirates in the West Indies must have spent their time when in their secret havens. The men who commanded these blockade-runners had probably never before in their lives received more than $50 to $75 a month. Now they received as high as $10,000 in gold for a round trip, besides being allowed cargo space to take in, for their own account, goods which could be sold at a fabulous price. In Bermuda these men seemed to suffer from a chronic thirst, which could be assuaged only by champagne, and one of their amusements was to sit in the windows with bags of shillings and throw handfuls to loafing Negroes to see them scramble.

It is a singular fact that it was not always the speedier craft that were the most successful. The *Kate* ran through the blockade fleets sixty times and she could not steam faster than seven or eight knots. That was the record, and no other vessel ever matched it.

As the war years went by, the blockade became tighter and tighter. Even so, however, Mr. Morgan tells us how some of them, like the *Lillian*, made port safely, although not before having lived through harrowing moments.

It was in the month of July 1864, and by this time the blockade of the coast was so complete that to get into a Southern port it was necessary to elude the United States war vessels three separate times on each trip.

At Saint George, Bermuda, our party of Confederate naval officers took passage on the *Lillian*, commanded by as big a braggart and blowhard as ever commanded a ship. Around the Bermuda Islands cruisers hovered to catch their prey when the blockade-runner was only a few miles from the neutral port, either coming or going. About fifty miles off the Southern coast other cruisers awaited them, and of course the channels leading into the Southern harbors were closely guarded. We passed out of the harbor of Saint George in daylight and then lingered until night, when we started at full speed for Wilmington. The *Lillian* was a very small paddle-wheel steamer whose deck was not more than three or four feet above the water line, and she drew only between seven and eight feet of water.

While we were still some fifty miles from the Cape Fear River, a big, bark-rigged, steam sloop of war, which we afterward learned was the U. S. *Shenandoah*, caught sight of us and gave chase.

Our captain, when in his cups, would swear by all the gods of the sea that the little *Lillian* could run seventeen knots an hour, but the heavy man-of-war gained rapidly on us. Our captain went below and stowed several big drinks of brandy under his vest and then, coming on deck, in a spirit of braggadocio, hoisted the Confederate flag. We put on our uniforms and side arms, as we wished to be captured, if captured we had to be, as officers of the Confederate navy.

Returning to the quarter-deck we awaited developments. The warship still steadily gained. Within an hour from the time she had sighted us she fired a shot. We naval officers knew that she was only trying to get the range, as we saw the projectile fall short several hundred yards from us, but our captain thought that was the best she could do, and with his habitual swagger he mounted to the little bridge and in the most dramatic manner said, "I want you naval officers to know that I am captain of her as long as a plank will float!"

Just then the *Shenandoah*, having got the range, sent a screaming rifled projectile through both paddle boxes, one shot passing only a foot or two under the bridge on which the captain was standing. With a yell of dismay he threw up his hands and came scampering down the ladder, screaming, "Haul that flag down! I will not have any more lives sacrificed!" Nothing besides the paddle boxes had as yet been touched, unless we except the captain's yellow streak.

Lieutenant Campbell who, as ranking officer, spoke for all of our little group, quietly said, "Captain, if you want to give up this boat, turn her over to me. I will not allow you to surrender her. These officers are branded as pirates, and may be hanged if captured."

Just then the man-of-war yawed and let fly her whole broadside, cutting the *Lillian* up considerably. The captain looked dazed for a moment, but was brought out of his mental stupor by a shot from a rifled gun which grazed the top of one of the boilers, letting the steam out with a roar. The engine-room force rushed on deck and gathered around us.

The chief engineer, a game little fellow, informed Mr. Campbell that the boilers could be disconnected from each other, a precaution against just such an accident as had happened, and that the boat, with the immense pressure of steam she was carrying, would run until the steam from the injured boiler cooled off sufficiently to allow the stokers to return to their duties. The crew gallantly cheered his remarks.

All this time the *Shenandoah* was yawing first to starboard and then to port, apparently so certain that she had us that she was amusing her crew at target practice. Mr. Campbell went into the pilothouse and took command of the *Lillian*. The first order he gave changed our course so that the man-of-war had to take in her sails, and after that we appeared to be holding our own in the contest of speed, but shots continued to fly over and around us.

All this time Lieutenant Campbell was edging the *Lillian* in toward the land, which we sighted between sundown and dark, and how we did pray that night would come soon! With our light draft we continued the "edging-in" maneuver until the heavy man-of-war had to change her course for fear of striking bottom. She hauled to the southward with the object of heading us off from Wilmington, from which port we were far to the northward by this time. We too had to change our course to the south, giving the broadside of the *Shenandoah* a fine target as we steamed in parallel lines down the coast, the *Lillian* being so close in to the beach that she was rolling on the curlers of the outer line of surf. Night at last came to our relief, and without further molestation we continued on our way to Wilmington.

We had hope of reaching the bar before daylight and thus elude the vigilance of the blockading fleet, but luck and the slow speed of the *Lillian* were against us. Day broke when we were still a couple of miles away, and the fleet at once saw us and opened fire. We had no choice but to go on, as the last few shovelfuls of coal on board were then being tossed into the furnaces. Fortunately none of the shots touched our remaining boiler or machinery. There was one small gunboat right in our path, inside of the bar, and very close to Fort Fisher. The people in the fort and on the gunboat must have been asleep. Lieutenant Campbell ordered the man at the wheel to steer for her, saying that she was so near the fort that she would not dare fire, as Fort Fisher would blow her out of the water if she did. He was right—for when she saw us coming she slipped her cable and scampered off without firing a shot, and a few minutes afterward we dropped our anchor in safety under the sheltering guns of the famous fortress.

An officer in the Union navy, Horatio L. Wait by name, who served on one of the blockading vessels outside Mobile harbor, remembered some of his experiences with mingled feelings.

The blockading service off the port of Mobile was difficult, because there were so many entrances to the harbor that could be used by the light-draft blockade-runners, while the blockaders were obliged to lie at a distance from the land. Violent gales spring up very suddenly there, yet we maintained our fleet without an interruption of a single hour for over three years. Our ship rode out several southeast winter gales lying at the inshore station, while we anxiously watched to see whether her anchors would hold.

The cruisers of the British navy and other foreign navies frequently entered the harbor and examined critically into the efficiency of the blockade. Of course they usually communicated with the senior officer of the blockading fleet before entering the port. The Confederate cruiser *Oreto*, or *Florida*, was built in England for the Rebels. She was the exact counterpart in appearance of the British men-of-war that had visited the blockading fleets and, owing to this circumstance, she was enabled to run the blockade into Mobile by flying the British naval ensign and maneuvering as if she were a man-of-war intending to communicate with the fleet.

The outward-bound blockade-runners sometimes made use of cotton saturated with turpentine to keep up their steam to a maximum point when closely pressed, though they preferred anthracite coal, as it made less of the telltale smoke that betrayed their presence when the vessel herself was invisible. They economized by limiting its use to the times when they were attempting to run through the blockading fleet. They would keep out of sight until they had run their steam up to the highest point, then make a dash at full speed through the fleet. For the rest of the voyage they would use the common British coal.

The horizon was unremittingly scanned by watchful eyes on board the blockaders, day in and day out, for indications of the suggestive black smoke. It happened several times that our ship saw steamers attempting to run past us. This was always at night, and usually when the weather was thick. We would pursue for hours, usually seeing enough smoke to be sure of the position of the vessel. The smoke would gradually increase in volume as if the pursued steamer was forcing her fires to the utmost; then we would do all we could to lift the speed of our ship. Suddenly no more smoke and no vessel could be seen.

We afterward learned from a captured officer that, when pursued in such circumstances, they would augment the volume of their smoke until it became quite dense; then, when so far from the pursuer that their hulls and spars were invisible in the darkness, they would suddenly close their dampers and shut off the smoke entirely, changing their course to one nearly at right angles to that previously steered.

It was a most successful maneuver.

> Conditions for the blockaders at Charleston were apparently as bad as, if not worse than, at Mobile, to judge from Mr. Wait's memoirs. He also narrates how the hunted at times unexpectedly changed places with the hunters.

The blockade of Charleston, South Carolina, was maintained under greater difficulties than at any other point. That coast is subject to storms of great severity in winter. We found in a Rebel newspaper a copy of a letter written by an old officer, expressing the belief that before long one of the old-fashioned gales would drive the whole fleet ashore.

The bar was a difficult one to blockade; in addition to the natural obstacles, the active and skillful defenders of the harbor were so aggressive in the use of their torpedoes, torpedo boats and other novel devices, that the calm weather brought more causes of anxiety to the blockaders than even the most violent gales. Through the long hours of the night watches, the anxious officers and the alert lookouts were speculating whether they would next be called on suddenly to contend with an ironclad ram, a torpedo or torpedo boat, or a swift blockade-runner at full speed. General Gabriel J. Rains, chief of the Confederate torpedo service, reported that his service destroyed fifty-eight of our vessels by torpedoes alone during the war.

The blockaders were in the habit of sending up rockets as signals when steamers tried to run in or out, the rockets being thrown in the direction in which the blockade-runner was going. Very soon the Rebels procured rockets of exactly the same kind, and then the runners would send up the signal rockets in the opposite direction, so that the fleet would be misled.

The ordinary duties of the blockading operations were liable to be disturbed by numerous accidents or incidents, and no service ever required more foresight in preparation or more perseverance in performance. The most careful precautions and sustained watchfulness were sometimes unavailing. On the night of June 3, 1864, the blockading steamer *Water Witch* was anchored inside the bar at Ossabaw Sound, below Savannah. The weather was so thick and hazy that objects could not be seen at any distance. Her boarding nettings were up, there was steam enough on to work the engines, and there were the usual number of lookouts at their stations. An attacking party of about double the number of the crew of the *Water Witch* came down from Savannah in eight cotton barges. They drifted noiselessly toward the *Water Witch* at about three o'clock in the morning, approaching within forty yards of her before they could be seen by the lookouts. The moment they were seen and hailed, they dashed alongside. The engines were started ahead, but the ship did not gather headway soon enough to prevent the Rebels boarding her. The crew made the best fight they could in the circumstances but, as they were so largely outnumbered and half of them asleep in their hammocks, the resistance was ineffectual.

The Rebels afterward ran the ship aground and she was subsequently destroyed.

Blockade-running was at best only a defensive weapon, and the South, never willing to forego an offensive, endeavored to acquire armed vessels for this purpose in foreign parts. Such ships as could be bought were fitted out as sea raiders to destroy the commerce of the United States.

International law forbade the open purchase of raiders in England, the most available of neutral countries, but the Confederate agents found ways to hoodwink the British authorities. Mr. Morgan relates how one raider, the *Georgia*, was loosed on the high seas and provided her crew with unusual adventures.

About half past nine in the evening we all took a train for White Haven, a little seaport about an hour's ride from London. There we met Commander Maury and were soon joined by others—all strangers to me. We waited at the inn for about a couple of hours. In those two hours it was to be decided whether our expedition was to be a success or a failure. If Mr. Adams, the American minister, was going to get in his fine work and balk us, now was his last opportunity.

A little after midnight, two by two we sauntered down to the quay, where we found a little seagoing tug called the *Alar*. We hurried on board, the lines were cast off, and the *Alar* shot out of the slip. For more than three days and nights, cold and wet, with no place to sleep and little to eat, we stumbled and tumbled down the English Channel. At last we saw on the horizon a trim-looking little brig-rigged steamer idly rolling on the swell of the sea, apparently waiting for something, and we steered for her. She proved to be the British steamer *Japan;* her papers said that she was bound from Glasgow to Nagasaki with an assorted cargo.

The vessel had not the slightest resemblance to a man-of-war; she belonged to a private person, and there was not an ounce of contraband in her cargo. Her captain himself did not know for what purpose she was intended.

When we had approached close enough Commander Maury asked her captain to send a boat. He then went aboard the brig, we were taken in tow and proceeded to the French island of Ushant, so that we might transfer our guns from the tug to the cruiser that was to be. We dropped anchor after dark in a little cove and commenced operations, despite the angry protests of the French coastguards from the shore.

The men worked most energetically, and by midnight we had our two 24-pounders and the two little 10-pounder Whitworth guns on board. We then stood out to sea, where, beyond the three-mile limit, we stopped. Captain Maury called all hands and read his orders, hoisted the Confederate flag and declared the Confederate States cruiser *Georgia* to be in commission.

His remarks were received with three lusty cheers. He then asked the men who were going with us to step forward and enlist for three years or the war, but alas, not a man came forward when told that the *Georgia* was a man-of-war and the pay was fixed by law. To our surprise nine men of the crew of the late merchantman *Japan* now said they would like to go with us, and of course they were accepted. With these men as a nucleus for a crew, we cast off the *Alar's* line and never saw or heard of her or the men on board of her again, and never wanted to.

It was the ninth of April, 1863, when this little friendless ship of only about 550 tons started on her long and hazardous cruise. She was as absolutely unfitted for the work as any vessel could conceivably be: she lay very low in the water and was very long for her beam; her engines were fitted with lignum-vitae cogs, and frequently these wooden cogs would break. When they did, it was worse than if a shrapnel shell had burst in the engine room, as they flew in every direction, endangering the lives of everyone within reach. Her sail power was insufficient and, owing to her length, it was impossible to put her about under canvas. She was slow under either sail or steam, or both together. Such was the little craft in which we got under way, bound we knew not where.

Day after day with a pleasant breeze we steered a course somewhat west of south, meeting but few ships, and those we saw displayed neutral colors. During the whole cruise we saw our Confederate flag only when we were in the act of making a capture or when we were in port. Usually we showed the Stars and Stripes. On April 25 about 4:00 P.M. we descried on the horizon a big full-rigged ship with long skysail poles—sure sign of the Yankee. She appeared unwilling to take any chances with us and cracked on more sail while we pursued her under steam. A little after five o'clock we hoisted the Confederate flag, and sent a shot bounding over the water just ahead of her, which was an order to heave to. In less time than it takes to tell, the main yard of the doomed ship swung around, and her sails on the main and mizzenmasts were thrown aback, as the American flag was broken out and fluttered from her peak. We immediately lowered a boat, and our second lieutenant and I rowed over to the prize which proved to be the splendid ship *Dictator* of between 3,000 and 4,000 tons from New York bound to Hong Kong with a cargo of coal. She carried no passengers.

After looking over the ship's papers we made her crew lower their boats and forced the captain, his three mates and the crew of twenty-seven men to get into them with their personal belongings. We then ordered them to pull for the *Georgia*, which they did with no enthusiasm whatever. On arriving alongside the cruiser they were allowed to come over the side one at a time and were then hurried below and placed in irons. It was not considered advisable to give them time enough to see how weak our force was. The captain was invited by our commander to share the cabin with him, and the first mate was confined in my room, but neither was allowed to go forward of the mainmast or to hold any communication with the men. On board the *Dictator* we found a fine assortment of provisions and sent several boatloads to our own ship. This was necessary, as we had now to feed the prize's crew as well as our own.

The *Georgia* made signal to burn the prize, and the lieutenant asked me if I would like to try my hand at setting her on fire. There were a large number of broken provision boxes lying about the deck which I gathered and, placing them against her rail, I lighted a match and applied it. The kindling wood burned beautifully, but when its flames expired, there was not a sign of fire on the ship. I was surprised and puzzled, and turned to seek an explanation from my superior officer. He told me not to mind; he would show me how it was done. I followed him into the cabin, where he pulled out several drawers from under the captain's berth and, filling them with old newspapers, he applied a match. The effect was almost instantaneous. Flames leaped up and caught the chintz curtains of the berth and the bedclothes, at the same time setting fire to the light woodwork. We hastily went down the ladder into our boat. By the time we reached the *Georgia* the prize was one seething mass of flames.

The *Dictator*, exclusive of her cargo, was valued at $86,000. By decree of the Confederate government we were to receive one-half of the value of every ship destroyed. Under the law regulating the distribution of prize money the total amount was divided into twentieths, of which the commanding officer got two, and the steerage officers got the same, the rest being shared by the wardroom officers and the crew. Since I was the only midshipman, or steerage officer, on board of the *Georgia*, the amount of prize money which I should have received would have almost equaled the share of the captain. It is still due me.

One of the strangest adventures that befell the *Georgia* is told by Mr. Morgan in this manner.

On October 9, 1863, in a light breeze we brought to the splendid American full-rigged ship *Bold Hunter*, of Boston, bound to Calcutta with a heavy cargo of coal. We hove to leeward of her and brought her captain and crew over to our ship. Being short of coal and provisions, we proceeded to supply our wants from the prize. After half a dozen trips one of our boats came very near being swamped, and the wind and sea rapidly rising, we gave it up as a bad job. We signaled our prize master to set fire to the *Bold Hunter* and to come aboard the *Georgia* at once, which he did.

We had hardly finished hoisting our boats when a great cloud of smoke burst from the hatches of the *Bold Hunter*, coming from the thousands of tons of burning coal in her hold. The wind had by this time increased to a gale, and the sea was running very high. When we had captured the ship she had hove to with all sails set. The flames leaped from her deck to her rigging and burned away her braces, her yards swung around, her sails filled, and the floating inferno, like a mad bull, bore down on us at full speed, rushing through the water as though she were bent on having her revenge.

The order was given on the *Georgia* to go ahead at full speed. The engine made two or three revolutions. Then there was a crash, followed by yells, as the engineers and oilers rushed to the deck, accompanied by a shower of lignum-vitae cogs and broken glass from the engine-room windows. The order to make sail was instantly given, but before the gaskets could be cast off, the burning ship was upon us. She had come for us with such directness that one could easily have imagined she was being steered by some demon.

We stood with bated breath awaiting the catastrophe. The *Bold Hunter* was rated at over 3,000 tons and had inside her a burning cargo of coal of even greater weight. The *Georgia* was scarcely one-sixth her size. Onward rushed the blazing ship, presenting an awesome spectacle with the flames leaping about her sails and rigging, while a huge mass of black smoke rolled out of her hatches. High above our heads her long, flying jib boom passed over our poop deck as she came down on our port quarter, her cutwater cleaving through the *Georgia's* fragile plates as cleanly as though they had been made of cheese. The force of the impact pushed the *Georgia* ahead, and for a moment we congratulated ourselves that we had escaped.

But the *Bold Hunter* was not yet satisfied. Recovering from the recoil, she again gathered way and struck us near the place she had previously damaged, but fortunately this was a glancing blow. The apparently infuriated inanimate object made a third attempt to destroy the *Georgia*, this time, fortunately, missing her mark and passing a few yards to leeward of us. Her sails having burned, she soon lost headway and helplessly lay wallowing in the trough of the sea while the fire ate through her sides, and her tall masts one after the other fell with a great splash into the sea.

Before she went down, surrounded by a cloud of steam, we had a good view through the great holes burned in her sides of the fire raging within. I imagine it was a very realistic imitation of what hell looks like when the forced drafts are turned on in honor of the arrival of a distinguished sinner.

The most famous of all Confederate raiders was the *Alabama*, and her commanding officer, Admiral Raphael Semmes, stood out as the foremost of all Confederate sea captains.

Raphael Semmes had lived in Mobile, Alabama, after serving with distinction in the United States Navy during the Mexican War. In 1861 he went to New Orleans, where he outfitted the raider *Sumter* with which he captured eighteen merchantmen.

Once while Semmes was lying inside the harbor of St. Pierre, the principal port of the French island of Martinique, the United States warship *Iroquois* threatened to bottle him up.

Semmes tells how he met this emergency and how, as usual, he came out triumphant.

It was known that the enemy's steam sloop *Iroquois*, Captain James S. Palmer, had been at the near-by island of Trinidad, and as a matter of course we might expect her presence very soon. When she did come in sight, it was ludicrous to witness her appearance. Her commander's idea seemingly was that the moment the *Sumter* caught sight of him, she would immediately try to escape, and hence he had made some attempts to disguise his ship. The Danish colors were flying from his peak, and his guns had all been run in. But the finely proportioned, taunt, saucy *Iroquois* looked no more like a merchant ship than a gay Lothario would look like a saint by donning a cassock. We had a small Confederate States flag flying, and it was amusing to witness the movements on board the *Iroquois* when this was discovered. The steamer, which had been hitherto cautiously creeping along as a stealthy tiger might be supposed to skirt a jungle, sprang forward under a full head of steam. At the same moment, down came the Danish and up went the United States flag. No doubt Captain Palmer thought to see, every moment, the little *Sumter* flying from her anchors. But the *Sumter* went on coaling and receiving on board some rum and sugar, as though no enemy were in sight.

The captain of the *Iroquois* was very much in earnest in endeavoring to capture me. He had left St. Thomas in a great hurry upon getting news of the *Sumter*. In a day or two after his arrival at St. Pierre, he took virtual possession of a small lumber schooner that lay a short distance from the *Sumter*—he used her as lookout ship. He arranged with the Yankee master a set of signals by which the *Sumter* was to be circumvented. Certain lights were to be exhibited in certain positions on board the Yankee schooner, to indicate to her consort that the *Sumter* was under way and the course she was running.

In the meantime the plot was thickening. Not only was the town agog, but the simple countrypeople, having heard what was going on and that a naval combat was expected, came in great numbers to see the show. Two parties were formed, the *Sumter* party and the *Iroquois* party. Young men boarded me in scores and volunteered to help me whip the *barbare*. I had no thought of fighting, but of running; but of course I did not tell *them* so.

The *Iroquois* had arrived on the fourteenth of November. It was now the twenty-third, and I had waited all this time for a dark night; unfortunately not only had the moon persisted in shining, but the stars looked, we thought, unusually bright. This night the moon would not rise until seven minutes past eleven, and that would be ample time in which to escape—or be captured. But time pressed, and it was absolutely necessary to be moving. Messengers had been sent hither and thither by the enemy to hunt up a reinforcement of gunboats, and if several of these should arrive, escape would be almost out of the question. The *Iroquois* was not only twice as heavy as the *Sumter* in men and metal, but she had as much as two or three knots per hour the speed of her. We must escape, if at all, unseen of the enemy.

I gave orders to the first lieutenant to make all the necessary preparations for getting up his anchor and putting the ship under steam at 8:00 P.M., the gun at the garrison to be the signal for moving. The crew were all to be at quarters a few minutes before the appointed hour of moving.

The engineer was standing, lever in hand, ready to start the engine, and a seaman with an uplifted ax was standing near the taffarel to cut the stern fast. One minute more! Everyone was listening eagerly for the sound. The *Iroquois* was quite visible through our glasses, watching for the *Sumter* like the spider for the fly. A flash, and the almost simultaneous boom of the eight o'clock gun! Without one word being uttered on board the *Sumter* the ax descended on the fast, the engineer's lever was turned, and the ship bounded forward under a full head of steam.

A prolonged and deafening cheer arose from the multitude in the market place. Skillful helmsmen brought the *Sumter's* head around to the south, where they held it so that she did not swerve a hairsbreadth. There was not a light visible on board. I had stationed a quick-sighted young officer to look out for the signals which I knew the Yankee schooner was to make. This officer now came running aft to me and said, "Look, sir, there are two red lights, one above the other," and I knew what they meant to say to the *Iroquois*: "Look out for the *Sumter*; she is under way, standing south!"

I ran a few hundred yards farther on my present course and then stopped. The island of Martinique is mountainous, and near the south end of the town, where I now was, the mountains run abruptly into the sea and cast quite a shadow on the waters for some distance out. I had the advantage of operating within this shadow. I now directed my glass toward the *Iroquois*. I have said that Captain Palmer was anxious to catch me and, to judge by the speed which the *Iroquois* was now making toward the south in obedience to her signals, his anxiety had not been abated by his patient watching of nine days. I now did what poor Reynard sometimes does when he is hard pressed by the hounds—I doubled. While the *Iroquois* was driving like mad for the south, this little craft was doing her level best for the north end of the island. It is safe to say that the next morning the two vessels were one hundred and fifty miles apart.

The *Sumter* was finally driven into Gibraltar, where she was blockaded by two United States warships. Semmes thereupon went to England where the *Alabama* was being built for him. She was put into commission in August 1862 and was destined to become a terror of the seas for any ship flying the flag of the United States.

Here is a typical capture of a merchant vessel by the *Alabama*, as related by Semmes himself.

Late one afternoon as we sailed along the shores of Flores, the most westerly of the Azores Islands, we chased a large ship looming up almost like a frigate. We had showed her the American colors, and she approached us without the least suspicion that she was running into the arms of an enemy. This ship proved to be the whaler *Ocean Rover*, of New Bedford, Massachusetts. She had been out three years and four months, had sent home one or two cargoes of oil and was now returning with another cargo of 1,100 barrels.

It being near night when the capture was made, I directed the prize to be hove to. In the meantime, however, the master, who had heard from some of my men that I had permitted the master of another ship and his crew to land in their own boats, requested permission to land in the same manner. I consented, and the delighted master returned to his ship. I gave him the usual permission to take what provisions he needed and the personal effects of himself and men. Not more than a couple of hours had elapsed before he was again alongside of the *Alabama*, with all his six boats, and six men in each. I could not but be amused at the amount of plunder that the rapacious fellow had packed in them. They were literally loaded down with all sorts of traps, from the seamen's chests and bedding to the tabby cat and parrot.

I said, to him, "Captain, your boats appear to be rather deeply laden. Are you not afraid to trust them?"

"Oh, no!" he replied. "They are as buoyant as ducks, and we shall not ship a drop of water."

The boats struck out for the shore. It was a beautiful spectacle. Moving swiftly and mysteriously toward the shore, they might have been mistaken for Venetian gondolas, with their peaked bows and sterns, especially when we heard coming over the sea a song sung by a powerful and musical voice and chorused by all the boats. Those merry fellows were proving that the sailor, after all, is a true philosopher. The echo of that night song lingered long in my memory. I little dreamed that four years afterward it would be alleged that I *compelled* my prisoners to depart for the shore at the hazard of their lives, desiring to drown them! And this was all the thanks I received for setting some of these fellows up as nabobs among the islanders. Why, the master of the *Ocean Rover*, with his six boats and their cargoes, when he landed in Flores, was richer than the governor of the island himself.

After almost two years of uninterrupted success the career of the *Alabama* came to an end.

It was in the summer of 1864 that the *Alabama* made port for the last time. One of her officers, Lieutenant Arthur Sinclair, recorded how she met her fate.

On the eleventh of June, 1864, we entered the harbor of Cherbourg, France.

We had cruised from the day of commission, August 24, 1862, to June 11, 1864, and during this time had visited two-thirds of the globe.

Immediately after arrival permission was asked for docking privileges. Some delay was experienced, the Emperor, whose permission must first be obtained, being absent from Paris. In the meantime, the captain of the U. S. warship *Kearsarge*, cruising near by, heard of our arrival and entered the harbor on the fourteenth. It seems the principal object of the visit was to ask permission to receive on board the *Kearsarge* prisoners recently landed by us. This would have seemed indeed the *sole* object of the visit, for it was generally understood that the *Alabama* was going in dock for thorough repairs. John A. Winslow, the captain of the *Kearsarge*, could hardly have contemplated waiting outside the harbor for us until our repairs were made; whether he knew Semmes so well as to be assured of a challenge has never transpired. The challenge alone is a matter of history.

Semmes lost no time, however. Through the United States consul he forwarded to Captain Winslow a communication to the effect that if he would wait until he could get his coal aboard he would go out and fight him. I have often been asked why Semmes should decide to fight in his disabled condition a ship so much his superior as to number of crew, armament and speed; with full knowledge, also, that the midship section of the *Kearsarge* was protected by chain cables hung over her sides. That is manifestly a question I cannot undertake to answer. But apart from the unquestioned gallantry of the man, the insinuations he had been forced to listen to regarding his avoidance of armed ships of his foe, he knew he had as gallant and perfectly trained a band supporting him as a commander ever had the good fortune to lead. He had two guns capable of quickly sinking any wooden gunboat of the period. He had no suspicion that his powder was damaged, and had no reason to think the *Kearsarge* would avoid, or even that she could avoid, his coming to close quarters. Had the 100-pound percussion shell, lodged so early in the action in the stern of the *Kearsarge*, exploded, who doubts that it must have proved her deathblow?

It being a settled thing that the fight was to take place, preparations were made for it. We were to enter the arena on Sunday the nineteenth. Our officers, other than the special ones engaged in the preparation of the ship for action, were determined to make the most of the days and hours at their disposal. A round of pleasures was inaugurated. We had been on the eternal "salt horse" for nearly three months and, as some wit put it, needed to be fattened for the slaughter.

The news that the *Alabama* was to fight on Sunday the nineteenth of June, 1864, was now the common property of Europe, indeed of all lands, the information having been wired to every available point, and the to-be-lookers-on were concentrating at Cherbourg from all points of the Continent.

The yacht *Deerhound* of the Royal Yacht Squadron had anchored in the harbor which was also graced with a powerful French fleet, among the number being one of the modern ironclads, the *Couronne*. This vessel was to accompany us beyond the marine league and then see that in the excitement of battle we did not stray.

Between ten and eleven o'clock we got under way and stood out of the harbor, passing the French liner *Napoleon* quite near. We were surprised and gratified as she manned the rigging and gave us three rousing cheers, her band at the same time playing a Confederate national air. It must have been a sort of private turnout of their own.

Our ship, as she steamed offshore for her antagonist, presented a brave appearance. The decks and brasswork shone in the bright morning sunlight from recent holystoning and polishing. The crew were all in muster uniform, as though just awaiting Sunday inspection, and Semmes, mounting a gun carriage, delivered a stirring address.

The *Kearsarge* suddenly turned her head inshore and steamed toward us, both ships being at this time about seven or eight miles from the shore. When at about one-mile distance from us, she seemed to have chosen this for her attack. We opened the engagement with our entire starboard battery, giving us six guns in broadside. The *Kearsarge* had pivoted to starboard also, and both ships with helms aport fought out the engagement, circling around a common center and gradually approaching each other. The enemy replied soon after our opening, but at that distance her pivot shell guns were at a disadvantage, not having the long range of our pivot guns and hence requiring judgment in guessing the distance and determining the proper elevation.

The battle was now on in earnest. After about fifteen minutes' fighting we lodged a 100-pound percussion shell in the quarter near her screw, but it failed to explode, though causing some temporary excitement and anxiety on board the enemy, most likely by the concussion of the blow. We found her soon after seeking closer quarters. We now

ourselves noted the advantage in speed possessed by our enemy.
Semmes felt her pulse, as to whether *very* close quarters would be agreeable, by sheering toward her to close the distance. But she had evidently reached the point wished for to fight out the remainder of the
action and demonstrated it by sheering off and resuming a parallel to us.
Semmes would have chosen to bring about yardarm quarters, fouling
and boarding, relying on the superior physique of his crew to over-
balance the superiority of numbers. But this was frustrated, though several times attempted.

Up to the time of shortening the first distance assumed, our ship had
received no damage of any account, and the enemy none that we could
discover. At the distance we were now fighting—point-blank range—
the effects of the 11-inch guns should have been severely felt, and
the little hurt done the enemy clearly proved the unserviceableness of
our powder.

The boarding tactics of Semmes having been frustrated, and we being
unable to pierce the enemy's hull with our fire, nothing could place
victory with us but some unforeseen and lucky turn. We could see the
splinters flying off from the armor covering of the enemy, but no pene-
tration occurred, the shot or shell rebounding from her side. The
Kearsarge, having now the range and being able with her superior speed
to hold it at ease, had us well in hand, and the fire from her was deliberate and hot. Our bulwarks were soon shot away in sections, and the
after pivot gun was disabled. The spar deck was by this time being
rapidly torn up by shell bursting on the between-decks, interfering with
working our battery, and the compartments below had all been knocked
into one. The *Alabama* was making water fast, showing severe punishment, but still the report came from the engine room that the ship was
being kept free to the safety point. She also had now become dull in
response to her helm. We were making a desperate but forlorn resistance, which soon culminated in the deathblow.

An 11-inch shell entered us at the water line and, passing on, exploded
in the engine room. Our ship trembled from stem to stern from the
blow. Semmes at once sent for the engineer on watch, who reported
the fires out and water beyond the control of the pumps. We had previously been aware our ship was whipped, and fore-and-aft sail was set
in an endeavor to reach the French coast. The enemy then moved inshore of us but did not attempt to close any nearer, simply steaming to
secure the shore side and await events.

It being now apparent that the *Alabama* could not float much longer, the colors were hauled down, and the pipe given, "All hands save yourselves!" Our waist boats had been shot to pieces, leaving us but two quarter-boats, and one of them much damaged. The wounded were dispatched in one of them to the enemy in charge of an officer, and this done we awaited developments. The *Kearsarge* evidently failed to discover our surrender at once, for she continued her fire after our colors had been struck.

The yacht *Deerhound* was now steaming full-power toward us both. The inaction of the *Kearsarge* from the time of the surrender until the last man was picked up will ever remain a mystery to all who were present and with whom the writer has since conversed. The fact is, the *Kearsarge* was increasing her distance slowly and surely all the time. Whether the drift of our ship under sail was accomplishing this alone I am not prepared to say, but the yacht was entitled to the greater credit in saving life. Few of the *Alabama's* men would have been saved but for its presence.

The officers and crew of our ship were now leaving at will, discipline and rule being temporarily at an end. The ship was settling to her spar deck, and her wounded spars were staggering in the "steps," held only by the rigging. The decks presented a woeful appearance, torn up in innumerable holes, and air bubbles rose and burst, producing a sound as though the boat were in agony. Just before she settled, it was a desolate sight for the three or four men left on her deck.

The ship had settled by the stern, almost submerging it and bringing the forward part of the hull out of water. We were all stripped for the swim and watched with catlike intensity the rise of air bubbles from the hatches indicating that the ship would yet float. From the wake of the *Alabama* and far astern, a long distinct line of wreckage could be seen winding with the tide like a snake, with here and there a human head appearing among it.

The *Alabama's* final plunge was a remarkable freak, witnessed by me about 100 yards off. She shot up out of the water bow first and descended on the same line, carrying away with her plunge two of her masts and making a whirlpool of considerable size and strength.

The action had lasted one hour and a half. It had taken only that long to end the career of a ship which had made history for the better part of two years, and whose gallant deeds have secured for her a permanent niche in the hall of maritime fame.

CHAPTER 14

Still Darker Days for the North

THE BATTLE OF CHANCELLORSVILLE

After Burnside's disastrous repulse at Fredericksburg in December 1862 the morale of the Army of the Potomac sank to the lowest point it reached during the war.

The Union boy Jesse B. Young thus described the mood of the men.

The army, driven back from the hills of Fredericksburg, settled down into camp life with a sad and heavy heart. The boys all knew that a blunder had been committed; that the attack against the frightful heights ought never to have been made; and although General Burnside gallantly took all the responsibility on himself yet there sprang up a brooding spirit of discontent, which soon spread throughout the entire army from the privates in the rear rank to the generals in command of corps and grand divisions. Soon after the battle an address from President Lincoln was read to the soldiers which began like this:

TO THE ARMY OF THE POTOMAC:
Although you were not successful the attempt was not an error, nor the failure other than an accident.

When this was read to our regiment, there was an undercurrent of comment which would have given the President some light on the situation, if he had overheard it.

Hoping to retrieve his fortune, Burnside decided on a new line of attack. His efforts resulted in the tragicomedy known as the "Mud March."

378

General Regis de Trobriand, then one of Burnside's brigadiers, took part in this queer military enterprise and reported on it.

Burnside's first thought after Fredericksburg was to try to obtain revenge. Keeping to himself his secret designs, he got ready for a new advance movement and set to work immediately. He himself carefully reconnoitered the banks of the Rappahannock above Falmouth and completed his preparations to cross all his forces at Banks' and United States fords—fords which were not passable at that season of the year; but he had pontoons with him.

We received the order to march on January 20. We had not expected it. What likelihood was there of commencing active operations in the middle of the winter?

In the evening of January 20 we arrived in rear of Banks' Ford. It was a dismal night, one of those sleepless nights when everything has a funereal aspect in which enthusiasm is extinguished, courage worn out, the will enfeebled and the mind stupefied.

The rain had been falling for twelve hours, and there were no indications of any cessation. A few fires were tolerated at first, then authorized. The soldier, benumbed with frost, soaked from head to foot, could at least prepare his coffee and warm his stomach, if not his limbs. Everyone understood that the passage of the river was out of the question.

The rain lasted thirty hours without cessation. To understand the effect one must have lived in Virginia through a winter. In vain had efforts been made to fill up the mudholes or open new side roads; in vain had whole companies dragged at the cannons, the caissons, the wagons carrying ammunition—all was useless. The powers of heaven and earth were against us.

This is how the "Mud March" lived on in the memory of a private soldier in the 118th Pennsylvania Volunteers.

On January 20 a flaming general order indicating prospective success was published to every regiment. But stirring appeals had lost their effectiveness; what was to be done, we considered, had better be done— and talked of afterward.

During the night a pouring, pelting rain set in, an undoubted indication of the commencement of the usual January thaw. The wind blew a gale; rest was out of the question. All the solid ground disappeared, and in its place, on the roads and in the fields, there was mud of a depth and consistency that held tight whatever penetrated it, so that release without assistance was almost impossible. It seemed scarcely conceivable that less than twenty-four hours should produce such a surprising change. The feed of men and animals, the wheels of gun, caisson, limber and wagon had so stirred and agitated the pasty substance that, as the nature of the soil varied, in one place it was a deep, sticky loam, and in another a thick fluid extract. Twelve horses could not move a gun. The wheels of vehicles disappeared entirely. Pontoons on their carriages stood fixed and helpless in the roadway. Human skill, strength and ingenuity were exhausted in the attempt to get forward the indispensable artillery, ammunition and bridges. The woods were resonant with "Heave! Ho, heave!" as if sailors were working away at the capstan. When night came on, the regiment, which had started in the early morning, had heaved itself along a distance of about three miles.

There was no improvement on the twenty-second; further progress was impracticable, and the command remained fastened to its uncomfortable bivouac. On the other side of the river the enemy had erected large boards, on which were displayed taunting phrases. On one: "Burnside stuck in the mud"; on another: "Yanks, if you can't place your pontoons yourself, we will send you help." They had impressed all the plows in the neighborhood and could be seen turning the sod in every direction, intending to assist the elements in their purpose to stop the progress of our army. They needed no such aid: their purpose had been fully accomplished unassisted.

On the twenty-third it was officially announced that the campaign was abandoned and the troops were ordered to return to their former camping grounds. Such directions were easy to publish, but their execution was not so easy. The army was fairly fast where it was—literally stuck in the mud. It was some twelve miles back to the nearest camp. Pontoons, artillery trains could not be moved. Subsistence was exhausted and the Army of the Potomac felt the pinch of hunger. To relieve this pressure the whole army was set to road-making, and by night a very creditable corduroy road had been completed all the way to the rear. Over it during the night all wheels were successfully moved. The troops followed on the twenty-fourth, the rain for the first time subsiding. Before evening the brigade was back to its old quarters, not to be disturbed until bud, blossom and flower indicated that the

elements had ceased to war with man, and that, freed from their inter-
ference, man might again make war against himself.

With the return of Burnside's men to their camps, his career
as commander of the Army of the Potomac came to an inglorious
end, and Lincoln chose General Joseph Hooker as his new leader.
Hooker was then forty-eight years old, but still the beau ideal of
a soldier. A graduate of West Point and a veteran of the Mexican War, he was tall, handsome, dashing, and gave the impression
of extreme self-confidence. He had distinguished himself in the
Peninsular Campaign, at Second Manassas, at South Mountain
and at Antietam where, shot in the foot, he had been carried from
the field.

His soldiers admired him and had bestowed on him the sobri-
quet "Fighting Joe." After the disaster of Fredericksburg, where
Hooker had obeyed orders although convinced of their unrea-
sonableness, he had criticized Burnside so severely that the latter
requested the removal of either "Fighting Joe" or himself. Lincoln chose to remove Burnside.

Under its new leadership the army picked up in spirit. After a
few weeks Hooker invited the President to Falmouth for a grand
parade.

One of Hooker's soldiers, Robert G. Carter, left us a lively narrative of this event.

The army had been looking forward to this parade for some time, and
great preparations had been made for a fine display. For several days
large parties had been busy with spade, pick and shovel, leveling, filling
ditches, removing stumps and stones, cutting down ridges and draining
puddles, until the country was more level than the inhabitants had ever
seen it before.

The men impatiently waited in the bitter, stinging cold until their
fingers grew numb. The wind swept across the open space. The horses
grew restless, but finally a salute from the guns of a battery announced
the approach of the President.

Whether intentionally or inadvertently, Mr. Lincoln had been furnished with a small, pony-built horse about fourteen hands high. The
President's legs looked longer than ever, and his toes seemed almost to
touch the ground. He wore the same solemn suit of black that he always

assumed, a tall silk hat, a little the worse for wear, with a long full-skirted black coat. Altogether he would have presented a comical picture, had it not been for those sad, anxious eyes, so full of melancholy foreboding, that peered forth from his shaggy eyebrows. He rode remarkably well, *i.e.*, with a wonderfully good seat, but with a loose, swaying, undulating movement, peculiar to the Western circuit rider.

It was a beautiful sight, this military pageant of over 100,000 veteran soldiers passing by in a steady stream. Hours went by. The drums and bands kept up their ceaseless music, and the light danced among the moving columns. But at last the rearmost regiment passed, dipped its flag and disappeared. The immense cavalcade of officers and orderlies rode slowly back to camp.

Leaving General Sedgwick with 40,000 men opposite Lee, who was still entrenched on the battlefield of Fredericksburg, Hooker struck out for the upper fords of the Rappahannock with the remainder of the army, some 80,000 men, to attack the Confederate flank. Sedgwick at the same time was ordered to hold himself ready for a frontal onslaught. Since Lee had only 62,000 men all told, he would either have to retreat or fight in the open on two fronts.

After the war General de Trobriand analyzed the plan and pronounced it admirable.

On April 27 Hooker began his movement on Chancellorsville. Chancellorsville was not a city, a village or even a hamlet. It was a solitary house in the midst of a cultivated clearing, surrounded on all sides by woods, which gave the region the name of the *Wilderness*. A veritable solitude, impenetrable for the deploying or quick maneuvering of an army. It was not there that Hooker had planned to give battle, but it was a well-chosen point for concentrating his forces. From that point he could strike the enemy, or at least force him to come out of his position, which was as weak from the rear as it was strong from the front. If the Confederate army fell back on Richmond, it presented its flank to our attack, and if Lee were stopped or delayed by some obstacle and pursued at the same time by a force strong enough to press his rear guard vigorously, his retreat might be changed to a rout. If, on the contrary, he marched toward Chancellorsville to meet us, he was forced to accept battle in the open field, in unforeseen conditions, exposed to attack by a pursuing army as much as on the Richmond road. Attacked at the same time both in front and rear, Lee ran the chance of being cut to pieces and would be very fortunate if he saved the remnant of his forces.

Such was Hooker's well-conceived plan, the secret of which was confided to no one, not even to his most intimate friends among the officers.

The campaign began auspiciously. The troops were full of confidence, as attested by a private in the Corn Exchange Regiment, which led the advance.

The army was in splendid health and buoyant spirits, secure in the knowledge of its strength, confident in the ability of its leader. General Hooker had popularized his administration by giving special attention to the commissariat. He directed a diet which in quantity, quality and variety was captivating, appetizing and nutritious. He also wisely permitted a judicious allowance of leaves of absence to officers and furloughs to enlisted men.

When the "general" sounded on the early morning of the twenty-seventh of April, the response was as ready as if the troops were starting from a night's bivouac.

At noon of April 29 the crossing of the Rappahannock was effected at Kelly's Ford on canvas pontoons, and then the march continued, steady and uninterrupted, to Ely's Ford on the Rapidan. The stream was waist-deep and rapid, and in crossing it the extra ammunition, haversacks, knapsacks and cartridge boxes were carried on the head and held in place by the rifle, pressed on them and grasped in both hands. At seven-thirty the men bivouacked near the river.

The march began with brisk, active gait, but its alacrity was soon checked. The skirmishers were much delayed in forcing their way through the thick underbrush, and their halts affected the movement of the whole column.

Nearing the Chancellorsville House, a most pretentious mansion, the skirmishers were brought to a temporary halt in front of a line of earthworks seen from the edge of the timber. As they entered the clearing, they speedily mounted the earthworks, while the enemy were leaving them. A few laggards were captured, and these indicated by their conversation and appearance such astonishment at the unexpected presence of an enemy as to assure the soldiery in their belief that they had really effected a complete surprise.

It was about eleven o'clock when a halt was made in front of the Chancellorsville House. It was a house of the Southern type, belonging to a well-known family of the neighborhood, still occupied by the women, and it stood there alone in a clearing. It was a large, commodious, two-story brick building, with peaked roof and a wing and pillared porches, about twelve miles from Fredericksburg and about six from Banks' Ford.

Upon the upper porch was quite a bevy of ladies in light, dressy, attractive spring costumes. They scolded audibly and reviled bitterly. They had little conception of the terrors in store for them. They were to see all the horrors of the battle, feel the hot blasts of shot and shell and, before another day was over, pitifully plead to be carried to a place of safety.

The Corn Exchange Regiment did not linger at the Chancellorsville mansion. The troops continued their march, eager to capitalize on their surprise movement and come to grips with the enemy.

Then something happened which was as incomprehensible to the soldier relating it as it was to all officers from lieutenants to major generals.

The march toward Fredericksburg was shortly resumed, and continued without incident for about two miles, when it was interrupted at the foot of a piece of high ground. Meanwhile our skirmishers had struck the enemy's line. There they stood facing each other, steady and silent, gazing, the one in apparent wonderment, and the other in real surprise at the unexpected situation.

Conceiving that this ridge was apparently the key of the position if a battle was to be fought in the vicinity, the soldiers awaited in earnest, anxious readiness the direction to occupy it. But it was decreed otherwise, and the spot that was the scene of the bloodiest, severest fight in the next day's struggle was permitted to remain in the loose grip of the enemy from whom, at that moment, it could have been readily wrested.

After several hours of impatient waiting, the whole division was withdrawn to the rifle pits near the Chancellorsville House. The soldiers were as discomfited as if they had been checked by a serious repulse.

All enthusiasm vanished, all the bright hopes of success disappeared. The belief that the campaign would culminate in the utter rout of the enemy was changed to sullen disappointment. Before the discharge of a single gun, before the firing of a single shot, somebody had again blundered.

General Regis de Trobriand was severely critical of Hooker's sudden change of plans.

The crux on which everything had depended was to assemble the army at Chancellorsville before the enemy could oppose us at that point. This part of the plan had been admirably executed, as it had been ably conceived, and it can be truly said that up to that point General Hooker had shown himself to be an able tactician.

So there, on the thirtieth of April, at night, the Confederates lay still motionless in their positions in rear of Fredericksburg, prepared for an attack on their right, while in rear of their left four of our corps were already united and were about to be joined by a fifth. On one side Sedgwick, on the other Hooker, in a position which seemed an assurance, in advance, of a victory. "Now," said Hooker in an order to the army, "the enemy must flee shamefully or come out of his defenses to our ground, where he is doomed to certain destruction!" Nobody doubted that before two days all our past reverses would be effaced by the annihilation of Lee's army.

What Hooker called "our ground" to give battle on was about half way from Chancellorsville to Fredericksburg. On that side the country was open and favorable for the maneuvering of an army. It was therefore important to get there at the earliest possible moment. Two broad roads led to it, coming together near a church called Tabernacle, while a third road, running near the river, led to Banks' Ford. By these three roads Hooker renewed his movement on Friday morning May 1. Henry W. Slocum with the 12th Corps held the right by the Plank Road; Sykes with a division of the 5th Corps advanced in the center, and George Meade led a column along the road near the river. The three other corps, the 2nd, the 3rd and the 11th, were to follow.

But before Hooker had left Chancellorsville, Lee had started to meet him, leaving behind him only Early's division reinforced by one brigade; he had hurried all the rest forward at midnight in the direction of Chancellorsville. Between ten and eleven o'clock in the morning his advance guard encountered our cavalry skirmishers and forced them back. But behind them Sykes had already deployed his division. He charged the enemy resolutely, drove them back in his turn and established himself in the center position which had been assigned to him by his instructions.

Everything went well with us. On the right Slocum had encountered no opposition; on the left Meade had arrived in full view of Banks' Ford without the least obstacle. He had only to form promptly in order

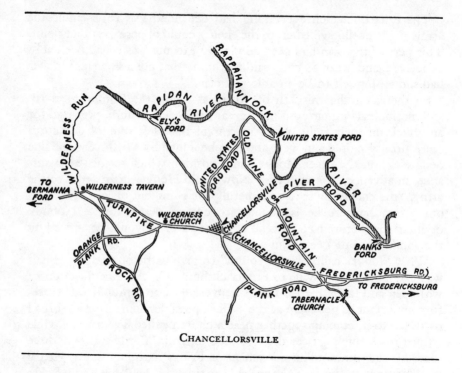

CHANCELLORSVILLE

of battle. The corps in the rear would have had time to get into line while the enemy made his disposition on his side, on the ground where General Hooker had devoted him to "certain destruction."

It was at this time and at this place that General Hooker virtually lost the battle of Chancellorsville by an error as unexpected as it was inexplicable.

Instead of pushing his forces forward, he hurriedly sent the order to the three columns to return to the positions they had occupied the night before. Among the generals who were in position to judge for themselves, I know not one who considered the measure otherwise than deplorable. Darius N. Couch, before withdrawing Hancock's division, sent word to pray the general in chief to countermand the order; Gouverneur K. Warren, who commanded the corps of topographical engineers, hurried to headquarters with the same errand. Nothing availed. The decision was maintained. The columns fell back uneasy, astonished above all that the first order given by Hooker as general in command in front of the enemy was to retreat without fighting. That did not at all resemble the Hooker when he had been commanding a division.

The position which we voluntarily abandoned to the enemy was excellent; the position which we took in place of it was detestable. In the first, we could have deployed and fought well; in the second, we were penned up in the midst of natural obstacles on low and flat ground. In the first, we barred to the enemy the only three routes by which he could penetrate into the Wilderness; in the second, we gave up to him the Plank Road, and it will soon be seen what use he made of it against us. Finally, in the first case, we preserved all the material and moral advantage of the offensive; in the second, we subjected ourselves to all the disadvantage of a defensive accepted without necessity, as it was without preparation.

The enemy took possession immediately of the position which we so benevolently had abandoned to him. He planted his guns there and followed our retreating troops closely.

General Lee had marched the bulk of his army toward Chancellorsville with the intention of selecting a good defensive position, there to await Hooker's assault. Such a position was yielded to him without a fight by Hooker's untimely retreat.

However, it was not in Lee's nature to remain on the defensive for long. How he changed to the offensive is told by Huntington W. Jackson, a Southern officer who heard the story from General Fitzhugh Lee, a nephew of Robert Lee and a distinguished cavalry leader.

On May 1 General Lee wished to cut Hooker off from the United States Ford, preventing his communication with Sedgwick, and rode down himself and examined the lands all the way to the river, but found no place where he could execute this movement. Returning at night, he found Jackson and asked him if he knew of any place to attack. Jackson said he had been inquiring about roads and soon returned with the Reverend Doctor B. T. Lacey, who said a circuit could be made around by the Wilderness Tavern. A young man living in the country, and then in the cavalry, was sent for to act as guide. Lee and Jackson took their seats on a log to the north side of the Plank Road and a little distant from the wood. "General," Lee said, "we must get ready to attack the enemy, and you must make arrangements to move around his right flank." General Lee then pointed out to Jackson the general direction of his route and the necessity of celerity and secrecy.

A captain on General Jackson's staff said that he had bivouacked in the woods, and about the middle of the night he awoke and saw Lee and Jackson seated and bending over a campfire which had almost died out; they were then planning for the flank attack. At daybreak the column was on the march.

> Lee's audacious plan involved the violation of an old military principle—not to divide an army in the face of the enemy, especially if the latter is the stronger. But the Confederate leaders believed that a successful surprise outweighed a textbook theory.
> Even Stonewall Jackson's own staff officers were left in ignorance of the coming move, as we learn from Major Heros von Borcke, who was one of them.

All was bustle and activity as I galloped along the lines on the morning of the second. Jackson's corps was marching in close columns in a direction which set us all wondering what could be his intentions, but we would as soon have thought of questioning the sagacity of our admired chief as of hesitating to follow him blindly wherever he should lead.

Thus commenced the famous flank march which, more than any other operation of the war, proved the brilliant strategical talents of General Lee and the consummate ability of his lieutenant. By about four o'clock we had completed our movement and reached a patch of wood in rear of the enemy's right wing, formed by the 11th Corps, which was encamped in a large open field not more than half a mile distant. Halting here, the cavalry threw forward a body of skirmishers to occupy the enemy's attention, while the divisions of Jackson's corps, numbering in all about 28,000 men, moved into line of battle as fast as they arrived.

Lieutenant Colonel H. W. Jackson, C.S.A., gives this graphic description of the view he had of the unsuspecting Federal 11th Corps.

Upon reaching the Plank Road some five miles west of Chancellorsville, while waiting for Stonewall to come up, I made a personal reconnoissance. What a sight presented itself to me! The soldiers were in groups, laughing, chatting, smoking, probably engaged here and there in games of cards and other amusements, feeling safe and comfortable. In the rear of them were other parties driving up and slaughtering beeves.

So impressed was I with my discovery that I rode rapidly back to the point on the Plank Road where I met Stonewall himself. "General," said I, "ride with me." He assented, and I rapidly conducted him to the point of observation. There had been no change in the picture. It was then about 2:00 P.M. I watched him closely. His eyes burned with a brilliant glow, lighting up a sad face; his expression was one of intense interest; his face was colored slightly with the sense of approaching battle and radiant at the success of his flank movement.

To my remarks he did not reply once during the five minutes he was on the hill; and yet his lips were moving.

One more look on the Federal lines, and then he rode rapidly down the hill, his arms flapping to the motions of his horse, over whose head it seemed, good rider as he was, he would certainly go.

Alas! I had looked on him for the last time.

Brilliant as the Confederate strategy was, it almost came to grief. The road over which Jackson had to travel ran fairly close to the Federal front, and his presence was discovered.

Regis de Trobriand, the Union general who came near upsetting Lee's plan, gave the following account of that day.

Hooker began to be troubled about what was going on in our front beyond that dense curtain of woods. He sent forward troops, and through an opening in the woods there appeared a column of Rebels marching rapidly from the left to the right, presenting its flank to our whole line of battle.

This movement threatened our right, which appeared to be unprepared for it. As it was the opposite side from that by which the enemy

had advanced from Fredericksburg, less disposition had been made
against an attack there than elsewhere. The whole 11th Corps prolonged
the general line parallel to the road. A small brigade thrown back
barred this road with two guns, resting on nothing, leaving our extreme
right completely in the air.

General Hooker had visited that part of the line without prescribing
any change. Only when the movement of the enemy revealed to him
the possibility of an attack from that direction, he sent some additional
instructions to General Howard, which had no other effect than to
cause an advance of the pickets. There was no change made in the
disposition of the troops. General Hooker did not believe in the danger
of such an attack and preferred to regard the movement we had discovered as a retreat of Lee on Gordonsville. Otherwise he would not
have telegraphed a few hours later to General Sedgwick, "Take Fredericksburg and everything you find there, and pursue the enemy vigorously. *We know that he is in full retreat,* endeavoring to save his trains.
Two of Sickles' divisions are upon him."

General Slocum was far from sharing that confidence. Toward noon
I met him visiting our front, which adjoined that of General Howard,
to see how we were placed and examining attentively the position of
the 11th Corps.

"Let me recommend you to fortify yourself as well as possible," he
said to me. "The enemy is massing a considerable force on our right.
In two or three hours he will fall on Howard, and you will have him
upon you in strong force."

I was about to follow his advice when the division received orders
to advance. We moved forward out of the woods and crossed the open
ground which extended in our front. It was an effort to cut in two the
column of the enemy, which continued to defile before us, and to sweep
away what must be his rear guard.

Our advance was delayed in the woods. We had to build or rebuild
bridges over some brooks. We had to cut our way painfully through
the thick underbrush, a network of branches and briars. Finally by
main force our first regiments reached the crossroads on which the rear
of the enemy's column was marching. A brisk fire was opened immediately; our men charged upon the enemy, who were surprised at seeing
an attack made upon them from a thicket which they thought absolutely
impenetrable. Some fled, others surrendered; the 27th Georgia resisted
stoutly, but it was soon surrounded and compelled to lay down its arms.

More than 500 prisoners remained in our hands and were immediately sent to the rear.

But we had been too late. The main column of the enemy had passed, and suddenly the noise of distant firing came through the air. Our ranks became silent, as if by magic. Each one listened and turned his head toward Chancellorsville.

In a moment the aides passed at a gallop along the front of our regiments. The command rang out from one end of the division to the other, "*Forward!* Double-quick! March!" And we were soon swiftly returning on the run by the road over which we had just come. Hurry up! Jackson has crushed our right; the 11th Corps is in utter rout. Hurry up! Quick, or we will be cut off!

Harassed and out of breath, we finally reached the edge of the open ground that we had first crossed on leaving our lines. Jackson's troops filled the entrenchments which the 11th Corps had raised, and the Rebel flag floated behind the abatis which in the morning had protected the front of our division.

All day long the Federal right wing had received warnings. Captain Hartwell Osborn, a cavalry officer in the menaced 11th Corps, relates the almost unbelievable indifference with which headquarters treated reports that were contrary to its preconceived opinions.

General Hooker had committed a most serious blunder in the part assigned to his cavalry. Instead of utilizing it to observe the movements of the enemy, he retained only a small division under General Alfred Pleasonton, the rest of the force, under General George Stoneman, being directed to make a raid upon the communications of the enemy. The force assigned to the 1st Division of the 11th Corps was just thirty-five men, a number barely enough for orderly duty. Never was there a situation where cavalry was more necessary, and never had a great army so small a force.

General Charles Devens' 1st Division of the 11th Corps formed the right flank of the army. Its 1st Brigade was posted on the extreme right. It had no reserve, and no protection except a slashing of small trees and bushes.

The movement of Jackson's force on roads parallel to our line had been noticed by our pickets, and the line advanced to observe it. The

Confederate forces appeared to be moving away from our front, and it was believed that the Confederates were in full retreat on Richmond. General Daniel E. Sickles hastened to get permission to follow the enemy. At this time most of Jackson's infantry had passed and were concealed in the dark recesses of the forest. Not having sufficient forces, as he thought, General Sickles called for and secured Francis C. Barlow's brigade of the 11th Corps, which was in reserve near the Wilderness Church. General Sickles' plan of following up, as he supposed, the retreating army and giving them battle had an important relation to the 11th Corps and resulted in the large force under his command moving off two miles out of line and out of touch with or supporting distance from the 11th Corps.

General Sickles had sent a captain of his staff to request from General Howard a brigade to co-operate in his attack. General Howard regretted that he had no brigade which he could properly spare, as Barlow's brigade was one of his largest and best and he could not think of detaching it. In about an hour, as I learned from a staff officer who was present, the captain returned with an order from General Hooker detaching Barlow's brigade and directing that it should report to General Sickles.

This removal of Barlow's brigade was one of the worst blunders of that fateful day. It not only deprived the 11th Corps of a strong brigade well commanded and in a position to meet an attack from the west and north, but it made the whole reserve artillery comparatively useless. Had all the guns of this splendid artillery enjoyed the infantry support which General Howard had planned, they would in all probability have held the enemy in check till night.

Barlow's brigade marched fully two miles south but discovered no enemy. Jackson's column pursued the march toward the west and upon reaching the Brock Road to Germanna Ford turned north, and at 2:30 P.M. the advance regiments began to form on the right rear of the Union force. From a hill General Jackson had a clear view of the lines of the 11th Corps and placed his force with exact knowledge of the position. Jackson had thus a force of about 30,000 men on the flank and rear of the 11th Corps, which, depleted of Barlow's brigade, numbered less than 9,000 men, only about 1,400 of whom were posted to resist an attack.

About noon General Hooker, superbly mounted, a picture of manly beauty, accompanied by a large staff, had come riding the lines. He was greeted with cheers as he passed, and we all were relieved as we felt that our position had been personally inspected by the commanding general.

General Howard directed General Hooker's attention to the fact that there was a wide gap between the right of the 11th Corps and the river. General Hooker replied that he would send a division of cavalry to occupy that gap. It need hardly be added that General Hooker never did this.

The colonels of the regiments in line were very anxious. As the afternoon wore away, the reports from the pickets came in often and were so specific and imperative that the colonel of the 55th Ohio took the men to brigade headquarters, and then to division headquarters, expressing his deep concern and requesting immediate action. General Devens received the information coldly and, upon the third visit, grew impatient and at last said, "You are frightened, sir," with another remark about western colonels being more scared than hurt. The colonel of the 24th Ohio brought in four scouts who had been far to the front and reported that the enemy was massing on our right. General Devens directed General Nathaniel McLean to send him back to his regiment. The colonel of the 75th Ohio sent a lieutenant colonel with an urgent message of like import, but General Devens said he did not believe it. The colonel then went to corps headquarters, where he was laughed at and warned not to bring on a panic.

But the most convincing evidence was from an artillery officer, Captain Hubert Dilger, prominent on account of his daredevil gallantry in action. About 2:00 P.M. Captain Dilger with an orderly rode west beyond our line. He soon ran into the enemy and had much difficulty in escaping capture. He went to see General Howard. A long-legged major of cavalry laughed at his story and refused to allow him to report. The army commander returned word to General Howard that the enemy was retreating, and that General Sickles was following him. Brigadier General James H. Van Alen, chief of Hooker's staff, wired at 4:10 P.M., "We know the enemy is fleeing and trying to save his trains." Captain Dilger returned sadly to his battery, and made preparations for the fight, even refusing to allow his horses to go to water.

Before he had completed his arrangements the storm broke. A shell from the right came down the road and burst right over our heads. This was the signal for Jackson's line to advance. Along our front deer and wild game came scurrying out of the woods. The firing increased and soon came nearer. The right was steadily falling back. The right regiment of the brigade, the 75th Ohio, having changed front, now began firing, and bullets began to hail down our line from right and rear. We had no enemy in front and yet had no orders to change front. It was the most trying experience the command ever endured. General Devens had been repeatedly urged to permit a change of front but had refused.

At last the storm signal reached us. From away to our rear and close at hand on our right came the Rebel yell. The men of the right brigade now began to come back in panic. The open ground to our rear was a mass of yelling Butternuts as the left of Jackson's line charged three batteries of reserve artillery. The 25th Ohio at last changed front and began to fire. The 55th formed behind it. After about three volleys the 25th broke. The 55th held for two volleys, and then broke back, and the whole clearing became one mass of panic-stricken soldiers flying at the top of their speed.

General Howard was the last man off the field. He sat on his horse in the roadway as cool as if on parade, but urging and insisting and entreating the flying men to go slower. General Carl Schurz had formed a line facing west, and although his line was afterward broken and went to the rear, the Rebel column was halted and reformed at this point. Adolphus Buschbeck's brigade held its ground the longest of all the corps; they climbed over to the reverse side of their entrenchments, steadily faced the overwhelming numbers and delivered their fire. They clung to the earthworks until their position was completely turned, and then retired in comparatively good order.

I was now helpless and my occupation was principally to observe the Rebel troops. They came on with very little attention to line formation, but they were all disciplined and eager to go on. I heard an officer cry, "Oh, for only one more hour of daylight!"

> Just as the panic of the 11th Corps threatened to engulf the entire Union army in disaster, an unusual combination of quick thinking and heroism stopped the onslaught.
>
> General de Trobriand, who was in the midst of the turmoil, rendered a good account of the turnabout.

At five o'clock the men appeared falling back hurriedly. A moment more, and the enemy, emerging from the woods in deep masses, with

Rebel yell threw himself upon the few regiments which still were opposing him. They were quickly swept away. The remainder of the
division, taken in flank, melted away and rolled upon the next division
which it carried with it. Along the road in the midst of the fleeing
multitude the wagons, the ambulances, horses and mules, which had
been imprudently left in that part of the field, were precipitated pell-
mell. It was not an engagement; it was a rout.

In the midst of the tumult Hooker hurried up. Very fortunately he
found at hand Berry's division, the one which he had so long commanded. "Forward," he cried, "with the bayonet!" The division advanced with a firm and steady step, cleaving the multitude of disbanded
men as the bow of a vessel cleaves the waves of the sea. It struck the
advance of the Confederates obliquely and stopped it with the aid of
the 12th Corps artillery.

Jackson's attack, arrested on the left and in front, was thrown toward
the right. Thus a new, terrible and imminent danger presented itself.
The division had left its artillery without protection. The guns were
there in full view under the guard of the cannoneers only. Multitudes
of flying men had taken this direction in the hope of finding, farther on,
an opportunity to get back into our lines. The moment was most
critical. Who should save the guns from almost certain capture?

At this instant General Pleasonton, who had accompanied us in our
forward movement, returned with two regiments of cavalry. On arriving he recognized at a glance the imminence of the peril. Then he
assumed the direct command of the artillery at that point.

To put it in position he must have at least ten or twelve minutes. He
called Major Keenan of the 8th Pennsylvania and said, "Major, charge
with your regiment and hold the Rebels in check until I can get these
pieces into position. It must be done at all hazards."

"General, I will do it," Major Keenan replied simply. It was certain
death. He knew it; but the honor of the duty assigned and the importance of the service to be done lighted up his features with a noble smile.
He had but 400 or 500 men. Riding at their head, he charged furiously
at the victoriously advancing enemy and fell lifeless on the line, whose
progress he seemed still to bar with his dead body. Pleasonton gained
the ten minutes which he required and had twenty-two guns in line,
loaded with double charges of canister and ready to open fire.

Soon the wood was full of Rebels. A moment later their flags appeared
behind the entrenchments, and a mass of men bounded over with a

fierce yell. Now was the time. The twenty-two pieces made but one detonation, followed by a deep silence. When the smoke rose, everything had disappeared. The mass of men had been annihilated.

This lightning stroke marked the limit of Stonewall Jackson's success. The firing still continued behind the cover of the entrenchments, and some attempts were even made to renew the charge against the guns, but Sickles soon arrived, followed by A. W. Whipple's division. D. B. Birney's division came back in its turn, and the contest ceased on both sides.

It might not have ceased, however, had not Stonewall Jackson tried to make a personal reconnaissance. What happened then, in the gathering dusk of the spring evening, is told by R. E. Wilbourne, Jackson's Chief Signal Officer.

From the order Jackson sent to General Stuart it was evident that his intention was to storm the enemy's works as soon as the lines were formed. While these orders were issued, Jackson started slowly along the pike toward the enemy. When we had ridden only a few rods, our little party was fired upon, the balls passing diagonally across the pike. I hardly think the troops saw us. At the firing our horses wheeled suddenly to the left, and General Jackson galloped away into the woods to get out of range of the bullets, but had not gone over twenty steps ere the brigade to the left of the turnpike fired a volley. It was by this fire that Jackson was wounded. We could distinctly hear General Hill calling, at the top of his voice, to his troops to cease firing. I was alongside of Jackson and saw his arm fall at his side, loosing the rein. The limb of a tree took off his cap and threw him flat on the back of his horse. I rode after him, but Jackson soon regained his seat, caught the bridle in his right hand, and turning his horse toward our men, somewhat checked his speed. I caught his horse as he reached the pike, and just as I caught the reins, Captain Wynn rode up on the opposite side. By this time the confusion was over and all was quiet; no living creature could be seen save us three.

I dismounted, and seeing that he was faint, I asked the General what I could do for him, or if he felt able to ride as far as into our lines. He answered, "You had best take me down," leaning as he spoke toward me and then falling, partially fainting from loss of blood. I caught him in my arms and held him until Captain Wynn could get his feet out of the stirrups, then we carried him a few steps and laid him on the ground.

The rest of the tragedy is told by James P. Smith, one of Jackson's aides, who tells a heartbreaking story of what befell the wounded general before an ambulance was reached.

I reached his side at that moment and made an unskilled attempt to stay the blood. Couriers were sent for a doctor and for an ambulance. Litter bearers were brought from the line, and we started to the rear. Twice men who were bearing the stretcher were shot down, and once the wounded, fainting general fell to the ground. At last, when it seemed an age of terrific fire, we reached an ambulance.

At the field hospital in the wilderness after midnight the left arm was amputated near the shoulder, and a ball taken from the right hand. A magnanimous note from General Lee came on the day following:

I cannot express my regret at this occurrence. Could I have directed events, I should have been disabled in your stead. I congratulate you upon the victory which is due your skill and energy.
                    Most truly yours,
                            R. E. LEE, General

When I read this dispatch to General Jackson, he turned his face away and said, "General Lee is very kind, but he should give the praise to God."

At Guinea's Station the next Sunday afternoon at 3:15 the famous soldier was content to die and saying, "Let us cross the river and rest under the shade of the trees!" he passed on.

The slaughter of May 2 was over. Then occurred a tragedy which in its weird frightfulness dwarfed even the terrible happenings that had preceded it.

We have the story from the soldier-correspondent George F. Williams, who since the days of the Peninsular Campaign had become an officer. One can sense the feeling of horror which still possessed him a quarter of a century later when he recalled that nerve-shaking night.

A dead silence had fallen on the woods. We had, however, been at rest only a few minutes when our ears were saluted by what seemed scattering musketry. No attack was made on our line, and I listened to the singular sounds, conjecturing what this strange, intermittent firing could be.

"I say, that's a queer sort of musketry," remarked the captain. "It don't sound much like picket firing, and there's not enough of it for breastwork fighting. I wonder what it means?"

As he spoke, a sergeant belonging to the pickets came scrambling over the pile of logs and earth.

"What's the matter, Sergeant? Are you wounded?" I asked.

"No, sir; I'm all right. But the woods are all on fire out there, and we're going to dig a trench to keep it from spreading; so I've come in for more men and some tools. Do you know the woods over there are full of wounded?"

"Good heavens! Is it possible?" I exclaimed in horror. "Can't you save them?"

"Too late, I'm afraid. That's been tried already. Why, we calculate there are 2,000 or 3,000 dead and wounded, both Federal and Confederate, lying there under the burning trees."

"That accounts for the queer musketry," remarked the captain. "It's the fire exploding the muskets lying on the ground."

On my telling the major the awful condition of affairs, he decided at once to rescue the wounded. With a force of nearly a hundred volunteers, he and I started for the abandoned battleground. Crossing the field of the engagement, we found it entirely deserted by both armies, but thickly strewn with debris. In the distance toward the Chancellorsville House I could distinguish a body of Confederate infantry. As we were not within range of their rifles, our party pushed boldly across the corner of the open ground. We found the irregularly dropping musketry fire still going on; and the ominous roar of the advancing flames betrayed the rapidity of their progress. I could hear the screams of pain and frenzied appeals for succor uttered by the hapless wounded, who seemed doomed to a dreadful fate.

"Come, men! Into the woods with you and pick up every live man you meet!" cried the major. "In with you, boys! Leave your muskets behind you. . . . Lieutenant, you remain here and see that the rescued are placed in safety."

The men quickly unslung their knapsacks and, sticking their bayoneted guns into the ground, disappeared among the trees. In a few minutes some of them returned, carrying groaning men, and I busied myself in seeing them comfortably disposed of at a safe distance from the fire. Our fellows were making no distinction: the blue and gray came side by side as they had fallen. The Confederate infantry we had seen now began firing at us, but after a few rounds they apparently discovered our errand, for they at once ceased, giving a wild sort of cheer to encourage us, their yell sounding strange amid the crackling of the flames. In a few minutes we had thirty or forty poor creatures in the field who loudly cried for water, water! We gave them what we had, and I sent for ambulances. As I gave the order, the major appeared, his face and hands black and grimy.

"It's no use. We can do no more. The fire has got such headway we can't face it and live. Heaven help those poor wretches! My God, it makes my blood run cold to hear them scream!" As he spoke, the stouthearted officer threw himself on the ground, tears coursing down his besmeared cheeks.

It was indeed a hopeless task. As our party reassembled, every man's face grave and awe-stricken, we listened silently to the cries of those beyond all mortal aid. Curses and yells of pain, piteous appeals and spasmodic prayers could be distinguished, but, though we could hear their voices, we were cut off from them by a wall of fire. The flames roared more fiercely, the cries grew fainter, until at last they were hushed. Looking into the burning forest, I saw that every shrub, tendril and sapling were being consumed; even the tree monarchs of that wild region were scorched and killed by the fire. And as the fiery torrent rolled on madly, swiftly, we stood and watched its progress, knowing that in those few fleeting moments hundreds of brave men who had struggled in mortal combat with one another had now passed into a horrible death together.

The early part of that fateful second of May had passed quietly at the Chancellorsville House, where Hooker had his headquarters. Lee was making demonstrations on the Union left to divert attention from Jackson's march, but they amounted to little more than skirmishing. One of Hooker's guards was John M. Gould and he tells what happened as the day progressed.

Early in the morning, say about six or seven o'clock, I was on guard in front of the main door of the house, at the foot of some steps leading up to a piazza. Some of General Hooker's staff were watching the fight on our left from the veranda, and the general himself frequently passed in and out. After a time he mounted his magnificent gray and remained near a fence enclosing the small front yard. A shell came from the Rebel right in direct range with the house, and in a few moments another. A third shell passed directly over General Hooker's head and burst scarcely twenty feet from him. Some small fragments, or perhaps the noise of the explosion, caused his horse to rear and plunge violently, but Hooker reined him in and then galloped off to the front.

At Gettysburg a few months later I met a captured lieutenant of a North Carolina regiment who avowed that he knew the shots to have been fired by the Rebel cavalry general Stuart. The lieutenant's regiment had seen General Hooker's horse and knew that its rider must be an officer of rank. He did pretty nearly put an end to Hooker's military career.

During the day twelve men were detailed from the battalion for duty at the headquarters of General Hooker. Two or three had been posted, and the remainder were lounging about the yard at the rear of the house, when a lively cannonade was opened from the extreme right of the Rebel line. The shells and solid shot flew thickly about the house and some entered the building. Attention was soon called to a still more vigorous artillery fire on our right, where lay the 11th Corps. It became evident that the attack upon the Union left was only a feint to divert attention from this new movement.

Fiercer and fiercer grew the fight, until it seemed as if the whole line was to be engaged. The assault was that of Stonewall Jackson upon the 11th Corps, resulting in its complete rout. The battalion was ordered up to assist in stopping the fugitives. Officers and men alike of the 11th Corps seemed to be seized with an irresistible panic. Away they rushed pell-mell, throwing off arms and clothing, nor did some of them, who succeeded in evading the guard, stop until they had crossed the Rappahannock at United States Ford, four miles distant, having done their best to spread the news of a terrible disaster.

At the center of the Union field the second of May passed uneventfully until the rout of the right made its repercussions felt. Then a shifting of positions took place, ending in a queer night struggle, which one of the participants later remembered with some embarrassment.

Just as the night of May 2 closed in completely, our division was rapidly moved toward the Chancellorsville House, where it was thrown into earthworks vacated the moment before by other troops. Then commenced a series of unauthorized, demoralizing and dispiriting tactics. Directions were first passed along the line from man to man to spread out and cover more ground, then to turn the visor of the cap to the rear so that the rays of the moon might not reflect on it. Then they were cautioned to keep perfectly still; then to lie down; then to stand up and come to a ready; and then to sit down. And so these and various other instructions, repeated and communicated in a whispering, quivering tone, continued until the men were so nervous and unstrung that to establish confidence many of the officers seized rifles and followed literally all the movements with them.

The engagement on Howard's front was over when, about nine o'clock, General Howard himself appeared, followed by a part of his discomfited corps. Their condition did not indicate need of much repair, but they were evidently to be placed well out of the reach of danger. An impressive silence followed. Even the insect world was hushed, and the night birds were voiceless.

The silence was soon disturbed as by the distant rumble of a mighty tempest. To the experienced ear this indescribable whir had another meaning. It was the hum and buzz and tramp of large bodies of men in motion, the rattle and jostle of arms and equipments. Nearer and nearer it approached, and louder and louder it swelled and spread until the veriest tyro could not mistake it. Disciplined battalions were massing for assault, and then distinct and audible came the voice of command, "Right shoulder shift arms! Forward march!" At once the stillness vanished. Off to the right and front instantly every part of the army was hotly engaged in the furies, terrors and uncertainties of a most determined night attack. This memorable assault at Chancellorsville on the night of the second of May, 1863, will ever be vividly recalled as what was then believed to be a repulse of the enemy's assault, but which history shows to have been "Sickles fighting his way home again." For it was not the enemy but Sickles' corps returning from a foolishly ordered night attack. Mistaken in the darkness for Confederates, they had tried to stumble back into our lines.

The Chancellorsville House continued to be the center of Confederate attacks on the following day, May 3. The right and left wings of the Southern army now again were reunited, and Lee saw a chance of delivering a *coup de grâce* to Hooker's demoralized forces. The bloodcurdling scenes enacted there are colorfully described by John M. Gould, who was an eyewitness.

About four o'clock Sunday morning May 3 the battle began in earnest. The brick house became the center of a furious cannonade, for battery after battery, Union and Rebel, from right to left, opened fire. Our battalion was placed on guard at the rear to prevent the escape of stragglers. It was not then under fire. The little handful at the brick house, however, was exposed to a most awful storm of solid shot and shell and even canister and musket balls. Many a missile pierced the walls; some stuck in the brick work; shells exploded in the upper rooms; the chimneys were demolished, and their fragments rained down on the wounded who had crawled near to the walls of the building. All this time the women and children (including some slaves) of the Chancellor family were in the cellar, which seemed to afford the only escape from the battle's fury.

Few private soldiers have such an opportunity to witness the details of a battle as was afforded those who were stationed at headquarters.

A young surgeon, half dead with fright, was binding up the wounds of the men who lay in the yard. His hands trembled so violently and his eyes were so constantly directed to the front that he made little progress and did very imperfect work.

A refreshing contrast to this was afforded by the bravery of some of the men and officers about the house, and especially of General Hooker himself, who was now on horseback, riding down into the very heaviest of the leaden rain; now on foot, coolly walking about from point to point constantly under fire.

The Union line was gradually beaten back until at one time it was very near to the house. The danger of capture by the Rebels seemed so imminent that the surgeons in the building gave orders not to resist if anyone appeared armed and determined to enter. But just then fair range was afforded for the Union batteries, which went hotly to work and soon drove back the Rebel forces.

Not long after this, in the afternoon, a man stationed on a line with the house was seen to make frantic motions as if some terrible calamity threatened the building and its occupants. The roar of the battle was so loud that what he said could not be distinguished. At last he ran nearer and gave us to understand that the house was in flames! Smoke poured down the stairways and out of the windows in heavy volume. Active preparations were at once begun to remove the wounded and prisoners. But while the guard was engaged in this work, a staff officer entered and in a most excited manner ordered the building to be cleared at once. Thus many helpless sufferers were left to perish.

The only avenue of escape that presented itself was the road leading to United States Ford. For a considerable distance the path extended through a large open field and then entered the woods. Across this field the deadly missiles of the Rebels were sweeping. One by one those who had been at the house, including the women and children, ran the gantlet of fire and reached the forest beyond—not all, however, unharmed.

Just at the edge of the woods a corps of Union troops lay on the ground. It was like *home* to a traveler just returned from dangers of shipwreck or worse calamity.

> While events were moving swiftly around the Chancellorsville House, Sedgwick and Early had been facing each other at Fredericksburg, occupying nearly the same relative positions as the two opposing forces had held when Burnside suffered his bloody defeat.
>
> It was only after Jackson had smashed through Howard's corps that Hooker ordered his troops at Fredericksburg to make a concerted supporting effort. General de Trobriand noted how Hooker's orders were carried into effect.

On the afternoon of the second, Hooker, seeing his right broken in, had thought immediately of making a diversion from the other side which would turn Lee. He sent an order to General Sedgwick to cross the Rappahannock as quickly as possible and march out on the Chancellorsville Road, attacking and destroying whatever force might bar his way. Sedgwick received the dispatch about midnight, having already crossed the river. He immediately marched on Fredericksburg without loss of time.

General Early, commanding the Confederate forces, was forewarned and prepared for an attack. Immediately on entering Fredericksburg Sedgwick sent four regiments to try the heights; they were received with a deadly fire and were compelled to retire. The preparations for a final assault occupied the last hours of the night. It was not till eleven o'clock in the morning of May 3 that the two attacking columns charged the entrenchments. In spite of the vigor of the defense, Marye's Heights were carried by main force. At the same time Howe's division carried the enemy's position on the left, and the whole line was ours, with a part of the artillery and a large number of prisoners.

Without loss of time the troops re-formed, and the 6th Corps advanced on the Chancellorsville Road. It was then about four o'clock in the afternoon (Sunday May 3). At this moment the army under the immediate command of Hooker was already inclosed behind a second entrenched line, and the battle there was virtually finished, entirely to the advantage of Lee.

Leaving in front of us at Chancellorsville what troops were necessary to hold us in the cramped position which we occupied, hardly able to move, Lee sent McLaws' division, strengthened by Mahone's brigade, against Sedgwick. Sedgwick's advance was arrested when night came to put an end to the engagement.

> Jackson's command had now passed to General Stuart, and it was feared that the absence of their beloved leader would impair the valor of his troops. A Southern officer, Colonel W. L. Goldsmith, relates first what happened on the evening of Jackson's wounding after the Confederate attack had been stopped by massed artillery, and then how his men fought the next morning.

I was just in time to catch the full benefit of that fearful cannonade of the Federals where, it is said, forty pieces of cannon were trained to sweep the Plank Road in order to check the victorious Confederates. Everybody lay flat on the ground. In a little while four litter bearers, carrying a wounded man, put him down so close to me that I could have touched him with my hand. I soon found it was Stonewall Jackson. He moaned frequently and piteously. When his friends proposed to move him out of the line of fire, he told them "not to mind him, but look out for themselves." The night attack was abandoned, and, as we lay down within a hundred yards of the enemy's line, I could plainly hear them cutting trees and building breastworks.

Next morning, the third of May, the order came to "charge and remember Jackson."

Instead of Jackson's approaching death casting a gloom and damper on the troops, it had just the opposite result. I never saw our soldiers act so much like insane demons; they moved forward utterly regardless of the blinding rain of bullets. The Federals also fought with great bravery. My company was the first to gain the breastworks, and I was the second man across them. In a few seconds fifty or a hundred men had crossed the breastworks of logs. These men I placed perpendicular to the works and enfilading them both ways, which soon caused the Federals to vacate the entire works north of the Plank Road. Our brigade moved forward some 200 or 300 yards within sight of the Chancellorsville House and held that advanced position until the battle ended. This enabled General J. E. B. Stuart to do the bravest act I ever saw. He led in person several batteries down the Plank Road, which was swept with the Federal artillery, and planted his guns on an eminence just to the right of the road and in advance of our infantry line. In a very short time the battle was won.

As soon as possible General Lee's army formed on and parallel to the Plank Road, looking north, with full intention to push the enemy and reap the fruits of our hard-won victory. My regiment was near the burning Chancellorsville House, and General Lee was just behind us, when a courier rode up and handed him a dispatch. He quietly and calmly ordered the line to remain where it was, and rode off down the Plank Road toward our right. We soon learned that General Sedgwick's command had broken our lines at Fredericksburg and was coming up on our right flank. We were thus forced to remain inactive all that and the next day, completely blocked in our game of pushing Hooker into the river.

> Major Robert Stiles, of Lee's staff, recorded an incident which throws an interesting light on the Confederate leader's behavior at a critical moment during the battle.
> The day was the third of May. The gray thin line which was to hold Sedgwick at Marye's Hill had been penetrated, and the Federal troops were menacing Lee's rear at a time when he was fully occupied in front with another force stronger than his own.

A horseman was coming at full speed, and as he drew near I saw it was the chaplain of the Mississippi Brigade, and that he was greatly excited. He did not have a saddle, and his horse was reeking with sweat and panting from exertion. When his eye fell on General Lee, he made directly for him. He dashed to the very feet of the commanding general, indeed almost on him, and, gasping for breath, his eyes starting from their sockets, began to tell of dire disaster at Fredericksburg—Sedgwick had smashed Early and was rapidly coming on in our rear.

I have never seen anything more majestically calm than General Lee was. Something very like a grave sweet smile began to express itself on the general's face, but he checked it, and raising his left hand gently, he interrupted the excited speaker.

"I thank you very much," he said, "but both you and your horse are fatigued and overheated. Take him to that shady tree yonder and rest a little. I'll call you as soon as we are through."

This is the way Sedgwick's attack on Marye's Heights and the opponents' subsequent movements looked to William M. Owen, who was one of the defenders.

General Lee had gone to meet Hooker with the bulk of the army, leaving Early's division and Barksdale's brigade at Fredericksburg, about 9,000 men.

On the second of May orders were received to move the Washington Artillery to the front, and their guns were placed in position in earthworks opposite Falmouth. Large bodies of Federal troops could be seen on our side of the Rappahannock.

To deceive the enemy, innumerable campfires were lighted all along Lee's Hill, to make it appear that there was a heavy force bivouacking there. There could not have been less than 20,000 men in front of us, perhaps more. A deserter came in and told us it was the corps of Sedgwick. We were evidently playing a big game of bluff to keep these 20,000 men off Lee at Chancellorsville.

At about ten o'clock, emboldened by the discovery of our weakness, the enemy suddenly appeared to spring out of the ground in line of battle. At the same time thirty or forty guns opened upon our positions from the Stafford Heights. It was a beautiful sight, but a terrible one for us. On the columns charged in a rush, with loud shouts and yells. The 17th Mississippi from behind the stone wall and the guns on the hill banged away as fast as they could be served to check the assaulting columns; but their efforts to stay the tide were unavailing against such great odds. General Barksdale cried out, "Fall back!"

Looking toward Marye's Hill, I saw it was crowded with the enemy; they had evidently overrun our small force. And our guns and the boys of the Washington Artillery—what of them? To my right the 13th and 17th Mississippi were marching off to the rear in good order; on the left General Barksdale was rallying the remnants of the 18th and 21st Mississippi. I was in a very belligerent state of mind and much excited. For the first time we had lost guns in action. We had approached the enemy too closely.

I rode over to where General Barksdale was rallying the infantry and asked him if he considered it safe to keep the battery where it then was. He replied, "Our center has been pierced, that's all. We will be all right in a little while." I rode back to the road, and there, to my amazement, the 2nd Company was going to the rear as fast as they could travel. A line of the enemy had climbed the hill right under the muzzles of their guns and appeared suddenly before their very faces.

One of our boys, who had stood by his gun until all hope was gone, was passing through General William N. Pendleton's reserve artillery. He was as mad as he could be, and his hands and face were covered with burned powder.

One of the reserves called out, "Hello, Washington Artillery! Where are your guns?"

He replied sharply, "Guns be damned! I reckon now the people of the South are satisfied that Barksdale's brigade and the Washington Artillery can't whip the whole damned Yankee army." He had about told the story of the fight. Of Early's 9,000 men, less than 2,000 had been engaged with Sedgwick's corps.

After driving our troops from Marye's Hill, Sedgwick took up his line of march along the Plank Road toward Chancellorsville to aid General Hooker, whose army General Lee was attacking furiously and successfully.

At sunrise on the fourth of May, in obedience to the orders of General Lee, Early moved forward and again occupied Marye's Hill. He thence followed Sedgwick with his division. The day before at Salem Church, Sedgwick had been met by General McLaws with five brigades detached by General Lee for this purpose.

General Early had connected with these troops, and in the afternoon Sedgwick was assailed, Early attacking the left, making the main assault.

At dusk the Federal general crossed back to the north side of the river. He never had got to Hooker at all and left Lee to finish off "the finest army on the planet."

Hooker had received a slight injury in the morning of May 3, and the command devolved on the officer next in rank, General Couch, who a few years later prepared an article on the last part of the battle for the *Philadelphia Times*. From this article some excerpts are presented.

On the morning of May 3 Hooker was standing on the porch of the Chancellor House when a cannon shot struck the pillar against which he was leaning and knocked him down. A report flew around that he was killed. I was at the time but a few yards to his left and, dismounting, ran to the porch. The shattered pillar was there, but I could not find him or anyone else. Hurrying through the house and finding no one, I continued my search through the back yard. All the time I was thinking, If he is killed, what shall I do with this disjointed army? Passing through the yard I came on him, to my great joy, mounted and with his staff also in their saddles. I briefly congratulated him on his escape—it was not the time to blubber or use soft expressions—and went about my own business.

This was the last I saw of my commanding general at the front. He probably left the field soon after his hurt, but he neither notified me of his going nor gave any orders to me.

Having, some little time before this, seen that the last stand would be about the Chancellor House, I had sent to the rear for some of the 2nd Corps batteries, but word came back that they were so jammed in that it was impossible to extricate them. General Meade, hearing of my wants, sent forward the 5th Maine Battery. It was posted in rear of the Chancellor House. With such precision did the artillery of Jackson's old corps play upon this battery that all of the officers and most of the noncommissioned officers and men were killed or wounded. The enemy, having thirty pieces in position on our right, now advanced some of his guns to within 500 or 600 yards of the Chancellor House, where there were only four of Rufus D. Pettit's 2nd Corps guns to oppose them, making a target of that building. Lee by this time knew well enough, if he had not known before, that the game was sure to fall into his hands and accordingly plied every gun and rifle that could be brought to bear upon us.

It was not then too late to save the day. Fifty pieces of artillery, or even forty, brought up and run in front and to the right of the Chancellor House, would have neutralized the thirty guns to the right which were pounding us so hard.

A few minutes later a staff officer from General Hooker rode up and requested my presence.

At the farther side of an open field half a mile in the rear of Chancellorsville I came on a few tents pitched, around which were a large number of staff officers. General Meade also was present, and perhaps other generals. General Hooker was lying down, I think, in a soldier's tent by himself. Raising himself a little as I entered, he said, "Couch, I turn the command of the army over to you. You will withdraw it and place it in the position designated on this map." He pointed to a line traced on a field sketch.

This was perhaps three-quarters of an hour after his hurt. He seemed rather dull, but possessed of his mental faculties. I do not think that one of those officers outside of the tent knew what orders I was to receive, for on stepping out, which I did immediately on getting my instructions, I met Meade looking inquiringly as if he expected that finally he would receive the order for which he had waited all that long morning—"to go in." Colonel N. H. Davis broke out, "We shall have some fighting now."

These incidents are mentioned to show the temper of that knot of officers.

No time was to be lost, as only Hancock's division now held Lee's army. After dispatching a major with orders for the front to retire, I rode back to the thicket accompanied by Meade and was soon joined by Sickles, and after a little while by Hooker, but he did not interfere with my dispositions. Hancock had a close shave to withdraw in safety, his line being three-fourths of a mile long, with an exultant enemy as close in as they dared or chose to be, firing and watching. But everything was brought off except 500 men of the 2nd Corps.

As to the charge that the battle was lost because the general was intoxicated, I have always stated that he probably abstained from the use of ardent spirits when it would have been far better for him to continue in his usual habit. The shock from being violently thrown to the ground, together with the physical exhaustion resulting from loss of sleep and the anxiety of mind incident to the last six days of the campaign, would tell on any man. The enemy did not press us

on the second line, Lee simply varying the monotony of watching us
by an occasional cannonade from the left.

At twelve o'clock on the night of May 4-5 General Hooker assembled his corps commanders in council. Meade, Sickles, Howard,
Reynolds and I were present. Hooker stated that his instructions
compelled him to cover Washington, not to jeopardize the army, etc.
It was seen by the most casual observer that he had made up his mind
to retreat. We were left by ourselves to consult. Meade, Reynolds
and Howard voted squarely for an advance, Sickles and I squarely no.
Upon this Hooker informed the council that he would take on himself
the responsibility of retiring the army to the other side of the river.

As I stepped out of the tent Reynolds, just behind me, broke out,
"What was the use of calling us together at this time of night when
he intended to retreat anyhow?"

Near midnight I got a note from Meade informing me that General
Hooker was on the other side of the river, which had risen over the
bridges, and that communication from him was cut off. I immediately
rode over to Hooker's headquarters and found that I was in command
of the army—if it had any commander. General Henry J. Hunt, of the
artillery, had brought the information as to the condition of the bridges,
and from the reports there we seemed to be in danger of losing them
entirely. After a short conference with Meade I told him that the
recrossing would be suspended, and that "we would stay where we
were and fight it out." I returned to my tent with the intention of
enjoying what I had not had since the night of the thirtieth—a good
sleep. But at 2:00 A.M., communication having been re-established, I
received a sharp message from Hooker to order the recrossing of the
army as he had directed, and everything was safely transferred to the
north bank of the Rappahannock.

> The Confederate Colonel Edward P. Alexander gives a short
> resume of what transpired on May 4 and 5—and fearfully con-
> templates what might have transpired on May 6, had Hooker not
> decided to retire across the Rappahannock.

The events of the morning of May 4 were as follows: No communication had been received by Sedgwick from Hooker, and he was
still under orders to come to Chancellorsville. But at an early hour
movements of Early's troops were discovered in his rear. Sedgwick

at once abandoned all idea of taking the aggressive and only wished himself safely across the river.

It was with great elation on the morning of the fifth that our guns fired the last shots across the Rappahannock at Sedgwick's retreating columns. Early was directed to remain in observation at Fredericksburg, while all the rest of the army was ordered to return to the front of Hooker's lines near Chancellorsville, which Lee intended to assault on the morrow with his whole force.

What was known of the enemy's position gave assurance that the task would be the heaviest which we had ever undertaken. Hooker now had his entire army concentrated and, allowing for his losses, must have had fully 90,000 men to defend about five miles of breastworks. These he had had forty-eight hours to prepare, with all the advantages for defense which the Wilderness offered. Lee would scarcely be able to bring into action 35,000 on the offensive. The attack would have to be made everywhere squarely in front, and our artillery would be unable to render any efficient help. When on the sixth we found the lines deserted and the enemy gone, our engineers were amazed at the strength and completeness of the enemy's entrenchments. Impenetrable abatis covered the entire front, and the crest everywhere carried head logs under which the men could fire as through loopholes. In the rear, separate structures were provided for officers, with protected outlooks whence they could see and direct without exposure.

Four of Hooker's corps had suffered casualties averaging twenty percent, but three, the 1st, 2nd and 5th, had scarcely been engaged. It must be conceded that Lee never in his life took a more audacious resolve than when he determined to assault Hooker's entrenchments. And it is the highest possible compliment to the army commanded by Lee to say that there were two persons who believed that, in spite of all the odds, it would have been victorious. These two persons were General Lee and General Hooker.

> The feelings of the men in Hooker's army and their morale during the retreat are well expressed by R. G. Carter, who was in the rear guard of the retiring troops.

That afternoon (Tuesday May 4) and night it poured down awfully. The mud and water were so deep that we could neither lie down nor sit down but slept on our guns standing, the rain driving through us at every step. Troops were moving, wet and despondent. We sat and took it, all worn out, no sleep for four nights, drenched to the skin, the cold wind sweeping through us.

We were in this condition until about four o'clock in the morning (Wednesday, May 5) when we started, and Heavens, what a retreat! We expected every moment a bloody fight, but it did not come. We wallowed through the mud up to our middles. The officers all got drunk (with a few worthy exceptions) from the general down to the line officers. The miserable fiends drew their swords and pistols, and fell off their horses, cursing. They say the Peninsular Campaign and retreat was nothing compared to this. That we should lose all and march away back to camp is enough to quench all hopes of victory!

Call it what you please, demoralization or discouragement, we cared not to sleep standing and fight running, when sure defeat always awaited such a *doomed* army.

> The editor of the Richmond *Examiner* also was disgusted, and took a very sober view of Lee's recent victories.

If this war were a tournament, we might desire nothing better than the manner in which it has been conducted. The Grand Army crosses over, a hundred thousand strong; fifty or sixty thousand Confederates fight with them; the Grand Army is whipped, loses 20,000 men, and then marches back to camp. After a month or more of recruiting it comes again, finds the same Confederates in the same fields, is whipped again, and marches back to camp in the same order.

If we could import shiploads of Irish and Dutch, no way of carrying on this war more favorably could be desired. But, while our army kills a great many Yankees, it also loses a considerable number of brave men. One of these is a greater loss to us than three to the enemy. If that loss were counter-balanced by some military advantages, which might serve as the foundation for future hopes, it would not be a loss, but a wise expenditure. Unfortunately, such victories change nothing.

> As soon as Hooker reached the safe side of the Rappahannock, he issued a congratulatory order to his troop which, in excerpt, read as follows:

Headquarters of the Army of the Potomac, May 6, 1863. The Major General Commanding tenders his army his congratulations on its achievements of the last seven days.

In withdrawing from the south bank of the Rappahannock before delivering a general battle to our adversaries, the army has given renewed evidence of its confidence in itself and its fidelity to the principles it represents.

By our celerity and secrecy of movement, our advance and passage of the rivers were undisputed, and on our withdrawal not a Rebel ventured to follow. The events of the last week may swell with pride the hearts of every officer and soldier of this army.

We have added new laurels to our army's former renown.

JOSEPH HOOKER,
Major General.

The newspapers had something to say about this order. What they said was more or less in line with these editorial words from the *New York World* of May 9, 1863.

Whoever knows the facts of the last two weeks will shudder as he reads this order. Whoever does not, let him credit it and believe that his ignorance is bliss.

What explanation or excuse did Hooker give for his strange conduct at Chancellorsville?

The answer was supplied by Hooker himself in a conversation which was overheard and reported by John Bigelow, Jr., a Union officer.

A couple of months after the battle, during the campaign of Gettysburg, Hooker was asked by General Doubleday, "Hooker, what was the matter with you at Chancellorsville? Some say you were injured by a shell, and others that you were drunk. Now tell me what it was."

Hooker answered frankly and good-naturedly, "Doubleday, I was not hurt by a shell, and I was not drunk. For once I lost confidence in Hooker, and that is all there is to it."

Despite Hooker's frank admission of his own delinquency, the public in general continued to blame General Howard and his 11th Corps for the debacle.

In his autobiography written many years later Howard argued his side of the controversy and then paid Lee and Jackson a fine and rare compliment.

It has been customary to blame me and my corps for the disaster. The imputations are far from true. My command was by positive orders riveted to that position. Stonewall Jackson was able to mass a large force a few miles off, whose exact whereabouts neither patrols, reconnaissances nor scouts ascertained. The enemy crossing the Plank Road was seen, but the interpretation of these movements was wrong.

There is always some theory which will forestall giving the credit of one's own defeat to one's enemy. But in our own hearts, as we take a candid view of everything that took place in the Wilderness around Chancellorsville, we impute our defeat to the successful efforts of Stonewall Jackson and Robert E. Lee.

CHAPTER 15

The Struggle for the Mississippi

GRANT'S VICKSBURG CAMPAIGNS

New Orleans had been occupied by Union forces in April, 1862; the fall of Memphis followed in June. But the Confederate batteries at Vicksburg still barred the way to hostile navigation. The strategic importance of the city, now fully recognized, was well set forth by E. A. Pollard.

Could the Federals obtain possession of Vicksburg, all the products of the Northwestern states would pass unmolested to the Gulf; the enemy would supply themselves with cotton, sugar and molasses, disjoin the east and west Mississippi states, divide our force, and open a new prospect of subjugation.

In the summer of 1862 General Earl Van Dorn found the city besieged by a powerful fleet and an army. While the enemy was completing his preparations, the Confederates had been engaged in the fitting out of a ram, called the *Arkansas*, near Yazoo City; and on the 15th of July this ungainly vessel commenced the fearful gauntlet of the enemy's vessels drawn up in parallel lines to receive her when she passed the channel to the Mississippi. A terrific fire from both the enemy's squadrons was poured on the *Arkansas*, but she moved on. Fighting at long range, the Federal fleet slowly followed, but the nearer she approached the bluff, the quicker she fought. At last finding her safe under the Confederate batteries, the enemy gave up the chase.

A Northern correspondent doffed his hat at the *Arkansas*.

Think of her—with twelve guns running the blockade of fourteen or fifteen vessels of war and several armed rams, with more than two hundred guns! Was it not delightfully, refreshingly daring?

From July, 1862, when Halleck was called to Washington, to October of that year, Grant had lain idle at Jackson, Tennessee. On October 16, however, he regained power of movement. His chief opponents, Generals Price and Van Dorn, had suffered a severe defeat at Corinth, and he set out to take Vicksburg. Before starting out on this campaign, Grant went to Cairo to see Admiral David D. Porter, who had been given command of the Mississippi squadron. Porter tells of the plans they discussed at the meeting.

I gave the General an account of my interviews with the President and with General McClernand, who was then raising troops in Illinois, and he inquired, "When can you move and what force have you?"

"I can move tomorrow with all the gunboats and five or six other vessels."

"Well," said General Grant, "I will start with a large force for Grenada. General Pemberton will meet me to check my advance. I will hold him while you and Sherman push down the Mississippi and make a landing somewhere on the Yazoo. The garrison at Vicksburg will be small, and Sherman will have no difficulty getting inside the works." (See map, page 419.)

Three days after, with all the naval forces, I started down the Mississippi, and at Memphis found General Sherman embarking his troops to proceed to the Yazoo and take possession of the landings.

Grant's plans were well laid, but they were unsuccessful after all. When he started from Holly Springs, he left behind him a large depot of stores, on which he depended for supplies. While he and Pemberton were marching toward each other, General Van Dorn got in Grant's rear and destroyed these supplies. That ended the campaign.

In the meantime Sherman had moved in accordance with the prearranged plans, unaware of the misadventure which had befallen Grant.

Horace Greeley, editor of the *New York Tribune*, gives a readable account of what happened to the Sherman expedition.

The day after the Holly Springs disaster General W. T. Sherman had left Memphis, some 30,000 strong, on boats which passed down the

Mississippi and twelve miles up the Yazoo, where the troops were debarked, and a general assault was made next day on the well-manned fortifications and batteries which defended Vicksburg on the north. The ground between the Yazoo and the precipitous bluffs whereon the Rebels were fortified is in the main a profound mire, resting on quicksand. Chickasaw Bayou, connecting the two rivers, is its most salient feature; but much of it was a cedar swamp. Expeditious as were Sherman's movements, most of the Rebel forces in that region were on hand to resist him (See map, page 433.)

On the twenty-sixth and twenty-seventh of December, 1862, our men were formed in four columns, gradually pushed foward and drove back the enemy's pickets toward the frowning bluffs. During the ensuing night the ground and obstacles in our front were carefully reconnoitered and found even more difficult than rumor had made them. Chickasaw Bayou was conclusively ascertained to be passable but at two points—one a narrow levee, the other a sand bar—each completely commanded by the enemy's sharpshooters, while batteries, trenches and rifle pits rose, tier above tier, up the steep bluffs beyond, which were crowned by still heavier batteries. Major General Frederick Steele, whose division had been debarked above the junction of the bayou with the Yazoo, found his progress barred by an impassable swamp, across which he could hardly hope to take half the men who made the attempt. This venture he properly declined and he was justified by Sherman.

Brigadier General George W. Morgan's division charged on the twenty-ninth, but what could valor avail against rifle pits filled with sharpshooters whose every bullet drew blood? Against gunners who poured grape and canister into our dauntless heroes, who could not advance and were stung by the consciousness that they were dying in vain?

This attempt on Vicksburg cost us no less than 2,000 men, while Pemberton reported his casualties at only 207.

Sherman was baffled but would not give up. He visited Admiral Porter on board his flagboat and concerted new efforts. The Rebel lines could not be broken. But might they not be turned? He proposed to the admiral a combined demonstration against the batteries some miles farther up the Yazoo: the admiral to bombard them, while 10,000 choice troops should attempt to carry them by assault, the residue of our army distracting the enemy's attention by menacing his front nearer Vicksburg with a fresh attack.

Porter as ever lent a prompt and hearty co-operation. The troops were accordingly embarked, the gunboats being directed to move at midnight slowly and silently up the Yazoo.

Sherman, who had left them at midnight, had by 4:00 A.M. every man at his post listening for the sound of Porter's guns, but no sound came. Fog on the river had been so dense that the admiral had been unable to move; the enterprise had to be postponed to the next night. But when the next night came, it was bright moonlight, rendering the proposed attack too hazardous. The swamp wherein our men were encamped would be drowned by the next heavy rain; there were rumors afloat that Grant had fallen back, leaving the Rebels free to concentrate 40,000 men at Vicksburg; so Sherman resolved to go, and by sunrise next morning, January 2, he had everything on board.

> Sherman's frontal attack at Chickasaw Bayou, the northern rampart of Vicksburg, had been so disastrous that the experiment was never repeated. Grant decided, when he arrived near Vicksburg a month later, that new ways had to be found to reduce the fortress. But the problems with which he was confronted were manifold. They are given here in his own words.

On the twenty-ninth of January 1863 I arrived at Young's Point, nearly opposite Vicksburg, and assumed command the following day.

The real work of the campaign of Vicksburg now began. *The main problem was to secure a footing on dry ground on the east side of the river from which the troops could operate against Vicksburg.* The Mississippi River from Cairo south runs through a rich alluvial valley of many miles in width. On the west side the highest land is but little above the highest water.

Marching across this country in the face of an enemy was impossible. The strategical way according to the rule, therefore, would have been to go back to Memphis, establish that as a base of supplies, fortify it and move from there along the line of railroad to the Yallabusha or to Jackson, Mississippi. At this time, however, the North had become very much discouraged. The elections of 1862 had gone against the party which was for the prosecution of the war. It was my judgment that to make a backward movement to Memphis would be interpreted as a defeat, and that the draft would be resisted, desertions ensue, and the power to capture deserters lost. There was nothing left to be done but to *go forward.*

CAIRO, ILL.

TENNESSEE RIVER

MISSISSIPPI RIVER

•JACKSON, TENN.

LA GRANGE

•MEMPHIS

COLDWATER RIVER

CORINTH •

HOLLY SPRINGS

TALLAHATCHIE R.

YAZOO PASS

YALLABUSHA R.

FORT PEMBERTON

•GRENADA

YAZOO RIVER

BIG BLACK RIVER

LAKE PROVIDENCE

VICKSBURG

•JACKSON

GRAND GULF

PORT GIBSON

BRUINSBURG

•PORT HUDSON, LA.

THE MISSISSIPPI

419

Vicksburg is on the first high land coming to the river's edge below Memphis. Haines' Bluff, eleven miles from Vicksburg on the Yazoo River, was strongly fortified. The whole distance from there to Vicksburg and thence to Warrenton was also entrenched, with batteries at suitable distances and rifle pits connecting them.

North of the Yazoo was all a marsh, heavily timbered, but cut up with bayous and much overflowed. The problem then was how to secure a landing on high ground east of the Mississippi without an apparent retreat. Thereupon commenced a series of experiments to divert the attention of the enemy, of my troops and of the public generally. I myself never felt great confidence that any of the experiments resorted to would prove successful. Nevertheless, I was always prepared to take advantage of them in case they did.

In 1862 General Thomas Williams had come up from New Orleans and cut a ditch ten or twelve feet wide and about as deep across Young's Point. It was Williams' expectation that, when the river rose, it would cut a navigable channel through. But the canal started in an eddy from both ends and, of course, it only filled up with water on the rise without doing any execution in the way of cutting. (See map, page 447.)

Even if the canal had proved navigable for steamers, it could not have been of much advantage to us. It runs in a direction almost perpendicular to the line of bluffs on the east bank of the river. As soon as the enemy discovered what we were doing, he established a battery commanding the canal throughout its length. This battery soon drove out our two dredges, which were doing the work of thousands of men. Had the canal been completed, it might have proved of some use in running transports through, under the cover of night, to use below; but they would yet have had to run the batteries, though for a much shorter distance.

The original canal scheme was abandoned on the twenty-seventh of March. In the meantime, we were trying to find available landing on high ground on the east bank of the river, or else to make waterways to get below the city, avoiding the batteries.

Grant had on his staff a young West Point graduate named James Harrison Wilson, a man of outstanding intellect and executive ability. He had been appointed inspector general of the Army of the Tennessee, but his preference was for strategical and engineering problems. In later life he would command an army corps in the Spanish-American War and be second in command of the American forces in the Chinese Boxer uprising, with many other honors awaiting him.

At the time of the Vicksburg campaign he was only twenty-six years old, but some important duties were already being assigned to him, all of which he discharged with skill and energy. As a close friend of John A. Rawlins, Grant's former Galena neighbor and intimate counselor, he was able to influence the thoughts of the commanding general to a greater extent than even Grant himself suspected.

Wilson explains how he found the situation at the beginning of the year 1863.

I had been sent in advance to look over the ground and prepare a report for General Grant on his arrival.

On the day Grant and his staff arrived at Milliken's Bend, he invited Sherman, McClernand, McPherson, Blair, Steele, Rawlins and me to accompany him across the point commanded by Vicksburg.

Rawlins and I rode together. I pointed out to him that there were only three possible plans for the capture of Vicksburg, namely:

First, to turn it by the left through the Yazoo River.

Second, to make a direct landing against the wharf and carry it by escalade.

Third, to run the batteries with the ironclads, gunboats, transports and barges, and march the troops across country to such a point below as might be selected as the base of operations.

All the plans for reaching a footing east of the Yazoo were to be tested. The second plan was dismissed as entirely too hazardous, and this brought us to the third plan. Rawlins favored it strongly but, recognizing that it might lead to a great disaster, wondered if it could be carried out. Before we got back to our steamboat, Rawlins said, "Wilson, I believe you are right."

That afternoon I was sent to lead the expedition through Yazoo Pass, the Coldwater and the Tallahatchie into the Yazoo.

The Confederates were fully aware of their vulnerability through the Yazoo and had erected strong fortifications along it, the most important of which was Fort Pemberton near the point where the Tallahatchie and the Yallabusha join to form the Yazoo.

Wilson put his ingenuity to work to overcome all hindrances
—with what success he himself tells us.

The Yazoo River expedition under my personal supervision was
covered by a detachment of light ironclads and gunboats and made its
way by the winding rivers more than 150 miles through the overhanging
forest. The Yazoo Pass to the Coldwater was about twenty miles long.
It was so narrow that the enemy cut it full of forest trees from the
banks. Many reached entirely across the stream, and many others were
felled diagonally across the first, so that for miles there was an entan-
glement so thick the troops could cross on it from bank to bank. I
thought at first that the trees could be trimmed up and hauled out by
block, tackle and capstan, but I soon found that this method was too
slow and that, as fast as we cleared out the obstructions above, the
enemy made new ones below.

The next plan tried was that of hitching steamboat hawsers, 500 or
600 feet long, to the ends of the logs, doubling them back and then
stringing out 400 or 500 men with orders to lay hold and march. This
plan proved entirely efficacious. Trees weighing thirty or forty tons,
covered with spreading limbs, were drawn out as fast as the men could
march. The working parties were multiplied till all our cables were in
use, and none who did not see it can understand with what speed the
trees were drawn out and the pass opened for navigation. The combined
strength of a full regiment was irresistible. As many officers and men
were woodsmen, they soon became most expert in the work.

But while the troops made good progress in the daytime, it was impossible to get the gunboats to move at night, even after they reached
the open river beyond the obstructions. The consequence was that the
enemy had time to construct and arm fortifications at the head of the
Yazoo and thereby make our entry into that river impossible. One of
our ironclads, after getting within range, was disabled by the shot of a
heavy gun from the fort, and this so alarmed the naval commander that
he refused to push others to closer quarters for fear that they might
also be injured, become unmanageable and prove a total loss. The expedition was therefore abandoned.

The approach to Vicksburg through the Yazoo having proved
impracticable, Grant next tried whether it was possible to by-pass
the fortress by a waterway which paralleled the Mississippi on
the opposite or Louisiana side.

Jefferson Davis gives his version of how the Confederates strove to circumvent this latest plan.

Another attempt to get into the Mississippi without passing the batteries at Vicksburg was by digging a canal to connect the river with the bayou in rear of Milliken's Bend, northwest of the city, so as to have water communication by way of Richmond to New Carthage. These indications of a purpose to get below Vicksburg caused General Pemberton early in February 1863 to detach Brigadier General John S. Bowen, with his Missouri Brigade, to Grand Gulf near the mouth of the Big Black and establish batteries there to command the mouth of that small river, which might be used to pass to the rear of Vicksburg and also by their fire to obstruct the navigation of the Mississippi.

> The contemplated passageway met with the same difficulties that had wrecked the Yazoo River project and eventually was shelved.
>
> Things had now reached an impasse. James Wilson, the young engineer on Grant's staff, relates how it was eventually broken.

One evening the principal generals dined with Grant, and the problems confronting the army came up again for discussion. Every suggestion, no matter who made it, received consideration, but none promised success. The meeting was about to break up when Rawlins said, "Wilson and I have a plan for taking Vicksburg."

"What is it, Rawlins—what is it?" asked Sherman.

Thereupon Rawlins explained my proposition to run the batteries under cover of darkness with the gunboats and transports, and march the troops below by land to the first feasible crossing.

Sherman at once and with emphasis declared, "It can't be done. The transports will be destroyed. The enemy's guns will sink them or set them afire." And that settled it for the time being, for although Rawlins gave the reasons clearly and emphatically for the faith that was in us, no one came to his support. Even Grant kept silent, though he tells us in his memoirs that it was his purpose from the first to carry that plan into effect if the others failed.

No one can say just when the plan first received Grant's approval, but he did not tell either Rawlins or me that he was going to carry it out, till he told us he would ask Admiral Porter to lead the transports with a section of his fleet by the batteries under cover of darkness.

Before committing his entire fleet to the risk of passing the batteries, Porter tried an experiment. Major William L. B. Jenney tells about it.

Admiral Porter first constructed a dummy gunboat from a large coal barge. This dummy was rigged up with smokestacks and sloping sides and covered black with a coat of coal tar so that in the dark, or even in moonlight, she looked like an ironclad. One dark night some smoke-making combustibles were lighted below the smokestack, the dummy was pushed down the river and floated silently and majestically with the current.

As soon as this dummy was discovered, the Confederate batteries opened fire, but it kept steadily on its course. General Pemberton sent a swift messenger down the river to where the ironclad *Indianola*, which had recently been captured by the Confederates, was being repaired. He had orders to blow her up, but when, later, the trick perpetrated by Porter was discovered, Pemberton sent another messenger to countermand the order. This messenger, however, was too late, for we heard the explosion which destroyed the *Indianola*.

Not long after this event Admiral Farragut came up the river. He was short of coal and provisions and, in order to supply him, Admiral Porter loaded some barges with coal and provisions and sent them down-river. They passed the Vicksburg batteries without notice. The next day a flag of truce on some other matter was received from Vicksburg with Major General Benjamin F. Cheatham in charge. After his business had been concluded, General Cheatham remarked, "You Yanks make very good dummy gunboats, and we wasted lots of powder and shot on one of them, but you must think us green if you expected to fool us a second time by the same trick. We saw your dummies last night, but we don't waste any more powder on such trash."

Thereupon we smiled pleasantly and bade him an affectionate good-by.

Before putting his plan of running the batteries into execution, Grant called a council of war. Among those present was Admiral Porter, who reports the decision which was reached.

General Grant was at last satisfied that he could not carry on military operations against Vicksburg in the way we had attempted heretofore.

"I will go below Vicksburg," he said, "and cross over, if I can depend on you, Admiral Porter, for a sufficient naval force. I will prepare some transports by packing them with cotton bales, and we'll start as soon as you are ready."

"I will be ready tomorrow night," I replied.

General Grant called a council of war that afternoon on board my flagship and, after informing the generals what he proposed to do, asked their opinions.

General McClernand did not attend the council but wrote to Grant approving the plan. I think General Sherman was present but did not favor it, as it would take the army a long distance from its base of supplies, and for other reasons.

All the other generals present at the council strongly objected to Grant's plan. He listened patiently and, when they had finished, remarked, "I have considered your arguments but continue in the same opinion. You will be ready to move at ten o'clock tomorrow morning. General McClernand will take the advance; General Sherman will remain here with his division and make an attack on Haines' Bluff in conjunction with such of the gunboats as the admiral may not want with him below." So ended the council.

Everything connected with this movement of General Grant's had been conducted with as much secrecy as possible, yet I believe the intended change of base was known in Vicksburg almost as soon as it was in the Union army. The Confederates had means of finding out what was going on, though we certainly supposed they would know nothing of the intended movement of the gunboats.

At the appointed hour we started down the Mississippi.

A staff officer, William E. Strong, watched the running of the batteries from Grant's headquarters boat and was deeply impressed.

The night was well chosen. It was black as the bottomless pit. The wind, which was blowing fresh at sunset, had died away, and not a breath of air fanned one's cheek.

The signal was given and one by one, at intervals of ten minutes, the boats dropped by. Like grim specters they one by one loomed up on our starboard quarter, came closer, swept on and were lost in the gloom and mist and darkness. Nothing could be seen but the dim shadowy outline of each transport as it drifted by with the current. There were no lights, no escape from steampipes, no ringing of bells, no throbbing of piston rods, no clang of machinery, no voices above a whisper. Every man stood grimly at his post, ready to do his full share and take his chances of life or death in the perilous and daring adventure.

At eleven o'clock the last transport of the fleet floated gracefully by and was lost in the darkness. As it disappeared from sight, we rounded to, swung into the current and followed slowly in her wake. The leading ship had been drifting for at least an hour and a quarter and must have been at this time near the Big Bend.

On the hurricane deck forward of the pilothouse stood the quiet, modest, unassuming commander of our army, U. S. Grant, and by his side Mrs. Grant and their two sons, Fred and Jesse, with John A. Rawlins, many other officers and me.

There was nothing in Grant's manner to indicate that anything unusual was about to occur. Cool and collected, he stood there, anxious without doubt but apparently quite unconcerned.

Five, ten or perhaps fifteen minutes passed, when suddenly from across the Big Bend came a single musket shot from the enemy's picket boats. This was followed by a rattling volley, and then a rocket of immense size shot out into the darkness, and then another, and still another. The reports from the guns were sharp, clear and very distinct; the flashes from guns and rockets lighted up for an instant the embattled heights of Vicksburg. We knew the critical moment was at hand.

Five minutes, possibly ten, passed, when a flash came from one of the 8-inch guns at the upper water battery, followed by a sharp, deafening report. One after another in quick succession the guns in this battery went into action. Those from the lower batteries joined rapidly in the cannonade on the approaching vessels, all of which now were rushing along at their utmost speed.

From the batteries along the river to the crest of the Vicksburg hills all was a mass of living flame.

As the fleet approached the city and passed it, fire was opened from batteries which had hitherto been unable to bring their guns to bear. Field batteries were hurried into position on the main streets near the river and on the sloping hillside, until it seemed as though every square foot of soil possessed a gun. Heavy bodies of infantry along the levee and wharf kept up a deadly fire upon the boats as long as these were within range.

Houses and barns on the shores were set on fire, and the bright glare, added to the incessant flashing of the guns, made the night as light as day. The men at the batteries and in the streets of Vicksburg could be distinctly seen from the vessels of the fleet when they were opposite the Vicksburg courthouse, and it was here that each vessel was exposed to the heaviest and most destructive fire. A storm of solid shot and shell, of almost every variety and size, poured upon the fleet, crashing through hull and pilothouse, shivering the machinery, cutting ropes and chimney guys and bursting in the cabins.

A grand ball was in progress in Vicksburg at the time, with General Pemberton and prominent officers of the garrison present. The ball-room was quickly deserted, the officers hastening to their respective commands, and the ladies in ball attire rushing into the streets to witness the grand spectacle. The entire population was awake, watching with intense interest the brilliant and indescribable scene on which the fate of Vicksburg depended.

The fleet was under fire for two and a half hours. But at length the last boat was out of range; the blazing bonfires burned low, flickered and went out. The heavy guns ceased firing, and silence once more reigned over the beleaguered city.

> One of the volunteer crewmen of the river fleet, S. H. M. Byers, gives a thrilling account of his experiences while being shot at, defenseless, by the cannon on the east side of the Mississippi.

It must have been some great event that was about to happen that night, for the Assistant Secretary of War was there, and General Grant and General Sherman were there, waiting and watching. Some 150 private soldiers were going to perform a deed that should help make American history. The success of a whole army and the capture of the best-fortified city on the American continent depended on this handful of private soldiers. Grant was to open the Mississippi River. "In my opinion," telegraphed General Halleck for the President, "*this is the most important operation of the war. To open the Mississippi River would be better than the capture of forty Richmonds.*"

For what had it availed to collect soldiers here? In front of Grant, in high flood, swept the mightiest river on the continent; he had not a boat to cross with, and the enemy laughed and dared him from the other side.

Without steamers on which to cross, the game was blocked: Vicksburg might stand there forever, and the Mississippi River be blockaded to the end of the war. Then the scheme was proposed to cover some of the wooden steamboats with cotton bales and on a dark night try to rush them past the batteries. The boat captains, however, would not risk it with their own crews, and so the army asked for volunteers. One hundred and fifty Union soldiers stepped forward. I was one of them.

We lay in the middle of the Mississippi a dozen miles above Vicksburg. Down in the dark hold of each vessel stood a dozen determined men. They had boards, pressed cotton and piles of gunny sacks beside them there to stop up holes made by the cannon of the enemy. They had none of war's excitement to keep them up. They were helpless. If anything happened they would go to the bottom of the river without a word. The boats must all move 200 yards apart. That was the order.

All was suspense. For a little while the night grew darker and more silent. There was no noise save the gurgling of the water as it ground past the hulls of the anchored vessels. All was ready.

Just then a lantern on the levee was moved slowly up and down. It was the signal to start. Quietly we lifted anchors and floated off with the current. Suddenly we were discovered. "Put on all steam!" called the captain, and our boats moved swiftly into the maelstrom of sulphur and iron, for the enemy opened fire vigorously.

The whole night seemed one terrific roar of cannon. Burning houses made the river almost as light as day. We saw the people in the streets of the town running and gesticulating as if all were mad. Their men at the batteries loaded and fired and yelled as if every shot sank a steamboat. On the west side of the river the lagoons and canebrakes looked weird and dangerous. The sky above was black, lighted only by sparks from the burning houses. Down on the river it was a sheet of flame. One of the steamers and a few of the barges had caught fire and were burning up, the men escaping in lifeboats and by swimming to the western shore.

The musketry on the shore barked and bit at the unprotected pilots on the boats. Ten-inch cannon and great columbiads hurled their shot and shell into the cotton breastworks of the barges or through the rigging of the steamers. The gunboats trembled from the impact of shot against their sides, and at times the little steamers were caught in the powerful eddies of the river and whirled three times around, right in front of the hot-firing batteries.

Amid all this roar and thunder and lightning and crash of cannon balls above, the men down in the holds of the boat stood in the dim candlelight waiting, ignorant of events, while sounds like the crash of worlds went on above their heads.

The enemy's shells set fire to cotton on board the transport *Henry Clay*, and the crew abandoned ship. It burned and later sank. The coal barges of the *Lafayette* and *Louisville* were cut loose, and several other coal barges were lost, but the rest of the ships passed the batteries, though not without suffering considerable damage.

Daylight saw the little fleet safe below Vicksburg, where the soldiers welcomed it with cheers.

On these same boats Grant's army would ferry across the Mississippi, and there on the other side fight his battles.

The fleet being safely past the batteries of Vicksburg, Grant now could proceed with his campaign and arrange to march his army overland on the Louisiana side of the Mississippi. It was a laborious march and many obstacles had to be conquered. Then a new problem arose: Where should Grant land below Vicksburg so as to be in a favorable position for attack?

James Wilson, in his capacity as engineer, again was called on for expert help and advice and, as usual, acquitted himself creditably.

The whole country was under water. Having no pontoon train, no boats except the flats gathered from the various plantations and no bridge materials except such as we obtained by tearing down plantation houses, our forward movement might well have been stopped at the very outset. With troops less capable and commanders less resolute and resourceful, we might well have been beaten before getting within reach of the enemy. But there was neither delay nor the thought of it. Three floating bridges, each over 300 feet long, were built of flatboats and ginhouse timbers, and in a few days we opened a practicable road, crossing bayous and threading one of the most difficult regions that ever tested the resources of an army.

Having given careful instructions, I left the details to my assistants, crossed the Mississippi with a regiment of infantry and made a reconnaissance of the country between the mouth of the Big Black and Warrenton to see whether we could find a landing from which we could reach the rear of Vicksburg. But the bottoms were several miles wide in places, and everywhere so much overflowed that it was impracticable to get to the highlands through them.

The most important discovery from the reconnaissance was that it assured us we would have to look for a landing farther down the river.

Accordingly the fleet and transports now moved down the river. The gunboats were to silence the Confederate batteries at Grand Gulf, after which the transports were to ferry the troops to Bruinsburg, the place which finally had been chosen for disembarkment.

The Confederate artillerist R. S. Bevier relates what occurred in the ensuing duel between the fleet and the guns at Grand Gulf.

The Federal fleet made its appearance above the batteries and anchored out of range. No movement was discovered until the twenty-eighth of April, when their transports arrived and their troops were rapidly disembarked on the Louisiana shore.

On the morning of the twenty-ninth the gunboats weighed anchor and rounded the point above out of sight, as if they were leaving, but almost immediately came down again, firing rapidly from their bow guns as they advanced, and took their stations at intervals near the center of the river. They extended along down in front of our batteries and rifle pits and delivered heavy broadsides as they fell into line. Our batteries, both siege and field, replied promptly and with spirit, and a terrific cannonading began. Two of the gunboats did not seem inclined to form in line with the others, but steamed up and down in front of our works and batteries, firing from their ports, plowing the works with both shot and shell, raking the ground occupied by the infantry with grape—a perfect storm of iron. But it produced comparatively little effect on a position strongly fortified and admirably protected.

We now discovered that the ironclads, which had kept such a respectful distance from our guns, were not afraid to come to close quarters. The two already mentioned, which were steaming up and down in every direction, determined to try the strength of our works at the closest possible range, and one of them, the *Pittsburgh*, ran within ten steps of the guns and fired a tremendous broadside immediately upon them. She lay so close under the bank that the muzzles of the guns in the battery could not be brought to bear upon her, but her smokestacks were riddled, and one of them shot almost entirely off, and she was soon forced to leave her position by our sharpshooters who poured a destructive fire into her portholes whenever opened. She also had sharpshooters aboard who fired upon our artillerymen with some effect.

The fire from all the boats was now furious. Our guns being skillfully handled, the enemy ships were struck repeatedly, but their iron sides appeared impervious, and our shot had little or no effect on them. Our field batteries, which were insufficiently protected, were partly abandoned, as pieces of such light caliber could render but little efficient service.

Only one of the gunboats had been crippled and compelled to withdraw from the action: it had its hog chains shot off, was damaged otherwise and was towed below out of range.

The bombardment was continued from the fleet until one o'clock, when they drew off up the river.

Empty transports were floated down the river at night, and Grant's army then crossed at Bruinsburg a few miles below Grand Gulf. Jefferson Davis appointed General Joseph E. Johnston commander of the entire Western theater of war. Johnston had recovered from the wounds he had suffered at Seven Pines but, being at odds with the Confederate President, had been left without a command. Even now his authority was so ill-defined that he was constantly defied by men nominally under his direction.

Johnston's contemplated strategy is set forth in his own language. His veiled contempt for General Pemberton, to whom he usually refers as "the Confederate general," can be readily discerned between the lines.

To be successful in this campaign it was necessary that the Confederate general should comprehend that he must defeat the invading army in the field, and that Vicksburg must fall if besieged.

The invading army could not be defeated without the concentration of the Confederate forces, but they were always more divided than the enemy. The whole course of the Confederate general indicates a determination, from the beginning, to be besieged in Vicksburg.

Our best opportunity to engage the Federal army was, manifestly, while it was divided during the passage of the Mississippi. Well convinced of it, I directed Lieutenant General Pemberton to attack the enemy on May 1 with all his force. This order was repeated on the second, only to be disregarded. Advantageous opportunities to engage the Federal army were offered continually.

Being confident that, should Vicksburg be besieged, a Confederate force sufficient to break the investment could not be assembled for the purpose, as well as of the fact that it had lost its importance since the occupation of the river by Federal vessels of war, I directed its evacuation. The order was received by General Pemberton, but set aside by advice of a council of war.

But without reference to the military value of Vicksburg, I directed that the army should not be exposed to investment in it; for the capture of the place would be the certain result. As the Confederate government had been unable to prevent a siege, it was certain that it could not break one. As the capture of the place could not be prevented, the army at least could be saved.

Grant's forces being necessarily scattered during and following their disembarkation, he endeavored to make Pemberton scatter the Confederates likewise. Toward this end he used various ruses, most of which proved successful. A Union officer, William L. B. Jenney, noted with glee how easily the commander of Vicksburg was led astray.

The Union cavalry General Grierson was at this time ordered to make a raid from La Grange to Baton Rouge, which caused Pemberton to send detachments from Vicksburg in several different directions in an effort to intercept and capture Grierson. This added to the confusion of Pemberton and the army under him.

In order to increase this perplexity further, Grant, before he attempted to cross the river with his troops, had written to Sherman at Milliken's Bend: "If you will make a demonstration against Haines' Bluff it will help to confuse the enemy as to my intentions. I do not give this as an order, for the papers will call it another failure of Sherman to capture Haines' Bluff."

When this letter was received by General Sherman he remarked, "Does General Grant think I care what the newspapers say?" and jumped into a boat at once and rowed to Porter's flagship, where Sherman and Porter then arranged a jolly lark.

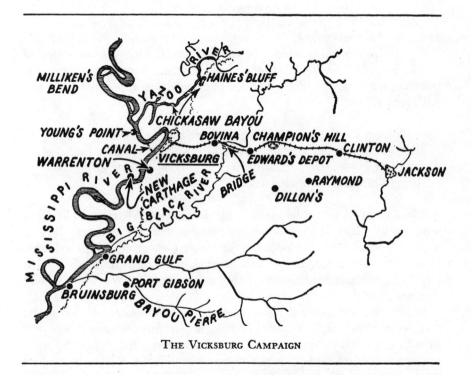

THE VICKSBURG CAMPAIGN

Sherman spread his command over the decks of the transports with orders that every man should be in sight and look as numerous as possible. Porter ordered every boat to get up steam, and even took a blacksmith shop in tow, with orders to make all the smoke possible. The gunboats and transports whistled and puffed and made all the noise they could. They showed themselves to the garrison at Haines' Bluff and then drifted back and landed the men, who were marched through the woods toward Haines' Bluff until they were seen by the enemy, marched a mile or so down the river and taken again on board the transports, to go through the same farce once more. The boats were kept in movement up and down the Yazoo all night, as if they were bringing up more and more troops. As soon as Grant had effected his landing he sent word to Sherman, "All right; join me below Vicksburg."

Later we learned the good effect of the demonstration of Sherman and Porter. The commander at Haines' Bluff had telegraphed to Pemberton: "The demonstration at Grand Gulf must be only a feint. Here is the real attack. Send me reinforcements." Pemberton recalled troops marching against Grant and sent them by forced marches to Haines' Bluff. When the nature of Sherman's maneuvers was discovered, these troops were marched back again, to arrive tired out and half demoralized.

> Among Pemberton's best troops were the 1st and 2nd Missouri
> Brigades under command of General John S. Bowen. At least one
> of these Missourians, R. S. Bevier, did not like General Pember-
> ton, to judge from his remarks.

After General Grant had landed his first troops, General Bowen was sent out by General Pemberton to resist the enemy's advance. Bowen urged on Pemberton the necessity of sending down all of his available force from Vicksburg to meet the enemy in detail as he landed. Had this been done, unquestionably the result would have been widely different.

Pemberton had come to us with no prestige of previous success: he was an untried man, it was his first important command, and the Missourians always distrusted him. He was rewarded by the most unstinted censure and with the most unqualified condemnation. We must, however, as a matter of simple justice to him, recall that he had a line of over 150 miles to defend, while operating against him was one of the best and most effective armies that have ever been created.

The blame which attaches to Pemberton is that he did not do with Grant's army what Grant subsequently did with his—defeat it in detail.

> Grant's original intention, after having left Vicksburg in his
> rear, had been to establish a base of supplies on the east bank of
> the Mississippi. An unforeseen difficulty arose but, instead of
> allowing it to interfere with his plans, he fitted it into an en-

tirely new mode of strategy, one destined to make his Vicksburg campaign famous in military annals.

Grant himself told how the novel plan was born and how it was executed.

My first problem after landing at Bruinsburg was to capture Grand Gulf. It was natural to expect the Confederates to meet us and prevent, if they could, our reaching a solid base.

McClernand's advance met the enemy about five miles west of Port Gibson, the nearest inland town. The enemy, numbering about 7,000 or 8,000 men, under General Bowen, had taken a strong natural position. His hope was to hold me in check until reinforcements could reach him from Vicksburg—but they did not come.

The enemy was sent in full retreat, and we followed up our victory until night overtook us about two miles from Port Gibson.

While at Grand Gulf I heard from General N. P. Banks, who was on the Red River, and who said that he could not join me before the tenth of May and then with only 15,000 men. Up to this time my intention had been to use Grand Gulf as a base of supplies, but the news from Banks forced on me a different plan of campaign. To wait for his co-operation would have detained me at least a month. I therefore determined to move independently of Banks, cut loose from my base, destroy the Rebel force in rear of Vicksburg and invest or capture the city.

Grand Gulf was accordingly given up as a base, and the authorities at Washington were notified. I knew well that Halleck's caution would lead him to disapprove of this course, but the time it would take to communicate with Washington would be so great that I could not be interfered with. We started from Bruinsburg with an average of about two days' rations and received no more from our own supplies for some days, but beef, mutton, poultry and forage were found in abundance. Quite a quantity of bacon and molasses was also secured from the country.

On the sixth of May Sherman arrived and the movement to Jackson commenced.

Pemberton was on my left, as I learned afterward, with nearly 50,000 men. A force was also collecting on my right, at Jackson, the point where the railroads communicating with Vicksburg connect. All the enemy's supplies of men and stores would come by that point. As I hoped in the end to besiege Vicksburg, I must first destroy all possibility of aid. I therefore determined to move swiftly toward Jackson, destroy or drive any force in that direction and then turn upon Pemberton.

I had been informed that General Joseph E. Johnston had arrived at Jackson in the night of May 13 from Tennessee and immediately had assumed command of all the Confederate troops in Mississippi.

That night McPherson was ordered to march upon Jackson, only fifteen miles away. Sherman was given the same order. I notified General Halleck that I should attack the state capital on the fourteenth.

Sherman and McPherson arranged to reach Jackson at about the same hour. By 9:00 A. M. McPherson's corps, now in advance, came on the enemy's pickets and speedily drove them in upon the main body. Johnston had been reinforced during the night by Georgia and South Carolina regiments, so that his force amounted to 11,000 men, and he was expecting still more.

Sherman also came on the Rebel pickets some distance out from the town and speedily drove them in.

I was with Sherman. He was confronted by a force sufficient to hold us back. Appearances did not justify an assault where we were. I rode to the right with my staff and soon found that the enemy had left. Johnston no doubt had given orders to retreat, leaving only the men at the guns to retard us while he was getting away. I rode immediately to the Statehouse, where I was soon followed by Sherman.

That night I slept in the room which Johnston was said to have occupied the night before.

Johnston saw at once that only a forceful attack on one of Grant's corps, before all of them could be united, offered a chance to turn the tide. Therefore he wanted all the Confederate forces, including the garrison of Vicksburg, combined into one strong and mobile fighting force.

Pemberton on the other hand wanted to protect and hold Vicksburg above anything else. His official report, from which the following extracts are taken, shows this clash of opinions between the two Confederate generals, which was bound to have disastrous consequences.

On the twelfth of May, 1863, I sent the following telegram to General Johnston: "The enemy is apparently moving his heavy force toward Edward's Depot; I will do all I can to meet him; that will be the battlefield, if I can forward a sufficient force, leaving troops enough to secure the safety of Vicksburg."

On the evening of that day I moved my headquarters to Bovina to be nearer the scene of active operations. The command arrived at Edward's Depot on the thirteenth and was placed in position covering all approaches from the south and east. This position was occupied from the night of the thirteenth until the morning of the fifteenth.

On the morning of the fourteenth I received the following dispatch, dated May thirteenth, from General Johnston, then at Jackson:

I have lately arrived and learn that General Sherman is between us with four divisions at Clinton. It is important to re-establish communications that you may be reinforced. If practicable, come up in his rear at once. To beat such a detachment would be of immense value. The troops here could co-operate. All the strength you could quickly assemble should be brought. Time is all important.

I immediately replied as follows:

I move at once with my whole available force, about 16,000. The men have been marching several days, are much fatigued, and I fear will straggle very much. In directing this move, I do not think you fully comprehend the position that Vicksburg will be left in, but I comply at once with your order.

I was firmly of the opinion that the movement indicated by General Johnston was extremely hazardous. I accordingly called a council of war and, placing the subject before them (including General Johnston's dispatch), asked their opinions. A majority expressed themselves favorable to the movement indicated by General Johnston. My own views were strongly expressed as unfavorable to any advance which might separate me farther from Vicksburg, which was my base.

Believing the only possibility of success to be in cutting the enemy's communications, I addressed the following to General Johnston:

I shall move early tomorrow morning with a column of 17,000 men to Dillon's, situated on the main road leading from Raymond to Port Gibson, seven and a half miles below Raymond. The object is to cut the enemy's communications and to force him to attack me, as I do not consider my force sufficient to justify an attack on the enemy in position or to attempt to cut my way to Jackson.

Grant now had maneuvered Pemberton into an impossible position. His army was stretched out over a distance of forty miles, and he was hopelessly separated from Johnston. He had been deluded in believing that Grant still depended on the Mississippi for his supplies, and hence tried to break a line of communications which no longer existed.

The result of Pemberton's decision was the Battle of Champion's Hill, to which Grant alludes in this manner.

I naturally expected that Pemberton would endeavor to obey the orders of his superior to attack us at Clinton. It turned out, however, that he had decided his superior's plans were impracticable and consequently determined to move south from Edward's Depot and get between me and my base. I, however, had no base, having abandoned it more than a week before.

Champion's Hill, where Pemberton had chosen his position to receive us, was well selected. It is one of the highest points in that section and commanded all the ground in range.

The Battle of Champion's Hill was one of the hardest-fought contests of the war. The Missouri soldier R. S. Bevier narrates the part he and his unit played in it.

On the fifteenth of May General Pemberton issued an order in which he exhorted the soldiers to do their duty nobly in the coming contest, stating that he had staked his reputation, his own fate and that of the army on the result of the battle which would probably be fought on the morrow.

A little after daylight we were startled by a cannonade directly in our front and close to us.

The most splendid artillery duel followed during which the guns on both sides were handled in the most skillful and scientific manner. Our metal proved too heavy for the enemy: great execution was done both among men and horses.

A lull then ensued during which Grant was massing heavily against our left, and at about one o'clock an overwhelming force moved against General C. L. Stevenson's division, which nobly sustained the fire for about an hour, when the men broke and fled in every direction.

At this critical moment General Bowen's division was ordered to redeem the day from utter disaster. The brave Missourians double-quicked to the point of danger, passing General Pemberton with cheers. The general seemed somewhat excited and looked at them with the hopeful gaze of one who expected them to do much. They moved quickly through the yard of Champion's House, where some lovely Southern ladies sang them "Dixie," to which they responded with resounding shouts. Stevenson's division had now given way en masse, while the Federals were advancing with triumphant cheers. The enemy had already captured two batteries of Stevenson's division, and his dense and formidable lines came pressing on, blazing with fire. Our 1st Brigade took position, a difficult maneuver, especially when performed under a murderous fire. Our colonel rode down the lines; in one hand he held the reins and a large magnolia flower, while with the other he waved his sword, and he gave the order to charge.

With a shout of defiance and with gleaming bayonets pointing to the front, the gray line leaped forward. Moving at quick time across the field, it dislodged the enemy with a heavy volley from the edge of the woods and pressed on. Cheers behind announced the coming up of a supporting brigade. The fighting now became desperate and bloody. The ground in dispute was a succession of high hills and deep hollows, heavily wooded, called "Champion's Hill." Our lines advanced steadily, though obstinately opposed, and within half a mile they recaptured the artillery lost by Stevenson's division and captured one of the enemy's batteries. The battle here raged fearfully—one unbroken, deafening roar of musketry was all that could be heard. The opposing lines were so much in the woods and so contiguous that artillery could not be used.

The ground was fought over three times. As the foe was borne back by us, we were confronted by fresh lines of troops, from which flashed and rolled the long, simultaneous and withering volleys that can come only from battalions just brought into action.

The numbers of the enemy seemed countless. Recoiling an instant, Bowen's division invariably renewed the attack and, taking advantage of every part of the ground with the practiced eye of soldiers accustomed to the field, they succeeded each time in beating back these new squadrons.

Once the enemy was driven so far before fresh forces were brought up that our men were in sight of his ordnance train, which was being turned and driven back under whip. Though the force in front was

vastly superior to ours, yet, if the fortunes of the day had depended
on the issue of the contest between them, victory might still have
remained on our side. Grant's center was undoubtedly pierced.

By this time, however, the hostile columns were closing in upon
the flanks of Bowen's lines. The Federal troops were threatening
their rear, and at the end of all this hard and desperate fighting, this
gallant and triumphant advance, it became necessary to fall back. In
front, on our flank and approaching the rear was now the whole of
the center and one wing of General Grant's army.

The enemy did not impede our retreat, which was pursued toward
Edward's Depot and the Big Black River.

S. H. M. Byers, now a corporal in the Federal army, had an
opportunity to watch Grant under fire.

It was a very hot day, and we had marched hard, slept little and
rested none. Among the magnolias on Champion's Hill the enemy
turned on us. We were in that most trying position of soldiers, being
fired on without permission to return the shots. A good many men
were falling, and the wounded were being borne to the rear, close to
an old well whose wooden curb seemed to offer the only protection.

"Colonel, move your men a little by the left flank," said a quiet
though commanding voice.

On looking around, I saw immediately behind us Grant, the commander in chief, mounted on a beautiful bay mare and followed by
perhaps half a dozen of his staff. For some reason he dismounted, and
most of his officers were sent off, bearing orders, to other quarters
of the field. It was Grant under fire.

The rattling musketry increased on our front and grew louder,
too, on the left flank. Grant had led his horse to the left and thus
kept near the company to which I belonged. He now stood leaning
complacently against his favorite steed, smoking the stump of a cigar.
His was the only horse near the line and must, naturally, have attracted some of the enemy's fire. I am sure everyone who recognized
him wished him away; but there he stood—clear, calm and immovable.
I was close enough to see his features. Earnest they were, but sign of
inward movement there was none. It was the same cool, calculating
face I had seen before; the same careful, half-cynical face I afterward
saw busied with affairs of state.

Whatever there may have been in his feelings there was no effort to conceal; there was no pretense, no trick; whatever that face was, it was natural. A man close by me had the bones of his leg shattered by a ball and was being helped to the rear. His cries of pain attracted Grant's attention, and I noticed the curious though sympathizing shades that crossed his quiet face as the bleeding soldier seemed to look toward him for help.

We had not waited many minutes when an orderly dashed up to Grant and handed him a communication. Then followed an order to move rapidly to the left and into the road. The fire grew heavier, and the air seemed too hot to be borne. I had been selected by the colonel to act as sergeant major, and I now ran behind and along the line, shouting at the top of my voice, "Fix bayonets!" The orders were not heard, and we were charging the enemy's position with bare muskets. A moment more and we were at the top of the ascent and among thinner wood and larger trees. The enemy had fallen back a few rods, forming a solid line parallel with our own, and now commenced in good earnest the fighting of the day. For half an hour we poured the hot lead into each others' faces. We had forty rounds each in our cartridge boxes, and probably nine-tenths of them were fired in that half hour.

"Stop! Halt! Surrender!" cried a hundred Rebels, whose voices seem to ring in my ears to this very day. But there was no stopping and no surrender. We ran and ran manfully. It was terribly hot, a hot afternoon under a Mississippi sun, and an enemy on flank and rear shouting and firing. The grass, the stones, the bushes, seemed melting under the shower of bullets that was following us to the rear. We tried to halt and tried to form. It was no use. Again we ran, and harder, and farther, and faster. We passed over the very spot where, half an hour before, we had left Grant leaning on his bay mare and smoking his cigar. Like ten thousand starving and howling wolves the enemy pursued, closer and closer, and we scarcely dared look back to face the fate that seemed certain.

Grant had seen it all, and in less time than I can tell it a line of cannon had been thrown across our path, which, as soon as we had passed, belched grapeshot and canister into the faces of our pursuers. They stopped, they turned, and they too ran and left their dead side by side with our own. Our lines, protected by the batteries, rallied and followed, and Champion's Hill was won, and with it was won the door to Vicksburg.

Grant passed along the lines after the fight as we stood in the narrow roads. Every hat was in the air, and the men cheered till they were hoarse. But speechless and almost without a bow he pushed on past, like an embarrassed man hurrying to get away from some defeat. Once he stopped near the colors and, without addressing himself to anyone in particular, said, "Well done!"

Pemberton's army retreated from Champion's Hill in fairly good order to occupy a strongly entrenched position in front of the Big Black River.

Missourian R. S. Bevier tells what happened there next morning.

The Big Black River formed an elbow in the rear of the army; the fortifications constituted a crescent in its front. The only means of crossing the stream was over a railroad bridge.

The 1st Missouri Brigade occupied the space to the right of the railroad, General Martin E. Green's brigade on the extreme left, General J. C. Vaughn's brigade of Tennesseeans and Mississippians in the center, while Stevenson's division on the opposite side of the river was held in reserve. Captain Landis' battery was placed on the western bluffs.

At daylight the enemy opened with their Parrott guns, which were briskly replied to. At 9:00 A.M. they made a determined assault, which was easily repulsed. Shortly after this General Sherman's whole corps in solid columns, six lines deep, advanced against our left wing. The veteran troops of Green's brigade received them with a withering fire and deadly aim, producing great gaps in their array and for a time staggering the assault. At this moment Vaughn's brigade became panic-stricken, broke, and fled in confusion, without firing a gun or striking a blow. On perceiving this, the Federals rallied and at double-quick darted past Green's men and occupied the place made vacant by the flying Mississippians.

The Yankees now occupied our center. Bowen's division was cut entirely in two, and Green's brigade was nearly surrounded and more than half of it captured. The rest threw their arms into the river and swam across—the only means of escape left to them.

Although the enemy immediately opened an enfilading fire on the 1st Brigade, it did not move from its rifle pits until ordered, and then they started with reluctance. But when they found a whole corps of the enemy making a race with them for the bridge, they "let out" and showed that they were as fleet-footed as they were courageous. A few of the artillerists remained at their pieces, loading and firing until they were captured.

By nightfall the fugitive and disordered troops were pouring into the streets of Vicksburg, and the citizens beheld with dismay the army that had gone out to fight for their safety returning to them in the character of a wild, tumultuous and mutinous mob.

> Chief-Engineer S. H. Lockett tells of Pemberton's despondency after the debacle.

I was the only Staff-officer with him. He was very much depressed, and for some time rode in silence. He finally said: "Just thirty years ago I began my military career at the United States Military Academy, and today that career is ended in disaster and disgrace." I strove to encourage him: that Vicksburg could not be carried by assault, and that Mr. Davis had telegraphed him "to hold Vicksburg at all hazards," adding that "if besieged we could be relieved." To all of which General Pemberton replied that my youth and hopes were the parents of my judgment; he himself did not think that our troops would stand the first shock of an attack.

On May 19 the Federals rushed upon the main line of defense with perfect confidence that there would be another "walk-over," such as they had had two days before, but this time they struck a rock. The men stood to their arms like true soldiers, and helped to restore the *morale* of our army.

> The main Federal attack at Big Black River had fallen to General Michael K. Lawler. How important his impetuous charge which started the enemy stampede would prove to be, even General Grant could not have known. The story is told by S. H. M. Byers, who was an eyewitness to the incident.

The night after our victory at Champion's Hill we marched ahead and in the morning bivouacked as a reserve at the Big Black River bridge. There it was that Grant reached the crisis of his career. While sitting on his horse, waiting to witness a charge by Lawler's brigade, a staff officer overtook him, bringing a peremptory order from Washington to abandon the campaign and take his army to Port Hudson, a fort below Vicksburg, to help General Banks, who was besieging it.

At that moment Grant saw a dashing officer suddenly come out of a cluster of woods leading his brigade to the assault. It was General

Michael K. Lawler. In five minutes the Rebel breastworks were carried, the enemy in flight or drowning in the rapid river. Then Grant turned to the staff officer and simply said, "See that charge! I think it is too late to abandon this campaign."

Had that order of Halleck's, written of course without knowledge of the recent victories, been followed, Banks, and not Grant, would have been first commander in the West. Had Lawler's charge failed just then and the battle been lost, Grant could have had no excuse for not obeying the order directing him to abandon what turned out to be a great military achievement.

> General Johnston's official report shows that he tried in vain to guide Pemberton and, after he had been disobeyed time and again, to save at least the remainder of his army.

On May seventeenth a letter was brought to me from General Pemberton. It contained intelligence of his engagement with the enemy on the sixteenth at Champion's Hill and of his having been compelled to withdraw, with heavy loss, to Big Black Bridge. He further expressed apprehension that he would be forced to fall back from that point, and said, "I have about sixty days' provisions at Vicksburg. I respectfully await your instructions."

I immediately replied, "If Haines' Bluff be untenable, Vicksburg is of no value and cannot be held. If you are invested in Vicksburg, you must ultimately surrender. Instead of losing both troops and place, save the troops. Evacuate Vicksburg and march to the northeast."

That night I was informed that General Pemberton had fallen back to Vicksburg.

> Grant now again takes up his story of the campaign.

The Battle of Champion's Hill had lasted about four hours. Had I known the ground, I cannot see how Pemberton could have escaped with any organized force. As it was, he lost over 3,000 killed and wounded and about 3,000 captured.

We were now assured of our position between Johnston and Pemberton, without a possibility of a junction of their forces. Pemberton might have made a night march to the Big Black, crossed the bridge there and, by moving north on the west side, have eluded us and finally returned to Johnston. But this would have given us Vicksburg. It would have been his proper move, however. In fact, it would have been in conformity with Johnston's orders.

But for the successful and complete destruction of the bridge, we should have followed the enemy so closely as to prevent his occupying his defenses around Vicksburg.

On the nineteenth of May there was constant skirmishing. The enemy had been much demoralized, and I believed he would not make much effort to hold Vicksburg. Accordingly at two o'clock I ordered an assault. It resulted in securing more advanced positions.

The twentieth and twenty-first were spent in strengthening our position and in making roads in the rear of the army.

I then determined on a second assault. Johnston was in my rear only fifty miles away, and I knew he was being reinforced. But the first consideration was—the troops believed they could carry the works in their front.

The attack was ordered to commence on all parts of the line at 2:00 A.M. on the twenty-second. Portions of each of our three corps succeeded in getting up to the very parapets of the enemy and in planting their battle flags upon them, but at no place were we able to enter. As soon as it was dark our troops were withdrawn. And thus ended the last assault upon Vicksburg.

The assault of May 22 was a bloody affair, as we learn from the testimony of one R. B. Scott of the 67th Indiana, who participated in it.

Our charge was to take place at ten o'clock. Early in the morning, and for five hours, the batteries all along the line vomited a torrent of shot and shell upon the Rebel minions, while Porter over on the river front was pouring upon the doomed city a heavy storm of iron hail. Meanwhile our skirmish line and sharpshooters were working their way well up to the forts.

When a few minutes before ten all the batteries ceased, and Porter's fleet stopped firing, a silence fell on the army. Every experienced soldier knew what this calm portended and, with every nerve strung up to high tension, awaited the signal. It came, and in a moment the troops sprang forward, clenching their guns as they started on the charge. But immediately the whole Rebel works and rifle pits were one blaze of fire. Twenty thousand muskets and 150 cannon belched forth death and destruction into our advancing lines. Our ranks were now becoming decimated, and McClernand called for support. The 59th Indiana boys came. The Rebels had reinforced this part of their line. And now the hill over which our columns had just passed was a field of death, where none could go and live. Our boys were seeking protection behind knolls and in the ditch beneath the Rebel fire. It was certain death to advance or retreat.

Now the lines were falling back all along. The charge was a bloody failure. Those in the ditch were left, and the hours slowly passed away as they watched for the going down of the sun that they might make their escape. One by one they crawled out, and sneaked their way through pools of blood and finally reached our lines.

Darkness spread over the terrible scene, and a drenching rain quenched the thirst of the wounded and cooled the brow of the dying.

> One of the defenders, Osborn H. Oldroyd, describes how quickly the hatreds of war disappeared when the combatants were allowed to meet as men to men.

In the afternoon of May 25 a flag of truce was sent into the lines for the purpose of burying the dead.

Now commenced a strange spectacle. The troops thronged the breastworks, gaily chatting with one another. Numbers of the Confederates accepted invitations to visit the enemy's lines, where they were hospitably entertained and warmly welcomed. Members of our regiment found numerous acquaintances and relatives among the Ohio, Illinois and Missouri regiments, and there were expressed mutal regrets that the issues of the war had made them enemies. At the expiration of the appointed time the men were all back in their places. The three hours of peace had scarcely expired ere those who had so lately mingled in friendly intercourse were once again engaged in deadly struggle.

> The direct assaults having failed, Grant tells how he resolved to proceed by a slower but safer method.

I now determined on a regular siege. With the navy holding the river, the investment of Vicksburg was complete. The enemy was limited in supplies of food, men and munitions of war. These could not last always. The work to be done was to make our position as strong against the enemy as his was against us. The problem was complicated by our wanting our line as near to that of the enemy as possible. We had but four engineer officers with us. We had no siege guns

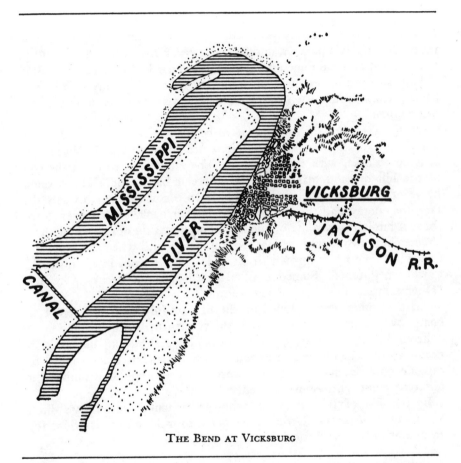

THE BEND AT VICKSBURG

except six 32-pounders, and there were none in the West to draw from. Admiral Porter, however, supplied us with a battery of navy guns of large caliber and, with these and the field artillery used in the campaign, the siege began.

In no place were our lines more than 600 yards from the enemy. It was necessary, therefore, to cover our men by something more than the ordinary parapet. Sandbags were placed along the tops of the parapets far enough apart to make loopholes for musketry. On top of these logs were put. By these means the men were enabled to walk about erect when off duty.

From the twenty-third of May the work of fortifying and pushing forward had been steadily progressing. At three points a sap was run up to the enemy's parapet, and by the twenty-fifth of June we had it undermined and the mine charged. The enemy had countermined but did not succeed in reaching our mine. At times the enemy threw over hand grenades, and often our men, catching them in their hands, returned them.

On the twenty-fifth of June at three o'clock, all being ready, our mine was exploded. A heavy artillery fire all along the line had been ordered to open with the explosion. The effect was to blow the top of the hill off and make a crater where it had stood. The breach, however, was not sufficient to enable us to pass a column through. In fact, the enemy had thrown up a line farther back. A few men were thrown into the air, some of them coming down on our side still alive. I remember one colored man, at work underground when the explosion took place, who was thrown to our side. He was not much hurt but terribly frightened. Someone asked him how high he had gone up. "Dunno, massa, but t'ink 'bout t'ree mile."

Another mine was exploded on the first of July, but no attempt to charge was made, the experience of the twenty-fifth admonishing us.

From this time forward the work of mining and pushing our position nearer to the enemy was prosecuted with vigor, but I determined to explode no more mines until we were ready to explode a number at different points and assault immediately after.

By the first of July our approaches had reached the enemy's ditch at a number of places. Orders were given to make all preparations for an assault on the sixth of July.

The besieged garrison soon began to feel the pinch of reduced rations. Sergeant Osborn Oldroyd relates what the men did to assuage their gnawing hunger.

The daily fighting, night work and disturbed rest began to exhibit their effects on the men. They were physically worn out and much reduced in flesh. Rations began to be shortened, and for the first time

(May 30) a mixture of ground peas and meal was issued. This food was very unhealthy, as it was almost impossible to bake the mixture thoroughly so that pea flour and meal would be fit for consumption. Yet these deficiencies were heroically endured, and the men succeeded, by an ingenious application of the culinary art, in rendering this unwholesome food palatable.

On June twenty-eighth orders were issued to select the finest and fattest mules and slaughter them. Mule flesh is coarse-grained and darker than beef, but really delicious, sweet and juicy. Besides this meat, traps were set for rats, which were consumed in such numbers that ere the termination of the siege they actually became a scarcity. I once made a hearty breakfast on fried rats and found the flesh very good.

A citizen of Vicksburg named Edward S. Gregory left us a picture of what life inside the city was like during the siege.

Hardly any part of the city was outside the range of the enemy's artillery except the south. The city was a target in itself and was hit every time. Just across the Mississippi, seven 11-inch and 13-inch mortars were put in position and trained directly on the homes of the people, and if any one of them ever was silent I fail to recall the occasion. All night long their deadly hail of iron dropped through roofs and tore up the deserted and denuded streets. For forty days and nights without interval the women and children of Vicksburg took calmly and bravely the iron storm. It became at last such an ordinary occurrence that I have seen ladies walk quietly along the streets while the shells burst above them, their heads protected only by a parasol held between them and the sun.

How people subsisted was another wonder. Business, of course, was suspended. There were some stores that had supplies, and prices climbed steadily, but first nobody had the money, and then nobody had the supplies.

A most interesting picture of life inside Vicksburg has come to us from the diary of a Southern lady, Mrs. James M. Loughborough, who voluntarily had come to the city to share her soldier-husband's fate. The excerpts given here begin on the day she arrived. The bombardment then was already in full swing.

Very few houses are without evidence of the bombardment, and yet the inhabitants live in their homes happy and contented, not knowing what moment the houses may be rent over their heads by the explosion of a shell.

"Ah!" said I to a friend, "how is it possible you live here?"

"After one is accustomed to the change," she answered, "we do not mind it. But becoming accustomed—that is the trial."

I was reminded of the poor man in an infected district who was met by a traveler and asked, "How do you live here?" "Sir, we die," was the laconic reply.

One night I was sleeping profoundly when the deep boom of the signal cannon awoke me. I sprang from my bed and went out on the veranda. The river was illuminated by large fires on the bank, and we plainly could discern huge black masses floating down with the current, now and then belching forth fire from their sides. We could hear the gallop of couriers on the paved streets. The rapid firing from the boats, the roar of the Confederate batteries, made a new and fearful scene to me. The boats were rapidly nearing the lower batteries, and the shells were beginning to fly unpleasantly near. The gentlemen urged the ladies to go down into a cave at the back of the house. While I hesitated, a shell exploded near by. Fear instantly decided me, and I ran. Breathless and terrified, I found the entrance and ran in, having left one of my slippers on the hillside.

The cave was an excavation in the earth the size of a large room, high enough for the tallest person to stand perfectly erect, provided with comfortable seats and altogether quite a large and habitable abode.

When the danger was over, we returned to the house and from the veranda looked on a burning boat, the only one, so far as we could ascertain, that had been injured. It was found that very few of the Confederate guns had been discharged at all. The fuses recently sent from Richmond had been found this night, of all others, to be defective.

Sunday, May 17, as we were dressing for church, we heard the loud booming of cannon. We passed groups of anxious men with troubled faces, but very few soldiers. Gloom seemed to hang over the men: a sorrowful waiting for tidings that all knew would tell of disaster. Soon wagons came rattling down the streets; now and then a worn and dusty soldier would be seen passing; then straggler after straggler came by; finally groups of soldiers, worn and dusty with a long march.

"What can be the matter?" we all cried.

"We are whipped, and the Federals are after us."

"It's all Pem's fault," said an awkward, long-limbed, weary-looking man. "We would ha' fit well, but General Pemberton came up and said, 'Stand your ground, boys! Your General Pemberton is with you.' And then, bless you, lady, the next we seed of him, he was sitting on his horse behind a house! And when we seed that, we thought 'tain't no use."

The caves were plainly becoming a necessity, as some persons had been killed by fragments of shells. The room that I had so lately slept in had been struck and a large hole made in the ceiling. Terror-stricken, we remained crouched in the cave while shell after shell followed one another in quick succession. My heart stood still as we would hear reports from the guns and the rushing and fearful sound of the shell as it came toward us. As it neared, the noise became more deafening; the air was full of the rushing sound; pains darted through my temples; my ears were bursting. And as it exploded, the report flashed through my head like an electric shock, leaving me in a quiet state of terror.

Even the dogs seemed to share the general fear. They would be seen in the midst of the noise to gallop up the street, and then to return, as if fear had maddened them. On hearing the descent of a shell, they would dart aside—then, as it exploded, sit down and howl in the most pitiful manner.

One evening I heard the most heart-rending screams and moans. I was told that a mother had taken a child into a cave about a hundred yards from us and laid it on its bed. A mortar shell entered the earth about it, crushing in the upper part of the little sleeping head.

A servant brought me one day a present from an officer that was acceptable indeed: two large, yellow, ripe June apples, sealed in a large envelope. Another gentlemen sent me four large slices of ham. While we were conversing, my little two-year-old daughter quietly secured them. When she had finished eating, she turned around to me, saying, "Mamma, it's so dood!"—the first intimation I had that my portion had disappeared. Fruits and vegetables were not to be procured at any price.

Already the men in the rifle pits were on half rations. Many of them ate it all at once and the next day fasted, preferring, as they said, to have one good meal. I often remarked how cheerfully the soldiers bore the hardships of the siege. I would see them pass, whistling and chatting pleasantly, as around them the balls and shells flew thick.

About this time the town was aroused by the arrival of a courier from General Johnston, who brought private dispatches to General Pemberton and letters to the inhabitants from friends without. His manner of entering the city was singular: he took a skiff in the Yazoo and proceeded to its confluence with the Mississippi, where he tied it up. At dark he took off his clothing, placed his dispatches securely within them, bound the package firmly to a plank and, going into the river, sustained his head above water by holding to the plank. In this manner he floated through the fleet to Vicksburg.

One evening I noticed one of the horses tied in the ravine writhing and struggling as if in pain. He had been very badly wounded in the flank by a Minié ball. The poor creature's agony was dreadful: he would reach his head up as far as possible into the tree to which he was tied, and cling with his mouth, while his neck and body quivered with pain. Every motion, instead of being violent as most horses' would have been when wounded, had a stately grace of eloquent suffering that is indescribable. How I wanted to go to him and pat and soothe him! His halter was taken off and he was turned free. He went to a tree, leaned his body against it and moaned, with half-closed eyes, shivering frequently throughout his huge body as if the pain were too great to bear.

Then he would turn his head entirely around and gaze at the group of soldiers that stood pityingly near, as if he were looking for human sympathy. The master refused to have him shot, hoping he would recover, but the noble black was doomed. Becoming restless with the pain, the poor brute staggered blindly on. My eyes filled with tears, for he fell with a weary moan, the bright intelligent eyes turned still on the men who had been his comrades in many a battle.

Poor fellow, you were far beyond human sympathy! In the midst of all the falling shells could not one reach him, giving him peace and death? I saw an ax handed to one of the bystanders and suddenly turned away from the scene. The glossy black body was being taken out from our sight, to be replaced by new sufferings and to be forgotten in new incidents.

The siege was drawing to a close. Let Grant himself tell the story of his final triumph.

On the third of July about ten o'clock white flags appeared on a portion of the Rebel works. Hostilities ceased at once. Soon two persons were seen coming toward our lines bearing a white flag. They proved to be General Bowen and Colonel L. M. Montgomery, aide-de-camp to Pemberton, bearing a letter to me proposing an armistice.

The news soon spread to all parts of the command. The troops felt that their weary marches and hard fighting were at last at an end.

I sent back an oral message saying that, if Pemberton desired it, I would meet him in front of McPherson's corps at three o'clock that afternoon. At the appointed time Pemberton appeared at the point suggested, accompanied by the same officers who had borne his letter of the morning. Several officers of my staff accompanied me. Our place of meeting was on a hillside within a few hundred feet of the Rebel line. Near by stood a stunted oak tree, which was made historical by the event. It was but a short time before the last vestige of its body, root and limb, had disappeared, the fragments having been taken as trophies.

Pemberton proposed that the Confederate army should be allowed to march out with the honors of war, carrying their small arms and field artillery. This was promptly and unceremoniously rejected. The interview here ended, I agreeing, however, to send a letter giving final terms by ten o'clock that night.

When I returned to my headquarters I sent for all my corps and division commanders. I informed them that I was ready to hear any suggestion but would hold the power of deciding entirely in my own hands. Against the general and almost unanimous judgment of the council I then sent the following letter to Pemberton:

You will be allowed to march out, the officers taking with them their side arms and clothing, and the field, staff and cavalry officers one horse each. The rank and file will be allowed all their clothing, but no other property.

Had I insisted on an unconditional surrender, there would have been over 30,000 men to transport to Cairo, very much to the inconvenience of the Army of the Mississippi. Thence the prisoners would have had to be transported by rail to Washington or Baltimore. Pemberton's army was largely composed of men whose homes were in the Southwest; I knew many of them were tired of the war and would go home.

Pemberton promptly accepted these terms.

The scene of the surrender was witnessed by William E. Strong, of Grant's staff. His account shows that the negotiations did not pass off as smoothly as Grant himself made it appear in his *Memoirs*.

Promptly at 3:00 P.M the commander in chief, accompanied by Major Generals James B. McPherson, E. O. C. Ord, A. J. Smith, John A. Logan, Lieutenant Colonels John A. Rawlins, James H. Wilson and me, rode through the Federal entrenchments, halted and dismounted near an oak tree, and the party patiently waited the arrival of Lieutenant General Pemberton. The day was hot and sultry; the silence was oppressive. Fifteen or twenty minutes passed, but the Rebel commander did not appear. General Grant was evidently annoyed at the delay, but said nothing.

At length there was a commotion, and the Rebel commander rode out, followed by Colonel Montgomery, one of his aides, and Major General Bowen, who were accompanied by their orderlies only. They halted within thirty feet of our party and immediately dismounted. General Grant advanced a few paces and stopped; General Pemberton did the same; but neither spoke, although they had known each other as young officers during the Mexican War. General Pemberton gave no sign of recognition and seemed determined that Grant should be the first to speak, but in this he was disappointed. The silence was extremely embarrassing.

At length Colonel Montgomery, who had met General Grant the evening before, formally introduced the two generals. They advanced and shook hands. General Pemberton then said in an insolent and overbearing manner, "What terms of capitulation do you propose to grant me?"

General Grant replied, "Those terms stated in my letter of this morning."

General Pemberton in an excited manner said, "If this is all you have to offer, the conference may as well terminate."

"Very well," said General Grant in his usual cool and collected way, "I am quite content to have it so," and, turning quickly away, called for his horse.

General Bowen, however, suggested that two or more of the officers retire and talk the matter over informally and suggest such terms as they might think proper. To this General Grant assented, but with the proviso that he should not be bound by any agreement of his subordinate officers.

Generals McPherson and A. J. Smith, General Bowen and Colonel Montgomery separated from the party and sat down to talk over the terms, while Grant and Pemberton went away by themselves and likewise sat down. Both were facing us. General Pemberton showed by his manner that he was laboring under great excitement; Grant was, as usual, perfectly cool and sat smoking his cigar and pulling up tufts of grass. Generals Grant and Pemberton had been engaged in conversation about fifteen minutes when they returned to the tree of rendezvous, and were soon joined by Generals McPherson, Smith, Bowen and Colonel Montgomery.

The proposition made by the Rebel officers and Smith was promptly declined by General Grant, but he agreed to send General Pemberton his final terms by ten o'clock that night. The interview then terminated, having lasted about an hour and a half.

The final terms agreed upon were along the lines which Grant had proposed in his first letter.

How the veterans inside the city reacted to the order for surrender is told by Sergeant Oldroyd.

On the fourth of July the order for surrender was promulgated. Its receipt was the signal for a fearful outburst of anger and indignation. The members of the 3rd Louisiana Infantry expressed their feeling in curses loud and deep. Many broke their trusty rifles against the trees and scattered the ammunition over the ground. In many instances the battle-worn flags were torn into shreds and distributed among the men as a sacred memento that they were no party to the surrender.

On July fifth rations for five days were issued to the Confederates from the commissariat of the Federals. These rations consisted of bacon, hominy, peas, coffee, sugar, soap, salt, candles and crackers. How the famished troops enjoyed such bounteous supplies it is needless to state. They grew jovial and hilarious over the change in their condition. The Yankees were unusually kind. They asked innumerable questions, were horrified at the fact of the men eating mules and rats and openly expressed their admiration for the unfaltering bravery of the Confederates.

General Sherman had not always agreed with Grant while the campaign had been in progress, but when its outcome justified his chief's strategy, he was not slow to render due homage to a military exploit which is now universally regarded as a masterpiece of clever and daring generalship.

The campaign of Vicksburg, in its conception and execution, belonged exclusively to General Grant, not only in the great whole, but in the thousands of its details.

The value of Vicksburg could not be measured by the list of prisoners, guns and small arms. The real value lay in the fact that its possession secured for us the navigation of the great central river of the continent and fatally bisected the Southern Confederacy.

CHAPTER 16

Lee Invades Pennsylvania

THE BATTLE OF GETTYSBURG

For several weeks after the Battle of Chancellorsville both armies rested. But the summer of 1863 was approaching, and with it the time for fresh campaigning. Which side would take the offensive?

Jefferson Davis explained why it was essential that Lee beat Hooker to the move.

In the spring of 1863 the enemy occupied his former position before Fredericksburg. He was in great strength and was preparing on the grandest scale for another advance against Richmond, which in political if not military circles was regarded as the objective point of the war.

The defense of our country's cause had already brought nearly all of the population fit for military service into the various armies then in the field, so that but little increase could be hoped for by the Army of Northern Virginia. To wait until the enemy should advance was to take the desperate hazard of his great superiority of numbers, as well as his ability to reinforce.

It was decided by a bold movement to transfer hostilities to the north by marching into Maryland and Pennsylvania, simultaneously driving the foe out of the Shenandoah Valley. Thus, it was hoped, General Hooker would be called from Virginia to meet our advance.

If, beyond the Potomac, some opportunity should be offered to enable us to defeat the enemy, the measure of our success would be full; but if the movement only resulted in freeing Virginia from the hostile army, it was more than could fairly be expected.

The details of Lee's plans were a secret known to only a few. Nevertheless, reports of an impending change in the *status quo* kept flitting across the river. They could be neither confirmed nor disproved by Hooker's scouts, but an observer in an army balloon, Huntington W. Jackson, easily penetrated the mystery.

One afternoon the writer made a balloon ascension for the purpose of reporting whether any movement could be detected across the river. A mile or more back from the shore, the entrenchments of the enemy could be plainly distinguished, and one glance in this direction through the powerful field glass told the whole story. Marching toward the left flank were seen long columns of infantry, artillery and wagon trains. The rumor of a movement had become a demonstrated fact.

Lee started out on June 3, 1863, brushed aside a Federal force under General R. H. Milroy in the Shenandoah Valley, crossed the Potomac, rapidly traversed Maryland and entered the state of Pennsylvania. (See maps, pages 467 and 504.)

Hooker set his army in motion at the same time, paralleling the movements of his opponent, always careful to shield Washington and the coast cities.

A reporter for the *Boston Journal* named Charles Carleton Coffin, who was in Harrisburg at that time, wrote of the panic there at Lee's approach.

Harrisburg was a bedlam when I entered it on the fifteenth of June. The railroad stations were crowded with trunks, boxes, bundles; packages tied up in bed blankets and quilts; mountains of baggage; mobs rushing here and there in a frantic manner, shouting, screaming, as if the Rebels were about to dash into the town and lay it in ashes. The railroads were removing their cars and engines. The merchants were packing up their goods; housewives were secreting their silver; everywhere there was a hurly-burly. The excitement was increased when a train of army wagons came rumbling in, accompanied by a squadron of cavalry. It was Milroy's train.

"The Rebels will be here tomorrow or next day," said the teamsters.

The Confederates swept through many Pennsylvania towns, meeting no opposition. When York fell to them, their entry, so we learn from Lieutenant Robert Stiles, did not produce the results which had been expected.

We were entering York, General William F. Smith's brigade in the lead. The population seemed to be in the streets, and I saw that General Smith—we called him the Old Governor—had blood in his eye. Turning to his aide, he told him to "go back and look up those tooting fellows," as he called the brigade band, "and tell them to march into town tooting 'Yankee Doodle.' "

The band got to the head of the column and struck up "Yankee Doodle." The Old Governor, riding alone and bareheaded in front, began bowing and saluting first to one side and then the other, and especially to every pretty girl he saw, with that manly, hearty smile which no man or woman ever resisted. The Yorkers seemed at first astounded, then pleased, and finally, by the time we reached the public square, they broke into enthusiastic cheers, till the Old Governor called a halt.

It was a rare scene—the vanguard of an invading army and the invaded population hobnobbing on the public green in an enthusiastic gathering. The general made a rattling, humorous speech, which both the Pennsylvanians and his own brigade applauded to the echo. He said substantially:

"What we all need on both sides is to mingle more with each other, so that we shall learn to know and appreciate each other. Now here's my brigade—I wish you knew them as I do. They are such a hospitable, wholehearted, fascinating lot of gentlemen. Why, just think of it—this part of Pennsylvania is ours today; we can do what we please with it. Yet we sincerely and heartily invite you to stay! Are we not a fine set of fellows?"

At the head of a Southern division belonging to Longstreet's corps rode General George E. Pickett, unaware that his name would soon be connected with one of the memorable events in American history. Pickett was then a man of thirty-eight, and very much in love with his fiancée, to whom he wrote frequently. In one letter he speaks of a quaint episode which occurred in the Pennsylvania town of Greencastle. Unlike the legendary incident of Barbara Fritchie, which it somewhat resembles, this episode actually happened, and appeals because of its surprise ending.

June 24, 1863.

Yesterday we were marching through the little town of Greencastle. The soldiers were happy, hopeful, making up for the welcome they were not receiving. As our band, playing "Dixie," passed a vine-bowered home, a young girl rushed out on the porch and waved a United States flag. Then she called out with all the strength of her brave young heart:

"Traitors—traitors—traitors, come and take this flag, the man of you who dares!"

I took off my hat and bowed to her, saluted her flag and then turned, facing the men who felt my unspoken order. And, don't you know, every man lifted his cap and cheered the little maiden who, though she kept on waving her flag, ceased calling us traitors, till she cried out:

"Oh, I wish—I wish I had a Rebel flag! I'd wave that too."

We left the little girl standing there with the flag gathered up in her arms as if too sacred to be waved, now that even the enemy had done it reverence.

> J. B. Polley of Hood's Texas Brigade, who had gone through the Maryland campaign of 1862, wrote a letter home which breathed a somewhat dissimilar spirit.

Where we are going now is a question concerning which a private soldier can only surmise. I have long ago gratified my thirst for gore and glory. Sometimes I feel inclined to echo the desire expressed by Jackson's man who, reprimanded by his general for running out of the fight "like a baby," broke into a big boohoo and exclaimed, "I don't care what you say, sir, but I wish I was a baby, and a girl baby at that!"

The plagued Yankees have such an ability and habit of outnumbering us that we are not prompt to join in any censure of the Texas Irishman who, sent out on the skirmish line, came back on a treble-quick and, when told by his lieutenant, "I'd rather die, Mike, than run out of a fight," fixed on the officer a withering look and replied, "The hell you would, sor, whin there was only a skirmish line of us boys, an' two rigiments and a battery of thim!"

Why can we not be better and more regularly supplied? Perhaps we are expected to live off the enemy; if so, we Texans will ask discharges. We are getting homesick, anyway. A comrade said the other day, "I wish to God I was at home."

"Oh," I replied. "You want to see the girl you left behind, don't you?"

"No, indeed," he blurted out. "I want something to eat."

A member of the New Orleans Washington Artillery contributes a pertinent observation on the behavior of the Confederate army during its march through the North.

The Northern farmers apparently did not know a war was going on. General Lee's orders were positive against any appropriation of private property; even chickens, milk and butter were sacred.

We passed many fine houses, and large barns full of grain and forage; but "Massa Robert" wouldn't permit any confiscations, and not a fence-rail was disturbed, much to the disgust of the Negro cooks, who could not understand why our army should act so differently from the Federal armies in Virginia.

Hooker's movements so far had given no cause for adverse criticism. He had shadowed Lee's march and kept him from debouching on the eastern plains. Both armies had now crossed the Potomac and drew closer toward each other. The Union commander, remembering the fate of Harpers Ferry in 1862, demanded its evacuation—with what results was reported by the correspondent Coffin.

General Hooker had waited in front of Washington till he was certain of Lee's intention, and then by a rapid march pushed on to Frederick. He asked that the troops at Harpers Ferry might be placed under his command. This was refused, whereupon he informed the War Department that, unless this condition were complied with, he wished to be relieved of his command. The matter was laid before the President, and Hooker's request was granted. General Meade was placed in command; and what was denied to Hooker was conceded to Meade.

It was a dismal day at Frederick when the news was promulgated that General Hooker was relieved of the command. Notwithstanding the result at Chancellorsville, the soldiers had a good degree of confidence in him. General Meade was unknown except to his own corps. He had entered the war as brigadier in the Pennsylvania Reserves and commanded a division at Antietam and at Fredericksburg, and the 5th Corps at Chancellorsville.

General Meade cared but little for the pomp and parade of war. His own soldiers respected him because he was always prepared to endure hardships. They saw a tall, slim, gray-bearded man, wearing a slouch hat, a plain blue blouse, with his pantaloons tucked into his boots. He was plain of speech and familiar in conversation.

I saw him soon after he was informed that the army was under his command. There was no elation, but on the contrary he seemed weighed down with a sense of responsibility. It was in the hotel at Frederick. He stood silent and thoughtful by himself. Few of all the noisy crowd around knew what had taken place. No change was made in the machinery of the army, and there was but a few hours' delay in its movement.

To change commanding generals while a great, perhaps decisive, battle was in the immediate offing, might easily have led to catastrophic consequences. But, fortunately for the Union side, Lee also had blundered. He had allowed General Stuart, with almost the entire cavalry, to go on a raid around Hooker, thereby, in the military language of the period, robbing his army of its eyes. Lee now had to depend almost entirely on scouts for information, and these were not always dependable.

The story of one scout, who became important to Lee at this juncture, is told by the Confederate staff officer G. Moxley Sorrel.

With us was a scout, more properly a spy, who was a man of about thirty, calling himself a Mississippian, and altogether an extraordinary character. His time seemed to be passed about equally within our lines and the enemy's. Harrison (such was his name) always brought us true information, and there was invariable confirmation of his reports afterward. He went everywhere, even through Stanton's War Office at Washington, and brought in much. We could never discover that he sold anything against us; besides, we did verify his account of himself as coming from Mississippi.

One night at the end of June, I was aroused by the provost guard bringing up a suspicious prisoner. It was Harrison, the scout, filthy and ragged, showing some rough work and exposure. His report was long and valuable. He brought it down to a day or two and described how the enemy were even then marching in great numbers in the direction of Gettysburg, with intention apparently of concentrating there. Harrison's report was so exceedingly important that I woke General

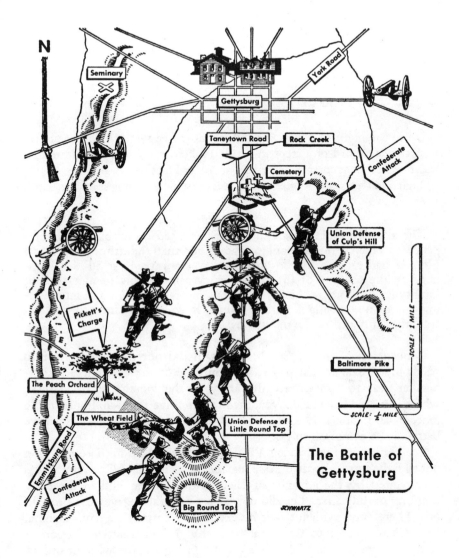

Cemetery Ridge was the burial place of the hopes of an army.

Longstreet, who immediately sent the scout to Lee. The general heard him with great composure and minuteness. It was on this, the report of a single scout, in the absence of cavalry, that the army moved.

What Lee's true intention was and how it was changed on the mere say-so of this one scout, is reported by a young staff officer, Lieutenant Randolph H. McKim.

Up to the night of June 28, at which time Lee was at Chambersburg, with the corps of Longstreet and A. P. Hill close at hand, Lee's intention had been to concentrate his entire army at Harrisburg.

That plan was abandoned for a reason which is thus stated in Lee's own report:

The advance against Harrisburg was arrested on account of intelligence received from a scout to the effect that the army of General Hooker had crossed the Potomac and was approaching South Mountain. In the absence of the cavalry it was impossible to ascertain his intentions; but to deter him from advancing farther west and interrupting our communications with Virginia, it was determined to concentrate the army east of the mountains.

Concentration east of South Mountain did not necessarily have to result in a battle at that place. The purpose of the Confederate commander was to concentrate the army in the vicinity of Cashtown, where it would have held a very strong defensive position, impregnable indeed—and where Lee, if attacked, could have fought a defensive battle, as he purposed to do.

Lee himself, before leaving Virginia, had expressed his determination not to fight a great battle unless attacked. The Battle of Gettysburg was precipitated by the advance of Lieutenant General Hill in the early morning of July first. Lee did not wish a general engagement brought on. There is no evidence that he expected a battle that day. General Lee was dragged into this great battle by the unauthorized action of one of his lieutenants in advancing and fighting a battle without orders.

General Meade had selected Pipe Creek, fifteen miles southeast of Gettysburg, as his line of defense. There he would have held a strong position, properly placed to protect Washington, Baltimore and Philadelphia. It was there that he hoped Lee would attack him.

But Lee, too, wanted to be attacked, convinced that the enemy sooner or later would have to take the offensive in order to drive him out of Pennsylvania. In the end both plans miscarried, because events intervened which took the decision out of the hands of the commanding generals and made Gettysburg the scene of the battle.

Gettysburg nestles between two ridges—Seminary Ridge on the west, Cemetery Ridge on the east. Up to that time the little town had dozed in obscurity, but presently the attention of the whole nation, if not the whole world, would be focused on it.

Charles Coffin, the reporter for the *Boston Journal*, advised his paper of the quickly moving developments from June 30 to the early morning hours of July 2.

On Tuesday evening the thirtieth of June General Reynolds, heretofore commanding the 1st Corps, received instructions from General Meade, assigning him to the command of the 1st, 11th and 3rd Corps. General Reynolds moved early in the morning to Gettysburg and sent orders to General Howard of the 11th Corps to follow. At 9:30 A.M. on Wednesday, July 1, A. P. Hill—on his way to Gettysburg in search of shoes for his soldiers, it was said—appeared in front of him, and skirmishing commenced. Buford's Federal cavalry kept Hill at bay for several hours against overwhelming odds. About ten o'clock in the morning of July 1, General Reynolds rode into Gettysburg in advance of the 1st Corps and turned toward the Seminary Ridge, deploying his divisions across the Chambersburg Road. General Archer's brigade of A. P. Hill's corps was advancing eastward, unaware of Reynolds' movement. The fight opened at once. Archer and several hundred of his men were captured. The contest increased. General Reynolds, while riding along the line, was killed in the field beyond the Seminary.

General Howard, on whom now the command devolved, had heard the cannonade and, riding rapidly, entered the town and sent messengers to General Reynolds, asking for instructions, not knowing that his superior officer had been killed. While waiting the return of his aides, he went to the top of the Seminary to reconnoiter the surrounding country.

It was now half past eleven. The Rebels were appearing in increased force. The prisoners taken said that the whole of A. P. Hill's corps was near by.

"You will have your hands full before night. Longstreet is near, and Ewell is coming," said one boastingly.

"I have come to the conclusion," said General Howard, "that the only tenable position for my limited force is on Seminary Ridge. From there my artillery can sweep the fields completely."

The head of Howard's 11th Corps reached Gettysburg about twelve o'clock, passed through the town and moved out beyond the college, adjoining the right of the 1st Corps.

Thus far success had attended the Union arms. A large number of prisoners had been taken, and the troops were holding their own against a superior force. About half past twelve, cavalry scouts reported that Ewell was coming down the York Road and was not more than four miles distant. General Howard sent an aide to General Sickles, of the 3rd Corps, who was at Emmitsburg, requesting him to come on with all haste. Another was sent down the Baltimore Pike to the Two Taverns, three miles distant, with a similar message to General Henry W. Slocum of the 2nd Corps, which was there, resting in the fields. They had heard the roar of the battle and could see the clouds of smoke rising over the intervening hills. General Slocum was the senior officer and not subject to Howard's orders. He received the message, but did not, for reasons best known to himself, see fit to accede to the request.

It was a quarter before three when Ewell's lines began to deploy on the York Road. The Rebel batteries were wheeled into position and opened on the Union forces. A battery in the cemetery replied.

"I sent again to General Slocum," said General Howard, "stating that my right flank was attacked, that it was in danger of being turned, and asking him if he was coming up, but General Slocum did not move."

Sickles, who, unlike Slocum, was under Howard's orders, was too far off to render assistance. Meanwhile Ewell was pressing on toward the college. Another division of Rebels under General William D. Pender came in from the southwest. An hour passed of close, desperate fighting. It wanted a quarter to four. Howard, confronted by four times his own force, was still holding his ground, waiting for Slocum. Another messenger rode to the Two Taverns, urging Slocum to advance.

"I must have reinforcements!" was the message Howard received from Doubleday on the left. "You must reinforce me!" was the word from the center.

"Hold out a little longer, if possible; I am expecting General Slocum every moment" was Howard's reply. Still another dispatch was sent to the Two Taverns, but General Slocum had not moved. The Rebel

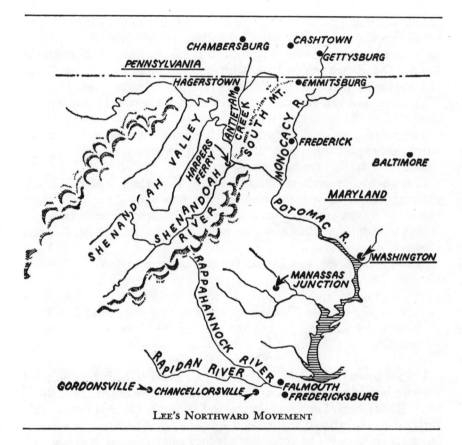

LEE'S NORTHWARD MOVEMENT

cannon were cutting the center line. Pender was sweeping round Doubleday; Ewell was enclosing part of Howard's own 11th Corps. Sickles was advancing as fast as he could. For six hours the ground had been held against a greatly superior force.

Major J. B. Howard, the general's brother, a member of his staff, dashed down the pike in search of Slocum with a request that he move at once and send one division to the right and the other to the left of Gettysburg. Slocum declined to go up to the front himself and take any responsibility, as he understood that General Meade did not wish to bring on a general engagement. He was willing, however, to send forward his troops as General Howard desired, and issued his orders accordingly.

But before the divisions of Slocum's 12th Corps could get in motion, the Rebels had completely enfolded both flanks of Howard's line. The order to retreat was given. The two corps came crowding through the town. The Rebels pressed on with cheers. Most of the 1st Corps reached the Cemetery Ridge and were rallied by Howard and Hancock. This officer had just arrived under direction of General Meade, to take charge of all the troops in front.

The Rebels, satisfied with the work of the day, made no further attack, although they greatly outnumbered the Union force.

So closed the first day at Gettysburg.

General Meade arrived on the battlefield at three o'clock on the morning of the second and had an interview with General Howard soon after by the cemetery gate. They rode along the lines together.

"I am confident that we can hold this position," said General Howard.

"I am glad to hear you say so, for it is too late to leave it," replied Meade.

> That the clash at Gettysburg really was a surprise to Lee is attested by General Longstreet, one of his three corps commanders.

On the morning of July 1, General Lee and I left his headquarters together and had ridden three or four miles when we heard heavy firing along Hill's front. The firing became so heavy that General Lee hurried forward to see what it meant, and I followed. The firing proceeded from the engagement between our advance and Reynolds' corps, which was totally unexpected on both sides. As an evidence of the doubt in which General Lee was enveloped, I quote from General R. H. Anderson the report of a conversation I had with him during the engagement.

About ten o'clock in the morning he received a message notifying him that General Lee desired to see him. He found General Lee intently listening to the fire of the guns, and very much disturbed and depressed. At length he said, more to himself than to General Anderson, "I cannot think what has become of Stuart. In his absence I am in ignorance as to what we have in front of us. It may be the whole Federal army, or it may be only a detachment. If it is the whole Federal force, we must fight a battle here; if we do not gain a victory, those defiles and gorges through which we passed this morning will shelter us from disaster."

When I overtook General Lee at five o'clock that afternoon, he said, to my surprise, that he thought of attacking General Meade on the heights the next day. I suggested that this course seemed to be at variance with his plan of the campaign. He said, "If the enemy is there tomorrow, we must attack him."

I replied, "If he is there, it will be because he is anxious that we should attack him—a good reason, in my judgment, for not doing so." I urged that we should move around by our right to the left of Meade and put our army between him and Washington, threatening his left and rear, and thus force him to attack us in such position as we might select. I called Lee's attention to the fact that the country was admirably adapted for a defensive battle, and that we should surely repulse Meade with crushing loss if we would take position so as to force him to attack us, and suggested that, even if we carried the heights in front of us, we should be so badly crippled that we could not reap the fruits of victory.

But General Lee was impressed with the idea that, by attacking the Federals, he could whip them in detail. I reminded him that if the Federals were there in the morning, it would be proof that they had their forces well in hand, and that, with Pickett in Chambersburg and Stuart out of reach, it was we who should be somewhat in detail. However, the sharp battle fought by Hill and Ewell on that day had given him a taste of victory.

When I left General Lee on the night of the first, I believed that he had made up his mind to attack.

Cannoneer Augustus Buell, of the United States regulars, gives a picture of the first day's fighting before the Union soldiers were driven back into the town and beyond it to Cemetery Ridge.

While we lay in bivouac during the afternoon and night of June 30, General N. B. Buford's cavalry passed up the road toward Gettysburg. They had plenty of exciting news for us. "We have found the Johnnies; they are just above and to the left of us, and the woods are full of 'em."

Our battery kept moving rapidly to the front along the Emmitsburg

Pike and halted in column just on the crest of Seminary Ridge. Our guns pointed due west, taking the Cashtown Pike *en écharpe*. There was infantry in our rear, in a railroad cut which ran behind us.

About noon of July 1, the infantry of the 1st Corps was struggling desperately in our front, and for a few moments we had nothing to do but witness the scene. Over across a creek (Willoughby's Run) we could see the gray masses of the Rebel infantry coming along all the roads and deploying in the fields, and it seemed that they were innumerable.

Our infantry was being slowly but surely forced in toward the Seminary. It was now considerably past noon. In addition to the struggle going on in our immediate front, the sounds of a heavy attack from the north side were heard, and away out beyond the creek to the south a strong force could be seen advancing and overlapping our left. Stray balls began to zip and whistle around our ears with unpleasant frequency. Then we saw the batteries in advance of us limber up and fall back toward the Seminary, and the enemy simultaneously advance his batteries down the road. All our infantry began to fall back.

The enemy did not press them but halted for nearly an hour to re-form his lines. At last he made his appearance in grand shape. His line stretched nearly a mile in length. First we could see the tips of their colorstaffs coming up over the little ridge, then the points of their bayonets, and then the Johnnies themselves, coming on with a steady tramp, tramp, and with loud yells. It was now apparent that the old battery's turn had come again, and that another page must be added to the record of Buena Vista and Antietam. The day was very hot, many of the boys had their jackets off, and they exchanged little words of cheer with one another as the gray line came on. In quick, sharp tones, like successive reports of a repeating rifle, came our captain's orders: "Load . . . Canister . . . Double!" There was a hustling of cannoneers, a few thumps of the rammer heads, and then "Ready! . . . By piece! . . . At will! . . . Fire!"

Directly in our front the Rebel infantry had been forced to halt and lie down, by the tornado of canister that we had given them. But the regiments to their right kept on, as if to cut us off from the rest of our troops.

Then ensued probably the most desperate fight ever waged between artillery and infantry at close range without a particle of cover on either side. They gave us volley after volley in front and flank, and we gave them double canister as fast as we could load. The 6th Wisconsin and 11th Pennsylvania men crawled up over the bank of the cut and joined their musketry to our canister.

The years have but softened in memory the picture of our burly corporal, bareheaded, his hair matted with blood from a scalp wound, and wiping the crimson fluid out of his eyes to sight the gun; of the steady orderly sergeant, moving calmly from gun to gun, now and then changing men about as one after another was hit and fell, stooping over a wounded man to help him up, or aiding another to stagger to the rear; of the dauntless commanding officer on foot among the guns, cheering the men, praising this one and that one, and ever and anon profanely exhorting to us to "feed it to 'em, God damn 'em! Feed it to 'em!"

The very guns became things of life—not implements, but comrades. Every man was doing the work of two or three. At our gun at the finish there were only the corporal and two drivers fetching ammunition. The water in the corporal's bucket was like ink. Up and down the line men were reeling and falling; splinters flying from wheels and axles where bullets hit; in rear, horses tearing and plunging, drivers yelling, shells bursting, shot shrieking overhead, howling about our ears or throwing up great clouds of dust where they struck; the musketry crashing on three sides of us; bullets hissing, humming and whistling everywhere; cannon roaring—all crash on crash and peal on peal, smoke, dust, splinters, blood, wreck and carnage indescribable. But not a man or boy flinched or faltered.

For a few moments the whole Rebel line seemed to waver, and we thought that maybe we could repulse them singlehanded. But their lines came steadily on. Orders were given to limber to the rear, the 6th Wisconsin and the 11th Pennsylvania behind us having begun to fall back down the railroad track toward the town, turning about and firing as they retreated.

The Rebels could have captured or destroyed our battery if they had made a sharp rush. But their general (Heth) has told me since the war that they were not able to conceive that a battery would hold such a position so long without adequate infantry support and were convinced that the railroad cut behind us must be full of concealed infantry.

We got off by the skin of our teeth and before sundown were in position on the north brow of Cemetery Hill.

The first day of the battle, July 1, had ended in a near-rout of the outnumbered Union forces. One of their officers pictures some exciting scenes during the hasty retreat.

A little before four o'clock in the afternoon the whole line of the enemy, extending between two and three miles, began to move and steadily advanced. The Eleventh Corps broke, followed by the entire line. As the troops hurried toward the town, the disorder increased. The First Corps retired more slowly, and as a portion of the two Corps met, the confusion was great. The Confederates poured volley after volley into the compact mass, and captured about 2500 prisoners. A sudden panic arose. Our regiment headed into an alley. Unfortunately, it offered no way out except a very narrow doorway; but the enemy had already piled a barrier of dead Union soldiers in its front, and two-thirds of the regiment was lost.

The rest of the Union Army did its best to reach the field, but its movements were beset with many hardships, as we glean from the recollections of Robert G. Carter.

The long tramp toward Gettysburg was unbroken in its monotony. Men became ragged, footsore and chafed. Many were marching in their drawers, some in their stocking feet, others barefooted. Sunstrokes were numerous, and every step seemed accompanied by a wail of anguish or a groan of exhaustion. In a few hours even the laugh and jest of the uncontrollable wag had died out.

In the afternoon we struck the border of Pennsylvania. Afar off was heard the sound of bugles, and every corps, division and brigade went into bivouac that night with increased numbers.

That the Confederates did not turn the retreat into a debacle was the fault of General Ewell, according to General Walter H. Taylor, Adjutant General of the Southern army.

General Lee witnessed the flight of the Federals and directed me to go to General Ewell and say that it was only necessary to press "those people" in order to secure possession of Cemetery Heights and that, if possible, he wished him to do this. General Ewell offered no objection. In the exercise of that discretion, however, which General

Lee was accustomed to accord to his lieutenants, and probably because of an undue regard for his admonition not to precipitate a general engagement, General Ewell deemed it unwise to make the pursuit, and the enemy proceeded to occupy and fortify the position which it was designed that General Ewell should seize.

A Confederate artillery officer was much puzzled about Ewell's failure to carry his attack to complete victory.

About three o'clock in the afternoon the whole Federal force gave way in utter rout. Our battery followed immediately. The pursuit was so close and hot that, though my gun came into battery several times, I could not get in a shot.

On no other occasion did I see any large body of troops, on either side, so completely routed and demoralized as were the two Federal corps who were beaten at Gettysburg the evening of July first. I am aware this statement sounds incredible, but the men had thrown away their arms and were cowering in abject terror in the streets and alleys.

Just at this climax a member of the staff galloped by and shouted, "Lieutenant, limber to the rear!"

"*To the front*, you mean, Major!"

"No," came the answer, "*to the rear!*"

Back, back, we went, and took position on a hill from which, next morning, we gazed on the earthworks which had sprung up in the night on Cemetery Ridge. The tide which might have led on to overwhelming victory had ebbed away forever.

According to one Union officer, Lieutenant Sidney Cooke, even Hancock, whom Meade had temporarily put in command of the forces in the immediate area of Gettysburg, could not have stopped a Southern onslaught on the night of July 1.

It was a most unmilitary crowd that Hancock and Howard rallied on Cemetery Hill. Organization had melted away. Here and there men would form on their flag, but many were unable to find either flag or officers. Company officers called loudly for their men to fall in, not yet realizing that all but a few had fallen out forever.

But if organization was lost, it needed but an organizer to restore it.

Hancock was there to meet the crisis. I happened to come near enough to note his bearing in that trying moment and to hear some of his remarks and orders. The enemy was emerging from the streets of the town below and forming line as if to charge and drive us from our position. Every man knew how hopeless resistance would be, but Hancock sat his horse, superb and calm as on review, imperturbable. It almost led us to doubt whether there had been cause for retreat at all. His dispositions were prompt. A skirmish line was at once organized and advanced down the hill in the face of the enemy. Others were quickly deployed to extend the line to the left and right.

To General Doubleday, who sat on his horse by his side, Hancock said, "General, move a brigade to the hill across the road on the right."

"But, General," Doubleday replied, "I have no brigade."

"Then take the first thousand men here. Never mind where they belong." No excitement in voice or manner; only cool, concise and positive directions, given in a steady voice and a conversational tone.

The tired and discouraged men responded to the will of their master. The show of strength impressed the enemy with the idea that we had received reinforcements. No charge was made. The terrible day's work was done.

And now to the ears of the exhausted troops came a welcome and inspiring sound. The notes of the bugle and the inspiring strains of bands drifted from the far rear to the heights of the Cemetery. The old 12th Corps was coming. The strongest defensive battle line in the North had been saved to the Union cause.

On July 2 Meade's army occupied the crest of Cemetery Ridge, ending in Culp's Hill on his right. At his left extremity stood two isolated elevations known as Big Round Top and Little Round Top. Big Round Top was a pyramided hill, rising some 300 feet above the level of the surrounding country. It was covered with immense granite boulders and wooded to the top. Directly north of it, and with only a slight depression between, was Little Round Top, rising about 150 to 200 feet.

Whoever occupied the Round Tops controlled the battlefield. Nevertheless, their importance, strangely enough, was not recognized by either side until late in the afternoon of the second day.

Lee's plan was to have Longstreet attack in the morning, on the right, and the battle was to sweep from there leftward, involving successively all of Hill's corps in the center.

Ewell, on the extreme left, opposite Culp's Hill, was instructed not to wait for the battle to reach him, but to attack with his corps the moment he heard Longstreet's guns. In this way Lee hoped to discover and take advantage of any weak spot in the long Federal line.

In the main, however, July 2 was to be Longstreet's day, for it was he to whom Lee had entrusted the initial assault, and the one promising the most decisive results. Early action was essential, before the Union army could be fully assembled; for while in the morning the Union left might have been overcome without too much difficulty, it rapidly increased in strength from then on, and every hour lost diminished the chances for a Southern victory.

Yet Longstreet did not attack until in the middle of the afternoon, and for the rest of his long life he would be blamed by the South for the slowness with which he made his thrust. He himself strenuously denied having been at fault and here gives his version of the day's struggle.

On the morning of July 2 I was confident that Lee had not yet decided when and where the attack should be made. He finally determined that I should make the main attack on the extreme right. It was fully eleven o'clock when General Lee arrived at this conclusion and ordered the movement. In the meantime, by General Lee's authority, E. McIver Law's brigade was ordered to rejoin my command and, on my suggestion that it would be better to await its arrival, General Lee assented. We waited about forty minutes for these troops and then moved forward. A delay of several hours occurred, because we had been ordered by General Lee to proceed cautiously so as to avoid being seen by the enemy. At length the column halted. Looking up toward Little Round Top, I saw a signal station in full view. It was apparent that our columns had been seen, and that further efforts to conceal ourselves would be a waste of time.

The troops were rapidly thrown into position, and preparations were made for the attack. Our army was stretched in an elliptical curve reaching from the front of the Round Tops around Seminary Ridge, and enveloping Cemetery Heights on the left, thus covering a space of four or five miles. The enemy occupied the high ground in front of us, being massed within a curve of about two miles, nearly concentric with the curve described by our forces. His line was about 1,400 yards from

ours. The proposition for our inferior forces to assault and drive out
the masses of troops on the heights was a very problematical one. My
orders from General Lee were to "envelop the enemy's left, and begin
the attack there."

My corps, with Pickett's division still absent, numbered hardly 13,000
men. At half past three o'clock the order was given General Hood to
advance and, hurrying to the head of McLaws' division, I moved with
his line.

Within a short time Longstreet was engaged in one of the bitterest fights of the war. What he encountered was Sickles' 3rd
Corps, which had left the crest of Cemetery Ridge and taken position in a peach orchard adjoining the Emmitsburg Road. The
reason why Sickles had moved away from the place originally
assigned to him is set forth by one of his regimental commanders,
Colonel Thomas Rafferty.

The low ground to our left was so faulty that it was impossible to
occupy it with any prospect of being able to hold it. The Emmitsburg
Road commands it and is in its turn overlooked and commanded by
both the Round Tops.

At early daylight of July 2 we began to take position. Our line extended from the left of the 2nd Corps, along the ridge, to the foot of
Little Round Top. This brought the left of the line into the low
ground, and into a position which enabled the Rebels to attack us with
every advantage in their favor. This was the original line which Meade
had designed us to occupy. How he came to design it I don't know, as
neither he nor any of his staff had ever seen it. Sickles was satisfied his
position was untenable should he be attacked, and he had every assurance that he would be, and in overwhelming force. At about 2:00 P.M.
our line was advanced to the new position. We had simply advanced
to the front.

General Lee had arranged all his plans. He had ordered Ewell to
demonstrate upon our extreme right early in the morning, which was
skillfully done. Bodies of troops were ostentatiously moved in that direction, a heavy artillery fire was opened upon our lines, and several
feints and one or two real attacks were made there for the purpose of
deceiving Meade as to Lee's real intentions. So well had he succeeded
in this that Meade became fully satisfied he would be compelled to

meet the main attack on his right. He utterly disregarded the information which Sickles so persistently urged on him, that the enemy was massing in heavy force on our left and that reinforcements should be sent to that flank; and so entirely did he ignore Sickles' representations that he did not even send an aide to ascertain whether the facts would bear out his assumptions.

I can excuse General Meade in the situation in which he was placed, arriving as he did at two o'clock in the morning. General Doubleday said, "When I saw him soon after daylight he seemed utterly worn out and hollow-eyed. Anxiety and want of sleep were evidently telling on him."

But the same excuse cannot be made for the staff of General Meade. His staff had been acting in that capacity under previous commanders of the army and should have known all about our line of battle. But they hardly knew whether there was any left flank until General Warren accidentally stumbled upon it and by his prompt and vigorous action saved and only just saved it. Certainly as late as 4:00 P.M. the position of Little Round Top was wholly unoccupied by our troops, and a single enemy battery there would have rendered untenable the whole position of our army, while the 5th Corps, with its splendid division of regulars, lay in reserve within a short distance of it.

Lieutenant (later Colonel) F. A. Haskell of the 2nd Corps looked on with dismay as General Sickles' forces detached themselves from the crest of Cemetery Ridge. He then watched with growing excitement the developments which followed. His description is so vivid that it is given here at length.

Somewhat after 1:00 P.M. a movement of the 3rd Corps occurred. I could not conjecture the reason for it. General Sickles commenced to advance his whole corps straight to the front. This movement had not been ordered by General Meade, as I heard him say, and he disapproved of it as soon as it was made known to him. Generals Hancock and John Gibbon criticized its propriety sharply, as I know, and foretold quite accurately what would be the result. This move of the 3rd Corps was an important one—it developed the battle. Oh, if this corps had kept its strong position on the crest and, supported by the rest of the army, had waited for the attack of the enemy!

It was magnificent to see these 10,000 or 12,000 men with their batteries, and some squadrons of cavalry on the left flank, all in battle order, sweep steadily down the slope, across the valley and up the next ascent toward their destined position. The 3rd Corps now became the absorbing object of interest of all eyes. The 2nd Corps took arms; and the 1st Division of this corps was ordered to be in readiness to support the 3rd Corps, should circumstances render support necessary. The 3rd Corps, as it advanced, became the extreme left of our line, and if the enemy was assembling to the west of Round Top with a view to turn our left, as we had heard, there would be nothing between the left flank of the corps and the enemy; and the enemy would be square upon its flank by the time it had attained the Emmitsburg Road. So when this advance line came near the road, and we saw the smoke of some guns, away to Sickles' left, anxiety became an element in our interest. The enemy opened slowly at first, and from long range, but he was square upon Sickles' left flank.

General John C. Caldwell was ordered at once to put his division—the first of the 2nd Corps, as mentioned—in motion and to take post in the woods at the west slope of Round Top in such a manner as to resist the enemy, should he attempt to come around Sickles' left and gain his rear. The division moved as ordered, toward the point indicated, between two and three o'clock in the afternoon. About the same time Sykes's 5th Corps of regulars, which had been held in reserve, could be seen marching by the flank from its position on the Baltimore Pike, heading to where the 1st Division of the 2nd Corps had gone. The 6th Corps had now come up and was halted on the Baltimore Pike. So the plot thickened.

It was now about five o'clock. The enemy batteries were opening and, as we watched, they pressed those of Sickles and pounded them until they began to retire to positions nearer the infantry. The enemy seemed fearfully in earnest. And, what was more ominous than the thunder of his advancing guns, far to Sickles' left appeared the long lines and the columns of the Rebel infantry, now unmistakably moving out to the attack. The position of the 3rd Corps became one of great peril, and it is probable that Sickles by this time began to realize his true situation. All was astir now on our crest. Generals and their staffs were galloping hither and thither; the men were all in their places, and you might have heard the rattle of 10,000 ramrods as they drove home the little globes and cones of lead. As the Confederates were advancing upon Sickles' flank, he commenced a change of front, or at least a partial one, by swinging back his left and throwing forward his right, in order that his lines might be parallel to those of his adversary, his batteries meantime doing what they could to check the enemy's advance. But this movement was not completely executed before new Rebel batteries opened upon Sickles' right flank—his former front—and in the same quarter appeared the Rebel infantry also.

Now came the dreadful battle picture, of which we for a time could be but spectators. Upon the front and right flank of Sickles came sweeping the infantry of Longstreet and Hill. Hitherto there had been skirmishing and artillery practice—now the battle started; for amid the heavier smokes and longer tongues of flame of the batteries began to appear the countless flashes and the long, fiery sheets of musket fire. We saw the long gray lines come sweeping down upon Sickles' front and mix with the battle smoke. Now the same colors emerged from the bushes and orchards on his right and enveloped his flank in the confusion of the conflict. Oh, the din and the roar, and these Rebel wolf cries! What a hell was there down in that valley! These 10,000 or 12,000 men of the 3rd Corps fought well, but it soon became apparent that they must be swept from the field or perish there. To move down and support them was out of the question, for this would be to do as Sickles did—relinquish a good position and advance to a bad one. There was no other alternative—the 3rd Corps must fight itself out of its position of destruction!

In the meantime some dispositions had to be made to meet the enemy in the event that Sickles was overpowered. With his corps out of the way, the enemy would have been in a position to advance upon our 2nd Corps, not in front, but obliquely from the left. To meet this contingency, the left of the 2nd Division of the 2nd Corps was thrown back slightly, and two regiments were advanced down to the Emmitsburg Road. This was all General Gibbon could do.

The enemy was still giving the 3rd Corps fierce battle. Sickles had been borne from the field minus one of his legs, and General D. B. Birney now commanded. We of the 2nd Corps, a thousand yards away with our guns, were, and had to remain, idle spectators. The Rebels, as anticipated, tried to gain the left of the 3rd Corps and were now moving into the woods at the west of Round Top. We knew what they would find there.

No sooner had the enemy got a considerable force into these woods than the roar of the conflict was heard there also. The 5th Corps and the 1st Division of the 2nd were there at the right time and promptly engaged him; and the battle soon became general and obstinate. Now its roar became twice the volume that it was before, and its rage extended over more than twice the space. The 3rd Corps had been pressed back considerably, and the wounded were streaming to the rear by hundreds, but still the battle there went on.

When the 1st Division of the 2nd Corps first engaged the enemy, for a time it was pressed back somewhat. After the 5th Corps became well engaged, fresh bodies of the Rebels continued to swell the numbers of the assailants. Our men there began to show signs of exhaustion; their ammunition was nearly expended; they had now been fighting more than an hour against greatly superior numbers. From the sound of the fighting and the place where the smoke rose above the treetops, we knew that the 5th Corps was still steady and holding its own there, and as we saw the 6th Corps marching and near at hand to that point, we had no longer fears for the left; we had more apparent reason to fear for ourselves.

The 3rd Corps was being overpowered. Here and there its lines started to break. The men began to pour back to the rear in confusion. The enemy were close upon them and among them. Guns and caissons were abandoned and in the hands of the enemy. The 3rd Corps, after a heroic but unfortunate fight, was being literally swept from the field. That corps gone, what was there between the 2nd Corps and those yelling masses of the enemy!

The time was at hand when we must be actors in this drama. Five or six hundred yards away the enemy was hotly pressing his advantage and throwing in fresh troops, whose line extended still more along our front, when Generals Hancock and Gibbon rode up.

Just at this time we saw another thing that made us glad: we looked to our rear, and there, and all up the hillside which had been the rear of the 3rd Corps before it went forward, were rapidly advancing large bodies of men from the extreme right of our line, coming to the support of the part now so hotly pressed. They formed lines of battle at the foot of the hill by the Taneytown Road, and when the broken fragments of the 3rd Corps were swarming by them toward the rear, they came swiftly up and with glorious cheers, under fire, took their places on the crest in line of battle to the left of the 2nd Corps. Now Sickles' blunder was repaired. Now we said to ourselves, "Rebel chief, hurl forward your howling lines and columns! Yell out your loudest and your last, for many of your host will never yell again!"

The 3rd Corps was out of the way. Now we were in for it. The battery men were ready by their loaded pieces. All along the crest everything was ready. Gun after gun, along the batteries, in rapid succession leaped where it stood and bellowed its canister upon the enemy. They still advanced. The infantry opened fire, and soon the whole crest, artillery and infantry, was one continuous sheet of fire. From Round Top to near the Cemetery stretched an uninterrupted field of conflict.

All senses for the time were dead but the one of sight. The roar of the discharges and the yells of the enemy all passed unheeded, but the impassioned soul was all eyes and saw all things that the smoke did not hide. How madly the battery men were driving the double charges of canister into those broad-mouthed Napoleons! How rapidly those long blue-coated lines of infantry delivered their fire down the slope! There was no faltering—the men stood nobly to their work. Men were dropping, dead or wounded, on all sides, by scores and by hundreds. Poor mutilated creatures, some with an arm dangling, some with a leg broken by a bullet, were limping and crawling toward the rear. They made no sound of pain but were as silent as if dumb and mute. A sublime heroism seemed to pervade all, and the intuition that to lose that crest was to lose everything.

Such fighting as this could not last long. It was now near sundown, and the battle had gone on wonderfully long already. But a change had occurred. The Rebel cry had ceased, and the men of the Union began to shout, and their lines to advance. The wave had rolled upon the rock, and the rock had smashed it.

Back down the slope, over the valley, across the Emmitsburg Road, shattered, without organization, in utter confusion the men in gray poured into the woods, and victory was with the arms of the Republic.

Toward the end of the afternoon, when Longstreet's attack was at its height, both sides suddenly recognized the vital importance of the Round Tops, and recognized it at exactly the same time. Then each army strove desperately to be the first to occupy them.

The Confederate Colonel William C. Oates narrates how near he came to winning this race.

General Law's brigade constituted the right of Hood's line which, in turn, was Longstreet's right wing, and my regiment, the 15th Alabama, was in the center, with the 44th and 48th Alabama Regiments to my right. About 3:30 P.M. both battalions of artillery opened fire. The Federals replied with their guns near Little Round Top, and our lines advanced through an open field.

General Law rode up to me as we were advancing and informed me that I was then on the extreme right of our line, and for me to hug the base of Big Round Top and go up the valley between the two mountains until I found the left of the Union line, to turn it and do all the damage I could. I looked to the rear for the 48th Alabama and saw it going, under General Law's order, across the rear of our line to the left. That left no one in my rear or on my right. The enemy was in the woods, and I did not know the number of them.

Seven companies of the 47th swung around with the 15th and kept in line with it. The other three companies of that regiment were sent forward as skirmishers. In places the men had to climb up Big Round Top, catching to the rocks and bushes and crawling over the boulders in the face of the fire of the enemy, who kept retreating, taking shelter and firing down on us from behind the rocks and crags which covered the side of the mountain thicker than gravestones in a city cemetery. As we advanced about halfway up the mountain, they ceased firing. I saw from the highest point of rocks that we were then on the most commanding elevation in that neighborhood. But I knew that my men were too much exhausted to make a good fight without a few minutes' rest.

About five minutes later Captain Terrell, assistant adjutant general to General Law, rode up by the only pathway on the southeast side of Big Round Top and inquired why I had halted. I told him. He then said for me to press on, turn the Union left and capture Little Round Top, if possible, and to lose no time.

I then called his attention to my position: a precipice on the east and north, right at my feet; a very steep, stony wooded mountainside on the west. The only approach to it by our enemy, a long wooded slope on the northwest. Within half an hour I could convert Big Round Top into a Gibraltar that I could hold against ten times the number of men I had; hence, in my judgment, it should be held and occupied by artillery as soon as possible, as it was higher than Little Round Top and would command the entire field. Terrell replied that probably I was right, but he had no authority to change or originate orders. He then repeated to lose no time but press forward. I felt confident that General Law did not know my position or he would not have me ordered from it.

Notwithstanding my conviction of the importance of holding and occupying Big Round Top with artillery, I considered it my duty to leave. It looked to me the key point of the field. But my order was to find and turn the left of the Union line.

Advancing rapidly, I saw no enemy until within forty or fifty steps of an irregular ledge of rocks on Little Round Top—a splendid line of natural breastworks. Vincent's Union brigade had reached this position ten minutes before my arrival and piled a few rocks from boulder to boulder, ready to receive us. They poured into us the most destructive fire I ever saw. Our line halted but did not break. I could see, through the smoke, men of the 20th Maine, in front of my right wing, running from tree to tree, and I advanced my right, swinging it around, overlapping and turning their left.

If I had had one more regiment, we would have completely turned the flank and won Little Round Top, which would have forced Meade's whole left wing to retire. Had the 48th Alabama not been transferred to the left, and had it followed my advance, we would have turned the tide of battle in favor of the Confederates. Another lost opportunity.

I now ordered my regiment to drive the Federals from the ledge of rocks and from the hill. My men advanced about halfway to the enemy's position, but the fire was so destructive that my line wavered like a man trying to walk against a strong wind, and then slowly, doggedly, gave back a little; then, with no one on the left or right of me, to stand there and die was sheer folly: either to retreat or advance became a necessity.

I again ordered the advance and, knowing the officers and men of that gallant old regiment, I felt sure that they would follow their commander anywhere in the line of duty. I passed through the line waving my sword, shouting, "Forward, men, to the ledge!" and was promptly followed by the command in splendid style. We drove the Federals from their strong defensive positions; five times they rallied and charged us, twice coming so near that some of my men had to use the bayonet, but in vain was their effort. It was our time now to deal death and destruction to a gallant foe, and the account was speedily settled.

The 20th Maine was driven back from this ledge, but not farther than to the next ledge on the mountainside. There never were harder fighters than the 20th Maine men and their gallant Colonel Joshua L. Chamberlain. His skill and persistency and the great bravery of his men saved Little Round Top and the Army of the Potomac from defeat. My position rapidly became untenable. Federal infantry were reported to be coming down on my right and certainly were closing in on my rear, while some dismounted cavalry were closing the only avenue of escape on my left. None of our troops were in sight. My dead and wounded were then nearly as great in number as those still on duty. The blood stood in puddles in some places on the rocks. I still hoped for reinforcements, or for the tide of success to turn my way. On reflection a few moments later, I found the undertaking to capture Little Round Top too great for my regiment unsupported. I waited until the next charge of the 20th Maine was repulsed, and then ordered retreat.

Had General Longstreet seen the necessity of protecting my flank, I would, with the 600 veterans I had, have reached Little Round Top before Vincent's brigade did and would easily have captured that place. Or had he seen my 15th and 48th Regiments when they reached the top of Big Round Top and ordered a battery and another regiment to aid my men in holding that mountain, it would have been held. Either success would have won the battle.

> On the Union side, it was General Gouverneur Kemble Warren, then chief engineer of Meade's army, who first recognized the vital importance of Little Round Top. On his own responsibility he took prompt measures to occupy it.
> Here is his own story of this exploit.

On July 2, I was with General Meade, near General Sickles, whose troops seemed very badly disposed on that part of the field. At my suggestion General Meade sent me to the left to examine the condition of affairs, and I continued on till I reached Little Round Top. There were no troops on it, and it was used as a signal station. I saw that this was the key of the whole position.

I immediately sent a hastily written dispatch to General Meade to send at least a division to me, and General Meade directed the 5th Army Corps to take position there. The battle was already beginning to rage at the Peach Orchard, and before a single man reached Little Round

Top the whole line of the enemy moved on us in splendid array, shouting in the most confident tones. While I was still all alone with the signal officer, the musket balls began to fly around us, and he was about to fold up his flags and withdraw, but remained, at my request, and kept waving them in defiance. I rode down the hill and fortunately met my old brigade. I took the responsibility to detach the first regiment I struck, whose colonel, on hearing my few words of explanation about the position, moved at once to the hilltop.

About this time First Lieutenant Charles E. Hazlett of the 5th Artillery, with his battery of rifled cannon, arrived. He comprehended the situation instantly and planted a gun on the summit of the hill.

The 20th Maine and its commander, Colonel Chamberlain, bore the brunt of the fighting on Little Round Top before it passed definitely into Federal possession.

A member of that regiment, Theodore Gerrish, gives a graphic account of the decisive conflict.

Little Round Top was the key to the entire position. A few batteries were scattered along its ragged side, but they had no infantry support. While the terrible charge was being made upon the line of General Sickles, Longstreet threw out a whole division, by extending his line to his right, for the purpose of seizing the coveted prize. The danger was seen by General Warren, and our brigade was ordered forward to hold the hill against the assault of the enemy.

Every soldier seemed to understand the situation and to be inspired by its danger. "Fall in! Fall in! By the right flank! Double-quick! March!" and away we went under the terrible artillery fire. Up the steep hillside we ran and reached the crest. "On the right by file into line!" was the command. We were on the extreme left of all our line of battle. The ground sloped to our front and left and was sparsely covered with a growth of oak trees, which were too small to afford any protection. Shells were crashing above our heads, making so much noise that we could hardly hear the commands of our officers. The air was filled with fragments of exploding shells and splinters torn from mangled trees. But our men appeared as cool and deliberate as on the parade ground. Our regiment mustered about 350 men.

Ten minutes had passed since we formed the line. The skirmishers must have advanced some thirty or forty rods through the rocks and trees, but we had seen no indications of the enemy. "But look!" "Look!" "Look!" exclaimed half a hundred men at the same moment—and no wonder, for right in our front, between us and our skirmishers whom they had probably captured, we saw the enemy. They were rushing on, determined to turn and crush the left of our line. Colonel Chamberlain, with rare sagacity, bent back the left flank of our regiment until the line formed almost a right angle with the colors at the point.

Imagine, if you can, 300 men on the extreme flank of an army, put there to hold the key of the entire position! Stand firm, ye boys from Maine, for not once in a century are men permitted to bear such responsibilities!

The conflict opened. Our regiment was mantled in fire and smoke. How rapidly the cartridges were torn from the boxes and stuffed in the smoking muzzles of the guns! How the steel rammers clashed and clanged in the heated barrels! How our little line reeled to and fro as it advanced or was pressed back! The lines at times were so near each other that the hostile gun barrels almost touched. As the contest continued, the Rebels grew desperately determined to sweep our regiment from the crest of Little Round Top.

The carnage went on. Our line was pressed back so far that our dead were within the lines of the enemy. Our ammunition was nearly all gone. We could remain as we were no longer: we must advance or retreat. Our colonel understood how it could be done. "Fix bayonets!" and the steel shanks of the bayonets rattled upon the rifle barrels. "Charge bayonets, charge!"

For a brief moment the order was not obeyed, and the little line seemed to quail. In that moment of supreme need, Lieutenant H. S. Melcher, with a cheer and a flash of his sword, sprang full ten paces to the front, more than half the distance between the hostile lines. "Come on! Come on! Come on, boys!" he shouted. With one wild yell of anguish wrung from its tortured heart, the regiment charged.

We struck the Rebels with a fearful shock. They recoiled, staggered, broke and ran, and like avenging demons our men pursued. The Rebels rushed toward a stone wall but, to their surprise and ours, two scores of rifle barrels gleamed over the rocks, and a murderous volley was poured in upon them at close quarters. A band of men leaped over the wall and captured at least 100 prisoners. Piscataquis had been heard from, and as usual it was a good report. This unlooked-for reinforcement were our skirmishers, who we supposed had all been captured.

Our colonel's commands were simply to hold the hill, and we did not follow the retreating Rebels.

Of our 350 men, 135 had been killed and wounded.

> While some of the heaviest fighting of the entire war had been going on between the Confederate right and the Union left, Hill's and Ewell's corps had failed to fulfill the tasks allotted to them. In spite of Lee's well-considered battle plan, the remainder of the field had remained fairly quiet all day long, with the exception of some isolated and halfhearted actions. This aroused the ire of Longstreet, whose corps had had to bear such a heavy burden in the second day's battle.

Notwithstanding the supreme order for a general battle, the Confederate 2nd and 3rd Corps had remained idle during all of my severe fight on the Confederate right, except the artillery, which was in practice only long enough on the extreme left to feel the superior metal of the enemy.

At eight o'clock in the evening one division on our extreme left, that of Edward Johnson, advanced. When it crossed Rock Creek it was night. The enemy's line to be assaulted was occupied by a brigade of the Union 12th Corps, reinforced by three regiments of James S. Wadsworth's division and three from the 11th Corps. After brave attack and defense, part of the line was carried, when the fight, after a severe fusillade between the infantry lines, quieted. Part of the enemy's trenches, vacated when the corps moved over to the left, General Johnson failed to occupy.

Before this, General Robert E. Rodes on our left had discovered that the enemy in front of his division was drawing off his artillery and infantry to my battle of the right, and suggested to General Early that the moment had come to attack. General Early ordered two brigades to do so. They made as gallant a fight as was ever made. Mounting to the top of the hill, they captured a battery and pushed on in brave order, taking some prisoners and colors, until they discovered that two brigades were advancing in a night affair against a grand army, and withdrew.

Thus the general engagement of the day was dwarfed into a battle of the right at three o'clock, one on the left at eight by a single division, and one on the left nearer to the center, at nine o'clock, by two brigades.

The second day of the battle had brought no decision, and the fateful third of July dawned with the issue at Gettysburg still in the balance. Lee's battle order once more directed the main Confederate attack to be made by Longstreet's corps, strengthened now by the arrival of Pickett's division, which had so far taken no part in the battle.

This time, however, Lee's entire army was to go into action simultaneously. Ewell was to start an attack from the trenches on Culp's Hill, which Edward Johnson the night before had occupied and still held, take the Federal right in reverse and try wresting that position from Meade. Culp's Hill was as vitally important on that end of the line as the Round Tops were on the other. Hill in the center was ordered to support Longstreet, with whose movements his own were to be closely co-ordinated. Thus the gross miscarriage of the previous day's plans was to be avoided and rectified.

When Longstreet received orders to use Pickett's force for a frontal attack, he felt grave misgivings.

I had not seen General Lee on the night of July second. On the next morning he came to see me and, fearing that he was still in his disposition to attack, I tried to anticipate him by saying, "General, I find that you still have an excellent opportunity to move around to the right of Meade's army and maneuver him into attacking us."

He replied, pointing with his fist at Cemetery Hill, "The enemy is there, and I am going to strike him."

I said, "General, I have been a soldier all my life. It is my opinion that no 15,000 men ever arrayed for battle can take that position."

General Lee in reply to this ordered me to prepare Pickett's men to get into position. The plan of assault was as follows: our artillery was to be massed in a wood from which Pickett was to charge, and it was to pour a continuous fire upon the cemetery. Under cover of this fire and supported by it, Pickett was to charge.

Our artillery was in command of Colonel E. P. Alexander, a brave and gifted officer. The arrangements were completed about one o'clock. Alexander had ordered a battery of seven 11-pound howitzers, with fresh horses and full caissons, to charge with Pickett, but General W. N. Pendleton, from whom the guns had been borrowed, recalled them and thus deranged this wise plan. Never was I so depressed as that day. Unwilling to trust myself with the entire responsibility, I had instructed Colonel Alexander to observe carefully the effect of the fire upon the enemy and, when it began to tell, to notify Pickett to begin the assault. I was so impressed with the hopelessness of the charge that I wrote the following note to Alexander:

If the artillery fire does not have the effect to drive off the enemy or greatly demoralize him, I would prefer that you should not advise General Pickett to make the charge. I shall rely a great deal on your judgment to determine the matter, and shall expect you to let Pickett know when the moment offers.

To my note the colonel replied as follows:

I will only be able to judge the effect of our fire upon the enemy by his return fire, for his infantry is but little exposed to view, and the smoke will obscure the whole field. If there is an alternative to this attack, it should be carefully considered before opening our fire, for it will take all the artillery ammunition we have left.

Colonel E. P. Alexander, chief of the Confederate artillery, to whom Longstreet tried to pass the responsibility of timing Pickett's charge, tells how he refused to accept it.

I was directed by Longstreet to post all of his artillery for a preliminary cannonade, and then to determine the proper moment to give the signal to Pickett to advance. The signal for the opening of the cannonade would be given by Longstreet himself. A clump of trees in the enemy's line was pointed out to me as the proposed point of our attack.

The Federal guns in position on their lines at the commencement of the cannonade were 166, and during it ten batteries were brought up from their reserves, raising the number engaged to 220, against 172 used on our side during the same time.

The formation of our infantry lines consumed a long time, and the formation used was not one suited for such a heavy task. Six brigades, say 10,000 men, were in the first line. Three brigades only were in the second line. The remaining brigade, Cadmus M. Wilcox', posted in rear of the right of the column, was not put in motion with the column. Both flanks of the assaulting column were in the air, and the left without any support in the rear. It was sure to crumble away rapidly under fire.

My guns had all been carefully located and made ready for an hour, while the infantry brigades were still not in their proper positions, and I was waiting for the signal to come from Longstreet.

Meanwhile, some half hour or more before the cannonade began, I was startled by the receipt of a note from Longstreet ordering me to judge whether or not the attack should be made at all.

Until that moment, though I fully recognized the strength of the enemy's position, I had not doubted that we would carry it, in my confidence that Lee was ordering it. But here was a proposition that I should decide the question. Overwhelming reasons against the assault at once seemed to stare me in the face.

But evidently the cannonade was to be allowed to begin. Then the responsibility would be on me to decide whether or not Pickett would charge. After an exchange of several notes, I wrote to Longstreet as follows:

General: When our fire is at its best, I will advise Gen. Pickett to advance.

It must have been with bitter disappointment that Longstreet saw the failure of his hope to avert a useless slaughter, for he was fully convinced of its hopelessness. Yet even he could have scarcely realized, until the event showed, how entirely unprepared were Hill and Ewell, the other two corps commanders, to render aid to his assault and to take prompt advantage of even temporary success. None of their guns had been posted with a view to co-operative fire, nor to follow the charge, and much of their ammunition had been prematurely wasted. Nowhere was there the slightest preparation to come to his assistance. The burden of the whole task fell on the ten brigades employed. The other brigades and guns were but widely scattered spectators.

It was just 1:00 P.M. by my watch when the signal guns were fired and the cannonade opened. The enemy replied rather slowly at first, though soon with increasing rapidity. It having been determined that Pickett should charge, I felt impatient to launch him as soon as I could see that our fire was accomplishing anything. I guessed that a half hour would elapse between my sending him the order and his column reaching close quarters. I dared not presume on using more ammunition than one hour's firing would consume, for we were far from supplies and had already fought for two days. So I determined to send Pickett the order at the very first favorable sign and not later than after thirty minutes' firing.

At the end of twenty minutes no favorable development had occurred. More guns had been added to the Federal line than at the beginning, and its whole length, about two miles, was blazing like a volcano. It seemed madness to order a column in the middle of a hot July day to undertake an advance of three-fourths of a mile over open ground against the center of that line.

But something had to be done. I wrote a last note and dispatched it to Pickett at 1:25:

General: If you are to advance at all, you must come at once, or we will not be able to support you as we ought. But the enemy's fire has not slackened materially, and there are still eighteen guns firing from the cemetery.

I had hardly sent this note when there was a decided falling off in the enemy's fire, and as I watched I saw other guns limbered up and withdrawn. The enemy had never heretofore practiced economy. After waiting a few minutes and seeing that no fresh guns replaced those withdrawn, I felt sure that the enemy was feeling the punishment, and at 1:40 I sent a note to Pickett as follows:

For God's sake come quick. The eighteen guns have gone. Come quick, or my ammunition will not let me support you properly.

This was followed by two oral messages to the same effect by an officer and sergeant from the nearest guns. The eighteen guns had occupied the point at which our charge was to be directed. Still Pickett's line had not come forward, though scarcely 300 yards behind my guns.

Longstreet, leaving his staff, rode out alone and joined me. He spoke sharply. "Go and stop Pickett where he is and replenish your ammunition."

I answered, "We can't do that, sir. The train has but little. It would take an hour to distribute it."

Longstreet seemed to stand irresolute—we were both dismounted—and then spoke slowly and with great emotion. "I do not want to make this charge. I do not see how it can succeed. I would not make it now, but that General Lee has ordered it."

General Pickett managed to scribble a few touching lines to his sweetheart a few minutes before he began his onslaught.

Gettysburg, July 3, 1863.

A summons came from Old Peter [General Longstreet], and I immediately rode where he and Marse Robert were making a reconnaissance of Meade's position.

"Great God!" said Old Peter as I came up. "Look, General Lee, at the insurmountable difficulties between our line and that of the Yankees —the steep hills, the tiers of artillery, the fences, the heavy skirmish line—and we'll have to fight our infantry against their batteries."

"The enemy is there, General Longstreet, and I am going to strike him," said Marse Robert in his firm, quiet, determined voice.

I rode with them along our line of prostrate infantry. The men had been forbidden to cheer, but they arose and lifted in reverential adoration their caps to our beloved commander. Oh, the responsibility for the lives of such men as these! Well, my darling, their fate and that of our beloved Southland will be settled ere your glorious brown eyes rest on these scraps of penciled paper.

Our line of battle faces Cemetery Ridge. The men are lying in the rear, and the hot July sun pours its scorching rays almost vertically down on them. The suffering is almost unbearable.

I have never seen Old Peter so grave and troubled. For several minutes after I had saluted him he looked at me without speaking. Then in an agonized voice, the reserve all gone, he said, "Pickett, I am being crucified. I have instructed Alexander to give you your orders, for I can't."

While he was yet speaking, a note was brought to me from Alexander. After reading it I handed it to Pete, asking if I should obey and go forward. He looked at me for a moment, then held out his hand. Presently, clasping his other hand over mine without speaking, he bowed his head on his breast. I shall never forget the look in his face nor the clasp of his hand, and I saw tears glistening on his cheeks and beard. The stern old war horse, God bless him, was weeping for his men and, I know, praying too that this cup might pass from them. It is almost three o'clock.

YOUR SOLDIER

A lieutenant-colonel in a New York regiment remembered the tension on Cemetery Hill on the forenoon of the third day.

Prior to ten o'clock the artillery fire had ceased; the firing on the skirmish line had quieted down, and a stillness that seemed oppressive had settled over the battlefield. It was like the hush which so often precedes the bursting of the storm. We waited. Another hour passed into history, and yet we waited. Eleven o'clock—twelve o'clock—one o'clock; then away to the enemy's right a single gun was fired. A minute or so passed, and then a gun in the enemy's center fired, and with it their entire line burst into flame. Our men rushed to their places and threw themselves on the ground, and none too soon.

A reporter for the *New York World* wrote of the artillery bombardment which preceded the assault.

Then the Rebel artillery began a terrific and concentrated fire. A flock of pigeons were scarcely thicker than the flock of horrible missiles that now descended on our position. The storm broke upon us so suddenly that soldiers and officers died, some with cigars between their teeth, some with pieces of food in their fingers, and one with a miniature of his sister in his hands. Horses fell, shrieking awful cries. The boards of fences flew in splinters through the air. The earth, torn up in clouds, blinded the eyes of hurrying men. As I groped for the shelter of the bluff, an old private was struck scarcely ten feet away by a cannon ball, which tore through him, extorting such a low, intense cry of mortal pain as I pray to God I may never again hear.

The Union private Warren Lee Goss, experienced soldier though he was, never forgot the terrible ordeal of the Confederate barrage.

Right, left and rear of us, caissons exploded, scudding fragments of wheels, woodwork, shell, and shot one hundred feet into the air, like the eruption of a volcano. Only eighty guns of the Union artillery could be crowded upon the ridge with which to make reply. For an hour and a half crash followed crash. Some of the shot shrieked and hissed, some whistled; some came with muffled growl; some with howls like rushing, circling winds. Some spat and sputtered; others uttered unearthly groans or hoarsely howled their mission of death. Holes like graves were gouged in the earth by exploding shells. The flowers in bloom upon the graves at the Cemetery were shot away. Tombs and monuments were knocked to pieces, and ordinary gravestones shattered in rows.

If a constellation of meteoric worlds had exploded above our heads, it would have scarcely been more terrible than this iron rain of death furiously hurled upon us. Over all these sounds were heard the shrieks and groans of the wounded and dying. The uproar of the day previous seemed silence when compared to this inferno.

The mounting tension within the Federal lines was aptly described by Richard S. Thompson, a soldier in an Illinois regiment.

The Confederate fire was concentrated upon a position occupied by part of two small divisions. Before it stopped, of the commanders of the five batteries in the two divisions, three had been killed, one wounded, while one alone escaped injury; 250 battery horses had been killed and eleven caissons exploded.

It seemed as though Old Time had halted in his unchangeable march. At last a soldier in the line cried out, "Thank God! There comes the infantry!" He voiced the feelings of his comrades. Anything that promised action was better than inaction under the horrors of that cannonade.

On a little hill behind Alexander's artillery stood two reporters of the *Richmond Enquirer*, waiting to see what the end of the cannonade would bring forth.

Surveying the scene before them, they saw, beneath shimmering heat waves, a gently declining slope, grown over with ripening grain, farther to the front a rise, another drop, then the last incline up Cemetery Ridge. There was no cover whatever for marching columns, but there were fences and stone walls which would have to be hurdled or broken down under enemy fire.

The reporters shook their heads, took out their books and started to write.

Where is that division which is to play so conspicuous a part in this day's tragedy? Just fronting that frowning hill from which heavy batteries are belching forth shell and shrapnel with fatal accuracy, the men are lying close to the ground, sweltering, almost suffocating in the murderous heat, only partially protected, powerless to fight back. Hours have passed and the deadly missiles have come thick and fast. See that shattered arm; that leg shot off; that headless body; and here the mangled form of a young and gallant lieutenant who had braved the perils of many battles.

That hill over there must be carried to rout the enemy. That is his stronghold. With that hill captured, his rout is inevitable; but the hill is exceedingly strong by nature, and rendered more so by the works thrown up the night before. It is a moment of the greatest emergency, but if unshrinking valor or human courage can carry those heights, it will be done.

Now the storming party is moved up, Pickett's division in advance, supported on the right by Wilcox' brigade and on the left by Henry Heth's division, commanded by James J. Pettigrew. I have seen brave men pass over that fated valley the day before. I have observed them return a bleeding mass, but with unstained banners. Now I see their valiant comrades prepare for the same bloody trial. They move forward; with steady, measured tread they advance upon the foe. Their banners float defiantly, as onward in beautiful order they press across the plain. I have never seen, since the war began, troops enter a fight in such splendid order as does this division of Pickett's.

Now Pettigrew's command emerges from the woods on Pickett's left and sweeps down the slope of the hill to the valley beneath, some 200 or 300 yards in rear of Pickett. But—wait—I notice by the wavering of his line as they enter the conflict that they want the firmness of nerve and steadiness of tread which so characterized Pickett's men! I fear that these men cannot, will not, stand the tremendous ordeal to which they will be soon subjected. They are mostly raw troops, have perhaps never been under fire—certainly never been in any severe fight—and I tremble for their conduct.

General Pickett receives the order to charge those batteries at the opportune moment. James L. Kemper, with as gallant men as ever trod beneath that flag, leads the right, Robert Garnett brings up the left, and the veteran Lewis A. Armistead, with his brave troops, moves forward in support. The distance is more than half a mile.

Our batteries have ceased firing. Why do not our guns reopen? is the inquiry that rises on every lip. Still our batteries are silent as death. But on press Pickett's brave Virginians.

The batteries on both sides now had stopped firing, and only a few musket shots, fired by skirmishers, broke the oppressive silence.

The two reporters watched, admiringly, Pickett's men keep up their steady tramp. Now and then small depressions hid the troops from view, but they emerged again on the other side, the uneven ground making their march more animated but also much more difficult for the troops. The grain of the fields beat gently against the soldiers as they waded through it. Some of the men, almost overcome by the sun, stumbled blindly forward but braced themselves each time they tore down fences or hurtled themselves over stone walls.

Then, suddenly, the silence vanished. Action had set in, and the pencils of the reporters once more raced across the pages of their notebooks.

And now the enemy opens upon them a terrible fire. Yet on, on they move in unbroken line, delivering a deadly fire as they advance. Now they have reached the Emmitsburg Road, and here they meet a severe fire from the enemy's infantry, posted behind a stone fence, while their artillery turn their whole fire upon this devoted band. Still they remain firm. That flag goes down. See how quickly it again mounts upward, borne by some gallant man who feels keenly the honor of his old Commonwealth in this hour which is to test her manhood.

The line moves onward, straight onward—cannon roaring, grape and canister plunging and plowing through the ranks—bullets whizzing as thick as hailstones in winter, and men falling as leaves fall when shaken by the blasts of autumn. In a double-quick, and with a shout which rises above the roar of battle, they charge. Now they pour in volleys of musketry—they reach the works—the contest rages with intense fury—men fight almost hand to hand—the red cross and gridiron wave defiantly in close proximity—the enemy are slowly yielding—a Federal officer dashes forward in front of his shrinking columns and, with flashing sword, urges them to stand.

General Pickett, seeing the splendid valor of his troops, moves among them as if courting death by his own daring intrepidity. The brave Kemper, with hat in hand, still cheering on his men, falls from his horse into the ranks of the enemy. His men rush forward, rescue their general, and he is borne mortally wounded from the field.

Again they advance. They storm the stone fence. The Yankees flee. The enemy's batteries are, one by one, silenced in quick succession as Pickett's men deliver their fire at the gunners and drive them from their pieces. I see them plant their banner in the enemy's works. I hear their glad shout of victory!

According to Lieutenant Haskell, fear gripped the hearts of the defenders of Cemetery Hill when they saw the enemy approaching their breastworks.

General H. J. Hunt, chief of artillery of the army, began swiftly moving about on horseback, giving some orders about the guns. Thought we, What could this mean? In a moment afterward we met a captain, pale and excited. "General, they say the enemy's infantry is advancing." We sprang into our saddles. A score of bounds brought us upon the all-seeing crest. To say that none grew pale at what we saw would not be true. Might not 6,000 men be brave and yet turn ashy white seeing a hostile horde of 18,000 less than five minutes away?

General Gibbon rode down the lines, cool and calm, and in an unimpassioned voice he said, "Do not hurry, men. Let them come up close before you fire, and then aim low." We could not be supported or reinforced until support would be too late. On the ability of two divisions of the 2nd Corps to hold the crest depended defeat or victory at Gettysburg.

The general said I had better go and tell General Meade of this advance. Great Heaven! Were my senses mad? The larger portion of A. S. Webb's brigade—my God, it was true!—there by the group of trees and the angles of the wall—was breaking from the cover of the works and, without order or reason, with no hand uplifted to check it, was falling back, a fear-stricken flock of confusion. The fate of Gettysburg hung on a spider's single thread.

A great, magnificent passion came on me at the instant. My sword that had always hung idle by my side, I drew, bright and gleaming, the symbol of command. As I met the flock of those rabbits, the red flags of the Rebels began to thicken and flaunt along the wall they had just deserted, and one was already waving over the guns. I ordered "Halt!" and "Face about!" and "Fire!" and they heard my voice, and gathered my meaning, and obeyed my commands. On some unpatriotic backs, or those not quick of comprehension, the flat of my saber fell, not lightly. And at its touch their love of country returned, and with a look at me as if I were the destroying angel they again faced the enemy.

This portion of the wall was lost to us, and the enemy gained the cover of the reverse side, where he now stormed with fire. But our men sent back as fierce a storm. Those red flags were accumulating at the wall every moment, and they maddened us as the same color does the bull. Webb's men were falling fast, and in not many minutes they would be overpowered.

Oh! where was Gibbon? Where was Hancock? Some general, anybody, with the power and the will to support this wasting, melting line? I thought of Alexander Hays on the right, but from the smoke and roar along his front it was evident he had enough on his hands. Doubleday on the left was too far off, and too slow.

Not a moment was to be lost. I found Colonel Norman J. Hall just in rear of his line, sword in hand, cool, vigilant, directing the battle of his brigade. The fire was constantly diminishing in his front.

"Webb is hotly pressed, and must have support."

"I will move my brigade at once."

In the briefest time I saw five friendly colors hurrying to the aid of the imperiled spot.

Before us the enemy was massed, his front at the stone wall. Between his front and us extended the very apex of the crest. Formation of companies and regiments was lost: companies, regiments and brigades were blended and intermixed. Although no abatement of the general conflict had at any time been appreciable, now it was as if a new battle, deadlier, stormier than before, had sprung from the body of the old. The jostling, swaying lines on either side boiled and roared, two hostile billows of a fiery ocean. Thick flashes streamed from the wall; thick volleys answered from the crest.

No threats or expostulations now. Individuality was drowned in a sea of clamor, and timid men, breathing the breath of the multitude, were brave. The dead and wounded lay where they had fallen; there was no humanity for them. The men did not cheer or shout—they growled.

Now the loyal wave rolled up as if to overleap its barrier, the crest. Pistols flashed with the muskets. My "Forward to the wall!" was answered by the Rebel countercommand, "Steady, men!" and the wave swung back. Again it surged, and again it sank.

These men of Pennsylvania, on the soil of their own homesteads, the first and only ones to flee the wall, must be the first to storm it. The line sprang. The crest of the solid ground, with a great roar, heaved forward its maddened load—men, arms, smoke, fire, a fighting mass. It rolled to the wall. Flash met flash. The wall was crossed. A moment of thrusts, yells, blows, shots, an indistinguishable conflict, followed by a shout, universal, that made the welkin ring again. The enemy had been repulsed, and the bloodiest fight of the great Battle of Gettysburg was ended.

Sad at heart, the correspondents of the *Richmond Enquirer* were watching the denouement from the opposite side.

While the victorious shout of the gallant Virginians was still ringing in my ears, I turned my eyes to the left, and there, all over the plain, in utmost confusion, was scattered Pettigrew's strong division. Their line was broken; they were flying, panic-stricken, to the rear. The gallant Pettigrew was wounded, but he still was vainly striving to rally his men. The moving mass rushed pell-mell to the rear, and Pickett was left alone to contend with the hordes of the enemy now pouring in upon him on every side. General Garnett fell, killed by a Minié ball, and Kemper, the brave and chivalrous, was mortally wounded. Now the enemy moved strong flanking bodies of infantry around and rapidly gained Pickett's rear.

The order was given to fall back, and our men commenced the movement, doggedly contending for every inch of ground. The enemy pressed heavily our retreating line, and many noble spirits who had passed safely through the fiery ordeal of the advance and charge fell on the right and on the left. Armistead was wounded and left in the enemy's hands. At this critical moment the shattered remnant of Ambrose R. Wright's Georgia brigade was moved forward to cover their retreat, and the fight closed here.

Lieutenant Haskell relates how General Meade himself appeared in time to see the last of the fight.

General Meade rode up, accompanied only by his son, who was his aide-de-camp. He was dressed in a serviceable summer suit of dark blue cloth, without badge or ornament save the shoulder straps of his trade. He wore heavy high-top boots and buff gauntlets, and his soft black felt hat was slouched down over his eyes. His face was very white, not pale, and the lines were marked and earnest and full of care.

As he arrived near me, coming up the hill, he asked in a sharp, eager voice, "How is it going here?"

"I believe, General, the enemy is repulsed," I answered.

A new light began to come on his face, and with a touch of incredulity he asked, "What! Is the assault entirely repulsed?" His voice was quicker and more eager than before.

"It is, sir," I replied.

By this time he was on the crest, and when his eye had taken in just a glance of the whole—the masses of prisoners, the numerous captured flags which the men were derisively flaunting about, the fugitives of the routed enemy disappearing with the speed of terror—he said impressively, and his face was lighted, "Thank God!" And then his right hand moved as if he would have caught his hat and waved it.

The glorious charge had failed. Bowed down in deepest sorrow, Pickett penned a few lines to his fiancée.

My brave boys were so full of hope and confident of victory as I led them forth! Over on Cemetery Ridge the Federals beheld a scene which has never previously been enacted—an army forming in line of battle in full view, under their very eyes—charging across a space nearly a mile in length, pride and glory soon to be crushed by an overwhelming heartbreak.

Well, it is all over now. The awful rain of shot and shell was a sob— a gasp.

I can still hear them cheering as I gave the order, "Forward!" the thrill of their joyous voices as they called out, "We'll follow you, Marse George, we'll follow you!" Oh, how faithfully they followed me on— on—to their death, and I led them on—on—on—Oh, God!

I can't write you a love letter today, my Sally. But for you, my darling, I would rather, a million times rather, sleep in an unknown grave.

Your sorrowing

SOLDIER

Lieutenant Colonel Arthur Lyon-Fremantle, English military observer in Lee's army, who had posted himself at its left wing where nothing of moment had happened, was unaware of the day's crucial event until later in the afternoon. Riding toward the center, he noted the effect of Pickett's repulse on the defeated men and on their commanders.

I rode on through the woods in the direction in which I had left Longstreet. When I got close up to him, I saw one of his regiments advancing through the woods in good order. So, thinking I was just in time to see the attack, I remarked, "I wouldn't have missed this for anything."

Longstreet was seated at the top of a snake fence, looking perfectly calm and unperturbed. He replied, "The devil you wouldn't! I would like to have missed it very much!"

The general told me that Pickett's division had succeeded in carrying the enemy's position and capturing the guns, but after remaining there twenty minutes it had been forced to retire. No person could have been more calm or self-possessed than General Longstreet in these trying circumstances, aggravated as they now were by the movements of the enemy, who began to show a strong disposition to advance.

The general was making the best arrangements in his power to resist the threat by advancing some artillery, rallying the stragglers, etc. I remember seeing a general come up to him and report that "he was unable to bring his men up again." Longstreet turned on him and replied with some sarcasm, "Never mind, then, General. Just let them remain where they are. The enemy will spare you the trouble."

If Longstreet's conduct was admirable, that of General Lee was perfectly sublime. He was engaged in rallying and in encouraging the broken troops, and was riding about a little in front of the wood, quite alone. His face, always placid and cheerful, did not show signs of the slightest disappointment, care or annoyance. He was addressing to every soldier he met a few words of encouragement, such as, "All this will come right in the end. We'll talk it over afterward, but in the meantime all good men must rally." He spoke to all the wounded men that passed him, and the slightly wounded he exhorted "to bind up their hurts and take up a musket" in this emergency. Very few failed to answer his appeal, and I saw many badly wounded men take off their hats and cheer him. He said to me, "This has been a sad day for us, Colonel—a sad day. But we can't expect always to gain victories."

General Lee seemed to observe everything, however trivial. When a mounted officer began licking his horse for shying at the bursting of a shell, General Lee called out, "Don't whip him, Captain. Don't whip him. I've just such a horse, and whipping does no good."

A Northern war correspondent got lost on the battlefield
that night, and noted the terrible aftermath of the slaughter.

I became possessed by a nameless horror. Once I tumbled over two
bodies and found my face close to the swollen, bloody features of the
man who lay uppermost, judging from the position of other bodies. A
shower of grape and canister must have torn the ranks of a regiment
into shreds, for 50 to 60 bodies lay there in a row. I came across the
corpse of a drummer-boy, his arms still clasped around his drum, his
head shattered by a shell. I realized what a price is paid for victories.

That Pickett's charge was not carried out in accordance with
Lee's plan is affirmed by his nephew Fitzhugh Lee.

A consummate master of war such as Lee would not drive en masse
a column of 14,000 men across an open terrain of 1,300 or 1,400 yards,
through a concentrated and converging fire of artillery, to attack an
army of 100,000 on fortified heights, and give his entering wedge no
support. Why, if every man in that assault had been bullet-proof, and
if the whole of those 14,000 splendid troops had arrived unharmed on
Cemetery Ridge, there still would have been time for the Federals to
seize them, tie them and take them prisoners before their supports could
have reached them.

It is fortunate that three of General Lee's trusted staff officers—
Walter H. Taylor, C. S. Venable and A. L. Long—have recorded that
the plan of assault involved an attack by Longstreet's whole corps, supported by one-half or all of Hill's. Long says the order was given
orally by General Lee in his presence. Venable states that he heard the
orders given, and that when he called General Lee's attention to it
afterward, he said, "I know it, I know it."

Aside from Pickett's charge, there was much other fighting at
Gettysburg on the third day, from Cemetery Hill on the north
to Big Round Top on the south, but again it was feeble and
disconnected. On the whole, the grave errors of the Confederates on the previous day were repeated, in spite of Lee's ex-
plicit orders for a concerted attack. Generals Early and Rodes

assaulted Cemetery Ridge through a ravine west of Culp's Hill, had some initial success, but were eventually driven back. Most of the Union troops who had been sent from that end of the line to help fight off Longstreet on July 2, had returned, and the position at Culp's Hill was no longer vulnerable. The bulk of Hill's corps acted as mere bystanders and scarcely took any part in the battle at all.

Meade kept strictly on the defensive, with one minor exception. In the late afternoon General Elon J. Farnsworth, with only 300 men, made a gallant and spectacular dash into the rear of the Confederate regiments fronting toward the Round Tops. But he only created some confusion, for which he and many of his troopers paid with their lives.

There was also a big battle in the afternoon between Jeb Stuart's cavalry, just returned from a rather fruitless ride around Meade's army, and the Federal cavalry under General David McM. Gregg, a few miles out from Gettysburg near the Hanover Road. It was a big fight, the biggest of its kind on American soil, but it resulted only in useless bloodshed and had no direct bearing on the outcome of the main battle.

There were renewed struggles in front of Little Round Top on and around the small wooded hill known as the Devil's Den, and isolated artillery duels or bloody infantry attacks.

But against Pickett's grand charge all these combats faded into insignificance.

The battle of July 3 ended in a stalemate, both sides retaining the approximate positions they had occupied the evening before. After a whole day of inactivity, during which Lee apparently dared the Union army to assume the offensive, he retreated toward Williamsport, where he hoped to cross the Potomac. Constant rains, however, made fording of the river impossible, and a new crisis seemed to be in the making. How Lee overcame it is recorded by Colonel E. P. Alexander.

In order to protect his retreat, Lee had maintained a pontoon bridge at Falling Waters, a few miles from Williamsport. But it was weakly guarded, and on June 5 a small enemy raiding party, sent from Frederick, had broken it and destroyed some boats, fortunately not all. The retreat of the army was, therefore, brought to a standstill just when forty-eight hours more would have placed it beyond pursuit. We were already nearly out of provisions, and now the army was about to be penned up on the riverbank and subjected to an attack at his leisure by Meade.

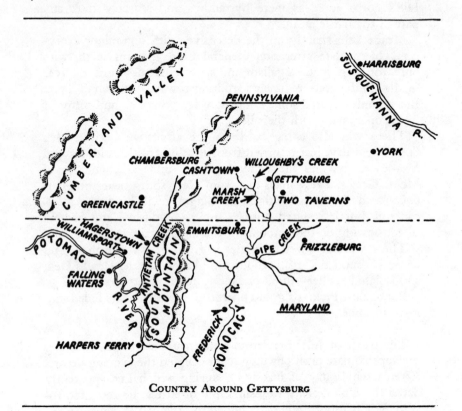

COUNTRY AROUND GETTYSBURG

All diligence was used to relieve the situation. The ferryboats were in use by day and by night carrying over, first, our wounded, and next, 5,000 Federal prisoners brought from Gettysburg. Warehouses on the canal were torn down, and from the timber new pontoon boats were being built to repair the bridge at Falling Waters.

Meanwhile, the engineers selected and fortified a line of battle on which we would make a last stand.

On July 11 the army was ordered into position on the selected line, but I never saw Lee so anxious as on this occasion.

General Doubleday clearly perceived Lee's predicament and
suggested a way to cut off his escape.

I do not see why a force could not have been formed on the Virginia side of the Potomac and have cut off the ammunition of which
Lee stood so much in need. The expedition from Frederick had destroyed the bridge at Falling Waters, the enemy had but few rounds
for his cannon, and our artillery could have opened fire on him from
a distance. Meade had Sedgwick's fresh corps, and was reinforced by
11,000 men. French's 4,000 and troops from Washington and Baltimore also were available. Meade, moreover, took a route twice as long
as that of Lee, who gained six days on him, during which to fortify
himself and renew his ammunition.

General Alfred Pleasonton, commanding the Federal cavalry,
also criticized Meade's hesitancy.

I was in a position to form a correct opinion of the failure to follow
General Lee, having been the constant companion of General Meade
since he assumed command. He had not that grasp to comprehend
quickly and decide on events as they occurred.
"How do you know Lee will not attack me again?" he asked. "We
have done well enough."
I answered that Lee had exhausted all his available men, had exhausted his ammunition, was far from his base of supplies. To this the
General did not reply, but as we rode along the troops cheered him in
a manner that plainly showed they expected an advance. Had Meade
followed the Confederates on the fourth of July, Lee's surrender
would have been unavoidable.

The dissatisfaction on the Northern side was equalled by that
of its opponents. A Confederate cavalryman named John N.
Opie condensed it into a few poignant words.

The plain truth is this: Lee blundered, Stuart blundered, Longstreet,
Ewell and Pickett blundered. The whole campaign was a blunder, but
Lee was the only man magnanimous enough to bear the burden. Here

we find the defensive general selecting his own battleground. General Lee should have declined battle, and drawn the Federal commander into the open where the ground was equal and victory more certain.

Lacerated and bleeding, the devoted army recrossed the Potomac; but Gettysburg was its Waterloo.

According to the War Department telegrapher Plum, Lincoln had grim forebodings that Meade would fail to seize the rare opportunity to destroy Lee's army.

On July twelfth Meade telegraphed the position of his own army and that of the enemy, as near as he could ascertain it, and said, "It is my intention to attack them tomorrow unless something intervenes to prevent it." The President called cipher operator Chandler to a map, and expressed the greatest astonishment that an attack had not been made before. He said it seemed to him that the rebels were *being driven across* instead of being *prevented* from crossing, and added bitterly, "They will be ready to fight a magnificent battle, when the enemy are over the river, and there is nobody left to fight."

On July 14, when Meade finally was ready to attack, he discovered that Lee had crossed the night before. On the same day Lincoln held a Cabinet meeting, the proceedings of which Secretary Welles duly recorded in his diary.

Stanton came in and asked to see the President alone. The two were absent about three minutes. When they returned, the President's countenance indicated distress; Stanton was disconcerted. Something was said that Lee had crossed the river. Stanton said curtly he knew nothing of Lee's crossing. "I do," said the President, with a look of painful rebuke to Stanton.

The President said he could not take up anything in Cabinet today. I retired slowly. The President overtook me. He said with a voice I shall never forget, that he had dreaded that Lee should escape with his force and plunder. "There is bad faith somewhere!" he exclaimed. "What does it mean? Great God! What does it mean?"

CHAPTER 17

Bloody Fighting in the West

THE BATTLES OF CHICKAMAUGA
AND MISSIONARY RIDGE

The Battle of Stone River, or Murfreesboro, which had ended in January, 1863, was followed by a long period of inactivity. Neither commander was anxious to take the offensive, but eventually it was Rosecrans who, late in summer, began to maneuver Bragg out of Tennessee, an attempt which was not too seriously contested.

Horace Greeley of the *New York Tribune* sketches the first moves of the campaign.

General Rosecrans' remaining inactive at Murfreesboro till late in the summer of 1863 was dictated by imperative necessity. His supplies were mainly drawn from Louisville, far distant, over a single railroad, traversing a semihostile country and requiring heavy guards at every depot, bridge and trestle.

Bragg held very strong positions at Shelbyville, Knoxville and Chattanooga. Perhaps 40,000 was the force he could concentrate for a battle, while Rosecrans had not less than 60,000; but then, if Bragg fell back, destroying the railroads and bridges, he would naturally be strengthened, while Rosecrans, protecting his communications, would be steadily becoming weaker.

At last, Rosecrans advanced on June 23, and in nine days, without a serious engagement, cleared Middle Tennessee of the Rebel army.

Bragg, having the use of a railroad (which he destroyed behind him), easily made good his retreat over the Cumberland Mountains and the Tennessee River.

Bragg had established his headquarters at Chattanooga, and Rosecrans' next goal was to dislodge him from there by a series of flanking movements. What followed is told by Horace Greeley and a Union officer, Lieutenant Colonel Arba N. Waterman.

The Union army now was, for practical offensive and defensive operations, at Bridgeport on the Tennessee River, to which point the railroad had been repaired, and where supplies had been accumulated.

Rosecrans determined to compel the evacuation of Chattanooga by threatening Bragg's line of supplies. To carry out this plan, on August 16 the 20th Army Corps under General Alexander McD. McCook and the 14th under General George H. Thomas crossed the river and mountain ranges south of Chattanooga, thus bringing themselves within striking distance of the railroad on which the Rebel commander depended. It was thought that Bragg would be forced either to fight in open field for his communications or to surrender Chattanooga.

He, however, determined to do neither. On September 7 he marched out of Chattanooga (which was immediately occupied by Thomas L. Crittenden's 21st Corps) and concentrated his army near Lafayette, about twenty-five miles to the south, from where he planned to annihilate in detail the corps of Thomas and McCook, as they emerged from the mountain passes, and then reoccupy Chattanooga. The scheme had many chances to succeed. (See map, page 515.)

McCook was already at Alpine, more than fifty miles from Chattanooga. Crittenden with his corps was still in the immediate vicinity of Chattanooga, while Thomas was in the mountains, midway between Crittenden and McCook, but within supporting distance of neither.

Unknown to Rosecrans, the Rebel forces in the vicinity of Lafayette were ready to strike, as might seem best, any one of the three Federal corps. McCook was the most isolated, and, had he obeyed instructions to move at once on Summerville, it is quite likely he would have speedily found on his flank and rear a superior force from whose attack there would have been no escape. He, however, became satisfied that the Rebel army was not retreating, and that he was in very deep water; so he commenced a rapid movement to connect with Thomas, away on his left. He closed up to Thomas only on September 17.

Crittenden, who had been ordered to follow up vigorously Bragg's supposed retreat, on September 10 moved two divisions to Ringgold but, encountering strong parties of the enemy on the way, retreated.

Thomas' Corps, advancing to Dug Gap, had found it decidedly held by the enemy and also wisely fell back.

Bragg had sprung his trap too soon. Had he permitted Thomas to force his way through Dug Gap, with barely a decent show of resistance, he might have crushed this and our other Corps in rapid succession, or he might, disregarding Thomas, have hurled his whole army upon Crittenden at Ringgold, crushed him, and then interposed between Thomas and Chattanooga. But when Thomas' division was forced back from Dug Gap, the game was too plain. Instead of a keen chase after a flying enemy, it was at once comprehended by our generals that they must concentrate and fight for their lives.

Disappointed, Bragg gave orders for the concentration of his army on the right bank of the Chickamauga River, intending to deliver battle there.

General D. H. Hill, one of the Confederate Corps commanders, discredited the claim that Bragg had intended to lay a clever trap for Rosecrans. Like most of his brothers-in arms, he had few kind words for this commanding officer.

The truth is, General Bragg was bewildered by "the popping out of the rats from so many holes." The wide dispersion of the Federal forces, and their confrontal of him at so many points, perplexed him, instead of being a source of congratulation that such grand opportunities were offered for crushing them one by one. He seems to have no well-organized system of independent scouts. For information in regard to the enemy, he apparently trusted alone to his cavalry. He only learned that he was encircled by foes.

Assistant Secretary of War Charles A. Dana, sent by Stanton to furnish him with confidential reports, thought differently.

I went at once to General Rosecrans' headquarters and presented my letter of introduction. The impression began to grow that Bragg had been playing possum and had not retreated at all. Rosecrans at once abandoned all idea of operations against the Confederate line of retreat and supply, drew his army in rapidly and began to look sharply after his own communications with Chattanooga, which had now become his base.

By noon of September 18 the concentration of his army was practically complete.

The next development was noteworthy because, for the first time since Bull Run in 1861, the Confederates made use of their interior lines. Support in the form of Longstreet's corps was sent to Bragg from the almost dormant Eastern front. This was no easy undertaking, as we may learn from the notes of G. Moxley Sorrel, one of General Longstreet's staff officers.

It was believed that Bragg, if reinforced, could strike Rosecrans a swift crushing blow and relieve a wide region from the presence of the enemy.

In the first half of September the details were settled. Longstreet was to take on the expedition his two splendid divisions, McLaws' and Hood's. The movement was to be wholly by train, and never before were so many troops moved over such worn-out railways. Never before were such crazy cars—passenger, baggage, mail, coal, box, platform, all and every sort—used for hauling good soldiers. But we got there nevertheless.

The journey through the states from Virginia was a continuous ovation to the troops. They were fed at every stopping place and must have hated the sight of food. Kisses and tokens of love and admiration for these war-worn heroes were ungrudgingly passed around and, as some troops were from states all south of Virginia, it was good for the men to show up in this fashion even for a few minutes with their home people.

September 18 found the Union army still on the march, desperately trying to concentrate its scattered forces, and these movements were continued throughout the night. When Bragg attacked on September 19, he found before him a solid Union front.

Lieutenant Colonel Waterman thus described the beginning of the battle which followed.

Bragg had intended to attack on the eighteenth, but was unable to cross the Chickamauga River in time. There was a sharp contest at Alexander's Bridge, and some skirmishing at other points. The enemy

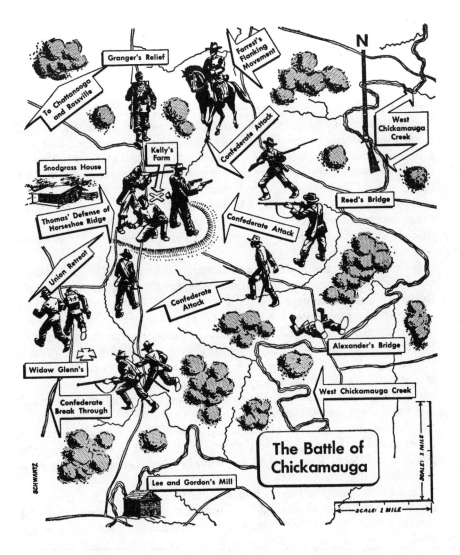

The Battle of Chickamauga

Here a great battle ended in a victory and an enigma.

made a feint of attacking at Lee and Gordon's Mill, but the day passed without other than movements preliminary to the coming battle. During the night preceding the nineteenth Thomas' corps moved steadily to the left, so that at daylight the head of his column was at Kelly's farm.

At this time each of the commanding generals was ignorant of the position of his opponent. Bragg, believing the Union left to be at Lee and Gordon's Mill, intended to crush it before Thomas and McCook could come to its aid. Rosecrans, on the other hand, was not aware that more than a brigade of Rebel infantry had crossed the river. He had, however, divined that the enemy would endeavor to move his right, and to meet this expected movement Thomas' corps had been moved during the night of the eighteenth. The entire country, with the exception of a few small fields, was broken and covered with heavy timber. Movements of large forces could therefore be made without observation.

Upon his arrival at Kelly's farm General Thomas was informed that a brigade of the enemy had crossed the evening previous at Reed's Bridge and might be captured. With this purpose in view, and also to determine the position of the enemy, General Thomas ordered a reconnaissance with two brigades. They advanced, encountering the enemy's cavalry, under Nathan B. Forrest, with strong infantry supports. These forces were pressed steadily back, until General Absalom Baird, one of the two brigade commanders, learned that a large force was advancing upon his right under cover of thick woods. Preparations to meet this force were speedily made, but before they could be completed, an enemy division assaulted with the accustomed vigor and fierceness of Rebel attacks, throwing Baird's right into disorder and capturing ten pieces of artillery. Reinforcements were, however, at hand and assisted in restoring the broken lines.

The battle was thus begun in a manner and at a time and place not intended by either commander. Rosecrans was not aware that the greater portion of the Rebel army had already crossed the Chickamauga, while Bragg was surprised to find that the Federal left, no longer at Lee and Gordon's Mill, extended beyond his right.

Bragg next determined to throw a column between the two Union wings and overwhelm each separately. To meet this movement, two Union brigades advanced to cover the wide space between Thomas and Crittenden. Gallantly they struggled against superior numbers, but, assailed in flank and front, they gradually gave way and would have been unable to prevent the consummation of the Rebel purpose had not other forces come to the rescue.

Foiled in the attempt to pass their columns between the two Union forces, the enemy renewed the attack upon General Thomas, endeavoring to crush and double back his right and thus to separate him from the remainder of the army. Under a most withering fire he was pressed back with somewhat disordered lines, but the lines were re-formed, and six batteries of artillery, fortunately posted, opened on the advancing array. Beneath this destructive fire Bragg's forces gave way. Each side knew that the conflict was to be renewed on the morrow.

The Union army had had some close calls during the day, one of which is recalled by James R. Carnahan, a captain in the 86th Indiana.

In the early morning of the nineteenth we were relieved from duty and sent back toward Lee and Gordon's Mill. Through that forenoon we saw the constantly moving columns of the enemy's infantry and saw battery after battery as they moved before us like a great panorama. In such moments men grow pale and lose their nerve. They are hungry, but they can not eat; they are tired, but they can not sit down. You speak to them, and they answer as if half asleep; they laugh, but the laugh has no joy in it.

Noonday had passed when suddenly from out the woods dashed an officer. "There come orders" were the words that passed from lip to lip. Without commands the lines were formed; the cannoneers stood by their guns; the drivers stood with hand on rein and foot in stirrup, ready to mount. The eye lighted up, the arm again grew strong, and the nerves were again growing steady. Nearer and nearer came the rider, and we could see the fearful earnestness that was written in his face. He reached our line, and the command came in quick, sharp words: "The general directs that you move your brigade at once. Our men are hard pressed."

It took almost no time for our brigade to get in motion. The whips of thirty-six drivers over the backs of as many horses sent that battery of six guns rattling and bounding over the road, while the infantry alongside was straining every nerve as they hastened to the relief. Our lines were scarcely formed when our advance was broken by a terrific charge of the enemy, and we were driven back in confusion.

On the crest of a ridge, without any kind of shelter, our troops were again hastily formed, and none too soon. The whistling of balls over our heads gave us warning that the advance of the enemy had begun, and in an instant a shout went up from the charging column as it started down in the woods. Our men were ready. The gunners were at their posts of duty, the tightly drawn lines in their faces showing their purpose. Officers passed the familiar command of caution: "Steady, men, steady!" The shout of the charging foe came rapidly on. Now they burst out of the woods. As if touched by an electric cord, so quick and so in unison, the rifles leaped to the shoulders. Now the enemy were in plain view, as, with cap visors drawn well down over their eyes, and with short, shrill shouts, they came. Quick and sharp rang out the command, "Ready! Fire!" Out from the rifles of the men and the mouths of those cannon leaped the death-dealing bullet and canister. Again and again, with almost lightning rapidity, they poured in their deadly, merciless fire. Now the enemy corps that had known little of defeat began to waver. No troops can long withstand such fire. Another volley, and they were broken.

A few logs and rails were hastily gathered together to form a slight breastwork. Soon scattering shots gave us warning that our foe was again moving on us. But with even greater courage did our men determine to hold their lines. The artillery was double-shotted with canister. Again the command "Fire!" and hotter, fiercer than before, the battle raged along our front. Shout was answered with shout, shot by shot tenfold, until once more our assailants were forced back. Again and again were the charges launched, only to be hurled back, broken and shattered.

It was absolute *desperation* of our men that held our lines. Each man felt the terrible weight of responsibility that rested on him personally for the results that day.

Charles A. Dana followed the beginning of the battle and its progress during the first day from reports received at Rosecrans' headquarters.

The army had not concentrated any too soon. During the night of September 18-19 it became pretty clear that Bragg's plan was to push

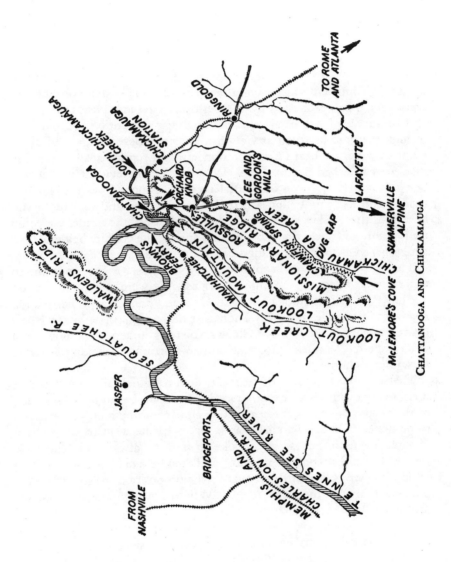

CHATTANOOGA AND CHICKAMAUGA

515

by our left into Chattanooga. This compelled another rapid movement
by the left down the Chickamauga. By a tiresome night march Thomas
moved down below Lee and Gordon's Mill, taking position on our
extreme left. Crittenden followed, connecting with Thomas' right
and thus taking position in the center. McCook's corps also extended
downstream to the left, but still covered the creek as high up as Crawfish Spring, while part of his troops acted as a reserve. These movements were hurriedly made, and the troops, especially those of Thomas,
were very much exhausted by their efforts to get into position.

Rosecrans had not been mistaken in Bragg's intention. About nine
o'clock the next morning at Crawfish Spring, where the general headquarters were, we heard firing on our left, and reports at once came in
that the battle had begun there. When it became evident that it was
being fought entirely on our left, Rosecrans removed his headquarters
nearer to the scene, taking a little house near Lee and Gordon's Mill
known as the Widow Glenn's. Although closer to the battle, we could
see no more of it here than at Crawfish Spring, the conflict being fought
altogether in a thick forest, invisible to outsiders.

That we were able to keep as well informed as we were was due to
our excellent telegraphic communications. We were in communication
not only with Chattanooga but with Gordon Granger, who headed the
reserves at Rossville, and with Thomas at his headquarters. When Rosecrans removed to the Widow Glenn's, the telegraphers went along, and
in an hour had connections made and an instrument clicking away in
Mrs. Glenn's house.

That evening a council of war was held to which all the corps and
division commanders were summoned. Rosecrans began by asking each
of the corps commanders for a report; also for his opinion of what was
to be done. General Thomas was so tired that he went to sleep every
minute. Each time Rosecrans spoke to him, he always said the same
thing: "I would strengthen the left," and then he would be asleep, sitting
up in his chair. General Rosecrans, to the proposition to strengthen the
left, made always the same reply: "Where are we going to take the
men from?"

While Rosecrans' council of war was in session, a similar conference took place at Bragg's headquarters, where Longstreet
had just arrived after a strenuous journey. Lieutenant Colonel
Sorrel tells the story.

It was about three o'clock in the afternoon of September 19 that our rickety train pulled up with jerks and bangs. Longstreet and some of his personal staff, including me, immediately took horse.

General Bragg should surely have had guides conduct us to the conference on which so much depended. A sharp action had taken place during the day, and it would appear that if Bragg wanted to see anybody, Longstreet was the man. But we were left to shift for ourselves. At one point in our hunt for him we narrowly escaped capture, being almost in the very center of a strong picket of the enemy before our danger was discovered.

Between ten and eleven o'clock that night we finally rode into the camp of General Bragg. He was asleep in his ambulance and, when roused, immediately entered into private conference with Longstreet.

An hour was quite enough to settle the plan and details, since nothing could be simpler than the operation proposed for Rosecrans' destruction.

Bragg's army was already occupying favorable ground. The enemy's force was not far off in our immediate front, seemingly easy to attack. Bragg made a good disposition of his separate divisions and commands, dividing the army into two wings, the right under Lieutenant General Polk and the left under Lieutenant General Longstreet. The order for the day was simple in the extreme.

There was no question about all the troops being in position by daylight, and at that hour the attack was to be opened by General Polk on the extreme right and followed up vigorously by the lines to the left, until the entire front of Bragg's fine army should be engaged and charging the enemy, exposed to an attack so furious it was not believed he could sustain it.

Horace Greeley gives a picture of the situation as it looked on the morning of September twentieth.

During the night Bragg had moved Breckinridge's division from his extreme left to his extreme right, being still intent on flanking our left and interposing between it and Chattanooga.

At daylight both armies stood to their arms, and the battle was to have opened by an attack on our left, but the fighting did not commence till 8:30 A.M. A dense fog filled the valley, rendering all objects indistinguishable at a few yards' distance. Thomas' corps (augmented by successive reinforcements till it was now more than half our army) improved the hours by throwing up rude breastworks of logs and rails, which stood it in good stead thereafter.

A young army surgeon who had just joined the army learned the difference in behavior between a recruit and an experienced soldier.

I had seen a book on the ground, and reading matter being scarce, I dismounted and picked it up. To my disgust I found it was an arithmetic. The colonel asked me for it, immediately began perusing the pages, and commenced figuring on a fly leaf. At this moment a rebel battery opened, and on came the shot, hissing, shrieking. I looked up and there the colonel sat on his horse, calmly figuring away. "There," he said, "is the length of the fish." "What fish?" the Lieutenant-Colonel inquired. "Why, the one given here." He had actually, amid all this—to me—frightful peril figured out a problem.
He had been under fire before. I hadn't.

The early morning of the second day, when fighting had barely begun, was recalled by Lieutenant R. M. Collins of a Texas regiment.

The boys all looked serious and determined. After a breakfast on blue Florida beef, cornbread washed down with cold water, and our canteens filled with Adam's ale, we were in line impatiently waiting, for certainty is preferable to suspense. Why all this delay? The battle was to begin at daylight. Finally we advanced, but one in authority came down the line and we were brought to a halt. General Longstreet was sitting on his horse; we did not know who he was, as he had no mark of an officer about him and wore a common hunting shirt and a slouch hat. A soldier came back leisurely from the front, when General Longstreet said to him, "Hello, my good fellow, you are not going to leave us, are you?"
The soldier stopped, looked up at him and said, "See here, you damned old hunting-shirt snoozer, do you know who you are talking to?" Longstreet laughed heartily and explained who he was. Then he and the private parted good friends.

The reason why the Confederate attack on September 20 was not begun much earlier is set forth by A. N. Waterman.

During the night Rosecrans and Bragg each had given orders for the morrow. Thomas was to maintain his position on the left at all hazards. Crittenden was placed in reserve, and McCook, commanding the right, was ordered to keep closed up toward the left, which was now recognized as the vital position, where the assault would be first made, and which was to be maintained even if the right had to be withdrawn altogether. Polk was to attack at daylight, the assault commencing on the right to be taken up in quick succession and pushed with vigor by each succeeding division on the left.

At daylight on the morning of the twentieth, the commanders of both armies were in the saddle waiting for the conflict to begin. Owing to the thick woods, neither could descry the lines or position of the other, and as the hours wore on without apparent movement each became anxious to learn the cause of the delay. A heavy fog, which during the early morning hours had hung over the battlefield, added to the uncertainty and afforded abundant room for conjecture. On the Confederate side, little groups of men, discussing the situation, concluded that the Yanks had "got their bellyful" the day before and were chiefly anxious to run away in the night. On the Union side, the opinion of the soldiers was that the "Johnnies" didn't want any more of "Rosy's pills."

Doubtless the man most angry and disappointed at the delay was General Bragg. Entirely ignorant of the cause, he began to think, in the light of his past experience, that he was fated never to have an attack made as he ordered it, and at last he sent Major Lee of his staff to ascertain the reason of the delay. Major Lee, instead of finding, as he expected, General Polk with his troops on the battle side of the Chickamauga, found him enjoying a good breakfast at a comfortable farmhouse on the opposite bank, and there delivered General Bragg's inquiry and renewed order for an immediate attack. The dignified bishop and general replied, "Do tell General Bragg that my heart is overflowing with anxiety for the attack—overflowing with anxiety, sir."

When this was reported to Bragg, he swore in a manner that would have powerfully assisted a mule team in getting up a mountain. He told Major Lee to ride along the line and order every captain to take his men into action. A quarter of an hour thereafter the battle was opened, as expected, by an attack upon our left.

The Confederate officer William Miller Owen gives us a glance at his immediate surroundings during the forenoon of September 20.

Our time came at last. An adjutant galloped up and said, "General Longstreet orders your division to move forward, keeping closed to the right." We advanced, swinging around on Polk's corps, which was now the pivot.

Our division, in advancing, passed the spot where General Bragg was seated on his horse on the Chattanooga Road. He looked pale and careworn, his features rendered more haggard by a white havelock he wore over his cap and neck.

During the heat of this battle General Henry Lewis Benning, of Georgia, one of the bravest men that ever lived, came charging up to General Longstreet in great agitation. He was riding an artillery horse and was using a rope trace for a whip. His hat was gone, and he was much disordered. "General," he said, "my brigade is utterly destroyed and scattered."

General Longstreet approached him and said quietly, "Don't you think you could find *one* man, General?"

"One man?" he said with astonishment. "I suppose I could. What do you want with him?"

"Go and get him," Longstreet said very quietly, laying his hand upon his arm, "and bring him here. Then you and I and he will charge together."

General Benning looked at General Longstreet curiously a moment, then laughed and, with an oath, lashed his horse with his rope trace and was off like a flash.

In a few moments he swept by at the head of a command that he had gathered together somehow or other, and he was in the fight once more.

The fight began late in the morning, and the afternoon found both sides embraced in a fierce struggle. Then sudden disaster came to the Union army.

Horace Greeley gives a good account of it.

The fog having lifted, Breckinridge, facing and overlapping our extreme left, advanced his fresh division, flanking our army, and pushed across the Rossville Road, fighting desperately. The movement was taken up in succession by the divisions farther and farther toward the Rebel center—Bragg thus renewing the attempt to interpose between our army and Chattanooga, which Thomas had disconcerted by his advance and attack of the previous day. Bragg's attempt was baffled by Thomas' firmness and that of the veterans under his command, while the struggle along our left center was equally desperate, equally sanguinary and equally indecisive.

Suddenly, however, our right became involved in fearful disaster. The movement of several divisions from right to left, after the battle had actually commenced, was at best hazardous, no matter how necessary, and was attended with the worst possible results. James S. Negley's and Horatio P. Van Cleve's divisions were successively ordered by Rosecrans to move to the support of Thomas on our left, while Thomas J. Wood was directed to close up to Joseph J. Reynolds on our right center, and J. C. Davis to close on Wood; McCook, commanding on this wing, being directed to close down on the left with all possible dispatch.

The hazard of such movements was in this instance increased by the fact that the orders were not clearly comprehended. Wood, understanding that he was ordered to *support* Reynolds, undertook to do so by withdrawing from the front and passing to the rear of John M. Brannan, thus opening a gap in our front into which Longstreet at once threw Hood's command.

The charge was decisive. Davis, by McCook's order, was just attempting to fill the gap made by Wood's withdrawal when Hood's charging column poured into it, striking Davis on the right, and Brannan on the left, and Sheridan, of Crittenden's corps, farther to the rear, cutting off five brigades from the rest of our army and pushing them to our right and rear, with a loss of 40 percent of their numbers.

In short, our right wing, struck heavily in flank while moving to the left, was crumbled into fragments and sent flying in impotent disorder toward Rossville and Chattanooga, with a loss of thousands in killed, wounded and prisoners. Rosecrans, McCook and many subordinate commanders were swept along in the wild rush. Sheridan and Davis rallied and re-formed the wreck of their divisions by the way and halted, with McCook, at Rossville. Rosecrans—prevented by the enemy from joining Thomas—hastened to Chattanooga, since it now looked as though our whole army was or would be routed, and that desperate efforts would be required to save what might be left from being captured or driven pell-mell into the Tennessee.

Charles A. Dana, who was at Rosecrans' headquarters, describes the break-through of Longstreet's men and the flight of the Union generals.

I had not slept much for two nights and lay down on the grass. I was awakened by the most infernal noise I ever heard. I sat up, and the first thing I saw was General Rosecrans crossing himself—he was a very devout Catholic. "Hello!" I said to myself. "If the general is crossing himself, we are in a desperate situation."

I looked around toward the front where all this din came from, and I saw our lines break and melt away like leaves before the wind. Then the headquarters around me disappeared. The graybacks came through with a rush, and soon the musket balls and the cannon shot began to reach the place where we stood. The whole right of the army had apparently been routed.

I turned my horse and, making my way over Missionary Ridge, rode to Chattanooga, twelve or fifteen miles away. The whole road was filled with flying soldiers. Here and there were pieces of artillery, caissons and baggage wagons. Everything was in the greatest disorder. When I reached Chattanooga a little before four o'clock, I found Rosecrans there. The two corps commanders, McCook and Crittenden, also both came into Chattanooga.

How the loosening of the Federal lines, caused by their sidewise movement and aggravated by Rosecrans' ambiguous order, was taken advantage of by Longstreet, is set forth by William M. Owen.

Longstreet discovered with his soldier's eye a gap in the enemy's already confused lines and, forming a solid column of attack, broke through and struck the enemy. Short and bloody was the work. We moved steadily forward, no halting. The men rushed over the hastily constructed breastworks of logs and rails of the foe, with the old-time familiar Rebel yell. Wheeling to the right, the column swept the enemy before it and pushed along the Chattanooga Road toward Missionary Ridge in pursuit. It was glorious!

Several thousand prisoners and fifty pieces of artillery were reported captured. At 2:45 P.M. our exultant troops were halted to rest. There was no enemy left except a small force on Horseshoe Ridge which, however, was in a very strong position.

At 3:00 P. M., while our division was resting at a halt, I rode to where Generals Longstreet and Simon B. Buckner, seated on a log, were eating their lunch. General Longstreet hailed me and asked for a pipeful of tobacco. I produced my little bag, and he filled his meerschaum pipe. I then asked him what he thought of the battle: was the enemy beaten or not? "Yes," he said, "all along his line; a few are holding out on the ridge up yonder—not many though. If we had had our Virginia army here, we could have whipped them in half the time."

At four o'clock, the remnant of the Federal army under Thomas still stubbornly held the Horseshoe Ridge, although they had been assaulted by Breckinridge, Bushrod Johnson, J. Patton Anderson, T. C. Hindman and lastly by James B. Kershaw, and all had lost heavily.

Longstreet determined to take the ridge and sent to Bragg for some of the troops of the right wing, but Bragg said, "They have been fought out and can do him no good."

The position held by the enemy was a very Gibraltar, its sides precipitous and difficult to climb, but the day was wearing away, and no time could be lost. Longstreet determined to put in his 10th Legion, William Preston's 5,000, sent for the general and ordered an immediate advance. "It shall be done," replied Preston, and the command "Attention!" was given down the lines of the three brigades. The young troops sprang to their arms. It was their first baptism of fire, and if they were whipped they wouldn't have known it.

At the command, "Forward! Forward!" the 5,000 moved on in beautiful order. The enemy opened a terrific fire, but up the hill our men advanced. Now the enemy's bullets began to tell upon the lines, and men fell to the right and left, dead and wounded. The fire was too hot for them and, halting under the crest where some protection was had, the lines were dressed. General Preston coolly examined each man's cartridge box and said, "Men, we must use the bayonet!"

With fierce yells the troops advanced—Archibald Gracie on the right, J. H. Kelly in the center and Robert C. Trigg on the left. It was a brave sight. Gracie and Kelly met a determined resistance, but Trigg, who had been pushed to the enemy's right in the hope of overlapping and flanking him, swept down on his flank and rear, capturing 500 prisoners. The enemy, assailed on front and flank, fell back, and the battle flags of Preston's division were planted upon the summit of Horseshoe Ridge. The battle was won.

The responsibility for creating the fatal gap in the Union lines became a matter of hot dispute. Major William J. Richards, a staff officer who was present when General Wood received the order, gives this version.

Generals McCook and Wood were sitting on their horses at the junction of their commands about 11:15 A. M. of the bloody twentieth, a part of the staff of each general being present, I among them. The attack, begun on the left some time before, was rapidly traveling toward our position on the extreme right, when an aide from Rosecrans dashed up to Wood with the following order: "You will immediately close up on Reynolds as fast as possible and support him."

Wood peered quizzingly at the order, turned to McCook and read it aloud, adding in the familiar vernacular indulged between these two generals, "Mack, I'll move out by the right flank and rear to hide my move from the enemy."

"No, Tom," said McCook, "just march out by the left flank."

As Brannan's whole division intervened between Wood and Reynolds, whom he had been ordered to support, no one present thought of any other meaning than that taken by Wood. Although Rosecrans admits the language of the order, and that at the instant he thought Wood, instead of Brannan, was next to Reynolds, yet he contends that Wood's action was mere blind obedience to orders, the execution of which he should have suspended pending a speedy report of the conditions under his immediate cognizance. But whatever the final equities, the direful result remains: the gap was made, and the rest is history, bordered in black.

Horace Greeley now again takes up his narrative of the fight, beginning with the break-through in the early afternoon. The spur of Horseshoe Ridge occupied by Thomas has since become better known as Snodgrass Hill, so named after the Snodgrass house which served as Thomas' temporary headquarters.

Matters, though bad enough, were not so bad as they seemed. Thomas was still fighting stoutly and holding his own on our left. Meantime, Wood came up and was directed to post his troops on the slope of Missionary Ridge, behind Thomas' line of battle.

General Gordon Granger, with his small reserve corps, moving without orders, reported at 3:00 P. M. to Thomas, who was holding the Horseshoe Ridge while the enemy in overwhelming force were pressing him in front and on both flanks. They held a ridge on his right running nearly at right angles with that he occupied and were advancing Hindman's division in a gorge of it, with intent to assail his right in flank and rear.

The moment was critical. Thomas had work for all his men and could spare none to confront this new peril. Instantly forming his brigades, Granger hurled them on the foe. Twenty minutes later Hindman had disappeared, and our men held both gorge and ridge.

There was a pause of half an hour while the enemy was forming and massing for a desperate charge on all points of our position. About 4:00 P.M. the storm burst in all its fury. The stampede of our right had swept with it nearly or quite all our ammunition trains, so that cartridges had become scarce, and the utmost economy in their use was indispensable. But for the fortunate arrival of Granger with a small supply, which afforded about ten rounds per man, many regiments would have been compelled to rely on their bayonets.

Longstreet was now here, in immediate command of his own corps. In fact, all but a fraction of the entire Rebel army was swarming around the foot of the ridge where Thomas, with what remained of seven divisions of ours, withstood and repelled assault after assault till sundown. Then by order from Rosecrans at Chattanooga, he commenced the withdrawal of his troops to Rossville.

General Thomas' resistance on Horseshoe Ridge might have crumbled, had it not been for the courageous decision by General Granger, who commanded the reserve corps. A. N. Waterman, serving under Thomas, tells about the acute danger to the Union cause.

Gradually the Rebel line was swinging round the ridge, and it seemed as if we were about to be enveloped, front, flank and rear. At last the

Union army seemed to be in the grasp of its persistent foe. Whence were to come the troops to meet this new danger?

Away off toward Rossville, a division of General Granger's corps was stationed, with orders to hold the place at all hazards. Hearing the heavy cannonade, the commander of this division had twice sent couriers to General Rosecrans, asking permission to move forward and join the troops engaged in battle. Neither of these couriers had returned—and neither, it may be remarked, ever reached General Rosecrans. But as the roar of battle gradually drew nearer and nearer, it became evident to Generals Granger and James B. Steedman, one of his division commanders, that our forces were being forced back, and the resolve was taken to move forward without orders.

General Thomas, who beheld the eager lines of Hindman already ascending the ridge, suddenly discovered, in the rear of our center, another column advancing. Was this another Rebel horde? There were a few moments of most intense anxiety when an officer rode toward this on-coming column to ascertain if they were friend or foe. He called out, "Whose troops are these?"

"Mine, sir" was the cautious reply of the general.

"General, may I inquire your name?" said the officer.

"I am General Steedman, commanding the 1st Division of the Union reserve corps."

"And I am serving on the staff of General Thomas."

As Steedman rode up to General Thomas, the latter remarked, "General, I never before was so glad to see you." Then, pointing to the ridge which Hindman's division had just occupied, he said, "You must drive the enemy off that ridge."

"It shall be done" was the reply. And it was.

The day was saved. The army was saved.

Bragg's victory was complete, but the Confederate staff officer Lieutenant Colonel G. Moxley Sorrel felt bitter.

It was a panic-stricken host that had fled. It was one of the greatest of the many Confederate successes. Yet there was probably only one man who did not believe that pursuit would be the word early next day, and that was our commander in chief. It is thought by some that General Bragg did not even know a victory had been gained. The next morning he asked Longstreet for suggestions. "Move instantly against Rosecrans' rear to destroy him" was the instant reply.

Apparently Bragg adopted this view, but did not give orders to march out until 4:00 P. M. The right wing then marched about eight miles; our men moved next day at daylight. At the close of the battle we could have strolled into Chattanooga; now it was vigorously defended. This was the fruit of the great battle, the pitiable end of the glorious victory that was ours.

> General Sheridan shared Sorrel's views of Bragg's failure to follow up his victory.

On the morning of September 21 the enemy failed to advance, and his inaction gave us the opportunity for getting the broken and disorganized army into shape. It took a large part of the day to accomplish this, and the chances of complete victory would have been greatly in Bragg's favor if he could have attacked us vigorously at this time.

> After Bragg had missed his best chance of taking Chattanooga, it looked for a while as if, in belated desperation, he were going to try storming the town's fortifications.
> Lieutenant L. D. Young describes the feeling among the rank and file of Bragg's army during these critical hours.

What next? We all expected that we would follow immediately on the heels of the retreating Federals and possibly capture them before they could get settled behind their fortifications.

We spent the night awaiting orders from Bragg, but he was spending his time sending congratulations to President Davis.

Next day my command was ordered toward the vicinity of Missionary Ridge, which we reached to find Rosecrans ready to receive and entertain us. We were formed in line of battle and expected to be flung against the forts to certain destruction.

Anathemas were hurled at the commander without stint for having held us back for this, the hour of our doom. It was an hour of dreadful suspense.

Thanks to a merciful Providence, which at the last moment changed the mind that commanded! But for this he who writes this story would doubtless now be "sleeping the sleep that knows no waking!"

> The Union army was besieged in Chattanooga. General Sheridan depicts the situation.

The enemy began at once to establish himself strongly on Lookout Mountain. This broke our direct communication with Bridgeport—our sub-depot—and forced us to bring supplies by way of the Sequatchee Valley and Waldens Ridge over a road most difficult even in summer, but now liable to be rendered impassable by autumn rains. The distance to Bridgeport by this circuitous route was sixty miles, and the numerous passes, coves and small valleys through which the road ran offered tempting opportunities for the destruction of trains, and the enemy was not slow to take advantage of them. General Rosecrans himself, in communicating with the President the day succeeding the Battle of Chickamauga, expressed doubts of his ability to hold Chattanooga.

In a few days rain began to fall, and the mountain roads were fast growing impracticable. Each succeeding train of wagons took longer to make the trip from Bridgeport, and the draft mules were dying by the hundreds. The artillery horses would soon go too, and there was every prospect that later the troops would starve, unless something could be done.

> Charles A. Dana found much fault with the behavior of General Rosecrans during the siege.

In the midst of all his difficulties General Rosecrans dawdled with trifles in a manner which scarcely can be imagined. Precious time was lost because our dazed and muzzy commander could not perceive the catastrophe that was close upon us, nor fix his mind on the means of preventing it. Our animals were starving, the men had starvation before them, and the enemy was bound soon to make desperate efforts to dislodge us. Yet the commanding general devoted that part of the time which was not employed in pleasant gossip to the composition of a long report, to prove that the government was to blame for his failure on September 20.

I have never seen a public man possessing less administrative power, less clearness and steadiness in difficulty, and greater practical incapacity than General Rosecrans. He had inventive fertility and knowledge, but his mind scattered; there was no system in the use of his busy days and restless nights, no courage against individuals in his composition and, with great love of command, he was a feeble commander.

While the Union troops were starving inside Chattanooga, their opponents were not faring too well as we learn from a letter written by the Texan J. B. Polley.

Appetite comes with eating, it is said, but to the Texans in Bragg's army it comes with fasting. Blue beef and musty corn meal have become monotonous. Anyhow, my comrade Jim Somerville and I decided to "varigate our eatin'," and we engaged in a search for quadrupeds of the porcine persuasion. Luck favored us, for about the middle of the afternoon we found ourselves in a secluded glade and in near proximity to a couple of fair-sized and well-fed hogs. Somerville took careful aim at the larger and fatter of the two and pulled the trigger.

But the cap on which the firing of the gun depended failed, and neither of us could find another. Even the hogs laughed at us—that is, if a constant turning up of dirty noses and a succession of seemingly contemptuous grunts may be called laughing. Suddenly a rapturous smile lighted up Jim's homely features, and he exclaimed, "By the great holy Moses, I found a cap way down in this old shirt pocket!"

And so, indeed, he had, and in less than half a minute the body of the larger hog lay lifeless on the sward. Twenty minutes later its carcass, skinned except as to head and feet, was tied up in a linen tent cloth and, suspended from a pole, was on the way to camp.

A dozen shining bayonets indicated the presence of provost guards. I decided to stop until they got out of the way. But when we resumed our journey, we ran plump into another squad.

The sergeant pointed at the swinging carcass and said, "I'll have to arrest you."

The moment we reached the provost-guard quarters, I requested the lieutenant to accompany us to General Micah Jenkins. Respectfully saluting, I began my plea.

"General, we are members of the 4th Texas, and every officer of that regiment will corroborate my assertion that we never shirk a duty. We come to you for release, sir. When a gentleman buys a hog and pays for it, he has a right to skin it."

At this juncture Colonel Sellers, the adjutant general of the division and a Texan, approached the fire, and I continued. "Although not personally known to Colonel Sellers, sir, I am sure he knows my people and will testify to their standing." Then I said, "Colonel, my name is Polley, and my father, an old Texan, used to live in Brazoria County."

"I knew him well," said the colonel, extending his hand with the utmost cordiality. "And I am glad to make the personal acquaintance of a son of his."

Colonel, soldier, gentleman and Texan to the core, he joined in pulling the wool over the commanding officer's eyes.

The general hastened to say, "I regret, Mr. Polley, that you have been subjected to the indignity of an arrest. But I shall request you to remain until morning, and then to go with the lieutenant and show him the party from whom you purchased the hog."

I replied, "Our comrades are hungry, pork is both scarce and high-priced and will spoil unless cut up and salted tonight."

"Oh, well," laughed the general, "take the meat to camp; but come back in the morning and save the good name of the division."

The advent of that hog marked an epoch in the annals of Company F, and was so timely that, while frying, broiling, boiling and roasting it, the boys loosened their purse strings, and in less than half an hour handed me a hundred dollars to be used in satisfying the owner, if he could be found. Next morning at daylight we found the right man and paid him twice the amount he demanded. Then we returned to camp, to be heartily congratulated on the hunger-satisfying issue of our adventure.

For the time being the private soldiers of both armies declared an informal armistice, as the following incident, related by the Confederate Colonel Sorrel, illustrates.

The pickets had resumed their posts and had become friendly, more given to trading than shooting one another at less than 100 yards. A fine Federal band came down to the riverbank one afternoon and began playing the Northern patriotic war songs. "Now give us some of ours!" shouted our pickets, and at once the music swelled into "Dixie," "My Maryland" and the "Bonnie Blue Flag." Then, after a mighty cheer, and a slight pause, the band again began. This time it was the tender, melting bars of "Home, Sweet Home." On both sides of the river there were joyous shouts, and soon many wet eyes could be found among those hardy warriors under the two flags.

In the midst of its troubles the unpopularity of its general in chief added to the perplexities of the Union army. Charles A.

Dana reports why it seemed expedient to change commanders.
and on whom fell the choice.

Rosecrans had fled to Chattanooga ahead of his men. He felt that he
could not clear himself either in his own eyes or in those of the army.

In writing to Mr. Stanton on September 27, I said that if it was decided to change the chief commander, I would suggest that some Western general of great prestige, like Grant, would be preferable as
Rosecrans' successor to one who had hitherto commanded in the East
alone.

The army, however, had its own candidate for Rosecrans' post. General Thomas had risen to the highest point in their esteem, and I saw
that there was no other man whose appointment would be so welcome.
I earnestly recommended that Thomas' merits be considered. He had
more the character of George Washington than any other man I ever
knew. At the same time he was a delightful man to be with.

Accordingly, I went at once over to General Thomas' headquarters.
I read to him the assenting telegram I had received in reply to my recommendation. He was too much affected by it to reply immediately.

After a moment he said, "Mr. Dana, I am greatly affected. I should
have long since liked to have an independent command, but I would not
like to be exposed to the imputation of having intrigued to supplant
my previous commander."

And so while he would gladly accept any other command, he could
not consent to become the successor of General Rosecrans.

After General Thomas' refusal he was put in temporary command of the army, pending the appointment of Rosecrans' successor. General Sheridan now takes up the story.

On October 16, 1863, General Grant was assigned to the command
of the "Military Division of the Mississippi," thus effecting a consoli-
dation of commands which might have been introduced most profitably
at an earlier date. The same order that assigned General Grant relieved General Rosecrans and placed General Thomas in command of
the Army of the Cumberland.

General Grant arrived at Chattanooga on October 23.

Grant's reception by the army was not very hearty, according
to Lieutenant Colonel John Atkinson, a Union officer.

The Army of the Cumberland was not enthusiastic about General Grant. They had heard of his great victories but knew less of him than those who had been at home and had read the papers. His appointment from another army seemed to be a reflection on their own. When he came to Chattanooga, he was crippled. His leg had been hurt by his horse falling. He was thin, and wore a look of intense anxiety on his face. He wore his uniform more like a civilian than a graduate of West Point. His military coat was never buttoned up to the neck. He sat on his horse carelessly, although securely. He walked with his head down and without the slightest suggestion of a military step. Neither his face nor his figure was imposing.

At Chattanooga, when he arrived, there was less left than a week's provisions, even on the short allowance of rations. Ten thousand animals had already perished hauling wagons over the road; those that remained had no strength.

> The Federal high command had decided to do as the Confederates had done—reinforce the Western armies by detaching troops from the East.
> General Oliver O. Howard, who commanded one of these Eastern divisions, met General Grant on his way west, and relates some interesting incidents.

The first week of October two divisions of the 11th and 20th Corps, under General Hooker, were transferred from the Army of the Potomac to the Western theater of war, and I, being one of Hooker's commanders, found myself on the same train with General Grant. He sat near the rear of the car, and I passed on at once to pay my respects to him. Without rising he extended his hand, smiled pleasantly and signified very briefly that it gave him pleasure to meet me.

Grant and staff went on with me to Bridgeport, where I was not a little anxious concerning my ability to entertain properly the distinguished guests.

After a sunrise breakfast General Rawlins lifted his general, as if he had been a child, into the saddle. The direct route across the Tennessee was held by Confederate Bragg, and the river road by way of Jasper, on our side, was exposed to sharpshooters from the other bank and to Confederate Joseph Wheeler's spasmodic raids. Yet almost without escort Grant risked the journey along the river through Jasper, across swollen streams, through deep mud and along roads that were already too wretched for the wagons. It would have been an awful journey for a well man—a journey of more than forty miles. The soldiers carried him in their arms across the roughest places. Yielding to no weariness or suffering, however, he pushed through to Chattanooga, reaching General Thomas on October 23.

In the evening several officers were sitting together when General Sherman arrived on the scene. He came bounding in after his usual buoyant manner. General Grant, whose bearing toward Sherman differed from that toward other officers, being free, affectionate and good-humored, greeted him most cordially and extended to him the ever-welcome cigar. This Sherman proceeded to light, but without stopping his ready flow of hearty words and not even pausing to sit down.

Grant arrested his attention by some apt remark and then said, "Take the chair of *honor*, Sherman," indicating a rocker with a high back.

That night I had the opportunity of hearing the proposed campaign discussed. Sherman evinced much previous knowledge and thought. Grant said that Sherman was accustomed while on horseback to "bone" his campaigns, *i.e.*, study them hard from morning till night.

General Thomas furnished them the ammunition of knowledge, positive and abundant, of the surrounding mountainous regions of East Tennessee and northern Georgia. General Grant appeared to listen with pleasant interest and now and then made a pointed remark. Thomas was like the solid judge, confident and fixed in his knowledge of law; Sherman, like the brilliant advocate; and Grant, rendering his verdict like an intelligent jury.

> The first thing Grant did was to continue efforts already begun to supply the besieged garrison with food and ammunition. On these efforts he reports himself.

The men had been on half rations for a considerable time. The beef was so poor that the soldiers were in the habit of saying that they were living on "half rations of hard bread and *beef dried on the hoof*." It looked, indeed, as if but two courses were open: the one to starve, the other to surrender or be captured.

As soon as I reached Chattanooga, I started out to make a personal inspection, taking Thomas with me. We crossed to the north side and reached the Tennessee at Brown's Ferry, some three miles below Lookout Mountain, unobserved by the enemy. Here we left our horses and approached the water on foot. There was a picket station of the enemy on the opposite side, in full view, and we were within easy range, but they did not fire upon us. They must have seen that we were all commissioned officers but, I suppose, they already looked on the garrison at Chattanooga as their prisoners of war.

That night I issued orders for opening the route to Bridgeport—*a cracker line*, as the soldiers appropriately termed it.

> The credit for the establishment of the "cracker line," according to Lieutenant Colonel Henry S. Dean of the 22nd Michigan, belonged to the chief engineer of the Army of the Cumberland.

The fate of the army at Chattanooga depended on the solution of the problem of supplies. At this time General William F. Smith, Chief Engineer of the Army of the Cumberland, conceived a plan, the successful execution of which would solve the problem. He submitted it to General Thomas, who gave his approval. General Grant authorized its execution.

Fortunately the preparations were far advanced and their completion required little time. The enemy had possession of the left bank of the river. General Smith's plan was to throw a force to that bank at Brown's Ferry, seize the entrance to Lookout Valley, lay a pontoon bridge and hold the position until General Hooker could come up with his forces from Bridgeport and thus restore to the besieged army at Chattanooga its short line of communication.

To accomplish this was no slight undertaking. From his position on Lookout Mountain the enemy could see every movement of our forces. To attempt to take a pontoon train from Chattanooga to Brown's Ferry, in plain view of the enemy, was to invite such a concentration of force at the contemplated place of crossing as to render the laying of a bridge impossible. It was decided that the boats for the bridge should be floated down the river to the point of crossing under cover of darkness. The rest of the material for the bridge was to be moved by night and concealed in the woods just above Brown's Ferry (See map, page 541.)

Fifty-two boats were required for the bridge. Each was provided with oars, one for steering and four for rowing. General William B. Hazen was in command of the landing force.

All the plans for the expedition were elaborated with the utmost secrecy. General Hazen selected 1,500 men who, under his command, were to constitute the first landing party.

This expedition must float past seven miles of the enemy's picket lines. Fortunately a fog settled down on the river. The boats, keeping close to the right bank, glided silently unpursued by pickets. At least they did not suspect what was passing them.

In the early dawn the first section neared the shore at its appointed place of landing. The surprised pickets fired their pieces and ran. The succeeding sections quickly landed. The men sprang on shore and charged up the hill, where they had a sharp, but brief, engagement with the small force which had rallied in response to the alarm given by the pickets. The boats immediately began to ferry the rest of the forces across. By daylight the balance of Hazen's brigade was across the river entrenching itself on the line of hills which commanded the entrance to Lookout Valley.

Under a vigorous artillery fire from the enemy's batteries, we immediately began laying the pontoon bridge. As soon as it was completed, we crossed the bridge and formed a junction with General Hooker's forces which had moved up the valley from Bridgeport.

Thus the problem of supplies for a starving army was solved.

> The importance of protecting Brown's Ferry against a Union surprise landing did not seem to have impressed the Confederate high command, but it was evident to Colonel William C. Oates.

Just after dark on October 27, 1863, a courier brought me a message that a heavy force of the enemy was attempting to cross the river near Bridgeport. A reinforcement of two army corps had been sent from the Army of the Potomac under "Fighting Joe" Hooker. These were the troops which were reported as in the act of crossing. On receiving the message I forwarded it, together with my apprehension that an attack on me was imminent, to General Longstreet, with the request to send reinforcements without delay. The courier returned before midnight and stated that he had delivered my communication and had a receipt for it. No other response came.

Some time before day a courier informed me that the Yankees were crossing the river near by and had driven a company away from Brown's Ferry. I had the long roll beaten, mounted my horse, and we moved off as rapidly as possible. Along the river at Brown's Ferry there is a ridge or little mountain. The gap through this leads to the ferry. When within twenty steps of it, I heard the invaders at work building breastworks. I came near riding into them. I then detailed two companies to walk right up to the foe, and for every man to place the muzzle of his rifle against the body of a Yankee when he fired. I waited in breathless silence, but when they did fire it must have done terrible execution, judging from the confusion of the enemy which followed.

My companies got inside their works and drove them, capturing eleven prisoners. But the Federal line to my right fired on us heavily, and to meet that I deployed another company and put it into action. I put in one company after another, until all six of my reserves were into it, and still I could not cover the enemy's front. I next sent a courier down the river to withdraw my other five companies and to bring them as speedily as possible, as I was contending with a force greatly superior to my own.

About this time General Law arrived with three regiments and the Texas Brigade. I told him that he was too late, that a heavy force had already crossed the river.

To give up the river and that valley utterly destroyed Bragg's policy by raising the siege of Chattanooga. General Longstreet had committed the defense of this valley (and the maintenance of the siege) to Law's brigade and never had ridden through it to see if Law was doing it. He and Law had become estranged, and the latter did not care whether he aided Longstreet in anything. Bragg, too, never had gone into that valley to see what was going on.

Whether I did right or not to report to him on the evening of October 27, it nevertheless gave him the information, and if he desired to hold Lookout Valley he should have ordered troops there at once.

> Grant, having made his communications secure, now explains his further campaign plans.

The enemy hastened to try to recover the line of supplies from us. On the night of the twenty-eighth and twenty-ninth an attack was made on our troops in Lookout Valley at Wauhatchie by Longstreet's corps. By four o'clock in the morning the battle had entirely ceased, and our "cracker line" was never afterward disturbed.

Having got the Army of the Cumberland in a comfortable position, I began to look after the remainder of my new command. Burnside was in Knoxville and in about as desperate a condition as the Army of the Cumberland had been, only he was not yet besieged.

On November 4 Longstreet had left our front with about 15,000 troops, besides Wheeler's cavalry, 5,000 more, to go against Burnside. Nothing could be done until Sherman should get up. The authorities at Washington were now more than ever anxious for the safety of Burnside's army and plied me with dispatches faster than ever, urging that something should be done for his relief. On the seventh, before Longstreet could possibly have reached Knoxville, I ordered Thomas to attack the enemy's right, so as to force the return of the troops that had gone up the valley. But he persisted in the declaration that he could not possibly comply with the order.

My orders for battle were all prepared. The possession of Lookout Mountain was of no special advantage to us now. Hooker was instructed to send Howard's corps to the north side of the Tennessee, thence up behind the hills on the north side, and to go into camp opposite Chattanooga. With the remainder of the command Hooker was, at a time to be afterward appointed, to ascend the western slope between the upper and lower palisades and so get into Chattanooga Valley.

The plan of battle was for Sherman to attack the enemy's right flank, extend our left over South Chickamauga River so as to threaten or hold the railroad in Bragg's rear, and thus force him either to weaken his lines elsewhere or lose his connection with his base at Chickamauga Station. Hooker was to perform like service on our right. His problem was to get from Lookout Valley to Chattanooga Valley in the most expeditious way possible; cross the latter valley rapidly to Rossville, south of Bragg's line on Missionary Ridge, thus threatening the enemy's rear on that flank and compelling him to reinforce this also. Thomas, with the Army of the Cumberland, occupied the center and was to assault while the enemy was engaged on his two flanks.

To carry out this plan, Sherman was to move east of Chattanooga to a point opposite the north end of Missionary Ridge and to place his command back of the foothills out of sight of the enemy on the ridge.

Hooker's position in Lookout Valley had been absolutely essential to us only so long as Chattanooga was besieged. It had been the key to our line for supplying the army. But it was not essential after the enemy had been dispersed from our front. By crossing the north face of Lookout the troops would come into Chattanooga Valley in rear of the line held by the enemy across the valley, and would necessarily force its evacuation. Orders were accordingly given to march by this route.

On November 23 Grant ordered a reconnaissance toward Orchard Knob, a slight elevation between Chattanooga and Missionary Ridge. This apparently unimportant episode, recorded by General Howard, was to have vital consequences.

On November 23 General Grant determined to make a reconnaissance. In plain sight of the enemy, and displayed before Generals Grant and Thomas and other officers, General Granger deployed one division and supported it by two others. "Only a reconnaissance!" The Confederates stood on their breastworks when, to their astonishment, our lines went forward with rapidity toward Orchard Knob. Soon all outward defenses for a mile ahead near the knob were in our hands. General Grant kept looking steadily toward the troops just engaged and beyond. He was slowly smoking a cigar. General Thomas, using his glasses, made no remark.

Rawlins seemed to be unusually urgent about something. He was heard to say, "It will have a bad effect to let them come back and try it over again."

When General Grant spoke at last, he said, "Entrench them and send up support."

Within a few minutes a new line of entrenchments was in process of construction, facing and parallel with Missionary Ridge, with Orchard Knob as a point of support.

In spite of having taken Orchard Knob, Grant could not move against Missionary Ridge until Sherman had crossed the Tennessee which, under conditions described by S. H. M. Byers, was not an easy task.

On November 23, 1863, my regiment was in Sherman's corps. We had marched twenty miles a day. Now this corps was to form the left of Grant's forces, cross a deep river in the darkness and assault the nearly inaccessible position of Bragg's army. That night we lay in bivouac in the woods close by the Tennessee River. We knew that 116 rude pontoon boats had been built for us and were lying hidden in a creek near by. We had almost no rations for the army. As for the horses and mules, they had already starved to death by the thousands and were lying around everywhere.

Midnight came, and all were still awake, though quiet, in the bivouac. At two o'clock we heard some splashing in the water. It was the sound of muffled oars. The boats had come for us. Every man seized his rifle, for we knew what was coming next. "Quietly, boys, fall in quietly," said the captains. Spades were handed to many of us. We did not ask for what, as we knew too well. Quietly, two by two, we slipped down to the water's edge and stepped into the rude flatboats. "There's room for thirty in a boat," said a tall man in a long waterproof coat who stood on the bank near us in the darkness. Few of us had ever before heard the voice of our beloved commander. Sherman's personal presence, his sharing the danger we were about to undertake, gave us confidence.

In a quarter of an hour a thousand of us were out in the middle of the river afloat in the darkness. Silently we sat there, our rifles and our spades across our knees. There was no sound but the swashing of the water against the boats.

In half an hour we were out on the opposite bank and creeping along through the thicket, a spade in one hand and a rifle in the other. What might happen any moment we knew not. Where was that escaped picket? And where was Bragg's army? Instantly we formed in line of battle and commenced digging holes for ourselves. We worked like beavers, turn about: no spade was idle for one moment. Daylight found us there, two thousand strong, with rifle pits a mile in length. Other brigades got over the river, pontoons soon were down; still other troops, whole divisions, were across, and forty cannon were massed close to the crossing to protect us. What a sight for General Bragg when he woke up that morning at his headquarters perch on top of Missionary Ridge!

> Grant was now ready to attack Bragg, who had so imprudently weakened his forces by detailing Longstreet's corps on the Knox-ville expedition. Sherman was to assault Missionary Ridge on the Union left, Hooker on the right, after passing Lookout Mountain.
>
> Grant reports on the beginning of these operations.

By the night of the twenty-third Sherman was in a position to move and at once formed his troops for assault on Missionary Ridge. By

1:00 P.M. on November twenty-fourth, he started. Soon the foot of the hill was reached. The skirmishers pushed directly up, followed closely by their supports. By half past three Sherman was in possession of the height without having sustained much loss. A brigade from each division was now brought up, and artillery was dragged to the top of the hill by hand. The enemy did not seem to be aware of this movement until the top of the hill was gained. There had been a drizzling rain during the day, and the clouds were so low that Lookout Mountain and the top of Missionary Ridge were obscured from the view of persons in the valley. But now the enemy opened fire upon their assailants and made several attempts with their skirmishers to drive them away, but without avail. Later in the day a more determined attack was made, but this, too, failed, and Sherman was left to fortify what he had gained.

Thomas having done on the twenty-third what was expected of him on the twenty-fourth, there was nothing for him to do this day except to strengthen his position.

While these operations were going on to the east of Chattanooga, Hooker was engaged on the west. His troops were all west of Lookout Creek. The enemy had the east bank of the creek strongly picketed and entrenched, and three brigades of troops in the rear to reinforce them if attacked. These brigades occupied the summit of the mountain. Why any troops, except artillery with a small infantry guard, were kept on the mountaintop, I do not see. A hundred men could have held the summit—which is a palisade for more than thirty feet down— against the assault of any number of men from the position Hooker occupied.

The side of Lookout Mountain confronting Hooker's command was rugged, heavily timbered and full of chasms, making it difficult to advance with troops, even in the absence of an opposing force. Farther up, the ground became more even and level and was in cultivation. On the east side the slope is much more gradual, and a good wagon road, zigzagging up it, connects the town of Chattanooga with the summit.

Early on the morning of the twenty-fourth Hooker moved John W. Geary's division up Lookout Creek to effect a crossing. A heavy mist obscured him from the view of the troops on the top of the mountain. He crossed the creek almost unobserved and then commenced ascending the mountain directly in his front.

Thomas and I were on the top of Orchard Knob. The day was hazy, so that Hooker's operations were not visible to us except at moments when the clouds would rise. But the sound of his artillery and musketry was heard incessantly. The enemy on his front was partially fortified but was soon driven out of his works. During the afternoon the clouds, which had so obscured the top of Lookout all day as to hide whatever

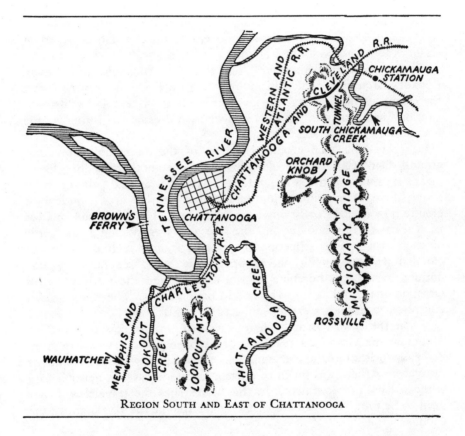

REGION SOUTH AND EAST OF CHATTANOOGA

was going on from the view of those below, settled down and made it so dark as to stop operations for the time. At four o'clock Hooker reported his position as impregnable.

In marching to his assigned position, Hooker took it upon himself to storm Lookout Mountain, which led to the spectacular "Battle above the Clouds," of which Brigadier General Charles P. Mattocks of Maine furnishes a glowing description.

Fourteen hundred feet above the plain, Lookout Mountain raises its massive head and looks out over five different states. At the foot of the mountain and between it and Missionary Ridge is a level plain where lay the Federal army, panting like hounds on a leash to be let loose. Confederate soldiers stretched along the tops and sides of the mountain ready to hurl death into the assaulting column. It had been determined to make an assault along the main line, but no one had dreamed of scaling the rugged sides of Lookout Mountain.

Hooker got permission from Grant to make a "demonstration" upon Lookout Mountain, which in military language would mean to divert the enemy while a general engagement is going on. Hooker's "demonstration" was something that had never been dreamed of by either the Federals or Confederates.

He moved his men around the base of the mountain. Towering around their heads were rocks piled upon one another, leading, like a giant's stairway, to the walls and pits of the plateau and palisades high above, these latter points being held by the Confederates. Suddenly a cloudy mist settled slowly down on the plateau. Hooker pushed on, his presence not being known until the two lines were within a few yards of each other. Then the opposing forces fought each other in the clouded darkness, while the troops below could see nothing, hear nothing except the booming of the artillery and the rattle of small arms; no one could dream what might be the result. The elements had conspired to make it a dreary and dismal night.

When the next morning there appeared on the top of Lookout Mountain the victorious standards of Hooker, a shout went up from the plain below to the very heavens above, and with the sound of many voices there was given to poets a scene such as was never before witnessed on the continent. In the future ages the traveler will not need to be told, "It was here that Hooker fought the Battle above the Clouds."

To the Confederate Lieutenant L. D. Young, the "Battle above the Clouds" appeared more spectacular than important, a view shared by many others, General Grant among them.

The extravagant talk about Hooker's "Battle above the Clouds" is a misnomer that has found its way into print and for a long time filled the papers and magazines. It is nothing but a magnified myth, unsupported by facts. At no time were the contending forces more than halfway up the mountain, and all the glory arrogated by the Federals was achieved over a light line deployed as skirmishers.

Although Grant's army had advanced successfully all along the line, Bragg was convinced that his main position on Missionary Ridge was impregnable, as appears from a story told by L. G. Bennett and William M. Haigh of the 36th Illinois Volunteers.

It was about 3:00 A.M. when Sherman ordered us to be ready for an advance at the firing of the signal. But what a task it was! We must charge across an open plain half a mile wide, in the very presence of the enemy, with sixty pieces of artillery playing on us. Then, when the foot of the ridge was reached, a heavy work packed with the enemy. That work carried, what then? A hill struggling up out of the valley 400 feet, another line of works, then up like a Gothic roof, rough with rocks, another ring of fire and iron, then the crest and then the enemy. No wonder the men had to brace themselves for such a journey.

Bragg stood near his headquarters and took the measurement of this new move. "Oh, General," said a woman who lived near by, "the Yankees are coming. What shall I do? Where shall I go?"

"Woman," said he, "are you mad? There are not Yankees enough in Chattanooga to come up here. Those are all my prisoners."

That Sherman had a most difficult task to perform is made clear by S. H. M. Byers.

The twenty-fifth of November, 1863, dawned clear and beautiful. Instantly whole divisions of Sherman's and Bragg's troops commenced slaughtering one another for the possession of single hills and spurs. At times the battle in front of Sherman was a hand-to-hand encounter. My own brigade was so close that the Rebels even threw stones down on us.

It was two o'clock when our division, my own regiment with it, received orders from Sherman to fix bayonets and join in the assault on Missionary Ridge. We had to charge over the open, and the storm of shot and shell became terrific. In front of us was a rail fence and, as it was in direct line of fire, its splinters and fragments flew in every direction. "Jump the fence, men! Tear it down!" cried the colonel. Never did men get over a fence more quickly.

We started on a charge, running across the open fields. I had heard the roaring of heavy battle before, but never such a shrieking of cannon balls and bursting of shell as met us on that charge. We could see the enemy working his guns, while in plain view other batteries galloped up, unlimbered and let loose at us. Behind us our own batteries—forty cannon—were firing at the enemy over our heads. Halfway over we had to leap a ditch, perhaps six feet wide and nearly as many deep. Some of our regiment fell into this ditch and could not get out. A few tumbled in intentionally and stayed there. All of the officers were screaming at the top of their voices. I, too, screamed, trying to make the men hear. "Steady! Steady! Bear to the right! Keep in line! Don't fire! Don't fire!" We shouted till we all were hoarse and the awful thunder of the cannon made all commands unheard and useless.

In ten minutes, possibly, we were across the field and at the beginning of the ascent of the ridge. Instantly the blaze of Rebel musketry was in our faces, and we began firing in return. It helped little, the foe was so hidden behind logs and stones and little breastworks. Still we charged, and climbed a fence in front of us and fired and charged again. Then the order was given to lie down and continue firing. That moment someone cried, "Look to the tunnel! They're coming through the tunnel." Sure enough, through a railway tunnel in the mountain the Graycoats were coming by hundreds. They were flanking us completely.

"Stop them!" cried our colonel to those of us at the right. "Push them back!" It was the work of but a few moments for four companies to rise to their feet and run to the tunnel's mouth, firing as they ran. Too late! An enfilading fire was soon cutting them to pieces. As I ran over I passed many of my comrades stretched out in death, others screaming in agony. For a few minutes the whole brigade faltered and gave way. Then I rose to my feet and surrendered.

General Grant now continues his narrative.

On the morning of November 25 the whole field was in full view from the top of Orchard Knob, where I stood with General Thomas. It remained so all day. At Bragg's headquarters officers could be seen coming and going constantly.

The point of ground which Sherman had carried on the twenty-fourth was almost disconnected from the main ridge occupied by the enemy. Sherman now threatened both Bragg's flank and his stores and made it necessary for him to weaken other points of his line to strengthen his right. From the position I occupied I could see column after column of Bragg's forces moving against Sherman. Every Confederate gun that could be brought to bear upon the Union forces was concentrated upon him, and he was compelled to fall back, followed by the foe.

Seeing the repulse, I directed Thomas to send a division to reinforce him. It had to march a considerable distance directly under the eyes of the enemy to reach its position. Bragg at once commenced massing in the same direction. This was what I wanted. But it had now got to be late in the afternoon, and I had expected before this to see Hooker crossing the right in the neighborhood of Rossville and compelling Bragg to mass in that direction also.

The enemy had evacuated Lookout Mountain during the night, as I expected he would. In crossing the valley he burned the bridge over Chattanooga Creek and did all he could to obstruct the roads behind him. Hooker was detained four hours crossing Chattanooga Creek, and thus was lost the immediate advantage I had expected from his forces. His reaching Bragg's flank and extending across it was to be the signal for Thomas' frontal assault of the ridge. But Sherman's condition was getting so critical that the assault for his relief could not be delayed any longer.

I now directed Thomas to order the charge at once. In an incredibly short time Generals Sheridan and Wood were driving the enemy before them toward Missionary Ridge. The Confederates were strongly entrenched on the crest of the ridge in front of us and had a second line halfway down and another at the base. Our men drove the troops in front of the lower line of rifle pits so rapidly, and followed them so closely, that Rebel and Union troops went over the first line of works almost at the same time. Many Rebels were captured and sent to the rear under the fire of their own friends higher up the hill. Those that were not captured retreated and were pursued. The retreating hordes being between friends and pursuers caused the enemy to fire high to avoid killing their own men. In fact, on that occasion the Union soldier nearest the enemy was in the safest position. Without awaiting further orders or stopping to re-form, our troops went to the second line of works, over that and on for the crest.

I watched their progress with intense interest. The fire along the

Rebel line was terrific, but the damage done was small. The pursuit continued until the crest was reached, and soon our men were seen climbing over the Confederate barriers. The retreat of the enemy was precipitate, and the panic so great that Bragg and his officers lost all control over their men. Many were captured, and thousands threw away their arms in their flight.

To the left, where Bragg's troops had massed against Sherman, the resistance was more stubborn and the contest lasted longer, but the enemy there, seeing everything to their left giving way, fled also.

The victory at Chattanooga was won more easily than was expected by reason of Bragg's grave mistakes: first, in sending away Longstreet, his ablest corps commander, with over 20,000 troops; second, in placing so much of a force on the plain in front of his impregnable position.

A colorful picture of the final assault on Missionary Ridge comes from the pen of Captain J. C. Donahower, serving in a Minnesota regiment.

The boom of a single cannon broke the stillness. Five more shots followed, and at the sixth the men marched forward. Suspense was at an end—the battle was on. The orders were: keep well aligned, march on quick time until the enemy open fire, and at the bugle's sound take the double-quickstep, charge and, without returning their fire, capture the lower works.

The line moved on, slowly at first, it seemed. It drew the fire of the skirmishers, who flew to the shelter of their barricades. Of the cannon on the summit a score or more let fly, in response to which the Union batteries in the rear sent shot and shell into the lower line of works. With steady step we moved on and, when within 300 yards, received a volley from the works. The piercing blast of the bugle, twice repeated, sounded the "charge." With arms apart the men assumed the double-quick. "That's the surgeon's call. The doctor wants you," yelled a waggish soldier.

The scene changed. From the summit above, forty guns, silent until now, almost simultaneously opened fire, terrific, awful, belching forth thick volumes of smoke, deluging the plain in a shower of exploding missiles. Even those proved of no avail. We got within fifty paces of the log barricade, and each right hand grasped the hammer and trigger in preparation for a shot. We reached it and saw the enemy fast leaving for the summit of the ridge. The assaulting column now fired, and men fell, but more succeeded in reaching the shelter of the timbered slope beyond. While reloading their pieces the men regained their breath and watched the animating scene enacted by comrades on their right, as brigade after brigade almost simultaneously captured the works in their front.

The second line, a marching target for Rebel cannoneers, was now approaching. Its phalanx of blue, gashed and rent by shot and shell, moved on, the gaps closing as they marched.

The commanding general's orders for the assault included in their scope the line of works just captured—no more. Himself a witness to its execution in spirit and to the very letter, no time was given him to promulgate further instructions. But standing still became unendurable. Regiment after regiment crossed the captured works and, with heads bowed toward the storm of seething, hissing shell, went forward.

The hill was steep and rifted, and the ascent was necessarily slow and retarded by the fire of the retiring Confederates, and from those behind the works above, but higher and still higher we moved toward those smoking cannon then almost within our grasp.

At last the crest was reached, the log barricade crossed at a bound, and there in the arena of strife and confusion for a brief moment we stood—dazed by the scene.

The enemy, those selfsame men who on other days and in open field had fairly met the shock in conflict and bravely hurled it back, gave way and yielded their works and cannon.

The historians of the 36th Illinois retained this impression of the final conquest.

Streams of surrendering and captured officers and men poured to the rear, while those defending the heights above grew more and more desperate as our men approached the top. They shouted "Chickamauga" as though the word itself were a weapon. They thrust cartridges into guns by handfuls. They lighted the fuses of shells and then rolled them down. They seized huge stones and threw them. But nothing could stop the force of the desperate charge, and one after another the regimental flags were borne over the parapet, and the ridge was ours.

The finest battery of guns in the Southern army, including the Lady

Buckner and Lady Breckinridge, etc., was there, the rammers halfway down the guns when captured. Bragg himself had stayed to the last moment and barely escaped as our men came up close to his headquarters. We threw our haversacks in the air until it was a cloud of black spots. Officers and men mingled indiscriminately in their joy. All distinction seemed lost for the time in the wild enthusiasm of success.

Soon General Sheridan appeared, mounted on his black horse, and the boys gathered around him and cheered. In a few moments our corps commander, General Gordon Granger, reached the top of the ridge, and a number of the boys shouted to him, "What do you think of this, General?"

"I think you disobeyed orders, you damned rascals!" was his reply.

Here is Bragg's own story of his debacle.

On Wednesday November twenty-fifth I visited the extreme right, now threatened by a heavy force. Another very heavy force in line of battle confronted our left and center.

About 11:00 A.M. the enemy's forces were being moved in heavy masses from Lookout and beyond to our front, while those in front extended to our right. They formed their lines just beyond the range of our guns and in plain view of our position.

Though we were greatly outnumbered, such was the strength of our position that no doubt was entertained of our ability to hold it, and every disposition was made for that purpose. During this time the enemy had made several attempts on our extreme right and had been handsomely repulsed with very heavy loss.

About half past three the immense force in the front of our left and center advanced in three lines, preceded by heavy skirmishers. Our batteries opened with fine effect, and much confusion was produced before they reached musket range. In a short time the roar of musketry became very heavy, and it was soon apparent that the enemy had been repulsed in my immediate front.

While I was riding along the crest congratulating the troops, intelligence reached me that our line was broken on my right, and the enemy had crowned the ridge. Assistance was promptly dispatched to that point, under Brigadier General William B. Bate, who had so successfully maintained the ground in my front, and I proceeded to the rear of the broken line to rally our retiring troops and return them to the crest to drive the enemy back. General Bate found the disaster so great that his small force could not repair it. About this time I learned that our extreme left had also given way, and that my position was almost surrounded. Bate was immediately directed to form a second line in the rear, where, by the efforts of my staff, a nucleus of stragglers had been formed on which to rally.

General Hardee moved toward the left when he heard the heavy firing in that direction. He reached there just in time to find it had nearly all fallen back. By a prompt and judicious movement he threw a portion of Cheatham's division directly across the ridge, facing the enemy. By a decided stand here the enemy was entirely checked, and that portion of our force remained intact. All else to the left, however, except a portion of Bate's division, was entirely routed and in rapid flight, nearly all the artillery having been shamefully abandoned by its infantry support. Every effort which could be made by me and my staff and by many other mounted officers availed but little. A panic such as I had never before witnessed seemed to have seized on officers and men, and each seemed to be struggling for his personal safety.

In this distressing and alarming state of affairs General Bate was ordered to hold his position, covering the road for the retreat, and orders were immediately sent to Generals Hardee and Breckinridge to retire their forces on the depot at Chickamauga. Fortunately it was now near nightfall, and the country and roads in our rear were fully known to us, but equally unknown to the enemy. The routed left made its way back in great disorder, effectually covered, however, by Bate's small command which had a sharp conflict with the enemy's advance, driving it back. After night, all being quiet, Bate retired in good order, the enemy attempting no pursuit. Lieutenant General Hardee's command, under his judicious management, retired in good order and unmolested.

As soon as all the troops had crossed, the bridges over the Chickamauga were destroyed to impede the enemy, though the stream was fordable in several places.

No satisfactory excuse can possibly be given for the shameful conduct of our troops on the left in allowing their line to be penetrated. The position was one which ought to have been held by a line of skirmishers against any assaulting column; wherever resistance was made, the enemy fled in disorder after suffering heavy loss. Those who reached the ridge did so in a condition of exhaustion, and the slightest effort would have destroyed them.

Had all parts of the line been maintained with equal gallantry and persistence, no enemy could ever have dislodged us. But one possible reason presents itself to my mind in explanation of such bad conduct in veteran troops who had never before failed in any duty assigned them, however difficult and hazardous. They had for two days confronted the enemy, marshaling his immense forces in plain view and exhibiting to their sight such a superiority in numbers as might have intimidated weak minds and untried soldiers.

Lieutenant L. D. Young of the Kentucky Orphan Brigade complained bitterly that his unit was taken from its position at a critical time.

On November 25 before daylight we were ordered to the extreme right. This move was a complete waste, for we, the Orphan Brigade, rendered practically no service at all on that eventful day. Had we kept our place in the line between and among Cobb's guns, "Lady Breckinridge," "Lady Buckner," "Lady Helm" and his other guns to which the Orphans were lovingly endeared, they would never have been surrendered while a man was on his feet. Lucky indeed for Sheridan and Wood that the Orphans were away from home, and perhaps equally lucky for some, if not all, of us, for we had sworn never to abandon this position while a man of us lived.

This, in my mind, was the strongest natural position with one exception ever held by the Confederate forces in the West, and its abandonment was a disgrace to Confederate arms. Imagine our mortification and deep chagrin when we learned that our battery—Cobb's—with the endearing names inscribed thereon, had been cowardly abandoned, after we had successfully defended them at Shiloh, Vicksburg, Baton Rouge, Murfreesboro, Jackson, Chickamauga and other places. It was enough to make an angel weep.

We never knew what had happened until about dark when we were ordered from our position toward Chickamauga Station. Then the truth took first the form of conjecture, then misgiving, and lastly the sad news that we were to cover the retreat of the army.

Lieutenant R. M. Collins of Bragg's army gave a good account of the Confederate retreat from Missionary Ridge.

About 11:00 P.M. the order was passed down the line in a whisper, from post to post, for us to move out by the left flank, and to be careful as to making any sort of noise and not to tread on any sticks that might break. We were old soldiers by this time, and knew what all this meant. We knew that the day had been lost. We moved as quietly as if there had been one man only. Up over the mountain and down through a deep gorge we went, wrapped in darkness inside and outside.

I was marching at the head of the column, and the first words I addressed to our captain were "This, Captain, is the death knell of the Confederacy, for if we cannot cope with those fellows with the advantages we had on this line, there is not a line between here and the Atlantic ocean where we can stop them."

He replied by saying, "Hush, Lieutenant, that is treason you are talking."

Doubtless such expressions in the presence of the men might have been wrong, but I thought it all right as between officers.

On we went, and pretty soon we came to where our division was camped in a sort of straggling, irregular manner in a great woodland. We lay down and rested an hour or two. About sunrise we arrived at Chickamauga Station. We were halted, built fires and were broiling bacon for breakfast. Looking in the direction the enemy would come, we saw, not more than 300 yards from us, a line of Federal cavalry. While the morale of Pat R. Cleburne's division was not the best in the world, yet it was the best in the Army of Tennessee. Fact is, every other division in the army was on a dead run for any place to get out of the reach of the Yankees. We did not stand on the order of our going but moved out at once. All day of the twenty-sixth and until late at night we were kept well in hand and on the move. About eleven o'clock at night we stopped on the banks of the Chickamauga, near Ringgold, Georgia, and oh, how tired and sleepy we were!

On we went down through the little town of Ringgold. General Bragg had sent orders to General Cleburne to hold this gap until twelve o'clock if possible, and told him that if he could do so, he could save the Army of Tennessee. Just about sunup came the Federals in high glee, down through the town, banners flying, drums beating, with heads up, as if they had nothing to do now but march right along through the country. On they came right up to within 100 yards of our hidden battery, when all at once the pine tops were thrown off, and six 12-pound Napoleon guns poured shot and shell into their ranks. They were utterly astonished and broke in great confusion, seeking shelter anywhere, behind dwellings, barns, outhouses, railroad embankment or anything else. But they were between the two wings of Cleburne's lines and we gave it to them good.

We fell back about a couple of miles and formed another line. The Federals came to where they could see us, but they did not want more. We had put a taste in their mouths that ended the campaign.

A Confederate wit managed to put the story of Bragg's recent up-and-down accomplishments into four lines of verse.

> For Bragg did well. Ah! who could tell,
> What merely human mind could augur,
> That they would run from Lookout Mount,
> Who fought so well at Chickamauga?

CHAPTER 18

Grant Takes the High Command

THE BATTLE OF THE WILDERNESS AND
THE SIEGE OF PETERSBURG

By his retreat after the battle of Gettysburg Lee had yielded
the initiative to the Union side. The summer and autumn of 1863
passed quietly, however, thus enabling Lee to send help to Bragg
at Chattanooga.

Some light is thrown on Meade's inactivity by one of his staff
officers, Lieutenant Colonel Theodore Lyman, in a letter he
wrote at that time.

September 24, 1863. I believe the whole of Lee's army should be
either cut to pieces or put in precipitate flight on Richmond. I accuse
nobody, but merely state my opinion. Bricks and mortar may be of the
best, but if there are three or four architects . . .

"Why doesn't Meade attack Lee?" Ah, I have already thrown out a
hint! Meade, though he expressly declares that he is *not* Napoleon, is a
thorough soldier, who does not move unless he knows where and how
many his men are; where and how many his enemy's men are; and what
sort of country he has to go through.

Meanwhile the papers say, "The fine autumn weather is slipping
away." Certainly; and shall we add, "Therefore let another Fredericksburg be fought?"

At the end of November 1863 Meade finally opened an offensive campaign. It began at Mine Run, a southern tributary of the
Rapidan, and ended there without an attack when it became plain
that it promised little hope for success.

Colonel Lyman explains and approves Meade's action.

553

December 12, 1863. . . . I am more and more struck with General Meade's self-control in refusing to attack. His plan was a definite one, and he had the firmness to say the blow has failed, and we shall only add disaster by persisting. It should be remembered, also, that this [straight] line [to Richmond] is *not* approved as a line of operations, and never has been; but we are forced to work on it.

How the officers in Meade's army spent the winter of 1863-1864 is told by one of them, Robert S. Robertson.

A winter in tents is monotonous; card playing, horse racing and kindred intellectual amusements become stale when made a steady occupation. Visits to distant camps, long rides, leaping fences or a chat with the Johnnies on their outposts failed to be exciting after a while.

Games of ball were played until all interest was lost in them. Beans were won on all sorts of games, until beans palled on the sight, as they had long before on the taste. For a time we amused ourselves with work. We found a dilapidated sawmill without saws and purchased saws. Soon we were sawing lumber to improve our tents and build cabins.

We celebrated Washington's birthday by a grand ball. Many of the officers' wives and daughters enlivened the camp. The Vice-President and a number of senators were there with their wives, and Governor Andrew G. Curtin of Pennsylvania and his wife acted as a convoy for a bevy of beauties.

Generals Meade, Hancock, Warren, Pleasonton, H. J. Kilpatrick and D. McM. Gregg were there, and so was one-legged Ulric Dahlgren, whose sad fate it was a few days later to be killed in a raid on Richmond.

However, all was not given up to revelry. There was reveille at daybreak, and roll call, after which came guard mounting, and squad and company drills until noon. Brigade and division drills occupied the afternoon, and dress parade at sundown finished the day. Intersperse this with details for picket duty, policing the camps and building miles of corduroy roads. and you have the ordinary routine of our winter camp.

In contrast, the Confederate Alexander Hunter has left a picture of how his regiment, the famous Black Horse Cavalry, spent the winter of 1863-64.

Time was chiefly spent in collecting wood and cooking things that might induce our meager rations to go as far as possible. But two crackers and a half pound of fat meat per day offered no great range for experiment; neither did it satisfy the hunger of able-bodied men.

Worse was to come: the crackers were changed to a pound of meal a day—meal it was called, but the God of Hungry Souls save the mark! A mixture of ground corncobs, husks and sawdust, it was so sour that any decent dog would reject it.

If the troopers were famishing, so were their horses. It was sad to see the wistful, half-human gaze the poor brutes cast on their owners, mutely imploring food. In their distress they would eat bushes, dried sticks and leaves. Fully one-half of them were incapable of getting up a gallop, a trembling trot being their fastest gait.

Yet in all this trying period I heard no word of discouragement from the soldiers; even among the unlettered countrypeople there was no cry of submission. They would only ask us with wan faces and sunken eyes, "For God's sake, drive the Yankees out—and soon, too, for we cannot stand it much longer!"

> On March 9, 1864, Grant was appointed Lieutenant General and put in command of all Federal armies. It was the first time since 1779 that Congress had bestowed this rank on a military leader. Grant immediately worked out a plan for an over-all campaign, on which he himself now enlarges.

When I assumed command of all the armies, the situation was about this: the Mississippi River was ours from St. Louis to New Orleans. East of the Mississippi we held substantially all of the state of Tennessee. Virginia north of the Rapidan and east of the Blue Ridge we also held. On the seacoast we had Fort Monroe and Norfolk in Virginia, and other ports or islands all the way to Key West. The balance of the Southern territory, an empire in extent, was still in the hands of the enemy.

In the East the opposing forces stood in substantially the same relations toward each other as when the war began: both were between the Federal and Confederate capitals.

That portion of the Army of the Potomac not engaged in guarding lines of communications was on the northern bank of the Rapidan. The Army of Northern Virginia confronted it on the opposite bank.

My plan now was to concentrate all the forces possible against the Confederate armies. There were but two—the Army of Northern Virginia, General Robert E. Lee commanding; the second, under General Joseph E. Johnston (who had succeeded Bragg) at Dalton, Georgia, opposed to Sherman, who was still at Chattanooga. Besides, the Confederates had to guard the Shenandoah Valley, a great storehouse to feed their armies from. Forrest, a brave and intrepid cavalry general, was in the West with a large force, making a larger command necessary to hold Middle and West Tennessee.

Since our forces could guard their special trusts as well when advancing from them as when remaining at them, I arranged for a simultaneous movement all along the line. Sherman was to move from Chattanooga, Johnston's army and Atlanta being his objective points. George Crook, commanding in West Virginia, had the Virginia and Tennessee Railroad as his objective. Sigel in the Shenandoah Valley was to advance up the valley, covering the North from an invasion through that channel. Butler was to advance by the James River, having Richmond and Petersburg as his objective. Banks in the Department of the Gulf had Mobile as his objective. [On orders from Washington, Banks was sent instead into Louisiana where he met defeat in what is known as the Red River Campaign.]

By April 27, 1864, spring had so far advanced as to justify me in fixing May 4 for the great move. Meade was notified to bring his troops forward. On the following day Butler was directed to move the same day and get as far up the James River as possible. Sherman was directed to get his forces ready to advance on the 5th. Sigel was notified to move in conjunction with the others.

This was the plan, and I will now endeavor to give the method of its execution, outlining first the operations of the detached columns.

Banks failed to accomplish what he had been sent to do on the Red River, and eliminated the use of 40,000 veteran troops. Sigel's record is almost equally brief. He moved out according to program but just when I was hoping to hear of good work being done in the valley I received instead the following announcement from Halleck: "Sigel is in full retreat on Strasburg. He will do nothing but run; never did anything else." The enemy had intercepted him at New Market and handled him roughly.

Butler embarked at Fort Monroe with all his command and seized City Point and Bermuda Hundred early in the day, very much to the surprise of the enemy. By the sixth of May he had begun entrenching, and on the seventh he sent out his cavalry to cut the Weldon Railroad and to destroy the railroad between Petersburg and Richmond but no great success attended these efforts. He neglected to attack Petersburg, which was almost defenseless. About the eleventh he advanced slowly until he reached the works at Drewry's Bluff, about halfway between Bermuda Hundred and Richmond. In the meantime Beauregard had

GRANT AND LEE IN VIRGINIA

been gathering reinforcements, and on the sixteenth he attacked Butler with such success as to limit very materially the further usefulness of the Army of the James as a factor in the campaign.

Soon after midnight, May 3-4, the Army of the Potomac started on the memorable Wilderness Campaign. (See map, page 573.)

The country over which the army had to operate was cut by numerous streams, which formed a considerable obstacle. The roads were narrow and poor. Most of the country was covered with a dense forest, almost impenetrable even for infantry.

All conditions were favorable for defensive operations.

> The bulk of Grant's army crossed the Rapidan at Germanna Ford on May 3 and 4. His plan was to traverse the Wilderness as quickly as possible, so as to gain open territory in which to operate more favorably, while Lee naturally tried to keep his opponents where their superiority in numbers and artillery would be minimized. The invading forces had to stretch out in a long line, while heading south, and were therefore vulnerable to a flank attack, which was not slow in forthcoming.
>
> The initial clash occurred on May 5, and Grant reports on it.

On May 4 Lee's headquarters were at Orange Court House. From there to Fredericksburg he had the use of two roads running nearly parallel to the Wilderness—the Orange Pike and the Orange Plank Road. This gave him unusual facilities for concentrating his forces. Both roads strike the road from Germanna Ford in the Wilderness.

On discovering the advance of the Army of the Potomac, Lee ordered Hill, Ewing and Longstreet, each commanding a corps, to move to attack us, Hill on the Orange Plank Road, Longstreet to follow on the same road. (Longstreet was at this time—the middle of the afternoon—at Gordonsville, twenty or more miles away.) Ewell, who was near by, was ordered forward by the Orange Pike.

My orders were for an early advance on the morning of the fifth. The Army of the Potomac was facing to the west, though our advance was made to the south, except when facing the enemy.

At 6:00 A.M., before reaching Parker's store, Warren discovered the enemy. He sent word back to this effect, and was ordered to attack. General H. G. Wright with his division of Sedgwick's corps was ordered, by any road he could find, to join onto Warren's right, and Major General George W. Getty with his division, also of Sedgwick's corps, was ordered to get on his left. This was the speediest way to reinforce Warren who was confronting the enemy on both the Orange Plank Road and the Pike.

Burnside, who was in the rear, had moved promptly on the fourth on receiving word that the Army of the Potomac had safely crossed the Rapidan. By making a night march, although some of his troops had to march forty miles to reach the river, he was crossing with the head of his column early on the morning of the fifth.

Neither party had any advantage of position. At nine o'clock Warren attacked with favorable though not decisive results. At 2:00 P.M. Hancock arrived, and immediately was ordered to attack the enemy. But the heavy timber and narrow roads prevented him from getting into position as promptly as he generally did when receiving such orders.

Fighting between Hancock and Hill continued until night put a close to it. Neither side had made any special progress.

> The Confederate General John B. Gordon took an important part in this struggle and gives his recollection in these words.

Having crossed the Rapidan with but little resistance, General Grant spent the fourth of May in placing his army in position and then pushed the head of his column toward Richmond in order to throw himself between Lee and the Confederate capital. Lee, in the meantime, was hurrying his columns along the narrow roads to check Grant's advance, but was unable to ascertain whether the heaviest assault was to be made on the Confederate center or upon either flank. Field glasses, scouts and cavalry were almost wholly useless in that dense woodland, which enabled General Grant to concentrate his forces at any point while their movements were entirely concealed.

My command brought up the rear of the extreme left of Lee's line, which was led by Ewell's corps. We hurried with quickened step toward the point of heaviest fighting. At one point the weird Confederate yell told us plainly that Ewell's men were advancing. At another the huzzas of the Union troops warned us that they had repelled the Confederate charge; and, as these ominous huzzas grew in volume, we knew that Grant's lines were moving forward. Our repulse had been so sudden and the confusion so great that practically no resistance was being made to the Union advance.

At this moment of dire extremity I saw General Ewell riding in furious gallop toward me, his thoroughbred charger bounding like a deer through the dense underbrush. With a quick jerk he checked his horse and rapped out his few words with characteristic impetuosity. "General Gordon, the fate of the day depends on you, sir," he said.

"These men will save it, sir," I replied.

I quickly wheeled a single regiment into line and ordered it forward in a countercharge, while I hurried the other troops into position. The sheer audacity and dash of that regimental charge checked, as I had hoped it would, the Union advance for a few moments, giving me time to throw other troops across the Union front. With a deafening yell, which must have been heard miles away, that glorious brigade rushed upon the hitherto advancing enemy and by the shock of their furious onset shattered into fragments all that portion of the compact Union line which confronted my troops.

While this movement was being executed, the Confederates who had been previously driven back rallied and moved in a spirited charge to the front and recovered the lost ground.

Both armies rested for the night near the points where the first collisions of the day had occurred. It would be more accurate to say they labored all night throwing up such breastworks as were possible—a most timely preparation for the next day's conflicts.

The Union officer Robert Robertson describes what fighting in the Wilderness was like.

The Wilderness is a densely wooded region of great extent, remarkable on account of its dreary and dismal woods. A dense undergrowth of scraggy pines, dwarfed oaks and laurel bushes has sprung up, while in the low points are sluggish streams and dank marshes choked with alders, twined closely with luxuriant tangled and prickly vines, making many places almost inaccessible.

At daybreak the reveille sounded and one could see men arising from amid stacks of arms. Evening shades fell fast in the gloomy recesses of these dark woods, and the darkness and undergrowth prevented any true alignment. Only by the flash of the volleys did we know where the enemy was with whom we were engaged. Night soon wrapped those gloomy woods in total darkness, and still the fight raged on. We saw no enemy, but we were so close that the flashes from their muskets and ours seemed to mingle, and we fired only at their line of fire and they at ours. It was a battle fought where maneuvering was impossible, where the lines of battle were invisible to their commanders, and where the enemy also was invisible.

Yet in that gloomy region of death nearly 200,000 men were grappling in one of the deadliest struggles of the war.

Another Union soldier, the cannoneer Augustus Buell, agreeing with his comrade, illustrates his narrative with some odd examples.

This Battle of the Wilderness was simply bushwhacking on a grand scale, in brush where all formation was soon lost, and where such a thing as a consistent line of battle on either side was impossible.

I knew a Wisconsin infantryman who walked right into the Rebel skirmish line. He surrendered, and a Rebel was sent to the rear with him. In two minutes he and his guard walked into our own lines, and that in broad daylight.

After dark one day, four or five of our soldiers, who had straggled, were halted by Union skirmishers, surrendered to them and had been started off under guard before it was discovered that they were Union men.

During the night of May 5 two men came back, both slightly wounded. One was a Rebel and the other was one of our men. They had got together in the brush. Both had lost their muskets and, as the brush was getting afire, they made their way out of it together, taking their chances which of the two lines they might fall into.

A man of the 44th New York, whom I knew, got lost in an attack in the afternoon of the fifth and after dark found himself away down among the troops of the 2nd Corps. He had passed at least two miles in the rear of the Rebel lines, and through them twice, unchallenged. He told me that when he came to the 2nd Corps front about ten o'clock at night and was halted, he answered, "I belong to the 44th New York. Who in hell are you?" He hadn't the remotest idea where he was.

One old fellow who was brought up out of the brush belonged to the 5th Texas and had been hit in the shin by a bullet. Some of the boys asked him what he thought of the battle. His reply was, "Battle be damned! It ain't no battle. It's a worse riot than Chickamauga was. At Chickamauga there was at least a rear, but here there ain't neither front nor rear. It's all a damned mess! And our two armies ain't nothing but howlin' mobs!"

In the morning of May 6 Lee was in great danger. The Union forces were threatening to overrun Hill's tired and weakened corps on the Plank Road, and time had to be gained at all hazards to allow Longstreet to come up. The Texan J. B. Polley tells of it.

Our position was on an open hill immediately in rear of a battery. Within 300 yards were the Yankees. Here General Lee, mounted on the same horse (a beautiful dapple-gray) that had carried him at Fredericksburg in 1862, rode up near us and gave his orders. "The Texas Brigade always has driven the enemy, and I expect them to do it today. Tell them, General, that I shall witness their conduct."

Galloping in front, General John Gregg delivered the message and shouted, "Forward, Texas Brigade!"

Just then Lee rode in front, as if intending to lead the charge, but a shout went up, "Lee to the rear!" A soldier sprang from the ranks and, seizing the dapple-gray by the reins, led him and his rider to the rear.

The Yankee sharpshooters soon discovered our approach, and some of our best men were killed and wounded before a chance was given them to fire a shot. Three hundred yards, and the leaden hail began to thin our ranks perceptibly; four hundred yards, and we were confronted by a line of blue which, however, fled before us without firing a single volley. Across the Plank Road stood another line, and against this we moved rapidly. The storm of battle became terrific. The Texas Brigade was alone: no support on our right, and not only none on the left, but a terrible enfilading fire poured on us from that direction. We crossed the road and pressed forward 200 yards farther when, learning that a column of Federals was double-quicking from the left and would soon have us surrounded, General Gregg gave the order to fall back. General Lee's object was gained, his trust in the Texans justified. Two divisions had been driven by one small brigade, of whose men more than one-half were killed and wounded.

Colonel William C. Oates of Longstreet's corps pictures some of the fighting that took place on that second day of the battle.

Lee's object manifestly was to have Longstreet turn Grant's left flank and attack him in the rear, but Longstreet was too slow. He had put his two divisions in bivouac on the night of the fifth more than six miles away from Hill. General Lee foresaw that Hill's troops could not withstand the assaults of the next morning from Hancock's veteran corps of 30,000, and that before Longstreet could reach Hancock's rear, the latter would beat Hill and drive him deep into the Wilderness, destroy the alignment and render a junction of our two corps difficult and hazardous. Longstreet had not moved down that parallel road with the celerity which Lee had expected, and hence could not turn Grant's left before the afternoon, although we had started our march at night to support Hill on time.

At about 2:00 A.M. on the sixth we had begun to move, but we progressed so slowly along the devious neighborhood road that it was daylight when the head of the column reached the Plank Road, about two miles in the rear of where the fighting had ceased the previous evening and where, just at this moment, it recommenced with great fury. In anticipation that his troops would be relieved early the next morning, Hill had not prepared to receive the attack which was made on him.

Longstreet's column reached the scene of action none too soon. Hancock was just turning Hill's right and driving his men from their positions, although they were manfully contesting every inch of ground. To reach our position we had to pass within a few feet of General Lee. He sat his fine gray horse Traveler, with the cape of his black cloak around his shoulders, his face flushed and full of animation. The balls were flying around him from two directions. His eyes were on the fight then going on south of the Plank Road between Kershaw's division and the flanking columns of the enemy. He had just returned from attempting to lead the Texas Brigade in a charge. He turned in his saddle and called to his chief of staff while pointing with his finger across the road, "Send an active young officer down there."

I thought him at that moment the grandest specimen of manhood I ever beheld. He looked as though he ought to have been, and was, the monarch of the world. He glanced his eye down on the ragged Rebels as they filed to their place in line, and inquired, "What troops are these?" and was answered "Law's Alabama brigade." He exclaimed in a strong voice, "God bless the Alabamians!" The men cheered and went into line with a whoop. The advance began.

It was now nearly nine o'clock in the morning. The Federal lines were some distance in front of the Brock Road, the most direct route to Spotsylvania Court House and to Richmond. They had constructed on it a triple line of fortifications. Situated as the armies were, it was the obvious policy of each commander to double back the wing of the opposing force. The success of General Grant would have opened an unobstructed road to Richmond and might have been decisive of the campaign. That of General Lee might have ended as did the Battle of Chancellorsville a year before. It would at least have interposed his army between General Grant and his objective point. The arrival of Longstreet's corps defeated the plan of Grant and threw him on the defensive.

The effort of General Lee was still to come. The plan of attack was to throw a force upon the flank and rear of Hancock and at the same time assail his front, so as to roll up and press back his entire left wing toward Fredericksburg. The left brigades were to conform their movements to those on their right, holding back, however, so as to constitute a movable pivot on which the whole line might wheel. The successful execution of such a movement would not only have disposed of Hancock for the day, but would have thrown a powerful force perpendicular to General Grant's center and right wing, already confronted by General Ewell.

There was a lull all along the line. It was the ominous stillness that precedes the tornado. Three brigades under Mahone—a dangerous man —were already in position for the flank attack, whose specter seemed to have been haunting Hancock from the beginning. A yell and a volley announced the opening of the tragedy. The din of battle rolled eastward; the enemy was giving way. It was a moment pregnant with momentous results and one of intense anxiety. The left brigades began to move forward. Already they had made considerable progress, and still eastward rolled the fiery billows of war. Could it be that we were on the eve of a great victory? But the fire began to slacken; the advance movement ceased. What could be the cause? Had that single line of attack expended its strength? Oh for a fresh division to be hurled upon that shattered, reeling flank! But no, there were no reserves. The firing ceased, and the victory, almost won, slipped from our grasp.

Longstreet with five brigades had been making the circuit around the enemy's left and had pretty well succeeded in reaching his rear. But the unseen intervened. He and General Micah Jenkins, whose brigade was the largest in the army, were riding together in front of their advancing lines when suddenly they came in view of the enemy. They turned and, while they were riding back through the dense forest, some of their own men mistook them for enemies, fired on them, killed Jenkins and severely wounded Longstreet. This put an end to that movement. What a striking similarity to the fatality which had taken Stonewall Jackson from us!

The Confederate Robert Stiles gives some details on the wounding of Longstreet.

I heard that General Longstreet had just been shot down and was being put into an ambulance. I could not learn anything definite as to the character of his wound, and, when the ambulance moved off, I followed it. The members of his staff surrounded the vehicle. One, I remember, stood upon the rear step of the ambulance, seeming to desire to be as near him as possible. All of them were in tears.

I rode up to the ambulance and looked in. They had taken off Longstreet's hat and coat and boots. The blood had paled out of his face, and its somewhat gross aspect was gone. I noticed how white and domelike his great forehead looked and, with scarcely less reverent admiration, how spotless white were his socks and his fine gauze undervest, save where the red gore from his breast and shoulder had stained it. While I gazed at his massive frame, his eyelids frayed apart, and he very quietly moved his unwounded arm, carefully lifted the saturated undershirt from his chest and heaved a deep sigh. He is not dead, I said to myself, and he is both greater and more attractive than I have heretofore thought him.

Longstreet's retirement from the field need not necessarily have stopped his promising attack. Lieutenant Colonel G. Moxley Sorrel tells of his efforts to have it continued.

The shot which had laid Longstreet low had entered near the throat, and he was almost choked with blood, but he directed me to hasten to General Lee, report what had been accomplished and urge him to continue the movement. The troops were ready, and Grant, he firmly believed, would be driven back across the Rapidan. I rode immediately to General Lee. He was most minute in his inquiries, and praised the handling of the flank attack. Longstreet's message was given, but the general was not in sufficient touch with the position of the troops to proceed with it; at least I received that impression, because activity came to a stop for the moment. A new attack with stronger forces was to be made directly on the enemy's works, lower down the Plank Road, in the hope of dislodging him.

But, meantime, the foe had not been idle. He had used the intervening hours in strengthening his position and making really formidable works across the road. When the Confederate troops assaulted them late in the afternoon, they met with a costly repulse, and with this the principal operations on our part of the field ceased for the day. It was coming on dark.

The rare opportunity on Lee's right had been lost, but Fortune that day once more beckoned to the Confederate cause, this time on the extreme other end of the battle line. The story is told by General Gordon.

The night of the fifth of May was far spent when my command reached its destination on the extreme Confederate left. Scouts were at once sent to the front to ascertain where the extreme right of Grant's line rested. At early dawn they had found it: it rested in the woods only a short distance in our front, was wholly unprotected, and the Confederate lines overlapped it. Moreover, the astounding information was brought that there was not a supporting force within several miles of it! These revelations filled me with confident anticipations of unprecedented victory.

What happened next is reported by Colonel William C. Oates.

Gordon asked leave of General Early, his division commander, to attack the exposed Union flank shortly after dawn. Early declined, giving as a reason that Burnside's corps was in the rear and would strike Gordon's column in the flank and destroy it. Gordon denied that Burnside was in support, and so informed Early, who refused to believe the report. Then Gordon brought it before General Ewell, who hesitated, but would not order the attack over Early's objection. That was a defect with General Ewell—he always desired the approval of some superior.

It was not until late in the afternoon, when Lee arrived on that part of the field and heard Gordon's statement, that he ordered him to attack at once.

Gordon himself now relates how the attack finally was made, and the results it produced.

My Georgia brigade was directed to make the assault, and Johnson's North Carolina brigade was ordered to move farther and gather up Sedgwick's men as they broke to the rear. In less than ten minutes my troops struck the Union flank, shattering regiments and brigades and throwing them into wildest confusion and panic. There was practically no resistance. There could be none. There was nothing for the Federals to do but to fly. The gallant Union leaders, Generals Truman Seymour and Alexander Shaler, with large numbers of their brigades, were quickly gathered as prisoners in the Confederate net, and nearly the whole of Sedgwick's corps was disorganized.

My troops were compelled to halt at last, not by the enemy's resistance, but solely by the darkness. Had daylight lasted one half hour longer, there would not have been left an organized company in Sedgwick's corps. Had the plan of battle I had proposed to Early and Ewell in the morning been accepted, can any impartial military critic suggest a maneuver which could possibly have saved General Grant's army from crushing defeat?

Colonel (later General) Horace Porter, who served as personal aide to Grant, describes how the news of Gordon's attack was received at Union headquarters.

It was about sundown; the storm of battle had been succeeded by a calm. Just then the stillness was broken by heavy volleys of musketry on our extreme right, which told that Sedgwick had been assaulted. The attack against which the general in chief, during the day, had ordered every precaution to be taken had now been made. Staff officers and couriers were soon seen galloping up to Meade's headquarters and his chief of staff, General Andrew A. Humphreys, sent word that a part of Sedgwick's line had been driven back in some confusion. Generals Grant and Meade, accompanied by me and one or two other staff officers, walked rapidly over to Meade's tent and found that the reports still coming in were bringing news of increasing disaster.

Aides came galloping in, laboring under intense excitement, talking wildly and giving the most exaggerated reports of the engagement. Some declared that a large force had scattered Sedgwick's entire corps. Others insisted that the enemy had turned our right completely and captured the wagon train.

A general officer came in at this juncture and said to the general in chief, speaking rapidly and excitedly, "General Grant, this is a crisis that cannot be looked on too seriously. I know Lee's methods well by past experience; he will throw his whole army between us and the Rapidan and cut us off completely."

The general rose, took his cigar out of his mouth and replied, with a degree of animation which he seldom manifested, "Oh, I am tired of hearing what Lee is going to do. Go back to your command and try to think what we are going to do ourselves."

> That Grant knew how closely he had escaped disaster is attested by General J. H. Wilson, then commanding one of Sheridan's cavalry divisions.

About 9:00 P.M. Sheridan's chief of staff came to my headquarters with the first news of the debacle which had befallen Sedgwick's 6th Corps. The situation was one of extraordinary gravity. I rode rapidly to army headquarters to see how Grant had borne the strain.

I found him surrounded by his staff in a state of perfect composure. A few minutes later I withdrew to a private conversation with J. A. Rawlins and T. S. Bowers, Grant's adjutants. They had been with him from the first of the war, had seen him in every battle and knew his idiosyncrasies better than anyone else. They told me that, although Grant had received the reports with his usual self-possession, the coming of officer after officer with additional details soon made it apparent that the general was confronted by the greatest crisis of his life. Still he gave his orders calmly and coherently, without any external sign of undue tension or agitation. But when all proper measures had been taken, Grant went into his tent, threw himself face downward on his cot and gave way to the greatest emotion, but without uttering any word of doubt or discouragement.

What was in his heart can only be inferred but, from what they said, nothing can be more certain than that he was stirred to the very depths of his soul. Rawlins and Bowers were emphatic in declaring that they had never before seen him so deeply moved, and that not till it became apparent that the enemy was not pressing his advantage did he recover his perfect composure.

During the first days in the Wilderness Grant experienced difficulties in communicating with Washington. A messenger, David B. Parker by name, relates how he brought the first dispatch to Lincoln.

I secured passage on one of the patrol boats, reached Washington very late at night and went at once to the War Department, where the lieutenant of the guard took me to the telegraphing room on the second floor, saying that Mr. Lincoln was there.

The lieutenant opened the door of the room and said, "An officer from General Grant."

Almost before I could get into the room Mr. Lincoln stepped forward and said, "Give me the dispatches."

I handed him the dispatch, which was in cipher. Mr. Lincoln expressed impatience, and I told him that I knew the contents of the dispatch which had been read to me so that I might destroy it if necessary. I repeated it to him as well as I could.

He said, "General Grant ought to keep us better informed. This is the first news we have had from him."

I said I knew that messengers had been dispatched each day overland, and that probably they would arrive soon.

He then plied me with questions about the army and its movements. I answered as well as I could, giving such information as I had obtained. Mr. Lincoln looked very haggard and careworn and had evidently arisen from his bed, pulled on some trousers and an old dressing sack and slippers and walked over, a short distance, to the War Department, to see if any news had arrived. His anxiety seemed very great.

He finally said, "Come back early in the morning, and dispatches will be prepared for you to take back."

"What time do you call early, Mr. Lincoln?"

"Five o'clock."

I went away, got a bath and something to eat and was back at the War Department at five o'clock. Mr. Lincoln was in Mr. Stanton's room, and General Halleck and Colonel James A. Hardie also were there. I was given a blue pencil and made to mark on a map the location of the army as well as I could, and to explain all that I knew. Dispatches were given me, and I returned immediately to General Grant.

> After his close call on May 6, Grant, being the aggressor, could be expected to make the next move which, in turn, would determine Lee's countermove. General Gordon vouches for an extraordinary feat performed by Lee that morning.

On the morning of May 7, I was invited by the commanding general to ride with him. I endeavored to learn what movements he had in contemplation. It was then that I learned for the first time of his intention to move at once to Spotsylvania. Reports had it that General Grant's army was retreating or preparing to retreat, but these had not made the slightest impression on his mind. He said in so many words, "General Grant is not going to retreat. He will move his army to Spotsylvania."

I asked him if he had information of such a contemplated change. "Not at all," said Lee, "not at all; but Spotsylvania is now General Grant's best strategic point. I am so sure of his next move that I have already made arrangements to march by the shortest practicable route, so that we may meet him there."

> From a report by Horace Porter:

On May 7 at 6:30 A.M. General Grant issued orders to prepare for a night march of the entire army toward Spotsylvania.

> Theodore Lyman, in a letter written at that time, records a similar attempt by Grant to read Lee's mind.

As General Grant sat under a pine tree, stoically smoking a brierwood pipe, I heard him say, "Tonight Lee will be retreating south." Ah! General, Robert Lee is not Pemberton; he will retreat south, but only far enough to get across your path. Grant had no longer a Pemberton—"his best friend," as he calls him!

The correspondent of the *Boston Journal,* C. C. Coffin, watched while Grant was pondering his next move, and reported the scene to his paper in this manner.

Grant and Meade had retired a little from the crowd and stood by the roadside in earnest conversation—Grant, thoughtful, a cigar in his mouth, a knife in one hand and a stick in the other, which he was whittling to a point. He whittled slowly toward him. His thoughts were not yet crystallized. Suddenly he commenced on the other end of the strick, whittled energetically from him, and word was at once sent to General Warren and the other corps to move in the direction of Spotsylvania.

General Richard H. Anderson, now commanding Longstreet's corps, beat Warren to Spotsylvania, and Grant records the first fighting there.

Anderson soon entrenched himself immediately across Warren's front. Warren assaulted at once, but was repulsed. He soon made a second attack, this time with his whole corps, and succeeded in gaining a position immediately in the enemy's front, where he entrenched.

I was anxious to crush Anderson before Lee could get a force to his support. To this end Sedgwick was ordered to Warren's support. Sedgwick was slow in getting up for some reason—probably unavoidable, because he was never at fault when serious work was to be done—so that it was near night before the combined forces were ready to attack. Even then all of Sedgwick's command did not get into the engagement. Warren led the last assault, one division at a time, and of course it failed.

How fierce this fighting was is indicated by the Union private Theodore Gerrish, who was in Sedgwick's corps.

Our regiment arrived at the scene of conflict at ten o'clock in the morning. We had heard for hours the roar of battle, and learned on our arrival that our own brigade had been desperately engaged and had suffered a severe loss. We changed our position several times on that day. At six o'clock in the evening we were again pushed up to the front, to assault the enemy's position. The troops were in three lines, our regiment being in the third. It was the design of our commander to make the assault under cover of darkness, but unbeknown to us, the Rebels also were preparing to make an assault.

Just at dark there was a heavy crash of musketry and a wild, savage yell as they rushed upon our first line of battle, which soon gave way and fell back upon the second. The confusion was indescribable: it was only with the greatest difficulty that we could tell friend from foe. As we reached the battle, our men gave way and fell back, leaving us in the breach. The Rebels came on with terrible energy. We were alone. The other regiments had all fallen back. Our men were in just the right mood to fight—weary, hungry, discouraged, mad. In such a condition it is as easy to die as to run. We were outnumbered, flanked, almost surrounded.

It was a hand-to-hand conflict, resembling a mob in its character. The contestants seemed to forget all the noble elements of manhood, and for that hour they were brutes, wild with passion and blood. Men were transformed to giants. The air was filled with shouts, cheers, commands, oaths, the sharp reports of rifles, the dull, heavy thuds of clubbed muskets, the swish of swords and sabers, groans and prayers. Occasionally our men would drop their guns and clench the enemy in single combat, until Federal and Confederate would roll on the ground in a death struggle. Our officers fought like demons. Revolvers and swords, which up to that hour had never seen actual service, received their baptism of blood. As the moments passed, the valor of the men increased. Many of those who were wounded refused to go to the rear but, with blood pouring from their wounds, continued to fight.

And thus Blue and Gray fought for victory. On the one side was the hot, brilliant, fiery blood of the South; on the other was the naturally cool and sluggish blood of the distant North, now inflamed to a boiling heat. The lumberman of the North crossed bayonets with the Southern planter, and both lay down to die together.

The country around Spotsylvania was more open than the Wilderness, and both armies were glad to note the change. Horace Porter illustrates this with an amusing incident.

Grant and Meade established their headquarters near Piney Branch Church, about two miles to the east of Todd's Tavern. It was Sunday, but the temple of prayer was voiceless.

A drum corps in passing caught sight of Grant and at once struck up

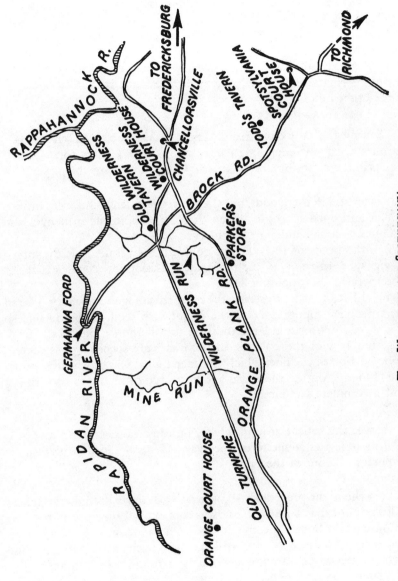

THE WILDERNESS AND SPOTSYLVANIA

a then popular Negro camp-meeting air. Everyone began to laugh, and Rawlins cried, "Good for the drummers!"

"What's the fun?" inquired the general.

"Why," was the reply, "they are playing, 'Ain't I glad to get out ob de wilderness!'"

The General smiled and said, "Well, with me a musical joke always requires explanation. I know only two tunes: one is 'Yankee Doodle,' and the other isn't."

During the next days, from May 8 to May 12, 1864, the two armies were entrenching their positions and feeling for weak spots in the opposing lines. General Gordon presents the picture.

We were still in the woods, but these were less dense and were broken by fields and open spaces in which there was room for maneuver and the more effective handling of artillery.

When the heads of the columns collided, the armies quickly spread into zigzag formation as each brigade, division or corps struck its counterpart in the opposing lines.

General Lee, in order to secure the most advantageous locality offered by the peculiar topography of the country, placed his battle line so that it should conform in large measure to the undulations of the field. Along the brow of these slopes earthworks were speedily constructed. On one portion of the line, which embraced what was afterward known as the "Bloody Angle," there was a long stretch of breastworks forming almost a complete semicircle.

It was this salient around which, on May 12, centered one of the bloodiest encounters of the war. General Gordon gives a colorful account of the event.

During the night preceding May 12, 1864, reports brought by scouts left little doubt that a heavy blow was soon to fall on some portion of the Confederate lines. It came at last, at a point on the salient from which a large portion of the artillery had been withdrawn for use elsewhere. It was held by General Edward Johnson of Virginia.

At about 5:00 A.M. one of the vedettes came hurriedly in from the front and said to me, "General, I think there's something wrong down in the woods near General Edward Johnson—something like officers giving commands, and a jumble of voices."

In the next few minutes there came the positive statement that the enemy had carried the outer angle on General Johnson's front and seemed to be moving in rear of our works. There had been, and still were, so few discharges of small arms—not a heavy gun had been fired —that it was difficult to believe the reports true. But they were accurate.

The surprise had been complete, and the assault practically unresisted. In all its details—its planning, its execution and its fearful import to Lee's army—this charge of Hancock was one of that great soldier's most brilliant achievements.

Meantime my command was rapidly moving toward the captured salient. The mist and fog were so heavy that it was impossible to see far. Before we had moved one-half the distance to the salient the head of my column butted squarely against Hancock's line of battle.

I placed my troops in line for a countercharge. On its success or failure the fate of the Confederate army seemed to hang. General Lee evidently thought so. His army had been cut in twain. Through that wide breach in the Confederate lines, which was becoming wider with every step, the Union forces were rushing like a swollen torrent through a broken milldam. General Lee knew that the Confederate army was in such imminent peril that nothing could rescue it except a countermovement, quick, impetuous and decisive. He resolved to save it, if need be, at the sacrifice of his own life. With perfect self-poise he rode to the margin of that breach and appeared on the scene just as I was in the act of moving in. With uncovered head he turned his face toward Hancock's advancing column. In a voice which I hoped might reach the ears of my troops, I called out, "General Lee, you shall not lead my men. They have never failed you. They will not fail you now."

With the fury of a cyclone my men rushed upon Hancock's advancing column. His leading lines were shivered and hurled back upon their supports. Before Hancock's lines could be reformed, all the officers on horseback in my division were riding among the troops, shouting in unison, "Forward, men, forward!" But the brave line needed no additional spur. Onward they swept, pouring their rapid volleys into Hancock's confused ranks. In the meantime the magnificent troops of Stephen D. Ramseur and Robert E. Rodes were rushing upon Hancock's dissolving corps from another point and were pouring a deadly fire into their ranks. Every foot of the lost salient and earthworks was retaken, except that small stretch which the Confederate line was too short to cover.

> Grant had entertained great hopes of breaking Lee's lines at the salient. Theodore Lyman describes the scene at Federal headquarters while the fighting was going on.

A little after daylight we were all gathered round General Grant's tent, waiting for news. At a little after five o'clock, General Williams approached from the telegraph tent. A smile was on his face: Hancock had carried the first line! Thirty minutes after, another dispatch: he had taken the main line with guns, prisoners and two generals! Great rejoicing now burst forth.

As I stood there waiting, I heard someone say, "Sir, this is General Johnson." I turned round and there was one of the captured major generals walking slowly up. He was a strongly built man of a stern face, and was dressed in a double-breasted blue-gray coat, high riding boots and a very bad felt hat. He was most horribly mortified at being taken and kept coughing to hide his emotion. Generals Meade and Grant shook hands with him, and good General Williams bore him off to breakfast. His demeanor was dignified and proper. Our attack had been a surprise: the assaulting columns rushed over the breastwork without firing a shot, and General Johnson, running out to see the reason of the noise, found himself surrounded by blue blouses.

That night the Rebels fell back from that part of their lines, leaving twenty-two guns, eighteen colors and an estimated 3,500 prisoners in our hands.

> While this fighting was going on, Sheridan made a raid on the Confederate lines of communications. Opposed to him was J. E. B. Stuart's much weaker cavalry. In an encounter on May 11, 1864, near a place called Yellow Tavern about six miles from Richmond, Stuart was wounded.
>
> His aide, Major Heros von Borcke, never forgot the tragic experience.

Stuart's brother-in-law, Dr. Brewer, informed me that my general had been wounded severely and was anxious to see me. I found him in a small room, surrounded by most of the members of his staff. He received me with a smile, saying, "I'm glad you've come, Von. I don't think I'm badly wounded, and hope I shall get over it."

He then recounted to me the manner in which he had been wounded. For more than six hours he had fought with 1,100 men against 8,000. At about four o'clock the Federals succeeded by a general charge in driving back one of our regiments which General Stuart was rallying in an open field. Seeing near him some of the dismounted Federal cavalry, Stuart rode up to them calling on them to surrender and firing at them as they continued their flight. He had just discharged the last barrel of his revolver when the hindmost of the fugitives fired his revolver at him, the ball taking effect in the lower part of the stomach and traversing the whole body. Stuart turned his charger round and galloped half a mile to the rear, where he was taken from his horse nearly insensible from loss of blood and sent in an ambulance to Richmond. During the early part of the morning the general felt comparatively easy, and the physician entertained great hope that the wound might not prove fatal. Toward noon, however, a change took place for the worse.

About this time President Davis visited the prostrate hero. Taking his hand, he said, "General, how do you feel?"

He replied, "Easy, but willing to die."

As evening approached, mortification set in. He became delirious, and his mind wandered over battlefields, then to his wife and children, and again to the front. About five o'clock the general asked Dr. Brewer how long he could live and, being told that death was rapidly approaching, he nodded and said, "I am resigned, if it be God's will."

At about seven o'clock death relieved the suffering hero from his agonies.

The attack on the Bloody Angle was repeated on May 18, after several days of comparative quiet. General Gordon tells with what success.

On the morning of May 18 Grant sent Hancock's corps, reinforced by fully 8,000 fresh troops, with Wright's corps to aid him, back to the point where the assault of May 12 had been made. The attack was to be made by daylight, and not upon the same breastworks, but upon new Confederate entrenchments which had been constructed behind them.

General Grant was to superintend the daring movement in person.

In superb style the Union army moved to the assault. The Confederates were ready for them and, as Hancock's and Wright's brave men climbed over the old abandoned works and debouched from the intervening bushes, a consuming fire of grape, canister and Minié balls was poured in incessant volleys upon them. Such a fire was too much for any troops. They first halted before it and staggered. Then they rallied, moved forward, halted again, wavered, bent into irregular zigzag lines, and at last broke in confusion and precipitate retreat. Again and again they renewed the charge, but each assault ended, as the first, in repulse and heavy slaughter.

Thus ended the second series of battles in which the Union commander had failed to drive the Confederate forces from the field.

For the time being Grant now gave up his frontal assaults and tried to outflank Lee by persistent night marches to the east. But wherever the Union army went, there also went the Confederates, who were always waiting in entrenchments for the arrival of their opponents.

The continuous sidling of both armies along parallel lines elicited these comments from Colonel Theodore Lyman.

May 18, 1864. The great feature of this campaign is the extraordinary use made of earthworks. Bayonets with a few picks and shovels, in the hands of men who work for their lives, soon suffice to make a cover, and within one hour there is a shelter against bullets, extending often for a mile or two. When our line advances, there is the line of the enemy, nothing showing but the bayonets and the battle flags stuck on the top of the work. It is a rule that, when the Rebels halt, the first day gives them a good rifle pit; the second, a regular infantry parapet with artillery in position; and the third a parapet with an abatis in front and entrenched batteries behind. Sometimes they put this three-days' work into the first twenty-four hours. Our men can do, and do the same. But remember, our object is offense—to advance.

Lee is *not* retreating. He is a brave and skillful soldier and will fight while he has a division or a day's rations left. These Rebels are not half-starved—a more sinewy, tawny, formidable-looking set of men could not be. In education they are certainly inferior to our native-born people, but they are usually very quick-witted, and they know enough to handle weapons with terrible effect. Their great characteristic is their stoical manliness: they never beg or whimper or complain but look you straight in the face, with as little animosity as if they had never heard a gun fired.

During these sideways movements there came a day on the North Anna when Grant might have been dealt a serious blow had not a sudden fever, accompanied by delirium, prevented Lee from issuing orders. By the time he recovered, Grant had discovered his perilous position and had withdrawn.

Finally, on June 1, Grant reached Cold Harbor, a place reminiscent of McClellan's Peninsular Campaign, and here he reverted once more to his hammering tactics, for reasons which General Horace Porter sets forth.

A serious problem now presented itself to General Grant—whether to attempt to crush Lee's army on the north side of the James, with the prospect of driving him into Richmond, capturing the city perhaps without siege, or to move the Union army south of the James without giving battle and transfer the field of operations to the vicinity of Petersburg. It was a nice question of judgment. After discussing the matter thoroughly with his principal officers and weighing all the chances, he decided to attack Lee's army in its present position. He had succeeded in breaking the enemy's line at other places in circumstances which were not more favorable, and the results to be obtained now would be so great that it seemed wise to make the attempt.

Horace Porter, continuing his narrative, shows that the Union soldiers were fully aware of what the contemplated frontal attack meant to them.

In passing along on foot among the troops the previous evening (June 2), I noticed that many of the soldiers had taken off their coats and seemed to be engaged in sewing up rents in them. On closer examination it was found that the men were calmly writing their names and home addresses on slips of paper and pinning them on the backs of their coats, so that their dead bodies might be recognized and their fate made known to their families at home.

At 4:30 A.M., June 3, three columns under Hancock, Wright and W. F. Smith, respectively, moved forward to the attack. Hancock's troops struck a salient of the enemy's works and after a desperate struggle captured it, taking a couple of hundred prisoners, three guns and a stand of colors. Then, turning the captured guns upon the enemy, they drove him from that part of the line into his main works, a short distance in the rear. Our second line, however, did not move up in time to support the first, which was finally driven back and forced out. Another division had rushed forward, but an impassable swamp divided the troops, who were now subjected to a galling fire of artillery and musketry and, although a portion of them gained the enemy's entrenchments, their ranks had become too much weakened and scattered to hold their position, and they were compelled to fall back.

Wright's corps had moved forward and carried the rifle pits in its front, and then assaulted the main line. This was too strong, however, to be captured, and our troops were compelled to retire. Nevertheless, they held a line and protected it as best they could, at a distance of only thirty or forty yards from the enemy.

Smith made his assault by taking advantage of a ravine, but the same cross fire from which Wright had suffered made further advances extremely hazardous. His troops were so cut up that there was no prospect of carrying the works in his front, unless the enfilading fire on his flank could be silenced.

At eleven o'clock General Grant rode out along the lines. Hancock reported that the position in his front could not be taken. Wright stated that a lodgment might be made in his front, but that nothing would be gained by it unless Hancock and Smith were to advance at the same time. Smith thought that he might be able to carry the works before him, but was not sanguine.

The general in chief at half past twelve wrote the following order to General Meade: "You may direct a suspension of farther advance for the present."

That evening the general said, "I regret this assault more than any one I have ever ordered. I regarded it as a stern necessity; but, as it has proved, no advantages have been gained sufficient to justify the heavy losses suffered." Subsequently the matter was seldom referred to in conversation.

James M. Nichols, a captain in the 48th New York Volunteers, a regiment whose men called themselves Perry's Saints, relates his experiences of the afternoon of June 3 after the main assault had broken down.

Arrived at Cold Harbor, we received the order to attack the enemy's works. The 47th New York Regiment, which was on our left, had already moved away, and still no word of command was given. What should we do? The greatest excitement prevailed. "Charge bayonets!" sounded across the field, and the first line of the enemy's rifle pits was occupied. In little more time than it takes to write it we had captured and occupied a section of the main line of Confederate works and had more prisoners marching to the rear than the whole number present in the regiment.

How much was crowded into the short time that we occupied that line of entrenchment! It was a dreadful place to hold, with the Rebels pouring in upon us a deadly flanking fire. Repeated messages were sent to the commanding general explaining our situation, but no help, and no word of any kind, was received. Efforts were made to induce the 47th New York, which was separated from us by a little ravine, to unite with us in a charge, but without avail. And so we were compelled to wait and suffer.

As the shadows deepened about us, there came a rush. The enemy was fairly upon us and, before we could gather ourselves, someone without authority had called out to retreat. Back through the woods we went, broken and dispirited. There we found the commander of a division reclining under a tree in a state of helplessness and demoralization. Completely beside himself because of the defeat and dispersion of his command, he insisted that our feeble line of officers and men should renew the attack, when a whole division had been defeated and scattered. We left him to his own reflections.

Already darkness had settled on us, and we lay down for a little rest in the field over which the regiment had so gallantly charged that afternoon.

The terrible Union losses at Cold Harbor, around 7,000 killed and wounded in less than one hour, are explained by the Confederate artillery officer Robert Stiles.

We were in line of battle at Cold Harbor from the first to the twelfth of June—say twelve days. The battle proper did not last perhaps that many minutes. In some respects at least it was one of the notable battles of history—certainly in its brevity measured in time and its length measured in slaughter, as also in the disproportion of the losses. For my own part, I could scarcely say whether it lasted eight or sixty minutes, or eight or sixty hours, all my powers being concentrated on keeping the guns supplied with ammunition.

Here, then, is the secret of the otherwise inexplicable butchery. A little after daylight on June 3, 1864, along the lines of our salient, our infantry and our artillery fired at very short range into a mass of men twenty-eight deep, who could neither advance nor retreat, and the most of whom could not even discharge their muskets at us.

Federal writers who have written about this battle speak about our works as bastions no troops could be expected to take, and *any troops* should be expected to hold.

About the works along our part of the line I can speak with exactness and certainty. I saw them, I helped with my own hands to make them, I fought behind them. They were a single line of earth about four feet high and three to five feet thick. It had no ditch or obstruction in front. There was no physical difficulty in walking right over that bank. I did it often myself, saw many others do it, and twice saw a line of Federal troops walk over it.

I wonder if it could have been the *men* behind the works!

The Cold Harbor defeat had a decided effect on Grant's future strategy, as General James H. Wilson points out.

At Grant's headquarters I found, in the early days of June, a feeling of despondency. Grant himself, while neither cast down nor discouraged, evidently felt disappointed at his failure to overwhelm Lee. Both Rawlins and Dana, able and experienced men, were disposed to hold Grant himself responsible for making head-on attacks against entrenched and almost impregnable positions. They feared that the policy of the direct and continuous attack, if persisted in, would ultimately so decimate and discourage the rank and file that they could not be induced to face the enemy at all.

Certain it is that the "smash-'em-up" policy was abandoned about that time and was never again favored at headquarters.

Horace Porter relates how Grant's decision to change his fighting style resulted in a complete alteration of his campaign plans.

The time had now come when Grant was to carry out his alternative movement of throwing the entire army south of the James River. Halleck, who was rather fertile in suggestions although few of them were ever practicable, had written Grant about the advisability of throwing his army round by the right flank, for the reason that it would better protect the capital. Grant said, "We can defend Washington best by keeping Lee so occupied that he cannot detach enough troops to capture it. I shall prepare at once to move across the James River."

General Grant was making careful preparations for the formidable movement he was about to undertake, for he was fully impressed with its hazardous nature. The army had to be withdrawn so quietly from its position that it would be able to gain a night's march before its absence should be discovered. The fact that the lines were within thirty or forty yards of each other at some points made this an exceedingly delicate task. Roads had to be constructed over the marshes leading to the lower Chickahominy, and bridges thrown over that stream preparatory to crossing. The army was then to move to the James, and cross upon pontoon bridges and improvised ferries. This would involve a march of about fifty miles in order to reach Butler's position, while Lee, holding interior lines, could arrive there by a march of less than half that distance.

In the afternoon of June 6 the general called Colonel C. B. Comstock and me into his tent and said with more impressiveness of manner than he usually manifested, "I want you to go to Bermuda Hundred, and explain the contemplated movement fully to General Butler and see that the necessary preparations are made by him to render his position secure against any attack from Lee's forces while the Army of the Potomac is making its movement. You will then select the best point on the river for the crossing."

Comstock and I had served on General McClellan's staff, and the country for many miles along the river was quite familiar to us. We returned to headquarters on June 12 and reported unhesitatingly in favor of a point about ten miles below City Point.

While listening to our report Grant showed the only nervousness he had ever manifested in my presence. After smoking his cigar vigorously for some minutes, he removed it from his mouth, put it on the table and allowed it to go out; then relighted it, gave a few puffs and laid it aside again. We could hardly get the words out of our mouths fast enough to suit him, and the numerous questions he asked were uttered with much greater rapidity than usual. At the close of the interview he informed us that he would begin the movement that night.

Porter reports how skillfully the transfer of the army to the south of the James was effected.

Warren's corps withdrew on the night of June 12-13 from the position to which it had advanced, and reached the James on the afternoon of the fourteenth.

Grant, with the bulk of his forces, was marching in an entirely different direction. On the fourteenth he ran up the river to Bermuda Hundred to have a personal interview with General Butler and arrange plans for an attack upon Petersburg. Grant knew now that he had stolen a march on Lee, and that Petersburg was almost undefended.

The work of laying the great pontoon bridge across the James began after 4:00 P.M. on June 14 and was finished by eleven o'clock that night. It was 2,100 feet in length and required 101 pontoons. Admiral Samuel P. Lee's fleet took position in the river and assisted in covering the passage of the troops.

By midnight of the sixteenth the army, with all its artillery and trains, had been safely transferred to the south side of the James.

Lee now decided to try once more the time-tested expedient of threatening Washington, in order to force a weakening of Grant's army.

General John B. Gordon recalls the beginning of this campaign.

As the Union army prepared to cross the James, it was decided that we should again threaten Washington. The Federal authorities sent General Lew Wallace to meet our command, under General Early, at Monocacy River, near Frederick, Maryland. His business was to check the Southern invaders and, if possible, to drive them back across the Potomac.

The Battle of Monocacy which ensued was short, decisive and bloody. Wallace's army, after the most stubborn resistance and heavy loss, was driven in the direction of Baltimore. The way to Washington was open.

On July 11, 1864, we were at the defenses of the capital. Undoubtedly we could have marched into Washington, but in the council of war called by General Early there was not a dissenting opinion as to the impolicy of entering the city.

Early himself subsequently declared that he had examined the fortifications confronting him, and had found them too strong for an assault by his weakened forces. One of his soldiers, however, John N. Opie, held a different opinion.

When we reached the suburbs, it could be easily seen that the men who occupied the works were not organized troops. A volley, a Rebel yell, and a vigorous charge would have given us Washington. Having captured the city, we could have easily marched across the bridge to Alexandria and back to Virginia. He was about the only man in the army who believed it impossible of accomplishment.

War correspondent Cadwallader of the *New York Herald* agreed with Opie.

I have always wondered at Early's inaction. Washington was never more helpless. Our lines in his front could have been carried at any point. Any such cavalry commander as Sheridan, Wilson, Hampton or Stuart could have burned the White House, the Capital and all public buildings. It has been stated that Early supposed Washington was fairly protected by Federal troops. But this is a very poor excuse. It was his business to inform himself.

Benjamin Taylor, correspondent of the *Chicago Evening Journal*, reported the tension in Washington at Early's approach.

Sunday, July 10. Newsboys singing out "Rebels a-marching on Washington" startle you. The city hears rumors; it whistles and tries to look unconcerned.

The President visits the works. Heavy artillery and reserve guards are moved to the northern fortification. I stroll along the Avenue. Everybody is saying "trenches . . . cavalry . . . defenses . . . Rebels." Night comes, and the tramp of marching regiments beats the pavements. It is the advance of the 6th Corps, General Wright commanding, en route for Fort Stevens, and not a minute too soon.

Tuesday morning found the Federal capital humming. Long guns sprouted with bayonets are going about in company with short clerks;

black-coated civilians take the beat of blue-coated guards. The clerks in the departments have "grounded" pens and shouldered arms, and everybody is tugging some sort of a death-dealing tool. The 6th Corps is in position; other troops are arriving; the enemy's opportunity, if he ever had one, is utterly gone.

In the morning the whole front, for miles out, is as empty as a drum.

Early's attempt to weaken Grant had failed, but he stayed on in the Shenandoah Valley to oppose Sheridan, who was threatening to destroy the supplies on which Richmond largely depended for its existence. General Gordon, who commanded one of Early's divisions, tells what happened during the remainder of the summer of 1864.

Thenceforward to the end of July, through the entire month of August and during more than half of September 1864, Early's little army was marching and countermarching toward every point of the compass in the Shenandoah Valley, with scarcely a day of rest, skirmishing, fighting, rushing hither and thither to meet and drive back cavalry raids, while General Sheridan gathered his army of more than double our numbers for his general advance up the valley.

The reports of the Federal approach, however, did not seem to impress General Early, and he delayed concentration until Sheridan was upon him in the vicinity of Winchester, ready to devour him piecemeal.

One division was nearly overwhelmed. Breckinridge's troops were furiously fighting on another part of the field, and they, too, were soon doubled up by charges in front and on the flank. This left not more than 6,000 men in all to contend with Sheridan's whole army of about 30,000 men, reaching in both directions far beyond our exposed right and left. The vast plain to our left was left open for the almost unobstructed sweep of the Federal horsemen, when night came and dropped her protecting curtains around us.

General Sheridan graciously granted us two days and a part of the third to rest and pull ourselves together for the struggle of September 22. The Battle of Fisher's Hill was so quickly ended that it may be described in a few words. Indeed, to all experienced soldiers the whole story is told in one word—"flanked."

The Confederates saw the hopelessness of their situation and realized that they had only the option of retreat or capture. They were not long in deciding. The retreat—it is always so—was at first stubborn and slow, then rapid, then—a rout.

> The Battle of Fisher's Hill seemed to have disposed of Early; but he received reinforcements, as a result of which matters took an unexpected turn. Alexander Hunter writes about them.

Sheridan, after administering a crushing defeat to Early at Fisher's Hill, went into camp. His officers and men sat at ease, enjoying the glorious Virginia autumn weather.

Sheridan's right was protected by his corps of superb cavalry, 10,000 strong; his left was perfectly secure; at least he and his subordinates thought so, as they gazed at the precipitous front of Massanutten Mountain and the swift-flowing river beneath.

General Gordon climbed to the top of the Massanutten and, from this aerie, with powerful field glasses saw every man, horse and gun at his feet, and the soldiery taking things as coolly as if there was not a Rebel nearer than Richmond. As he gazed on the scene, he must have felt the same fierce joy that Stonewall Jackson did when he saw Hooker's right wing at Chancellorsville. If Early approved of his plan and let him follow it to the end, the total destruction of Sheridan was inevitable.

There was a narrow path that zigzagged down the rocky fastness of Massanutten, and all that night the hardy infantry crept and glided in single file along this low tract, and forded and swam the Shenandoah, and at dawn of day formed in line of battle within pistolshot of Sheridan's sleeping army.

Gordon gave the word "Forward!"

The silence of the solemn calm morn was broken by the Rebel yell issuing from thousands of throats.

Never was a surprise more complete, never was there a success more quickly earned. The Federal soldiers who were not shot down had either to surrender or seek safety in flight.

An hour after sunrise the Federal camp was captured, and nearly all their artillery was seized. Their fine cavalry force was panic-stricken and retreated before Thomas L. Rosser's attack. The 6th Corps of Sheridan's army alone kept its formation, but was badly rattled.

Gordon now made his final preparations for the coup; his army was fresh, united, and wild with victory. Gordon being ready, he drew back his arm to strike. His lips were parted to give the signal to advance when that evil genius of the South stopped the blow.

> The Union general A. B. Nettleton gives us the next chapter of the story, having lived through it.

On October 12 our scouts reported that Early's infantry force had advanced to Fisher's Hill, their old Gibraltar, six miles south of our position at Cedar Creek, which intelligence caused Sheridan to halt the 6th Corps near Front Royal to await developments. Lieutenant General Grant had recommended that a part of Sheridan's force should establish a strong position in the vicinity of Manassas Gap. To this Sheridan demurred and was summoned to Washington for a conference. He started out on the sixteenth.

Midnight of October 18-19 came, and with it no sound but the tramp of the tired sentinels. One o'clock, and all was tranquil as a peace convention; two, three o'clock, and yet the soldiers slept. At four the silence was broken by sharp firing toward the western side of the valley, suggesting an attack in force by cavalry. General G. A. Custer quietly dispatched a regiment to support our outposts. Fifteen minutes later heavy skirmish firing was heard on the left of the infantry.

As we came into full view of the field, the whole sickening truth flashed upon us—the infantry had been surprised in their beds by Early's reinforced army; our best artillery was already in the hands of the Confederates and turned against us; thousands of our men had been killed, wounded or captured before they could even offer resistance; Sheridan's victorious and hitherto invincible army was routed and in disorderly retreat before a confident, yelling and pursuing enemy. A brave nucleus of the army was fighting with determined pluck to prevent disaster from becoming disgrace.

At 9:00 A.M. a portion of the enemy's troops were plundering the camps where the 6th Corps had slept the night before; our left was being pressed with great vigor by a flanking force which seemed determined to reach the pike and thus strike our wagon trains. General Wright had resolved on a retreat to a new line near Winchester, and the best we hoped for was that our mounted troops could so retard the pursuit as to prevent the annihilation of the broken army and the exposure of Washington.

Gordon himself now tells of the fatal blunder by "the evil genius of the South," General Early.

Sheridan's 6th Corps was at that hour largely outnumbered and I had directed every Confederate command then subject to my orders to assail it in front and upon both flanks simultaneously.

Just then General Early came upon the field, and said, "Well, Gordon, this is glory enough for one day. This is the nineteenth. Precisely one month ago today we were going in the opposite direction."

I pointed to the 6th Corps and explained the movements I had ordered. When I had finished, he said, "No use, they will all go directly." And so it came to pass that the fatal halting in the face of the sullen and orderly retreat of this superb Federal corps lost us the great opportunity. The 6th Corps could not possibly have escaped had the proposed concentration upon it and around it been permitted.

General Nettleton describes how the battle ended.

Suddenly we heard, far to the rear of us, a faint cheer go up, as a hurrying horseman dashed down that historic road toward our line of battle. As he drew nearer we could see that the coal-black horse was flecked with foam, both horse and rider grimed with dust. A moment more, and a deafening cheer broke from the troops as they recognized in the coming horseman their longed-for Sheridan. The news flashed from brigade to brigade along our front, and then, as Sheridan, cap in hand, dashed along the rear of the struggling line, hope took the place of fear. The entire aspect of things changed in a moment. Further retreat was no longer thought of. At all points to the rear, stragglers could be seen by hundreds voluntarily rejoining their regiments with such arms as they could hastily find. Order seemed to have come spontaneously out of chaos, an army out of a rabble.

The enemy, believing the continued cheers announced the arrival of Federal reinforcements, became more cautious and threw up breastworks. Our commander instantly sent orders to the 6th and 19th Corps to hasten up to our support. By two o'clock our lines were fully reformed. By this time Early made a confident assault upon our lines. The attack was repulsed at every point.

At 4:00 P.M. the command was sent to prepare for a general forward movement. Two hundred bugles sounded the advance. All our artillery opened on the enemy with shot and shell, and the long line of cavalry and infantry moved steadily forward under a heavy fire toward the Rebel position. To one who had seen the rout and panic and loss of the morning, it seemed impossible that this was the same army.

As soon as the Confederate infantry was fully engaged with ours in the center, the order was given for the cavalry divisions to charge both flanks of the enemy's line.

The effect was magical. The enemy's mounted troops first made a stout resistance, then scattered to the hills, and his infantry line, having both flanks turned back upon itself and its center crushed by a final magnificent charge of our infantry, broke in confusion. Panic seized every part of the Rebel force. Infantry vied with artillery and both with the wagon trains, in a harum-scarum race and, as the sun went down, the army which at daybreak had gained one of the most dramatic and overwhelming victories of the war was a frantic rabble, flying before the same army it had twelve hours before so completely surprised and routed.

> With Early's defeat at Cedar Creek possession of the Shenandoah Valley definitely passed into Union hands, and eventually Early was recalled. The war in the East from now on centered on Petersburg.
> Petersburg, about twenty-two miles south of Richmond, was the key to the Confederate capital.
> The editors of *Harper's Weekly*, Alfred H. Guernsey and Henry M. Alden, point out its importance.

Petersburg itself was of little consequence to either army. Its military importance arose solely from its relations to the system of railroads which connected Richmond with the region from which its supplies were drawn. Had the Confederate capital been provisioned for a siege, Petersburg might safely have been abandoned. But at no time were full rations for a fortnight in advance ever accumulated—oftener there was not three-days' supply in depot. The possession of Petersburg would insure the capture of Richmond by giving to the assailants the absolute control of the Weldon and Southside Railroads, and rendering almost certain that of the Danville Railway: two certainly, and almost inevitably a third, of the five avenues of supply for the Confederate army.

Grant had convinced himself that, due to Butler's ineptitude, the opportunity of taking Petersburg by a quick assault had been lost. Jefferson Davis cites by what other means Richmond was next to be menaced.

General Grant now determined on the method of slow approaches and proceeded to confront the city with a line of earthworks. By gradually extending the line to his left he hoped to reach out toward the Weldon and Southside Railroads.

The line of General Lee conformed to that of General Grant. Besides the works east and southeast of Richmond, an exterior line of defense had been constructed against the hostile forces at Deep Bottom and, in addition to a fortification of some strength at Drewry's Bluff, obstructions were placed in the river to prevent the ascent of the Federal gunboats. The lines thence continued facing those of the enemy north of the Appomattox, crossing that stream, extending around the city of Petersburg, gradually moving westward with the works of the enemy. The struggle that ensued consisted chiefly of attempts to break through our lines.

Siege operations were slow, and a direct assault on Petersburg would have been too costly. Hence a different scheme was proposed to break through the town's defenses. General Regis de Trobriand tells about it.

The project proposed was the laying of a mine, by means of which a part of the enemy entrenchments were to be blown up. This plan had occurred to Lieutenant Colonel Henry Pleasants, an old civil engineer, now commanding the 48th Pennsylvania. General Burnside approved, and the next morning Colonel Pleasants set to work.

The chief engineers of the army declared that the project was foolish; that a mine as long as that had never been dug; that it could not be done. But Colonel Pleasants, left to himself, continued his work with unshakable perseverance. He was refused timber; he sent for it to a sawmill out of the lines. They refused him mining picks; he had the common picks in the division fixed over. They refused him wheelbarrows; he had the earth carried out in cracker boxes.

The work, begun June 25, was finished on July 23, without accident. Everything promised success.

Immediately after the explosion two brigades were to pass through the opening made in the enemy's works, in two columns, one to turn to the right, and the other to the left. Three other divisions would charge directly for the summit of the hill. After them would advance the 18th Corps, and our success seemed assured. Once established on the hill, Petersburg would be ours on July 30.

The hour set for the explosion was half past three in the morning. Everyone was up, the officers watch in hand, eyes fixed on the fated redan. From after three the minutes were counted. . . . It is still too dark, it was said. . . . At four o'clock it was daylight; nothing stirred as yet. At a quarter past four a murmur of impatience ran through the ranks. What has happened? Has there been a counterorder or an accident?

What had happened was that the fuse, which was ninety feet long, had gone out at a splice about halfway of its length. Two intrepid men volunteered to relight it. Suddenly the earth trembled under our feet. An enormous mass sprang into the air. Without form or shape, full of red flames and carried on a bed of lightning flashes, it mounted toward heaven with a detonation of thunder. It spread out like an immense mushroom whose stem seemed to be of fire and its head of smoke.

Then everything appeared to break up and fall back in a rain of earth mixed with rocks, beams, timbers and mangled human bodies, leaving floating in the air a cloud of white smoke and a cloud of gray dust, which fell slowly toward the earth. The redan had disappeared. In its place had opened a gaping gulf more than 200 feet long and 50 wide and 25 to 30 feet deep.

All our batteries opened at once on the enemy's entrenchments, and the 1st Brigade advanced to the assault.

It had nothing in front of it. The Confederate troops occupying the lines in the immediate vicinity of the mine had fled precipitately. The way was completely open to the summit of the hill.

The column marched to the crater but instead of turning around it, descended into it. Once at the bottom, finding itself sheltered, it stayed there. The general commanding the division had remained within our lines, in a bombproof.

The 2nd Brigade was soon mixed up with the other. Several regiments descended into the crater, but only one brigade succeeded in making its way through so as to advance beyond. It found itself then engaged in ground cut up by trenches, by covered ways, by sheltered pits dug in the ground. Worse than that, the enemy, recovering from his surprise, had already placed his guns in position and formed his infantry so as to throw a concentrated fire upon the opening made in his works. The brigade, seeing that it was neither supported nor reinforced, was compelled to fall back with loss.

The 3rd Brigade had not even made a like attempt. Mingling with the first, it had simply increased the confusion.

Time was flying; the chances of success were disappearing as we were looking on. Nothing could force the troops, crowded together in the crater, to leave their positions. The greater part of the officers remained, like the men, motionless in a state of paralysis.

Toward seven o'clock a colored brigade received orders to advance in its turn. The Negroes advanced resolutely, passed over the passive mass of white troops, not a company of whom followed them, and charged under a deadly fire of artillery and musketry, which reached them from all sides at once. They even reached the enemy, took from him 250 prisoners, captured a flag and recovered one of ours taken by him. But they were not sustained. They were driven back by a counter-charge and returned running in confusion to our lines where, by this time, a large number of the white troops were eager to return with them.

In a moment it was a general *devil-take-the-hindmost*, a confused rush in which those who could run fast enough and escape the Rebel fire returned to our lines. Those who endeavored to resist, or were delayed, were taken prisoners.

Thus passed away the finest opportunity which could have been given us to capture Petersburg.

> The Union army now again settled down to regular siege operations. The private Theodore Gerrish recalls his routine life in the trenches.

The defenses of Petersburg consisted of redans, redoubts and infantry parapets, with an outer line of defenses, abatis, stakes and *chevaux-de-frise*, constructed by the most skillful engineers. To hold Lee's army in check we must have defenses equally elaborate, and quickly the work of construction began.

A battle would be raging at some point along our extensive line nearly every day. One day all would be peaceable: the Rebels would come outside their works, and we would clamber out over ours, and not a shot would be fired from either line. In two hours from that time, perhaps, the great shells would be flying from either side and, if a man put his head above the breastworks, it was certain death.

We learned to tell by the sound the nature of every missile and knew just which ones to dodge. The mortar shells had the most terror for us. The ordinary fieldpieces or siege guns did not disturb us much, but those confounded mortars, whose shells would descend plump within our lines! The bombproofs were damp and unhealthy, so we had our tents out in the open air and fled to the bombproofs when danger threatened us.

The only way in which we could hope to drive the Rebels from their positions was to extend our lines to the left and get possession of the great lines of railway, but it was a most difficult task to perform. Lee had the inside of the circle, and consequently his lines were much more contracted than ours. He was also acting on the defensive and in such a position that he could see any movement that was being made by our troops. If Grant moved any portion of his army to the extreme left, he would weaken some other point in the line. Lee, knowing this, would hurl his troops either upon this weakened point or upon the force moving to the left, and a success to him in either case would be very disastrous to us.

The idea of the mine brought in its wake proposals for other novel methods of warfare. Among those who favored them was General Benjamin Butler, about whom Colonel Theodore Lyman, General Meade's personal aide, made some pungent remarks in a letter dated November 29, 1864.

Butler never is happy unless he has half a dozen contrivances on hand. An idea that Benjamin considered highly practicable was a fire engine, wherewith he proposed to squirt water on earthworks and wash them all down. Then, with Greek fire, he proposed to hold a redoubt with only five men and a small garden engine. "Certainly," said General Meade. "Only your engine fires thirty feet, and a rifle 3,000 yards, and I am afraid your five men might be killed before they had a chance to burn up their adversaries!" Butler also was going to get a gun that would shoot seven miles and, taking direction by compass, burn the city of Richmond with shells of Greek fire. If that didn't do, he had an auger to bore a tunnel five feet in diameter, and he was going to bore to

Richmond and suddenly pop up in somebody's basement while the family were at breakfast! So, you see, he is ingenious.

Both armies did, however, have real down-to-earth inventors in their ranks. Foremost among those in the Confederate army, according to William M. Owen, was Colonel E. P. Alexander, chief of artillery of Longstreet's corps.

Colonel Alexander was always doing and suggesting something new. During the siege of Petersburg he invented all sorts of contraptions, such as wooden mortars, sharpshooters' boxes, which were so placed on the works that the men could get an oblique fire and not run the risk of a direct shot from the enemy's quick-eyed marksmen. He also furnished the guns along the lines with bulletproof oak shields.

He introduced a system of awards for the men who could collect the largest amount of leaden bullets and fragments of shell fired by the enemy, and would have the men chasing projectiles and fragments even before the former exploded.

It was while collecting bullets himself one day, in sight of the enemy, that he was dangerously wounded.

A few sidelights on the food situation inside Richmond during the siege may be gathered from the diary of the war clerk J. B. Jones.

July 31, 1864. This morning a chicken was found in my yard brought hither by a cat. A portion of the breast only had been eaten, and our cook seized upon the remains. To such straits are we reduced by this cruel war!

August 4. Public meetings and the press continue to denounce in unmeasured terms the high schedule of prices.

August 30. The Secretaries of State, Navy, and the Postmaster General are getting to be as fat as bears, while some of the subordinates I know of are becoming mere shadows from scarcity of food.

January 12, 1865. General Lee says he has not *two days'* rations for his army!

William M. Owen in a buoyant spirit tells about lighter moments during the siege.

While we were in the trenches and matters comparatively quiet, we would often slip into town and get the girls together and have a dance. On several occasions while we were thus enjoying ourselves, furious firing would break out, and the officers would have to scamper, but not without securing a partner for a dance after their return.

An hour or so would pass, and we would return and say, "You have kept the dance for me, Miss——? Only a small affair: one man killed, that's all."

"Oh, is that all!" she would reply. "Come, they are forming the set."

The same officer also relates an amusing incident which happened during the intermittent fighting between the two armies.

During one of the battles around Petersburg, Colonel Charles Marshall, of General Lee's staff, was riding a horse that he had lately purchased. He happened to be riding through a field that had some large stumps in it. Marshall found his horse capering about in a queer fashion. Espying a large stump, the steed placed his forefeet on it and began moving around in a sort of waltz. The hotter the fire, the more he would waltz. The colonel had no desire to keep the thing up—it was getting monotonous—but all at once there was a lull in the conflict, and then the horse was as easily guided as the colonel wished.

The mystery was solved shortly afterward. The horse Colonel Marshall had bought was a circus horse.

On the Federal side this winter also brought some humor-filled moments, to judge by what Colonel Lyman wrote home.

As we sat at breakfast one morning, there came a dispatch saying that Honorable Secretary Stanton, with a long tail, might be looked for, per rail, very presently. General Meade thus expressed his gratification at this deep honor. "The devil! I shan't have time to smoke my cigar."

Immediately I got on my double-barreled coat and a pair of white cotton gloves, but there was plenty of time to smoke a cigar, for they didn't get along for an hour or two, and then came the greatest posse of large bugs! First, on horseback, Generals Grant, M. C. Meigs (Quartermaster General), John G. Barnard, John Eaton (Commissary General), Joseph K. Barnes (Surgeon General), young Fessenden. Then, in ambulances, Fessenden's papa, the Secretary of the Treasury, a sharp, keen, quiet-looking man, and Honorable Secretary Stanton, who looks like his photographs, only more so.

General Meade received them with his usual high ceremony. He walked out of his tent, with his hands in his pockets, said, "Hullo, how are you?" and removed one hand for the purpose of extending it to Grant, who lighted down from his horse, put his hands in his pockets and sat down on a camp chair. We carted them all to see Fort Wadsworth, where Mr. Stanton, on being informed that there was only a picket line between him and the enemy, pulled out his watch and said they really must be going back! Which indeed they did.

> The food situation of Lee's army once was temporarily relieved in an unusual way, as telegrapher Plum tells us.

In September 1864 the most successful wire-tapping of the war was accomplished by one of Lee's operators named Gaston, who had been chosen for the hazardous undertaking of tapping Grant's wires. He was accompanied by a few men under General Roger A. Pryor, who were, so far as appeared, peaceable citizens engaged in chopping wood. Gaston opened his office on the military line connecting City Point with the Federal War Department, but for six weeks but one intercepted message was worthwhile, but this one proved of incalculable value. It was from the Quartermaster in Washington, and requested a guard to meet 2,486 cattle where they would be landed. Instead, Wade Hampton with a large body of rebel cavalry arrived there in time to receive the cattle and convoy them to the Confederate army, which thus was supplied for about forty days.

> During idle hours some soldiers, like the Confederate Lieutenant R. M. Collins, fell to meditating.

As we lay there watching the bright stars and listening to the twitter of the little birds in their nests, many a soldier asked himself the questions: What is all this about? Why is it that 200,000 men of one blood and one tongue, believing as one man in the fatherhood of God and the universal brotherhood of man, should in the nineteenth century of the Christian era be thus armed with all the improved appliances of modern warfare and seeking one another's lives? We could settle our differences by compromising and all be at home in ten days.

On the Federal side, Colonel Lyman expressed ideas which were not much different.

Sometimes I feel like saying to the Rebels, "You're as brave a set of men as ever were, and honest—the mass of you. Take what territory you have left, and go and live with your own delusions." Instead of being exasperated at the Southerners by fighting against them, I have a great deal more respect for them than ever I had in peacetime. There is no shadow of doubt that the body of the Southerners are as honestly, as earnestly and as religiously interested in this war as the body of the Northerners.

To his paper Cadwallader wrote about the bad effect of the prevailing inactivity on the morale of the Union army.

The soldier who will face instant and almost certain death under the excitement of the battle, becomes the most restless mortal when confined to the daily routine. He becomes morbidly discontented and homesick.

During the fall and winter desertions became alarming. Some went over to the enemy, thinking, no doubt, that escape from there to their homes would be easier. But the Confederates induced or compelled some to enter the rebel service, and several were captured bearing arms against the United States.

Inside the Confederacy dissension was becoming plainly visible to war clerk Jones, who also noted President Davis' attention to trivialities.

September 26, 1864. A long letter was received today from Governor Brown, of Georgia. He says if the President won't send reinforcements, he demands the return of Georgia troops to defend his state.

December 3. A "peace resolution" has been introduced in the North Carolina Legislature.

November 1, 1864. The President attends to many little matters, such as solicitations for passports; and the ladies who address him, knowing his religious bias, frame their phraseology accordingly.

December 5. Congress has passed a resolution declaring that it was not meant, in calling for the ages of the clerks in the departments, to include the ladies.

December 23. The President is hard at work making majors.

While the President is incapacitated both mentally and physically by disease, disaster and an inflexible defiance of his opponents, Congress wastes its time in discussions on the adoption of a *flag* for future generations!

The year 1864 had come to an end, and outwardly the position of the two opposing armies before Petersburg was much the same as it had been six months before. As Grant looked over the situation before him, he found much to worry about.

One of the most anxious periods of my experience during the Rebellion was the last few weeks before Petersburg. I felt that the situation of the Confederate army was such that they would try to make an escape at the earliest practicable moment, and I was afraid, every morning, that I would awake to hear that Lee had gone. He had his railroad by the way of Danville south, and I knew he could move much more lightly and more rapidly than I. If he got the start, the war might be prolonged another year.

I could not see how it was possible for the Confederates to hold out much longer where they were. Desertions were taking place throughout the whole Confederacy. It was my belief that the enemy were losing at least a regiment a day by desertions alone. It was a mere question of arithmetic to calculate how long they could hold out.

For these and other reasons I was naturally very impatient to commence the spring campaign.

There were two considerations I had to observe, however, which detained me. One was the fact that the roads were impassable for artillery and teams. The other was that I should have Sheridan's cavalry with me, and was therefore obliged to wait until he could join me.

This time Grant had read Lee's mind correctly, as we learn from Jefferson Davis.

During the months of February and March Lee's army was materially reduced by the casualties of battle and the frequency of absence without leave.

In the early part of March General Lee held a long and free conference with me. He stated that circumstances had forced on him the conclusion that the evacuation of Petersburg was but a question of time. He appreciated the embarrassment which would result from losing the workshops at Richmond, which had been our main reliance for the manufacture of arms as well as ammunition. To my inquiry whether it would not be better to withdraw at once, he said that his artillery and draft horses were too weak for the roads in their soft condition, and that he would have to wait until they became firmer.

Long before this, late in 1864, the Confederate Congress had passed a law forcing all able-bodied men up to the age of fifty to bear arms.

This decree, together with the definition of able-bodied men, led to some queer incidents, according to diarist Jones.

September 30, 1864. Every device of the military authorities has been employed to put the people here in the ranks. Guards everywhere are arresting pedestrians who, if they have no passes, are confined until marched to the field or released.

Today the guards arrested Judges John H. Reagan and George C. Davis, Postmaster General and Attorney General, because neither of them was over fifty years old. Judge Reagan grew angry and stormed a little; both were released immediately.

October 10. General W. M. Gardner reports that of the citizens taken from the streets to the front, last week, *a majority have deserted.*

October 13. The medical boards have been instructed to put in all men that come before them capable of bearing arms *ten days.* One died in the trenches, on the eleventh day, of consumption!

Into the midst of Mr. Jones's discouragement burst the news that peace commissioners had been appointed, and that a meeting with Northern representatives had been arranged.

January 29, 1865. Three commissioners start for Washington on a mission of peace. They are Vice-President Alexander H. Stephens, Senator R. M. T. Hunter and James A. Campbell, Assistant Secretary of War and formerly a judge on the bench of the Supreme Court of the United States, all of them heartily sick of war and languishing for peace.

If *they* cannot devise a mode of putting an end to the war, none can. Of course they have the instructions of the President, with his ultimata.

January 31. The peace commissioners proceeded on their way yesterday morning. As they passed our lines, our troops cheered them very heartily and, when they reached the enemy's lines, they were cheered more vociferously than ever. Is not this an evidence of a mutual desire for peace?

February 5. Our commissioners are back again! It is said Lincoln and Seward met them at Fort Monroe. No basis of negotiation but reconstruction could be listened to by the Federal authorities. How could it be otherwise, when their armies are marching without resistance from one triumph to another?

General Lee, as Grant had reasoned, was anxious to evacuate Richmond and reach the Danville Railroad. In order to secure a wider opening for his troops he determined on an aggressive move, about which Jefferson Davis wrote this account.

In a week or two after our first conference General Lee presented to me the idea of a sortie. If entirely successful, it would threaten Grant's line of communication with his base, City Point, and might compel him to move his forces around ours to protect it. If only so far successful as to cause the transfer of his troops from his left to his right, it would relieve our right and delay the impending disaster until the more convenient season for retreat.

Fort Stedman was the point against which the sortie was directed. Its distance from our lines was less than 200 yards. For this service, requiring equal daring and steadiness, General John B. Gordon was selected. Before daylifht on the morning of the twenty-fifth of March Gordon moved his command silently forward. The troops surprised and captured the garrison, then turned the guns upon the adjacent works and soon drove the enemy from them. A detachment was now sent to seize the commanding ground and works in the rear, the batteries of which, firing into the gorges of the forts on the right and left, would soon make a wide opening in Grant's line. But the guides to this detachment misled it in the darkness of a foggy dawn.

In the meantime the enemy, recovering from his surprise, rallied and with overwhelming power concentrated both artillery and infantry upon Gordon's command. The supporting forces failed to come forward, and Gordon's brilliant success was turned to ashes.

At the end of March, almost coincident with Lee's last sortie, Sheridan had come from the Shenandoah, and now Grant at last could make an attempt to close Lee's avenues of escape. Grant himself relates the military measures he took with that end in view.

Sheridan reached City Point on the twenty-sixth day of March. His horses, of course, were jaded and many of them had lost their shoes. A few days of rest were necessary to recuperate. Immediately I prepared his instructions for the move which I had decided on, and which was to commence on the twenty-ninth of the month.

In preparing his instructions I contemplated capturing Five Forks, driving the enemy from Petersburg and Richmond and terminating the contest.

Finally the twenty-ninth of March came, and I moved out with all the army available, after leaving a sufficient force to hold the line about Petersburg. The next day, March 30, we had made sufficient progress to the southwest to warrant me in starting Sheridan with his cavalry over by Dinwiddie, with instructions to come up by the road leading northwest to Five Forks, thus menacing the right of Lee's line.

My hope was that Sheridan would be able to carry Five Forks, get on the enemy's right flank and rear and force them to weaken their center to protect their right, so that an assault in the center might be successfully made.

Lee would understand my design to get up to the Southside Railroad and ultimately to the Danville Railroad. These roads were so important to his very existence while he remained in Richmond and Petersburg, and of such vital importance to him even in case of retreat, that naturally he would make most strenuous efforts to defend them. He did, and on the thirtieth sent Pickett with five brigades to reinforce Five Forks.

The outcome of the battle at Five Forks could no longer influence the fate of Richmond, but it would decide the success or failure of its evacuation. General Pickett, of Gettysburg fame, who had command of the Confederate forces at that point, wrote about the fight to his erstwhile sweetheart, now his wife.

Just after mailing my letter to you at Five Forks telling you of our long continuous march of eighteen hours, I received a dispatch from the great Tyee telling me to "hold Five Forks at all hazards to prevent the enemy from striking the Southside Railroad."

I immediately formed line of battle and set my men to throwing up temporary breastworks. The men, God bless them, though weary and hungry, sang as they felled and dug. Three times in the three hours their labors were suspended because of attack from the front, but they as cheerily returned to their digging and to their "Annie Laurie" and "Dixie" as if they were banking roses for a festival.

Five Forks is situated in a flat, thickly wooded country and is simply a crossing at right angles of two country roads and a deflection of a third bisecting one of these angles. Our line of battle, short as four small brigades' front must be, could readily be turned on either flank by a larger attacking force. Do you understand, my dear? If not, you will some day.

Well, I made the best arrangements of which the ground admitted. About two o'clock in the afternoon Sheridan made a heavy demonstration with his cavalry, threatening also the right flank. Meantime Warren's corps swept around the left flank and rear of the infantry line, and the attack became general.

I succeeded in getting a sergeant and enough men to man one piece, but after their firing eight rounds the axle broke. One regiment fought hand to hand after all their cartridges had been used. The small cavalry force, which had got into place, gave way, and the enemy poured in. Charge after charge was made and repulsed, and division after division of the enemy advanced upon us. We were completely entrapped. Their cavalry enveloped us front and right and, sweeping down upon our rear, held us as in a vise.

My darling, overpowered, defeated, cut in pieces, starving, captured, as we were, those that were left of us formed front north and south and met with sullen desperation their double onset. With the members of my own staff and the general officers and their staff officers we compelled a rally enabling many of us to escape capture.

The birds were hushed in the woods when I started to write, and now one calls to its mate, "Cheer up—cheer up." Let's listen and obey the birds, my darling.

Faithfully

YOUR SOLDIER.

The end was now in sight, as even Jefferson Davis was forced to admit.

Grant's massive columns, advancing on right, left and center, compelled our forces to retire to the inner line of defense, so that on the morning of April 2 the enemy was in a condition to besiege Petersburg in the true sense of that term. Battery Gregg made an obstinate defense and, with a garrison of about 250 men, held a corps in check for a large part of the day. The arrival of Longstreet's troops, and the strength of the shorter line now held by Lee, enabled him to make several attempts to dislodge his assailant from positions he had gained.

But retreat was now a present necessity. All that could be done was to hold the inner lines during the day and make needful preparations to withdraw at night.

In despairing haste war clerk Jones made the last entries in his diary.

April 2. The absence of dispatches is now interpreted as bad news! The marching of veteran troops from the defenses of Richmond and replacing them hurriedly with militia can only indicate an emergency of alarming importance.

Mrs. Davis sold nearly all her movables—including presents—before leaving the city. Intense excitement prevails. Our pastor, Dr. Minnegerode, gave notice that General Ewell desired the local forces to assemble at 3:00 P.M.—and afternoon services will not be held.

It is true! The enemy has broken through our lines and attained the Southside Road. General Lee has dispatched the Secretary of War to have everything in readiness to *evacuate the city tonight.*

CHAPTER 19

Sherman's Georgia Campaign

ATLANTA AND THE MARCH TO THE SEA

As Grant began his campaign against Lee in the East, Sherman was ordered to proceed against Johnston in a co-ordinated movement. While Grant was to hold Lee in front of Richmond, Sherman's object was to penetrate into the deep South and split it off from the rest of the Confederacy.

Sherman tells of his plans and the beginning of his campaign.

On the eighteenth of March, 1864, I relieved Lieutenant General Grant in command of the Military Division of the Mississippi and addressed myself to the task of organizing a large army to move into Georgia.

The great question of the campaign was one of supplies. Nashville, our chief depot, was itself partially in a hostile country, and even the routes from Louisville to Nashville had to be guarded. Chattanooga, our starting point, was 136 miles in front of Nashville, and every foot of the way had to be strongly guarded against a hostile population and the enemy's cavalry.

About the early part of April, I was much disturbed by a bold raid made by the Rebel general Nathan B. Forrest between the Mississippi and Tennessee rivers. He reached the Ohio River at Paducah, then swung down toward Memphis and successfully assaulted Fort Pillow.

I also had another serious cause of disturbance about that time. I wanted badly the two divisions of troops which had been loaned to General Banks for his Red River Campaign, with the express understanding that their absence was to endure only one month. But rumors were reaching us of defeat and disaster in that quarter, and General Banks could or would not spare those two divisions. This was a serious loss.

605

My three armies, by the first of May, 1864, totaled 100,000 men. In Generals Thomas, McPherson and Schofield I had three generals of education and experience, admirably qualified for the work before us.

General Grant had indicated May 5 as the day for our simultaneous advance. The sixth of May was given to Schofield and McPherson to get into position, and on the seventh General Thomas moved in force against Tunnel Hill, from where I could look into the gorge called the Buzzard Roost through which the railroad passed.

Mill Creek, which formed the gorge, had been dammed up, filling the road, and the enemy's batteries crowned the cliffs on either side. The position was very strong, and I knew that such a general as Joe Johnston had fortified it to the maximum. Therefore I had no intention to attack the position seriously in front but depended on McPherson to capture the railroad to its rear, which would force Johnston to evacuate his position at Dalton. My orders to Generals Thomas and Schofield were merely to press strongly at all points, ready to rush in on the first appearance of "Let go."

On the ninth McPherson's head of column entered and passed through a narrow pass named Snake Creek Gap, which was undefended, and accomplished a complete surprise to the enemy. A Confederate cavalry brigade, retreating hastily north toward Dalton, doubtless carried to Johnston the first intimation that a heavy force was to his rear near Resaca and within a few miles of his railroad. I renewed orders to Thomas and Schofield to be ready for the pursuit of what I expected to be a broken and disordered army.

But that night I received notice from McPherson that he had found Resaca too strong for a surprise; that in consequence he had fallen back three miles to the mouth of Snake Creek Gap and was there fortified (See map, page 610.)

McPherson had not done the full measure of his work. He could have walked into Resaca, then held only by a small brigade, or he could have placed his whole force astride the railroad above Resaca and there have easily withstood an attack of Johnston's army, with the knowledge that Thomas and Schofield were on his heels. Had he done so, I am certain that Johnston would have retreated eastward, and we should have captured half his army and all his artillery and wagons. Such an opportunity does not occur twice in a single life.

I now determined to pass the whole army through Snake Creek Gap and to move with it on Resaca.

Why the Confederates had left Snake Creek Gap unguarded puzzled the Confederate Colonel W. P. C. Breckinridge, as it has puzzled others then and since.

McPherson had steadily marched toward Snake Creek Gap, to protect which no steps had been taken. That this gave Sherman the easy means of causing the evacuation of Dalton and the retreat of Resaca, is undoubtedly true. If a cavalry force had been started to Snake Creek Gap, it would have reached there before McPherson, and held it during the night of the eighth, during which time infantry support could have reached them.

General Bragg, after his defeat at Missionary Ridge, had been superseded by General Joseph E. Johnston. The effect of this change in command is commented on by Sam R. Watkins, a private in the 1st Tennessee Regiment.

Allow me to introduce you to old Joe. Fancy a man about fifty years old, rather small, but compactly built, with an open and honest countenance and a keen but restless black eye that seemed to read your very inmost thought. In his dress he was a perfect dandy. He ever wore the very finest clothes, never omitting anything, even to the trappings of his horse, bridle and saddle. He was the very picture of a general.

But he found the army depleted by battles, and worse, the men were deserting by thousands. The spirit of the soldiers was crushed. They would not answer at roll call. Discipline had gone. A feeling of mistrust pervaded the whole army.

When Johnston took command, men returned to their companies and order was restored. He ordered his soldiers new suits of clothes, shoes and hats. He allowed us what General Bragg had never allowed —a furlough. He passed through the ranks, shaking hands with everyone. He brought the manhood back to the private's bosom. He was loved, respected, admired. I do not believe there was a soldier in his army but would gladly have died for him.

General Johnston now expounds his plans of defense against the coming invasion.

Dalton had not been selected by General Bragg for its value as a defensive position but because the retreat from Missionary Ridge had ceased at that point. The position had little to recommend it. At Dalton the Federal army, even if beaten, would have had a secure place of refuge in Chattanooga, while our only place of safety was Atlanta, a hundred miles off with three rivers intervening. Therefore, a victory gained by us could not have been decisive while defeat would have been disastrous.

I therefore decided to remain on the defensive. Fighting under cover, we would have trifling losses compared with those inflicted. Moreover, due to its lengthening lines the numerical superiority of the Federal army would be reduced daily so that we might hope to cope with it on equal terms beyond the Chattahoochee, where defeat would be its destruction while the Confederate army had a place of refuge in Atlanta, too strong to be taken by assault, too extensive to be invested. I also hoped to be able to break the railroad by which the invading army was supplied.

Sherman's men were of good spirits and full of mischief, as we may read in the notes of an Illinois lieutenant named Charles W. Wills.

May 2, 1864. A surgeon rode past us. His horse got into a hole four feet deep, stumbled, fell, rolled over and almost finished the doctor. He was under both water and horse. The boys consoled him with cheers and groans. Anything short of death is a capital joke now.

May 7. The boys have started a new dodge on the citizens. One of my men told me of it. When we camped for the night he went to a house and found out one who had relatives North and something of the family history. Then he called and represented himself as belonging to the northern branch of the family, got to kiss the young lady *cousins*, had a pleasant time generally and returned with his haversack full of knickknacks.

May 13. We have had a perfect rush of generals along the line today: Hooker, McPherson, Thomas, Sherman and a dozen of smaller fry. The boys crowded around Sherman, and he could not help hearing such expressions as "Where's Pap?" . . . "Let's see old Pap," nor could he help laughing, either. The men think more of Sherman than of any general who ever commanded them.

When Sherman reached Resaca, he found Johnston ready for him. General O. O. Howard, who played a prominent part on the Union side throughout this campaign, looked on the battle which followed as a relatively unimportant episode.

As soon as Johnston reached the little town of Resaca, he formed a horseshoe-shaped line, something like ours at Gettysburg. The position was as strong as Marye's Heights had been against direct attack. We spent a part of the fourteenth of May creeping up among the bushes, rocks and ravines.

Early that morning Sherman, who had worked all night, was sitting on a log with his back against a tree, fast asleep. Some men marching by saw him, and one fellow ended a slurring remark by, "A pretty way we are commanded!"

Sherman, awakened by the noise, heard the last words. "Stop, my man," he cried. "While you were sleeping last night, I was planning for you; and now I was taking a nap." Thus, familiarly and kindly, the general gave reprimands and won confidence.

Our fighting at Resaca did not effect much. There might possibly have been as much accomplished if we had used skirmish lines alone.

While the main battle was in progress, General Grenville Dodge had sent a division to Lay's Ferry, a point below Resaca. He laid a bridge, threw over his whole force and fought a successful battle against Confederate cavalry. There was nothing left to the Confederate commander but to withdraw his whole army from Resaca. This was effected during the night of the fifteenth, while our weary men were sound asleep.

Lieutenant L. D. Young viewed the battle of Resaca from the Confederate side.

At Resaca was fought the first battle of magnitude in the celebrated Georgia Campaign. From then on there was not a day or night, yes, scarcely an hour, that we did not hear the crack of a rifle or roar of a cannon. To their music we slept, by their thunderings we were awakened and to the accompanying call of the bugle we responded on the morning of May 14 to engage in the death grapple with Sherman's well-clothed, well-fed and thoroughly rested veterans who moved against us in perfect step, with banners flying and bands playing, as though expecting to charm us.

When they had come within seventy-five or eighty yards, our lines opened a murderous fire from both infantry and double-shotted artillery. Having retired in disorder to their original position in the woods, they rallied and again moved to the attack to be met in the

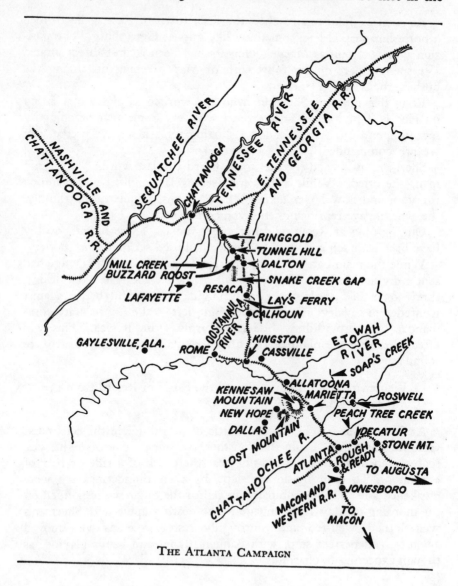

The Atlanta Campaign

same manner and with similar results. Three times during the morning and early afternoon were these attacks made upon our lines. It was a veritable picnic for the Confederates, protected as we were by earthworks with clear and open ground in front. Had Sherman continued this business during the entire day (as we hoped he would) the campaign would have ended right there.

This day's work, however, was a clever ruse of Sherman's for, while he was entertaining us with the main part of his army, he was planning our undoing by sending down the river to our rear Dodge's corps to cut our communications and intercept our retreat. But Johnston had foreseen this move, and we were the first to cross the Oostanaula.

Sherman now reports on the next steps in his campaign.

Johnston having retreated from Resaca in the night of May 15, immediate pursuit was begun. It was continued to Kingston, which we reached on the nineteenth.

About noon I got a message that the enemy had drawn up in line of battle about halfway between Kingston and Cassville and that appearances indicated his willingness and preparation for battle. But when day broke the next morning, May 20, the enemy was gone, and our cavalry reported him beyond the Etowah River. I found at Cassville many evidences of preparation for a grand battle and could not then imagine why Johnston had declined it.

The reasons why the Confederates failed to give battle at Cassville are revealed by General Johnston.

At Cassville we were about to give battle to the enemy. The position I remember as the best that I saw during the war—a ridge immediately south of the town with a broad, open, elevated valley in front of it completely commanded by the troops occupying its crest. Its length was just sufficient for Hood's and Polk's corps and half of Hardee's. The other half of Hardee's troops, prolonging this line, were on undulating ground on which they had only such advantage as their own labor could give them. They worked with great spirit, though, and were evidently full of confidence.

On reaching my tent soon after dark, I found an invitation to meet General Polk at his quarters. General Hood was with him but not

General Hardee. The two officers expressed the opinion very positively that neither of their corps would be able to hold its position next day, because, they said, a part of each was enfiladed by Federal artillery. They urged me to abandon the ground immediately and cross the Etowah.

Although the position was the best we had yet occupied, I yielded at last in the belief that this lack of confidence of two corps commanders would be communicated to their troops. General Hardee, who arrived after this decision, remonstrated strongly and was confident that his corps could hold its ground, although less favorably posted. The error was adhered to, however, and the position abandoned before daybreak.

Next day the army was led to the Etowah and crossed it about noon.

> Sam Watkins, who seemed the typical Southern soldier, had this to say about the near-battle of Cassville and the fighting that led up to it.

It seemed that both Confederate and Federal armies were celebrating a Fourth of July. Two hundred cannon were roaring and belching like blue blazes. It seemed as though the Confederate and Federal cannons were talking to each other. Sometimes a ball passing over would seem to be mad, then again some would seem to be laughing, some would be mild, some sad, some gay, some sorrowful, some rollicking and jolly, and some would scream like the ghosts of the dead. But all through that storm of battle, every soldier stood firm, for we knew that old Joe was at the helm.

At Kingston General Johnston issued his first battle order, that thus far he had gone and intended to go no farther. His line of battle was formed; his skirmish line was engaged. There were no earthworks on either side. It was to be an open field and a fair fight, when—"Fall back!" What's the matter? Here is what is told us—and so it was, every position we ever took. When we fell back the news would be, "Hood's line is being enfiladed, and he can't hold his position."

We fell back and took a position at Cassville. I never saw our troops happier or more certain of success. A sort of grand halo illumined every soldier's face. You could see self-confidence in the features of every private soldier. We were confident of victory and success. It was like going to a frolic or a wedding. Joy was welling up in every heart. We were going to whip and rout the Yankees. It seemed to be anything else than a fight. The soldiers were jubilant. Gladness was depicted on every countenance. I believe a sort of fanaticism had entered our souls. It seemed that whoever was killed would at once be carried to the seventh heaven. Then "Halt!" "Retreat!" "What is the matter?" "General Hood says they are enfilading his line, and he can't hold his position."

> The next part in the campaign consisted of continuous moves and countermoves, both executed with great skill. It was Sherman's object to bring the Confederates to battle in the open, and Johnston's to keep fighting behind breastworks. As soon as Johnston was entrenched, Sherman tried to flank him, but Johnston never was caught napping and always had new and strong positions to fall back on. Sherman's attacks led to the battles of New Hope Church, Pickett's Mill, Pumpkin Vine Creek and Dallas, all similar to the battle of Resaca, and ending similarly.
>
> The notes of Sam Watkins written some twenty years later, show the spirit of Joe Johnston's army during the Spring campaign of 1864.

Now for Old Joe's generalship. We have seen him in camp, now we will see him in action. Come on, Mister Yank—we are keen for an engagement. It is like a picnic; the soldiers are ruddy and fat and strong; whoop! whoop! hurrah! come on, Mr. Yank. Why don't you unbottle your thunderbolts and dash us to pieces?

We are ordered to march somewhere. Old Joe knows what he is up to. Every night we change our position. The troops are in excellent spirits. Yonder are our "big guns," our cavalry—Forrest and Wheeler—our sharpshooters, and here is our wagon and supply train, right in our very midst. The private's tread is light—his soul is happy.

Another flank movement. Tomorrow finds us face to face. Well, you have come here to fight us; why don't you come on? We are ready; always ready. You say Old Joe has got the brains and you have got the men; you are going to flank us out of the Southern Confederacy. That's your plan, is it? Well, look out; we are going to decimate your men every day. You will be a picked chicken before you do that.

It was fighting, fighting, every day. When we awoke in the morning, the firing of guns was our reveille, and when the sun went down it was our "retreat and our lights out." Fighting, fighting, fighting, all day and all night long. In one respect we always had the advantage; they were the attacking party, and we always had good breastworks thrown up during the night.

The soldiers drew their regular rations of biscuit and bacon, sugar and coffee, whisky and tobacco. When we went to sleep we felt that Old Joe, the faithful old watch dog, had his eye on the enemy.

It was not until the Kennesaw Mountain line was reached that Sherman decided to change from his flanking tactics to a frontal attack.

On June 15 we advanced our lines, intending to attack at any weak point discovered between Kennesaw and Pine Mountain; but Pine Mountain was found to be abandoned, and Johnston had contracted his front somewhat on a direct line connecting Kennesaw with Lost Mountain. On the sixteenth Lost Mountain was abandoned by the enemy.

I had consulted Generals Thomas, McPherson and Schofield, and we all agreed that we could not with prudence stretch out any more, and therefore there was no alternative but to attack "fortified lines," a thing carefully avoided up to that time. The twenty-seventh of June was fixed as the day for the attempt.

The Confederate position on Kennesaw Mountain was strongly entrenched. R. M. Collins of the 15th Texas describes his daily life there while awaiting the Federal attack.

We had been on the main Kennesaw line fourteen days, and the booming of cannon and crack of the rifles was kept up day and night except as the men would get up an armistice on their own hook. When conditions were favorable, a Yankee soldier would step out, shake a newspaper and say, "Hello, Johnny Reb."

"Hello, Yank, what do you want."

"Let's hold awhile—we want to swap some of our Lincoln coffee for yer flat tobacco."

"All right, lay down yer gun and meet us halfway."

Thus we would meet, crack jokes, swap tobacco and coffee and have a jolly good time until some officer would come along, when all hands would scamper back to their holes in the ground.

We had now been on the march, or in battle, quite sixty days, and hard service with poor rations was telling on the health of the army. The scurvy broke out among us, and some of the boys' legs were as black and brown as navy tobacco. General Johnston had several car-loads of tomatoes shipped up as an antiscorbutic; but as I took in the careworn looks of the officers and men, I wondered what was coming next.

> Sherman's men, so Lieutenant C. W. Wills's diary tells us, also were curious what was to come next. They did not have much longer to wait.

June 20, 1864. I would like to date my next from a new place, but Sherman and Johnston will decide that matter.

This is becoming tedious. Johnston has no regard for one's feelings. We are all exceedingly anxious to see what is on the other side of these mountains, but he has no idea of letting us take a look.

June 27. The battle comes off today. We do not commence until 8:00 A. M. Our brigade and one from each of the other two divisions of the corps are selected to charge the mountain. If we are successful with a loss of only half our number, we will think our loss more than repaid.

> The experiences of F. Y. Hedley, a Union adjutant, show what it meant to storm Kennesaw Mountain.

Early after breakfast three guns gave the signal for the advance, and our assaulting column dashed from under cover. The enemy's batteries opened with grape and canister, and over their heads the Union gunners poured answering volleys.

On went the blue lines at a keen run, passing beyond the rifle pits of their own skirmishers. Still on they pressed at a rapid pace, firing scarcely a shot, reserving all their energies for the supreme effort. They ran over the rifle pits of the enemy's skirmishers without a thought of the fleeing occupants. Their goal was five hundred yards farther on. And then, from the light red line of earth came a storm of lead which, united with the volleys of artillery on either flank, bore down countless scores. At every pace of their magnificent advance men dropped, mangled or dead. None stopped to see who had fallen—looking neither to the right nor the left, they instinctively sought one another's side, closing up the gaps and continually shortening the line but resolutely pressing on. The only instinct left alive was that of destruction.

And now they came upon the abatis in front of the enemy's position, reaching up the steep ascent of the foothill of Kennesaw Mountain. The men tore through, climbing over or under the entangling treetops and twisted vines as best they could. It was slow and painful work. From front and flanks came a fire of musketry, tenfold fiercer than before, and every missile that artillery could throw. Our lines were irretrievably crushed, and the men sought such shelter as the ground afforded. Afterward they fell back and occupied the enemy's late skirmish line.

Other assaults were made and all failed.

General Sherman, however, successfully defended the experiment. "All looked to me," he said, "to 'outflank.' An army, to be efficient, must not settle down to one single mode of offense but must be prepared to execute any plan which promises success."

Sam R. Watkins of the 1st Tennessee relates how he helped defend Kennesaw Mountain.

Well, on the fatal morning of June 27, all at once a hundred guns from the Federal line opened upon us. All of a sudden our pickets jumped into our works. Almost at the same time a solid line of blue coats came up the hill. My pen is unable to describe the scene of carnage that ensued in the next two hours. Column after column of Federal soldiers were crowded upon that line. No sooner would a regiment mount our works than they were shot down or surrendered. Yet still they came. It seemed impossible to check the onslaught, but every man seemed to think that at that moment the whole responsibility of the Confederate government was upon his shoulders.

I am satisfied that every man in our regiment killed from onescore to fourscore, yea, fivescore men. All that was necessary was to load and shoot. In fact, I will ever think that the reason they did not capture our works was the impossibility of their living men to pass over the bodies of their dead.

After Sherman's failure at Kennesaw Mountain, events followed one another in rapid succession. They are aptly reported by Horace Greeley of the *New York Tribune.*

Sherman did not choose to rest on his bloody repulse; but, having waited only to bury the dead and care for the wounded, he again threw forward his right. McPherson was ordered to move rapidly down to the Chattahoochee and to threaten a crossing at or near Turner's Ferry. The success of this maneuver was instantaneous. Though its execution began at nightfall, Kennesaw was forthwith evacuated by Johnston; our skirmishers stood on the summit at dawn; and—our whole army pressing forward—General Sherman rode into Marietta on the heels of the Rebel rearguard.

Sherman expected to catch Johnston crossing the Chattahoochee and destroy half his army, but the wary Confederate had, ere this, strongly entrenched a position on the west side, covering the passage of the river, and stood here awaiting—in fact, inviting—an assault. Sherman paused and cautiously approached. He sent forward at length a strong skirmish line, which carried the enemy's outer line of rifle pits, taking some prisoners. Next morning, July 5, Johnston was partly over the river, and our army advanced in triumph to its bank at several points, with Atlanta just at hand.

But the Chattahoochee is here a large stream, rapid as well as deep, and barely fordable at one or two points. The railroad and other bridges, of course, were covered by the enemy's strong work on our side which they still held.

Sherman now carries the story of his campaign through its next steps.

I knew that Johnston would not remain long on our bank of the Chattahoochee, for I could entrench a goodly force in his front and with the rest of our army cross the river and threaten either his rear or the city of Atlanta itself.

Schofield effected a crossing at Soap Creek very handsomely on July 9. By night he was on the high ground beyond, strongly entrenched, with two good pontoon bridges finished, and was prepared, if necessary, for an assault by the whole Confederate army.

That night Johnston evacuated his trenches, crossed over the Chattahoochee, burned the railroad bridge and his pontoon and trestle bridges and left us in full possession of the north bank.

General Grenville M. Dodge, entrusted with throwing a bridge across the Chattahoochee, relates an interesting episode coincident with this task.

Before General Sherman crossed the Chattahoochee, he came to my headquarters and asked how long it would take me to construct a bridge at Roswell. I told him it would require at least a week. He had not gone more than an hour when I received orders to move to Roswell.

Roswell had cotton and woolen factories, and over the proprietor's house flew a French flag. I saw immediately that if I utilized his buildings I could erect the bridge in half the time and instructed the detail which was to build the bridge to tear them down. The proprietor made a strong protest and told me that I was liable to get into trouble on account of international law. I thought it best to write General Sherman what I had done. Sherman answered in the following characteristic manner: "July 11, 1864. The bridge at Roswell is important, and you may destroy all Georgia to make it good and strong."

On July 12, just three days after I had arrived there, I notified General Sherman that the bridge was completed.

Hardly had Sherman crossed the Chattahoochee, when he received news of a startling character.

About 10:00 A.M. of July 18 one of General Thomas' staff officers brought me a newspaper containing Johnston's order relinquishing the command of the Confederate forces, Hood assuming the command. Hood was bold even to rashness and courageous in the extreme. I inferred that the change of commanders meant "fight." This was just what we wanted, to fight in open ground instead of being forced to run up against prepared entrenchments.

Author DeLeon was outraged and chagrined at Johnston's dismissal.

There is no stronger proof of the people's confidence in General Johnston than their reception of this news. They had watched his long retreat without a fight, and yet they never murmured. There was an unshaken belief that he was doing his best; that his best was *the* best. Feeling that the fate of the whole cause was vested in the little army left to him, he was great enough to resist the opportunities for glorious battle, to offer himself to the condemnation of the unthinking censure to insure the safety of Confederate life.

Senator Benjamin H. Hill of Georgia, who was in Richmond
at that time, had this to say about Johnston's removal.

The President had appointed Johnston against his own convictions,
but would not remove him now if he could have any assurance that
General Johnston would not surrender Atlanta without a battle.

The situation was referred to General Lee, but he declined to give
any positive advice and expressed regret that the removal of General
Johnston, in the circumstances existing, should be found necessary.

During all the time, a telegraphic correspondence was kept up with
General Johnston, the object being to ascertain if he would make a
determined fight to save Atlanta. His answers were thought to be
evasive. "This evasive answer," said one member of the Cabinet to me,
"brought the President over. He yielded very reluctantly."

This is Johnston's own story of his dismissal.

On July 17 the Federal army had crossed the Chattahoochee. At
10:00 P.M. the following telegram was received:

I am directed to inform you that, as you have failed to arrest the
advance of the enemy and express no confidence that you can defeat
or repel him, you are hereby relieved from the command of the Army
of Tennessee, which you will immediately turn over to General Hood.

Next morning I replied:

Your dispatch of yesterday received and obeyed. Confident language by a military commander is not usually regarded as evidence of
competence.

The Confederate lieutenant R. M. Collins tells how he and his
company felt about the change in their high command.

Along with a majority of my company I was playing a game of
draw poker in the shade of a great oak when an adjutant read the order
removing General Johnston. The boys threw down their cards and collected in little groups. They were all dissatisfied. President Davis could

not have suited General Sherman better had he commissioned him to make the appointment himself.

The Virginia soldier Alexander Hunter was still more out-spoken.

Had Mr. Davis died or resigned at the commencement of the 1864 campaign, affairs would have worn a different aspect.

The Fabius of the Southern Revolution had been removed by the President. When Mr. Davis, who thought himself infallible, took a dislike, he became stone-blind in his hatred.

When the Autocrat of Richmond removed Johnston from the head of the Army of the Tennessee, he dealt a stab deep in the vitals of the Confederacy.

Sherman now relates what happened after Hood had been put in command of the Confederate army.

On July 19 our three armies were converging toward Atlanta, meeting such feeble resistance that I really thought the enemy intended to evacuate the place. On the twentieth soon after noon I heard heavy firing which lasted an hour or so and then ceased. I soon learned that the enemy had made a furious sally, the blow falling mainly on Hooker's corps (the 20th).

Our troops had crossed Peach Tree Creek, were deployed but at the time were resting for noon when, without notice, the enemy came down upon them. They became commingled and fought in many places hand-to-hand. General Thomas happened to be near and got some field batteries in a good position from which he directed a furious fire. After a couple of hours of hard and close conflict the enemy retired slowly within his trenches. We had met successfully a bold sally and were also put on our guard.

During the night of July 21-22, finding that McPherson was stretching out too much on his left flank, I wrote him a note early in the morning not to extend so much by his left, for we had not troops enough to invest Atlanta completely.

McPherson came over to see me. While we sat there we could hear lively skirmishing going on near us and could hear similar sounds all along down the lines to our right. The firing was too far to our left rear to be explained by known facts, and he hastily called for his horse, saying he would send me back word. I was walking up and down listening, when an aide dashed up and reported that McPherson's horse had come back, bleeding and riderless.

The story told mutely by General McPherson's riderless horse is unfolded in full by Captain Richard Beard of Hood's army. McPherson had been considered one of the most promising young military leaders in the Union army.

I had been in command of a brigade line of skirmishers, and early on the morning of July 22 we were furnished with sixty additional rounds of ammunition and were told that there was a hard day's work before us.

We were placed in line of battle about twelve or one o'clock in the day. Shortly afterward a heavy and rapid cannonading commenced which announced that the ball was about to open in good earnest. We commenced a double-quick through a forest covered with dense underbrush. Suddenly we came up to the edge of a little wagon road running parallel with our line of march and down which General McPherson came thundering at the head of his staff and, according to the best of my recollection, followed by his bodyguard. He had evidently just left the last conference he ever had with General Sherman and was on his way to see what the sudden and rapid firing on his left meant. I estimated his rank not only by his personal appearance but by the size of his retinue, and in that estimate I fixed his rank as nothing less than a corps commander.

He was certainly surprised to find himself suddenly within a few feet of where we stood. I threw up my sword to him as a signal to surrender. Not a word was spoken. He checked his horse slightly, raised his hat as politely as if he were saluting a lady, wheeled his horse's head directly to the right and dashed off to the rear in a full gallop. Young Corporal Coleman who was standing near me was ordered to fire on him. He did so and brought General McPherson down. He was shot as he was bending over his horse's neck in order to pass under the thick branches of a tree. He was shot in the back and the ball ranged upward across the body and passed through his heart.

I ran immediately up to where the general lay just as he had fallen upon his knees and face. There was not a quiver of his body to be seen, not a sign of life. Even as he lay there in his major general's uniform with his face in the dust, he was as magnificent a specimen of manhood as I ever saw.

Right by his side lay a man who was but slightly wounded. I took him to be the adjutant or inspector general of the staff. Pointing to the dead man I asked him, "Who is this lying here?"

He answered with tears in his eyes, "Sir, it is General McPherson. You have killed the best man in our army."

Here Sherman again takes up his account of the battle.

Meantime the sounds of the battle had become more and more furious on our extreme left.

The reports that came to me revealed clearly the game of my antagonist. Hood, during the night of July 21, had withdrawn from his Peach Tree line, had marched out to the road leading to Decatur and had turned so as to strike the left and rear of McPherson's line "in air." At the same time he had sent Wheeler's division of cavalry against the trains parked in Decatur.

The enemy had been enabled, under cover of the forest, to approach quite near before he was discovered. The right of his line struck Dodge's troops in motion; but, fortunately, this corps (the 16th) had only to halt, face to the left and was in line of battle. It not only held the enemy in check but drove him back. One or two brigades of the 15th Corps came rapidly across the open field to the rear and filled up the gap, thus forming a strong left flank, at right angles to the original line of battle. The enemy attacked, boldly and repeatedly, the whole of this flank but met an equally fierce resistance, and a bloody battle raged from little after noon till into the night.

A part of Hood's plan of action had been to sally from Atlanta at the same moment, but this sally was not made simultaneously. I urged Generals Thomas and Schofield to take advantage of the absence of so considerable a body and to make a lodgment in Atlanta itself, but they reported that the lines to their front were strong and fully manned. About 4:00 P. M. the expected sally came from Atlanta, directed mainly against Leggett's Hill and along the Decatur Road. At Leggett's Hill they were met and bloodily repulsed. Along the railroad they were more successful. Sweeping over a small force with two guns, they reached our main line and broke through it. General Charles R. Woods reported to me in person that the line on his left had been swept back and that his connection with General Logan on Leggett's Hill was broken. I ordered him to wheel his brigades to the left, to advance in echelon and to catch the enemy in flank. General Schofield brought forward all his available batteries, to the number of twenty guns, and directed a heavy fire over the heads of General Woods's men against the enemy; and we saw Woods's troops advance and encounter the enemy, who had secured possession of the parapets which had been held by our men. These forces drove the enemy back into Atlanta.

This battle of July 22 is usually called the Battle of Atlanta.

A stirring picture of the Battle of Atlanta comes to us from the pen of R. S. Tuthill, a Federal artillerist.

I remember that I had finished my noonday bean soup, hardtack and coffee and had started to write a letter. I had but fairly begun it when artillery firing was heard from the direction of the city. Musketry firing in our rear had become startling by its nearness. Hardee's corps had got on our flank and in our rear and was marching, as it confidently believed, to our certain destruction. Great numbers of our own men, driven from their positions on our left, many of them panic-stricken, passed by us and among us.

Hardee had struck us "endways" and his men could be seen occupying the works from which ours had just been driven. A battery of regulars had been captured, and soon their shot came plowing through our line in direct enfilade.

I have heard it said that then an order for a change of position was given. I doubt it. There was no time to give orders, and I saw neither general nor staff officer there to give them. All I know is that we limbered up our guns and sullenly moved back.

Some distance to the rear of us was a rail fence. Consternation, I have been told, fell upon General Sherman, as with his glass he saw half of General Mortimer D. Leggett's division drop their guns and run to the rear. But when he saw them stop at the rail fence and each man pick up two, three and even four rails and run back, carrying them to the place where they had left their guns, he smiled grimly. The rails were placed lengthways along our front; with bayonets, knives and tin plates taken from haversacks, the earth was dug up and the rails covered until a very fair protection for men lying on their bellies was made.

In front of us lay an open field beyond which were woods and Pat.

Cleburne's Texans. Their line emerged and, yelling as only the steer drivers of Texas could yell, charged. They were met by musketry and shrapnel; yet, still yelling, again and again they attempted the impossible.

The exact sequence of events that afternoon I cannot give, nor do I believe any man can. One thing I remember: a general called for a flag. Some frightened young officer ran hither and thither to get a white handkerchief or shirt. The general shouted, "Damn you, sir! I don't want a flag of *truce*; I want the American flag!" A flag was soon obtained and planted upon the highest point in our earthworks.

In the end, the attack was repulsed bloodily.

Here is Hood's own version of the battles around Atlanta.

On the night of the eighteenth and morning of the nineteenth I formed line of battle facing Peach Tree Creek. I perceived at once that the Federal commander had committed a serious blunder in separating his corps so as to allow me to concentrate the main body of our army upon his right wing while his left was too far removed to render assistance.

General Stewart carried out his instructions to the letter, but the troops of Hardee did nothing more than skirmish with the enemy. Instead of charging down upon the foe as Stewart's men did, many, when they discovered that they had come into contact with breastworks, lay down and consequently this attempt proved abortive.

During the night of the twentieth I received information of the exposed position of McPherson's left flank; it was standing out in air, near the Georgia Railroad between Decatur and Atlanta. The roads were in good condition and ran in the direction to enable a large body of our army to march, under cover of darkness, around this exposed flank and attack in rear.

The Federal army at the close of night on the twenty-first was but partially entrenched; Schofield and McPherson were still separated from Thomas, and at such distance as to compel them to make a detour of about twelve miles in order to reach the latter in time of need.

Every preparation had been carefully made during the twenty-first. I hoped each officer would know what support to expect from his neighbor in the hour of battle.

Orders were given to attack from right to left and to press the Federal army down and against the deep and muddy stream in their rear. These orders were carefully explained again and again, till each officer present gave assurance that he fully comprehended his duties.

After waiting nearly the entire morning, I heard about ten o'clock skirmishing going on directly opposite the left of the enemy. I at once perceived that Hardee had not only failed to turn McPherson's left, according to positive orders, but had thrown his men against the enemy's breastworks, thereby occasioning unnecessary loss to us and rendering doubtful the great result desired. In lieu of completely turning the Federal left and taking the entrenched line of the enemy in reverse, he attacked the retired wing of their flank. It had rested in his power to rout McPherson's army by simply moving a little farther to the right. I hoped, nevertheless, this blunder would be remedied, at least in part, by the extreme right of his line lapping round, during the attack, to the rear of McPherson.

Although the troops of Hardee fought, seemingly, with determination and spirit, there were indications that the desired end was not being accomplished. The roar of musketry occurring only at intervals strengthened this impression.

Fearing a concentration of the enemy upon Hardee, I commanded General Cheatham, about 3:00 P.M., to move forward with his corps and attack the position in his front, so as to create a diversion at least. The order was promptly executed, and our troops succeeded in taking possession of the enemy's defenses in that part of the field. A heavy enfilade fire, however, forced Cheatham to abandon the works he had captured.

The partial success of that day greatly improved the morale of the troops and demonstrated to the foe our determination to abandon no more territory without a manful effort to retain it.

But the holding of Atlanta itself depended on our ability to hold intact the road to Macon.

In his official report General Hardee bitterly resented the intimation that he had disobeyed instructions, and thereby contributed to the failure of the Confederate sortie on July 22.

The publication of General Hood's report makes it a duty to record a correction of the misrepresentations which he has made with respect to myself and the corps which I commanded. It is well known that I felt unwilling to serve under General Hood, because I believed him to be unequal in both experience and natural ability to so important a command.

That I committed errors is very possible, but that I failed in any instance to carry out in good faith his orders I utterly deny; nor during our official connection did General Hood ever evince a belief that I had in any respect failed in the execution of such parts of his military plans as were intrusted to me. On the contrary, by frequent and exclusive consultation of my opinions, by the selection of my corps for important operations and by assigning me on several occasions to the command of two-thirds of his army, he gave every proof of implicit confidence in me.

In proof that General Hood's instructions were obeyed, I have only to mention that when my dispatch informing him of the position I had taken and the dispositions I had made for the attack was received, he exclaimed to Brigadier General Mackall, his chief of staff, with his finger on the map, "Hardee is just where I wanted him."

The desperate fighting of Hood's troops on July 22 is graphically described by the Union captain, George W. Pepper.

The entire Rebel forces were advancing, and all our available strength was required to prevent being overwhelmed by the terrible onset. Charge after charge was made upon the Rebels to regain the ground we had lost.

The balance of victory now inclined to this side, now to that. Men glared at one another like wild beasts and, when a shell burst among the advancing foe and arms, legs and heads were torn off, a smile of pleasure lighted up our smoke-begrimed faces. Soldiers were wounded and knew it not, so intense was their excitement. Men with knitted brows and flushed cheeks fought madly over ridges, along ravines and up steep ascents, with blood and perspiration streaming down their faces. Men with shattered fingers changed their muskets to the left hands. Commanders galloped wildly to the front of their regiments, using their sabers, and urging on their troops wherever they were falling back.

A crisis had arrived. Sherman ordered two batteries to a position commanding a flank fire upon the enemy. The charges of our men were stubbornly resisted, but the determination of the onset overwhelmed everything. Captains, majors, colonels and generals fought like common soldiers. Our boys rushed on the enemy's rifle pits, bayoneting them in their works, careless of their own lives as if they had a million souls to spare.

No life was worth a farthing. Whole heaps of corpses lay on the bloody ground, and fixed eyes stared at the surrounding strife with the awful stare of death. The Rebels fought with a fierceness seldom if ever equaled. They stood firm as a rock and, though our artillery swept down their ranks, they manifested no trepidation. The musket that had fallen from a lifeless hand was seized at once, and the hideous strife went on as before. The force of the enemy appeared increasing and, where the greatest havoc was made, there the strongest opposition was shown. There was little shouting—the warriors were too much in earnest. Men seemed to feast on the sight of blood.

Now came the grand *coup de main*. Two Rebel lines came on exultant and sure of victory. All our artillery was opened upon them. Words cannot describe the awful effects of this discharge: 17,000 rifles and several batteries of artillery, each gun loaded to the muzzle with grape and canister, were fired simultaneously, and the whole center of the Rebel line was crushed down as a field of wheat through which a tornado has passed. The Rebel column gave way, and thus ended the fearful and bloody struggle of the twenty-second of July.

Having repulsed the sorties of July 20 and July 22, Sherman now explains his plan to take possession of the all-important Macon Road.

My next plan of action was to move the Army of the Tennessee to the right against the railroad below Atlanta, and at the same time send all the cavalry to make a lodgment on the Macon Road about Jonesboro.

The morning of July 27 was fixed for commencing the movement. On the morning of the twenty-eighth, the sound of cannon and musketry denoted a severe battle in progress, which began seriously at 11:30 A.M., and ended substantially by 4:00 P.M. It was a fierce attack by the enemy on our extreme right flank.

At no instant of time did I feel the least uneasiness about the result. Our men were unusually encouraged, for they realized that we could compel Hood to come out from behind his fortified lines to attack us at a disadvantage. The soldiers spoke of the affair of the twenty-eighth as the easiest thing in the world, but, in fact, it was a slaughter.

The enemy, though evidently somewhat intimidated by the results of their defeats on the twentieth, twenty-second and twenty-eighth, still presented a bold front at all points, with fortified lines that defied a direct assault.

Edward A. Pollard, editor of the *Richmond Examiner*, analyzed the situation as he saw it after Hood's abortive sorties, and bitterly criticized the Confederate general's strategy.

Hood's attacks were the most reckless, massive and headlong charges of the war, where immense prices were paid for momentary successes. This had been the great point in Johnston's calculations: Sherman's army was not large enough to encircle Atlanta completely without making his lines too thin and assailable. He never had contemplated an assault upon its strong works. It was his object to get possession of the Macon Road and thus sever Atlanta entirely from its supplies. The road must be kept broken, and to accomplish this it was necessary to plant a sufficient force south of Atlanta.

While Sherman meditated such a movement, Hood thrust into the hands of his adversary the opportunity he had waited for. He sent off his entire cavalry toward Chattanooga to raid the enemy's line of communication—a most absurd excursion since Sherman had enough provisions accumulated this side of that place.

Even the privates in Hood's army felt that to send all the cavalry away, at this juncture, was a highly dangerous undertaking. Sam Watkins of the 1st Tennessee still winced when he wrote about it sixteen years later.

Now Hood sent all his cavalry away. O ye gods! I get sick at heart even at this late day when I think of it.

I remember the morning that Wheeler's cavalry filed by our brigade. I cried. I remember stopping the command and begging them not to leave us; that if they did, Atlanta would surrender in a few days. The most ignorant private in the whole army saw everything that we had been fighting for scattered like chaff to the winds. Generals resigned and those who did not resign were promoted; colonels were made brigadier generals, captains were made colonels, and the private soldier—well, he deserted.

The cavalry which Sherman had sent out to take the Macon Road suffered a defeat and, as he wrote to his wife, there were other matters troubling him.

I fear we have sustained a reverse in some cavalry that I sent around by the rear to break the Macon Road.

My army is much reduced in strength by deaths, sickness and expiration of service. It is hard to see regiments march away when their time is up. No recruits are coming, for the draft is not till September, and then I suppose it will consist mostly of bought recruits that must be kept well to the rear. I sometimes think our people do not deserve to succeed in war: they are so apathetic.

Good news has just come that Farragut's fleet is in Mobile Bay and has captured the Rebel fleet there; also that Fort Gaines which guards the west entrance to the Bay has surrendered. So perhaps all is coming round well.

Sherman now had to choose among three moves to force an early decision. The first, a direct assault on Atlanta, was discarded for a reason set forth by Sherman's aide-de-camp Major George Nichols in seventeen words.

Had it been necessary to capture Atlanta by direct attack, it would have taken months or years.

This left two more plans to be considered. As it happened, both of them succeeded simultaneously, as Sherman explains.

It was evident that we must decoy Hood out to fight us or else, with the whole army, attack his communications. Accordingly, on the thirteenth of August, I gave general orders for the 20th Corps to draw back to the railroad bridge at the Chattahoochee to protect our trains while the rest of the army should move bodily to some point on the Macon Railroad.

Luckily, I learned just then that Hood had sent *all* his cavalry under Wheeler to raid upon our railroads. That same evening I telegraphed to General Halleck as follows:

I will commence the movement around Atlanta by the south tomorrow night and for some time you will hear little of us. The 20th Corps will hold the railroad bridge, and I will move with the balance of the army, provisioned for twenty days.

On August 26 the 15th and 17th Corps drew out of their trenches and made a wide circuit. The enemy seemed to suspect we were going to retreat altogether. There was great rejoicing in Atlanta "that the Yankees were gone"; the fact was telegraphed all over the South, and several trains of cars with ladies came up from Macon to assist in the celebration.

On August 31 we all moved straight for the railroad. Schofield reached it near Rough and Ready, and Thomas at two points between there and Jonesboro. About 3:00 P.M. the enemy sallied from Jonesboro against the 15th Corps, but was easily repulsed. All hands were kept busy tearing up the railroad.

Meantime General Slocum had been sent to feel forward toward Atlanta. That night I was so restless and impatient that I could not sleep, and about midnight there arose toward Atlanta sounds of shells exploding and other sounds.

The next morning rumors came that the enemy had evacuated Atlanta, and later in the day I received a note in Slocum's own handwriting, stating that he had entered Atlanta unopposed. I sent one of my staff officers to show Thomas the note. He snapped his fingers, whistled and almost danced, and, as the news spread to the army, the shouts, the wild hallooing and glorious laughter were a full recompense for the labor and toils and hardships through which we had passed in the previous three months.

General Hardee relates how woefully Hood misinterpreted Sherman's turning movements from August 26 to the end of the month.

On the twenty-sixth of August the enemy drew in his left on the north front of Atlanta in pursuance of a plan to turn our position and move upon our railroad communications. Wheeler had cut the railroad between Atlanta and Chattanooga, and General Hood believed the enemy to be retreating for want of supplies. He even ordered General W. H. Jackson, then commanding the cavalry of the army, to harass the rear of the retreating enemy. General Jackson endeavored to convince him of his error but to no purpose. The opportunity to strike the exposed flank of the enemy during the five days occupied in the movement from Atlanta to Jonesboro was neglected and lost. It was not until the thirtieth of August, in the evening of the day the enemy actually reached the vicinity of Jonesboro, that General Hood was convinced by information sent him by me that the enemy was moving upon that place. He then determined to attack what he believed to be only two corps of the enemy at Jonesboro.

General Hardee now describes the Confederate failure to break Sherman's hold on the Macon Railroad at Jonesboro, and then continues:

On the morning of September 1 the situation was as follows: General Hood was at Atlanta with Stewart's corps and the Georgia militia; my corps was at Jonesboro thirty miles distant; and Stephen D. Lee's corps on the road from Jonesboro to Atlanta, fifteen miles from each place, and in supporting distance of neither. The Federal commander, on the other hand, had concentrated his whole army upon my corps at Jonesboro, except the one corps left in front of Atlanta, and was now in position to crush in detail the scattered corps of his unwary antagonist. It was absolutely necessary for me to hold my position through the day to secure the evacuation of Atlanta which had now become a necessity. To add to my embarrassment, I was encumbered by the immense subsistence and ordnance trains of the army which had been sent for safety from Atlanta to Jonesboro and could not now be sent farther to the rear because the superiority of the enemy in cavalry made it necessary for their safety that they should remain under the protection of the infantry. It is difficult to imagine a more perplexing or perilous situation: my corps was attacked by six corps commanded by General Sherman in person, and on my ability to hold the position through the day depended the very existence of the remainder of the army. If the enemy had crushed my corps, or even driven it from its position at Jonesboro on the first of September, no organized body of the other two corps could have escaped destruction.

With the Macon Road definitely in enemy hands, there was nothing left for Hood but to evacuate Atlanta, which was immediately occupied by Sherman.

Edward A. Pollard expressed the views of the South when he recounted the decrees prescribed by Atlanta's conqueror, and their effect.

Sherman entered Atlanta on the morning of September 2 and rode through the streets to his headquarters without parade or ostentation. He declared that his army, wearied by an arduous campaign, needed rest. But the period of military inaction was to be employed in launching measures of the most extraordinary cruelty against the noncombatant people of Atlanta. General Sherman was the author of the sentiment, "War is cruelty, and you cannot refine it." This extraordinary doctrine Sherman at once proceeded to put in practice by depopulating Atlanta and driving from their homes thousands of helpless women and children. It was the most cruel and savage act of the war.

In vain the mayor of Atlanta pointed out to General Sherman that the country south of the city was crowded already with refugees and without houses to accommodate the people, that the consequences would be woe, horror and suffering, which could not be described by words. Sherman was inexorable. He affected the belief that Atlanta might again be rendered formidable in the hands of the Confederates and resolved, in his own words, "to wipe it out." The old and decrepit were packed into railroad cars; wagons were filled with wrecks of household goods; and, the trains having deposited their medley freight, the exiles were left to shift for themselves.

To justify his admitted departure from the accepted methods of warfare, Sherman advanced these arguments.

I was resolved to make Atlanta a pure military depot, with no civil population to influence military measures. I had seen Memphis, Vicksburg, Natchez and New Orleans captured from the enemy, and each at once was garrisoned by a full division of troops, if not more. Success was actually crippling our armies by detachments to protect the interests of a hostile population.

I gave notice of this purpose to General Halleck, concluding with these words: "If the people raise a howl against my barbarity and cruelty, I will answer that war is war, and not popularity seeking. If they want peace, they and their relatives must stop the war."

With Atlanta in Sherman's hands, the Confederates worked out a new plan by which they hoped, as Jefferson Davis explains, to nullify all that the Union armies in Georgia had accomplished.

It was not to be expected that General Sherman would remain long inactive. The rapidity with which he was collecting recruits and supplies indicated that he contemplated a movement farther south, making Atlanta a secondary base. To rescue Georgia and save the Gulf States, the railroads in his rear must be effectually torn up. Could this be accomplished, all the fruits of Sherman's successful campaign in Georgia would be blighted, his capture of Atlanta would become a barren victory and he would probably be compelled to make a retreat toward Tennessee. Or, should he push forward through Georgia to the Atlantic coast, our army, having cut his communications north of Atlanta, could fall upon his rear. With the advantages of a better knowledge of the country, of a devoted population and of the auxiliary force to be expected in the circumstances, it was not unreasonable to hope that retributive justice might overtake the ruthless invader.

General Richard Taylor, who had been assigned a roving commission after his notable victories over Banks in the Red River Campaign, tells of an interesting meeting he had with President Davis in Montgomery, shortly after the fall of Atlanta.

Late in the afternoon a dispatch was received from President Davis, announcing his arrival for the following morning. It was ten o'clock at night when he took me to his chamber, locked the door and began by saying that he had visited Hood and his army on his way to Montgomery and was gratified to find officers and men in excellent spirits, not at all depressed by recent disasters, and that he thought well of a movement north toward Nashville. I expressed surprise at his statement as entirely opposed to the conclusions forced on me by all the evidence I could get and warned him of the danger of listening to narrators who were more disposed to tell what was agreeable than what was true. I thought it a serious matter to undertake a campaign into Tennessee in the autumn with troops so badly equipped as were ours for the approaching winter. Every mile the army marched north, it was removing farther from supplies, and no reinforcements were to be hoped for from any quarter.

The President asked what assistance might be expected from the trans-Mississippi. I replied, none. The difficulty of bringing over organized bodies of men was explained, with the addition of their unwillingness to come. So far from desiring to send any more men to the east, they clamored for the return of those already there. Certain senators and representatives, who had bitterly opposed the administration at Richmond, talked about setting up a government west of the Mississippi, uniting with Maximilian in Mexico and calling on Louis Napoleon for assistance.

The President listened attentively to this, and asked, "What then?" As Johnston had been so recently removed from command, I would not venture to recommend his return but believed that our chances would be increased by the assignment of Beauregard to the army. At the same time, I did not disguise my conviction that the best we could hope for was to protract the struggle until spring. It was for statesmen, not soldiers, to deal with the future. The President said Beauregard should come, but that he was distressed to hear such gloomy sentiments from me. I replied that it was my duty to express my opinions frankly to him. With much other talk we wore through the night. In the morning he left.

My next meeting with President Davis was when he was a prisoner at Fort Monroe.

In accordance with the plan outlined by Davis, Hood decided to join his cavalry with the rest of the army and destroy Sherman's communications and depots.

General O. O. Howard, who had been ordered to pursue the Confederates, reports on his movements and how, by the pressure of events, the famous March to the Sea followed as a necessary sequence.

On September 29, 1864, Hood left his position near Palmetto, Georgia, crossed the Chattahoochee and reached Lost Mountain.

Hood had heard that we had an extensive subdepot at Allatoona Pass, so he directed Lieutenant General Alexander P. Stewart to have it broken up. If this redoubt could be taken, what a clean sweep there would be of Sherman's line of communications between the Chattahoochee Bridge and the crossing of the Etowah!

As soon as Sherman found out what Hood was undertaking, he set his whole force in motion northward, except Slocum, with his 20th Corps, who was left back to keep Atlanta for our return.

We commenced the pursuit from Atlanta the morning of October 3. By the fifth we had reached the vicinity of the battlefield of Kennesaw Mountain.

Sherman divined that the subdepot at Allatoona Pass was Hood's coveted prize. Colonel John E. Tourtelotte at Allatoona and his brave men had held on against all preliminary skirmishing, and reinforcements under General John M. Corse gave new courage to them. Corse's arrangements were scarcely completed before the battle began in earnest and raged with great severity.

French's Confederates worked themselves entirely around the trenches and, though not rapidly yet constantly, were picking off our men. About one o'clock Corse himself received a wound from a rifle ball. For half an hour the gallant commander seemed unconscious. Then, thinking he heard somebody cry, "Cease firing!" he revived and instantly encouraged the officers around him to keep up their resistance. Corse's words had the desired effect, and the Confederates were repelled by the quick fire from the waiting rifles of our men. By four o'clock every front had been thoroughly cleared of living Confederates.

As soon as the news of the failure was brought to Hood, he continued his march northward. He went above Resaca and destroyed the railroad all the way along toward Chattanooga. He captured our posts at Dalton and Buzzard Roost, securing at least 1,000 prisoners.

My army was near Kennesaw on October 5, pulling northward as rapidly as possible. During the night of the twelfth we all reached the vicinity of Resaca, having, in fact, recovered all of our stations up to that point, and commenced the speedy repair of the culvert and railroad tracks.

On the morning of the thirteenth we found that every detachment of the enemy had disappeared. Sherman desired me to push rapidly after Hood and I was eager enough myself. We proceeded as rapidly as we could as far as the town of Gaylesville, Alabama. There we halted October twenty-first.

From that time on the Confederates were moving rapidly away from us. From the twenty-first to the twenty-eighth of October we remained at Gaylesville or in that vicinity, while Sherman was communicating with his commanders at Chattanooga and Nashville and with his commander in chief at Washington concerning the future.

Our return march was made by short stages. November 5 brought the Army of the Tennessee back to Smyrna Camp Ground. There we remained until November 13.

General Sherman himself, as early as November 2, had changed his headquarters again to the little hamlet of Kingston, Georgia. From this point that same day was sent the significant dispatch to Grant:

If I turn back, the whole effect of my campaign will be lost. . . . I am clearly of the opinion that the best results will follow a movement through Georgia.

This was Grant's reply:

I do not see that you can withdraw from where you are to follow Hood without giving up all we have gained in the territory; I say, then, go on as you propose.

> Soon after Sherman had given up his pursuit, Hood started out with Nashville as his goal. (See map, page 640.)
> Schofield with his corps had been sent to reinforce Thomas there. If he could be beaten or destroyed, Thomas might be an easy prey. The whole campaign centered on this issue. Hood now narrates how his plan worked out.

Information had reached me that Sherman was advancing south from Atlanta, and November 21 found my army in full motion. I hoped, by a rapid march, to get in the rear of Schofield's forces before they were able to reach Duck River. The Federals became alarmed and by forced marches reached Columbia just in time to prevent our troops from cutting them off.

I then endeavored to place the main body of my army at Spring Hill, twelve miles directly in the enemy's rear, to attack and capture their army, which was the only barrier to the success of the campaign. The situation presented an occasion for one of those beautiful moves for which I had often desired an opportunity.

Thus I led the main body of the army to within about two miles and in full view of the pike from Columbia to Spring Hill and Franklin. I here halted about 3:00 P.M. on November 29, and had in sight the enemy's wagons and men passing at double-quick along the Franklin Pike. I told General Cheatham, commanding the leading corps, to "take possession of that pike at Spring Hill." Then, addressing Cleburne, I said, "General, you have one of my best divisions. Go with General Cheatham, assist him in every way you can. Do this at once."

They immediately moved off with their troops at a quick pace in the direction of the enemy.

Within about half an hour skirmishing began, when I rode forward at a point nearer the pike and sent a staff officer to General Cheatham to lose no time in gaining possession of the pike at Spring Hill. It was reported back that he was about to do so.

Listening attentively to the fire in that direction, I discovered there was no continued roar of musketry. I became uneasy and again ordered an officer to General Cheatham to inform him that he must attack at once. At this juncture the last messenger returned with the report that the road had not been taken possession of.

By this hour, however, twilight being upon us, General Cheatham rode up in person. Turning to him, I exclaimed with deep emotion, as I felt the opportunity fast slipping from me, "General, why in the name of God have you not taken possession of that pike?" He replied that the line looked a little too long for him. I could hardly believe it possible that this brave old soldier, who had given proof of such courage and ability upon so many hard-fought fields, would ever make such a report. Darkness now closed upon us, and Stewart's corps went into bivouac for the night, near but not across the pike.

It was reported to me after this hour that the enemy was marching almost under the light of the campfires of the main body of our army. I sent anew to General Cheatham to delay their march and allow us a chance to attack in the morning. Nothing was done. The Federals, with immense wagon trains, were permitted to march by us the remainder of the night within gunshot of our lines. I could not succeed in arousing the troops to action, when one good division would have sufficed to do the work. General Forrest gallantly opposed the enemy to the full extent of his power. Beyond this effort, nothing whatever was done, although never was a grander opportunity offered to rout and utterly destroy the Federal army.

The best move in my career as a soldier I was thus destined to behold come to naught. I thereupon decided, before the enemy would be able to reach his stronghold at Nashville, to make another and final effort to overtake and rout him and drive him into the Harpeth River at Franklin since I could no longer hope to get between him and Nashville.

The Illinois captain Thomas E. Milchrist of Schofield's corps, who was present at the Spring Hill affair, was glad that his forebodings failed to materialize.

Hood's failure at Spring Hill utterly to destroy Schofield's army has never been satisfactorily explained and never will be. Almost his entire army was within a mile of the Columbia-Franklin Pike, and in full view of it, when the 23rd Corps passed through that village. I fully expected that I would diet in Libby or Andersonville before I saw old friends again.

The Confederate lieutenant, R. M. Collins, offered a charitable explanation for Hood's blunder.

All day we had heard our guns pressing Schofield, and we knew that we had him. Just south of Spring Hill was a farm extending up to the pike, and our line, Cleburne's division, was formed at once and moved forward through the field. When we got in sight of the pike, it was lined as far as we could see with a Yankee train of wagons and, best of all, there was only a line of Federal skirmishers between it and us. The hearts of the boys beat high with joy, when all at once we were commanded to halt, and we went back over the ground we had just come over. By this time it was dark. We were all astonished at our line not being thrown across the pike, capturing this whole train and completely cutting off Schofield's retreat.

We built fires, ate our supper and went to sleep. While we slept Schofield's army passed by on its way to Franklin. We were actually so close to the pike that many Federal soldiers came out to our fires to light their pipes and were captured.

Generals Hood, Cheatham, Bate and others in high places have said a good deal in trying to fix the blame for this disgraceful failure; but the most charitable explanation is that the gods of battle injected confusion into the heads of our leaders.

Hood now reports what happened when, at the town of Franklin, his troops caught up with Schofield's retreating corps.

At early dawn on November 30 the troops were put in motion in the direction of Franklin, marching as rapidly as possible to overtake the enemy before he crossed the Harpeth, eighteen miles from Spring Hill. The troops appeared to recognize that a rare opportunity had been totally disregarded and manifested a determination to retrieve the fearful blunder of the previous night.

Within about three miles of Franklin, the enemy was discovered on the ridge over which passes the turnpike. As soon as the Confederate troops began to deploy, the Federals withdrew slowly to the environs of the town.

It was about 3:00 P.M. when we began to establish our position in front of the enemy. Schofield's position was rendered favorable for defense by open ground in front and temporary entrenchments which the Federals had had time to throw up. Shortly afterward, the men received orders to drive the enemy into the river *at all hazards*.

About that time General Cleburne came to me and, expressing himself with an enthusiasm which he had never before betrayed, said, "General, I have more hope in the final success of our cause than I have had at any time."

I replied, "God grant it!"

Within forty minutes he lay lifeless upon the breastworks of the foe. The conflict raged with intense fury. Our troops succeeded in breaking the main line at one or more points, capturing and turning some of the guns on their opponents.

Just at this critical moment a brigade of the enemy gallantly charged and restored the Federal line, capturing at the same time about 1,000 of our troops within the entrenchments. Still the ground was obstinately contested.

The struggle continued with more or less violence until 9:00 P.M. The enemy then withdrew, leaving his dead and wounded on the field. Thus terminated one of the fiercest conflicts of the war.

> According to the Union captain John K. Shellenberger, the outcome of the battle was largely due to a disobedience of orders by a Federal colonel.

I was commanding a company in the rear guard on our retreat to Franklin, and General G. D. Wagner, our commander, was ordered to take up a position in front of the breastworks which had been thrown up around Franklin.

When Emerson Opdycke's brigade, the last to withdraw, came up, Wagner ordered Colonel Opdycke into line with us. Opdycke strenuously objected. He declared that troops out in front of the breastworks were only an aid to the enemy, and to nobody else. Wagner turned away with the remark, "Well, Opdycke, fight when and where you damn please; we all know you'll fight." Opdycke marched his brigade inside the breastworks, and that proved to be the salvation of our army.

When the enemy were coming on the run, I shouted to my company, "Fall back! Fall back!" and gave an example of how to do it by running for the breastworks.

HOOD'S NASHVILLE CAMPAIGN

It seemed bullets had never before hissed with such diabolical venom. The cry of our wounded, knowing they would have to lie there exposed to the fire from our own line, had a pathetic note of despair I had never heard before. The next morning some of them were found with their thumbs chewed to a pulp. Their agony had been so great that they had stuck their thumbs in their mouths and bit on them to keep from bleating like calves. Many of the bodies thus exposed were hit so frequently that they were literally riddled with holes.

The Rebels broke through the breastworks but held possession of the inside only for a brief period. Opdycke was directly in the rear of where the break had occurred. As soon as he saw that a stampede was coming, he instantly led his men forward, and his brigade restored the break, after a desperate hand-to-hand encounter. If Opdycke's brigade had not been where it was, the day undoubtedly would have closed with our utter rout and ruin. When General Jacob D. Cox met Opdycke on the field immediately after, he took him by the hand and fervently exclaimed, "Opdycke, that charge of yours saved the day."

> Defeated at Franklin with fearful losses, Hood now relates why he decided on his next move and how he carried it out.

After the failure to crush Schofield's army before it reached Nashville, I remained with an effective force of only 23,000. The only remaining chance of success in the campaign was to entrench around Nashville and await Thomas' attack which, if handsomely repulsed, might afford us an opportunity to follow up our advantage on the spot and enter the city on the heels of the enemy.

In accordance with these convictions I ordered the army to move forward on the first of December in the direction of Nashville. On the morning of the second the line of battle was formed.

> Hood's opponent at Nashville, General George Thomas, although entrenched and now reinforced by Schofield's corps, was not without difficulties of his own, as we learn from the notes of Captain Thomas E. Milchrist.

Thomas' army outnumbered Hood's by a number of thousand, but about ten or twelve thousand were new troops, who had never seen service, and four or five thousand were employees of the quarter-master's department.

As Hood was in our immediate presence, Thomas prudently sought a little time in which to strengthen and equip before making an attack. On December 6, orders were issued to prepare for action on the eighth and a plan of battle was given to the corps commanders, but on the morning of the eighth the ground was covered with a frozen sleet that made it impossible to warrant an advance. For this delay Thomas was severely criticized by the War Department and by General Grant, and General Logan was on his way to Nashville to relieve Thomas. But on the morning of the fifteenth, the snow and ice having melted, Thomas ordered the attack.

Hood now narrates the course of the battle.

The enemy attacked on the morning of the fifteenth. Throughout that day they were repulsed at all points with heavy loss and only succeeded toward evening in capturing the infantry outposts on our left.

The morning of the sixteenth the enemy made a general attack along our front and were again and again repulsed. About 3:30 P.M., however, the Federals concentrated a number of guns against a portion of our line. This point was favorable for massing troops for an assault under cover of artillery. Accordingly the enemy made a sudden and gallant charge up to and over our entrenchments. Our line, thus pierced, gave way. Soon thereafter it broke at all points, and I beheld for the first and only time a Confederate army abandon a field in confusion.

I was seated on my horse not far in rear when the breach was effected and soon discovered that all hope to rally the troops was vain.

Order was in a measure restored at Brentwood, a few miles in rear of the scene of disaster. The result was that after the army had passed the Harpeth at Franklin the brigades and divisions were again marching in regular order. General Forrest had been informed of our misfortune, and his cavalry covered our retreat.

The army bivouacked in line of battle near Duck River on the night of the eighteenth. The following day we crossed, and the march was continued in the direction of Tupelo at which place Cheatham's corps, the last in the line of march, went into camp on the tenth of January, 1865.

Here is how Sam Watkins lived through the battle of Nashville and the days preceding it.

Where were our generals? Alas! there was none. After the battle of Franklin, not one single general out of Cheatham's division was left— not one. Nearly all our captains and colonels were gone too. Companies mingled with companies, regiments with regiments and brigades with brigades. A few rawboned horses stood shivering under the ice-covered trees, nibbling the short, scanty grass. We were not allowed to have fires at night, and our thin and ragged blankets were but poor protection against the cold, raw blasts of December weather.

One morning about daylight our army began to move. The battle had begun. We would build little temporary breastworks, then we would be moved to another place. Our line kept on widening out until it was not more than a skeleton of a skirmish line from one end to the other. Not more than a thousand yards off, we could see the Yankee cavalry, artillery and infantry marching.

We were willing to go anywhere or to follow anyone who would lead us. I have never seen an army so confused and demoralized. The whole thing seemed to be trembling and tottering.

Every soldier mistrusted General Hood's judgment. I remember when passing by Hood how feeble and decrepit he looked, with an arm in a sling and a crutch in the other hand, trying to guide and control his horse. I prayed in my heart that day for General Hood. Poor fellow!

We continued marching, our battle line getting thinner and thinner. We could see the Federals advancing. I heard, "Surrender, surrender!" I picked up my gun and ran.

The whole army had broken and were running in every direction. Such a scene I never saw. The woods everywhere were full of running soldiers. Our officers were crying, "Halt! Halt!" and trying to rally and re-form their broken ranks. The Federals would dash their cavalry in among us, and even their cannon joined in the charge.

Wagon trains, cannon, artillery, cavalry and infantry were all blended in inextricable confusion. Broken-down and jaded horses and mules refused to pull, and the badly scared drivers looked like their eyes would pop out of their heads from fright. The officers soon became affected with the demoralization of their troops and rode on in dogged indifference. Generals Cheatham and W. W. Loring tried to form a line at Brentwood, but it was like trying to stop Duck River with a fish net. I saw a wagon abandoned, and unhitched one of the horses and rode to Franklin, General Hood's headquarters. He was much agitated and affected, pulling his hair with his one hand and crying as though his heart would break. The citizens seemed to shrink and hide from us as we approached them. The once proud Army of Tennessee had degenerated into a mob. Our country was gone, our cause lost.

Lieutenant R. M. Collins, who was caught in the debacle, had not lost his humor, as demonstrated by his account of the retreat.

About three o'clock we marched off in the direction of Franklin. I looked to the right and saw our men running like wild cattle, throwing away everything that would impede their flight.

A long, slim Tennessee mule came running diagonally toward the pike. He had been slightly wounded and was running for his life. As he passed me I made a leap for him, caught the piece of rope around his neck and climbed onto him. The pike was full of wagons of every description, and my mule would sail through between the lead and wheel horses, back and forth, yet I "sot" as tight as if I had been a part of him. On either side of the pike were the foot people, and time and again I heard them say, "Shoot that blasted feller on the mule." This did not alarm me in the least, for I much preferred being shot by our own men to going to a Northern prison. About dark we struck Brentwood, a little station in the mountain, where the railroad passed.

Here we found General Hood, and all other generals who had not been captured, making a desperate effort to rally the men, but they would walk around him and all the other big officers just as if they had been common mortals. They were marching as if they had a thirty-days' furlough in their pocket.

The Yankees seemed to think that liberty of speech and freedom of the press depended on their keeping us on the run night and day. On the high hill about four miles north of Columbia we made a stand and gave them a fight that convinced them there was more to be done than catching us.

The next stand we made was at Pulaski, Tennessee. We were now approaching that part of Tennessee where bushwhackers did abound, and hatred for the Southern Confederacy abounded much more; therefore we kept pretty well together and in the middle of the road.

About the fifth of January, 1865, we were moved down to Corinth, Mississippi. The few people remaining there seemed to hate a Confederate soldier about as much as they did a Federal. Even the women had fallen from their patriotism of the earlier days of the war. The people had seen to their fill the empty foolishness of the so-called "pomp and circumstance of glorious war."

Hood's men, discouraged as they were, still had kept singing on their march south, and to the tune of "The Yellow Rose of Texas" someone had made up this ditty:

And now I'm going southward,
  For my heart is full of woe,
I'm going back to Georgia
  To find my 'Uncle Joe.'
You may sing about your dearest maid,
  And sing of Rosalie,
But the gallant Hood of Texas
  Played Hell in Tennessee.

* * *

Sherman, having received Grant's approval of his March to the Sea, now describes his departure from Atlanta.

On the twelfth of November the railroad and telegraph communications with the rear were broken, and the army stood detached, dependent on its own resources. The troops were grouped into two wings, commanded respectively by Major Generals O. O. Howard and H. W. Slocum, both young men but fully competent to command.

The march from Atlanta began on the morning of November 15. I remained behind to complete the destruction of the buildings which could be converted to hostile uses.

The burning of Atlanta was not an indiscriminate affair, according to Adjutant Henry Hitchcock, whose notes, made on the ground, show what Sherman's orders were.

Orders are to destroy all railroad depots, warehouses, machine shops, etc., including all buildings of use to the enemy; but no *dwellings* are to be injured.

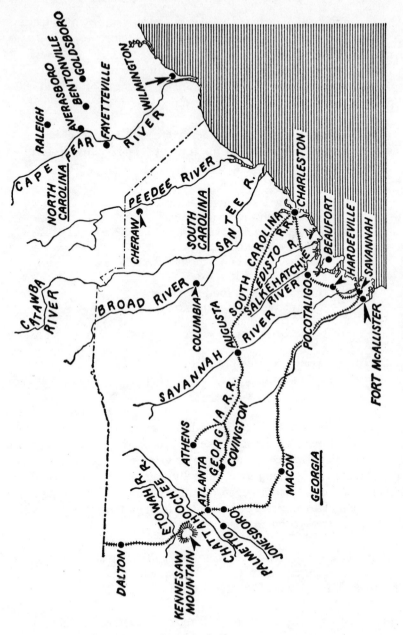

From Atlanta to the Coast

646

Sentries were posted in front of the two churches near our Head-quarters, with orders so strict that, on returning with other officers, they would not let us pass on the sidewalk but ordered us out into the street. I note these and preceding facts, because General Sherman will hereafter be charged with indiscriminate burning, which is not true. His orders are to destroy only such buildings as are used or useful for war purposes; but all others are to be spared, and *no dwellings touched.* He talked to me again today about this.

His special field order expressly defines and limits the discretion of army corps commanders to whom *alone* is committed the question of destruction, and all private soldiers are expressly forbidden *to enter any house,* even to forage.

The only danger yet is from stragglers and teamsters, after the guards are withdrawn, which they must be tomorrow.

> Edward A. Pollard presents the Southern view of the destruction of Atlanta.

On the night of the fifteenth the torch was applied to Atlanta; and where the merciless commander had already created a solitude he determined to make a conflagration, by the light of which his marching columns might commence their journey to the sea. The work was done with terrible completeness; buildings covering 200 acres were in flames at one time; the heavens were an expanse of lurid fire; and amid the wild and terrific scene the Federal bands played "John Brown's soul goes marching on." The next morning Sherman's army moved from a scene of desolation such as had occurred in no modern picture of civilized war. From 4,000 to 5,000 houses were reduced to ruins; 400 left standing were the melancholy remnant of Atlanta. Nearly all the shade trees in the park and city had been destroyed, and the suburbs, stripped of timber, presented to the eye one vast, naked, ruined, deserted camp.

> F. Y. Hedley, one of Sherman's aides, gives us an idea of the kind of soldiers who composed his army at that time.

Sherman's army was now a remarkable body of men. Sixty thousand in round numbers, it was an army of veterans, who had learned far more than their generals had known three years before.

The old men and the big men had been sent home. It was the "little devils" (as Sherman called them) who remained and could be depended on to march all day and be ready for a frolic at night.

The average soldier cared only for a blanket, carried in a roll swung over his shoulder. A majority of the men discarded knapsacks altogether. Each had forty rounds of ammunition in his cartridge box, and one hundred and sixty more elsewhere upon his person. His cooking utensils were a tin oyster can, in which to make his coffee, and sometimes one-half of a canteen to serve as a frying pan. His haversack contained a liberal amount of coffee, sugar and salt, a very small fragment of salt pork and three days' rations of hard bread. This supply was to last him ten days. The soldier's outfit was not complete without a deck of cards.

The army marched in four columns, pursuing parallel roads. These columns were sometimes five, sometimes fifteen miles apart. Their combined front was from forty to sixty miles.

In front of each corps marched a regiment of cavalry or mounted infantry. Frequently these troops, with the aid of the infantry brigade at the head of the column, were able to brush aside the enemy without much trouble and without halting the main column, and it was only when crossing a stream, where the passage was contested, that anything like a general line of battle was ever formed.

Here are some observations made during the march by a Union soldier named Charles Sheldon Sargeant.

Our departure from Atlanta had occasioned a tremendous sensation all over the Confederacy. The Georgia legislature had ordered a levy "en masse," and General Beauregard had followed with a volley of "General Orders" commanding the people to destroy all their property to prevent our troops from getting the benefit of it. The Southern papers were full of hysterical shrieks—"we are drawing the Yankees into the swamps; when we get them far enough in, we will destroy every one of them."

As one of the principal objects of this march was to break up railroad communication between the East and West, General Sherman made arrangements to have it thoroughly done. Little was left undestroyed. Generally a corps was detailed for the work, and, as it was always one of the "center corps" (having a full corps marching on each flank), it was safe from attack.

General Sherman took great interest in the destruction of the railroad and, as he rode along the line watching the work and looking like anybody excepting the commanding general, the boys, who always hailed him as "Uncle Billy," had a great many remarks to make as to our destination. He always took everything good-naturedly, but I never heard of anyone getting any information on that subject. When one, more daring than the rest, remarked, "I guess Grant is waiting for us at Richmond, Uncle Billy," he only laughed and suggested "a little more twist on that rail."

One incident I may recall as showing General Sherman's prompt method of dealing with what he considered violations of the laws of war. When nearing a city, we found that the main road at a certain point had been planted with torpedoes and several of our men were killed and wounded. General Sherman promptly ordered the prisoners to be brought to the front and forced them at the point of the bayonet to march in advance of the troops until the danger was passed. He then paroled an officer and sent him through the lines with a message of such a character that this act was not repeated.

When Sherman's aims, after his departure from Atlanta, became clearly defined, the Confederate authorities made frantic efforts to hinder his progress. Various proclamations were issued, of which the following are examples. None of them accomplished their purpose, if for no other reason than that they came too late. Raw recruits could not be molded into an efficient fighting force in a few days.

November 18, 1864

To the People of Georgia:

Arise for the defence of your native soil! Rally around your patriotic Governor and gallant soldiers. Obstruct and destroy all the roads in Sherman's front, flank, and rear, and his army will soon starve in your midst. Be confident. Be resolute. Trust in an overruling Providence, and success will soon crown your efforts. I hasten to join you in the defence of your homes and firesides.

G. T. BEAUREGARD

To the People of Georgia:

You have now the best opportunity ever yet presented to destroy the enemy.

Every citizen with his gun and every Negro with his spade and axe can do the work of a soldier. You can destroy the enemy by retarding his march.

Georgians be firm, act promptly, and fear not.

B. H. Hill, Senator

> One of the most spectacular developments during Sherman's March to the Sea, and one which was to leave the deepest resentment in the South, was the creation of a type known as "bummers." Sherman explains how they came into existence.

The skill and success of the men in collecting forage was one of the features of this march. Each brigade commander had authority to detail a company of foragers. They would usually procure a wagon or family carriage, load it with bacon, corn meal, turkeys, chickens, ducks and everything that could be used as food. Although this foraging was attended with great danger and hard work, there seemed to be a charm about it that attracted the soldiers. No doubt many acts of pillage, robbery and violence were committed by these foragers, usually called "bummers"; for I have since heard of jewelry taken from women and the plunder of articles that never reached the commissary; but these acts were exceptional and incidental.

> What the South thought—and remembered—of Sherman's bummers is expressed by Mr. Pollard of the *Richmond Examiner.*

For a hundred miles Sherman left behind him a wreck of railroads and a desolated country. He had consumed the fat of the land, and he had strewn every mile of his march with the evidences of savage warfare. His army had been permitted to do whatever crime could compass and cruelty invent. Even crockery, bedcovering, or clothes were fair spoils. As for plate, or jewelry or watches, these were things Rebels had no use for. If the spoils were ample, the depredators were satisfied and went off in peace; if not, everything was torn and destroyed and most likely the owner was tickled with sharp bayonets into confessing where he had his treasures hid. Furniture was smashed to pieces, music was pounded out of 400-dollar pianos with the ends of muskets. Rich cushions and carpets were carried off to adorn teams and war steeds. After all was cleared out, most likely some stragglers set the house and all the surroundings ablaze. This is the way Sherman's army lived on the country.

The bummers sometimes indulged in what they considered humorous performances, so Captain Daniel Oakey of the 2nd Massachusetts Volunteers reports.

If antiquated uniforms were discovered on a plantation, the booty was escorted to the point where the brigade was expected to bivouac for the night. On one occasion, when our regiment had the advance, it was confronted by a picket dressed in continental uniform, who waved his plumed hat, and galloped away on his bareback mule to apprise his comrades of our approach. We marched into town and rested. Presently a forager in ancient militia uniform, indicating high rank, debouched from a side street to do the honors. He was mounted on a raw-boned horse with a bit of carpet for a saddle. His old chapeau in hand, he rode with gracious dignity through the street, as if reviewing the brigade. After him came a carriage laden with hams, sweet potatoes, and other provisions, drawn by two horses, a mule and a cow, the latter two ridden by postillons.

The Northern captain George Pepper described the ways of a bummer in a manner which did not differ materially from that of the Southern journalist Pollard.

Fancy a ragged man, blackened by smoke, mounted on a scrawny mule without a saddle, with a gun, a knapsack, a butcher knife and a plug hat, stealing his way far out on the flanks of a column. Keen on the scent of Rebels, or bacon, or silver spoons, or corn, or anything valuable, and he will be in your mind. Think how you would admire him if you were a lone woman, far from help, when he blandly inquired where you kept your valuables. Think how you would smile when he pried open your chests with his bayonet or knocked to pieces your tables, pianos and chairs, tore your bed clothing in three-inch strips and scattered the strips. They go through a Negro cabin with as much vivacity as they loot the dwelling of a wealthy planter. They appear to be possessed of a spirit of pure cussedness.

One incident of many will illustrate. A bummer stepped into a house and inquired for sorghum. The lady of the house presented a jug which he said was too heavy, so he merely filled his canteen. Then, taking a huge wad of tobacco from his mouth, he thrust it into the jug. The lady inquired why he spoiled that which he did not want. "Oh, some feller'll come along and taste that sorghum and think you've poisoned him; then he'll burn your damned old house." There are hundreds of these mounted men, and they go everywhere. Some of them are loaded down with silverware, gold coin and other valuables. I hazard nothing in saying that three-fifths (in value) of the personal property of the country we passed through was taken.

On a plantation near Covington, Georgia, there lived at that time a woman named Dolly Sumner Lunt. On November 19, 1864, Sherman's army passed by her property, and while the events of that memorable day were still fresh in her mind she recorded them in her diary.

Mrs. Lunt's observations are noteworthy, because in her estimation the damage she sustained was the work of Sherman's own advance columns, not that of irresponsible and power-drunk bummers.

There the Yankees came filing up. I hastened to my frightened servants and told them that they had better hide, and then went back to the gate to claim protection and a guard. But like demons they rushed in! My yards were full. To my smokehouse, my dairy, pantry, kitchen and cellar like famished wolves they came, breaking locks and whatever was in their way. The thousand pounds of meat in my smokehouse were gone in a twinkling, my flour, my meat, my lard, butter, eggs, pickles of various kinds—both in vinegar and brine—wine, jars and jugs were all gone. My eighteen fat turkeys, my hens, chickens, and fowls, my young pigs, were shot down in my yard and hunted as if they were Rebels themselves. Utterly powerless I ran out and appealed to the guard.

"I cannot help you, Madam; it is orders."

As I stood there, from my lot I saw driven, first, old Dutch, my dear old buggy horse, who had carried my beloved husband so many miles, and who would so quietly wait at the block for him to mount and dismount and who at last drew him to his grave; then came old Mary, my brood mare, who for years had been too old and stiff for work, with her three-year-old colt and her last little baby colt. There they went! There went my mules, my sheep and, worse than all, my boys [slaves]!

Alas! Little did I think while trying to save my house from plunder and fire that they were forcing my boys from home at the point of the bayonet. One jumped into bed in his cabin and declared himself sick. Another crawled under the floor—a lame boy he was—but they pulled him out, placed him on a horse and drove him off.

I had not believed they would force from their homes the poor, doomed Negroes, but such has been the fact here, cursing them and saying that "Jeff Davis wanted to put them in his army, but that they should not fight for him but for the Union." No! Indeed no! They are not friends to the slave. We have never made the poor Negro fight, and it is strange, passing strange, that the all-powerful Yankee nation with the whole world to back it, its ports open, its armies filled with soldiers from all nations, should at last take the poor Negro to help it out against this little Confederacy which was to have been brought back into the Union in sixty days' time!

My poor boys! My poor boys!

Sherman himself and a greater portion of his army passed my house that day. All day, as the sad moments rolled on, were they passing not only in front of my house, but behind. They tore down my garden palings, made a road through my back yard and lot field, driving their stock and riding through, tearing down my fences and desolating my home—wantonly doing it when there was no necessity for it.

Such a day, if I live to the age of Methuselah, may God spare me from ever seeing again!

　　Bumming, however, was done by both sides, so we are told by a Federal bummer named Charles E. Belknap.

One day we captured a plantation rich in chickens and other articles. While the men were busy twisting necks and gathering eggs, a troop of Wheeler's men came down on us like a whirlwind and drove the boys to the woods near by. Hasty preparations were made for a fight. The lady of the house came out and, shaking her first, shouted, "You miserable Yankees! You have taken every chicken on the place."

"What's that?" said the Confederate. "Taken all the chickens? Then there's nothing left worth fighting for." He called his men and rode away, leaving the woman calling names and shaking fists until the miserable Yankees returned to gather up the odds and ends.

Resistance by the Georgia militia was encountered by Sherman's men now and then. Lieutenant C. W. Wills noted a case of this kind in his diary.

November 22, 1864, has been a heyday for our brigade. We were getting dinner, not dreaming of a fight, when a fine line of Johnnies pushed out of the woods and started for us. By the time their first line had got within 250 yards of us, three other lines had emerged from the woods and they had run two batteries out on the field. Our artillery was silenced almost immediately. We then let loose on them with our muskets, and one after another their lines crumbled to pieces, and they ran. Our little brigade had 1,100 muskets engaged, while the Rebels had about 6,000. But the four brigades were militia.

Old gray-haired and weakly-looking men and little boys not over fifteen years old lay dead or writhing in pain. I hope we will never have to shoot at such men again.

Sherman was now approaching Savannah and hoped to make contact there with a Federal fleet. From the land side Fort Mc-Allister was the key to the city and had to be taken.

Richmond Smith, Sherman's chief telegraph operator, thus recorded the last chapter in the March to the Sea.

Last evening General Sherman disappeared from headquarters, but made his appearance early next morning on his way to our extreme right. At that place there is a large rice mill, from which Fort McAllister could be seen. Hearing about what was going on, I hurried to the mill, twenty-one miles distant from headquarters. I reached there just in time. With the use of a field glass I could see the fort, rebel flag, and even the men, very distinctly. Affairs were evidently drawing to a focus rapidly, as the General was beginning to get somewhat excited. Our skirmishers were getting so close to the fort that they could do little or no service at firing on the enemy. All at once the guns of the fort burst forth with a fearful fire of grape and canister. Our boys shot out of the woods over the *cheveaux-de-frise*, and quickly mounted the parapets. This was the moment the General had been looking for. We could no longer discern our boys, but the old flags, two of which were held upon the parapets, could be seen, and we knew that as long as they stood up so proudly, all was well. Volley after volley continued to be showered upon the rebels; still they did not surrender, nor did they until every gun was taken from them. They were evidently the best men the South could boast of. The first evidence that the fight had ended was our flag waving to and fro, a sign evidently agreed on. General Sherman was almost beside himself.

This was the key to the river, and in fact had been the only obstruction to our communication with the fleet.

After the fall of Fort McAllister, the conquest of Savannah, according to Sherman's account, proved easy.

Fort McAllister had been captured late in the evening of December 13. On the eighteenth I received General Hardee's letter declining to surrender, and nothing remained but to assault. The ground was difficult, and I concluded to make one more effort to surround Savannah completely on all sides. But toward evening of December 21, a tug arrived, reporting that the city of Savannah had been found evacuated on the morning of that day and was then in our possession. General Hardee had crossed the Savannah River by a pontoon bridge, carrying off his men and light artillery, blowing up his ironclads and navy yard, but leaving for us all the heavy guns, stores, cotton, railway cars, steamboats and an immense amount of public and private property.

Sherman presented Savannah to President Lincoln as a Christmas gift and then prepared for further exploits. He now could either join Grant by water or else march by land through the Carolinas. He preferred the latter.

I had not yet received from General Grant any modification of the orders to embark my command for Virginia by sea; but on the second of January, 1865, I was authorized to march with my entire army north by land. I still remained in doubt, however, whether I should take Charleston en route or confine my whole attention to breaking up the railways of South and North Carolina and the greater object of uniting my army with that of General Grant before Richmond.

By the tenth General Howard began his march for Pocotaligo, twenty-five miles inland. About the same time General Slocum crossed over the Savannah River, occupying Hardeeville. Thus by the middle of January we had effected a lodgment in South Carolina and were ready to resume the march northward.

On the twenty-first of January, I embarked for Beaufort, South Carolina. All the country between Beaufort and Pocotaligo was low alluvial land, cut up by an infinite number of salt-water sloughs and fresh-water creeks, easily susceptible of defense by a small force. Why the enemy had allowed us to make a lodgment at Pocotaligo so easily I did not understand, unless it resulted from fear or ignorance. Somehow our men had got the idea that South Carolina was the cause of all our troubles, and therefore on its people should fall the scourge of war in its worst form. I saw and felt that we would not be able longer to restrain our men as we had done in Georgia.

The enemy occupied the cities of Charleston and Augusta with garrisons capable of making a respectable, if not successful, defense but utterly unable to meet our veteran columns in the open field. To resist or delay our progress north, General Wheeler had his division of cavalry (reduced to the size of a brigade), and General Wade Hampton had been dispatched from the Army of Virginia to his native South Carolina with extraordinary powers to raise men, money and horses with which "to stay the progress of the invader."

Of course, I had a species of contempt for these scattered and inconsiderable forces, and the only serious question was: Would General Lee permit us, almost unopposed, to pass through South and North Carolina, cutting off and consuming the very supplies on which he depended to feed his army, or would he make an effort to escape from General Grant and endeavor to catch us inland somewhere between Columbia and Raleigh? I knew that the broken fragments of Hood's army were being hurried rapidly across Georgia to make junction in my front. Estimating them at the maximum 25,000 men, and Hardee's, Wheeler's and Hampton's forces at 15,000, made 40,000, which, if handled with spirit and energy, would constitute a formidable force and might make the passage of such rivers as the Santee and Cape Fear a difficult undertaking.

On February 3 the 17th Corps was on the Salkehatchie, which was over its banks and presented a most formidable obstacle. The enemy appeared in some force on the opposite bank. Generals Joseph A. Mower and Giles A. Smith, however, led their heads of column through a swamp, the water up to their shoulders, turned upon the Rebel brigade which defended the passage and routed it in utter disorder.

On February 5 I gave orders for the march straight for the South Carolina Railroad. I expected severe resistance there, for its loss would sever all the communications of Charleston with Augusta.

Early on the seventh we reached the railroad, almost unopposed. General Howard told me a good story concerning this. When about five miles from the railroad, he got ready for battle. Sitting on his horse by the roadside, he saw a man coming down the road, riding as hard as he could, and recognized him as one of his own "foragers." The man called out, "Hurry up, General; we have got the railroad!" So, while we, the generals, were proceeding deliberately to prepare for a serious battle, a parcel of our foragers, in search of plunder, had actually captured the South Carolina Railroad.

On the tenth I made out orders for the movement to Columbia. During the sixteenth of February, the 15th Corps reached the point opposite Columbia, crossed the Broad River, and the head of the column reached there just in time to find the bridge in flames.

Sherman's march through the Carolinas was no holiday affair, as may be gleaned from the observations of General M. F. Force.

The soil melted away under rain. Even where the surface looked firm and solid, wagon wheels would break through and sink to the hubs. The sluggish rivers, swollen with winter rains, spread far beyond their borders, branching into a dozen channels creeping through a wide belt of swamp.

Instead of finding streams with well-defined, solid banks, we came upon tangled swamps, miles across, dense with trees, vines and thickets and full of icy water. The regular crossing was by roads, at long intervals, built through the swamps on raised causeways with bridges over the stream. As every crossing was defended by batteries which swept it, advance over the causeway was impossible. Sometimes a place above or below could be found where the streams were fordable, and the troops waded through and then bridged the streams. Sometimes all the streams united in one channel, with a firm bank on our side and a swamp beyond. There we could lay pontoons and cross. Always, to the very last, we crossed unobserved, and the enemy, surprised to see a line of battle emerge from the woods on their flanks, abandoned their works precipitately and fell back behind the next river. We would rebuild the burned bridges, move the trains over the regular road and pursue.

It rained most of the time, day and night. Every division had a regularly organized pioneer corps, which toiled all day building roads and bridges. Parties were detailed every day to lift wagons out of the mud when the teams could not pull them through. Sometimes a brigade, sometimes a regiment, was turned into a pioneer detail.

The march across South Carolina was devastating. There was much burning and destruction; and there was pillage, undoubtedly. But soldiers who threw away every unnecessary inch of blanket in order to save the weight would not incumber themselves with plunder. At a place where we halted for a day, the provost marshals of the 17th Corps, without warning, inspected the camps to find stolen articles. The result was a little clothing and some tobacco. Even in South Carolina I never heard of any case of personal abuse. The people said both armies, the National and the Confederate, were alike in taking their property; that the difference was we also burned their houses, while their own soldiers abused and insulted them.

On February 17, 1865, Sherman entered Columbia, the capital of South Carolina. The trouble he met there, so he stoutly avers, was not of his making.

As soon as the bridge over the Broad River was done, I led my horse over it, followed by my whole staff. A high and boisterous wind was prevailing, and flakes of cotton were flying about in the air. Near the market square we found some citizens with an old fire engine, trying to put out the fire in a pile of burning cotton bales.

I strolled through the streets, found sentinels posted at the principal intersections and generally good order prevailing. In the evening of that day, February 17, I lay down to rest. Soon after dark I became conscious that a bright light was shining on the walls and called someone of my staff to inquire the cause. The same high wind still prevailed, and I bade him go in person to see if the provost guard was doing its duty. He soon returned and reported that the block of buildings directly opposite the cotton burning that morning was on fire and that it was spreading; but he had found General Woods on the ground, with plenty of men trying to put the fire out, or at least, to prevent its extension.

The fire continued to increase, though. I dispatched messenger after messenger to Generals Howard, Logan and Woods and received from them repeated assurance that all was being done that could be done, but that the high wind was spreading the flames beyond all control. The whole air was full of sparks and of flying masses of cotton, shingles, etc., some of which were carried four or five blocks and started new fires. The men seemed generally under good control and certainly labored hard to girdle the fire. Fortunately, about 3:00 or 4:00 A.M., the wind moderated and gradually the fire was got under control, but it had burned out the very heart of the city, embracing several churches, the old Statehouse and the school of the Sisters of Charity. Many people thought that this fire was deliberately planned and executed. This is not true. It was accidental, and in my judgment began with the cotton which General Hampton's men had set fire to on leaving the city.

Wade Hampton, replying to this accusation, put the blame for the destruction of Columbia squarely on Sherman's shoulders.

I deny emphatically that any cotton was fired in Columbia by my order. I deny that the citizens set fire to thousands of bales rolled out into the streets. I deny that any cotton was on fire when the Federal troops entered the city. I pledge myself to prove that General Sherman burned the city to the ground, deliberately, systematically and atrociously.

S. H. M. Byers, who had just rejoined Sherman's army after some months in a Confederate prison camp, allows us a glance at the horror of the burning city.

The sights of that awful night will never fade from my memory. Most of the citizens of Columbia had sons or relations in the Rebel army. Half of them were dead, and in the blackness of this terrible night their fortunes were all lost. Many wandered about wringing their hands and crying; some sat stolid and speechless in the street, watching everything that they had go to destruction. A few rambled around, wholly demented. Some of the invading soldiers tried earnestly to extinguish the flames; others broke into houses and added to the conflagration. Numbers of Federal prisoners, who only a few weeks before had been marched through the streets like felons, had escaped, and what average human nature led them to do never will be known. There were fearful things going on everywhere. Most of the people of Columbia would have been willing to die that night, then and there. What had they left to live for? *This, too, was war.*

With Columbia at his back, Sherman now describes his further progress.

The right wing of the army resumed its march northward on February 20. It was to move rapidly toward Fayetteville, North Carolina.

While in camp one night, two prisoners were brought to me. General Hardee was, they said, evacuating Charleston; Wilmington, North Carolina, was reported in possession of the Yankee troops; so that I had every reason to be satisfied that our march was reaping all the fruits we could possibly ask for. Charleston was, in fact, evacuated on the eighteenth of February, and Wilmington was captured on the twenty-second.

By March 12 I was again in full communication with the outside world. I was anxious to reach Goldsboro, so as to be ready for the next and last stage of the war. I then knew that General Joseph Johnston was back with part of his old army, that he would not be misled by feints and false reports and would compel me to exercise more caution than I had hitherto done.

On the night of March 18 we were within twenty-seven miles of Goldsboro, and five from Bentonville. Supposing that all danger was over, I crossed over to join Howard's column to the right, so as to be nearer to Goldsboro.

On the twenty-third of March we rode into Goldsboro, where I found General Schofield with the 23rd Corps, thus effecting a perfect junction of all the army at that point, as originally contemplated.

Thus was concluded one of the longest and most important marches ever made by an organized army in a civilized country. The distance from Savannah to Goldsboro is 425 miles, and the route traversed embraced five large navigable rivers, viz., the Edisto, Broad, Catawba, Pee Dee and Cape Fear. We had captured Columbia, Cheraw and Fayetteville, important cities and depots of supplies, had compelled the evacuation of Charleston, had broken up all the railroads of South Carolina and had consumed a vast amount of food and forage essential to the enemy for the support of his own armies. We had in midwinter accomplished the whole journey of 425 miles in fifty days, averaging ten miles per day, allowing ten lay days, and had reached Goldsboro with the army in superb order.

It was manifest to me that we could come within the theater of General Grant's field of operations in April and that there was no force in existence that could delay our progress, unless General Lee should succeed in eluding General Grant at Petersburg, make junction with General Johnston and thus united meet me alone; and I had no fear even of that.

As Sherman approached the North Carolina town of Bentonville, he was once more made to feel the prowess of his old adversary, General Johnston.

Alexander C. McClurg of the Union army narrates the event.

It was the nineteenth of March, 1865. A part of the 20th Corps, supported by the 14th, had had a sharp engagement with the enemy, under Hardee, at Averasboro and had chased him northward toward Raleigh. General Sherman made his disposition for a rapid march to Goldsboro, supposing that all danger was over.

But for once General Sherman had reckoned without his host; and that host was Joseph E. Johnston, whose forces had, unbeknown to Sherman, concentrated on his left flank and front and within striking distance.

Sherman's army consisted of between 57,000 and 58,000 men. Two divisions of the 14th Army Corps, numbering a little over 8,000 men, were on the direct road from Averysboro to Goldsboro. Two divisions of the 20th Corps, also about 8,000 men, had encamped eight miles in the rear on the same road, a terrible stretch of almost impassable mud lying between the two commands. The 15th and 17th Corps, constituting the right wing of the army, were scattered out on roads lying five to ten miles to the south.

General Sherman had himself been riding for several days with the left and exposed wing, and at about 7:30 A.M. he and General Slocum, with General Jefferson C. Davis, who commanded the 14th Army Corps, were listening to the signs of skirmishing which came back from the front. Something impressed the soldierly instinct of General Davis with the belief that he was likely to encounter more than the usual cavalry opposition, and he frankly said so to General Sherman. The latter, after listening attentively a moment or two, replied in his usual brisk, nervous, and positive way, "No, Jeff; there is nothing there but cavalry. Brush them out of the way. Good morning. I'll meet you tomorrow morning at Cox's Bridge." It turned out that three days and a desperate fight yet lay between us and Cox's bridge.

The men found in their front, as they always did, the enemy's cavalry. But this time it did not yield. The old expression was brought out again: "They won't drive worth a damn."

At length the whole 1st Brigade was pushed forward; but still the resistance of the enemy was determined. Ten o'clock came, and we had moved but five miles. Soon the enemy overlapped us on our right flank. The right and left of our line were ordered to advance but, to the surprise of everyone, they dashed, all unprepared, against a line of earthworks manned with infantry and artillery. The enemy opened upon them such a destructive fire that they were compelled to fall back with severe loss.

It was now about half past one o'clock, and Generals Slocum and Davis were in consultation in the woods when a deserter from the enemy was sent to them. He belonged to that limited class of "galvanized Yankee" men who had been captured and who, rather than endure prison life, had taken service in the Rebel army. This man told a startling story. General Johnston's army had by night marches been concentrated in our immediate front and was strongly entrenched. At first his story was doubted; but a young officer recognized him as a fellow townsman and former playfellow. There could be little doubt that he was telling the truth.

It was certain the enemy would attack at once and in overwhelming numbers. It was too late to withdraw; the men all were working like beavers, throwing up hasty field works, when the attack came on us like a whirlwind. I had gone to the rear, and as I again started for the front I met large masses of men doggedly falling back. They were retreating but they were not demoralized.

The Rebel regiments in front were in full view, stretching through the fields as far as one could see, advancing rapidly and firing as they came. It was a gallant sight and contrasted signally with our center and left, where our thin line seemed to have been nearly wiped out of existence. The onward sweep of the Rebel lines was like the waves of the ocean, resistless.

One of James D. Morgan's brigades had not been engaged. General Davis sent instructions to hold this brigade in readiness. A few moments later, when our left and center were falling back, General Davis came plunging through the swamp on his fiery white mare toward the reserve. "Where is that brigade?"

"Here it is, sir, ready to march."

Ordering it swung around to the left, General Davis shouted, "Advance upon their flank; strike them wherever you find them!"

The words seem cold in print, but when uttered by a man born to command, they were electric. The men struck the unsuspecting enemy with impetuosity and were quickly engaged in a desperate conflict. On this movement, in all probability, turned the fortunes of the day. It was the right thing, done at the right time.

General Davis sent to General Slocum, begging for another brigade to support him. Fortunately Cogswell's fine brigade of the 20th Corps arrived on the field about this time. Not often does an officer, coming upon the field with tired troops, display the alacrity which Colonel William Cogswell showed. He and his men soon too were enveloped in fire and smoke. The flushed and victorious troops of the enemy, thus taken in the flank, in their turn fell back in confusion and re-entered their works.

And now there was a lull of an hour along the whole front. It was about five o'clock before their long line was again seen sweeping across the open fields. As soon as they appeared, our artillery opened upon them with most destructive effect. Still they moved gallantly on, only to be met with a well-delivered fire from our infantry, securely posted behind hastily improvised field works. Attack after attack was gallantly met and repulsed, and the best opportunity of the enemy was lost.

After a while a slight cessation was noticed in the firing, and by direction of General Davis I rode forward to ascertain how matters stood. I had gone but a few rods when I caught a glimpse of a Confederate column moving directly in rear of our line. Hardee's corps, or a considerable part of it, had passed through an opening in our line.

General Morgan was thoroughly aware of his perilous situation. He quickly got his men so they were now prepared to sustain an attack from the rear.

The enemy attacked vigorously, but instead of taking Morgan by surprise, as they had expected, they found him ready. Again the struggle was sharp and bloody, but it was brief. Nothing could stand that day before the veterans of the old 2nd Division. Hardee was repulsed with severe loss.

At length daylight faded. Seldom was coming darkness more heartily welcome to wearied soldiers. Before morning the troops of the right wing would march to our assistance.

Never before had fortune and circumstances so united to favor Johnston, and never before had hope shone so brightly for him and his Confederate troops. If Sherman's army had been destroyed in the Battle of Bentonville, the Confederacy might yet have been inspired with new spirit and ultimate success might at least have been probable. But as the sun went down that night, it carried with it the last hopes of the Southern Confederacy.

A young aide to the Confederate general A. P. Stewart kept a diary during the last days of the Carolina campaign, and from it the following excerpts seem worth quoting.

March 16, 1865. General J. E. Johnston took command yesterday of the Army of the South.

March 17. Conducted General Johnston to our headquarters, found him surprisingly social. He endeavors to conceal his greatness rather than to impress you with it. I expressed to him the joy the Army of Tennessee manifested on hearing of his restoration to command. He said that he was equally gratified to be with them as they were at his coming, but he feared it "too late to make it the same army."

March 19. Both armies commenced the march. Three miles beyond Bentonville, at Cole's farm, we met and skirmished heavily for a short time. Armies went into position—Bragg commanded left wing, Stewart the center, and Hardee the right. At one o'clock the enemy charged Clayton's division and was repulsed handsomely. General Johnston now ordered an advance. The hour for attack agreed upon was fifteen minutes to three o'clock. With a Rebel shout we drove the enemy nearly a mile and routed them from two lines of breastworks, capturing eight pieces of artillery and 417 prisoners. The excitement of the occasion and the many ravines we had to cross broke our line to such an extent that we halted and re-formed. While doing this, the enemy rallied, reinforced and charged repeatedy upon our lines until nightfall but with no effect. The brunt of this battle was on the Army of Tennessee, and the more praise should be accorded them for their quick recuperation from the disaster at Nashville. "Old Joe" drove back Sherman's disciplined veterans with a demoralized army of not exceeding 12,000 men. In consequence of a flank movement to our left, we were ordered to retire.

March 27. We saw a squad of forty Yanks. From their brazen looks, they consider us virtually whipped and our complete overthrow only a question of time. Numbers may subdue but cannot conquer.

April 4. I witnessed today the saddest spectacle of my life, the review of the skeleton Army of Tennessee. But one year ago replete with men, it now filed by with tattered garments, barefooted and with ranks so depleted that each color was supported by only thirty or forty men. The march of the remnant was so slow—colors tattered and torn with bullets—that it looked like a funeral procession. Oh, it is beginning to look dark in the east, gloomy in the west and almost like a lost hope when we reflect on the review of today!

CHAPTER 20

The Curtain Falls

THE APPOMATTOX CAMPAIGN AND LEE'S SURRENDER

In Virginia, Lee's long thin line had at last been broken. His defeat at Five Forks had made Petersburg and Richmond untenable. Grant, as Regis de Trobriand relates, was determined to overtake Lee's army and prevent its union with Johnston.

After the Battle of Five Forks General Grant had one fear: that the enemy would take advantage of the night to evacuate his works. He therefore kept up a continual attack along the whole line. At 4:00 A.M. on April 2 the 6th Corps and the 9th were to assault. The great day had arrived.

Punctually at four o'clock the two corps threw forward their assaulting columns, carrying everything before them. United, they then turned their faces toward Petersburg. Two closed redoubts were found in the plain. Both were captured, but not without the most intrepid resistance from one of them.

We now hurried on toward Petersburg. It was a beautiful day. The spring sun laughed among the new foliage. The men marched with a joyous step, running and laughing.

On approaching the city we arrived near a house of poor appearance, when a movement ran through the ranks. There is General Grant! Everyone straightened himself up, adjusted his equipment. The general, seated on a front veranda, his legendary cigar in his mouth, looked on us passing by. All was motion and life. He alone preserved his habitual calm, but through it shone the pride of triumph.

Everything, however, was not yet over. Between us and Petersburg there was still a line of works. In order to strengthen his position the enemy had even endeavored to recapture some positions from the 9th Corps. It was in one of these offensive efforts, unsuccessful though vigorously made, that General A. P. Hill was killed.

The remainder of the day passed in putting the artillery in position so as to carry the city by assault if the enemy persisted in defending it.

> With the fall of Petersburg in sight, Horace Porter, now a brigadier general, narrates what happened at Grant's headquarters.

Prominent officers urged Grant to make an assault on the inner lines and capture Petersburg that afternoon, but he was firm in his resolve not to sacrifice lives. He said the city would undoubtedly be evacuated during the night.

General Grant's prediction was fully verified. The evacuation had begun about ten the night before and was completed on the morning of April 3.

Mr. Lincoln soon after arrived at the house which Grant occupied, accompanied by Robert, by his little son Tad and Admiral Porter. He came in through the front gate with long and rapid strides, his face beaming with delight. He seized General Grant's hand and stood shaking it for some time, pouring out his thanks and congratulations.

Mr. Lincoln then began to talk about the civil complications that would follow the destruction of the Confederate armies and showed plainly his anxiety regarding the great problems which would soon be thrust on him. He intimated very plainly that thoughts of leniency to the conquered were uppermost in his heart.

> Jefferson Davis' reaction to the bad news from Petersburg is reported by himself.

On Sunday the second of April, while I was in St. Paul's church, a telegram from General Lee was handed to me, announcing his speedy withdrawal from Petersburg and the consequent necessity for evacuating Richmond. I quietly rose and left the church. I went to my office and assembled the heads of departments and bureaus, as far as they could be found, and gave instructions for our removal that night simultaneously with General Lee's withdrawal from Petersburg.

The few arrangements needful for my personal wants were soon made. I waited until the time when the train would depart. Then I went to the station and started for Danville, whither I supposed General Lee would proceed with his army.

> This is how the news of the victory was received by the Union army, according to the infantryman Theodore Gerrish.

A staff officer came dashing back along the line, swinging his hat and shouting, "Petersburg and Richmond are evacuated, and General Lee is in full retreat!"

The news was too good to believe. We remembered how often we had been told of great victories when they wanted us to make some great exertion. So we shouted back, "That's played out!" . . . "Tell it to the recruits!" . . . "Give him a hard tack!"

Our own colonel, however, soon told us that the news was true. In a moment our caps went up in the air, we shook one another's hands and cheered until we were hoarse. And all the time our line was sweeping on in swift pursuit of the fleeing foe.

> All Confederate outposts were quickly called in to join in the retreat. Colonel E. M. Boykin of the 7th Georgia, whose regiment stood six miles east of Richmond, describes his experiences that morning.

It was out now: there had been a heavy fight near Petersburg, and the army was in full retreat. We started to move on to the city at once.

In a short time a tremendous explosion took place toward the river. This was the ironclad *Virginia*, as we afterward heard, just completed. She burst like a bombshell, and the explosion told, in anything but a whisper, the desperate condition of things.

We passed into the "Rockets," the southern suburb of Richmond, at an easy marching gait. One strapping virago stood on the edge of the pavement with her arms akimbo, looking at us with intense scorn. "Yes," said she, "afther fighting them for four years ye're running like dawgs!" I could not stop to explain that General Longstreet's orders were not to make a fight in the city.

On we went. We met a motley crowd loaded with every species of plunder. Women, their arms filled with goods plundered from warehouses and shops, their hair hanging about their ears, were rushing one way, while a current of the empty-handed surged in a contrary direction. This, together with the roaring and crackling of burning houses, made a scene which I hope never to see again: a city undergoing pillage at the hands of its own mob, while the tramp of a victorious enemy could be heard at its gates!

As we reached the high hill on which Manchester is built, we looked down on Richmond. By this time the fire appeared to be general. Some magazine or depot was on fire about the center of the city; from it would come the roar of bursting shells and boxes of fixed ammunition, with flashes that gave it the appearance of a thundercloud with lightning playing through it. On our right was the navy yard. Several steamers and gunboats were on fire there, from which the cannon were thundering as the flames reached them. The old war-scarred city seemed to prefer annihilation to conquest—a useless sacrifice, however much it may have added to the grandeur of the closing act.

Through T. C. DeLeon we have a picture of the fall of Richmond as seen by one of its inhabitants.

The morning after Richmond's evacuation, just as dawn broke, two carriages crept through the empty streets toward the fortifications. In them—grave-faced and sad—sat the mayor of Richmond and a committee of her council carrying the formal surrender to the Federal commander.

Before long came the clatter of cavalry, sabers drawn and at a trot. Behind followed artillery and infantry in compact column. The troops were quiet, their officers watchful. Not a cheer broke the stillness.

A dense pall of smoke hovered low over the entire city, and through it shone huge eddies of flames and sparks, carrying great blazing planks and rafters whirling over the shriveling buildings. Should the wind shift, that fire would devour the whole city, but, while the few men left looked on in dismayed apathy, deliverance came from the enemy. What we received from the enemy that day was aid—protection—safety! Richmond's population might have been houseless that night but for the disciplined promptitude of the Union troops. If the fire could not be stayed at any particular point, a squad entered each house and bore its contents to a safe distance; then a guard was placed over them.

For two days the ladies of Richmond remained close prisoners. Then necessity drove them out. Clad in deep mourning, the brokenhearted daughters of the capital moved like shadows of the past. And, to their credit be it spoken, the soldiers of the North respected the distress they could see, the bitterness they could not misunderstand.

To Admiral Porter, who was with Lincoln at that time, we owe the story of the President's visit to Richmond.

"Thank God," said the President fervently, "that I have lived to see this! I want to see Richmond."

I proceeded up to Richmond in the *Malvern*, with President Lincoln on board the *River Queen*, and a heavy feeling of responsibility was on my mind.

We landed at a point where the city was entirely deserted, but within a few minutes the streets were suddenly alive with the colored race. They seemed to spring from the earth. We needed our marines to keep them off. I don't think I ever looked on a scene where there were so many passionately happy faces.

I got twelve seamen with fixed bayonets around the President to keep him from being crushed. It never struck me that there was anyone in that multitude who would injure him.

In a short time we reached the mansion of Mr. Davis, President of the Confederacy. It was quite a small affair and modest in all its appointments, showing that Davis was living in a modest way, like any other citizen. Amid all his surroundings the refined taste of his wife was apparent.

After lunch we visited the Statehouse, the last seat of the Confederate Congress. It was in dreadful disorder, and many official documents were scattered about.

After this inspection I urged the President to go on board the *Malvern*. He was glad to go.

General de Trobriand, who took an active part in this campaign, outlines the routes of the two hostile armies after the fall of Richmond. (See map, page 672.)

The route selected by General Lee was to cross the Appomattox at Goode's Bridge, in order to strike the Danville Railroad at Amelia

Court House. From there he hoped to precede us to Burkeville, the point of intersection with the Lynchburg Railroad. If he succeeded in passing that point before we were able to oppose him, he was nearly certain to effect a junction with Johnston, who was stretching out his left from Smithfield to meet him. The common objective, then, was Burkeville. Pursuers and pursued hurried in that direction with equal ardor.

The two armies started on the race by parallel roads, Lee to the north and Grant to the south of the Appomattox. Sheridan took the lead, General Edward O. C. Ord, with the greater part of the Army of the James, marched along the line of the Lynchburg Railroad.

The retreat of Lee's army was soon in full swing. General John B. Gordon tells of the difficulties encountered in this movement.

My command was to cover the retreat of Lee's brave but shattered little army.

The old corps of Stonewall Jackson, which it was my privilege to command, was the last to abandon those mortar-battered lines around Petersburg. After all other troops were safely on the march to the rear, we sadly withdrew.

To bring up the rear and adequately protect the retreating army was an impossible task. Fighting all day, marching all night, with exhaustion and hunger claiming their victims, with charges of infantry in rear and of cavalry on the flanks, it seemed the war-god had turned loose all his furies to revel in havoc. On and on, hour after hour, from hilltop to hilltop, the lines were alternately forming, fighting and retreating, making one almost continuous shifting battle.

Here a battery of artillery became involved; there a blocked ammunition train required rescue, while the different divisions of Lee's lionhearted army were being scattered or captured. Out of one of these whirlwinds there came running a boy soldier. When asked why he was running, he shouted back:

"Golly, I'm running 'cause I can't fly!"

Here is the simple story of the Confederate private Carlton McCarthy, who participated in the last march of the Army of Northern Virginia.

The march was almost continuous, day and night, and it is with the greatest difficulty that a private in the ranks can recall with accuracy dates and places. Night was day—day was night. There was no stated time to sleep, eat or rest, and the events of morning became

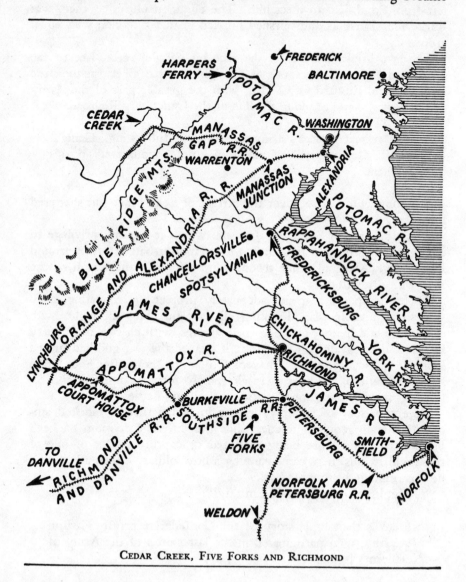

CEDAR CREEK, FIVE FORKS AND RICHMOND

strangely intermingled with the events of evening. Breakfast, dinner and supper were merged into "something to eat," whenever and wherever it could be had.

When it was found that the last morsel had been issued, the battalion was again thrown on its own resources, to wit: corn on the cob intended for the horses. It was parched in the coals, mixed with salt, stored in the pockets and eaten on the road. Chewing the corn was hard work. It made the jaws ache, and the gums so sore as to cause almost unendurable pain.

I recall one incident of the march. In the rear of the battalion, on the road, was General Lee, surrounded by officers. After a short while the enemy appeared, and stampeded troops came rushing by. Officers galloped about, begging the fleeing men to halt, but in vain. Several of the fugitives were collared by the squad, relieved of their muskets and ammunition and with a kick allowed to proceed. There was now between the group in the road and the enemy only a battalion of improvised infantry. Someone said, "Forward!" With cheers, the battalion moved rapidly to meet the enemy. A courier came with orders to stop the advance, but they heeded him not. Finally General Lee in person rode up and addressed himself directly to the men in ranks—a thing very unusual with him. "That is right, men. Just keep *those people* back awhile."

As night came on, the signs of disaster increased. At several places whole trains were standing in the road abandoned; artillery, chopped down and burning, blocked the way, and wagonloads of ammunition were dumped out in the road and trampled under foot.

> Another of Lee's veterans, George S. Bernard, also noted with breaking heart the dissolution of the once proud Army of Northern Virginia.

There were increased signs of demoralization and disintegration all along the roads. Soldiers whom I had known for steadiness and courage were straggling and sleeping, unarmed and apparently unconcerned; I attributed it to fatigue and hunger and exhaustion. Officers seemed to be doing the same thing—colonels, generals, even lieutenant generals. I saw one of them throw himself on the ground and swear on oath that he would never draw his sword from its scabbard again.

There were a great number of muskets stuck in the ground by the bayonets, whose owners, heartsick and fainting of hunger and fatigue, had thrown them away and gone none knew whither. Gaunt hunger had at last overcome their manhood, and they had scattered throughout the country to any house or hut that promised a piece of bread.

The misery of the retreat was broken by some incidents of touching human interest.

Robert Stiles relates an instance of this kind.

We halted at daylight at a country crossroad to allow other bodies of troops to pass.

I sat on the porch of a house, where an old couple were also sitting, when the door of the house opened and a young woman appeared. She was beautiful, plainly but neatly dressed, and had evidently been weeping. Her face was deadly pale. Turning to the old woman, she said, "Mother, tell him if he passes here instead of coming in, he is no husband of mine," and she started to leave.

I rose and extended my arm to prevent her escape. She drew back with surprise and indignation. "What do you mean, sir?" she cried.

"I mean, madam," I replied, "that you are sending your husband word to desert, and that I cannot permit you to do."

"Indeed! And who asked your permission, sir? Is he your husband or mine?"

"He is your husband, madam, but these are my soldiers. They and I belong to the same army with your husband."

"Army! Do you call this mob of retreating cowards an army? Soldiers! If you are soldiers, why don't you stand and fight the savage wolves that are coming upon us defenseless women and children?"

"We don't stand and fight, madam, because we have to obey orders."

"Quite a fine speech, sir, but this thing is over. The government has run off, bag and baggage, and there is no longer any country for my husband to owe allegiance to. He does owe allegiance to me and to his starving children."

The woman was getting the better of me. She saw it, I felt it, and, worst of all, the men saw and felt it too.

I tried every avenue of approach to that woman's heart. It was congealed by suffering. With the nonchalance of pure desperation I asked the soldier-question: "What command does your husband belong to?"

She started a little, and there was a trace of color in her face as she proudly replied, "He belongs to the Stonewall Brigade, sir."

"When did he join it?"

A little deeper flush, a little stronger emphasis of pride. "He joined it in the spring of '61, sir."

Turning to the men, I said, "Men, if her husband joined the Stonewall Brigade in '61 and has been in the army ever since, I reckon he's a good soldier."

I looked at her. It was all over. She answered instantly, with head raised high, face flushing, eyes flashing, "General Lee hasn't a better in his army!"

She put her hand in her bosom and, drawing out a folded paper, extended it toward me. It had been much thumbed and was hardly legible, but I made it out.

"Take off your hats, boys. I want you to hear this with uncovered heads." And then I read an endorsement on application for furlough, in which General Lee himself had signed a recommendation of the woman's husband for a furlough of special length on account of extraordinary gallantry in battle.

During the reading of this paper the woman was transfigured, glorified. Her bosom rose and fell with deep, quiet sighs; her eyes rained gentle, happy tears.

The men were all gazing on her. I turned once more to the soldier's wife. "This little paper is your most precious treasure, isn't it?"

"It is."

"And yet you would disgrace this husband of yours, for the rear guard would hunt him from his own cottage in half an hour, a deserter and a coward."

Not a sound could be heard save her hurried breathing. The rest of us held our breath.

Suddenly with a gasp she snatched the paper from my hand and, turning once more to her mother, said, "Mother, tell him not to come in."

Amelia Court House, an obscure cluster of little houses, was to play an important part in Lee's plans, as explained by General Fitzhugh Lee.

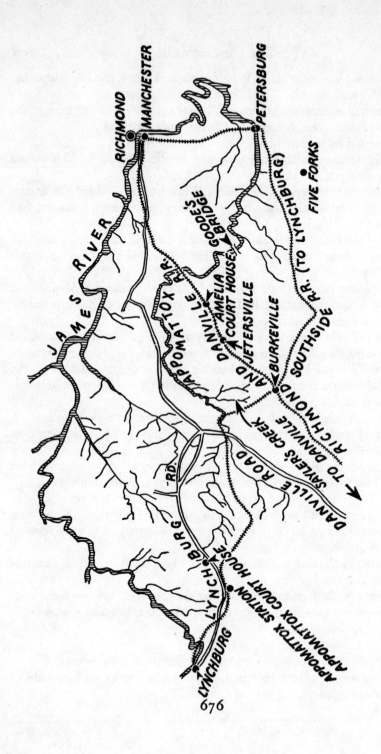

From Richmond to Appomattox

Amelia Court House is on the Richmond and Danville Railroad, thirty-eight miles southwest of Richmond. At that point it had been determined to issue abundant rations to the troops. We reached there on April 5. Sheridan had arrived at Jetersville—on the Danville Railroad, seven miles from Amelia Court House—on the afternoon of the fourth, with some 18,000 troops of all arms, and entrenched. If Lee's supplies had been at Amelia Court House as ordered, he might have moved against Sheridan at Jetersville early on the fifth with his whole force, except Ewell who was somewhat behind, of over 20,000 men, defeated Sheridan and reached Burkeville, thirteen miles farther, before Ord, who arrived there late that night, could have come up. Had Lee once passed beyond Burkeville, the Danville Road could have supplied his men, its trains transported them to Danville, and to Raleigh and Goldsboro, or wherever Johnston was.

But when we reached Amelia Court House, the supplies ordered were not there. Nearly twenty-four hours were lost in endeavoring to collect in the country subsistence for men and horses. The delay was fatal and could not be retrieved.

> In consequence of Lee's delay at Amelia Court House, Sheridan was enabled to strike Ewell's corps at Sayler's Creek. Of the battle which ensued there, Edward Pollard of the *Richmond Examiner* gives this description.

On April 6 Sheridan struck in upon the Confederate line of retreat just south of Sayler's Creek, a small tributary of the Appomattox. Ewell's corps, consisting of about 4,200 men, was called on to support Pickett who, with his division reduced to about 800 men, was being pressed by Sheridan. Gordon's division, which formed the rear guard of the army, had taken another road, and the Federal forces had already occupied the high ground in Ewell's rear, opening upon his troops a rapid and deadly fire of artillery. The appearance of a very heavy force of infantry also in the rear rendered it necessary to face about the Confederate line and prepare for another conflict on the ground over which it had just passed. Without being able to assist Pickett, Ewell, with his small force, was compelled to hold his ground against overwhelming numbers.

At this critical juncture fresh troops were brought up against Pickett and, charging impetuously on his line, easily broke it, and it was never again to be reformed. The enemy's forces were now hurled upon Ewell's corps, and the unequal contest was terminated. General Ewell was captured, and the greater portion of the command surrendered.

General Regis de Trobriand sketches the battle at Sayler's Creek from the Federal point of view.

During the night from April 5 to 6 we were upon the enemy. Our line had just passed the highest point of a hill when an unexpected sight was presented to us. At the bottom of a narrow valley, divided throughout its length by a small stream called Sayler's Creek, more than 200 wagons were hurrying pell-mell to cross the stream on a bridge half destroyed. We fell upon the prey with enthusiastic cries. This, however, was among the least of our successes.

Three divisions of cavalry struck the trains on Sayler's Creek a few miles above the point where we had captured a part. They destroyed 400 wagons *en bloc*, captured sixteen pieces of artillery and made a large number of prisoners.

This battle of the sixth of April, known generally as the Battle of Sayler's Creek, gave the *coup de grace* to Lee's army.

The pursuit was now rapidly approaching a crisis. General Horace Porter reports how Grant met it.

It was now the seventh of April. General Ewell, after his capture at Sayler's Creek, had said in conversation that their cause was lost, and that every man killed after this would be little better than murder. He hoped that Lee would at once surrender his army. This statement induced the general to write the following communication:

> Headquarters, Armies of the U. S.
> 5 P.M., April 7, 1865.
>
> General R. E. Lee, Commanding C. S. A.:
>
> The results of the last week must convince you of the hopelessness of further resistance on the part of the Army of Northern Virginia in this struggle. I feel that it is so, and regard it as my duty to shift from myself the responsibility of any further effusion of blood by asking of you

the surrender of that portion of the Confederate States army known as the Army of Northern Virginia.

> Very respectfully, your obedient servant,
> U. S. GRANT,
> Lieutenant-General.

Lee wrote the following reply within an hour after he received General Grant's letter:

> April 7, 1865.
> General: I have received your note of this date. Though not entertaining the opinion you express of the hopelessness of further resistance on the part of the Army of Northern Virginia, I reciprocate your desire to avoid useless effusion of blood, and therefore, before considering your proposition, ask the terms you will offer on condition of its surrender.
>
> R. E. LEE,
> General.

The next morning this following reply was transmitted to Lee:

> April 8, 1865.
> General R. E. Lee, Commanding C. S. A.:
> Your note of last evening just received. In reply would say that there is but one condition I would insist upon—namely, that the men and officers surrendered shall be disqualified for taking up arms against the Government of the United States until properly exchanged. I will meet you at any point agreeable to you, for the purpose of arranging definitely the terms upon which the surrender of the Army of Northern Virginia will be received.
>
> U. S. GRANT,
> Lieutenant-General.

Lee called together his generals to discuss the situation and decide on a course of action. General Gordon has left us a pathetic picture of the meeting.

On the evening of April 8 came the last sad Confederate council of war. It met in the woods at Lee's headquarters by a low-burning bivouac fire. There were no tents there, no table, no chairs, no campstools. On blankets spread on the ground or on saddles at the roots of the trees, we sat around the great commander. No tongue or pen will ever be able to describe the unutterable anguish of Lee's lieutenants as they looked into the clouded face of their beloved leader and sought to draw from it some ray of hope.

It would be impossible to give the words that were spoken or the suggestions that were made. The letters of General Grant asking surrender, and the replies thereto, evoked a discussion as to the fate of the Southern people, and the condition in which the failure of our cause would leave them. There was also some discussion as to the possibility of forcing a passage through Grant's lines and continuing a desultory warfare. In no hour of the great war did General Lee's masterful characteristics appear so conspicuous as they did in that last council. We knew by our own aching hearts that his was breaking. Yet he stood calmly facing the long-dreaded inevitable.

It was finally determined that we should attempt at daylight the next morning to cut through Grant's lines.

The attack which had been decided on was carried into effect. How it ended is again related by General Gordon.

The audacious movement of our troops was begun at dawn. The dashing cavalry leader Fitzhugh Lee swept around the Union left flank, while the infantry and artillery attacked the front. This last charge of the war was made by the footsore and starving men of my command with a spirit worthy the best days of Lee's army. The Union breastworks were carried. Two pieces of artillery were captured. The Federals were driven from all that portion of the field, and the brave boys in tattered gray cheered as their battle flags waved in triumph.

Our lines were still advancing when I discovered a heavy column of Union infantry coming from the right end upon my rear. Longstreet was being assailed by other portions of the Federal army. He was so hard pressed that he could not join in the effort to break the cordon of men and metal around us.

Such was the situation when I received a significant inquiry from General Lee. The commander wished me to report as to the conditions on my portion of the field. I said, "Tell General Lee that my command has been fought to a frazzle, and I cannot long go forward."

When General Lee received my message, he said, "There is nothing left me but to go and see General Grant, and I had rather die a thousand deaths."

My troops were still fighting when a note from General Lee reached me that there was a flag of truce between General Grant and himself, and that I could communicate that fact to the commander of the Union forces in my front. I called Colonel Green Peyton of my staff to take a flag of truce and bear the message to General Ord. Colonel Peyton informed me that we had no flag of truce. I said, "Well, take your handkerchief and tie that on a stick."

He felt in his pockets and said, "General, I have no handkerchief."

"Then tear your shirt, sir, and tie that to a stick."

He looked at his shirt, and then at mine, and said, "I don't believe there is a white shirt in the army."

Finally he did secure a rag of some sort, however, and rode rapidly away.

That the Union troops also recognized finality in this fight appears clearly in almost every line of an account written by Major General Joshua L. Chamberlain.

By sunrise we had reached Appomattox Station. A staff officer was here to turn us to the Appomattox River, where we might cut Lee's retreat. Already we heard the sharp ring of the horse artillery. There was no mistake. Sheridan was square across the enemy's front, holding at bay all that was left of the proudest army of the Confederacy. It had come at last—the supreme hour! No thought of human wants or weakness now: all for the front!

Dashing out of a woods road came a cavalry staff officer. With sharp salutation he exclaimed, "General Sheridan wishes you to come to his support! The Rebel infantry is pressing him hard!"

Sharp work now! At cavalry speed we pushed through the woods, right on Sheridan's battle flag gleaming in an open field. Weird-looking flag it was: fork-tailed, red and white, the two bands that composed it each charged with a star of the contrasting color; two eyes sternly glaring through the cannon cloud. Beneath it, that storm center spirit, that form of condensed energies, mounted on the grim charger Rienzi, who had turned the battle on Cedar Creek.

Right before us our cavalry gallantly was stemming the surges of the old Stonewall Brigade, desperate to beat its way through. I rode straight to Sheridan. A dark smile and impetuous gesture were my only orders. Forward into double lines of battle, past Sheridan, his guns, his cavalry, and on for the quivering crest! For a moment it was a glorious sight: every arm of the service in full play—cavalry, artillery, infantry. Then a sudden shifting scene as the cavalry, disengaged by successive squadrons, rallied under their bugle calls with beautiful precision and promptitude and swept like a storm cloud beyond our right, to close in on the enemy's left and complete the fateful envelopment.

In a few minutes the tide was turned: the incoming wave was at high flood; it receded. Their last hope was gone. It was the end! They were now giving way but kept a good front by force of old habit. Halfway up the slope they made a stand, with what perhaps they thought a good omen—behind a stone wall.

Suddenly rose to sight another form—a soldierly young figure, a Confederate staff officer undoubtedly, to whom someone in my advanced line seemed to be pointing out my position. Now I saw the white flag, and its possible purport swept before my inner vision. I could even smile at the material of the flag, wondering where in either army had been found a towel, and one so white. But that simple emblem of homely service bore a mighty message.

The messenger drew near, dismounted. "Sir, I am from General Gordon. General Lee desires a cessation of hostilities until he can hear from General Grant as to the proposed surrender."

One o'clock came. I turned about. There behind me appeared a commanding form, superbly mounted, richly accoutered, of imposing bearing, noble countenance, with expression of deep sadness overmastered by deeper strength. It was no other than Robert E. Lee! He was coming with a single staff officer, for the meeting which was to determine a momentous issue.

Not long after, by another road, appeared another form—plain, unassuming, simple, and familiar to our eyes, but as awe-inspiring as Lee in his splendor and sadness. It was Grant! He too came with a single aide. Slouched hat without cord; common soldier's blouse, unbuttoned, on which, however, were four stars; high boots mud-splashed to the top, trousers tucked inside; no sword, but the sword hand deep in the pocket; sitting his saddle with the ease of a born master; taking no notice of anything, all his faculties gathered into intense thought. He seemed greater than I had ever seen him—a look as of another world about him.

Staff officers were flying about crying, "Lee surrenders!"

William Miller Owen of the famous Washington Artillery tells how the morning of the surrender brought both comedy and pathos to the remainder of Lee's army.

At nine o'clock on the morning of April 9 the battalion was moved out into the road to resume the march. Just as we emerged General Lee was riding by, going toward the rear, accompanied by Colonels Marshall and Taylor of his staff. I noted particularly his dress. He was in full uniform. His horse, Old Traveler, was finely groomed, and his equipment—bridle, bit, etc.—were polished until they shone like silver.

All this seemed peculiar. I had never seen him before in full rig and began to think something strange was to happen. He always wore during the campaigns a gray sack coat with side pockets, quite like the costume of a businessman in cities; and after the Second Manassas I had never seen him carry a sword.

I moved the battalion forward toward the hill. There I espied General Longstreet and General Alexander, chief of artillery, sitting on a log. Alexander got up and came toward me. I said to him, "General Lee instructed me to stop here for orders. What do you want me to do?"

He replied, "Turn into that field on the right and park your guns." Then he added, in a low tone, "We are going to surrender today."

Presently a Federal cavalry officer was observed coming down the road toward our forces. He wore his hair very long, and it was of a light or reddish color. In his hand he carried a white handkerchief, which he constantly waved up and down. Upon approaching he dismounted and said, "General Longstreet, in the name of General Sheridan and myself, I demand the surrender of this army. I am General Custer."

General Longstreet replied, "I am not in command of this army. General Lee is, and he has gone back to meet General Grant in regard to a surrender."

"Well," said Custer, "no matter about General Grant. We demand the surrender be made to us. If you do not do so, we will renew hostilities."

"Oh, well!" said Longstreet, "I will do my best to meet you." Then, turning to his staff, he said, "Colonel Manning, please order General Johnson to move his division to the front, to the right of General Gordon. Colonel Latrobe, please order General Pickett's division forward to General Gordon's left."

Custer listened with surprise; he had not thought so many of our troops were at hand. Cooling off immediately, he said, "General, probably we had better wait until we hear from Grant and Lee. I will speak to General Sheridan about it. Don't move your troops yet." And he mounted and withdrew in a much quieter style.

As he passed out of hearing Longstreet gave that peculiar chuckle of his. The divisions of Johnson and Pickett had had no existence since the fight at Five Forks.

In modest words Grant himself now relates the story of the surrender.

On April 8 I had followed the Army of the Potomac in rear of Lee. I was suffering very severely with a sick headache and stopped at a farmhouse on the road some distance in rear of the main body of the army.

Next morning I proceeded at an early hour, still suffering with the headache, to get to the head of the column. I was not more than two or three miles from Appomattox Court House at the time, but to go directly I would have to pass through Lee's army, or a portion of it.

Lee, therefore, sent an escort with the officer bearing this message through his lines to me.

April 9, 1865.

General:— I received your note of this morning . . . with reference to the surrender of this army. I now request an interview in accordance with the offer contained in your letter of yesterday for that purpose.
R. E. Lee, General.

When the officer reached me I was still suffering with the sick headache, but the instant I saw the contents of the note I was cured. I wrote the following note in reply and hastened on:

April 9, 1865.

General R. E. Lee:— Your note of this date is but this moment (11:50 A.M.) received. . . . I am at this writing about four miles west of Walker's Church, and will push forward to the front for the purpose of meeting you. Notice sent to me on this road where you wish the interview to take place will meet me.

U. S. GRANT.

Before stating what took place between General Lee and me, I will give all there is of the story of the famous apple tree.

It is fiction based on a slight foundation of fact. There was an apple orchard on the side of the hill occupied by the Confederate forces. Colonel Orville E. Babcock, of my staff, reported to me that when he first met General Lee he was sitting with his back resting against an apple tree. The story has no other foundation than that.

When I went into the house where the meeting had been arranged, I found General Lee there. We greeted each other and after shaking hands took our seats. A good portion of my staff came into the room during the interview.

What General Lee's feelings were I do not know. As he was a man of much dignity, it was impossible to say whether he felt inwardly glad, or felt sad and was too manly to show it. My own feelings, which had been quite jubilant on the receipt of his letter, were sad and depressed.

We soon fell into a conversation about old army times. He remarked that he remembered me very well in the old army, and I told him that I remembered him perfectly but thought it very unlikely that I had attracted his attention sufficiently to be remembered by him. Our conversation grew so pleasant that I almost forgot the object of our meeting. After some time General Lee said that he had asked for this interview for the purpose of getting the terms I proposed to give his army. I said that his men should lay down their arms, not to take them up again during the continuance of the war unless duly and properly exchanged. He said that he had so understood my letter.

Then we gradually fell off again into conversation about matters foreign to the subject which had brought us together, when General Lee again interrupted by suggesting that the terms ought to be written out. I called to Colonel Ely S. Parker, secretary on my staff, for writing materials and commenced writing out the terms.

When I put my pen to the paper, the thought occurred to me that the officers had their own private horses and effects, which were important to them but of no value to us; also that it would be an unnecessary humiliation to call on them to deliver their side arms.

When General Lee read over that part about side arms, horses and private property of the officers, he remarked, with some feeling I thought, that this would have a happy effect on his army.

I then said that the whole country had been so raided by the two armies that it was doubtful whether the men in the ranks would be able to put in a crop without the aid of the horses they were then riding. I therefore instructed the officers to let every man of the Confederate army who claimed to own a horse or mule take the animal to his home. Lee remarked again that this would have a happy effect.

General Lee, before taking his leave, remarked that his army was in a very bad condition for want of food, and that he would have to ask me for rations and forage. I told him, "Certainly," and asked for how many men he wanted rations. His answer was "About 25,000," and I authorized him to send his own commissary and quartermaster to Appomattox Station, two or three miles away, where he could have all the provisions wanted.

Lee and I then separated as cordially as we had met.

When news of the surrender reached our lines, our men commenced firing a salute. I at once sent word to have it stopped. The Confederates were now our prisoners, and we did not want to exult over their downfall.

To this conversation between the two commanding generals as reported by Grant, Porter adds some interesting details.

When Grant had finished the letter, he called Colonel Parker to his side and directed him to interline six or seven words. General Grant then started to rise from his chair to hand the book to him. I stepped forward, took the book and passed it on.

Lee pushed aside some books and two brass candlesticks which were on the table, then took the book and laid it down before him. He drew from his pocket a pair of steel-rimmed spectacles and wiped the glasses carefully with his handkerchief. He crossed his legs, adjusted the spectacles very slowly and deliberately, took up the draft and proceeded to read it attentively. When he reached the top line of the second page, he looked up and said to General Grant, "After the words 'until properly' the word 'exchanged' seems to be omitted. You doubtless intended to use that word."

"Why, yes," said Grant. "I thought I had put it in."

"With your permission I will mark where it should be inserted," continued Lee.

"Certainly," Grant replied.

After rereading the draft, Lee handed it over to Colonel Parker, whose handwriting presented a better appearance than that of anyone else on the staff. Parker sat down to write, but it was found that the contents of the conical-shaped stoneware inkstand had disappeared. Colonel Marshall of Lee's staff now took from his pocket a small box-wood inkstand, so that, after all, we had to fall back on the resources of the enemy for the final scene in the memorable military drama.

> Colonel Ely S. Parker, who was a full-blooded Indian, now breaks into the story.

Having finished the transcription, I brought it to General Grant, who signed it, sealed it, and handed it to General Lee, who asked me if I had any paper without a printed heading. He extended his hand, and said, "I am glad to see one real American here." I shook his hand and said, "We are all Americans."

> At this point Porter takes up the story again.

A little before four o'clock General Lee shook hands with General Grant, bowed to the other officers and with Colonel Marshall left the room. He gazed sadly in the direction of the valley beyond, where his army lay—now an army of prisoners. He thrice smote the palm of his left hand slowly with his right fist in an absent sort of way, seemed not to see the group of Union officers in the yard, who rose respectfully at his approach, and appeared unaware of everything about him. The approach of his horse seemed to recall him from his reverie. General Grant now stepped down from the porch, moving toward him, and saluted him by raising his hat. He was followed in this act of courtesy by all our officers present. Lee raised his hat respectfully and rode off at a slow trot.

> The final act at Appomattox was held in sacred memory by General Fitzhugh Lee.

When the Confederate commander left, he rode away to break the sad news to the brave troops he had so long commanded.

His presence in their midst was an exhibition of the utmost devotion. The troops crowded around him, eagerly desiring to shake his hand. They had seen him when his eye calmly surveyed miles of fierce, raging conflict; had observed him when, tranquil, composed, undisturbed, he had heard the wild shouts of victory. Now they saw their beloved chieftain a prisoner of war, and sympathy, boundless admiration and love for him filled their brave hearts. They pressed up to him, anxious to touch his person or even his horse, and copious tears washed from strong men's cheeks the stains of powder.

Slowly and painfully he turned to his soldiers and, with voice quivering with emotion, said, "Men, we have fought through the war together. I have done my best for you. My heart is too full to say more." It was a simple but most affecting scene.

On the next day this leave of his army was taken by General Lee:

Headquarters Army Northern Virginia
April 10, 1865.

After four years of arduous service marked by unsurpassed courage and fortitude the Army of Northern Virginia has been compelled to yield to overwhelming numbers and resources.

I need not tell the survivors of so many hard fought battles who have remained steadfast to the last that I have consented to this result from no distrust of them.

But feeling that valor and devotion could accomplish nothing that could compensate for the loss that would have attended the continuance of the contest I determined to avoid the useless sacrifice of those whose past services have endeared them to their country.

By the terms of agreement officers and men can return to their homes and remain until exchanged. You will take with you the satisfaction that proceeds from the consciousness of duty faithfully performed, and I earnestly pray that a merciful God will extend to you his blessing and protection. With an unceasing admiration of your constancy and devotion to your country and a grateful remembrance of your kind and generous consideration for myself, I bid you an affectionate farewell.

R. E. LEE
Gen.

Before taking his final departure, Lee stopped his horse and once more read the notice, which had been posted so all could see it. And then in silence, with lifted hat, he rode through a weeping army to his home in Richmond.

EPILOGUE

With Lee's surrender the great struggle ended. A few days after, Johnston handed his sword to Sherman, and the remaining Confederate detachments soon followed.

Almost forgotten, and accompanied only by a small loyal squad, Jefferson Davis tried to make his escape, but in the early days of May was captured in the pine forests of Georgia.

The paroled Southern soldiers, as Colonel E. M. Boykin put it, "stood on the bare hills, men without a country." Then they slowly and painfully made their way homeward. The Northern armies assembled in Washington for a grand parade, and then they, too, disbanded.

And with that the cover closed on the last page of the *American Iliad*.

But although the war was over for those who had lived through it, the poet Walt Whitman foresaw that it would forever linger in the memory of the American people.

A great literature will yet arise out of the era of those four years, compressing centuries of native passions, first-class pictures, tempests of life and death—an inexhaustible mine for the histories, romance and even philosophy of people to come,—far more grand, in my opinion, than Homer's Siege of Troy.

BIBLIOGRAPHY

This bibliography lists the source for each of the selections used in this volume. The books are arranged alphabetically under the name of the narrator whose contribution appears in the text. Where several persons' contributions originally appeared in the same book, the work is listed under the title and under the name of each contributor. Where permission was obtained to quote material from any book, the name of the person or firm through whose kindness we have been permitted to use the selection is recorded.

AGASSIZ, GEORGE R. See LYMAN, THEODORE.

ALDEN, HENRY M. See *Harper's Pictorial History of the Great Rebellion*.

ALEXANDER, EDWARD P., *Military Memoirs of a Confederate*. New York: Chas. Scribner's Sons, 1907. (By permission of Charles Scribner's Sons.)

ANDERSON, WILLIAM H., *Blockade Life*. See M. O. L. L. U. S., Maine Commandery, *War Papers*, Volume II.

The Annals of the War, by Leading Participants North and South. Phila.: The Times Pub. Co., 1879.

Appleton's Cyclopedia of American Biography, edited by James Grant Wilson and John Fiske. New York: D. Appleton & Co., 1892. 6 volumes and supplement. (By permission of D. Appleton-Century Company, Inc.)

ATKINSON, JOHN, *The Story of Lookout Mountain and Missionary Ridge*. Detroit: Winn & Hammond, 1893.

BANKHEAD, J. P., *Report to Acting Rear-Admiral S. P. Lee*. See Rogers, William. (In M. O. L. L. U. S., Maine Commandery, *War Papers*, Volume II.)

BATES, EDWARD, *The Diary of Edward Bates, 1859-1866*. Edited by Howard K. Beale. (Annual Report Amer. Hist. Ass'n, 1930.) Washington: Govt. Ptg. Office, 1933.

Battle Fields of the South, from Bull Run to Fredericksburg, with sketches of Confederate Commanders . . . By an English Combatant. New York: John Bradburn, 1864.

Battles and Leaders of the Civil War. Edited by Robert Underwood Johnson and Clarence Clough Buel. New York: The Century Co., 1884-1888. 4 volumes.

BEALE, HOWARD K. See BATES, EDWARD.

BEARD, RICHARD, *An Incident of the Battle of Atlanta, July 26, 1864*. See RIDLEY, *Battles and Sketches of the Army of Tennessee*.

BEAUREGARD, P. G. T., *The First Battle of Bull Run*. See *Century Magazine*, Volume XXIX.

BEAUREGARD, P. G. T., *The Military Operations of General Beauregard in the War Between the States, 1861 to 1865*. By Alfred Roman. New York: Harper & Bros., 1884. 2 volumes. (Though Roman is recorded as the author, this is actually Beauregard's story and we have therefore transposed the writing from the third person to first person.)

BELKNAP, CHARLES E., *Recollections of a Bummer*. See HUTCHINS, *The War of the Sixties*.

BENNETT, L. G., and HAIGH, WILLIAM M., *History of 36th Regiment, Illinois Volunteers . . .* Aurora: Knickerbocker & Hodder, 1876.

BERNARD, GEORGE S., editor, *War Talks of the Confederate Veterans*. Petersburg, Va.: Fenn & Owen, 1892.

BEVIER, R. S., *The Confederate 1st and 2nd Missouri Brigades, 1861-1865* . . . St. Louis: Bryan, Brand & Co., 1879.

BICKHAM, WILLIAM D., *Rosecrans' Campaign with the Fourteenth Army Corps, or The Army of the Cumberland* . . . Cincinnati: Moore, Wilstach, Keys & Co., 1863.

BIGELOW, JOHN, JR., *The Campaign of Chancellorsville*. New Haven: Yale Univ. Press, 1908. (By permission of Yale University Press.)

BILLINGS, JOHN D., *Hardtack & Coffee*. Boston: Geo. M. Smith & Co., 1888.

BLACKFORD, CHARLES M. See BLACKFORD, SUSAN LEIGH.

BLACKFORD, CHARLES MINOR III. See BLACKFORD, SUSAN LEIGH.

BLACKFORD, SUSAN LEIGH, *Letters from Lee's Army or Memoirs of Life In and Out of The Army in Virginia During the War Between the States*. Compiled by Susan Leigh Blackford . . . , Annotated by her husband, Charles Minor Blackford. Edited and abridged for publication by Charles Minor Blackford III. New York: Charles Scribner's Sons, 1947. (By permission of Charles Scribner's Sons.)

BLOSS, JOHN M., *Antietam and the Lost Dispatch*. See M. O. L. L. U. S., Kansas Commandery, *War Talks in Kansas*, Volume I.

BOYKIN, E. M., *The Falling Flag. Evacuation of Richmond, Retreat and Surrender at Appomattox*. New York: E. J. Hale & Sons, 1874.

BRAGG, BRAXTON, *Report to General S. Cooper*. See *Harper's Pictorial History of the Great Rebellion*.

BRECKINRIDGE, W. P. C., *The Opening of the Atlanta Campaign*. See *Battles and Leaders of the Civil War*, Volume IV.

BRINTON, JOHN H., *Personal Memoirs of John H. Brinton* . . . Introductory note by S. Weir Mitchell. New York: The Neale Pub. Co., 1914.

BROWNE, DUNN. See FISKE, SAMUEL.

BROWNE, JUNIUS HENRI, *Four Years in Secessia: Adventures Within and Beyond the Union Lines* . . . Hartford: O. D. Case and Company, 1865.

BUEL, CLARENCE CLOUGH. See *Battles and Leaders of the Civil War*.

BUELL, AUGUSTUS, *The Cannoneer—Story of a Private Soldier* . . . Washington: The National Tribune, 1890.

BYERS, S. H. M., *With Fire and Sword*. New York: The Neale Pub. Co., 1911.

CADWALLADER, SYLVANUS, *Three Years with Grant, As Recalled by War Correspondent Sylvanus Cadwallader*. Edited, and with an Introduction and Notes by Benjamin P. Thomas. New York: Alfred A. Knopf, 1955. (By permission of Alfred A. Knopf, Inc.)

CANNON, LE GRAND B., *Personal Reminiscences of the Rebellion 1861-1865*. New York: [Privately Printed], 1895.

CARNAHAN, JAMES R., *Personal Recollections of Chickamauga*. See M. O. L. L. U. S., Ohio Commandery, *Sketches of War History, 1861-1865*, Volume I.

CARPENTER, S. D., *Logic of History. Five Hundred Political Texts* . . . [*Scraps from My Scrap-Book*]. Second Edition. Madison: S. D. Carpenter, 1864.

CARTER, ROBERT G., *Reminiscences of the Campaign and Battle of Gettysburg*. See M. O. L. L. U. S., Maine Commandery, *War Papers*, Volume II.

CARTER, ROBERT GOLDTHWAITE, *Four Brothers in Blue. A True Story of the Great Civil War from Bull Run to Appomattox* . . . Washington: Gibson Bros., 1913.

CASLER, JOHN O., *Four Years in the Stonewall Brigade*. Guthrie, Okla.: State Capital Ptg. Co., 1893.

CASTLE, HENRY A., *Some Experiences of an Enlisted Man.* See M. O. L. L. U. S., Minnesota Commandery, *Glimpses of the Nation's Struggle.*

The Century Magazine, Nov.-April, 1884-1885. Volume XXIX. New Series Volume VII. New York: The Century Co., 1885.

Charleston Mercury, April 13, 1861.

CHESNUT, MARY BOYKIN, *A Diary from Dixie.* New York: D. Appleton & Co., 1905. (By permission of D. Appleton-Century Company, Inc.)

CHAMBERLAIN, JOSHUA L., *Appomattox.* See M. O. L. L. U. S., New York Commandery, *Personal Recollections of the War of the Rebellion*, Third Series.

CHAMBERLAIN, JOSHUA L., *Night on the Field of Fredericksburg.* See King & Derby, *Camp-Fire Sketches and Battle-Field Echoes.*

Chicago Tribune, April 10, 1865.

COFFIN, CHARLES CARLETON, *The Boys of '61, or Four Years of Fighting.* Boston: Estes & Lauriat, 1885.

COLLINS, R. M., *Chapters from the Unwritten History of the War Between the States.* St. Louis: Nixon-Jones Ptg. Co., 1893.

COOKE, SIDNEY G., *The First Day at Gettysburg.* See M. O. L. L. U. S., Kansas Commandery, *War Talks in Kansas*, Volume I.

COUCH, DARIUS N., *The Chancellorsville Campaign.* (Article originally published in the *Philadelphia Times* and reprinted in *Battles and Leaders of the Civil War.*)

COX, JACOB D., *War Preparations in the North.* See *Battles and Leaders of the Civil War*, Volume I.

CRANE, WILLIAM E., *Bugle Blasts.* See M. O. L. L. U. S., Ohio Commandery, *Sketches of War History, 1861-1865*, Volume I.

CRAWFORD, SAMUEL WYLIE, *The Genesis of the Civil War.* New York: Chas. L. Webster & Co., 1887.

DAGGETT, GEORGE H., *Thrilling Moments.* See M. O. L. L. U. S., Minnesota Commandery, *Glimpses of the Nation's Struggle*, Fifth Series.

DANA, CHARLES A., *Recollections of the Civil War* . . . New York: D. Appleton & Co., 1898. (By permission of D. Appleton-Century Company, Inc.)

DANFORTH, WILLIS, *How I Came to Be in the Army.* See M. O. L. L. U. S., Wisconsin Commandery, *War Papers*, Volume I.

DAVIS, JEFFERSON, *The Rise and Fall of the Confederate Government.* New York: D. Appleton & Co., 1881. 2 volumes.

DAVIS, VARINA HOWELL, *Jefferson Davis, Ex-President of the Confederate States of America. A Memoir by His Wife.* New York: Belford Company, 1890. 2 volumes.

DAVIS. W. W. H., *History of the 104th Pennsylvania Regiment* . . . Phila.: Jas. B. Rodgers, 1866.

DEAN, HENRY S., *The Relief of Chattanooga.* Detroit: Winn & Hammond, 1893.

DELEON, T. C., *Four Years in Rebel Capitals.* Mobile: The Gossip Ptg. Co., 1890.

DERBY, W. P. See KING, W. C.

DE TROBRIAND, REGIS, *Four Years with the Army of the Potomac.* Translated by George K. Dauchy. Boston: Ticknor & Co., 1889.

DODGE, GRENVILLE M., *Personal Recollections of Some of our Great Commanders in the Civil War.* See M. O. L. L. U. S., New York Commandery, *Personal Recollections of the War of the Rebellion*, Third Series.

DONAHOWER, J. C., *Lookout Mountain and Missionary Ridge.* See M. O. L. L. U. S., Minnesota Commandery, *Glimpses of the Nation's Struggle*, Fifth Series.

DOUBLEDAY, ABNER, *Reminiscences of Fort Sumter and Moultrie, 1860-1861.* New York: Harper & Bros., 1876.

DOUBLEDAY, ABNER, *Chancellorsville and Gettysburg.* (Campaigns of the Civil War, Volume VI.) New York: Charles Scribner's Sons, 1882.

DOUGLAS, HENRY KYD, *I Rode with Stonewall.* Chapel Hill: The University of North Carolina Press, 1940. (By permission of The University of North Carolina Press.)

EARLY, JUBAL ANDERSON, *Autobiographical Sketch and Narrative of the War Between the States.* With Notes by R. H. Early. Philadelphia: J. B. Lippincott Company, 1912. (By permission of J. B. Lippincott Company.)

EARLY, R. H. See EARLY, JUBAL ANDERSON.

ELLIS, THOMAS T., *Leaves from the Diary of an Army Surgeon; or, Incidents of Field, Camp, and Hospital Life.* New York: John Bradburn, 1862.

An English Combatant. See *Battle Fields of the South.*

FISKE, JOHN. See *Appleton's Cyclopedia of American Biography.*

FISKE, SAMUEL, *Mr. Dunn Browne's Experiences in the Army.* Boston: Nichols and Noyes, 1866.

FORCE, MANNING F., *Marching Across Carolina.* See M. O. L. L. U. S., Ohio Commandery, *Sketches of War History,* Volume I.

FOSTER, WILBUR F., *The Building of Forts Henry and Donelson.* See RIDLEY, *Battles and Sketches of the Army of Tennessee.*

FREMANTLE, ARTHUR LYON-, *Three Months in the Southern States, April-June, 1863.* London: Wm. Blackwood & Sons, 1863.

GALWEY, THOMAS F. DeBURGH, *At the Battle of Antietam with the Eighth Ohio Infantry.* See M. O. L. L. U. S., New York Commandery, *Personal Recollections of the War of the Rebellion,* Third Series.

GATES, THEODORE B., and TYRREL, BENJAMIN H., *The Ulster Guard, 20th New York State Militia* . . . New York: Benj. H. Tyrrel, 1879.

GERRISH, THEODORE, *Army Life. A Private's Reminiscences of the War* . . . With an introduction by Josiah H. Drummond. Portland, Me.: Hoyt, Fogg and Donham, 1882.

GOLDSBOROUGH, W. W., *The Maryland Line in the Confederate States Army.* Baltimore: Kelly, Piet & Co., 1869.

GOLDSMITH, W. L., editor. See *Under Both Flags.*

GORDON, GEORGE H., *Brook Farm to Cedar Mountain in the War of the Great Rebellion, 1861-1862.* Cambridge: The Riverside Press, 1883.

GORDON, JOHN B., *Reminiscences of the Civil War.* New York: Chas. Scribner's Sons, 1903. (By permission of Charles Scribner's Sons.)

GOSS, WARREN LEE, *Recollections of a Private.* See *Century Magazine,* Volume XXIX.

GOSS, WARREN LEE, *Recollections of a Private. A Story of the Army of the Potomac.* New York: Thos. Y. Crowell & Co., 1890.

GOULD, JOHN M., *History of the 1st-10th-29th Maine Regiments in Service of the United States from May 3, 1861 to June 21, 1866* . . . *History of the 10th Maine Battalion* . . . by Rev. Leonard G. Jordan. Portland: Stephen Berry, n.d.

GRANT, ULYSSES S., *Personal Memoirs of U. S. Grant.* New York: Chas. L. Webster & Co., 1885. 2 volumes.

GREELEY, HORACE, *The American Conflict.* Hartford: O. D. Case & Co., 1866. 2 volumes.

GREELEY, HORACE. See *New York Tribune,* December 17, 1860.

GREENE, CHARLES SHIEL, *Thrilling Stories of the Great Rebellion* . . . Philadelphia: John E. Potter, 1866.

GREGORY, EDWARD D., *Vicksburg during the Siege.* See *The Annals of the War.*

GUERNSEY, ALFRED H. See *Harper's Pictorial History of the Great Rebellion.*

HAIGH, WILLIAM M. See BENNETT, L. G.

HARDEE, WILLIAM J., *Battles around Jonesborough, Lovejoy Station and Atlanta.* See RIDLEY, *Battles and Sketches of the Army of Tennessee.*

Harper's Pictorial History of the Great Rebellion. By ALFRED H. GUERNSEY and HENRY M. ALDEN. New York: Harper & Bros., 1866. 2 volumes.

HASCALL, MILO S., *Personal Recollections and Experiences concerning the Battle of Stone River.* See M. O. L. L. U. S., Illinois Commandery, *Military Essays and Recollections,* Volume IV.

HASKELL, FRANK ARETAS, *The Battle of Gettysburg.* Boston: The Mudge Press, 1908.

HAUPT, HERMAN, *Reminiscences of General Herman Haupt.* With notes and a personal sketch by FRANK ABIAL FLOWER. Milwaukee: Wright & Joys Co., 1901.

HEDLEY, F. Y., *Marching Through Georgia. Pen-Pictures of Every-Day Life.* Chicago: Donohue, Henneberry & Co., 1890.

HENRY, ROBERT S., *The Story of the Confederacy.* Indianapolis: The Bobbs-Merrill Co., 1931.

HICKENLOOPER, ANDREW, *The Battle of Shiloh.* See M. O. L. L. U. S., Ohio Commandery, *Sketches of War History, 1861-1865,* Volume V.

HILL, DANIEL HARVEY, *Chickamauga—The Great Battle of the West.* See *Battles and Leaders of the Civil War,* Volume III.

HITCHCOCK, HENRY, *Marching with Sherman, Passages from the Letters and Campaign Diaries* . . . Edited, with an introduction, by M. A. DEWOLFE HOWE. New Haven: Yale Univ. Press, 1927. (By permission of Yale University Press.)

HOOD, J. B., *Advance and Retreat. Personal Experiences in the United States and Confederate States Armies.* New Orleans: G. T. Beauregard, 1880.

HOWARD, OLIVER OTIS, *The Struggle for Atlanta.* See *Battles and Leaders of the Civil War,* Volume IV.

HOWARD, OLIVER OTIS, *Grant at Chattanooga.* See M. O. L. L. U. S., New York Commandery, *Personal Recollections of the War of the Rebellion.*

HOWARD, OLIVER OTIS, *Autobiography of Oliver Otis Howard.* New York: The Baker & Taylor Co., 1908. 2 volumes.

HOWE, M. A. DEWOLFE. See HITCHCOCK, HENRY, and SHERMAN, WILLIAM T.

HUNTER, ALEXANDER, *Johnny Reb and Billy Yank.* New York: The Neale Pub. Co., 1904.

HUTCHINS, E. R., *The War of the 'Sixties.* New York: The Neale Pub. Co., 1912.

JACKSON, HUNTINGTON W., *The Battle of Chancellorsville.* See M. O. L. L. U. S., Illinois Commandery, *Military Essays and Recollections,* Volume II.

JACKSON, HUNTINGTON W., *The Battle of Gettysburg.* See M. O. L. L. U. S., Illinois Commandery, *Military Essays and Recollections,* Volume I.

JENNEY, WILLIAM L. B., *Personal Recollections of Vicksburg.* See M. O. L. L. U. S., Illinois Commandery, *Military Essays and Recollections,* Volume III.

JENNINGS, WILLIAM, *Personal Reminiscences of the North Atlantic Blockading Squadron.* See M. O. L. L. U. S., Minnesota Commandery, *Glimpses of the Nation's Struggle,* Fifth Series.

JOHNSON, ROBERT UNDERWOOD. See *Battles and Leaders of the Civil War.*

JOHNSON, R. W., *A Soldier's Reminiscences*. Philadelphia: J. B. Lippincott Company, 1886.

JOHNSTON, JOSEPH E., *Report, November 1, 1863*. (*To General S. Cooper*.) See MOORE, *The Rebellion Record* . . . Volume X.

JOHNSTON, JOSEPH E., *Johnston's Narrative of Military Operations, Directed during the Late War Between the States*. New York: D. Appleton &. Co., 1874.

JOINVILLE, FRANCOIS FERDINAND PHILLIPPE LOUIS MARIE D'ORLEAN, PRINCE DE. See TENNEY, *The Military and Naval History of the Rebellion in the United States*.

JONES, J. B., *A Rebel War Clerk's Diary, at the Confederate States Capital*. Phila.: J. B. Lippincott & Co., 1866. 2 volumes.

JORDAN, LEONARD G. See GOULD, JOHN M.

KELLOGG, MARY E. See WILLS, CHARLES W.

KING, W. C., and DERBY, W. P., *Camp-Fire Sketches and Battle-Field Echoes*. Springfield, Mass.: W. C. King & Co., 1887.

LAWRENCE, ELIJAH C., *Stuart's Brigade at Shiloh*. See M. O. L. L. U. S., Massachusetts Commandery, *Civil War Papers*, Volume II.

LEASURE, DANIEL, *Personal Observations and Experiences in the Pope Campaign in Virginia*. See M. O. L. L. U. S., Minnesota Commandery, *Glimpses of the Nation's Struggle*.

LEE, FITZHUGH, *General Lee*. (Great Commanders Series, edited by JAMES GRANT WILSON.) New York: D. Appleton & Co., 1894. (By permission of D. Appleton-Century Company, Inc.)

LEWIS, SAMUEL ("Peter Truskitt"), *Life on the Monitor. A Seaman's Story of the Fight with the Merrimac* . . . See KING and DERBY, *Camp-Fire Sketches and Battle-Field Echoes*.

LITTLEPAGE, LIEUTENANT, *Merrimac vs. Monitor. A Midshipman's Account of the Battle with the "Cheese Box."* See KING and DERBY, *Camp-Fire Sketches and Battle-Field Echoes*.

LOCKETT, S. H., *The Defense of Vicksburg*. See *Battles and Leaders of the Civil War*, Volume III.

LONGSTREET, JAMES, *Lee in Pennsylvania*. See *The Annals of the War*.

LONGSTREET, JAMES, *Battle of Antietam, Sept. 17, 1862*. See KING and DERBY, *Camp-Fire Sketches and Battle-Field Echoes*.

LONGSTREET, JAMES, *The Battle of Fredericksburg*. See *Battles and Leaders of the Civil War*, Volume III.

LONGSTREET, JAMES, *From Manassas to Appomattox*, 2nd Edition, Revised. Phila.: J. B. Lippincott & Co., 1903. (By permission of Mrs. Helen Dortch Longstreet.)

LOUGHBOROUGH, MRS. JAMES M., *My Cave Life in Vicksburg* . . . New York: D. Appleton & Co., 1864.

LUNT, DOLLY SUMNER, *A Woman's Wartime Journal*. New York: The Century Co., 1918. (By permission of Mrs. Louis D. Bolton.)

LYMAN, THEODORE, *Meade's Headquarters, 1863-1865. Letters of Colonel Theodore Lyman* . . . Selected and edited by GEORGE R. AGASSIZ. Boston: The Atlantic Monthly Press, 1922. (By permission of George R. Agassiz and the Massachusetts Historical Society.)

McCARTHY, CARLTON, *Detailed Minutiae of Soldier Life in the Army of Northern Virginia, 1861-1865*. Richmond: Carlton McCarthy Co., 1882.

McCLELLAN, GEORGE B., *McClellan's Own Story* . . . New York: Chas. L. Webster & Co., 1887.

McClurg, Alexander C., *The Last Chance of the Confederacy.* See M. O. L. L. U. S., Illinois Commandery, *Military Essays and Recollections,* Volume I.

McDowell, Irvin M., *Report, June 24, 1861.* See *Battles and Leaders of the Civil War,* Volume I.

McGuire, Judith W., *Diary of a Southern Refugee during the War, by a Lady of Virginia.* Richmond: J. W. Randolph & English, 1889. 3rd Edition.

McKim, Randolph H., *A Soldier's Recollections. Leaves from Diary of a Young Confederate.* New York: Longmans, Green & Co., 1910.

Marshall, Charles, *An Aide-de-Camp of Lee, being the papers of Colonel Charles Marshall* . . . Edited by Major General Sir Frederick Maurice. Boston: Little, Brown & Co., 1927. (By permission of Major General Sir Frederick Maurice.)

Mattocks, Charles P., *Major General Joseph Hooker.* See M. O. L. L. U. S., Maine Commandery, *War Papers,* Volume III.

Maurice, Frederick. See Marshall, Charles.

Meade, George, *The Life and Letters of General George Gordon Meade.* New York: Chas. Scribner's Sons, 1913. 2 volumes. (By permission of Charles Scribner's Sons.)

Milchrist, Thomas E., *Reflections of a Subaltern on the Hood-Thomas Campaign in Tennessee.* See M. O. L. L. U. S., Illinois Commandery, *Military Essays and Recollections,* Volume IV.

Military Order of the Loyal Legion of the United States. See M. O. L. L. U. S.

M. O. L. L. U. S., Illinois Commandery, *Military Essays and Recollections,* Volume I. Chicago: A. C. McClurg & Co., 1891.

M. O. L. L. U. S., Illinois Commandery, *Military Essays and Recollections,* Volume II. Chicago: A. C. McClurg & Co., 1894.

M. O. L. L. U. S., Illinois Commandery, *Military Essays and Recollections,* Volume III. Chicago: The Dial Press, 1899.

M. O. L. L. U. S., Illinois Commandery, *Military Essays and Recollections,* Volume IV. Chicago: Cozzens & Beaton Co., 1907. (By permission of Illinois Commandery, Military Order of the Loyal Legion of the United States.)

M. O. L. L. U. S., Indiana Commandery, *War Papers,* Volume I. Indianapolis: Levey Bros., 1898. (By permission of the Indiana Commandery, Military Order of the Loyal Legion of the United States.)

M. O. L. L. U. S., Kansas Commandery, *War Talks in Kansas,* Volume I. Kansas City: Franklin Hudson Pub. Co., 1906.

M. O. L. L. U. S., Maine Commandery, *War Papers,* Volume I. Portland: The Thurston Print, 1898.

M. O. L. L. U. S., Maine Commandery, *War Papers,* Volume II. Portland: Lefavor-Tower Co., 1902.

M. O. L. L. U. S., Maine Commandery, *War Papers,* Volume III. Portland: Lefavor-Tower Co., 1908. (By permission of Maine Commandery, Military Order of the Loyal Legion of the United States.)

M. O. L. L. U. S., Massachusetts Commandery, *Civil War Papers,* Volume II. Boston: F. H. Gibson Co., 1900. (By permission of Massachusetts Commandery, Military Order of the Loyal Legion of the United States.)

M. O. L. L. U. S., Minnesota Commandery, *Glimpses of the Nation's Struggle.* St. Paul: St. Paul Book & Stat'y Co., 1887.

M. O. L. L. U. S., Minnesota Commandery, *Glimpses of the Nation's Struggle*, Fifth Series. St. Paul: The Review Pub. Co., 1903.

M. O. L. L. U. S., New York Commandery, *Personal Recollections of the War of the Rebellion*. New York: The Commandery, 1891.

M. O. L. L. U. S., New York Commandery, *Personal Recollections of the War of the Rebellion*, Third Series. New York: G. P. Putnam's Sons, 1907.

M. O. L. L. U. S., Ohio Commandery, *Sketches of War History, 1861-1865*, Volume I. Cincinnati: Robt. Clarke & Co., 1888.

M. O. L. L. U. S., Ohio Commandery, *Sketches of War History, 1861-1865*, Volume V. Cincinnati: The Robt. Clarke Co., 1903. (By permission of Ohio Commandery, Military Order of the Loyal Legion of the United States.)

M. O. L. L. U. S., Wisconsin Commandery, *War Papers*, Volume I. Milwaukee: The Commandery, 1891. (By permission of Wisconsin Commandery, Military Order of the Loyal Legion of the United States.)

MILLER, MADISON. See SARGEANT, CHARLES SHELDON.

MOORE, EDWARD A., *The Story of a Cannoneer under Stonewall Jackson*. Lynchburg, Va.: J. P. Bell Co., 1910.

MOORE, FRANK, editor, *Putnam's Record of the Rebellion*, Volume VI. New York: G. P. Putnam, 1863.

MOORE, FRANK, editor, *The Rebellion Record* . . . Volume VII. New York: D. Van Nostrand, 1864.

MOORE, FRANK, editor, *The Rebellion Record* . . . Volume X. New York: D. Van Nostrand, 1867.

MORGAN, JAMES MORRIS, *Recollections of a Rebel Reefer*. Boston: Houghton Mifflin Co., 1917. (By permission of Mrs. Daniel Hunter Wallace.)

MORSE, JOHN T., JR. See WELLES, GIDEON.

MORTON, CHARLES, *A Boy at Shiloh*. See M. O. L. L. U. S., New York Commandery, *Personal Recollections of the War of the Rebellion*, Third Series.

NEESE, GEORGE M., *Three Years in the Confederate Horse Artillery*. New York: The Neale Pub. Co., 1911.

NETTLETON, ALVRED BAYARD, *How the Day Was Saved at the Battle of Cedar Creek*. See M. O. L. L. U. S., Minnesota Commandery, *Glimpses of the Nation's Struggle*.

New York Tribune, November 9, 1860.

New York Tribune, December 17, 1860.

New York Tribune, February 20, 1862.

New York Tribune, April 15, 1879.

New York World, May 9, 1863.

New York World, July 6, 1863. (As quoted in MOORE, *The Rebellion Record*, Volume VII.)

NICOLAY, JOHN G., *The Outbreak of the Rebellion*. (*Campaigns of the Civil War.* Volume I.) New York: Chas. Scribner's Sons, 1881.

NICHOLS, GEORGE WARD, *The Story of the Great March, from the Diary of the Staff Officer*. New York: Harper & Bros., 1865.

NICHOLS, JAMES M., *Perry's Saints*. Boston: D. Lothrop & Co., 1886.

A Northern Writer. See *Battle Fields of the South*.

NORTON, OLIVER WILLCOX, *Army Letters, 1861-1865. Extracts from Private Letters, etc.* Chicago: O. L. Deming, 1903.

OAKEY, DANIEL, *Marching Through Georgia and the Carolinas*. See *Battles and Leaders of the Civil War*, Volume IV.

OATES, WILLIAM C., *The War Between the Union and the Confederacy* . . . New York: The Neale Pub. Co., 1905.

OLDROYD, OSBORN H., *A Soldier's Story of the Siege of Vicksburg* . . . Springfield, Ill.: The Author, 1905.

OPIE, JOHN N., *A Rebel Cavalryman with Lee, Stuart, and Jackson.* Chicago: 1899.

OSBORN, HARTWELL, *On the Right of Chancellorsville.* See M. O. L. L. U. S., Illinois Commandery, *Military Essays and Recollections,* Volume IV.

OTIS, EPHRAIM ALLEN, *Recollections of the Kentucky Campaign of 1862.* See M. O. L. L. U. S., Illinois Commandery, *Military Essays and Recollections,* Volume IV.

OWEN, WILLIAM MILLER, *In Camp & Battle with the Washington Artillery Battery of New Orleans.* Boston: Ticknor & Co., 1885.

Papers of Military Historical Society of Massachusetts. See *Petersburg, Chancellorsville, Gettysburg.*

PARKER, A. C., *Life of General Ely S. Parker.* Buffalo: Buffalo Historical Society, 1919. (By permission of Buffalo Historical Society.)

PARKER, DAVID B., *A Chautauqua Boy in '61 and Afterward* . . . Edited by TORRENCE PARKER. Introduction by ALBERT BUSHNELL HART. Boston: Small, Maynard & Co., 1912.

PARKER, ELY S. See PARKER, A. C.

PARKER, TORRENCE. See PARKER, DAVID B.

PEMBERTON, J. C., *The Siege of Vicksburg, Mississippi.* See MOORE, *The Rebellion Record* . . . Volume X.

PEPPER, GEORGE W., *Personal Recollections of Sherman's Campaigns in Georgia and the Carolinas.* Zanesville, Ohio: Hugh Dunne, 1866.

Petersburg, Chancellorsville, Gettysburg. Volume V. Papers of Military Historical Society of Massachusetts. Boston: The Society, 1906. (By permission of Military Historical Society of Massachusetts.)

PICKETT, GEORGE E., *The Heart of a Soldier, as Revealed in the Intimate Letters of General George E. Pickett, C. S. A.* New York: Seth Moyle, Inc., 1913.

PLEASONTON, ALFRED, *The Campaign of Gettysburg.* See *The Annals of the War.*

PLUM, WILLIAM R., *The Military Telegraph during the Civil War in the United States* . . . also a Running Account of the War between the States. Chicago: Jansen, McClurg & Company, 1882. 2 volumes.

POLLARD, EDWARD A., *The Lost Cause.* Richmond: E. B. Treat & Co., 1866.

POLLARD, EDWARD A., *Life of Jefferson Davis, with a Secret History of the Southern Confederacy* . . . Philadelphia: National Publishing Company, 1869.

POLLEY, J. B., *A Soldier's Letters to Charming Nellie.* New York: The Neale Pub. Co., 1908.

PORTER, DAVID D., *Incidents and Anecdotes of the Civil War.* New York: D. Appleton & Co., 1886.

PORTER, FITZ JOHN, *The Battle of Malvern Hill.* See *Battles and Leaders of the Civil War,* Volume II.

PORTER, HORACE, *Campaigning with Grant.* New York: The Century Co., 1897. (By permission of D. Appleton-Century Company, Inc.)

PRYOR, MRS. ROGER A., *Reminiscences of Peace and War.* Revised and Enlarged Edition. New York: The Macmillan Company, 1905. (By permission of The Macmillan Company.)

Putnam's Record of the Rebellion. See MOORE, FRANK.

RAFFERTY, THOMAS, *Gettysburg*. See M. O. L. L. U. S., New York Commandery, *Personal Recollections of the War of the Rebellion*.

The Rebellion Record . . . See MOORE, FRANK.

REDFIELD, H. V., *Characteristics of the Armies*. See *The Annals of the War*.

RICHARDS, WILLIAM J., *Rosecrans and the Chickamauga Campaign*. See M. O. L. L. U. S., Indiana Commandery, *War Papers*, Volume I.

RICHARDSON, ALBERT D., *History of the Secret Service, the Field, the Dungeon, and the Escape*. Hartford: American Pub. Co., 1865.

Richmond Enquirer, July 9, 1863. (As quoted in MOORE, *The Rebellion Record* . . . Volume VII.)

Richmond Examiner, September 12, 1862.

RIDLEY, BROMFIELD L., *Battles and Sketches of the Army of Tennessee—1861-65*. Mexico, Mo.: Missouri Ptg. & Pub. Co., 1906.

ROBERTS, CAPTAIN, *Never Caught* . . . *Blockade Running during the American Civil War*. London: John Camden Hotten, 1867. Reprinted, *The Magazine of History*, Extra No. 3. New York: William Abbatt, 1908.

ROBERTSON, ROBERT STODDART, *From the Wilderness of Spotsylvania*. See M. O. L. L. U. S., Ohio Commandery, *Sketches of War History, 1861-1865*, Volume I.

ROBINS, RICHARD, *The Battles of Groveton and Second Bull Run*. See M. O. L. L. U. S., Illinois Commandery, *Military Essays and Recollections*, Volume III.

ROGERS, WILLIAM, *The Loss of the Monitor*. See M. O. L. L. U. S., Maine Commandery, *War Papers*, Volume II.

ROMAN, ALFRED. See BEAUREGARD, P. G. T.

RUSSELL, WILLIAM HOWARD, *My Diary North and South*. Boston: T. O. H. P. Burnham, 1863.

SARGEANT, CHARLES SHELDON, *Personal Recollections of the 18th Missouri Infantry in the War for the Union* . . . Addenda by GENERAL MADISON MILLER. Unionville, Mo.: Stille & Lincoln, 1891.

SAWYER, B. F., *Battle Scenes at Shiloh*. See KING and DERBY, *Camp-Fire Sketches and Battle-Field Echoes*.

SCOTT, R. B., *History of the 67th Indiana Regiment* . . . Bedford, Ind.: Herald Book & Job Print, 1892.

SEMMES, RAFAEL, *Service Afloat, or the Remarkable Career of the Confederate Cruisers, Sumter and Alabama* . . . Baltimore: The Baltimore Pub. Co., 1887.

SHELLENBURGER, JOHN K., *The Battle of Franklin, Tenn., November 30, 1864*. Cleveland: Arthur H. Clark Co., 1915.

SHERIDAN, PHILIP H., *Personal Memoirs of P. H. Sheridan*. New York: Chas. L. Webster & Co., 1888. 2 volumes.

SHERMAN, WILLIAM T., *Memoirs of General W. T. Sherman, Written by Himself*. New York: D. Appleton & Co., 1875. 2 volumes.

SHERMAN, WILLIAM T., *Home Letters of General Sherman*. Edited by M. A. DE-WOLFE HOWE. New York: Chas. Scribner's Sons, 1909. (By permission of Charles Scribner's Sons.)

SINCLAIR, ARTHUR, *Two Years on the Alabama*. Boston: Lee & Shepard, 1896. (By permission of Lothrop, Lee & Shepard Co.)

SMITH, J. L., *Philadelphia's Corn Exchange Regiment, History of the 118th Pennsylvania Regiment Volunteers—from Antietam to Appomattox* . . . Phila.: J. L. Smith, 1888.

SOLEY, JAMES RUSSELL, *The Blockade and the Cruisers*. New York: Charles Scribner's Sons, 1883.

SORREL, G. MOXLEY, *Recollections of a Confederate Staff Officer*, with an introduction by JOHN W. DANIEL. New York: The Neale Pub. Co., 1905.

STANLEY, Dorothy. See STANLEY, HENRY M.

STANLEY, HENRY M., *The Autiobiography of Sir Henry Morton Stanley*. Edited by his wife DOROTHY STANLEY. Boston: Houghton Mifflin Co., 1911. (By permission of Houghton Mifflin Company.)

STEVENSON, ALEXANDER F., *The Battle of Stone's River, near Murfreesboro, Tennessee*. Boston: James R. Osgood & Co., 1884.

STEVENSON, WILLIAM G., *Thirteen Months in the Rebel Army . . . By an Impressed New Yorker*. New York: A. S. Barnes & Burr, 1862.

STILES, ISRAEL, *The Merrimac and the Monitor*. See M. O. L. L. U. S., Illinois Commandery, *Military Essays and Recollections*, Volume I.

STILES, ROBERT, *Four Years under Marse Robert*. New York: The Neale Pub. Co., 1903.

STILLWELL, LEANDER, *In the Ranks at Shiloh*. See M. O. L. L. U. S., Kansas Commandery, *War Talks in Kansas*, Volume I.

STRONG, WILLIAM E., *The Campaign against Vicksburg*. See M. O. L. L. U. S., Illinois Commandery, *Military Essays and Recollections*, Volume II.

TAYLOR, BENJAMIN F., *In Camp & Field, Mission Ridge and Lookout Mountain . . .* New York: D. Appleton & Co., 1872.

TAYLOR, RICHARD, *Destruction and Reconstruction. Personal Experiences of the Late War*. New York: D. Appleton & Co., 1879.

TAYLOR, WALTER, *Four Years with General Lee*. New York: D. Appleton & Co., 1878.

TENNEY, W. J., *The Military and Naval History of the Rebellion in the United States . . .* New York: D. Appleton & Co., 1868.

THAXTER, SIDNEY W., *Stonewall Jackson*. See M. O. L. L. U. S., Maine Commandery, *War Papers*, Volume III.

THOMAS, BENJAMIN P. See CADWALLADER, SYLVANUS.

THOMAS, HORACE H., *What I Saw under a Flag of Truce*. See M. O. L. L. U. S., Illinois Commandery, *Military Essays and Recollections*, Volume I.

THOMPSON, RICHARD S., *A Scrap of Gettysburg*. See M. O. L. L. U. S., Illinois Commandery, *Military Essays and Recollections*, Volume III.

TRUSKITT, PETER. See LEWIS, SAMUEL.

TUTHILL, RICHARD S., *An Artilleryman's Recollections of the Battle of Atlanta*. See M. O. L. L. U. S., Illinois Commandery, *Military Essays and Recollections*, Volume I.

TYRREL, BENJAMIN H. See GATES, THEODORE B.

Under Both Flags, A Panorama of the Great Civil War. By Celebrities of Both Sides. Edited by W. L. GOLDSMITH, n.p.: C. R. GRAHAM, 1896.

VON BORCKE, HEROS: *Memoirs of the Confederate War for Independence*. London: Blackwood, 1866. 2 volumes.

WAIT, HORATIO L., *The Blockading Service*. See M. O. L. L. U. S., Illinois Commandery, *Military Essays and Recollections*, Volume II.

WALKER, JOHN G., *Sharpsburg*. See *Battles and Leaders of the Civil War*, Volume II.

WALLACE, LEW, *Lew Wallace, An Autobiography*. New York: Harper & Bros., 1906. 2 volumes. (By permission of Harper & Bros.)

The War of the Rebellion . . . Official Records of the Union and Confederate Armies. Washington: Govt. Ptg. Office, 1890-1901. 128 volumes.

The War of the Rebellion . . . Official Records of the Union and Confederate Navies. Washington: Govt. Ptg. Office, 1894-1922. 30 volumes.

WARREN, GOUVERNEUR KEMBLE, *Letter, July 13, 1862.* See *Battles and Leaders of the Civil War,* Volume III.

WATERMAN, ARBA N., *The Battle of Chickamauga.* See M. O. L. L. U. S., Illinois Commandery, *Military Essays and Recollections,* Volume I.

WATKINS, SAM R., *"Co. Aytch," Maury Grays, First Tennessee Regiment, or a Side Show of the Big Show.* Nashville: Cumberland Presbyterian Pub. House, 1882.

WELLES, GIDEON, *The First Iron-Clad Monitor.* See *The Annals of War.*

WELLES, GIDEON, *The Diary of Gideon Welles, Secretary of the Navy under Lincoln and Johnson.* Edited, with an introduction by JOHN T. MORSE, JR. Boston: Houghton Mifflin Co., 1911. 3 volumes. (By permission of Houghton Mifflin Co.)

WHITMAN, WALT, *The Death of Lincoln, A Lecture by Walt Whitman.* See *New York Tribune,* April 15, 1879.

WILLIAMS, GEORGE F., *Bullet and Shell. War, As the Soldier Saw It.* New York: Fords, Howard & Hulbert, 1888.

WILLS, CHARLES W., *Army Life of an Illinois Soldier . . . Letters and Diary . . .* Compiled by his sister, MARY E. KELLOGG. Washington: Globe Ptg. Co., 1906.

WILSON, JAMES GRANT. See *Appleton's Cyclopedia of American Biography* and LEE, FITZHUGH.

WILSON, JAMES HARRISON, *Under the Old Flag.* New York: D. Appleton & Co., 1912. 2 volumes. (By permission of D. Appleton-Century Company, Inc.)

WILSON, WILLIAM BENDER, *A Few Acts and Actors in the Tragedy of the Civil War in the United States.* Philadelphia: Published by the Author, 1892.

WOODS, JOSEPH T., *Services of the Ninety-sixth Ohio Volunteers.* Toledo: Blade Printing & Paper Co., 1874.

YARYAN, JOHN LEE, *Stone River.* See M. O. L. L. U. S., Indiana Commandery, *War Papers,* Volume I.

YOUNG, JESSE BOWMAN, *What a Boy Saw in the Army.* New York: Hunt & Eaton, 1894.

YOUNG, L. D., *Reminiscences of a Soldier of the Orphan Brigade.* Louisville: Courier-Journal Job Ptg. Co., n.d.

INDEX